# Composers of North America

*Series Editors:* Sam Dennison, William C. Loring, Margery Lowens, Ezra Schabas

*Arthur George Farwell*
*1872 - 1952*

# HE HEARD AMERICA SINGING

## Arthur Farwell

### composer and crusading music educator

by
**Evelyn Davis Culbertson**

*Composers of North America, No. 9*

The Scarecrow Press, Inc.
Metuchen, N.J., & London
1992

All music appearing herein composed by Arthur Farwell, shown as image of his handwriting, and not otherwise published, is copyright 1975 by Betty Richardson Farwell, Brice Farwell, Arthur Bragdon Farwell, Beatrice Farwell, Sara Emerson Farwell, Emerson Farwell, Jonathan Kirkpatrick Farwell, Cynthia Farwell Hensch, and is used by special permission of the copyright owners. Similar music previously first published by Brice Farwell is copyright 1972 by Brice Farwell and is used by special permission of the publisher.

Permission has been gratefully received for the use of the drawing of Arthur Farwell by Kahlil Gibran (J0013450) from the Peter A. Juley & Son Collection, National Museum of American Art, Smithsonian Institution.

The photograph of Arthur Farwell taken by Charles Lummis (Photo N.24535), is courtesy of the Southwest Museum, Los Angeles.

(Acknowledgements continued on next page)

British Library Cataloguing-in-Publication data available

Library of Congress Cataloging-in-Publication Data

Culbertson, Evelyn Davis.
    He Heard America Singing: Arthur Farwell, Composer and Crusading Music Educator / by Evelyn Davis Culbertson
        p.   cm. -- (Composers of North America; no. 9.)
    Includes bibliographical references, discography, and index.
    ISBN 0-8108-2580-5
    1. Farwell, Arthur, 1872-1952. 2. Composers--United States--Biography. 3. Music teachers--United States--Biography.
4. Farwell, Arthur, 1872-1952--Criticism and interpretation.
I. Title. II. Series.
ML410.F228C8 1992
780' .92 -- dc20
[B]                                       92-11172

The author gratefully acknowledges the following publisher for granting permission
to reprint excerpts from these songs:

THIRTY-FOUR SONGS ON POEMS BY EMILY DICKINSON (VOLUME I)

    1) "UNTO ME"
    2) "SAFE IN THEIR ALABASTER CHAMBERS"
    3) "THE SABBATH"
    4) "THE LITTLE TIPPLER"

© Copyright 1983 by Boosey & Hawkes, Inc.
Reprinted by permission of Boosey & Hawkes, Inc.

THIRTY-FOUR SONGS ON POEMS BY EMILY DICKINSON (VOLUME II)

    1) "TIE THE STRINGS TO MY LIFE"
    2) "ON THIS WONDROUS SEA"
    3) "HEART, WE WILL FORGET HIM"
    4) "I'M NOBODY! WHO ARE YOU?"
    5) "WILD NIGHTS! WILD NIGHTS!"
    6) "THE GRASS SO LITTLE HAS TO DO"
    7) "AN AWFUL TEMPEST MASHED THE AIR."

© Copyright 1983 by Boosey & Hawkes, Inc.
Reprinted by permission of Boosey & Hawkes, Inc.

*He Heard America Singing* is dedicated to:

My deceased husband, Floyd Culbertson;
and my sons,
Bryan, Allan, and Darrell Davis.

# CONTENTS

# Photographs and Illustrations

# Musical Examples

**Chapter 19, Piano Music**

**Chapter 20, Chamber Music**

**Chapter 21, Theater Music**

**Chapter 22, Orchestral Works**

# Foreword

This series on Composers of North America is designed to focus attention on the development of art music and folk music from colonial times to the present. Few composers of art music before 1975 had their works performed frequently during their lifetime. Many suffered undeserved neglect.

Each volume consists of a substantial essay about the composer and a complete catalog of compositions, published and unpublished. Part I deals with the composer's life and works in the context of the artistic thought and the musical world of his or her time. In Part II the goals of the composer and the critical comments by contemporaries are included, as are illustrations and musical examples. Some works which merit performance today are singled out for analysis and discussion. In Part III the catalog of the composer's output has full publication details and locations of unpublished works. We hope that the Series will make readers conscious and appreciative of our North American musical heritage to date.

The books are also intended to help performers and teachers seeking works to use. For them we designed the Part III catalog of the composer's music to allow a quick search for works the author finds of historic or current interest that may be considered for readings and hearings.

Sam Dennison
William C. Loring, Jr.
Margery M. Lowens
Ezra Schabas
Martha Furman Schleifer
Series Editors

\*\*\*\*\*\*\*\*\*\*\*

As Series Editor for this book, it has been my delight to see this volume grow over several years. Dr. Evelyn Davis Culbertson presents here a typical history of an American composer, who, once he or she had a family, had to find a way to earn a livelihood other than solely by composing. Arthur Farwell did this by putting time into artistic and money-earning pursuits while also promoting the cause of American Music. He generated and filed much written evidence of the problems that faced him and his fellow artists in music, as he directed pageants and taught in universities and a settlement school on the east coast, the west coast, and in the midwest. Through unusual circumstances our author acquired these files giving her many authentic primary source materials to write this definitive book on Arthur Farwell as a composer and a unique person.

Series Editor:    William C. Loring, Jr., Ph.D.
                         Bethesda, Maryland

# Preface

Nineteen hundred seventy-two was an Arthur Farwell milestone that marked the centennial of his birth. It was commemorated by his family with the publication of *The Guide to the Music of Arthur Farwell and the Microfilm Collection of his Work*. This was based in part on the loan of my Farwell Collection manuscripts to Brice Farwell for the microfilming. A number of libraries across the country have purchased these microfilms and many more the Guide. Scholars have benefited from the use of these resources.

The same year also saw the completion of my dissertation *The Significance of Arthur Farwell as an American Music Educator* and the conferring of my PhD. Prior to my study was the groundbreaking dissertation in musicology in 1958 by Edgar Lee Kirk, *Toward American Music - A Study of the Life and Music of Arthur Farwell*. Vernon H. Mueller's M.M. thesis in 1979 dealt with *Theoretical Aspects of Arthur Farwell's Musical Settings of Poems by Emily Dickinson*. Linda Sue Richer prepared an analysis of Farwell's *Piano Quintet* for her thesis in 1987. Patricia Harper edited Farwell's *Suite for Flute and Piano* and presented a lecture-recital on this work in 1991.

Other scholars have written or lectured on different phases of Farwell's work, but no comprehensive biography of his life has been published. Rose Marie Grentzer Spivak warned me during my graduate studies that the day would come when I would have to write Farwell's biography. Thanks to the challenge by Scarecrow Press, I have been prodded to do so. I have gained new insights from family members, from further delving into Farwell's writings, and other sources to enrich my own perspective during the past 20 years. The problem has been to find a stopping place, as there is too much material for one book. The first two years of writing and research for the book were undertaken while I endured my dear husband's losing battle with cancer. It was Floyd who urged me to accept the offered contract before he became ill.

In addition to Floyd's steady encouragement, I am grateful especially to the Farwell family. I cannot express enough appreciation for their generous and loyal support, without which I could not have undertaken this writing. As archivist for the family memorabilia, Brice Farwell contributed the most continuous help, providing the basis for the Catalog and Discography in Part III. Sara spoke for her mother and added fresh glimpses of her father. Beatrice, Emerson and Jonathan also gave valuable information.

With the help of these wonderful people and many others named below, I have tried to present the personal story of a composer whose visionary stance and crusading zeal for the American composer and the American people should be known. I do not pretend this biography to be the definitive one, but I have drawn heavily on Farwell's journals, letters and speeches to reveal the human side of the man as he expressed his own ideas and times. The title of the book comes from the Walt Whitman phrase Farwell used as a motto for his Wa-Wan Press, "I hear America singing."

Because so much of Farwell's music is now out of print or still in manuscript form, I have included over seventy music examples - some of them in complete score. My hope is that other music lovers and performers will be encouraged to secure copies of the originals from the sources given.

Enjoy Farwell's efforts and discover how Farwell heard America singing!

## Acknowledgments

Many scholars have given their unselfish assistance: Naima Prevots, on pageantry; David Hall helped determine the dates on the Roy Harris correspondence; Dan Stehman also helped with Roy Harris details; Daniel Pinkham for his music and information on Emily Dickinson; Carlton Lowenberg also on Dickinson's poems set to music; Edward N. Waters for his early encouragement and the copy of his *Wa-Wan Press: An Adventure in Musical Idealism*; Howard Hanson shared memories of conducting a Farwell work. Thomas Stoner, Anne Simpson, Jo Ann Sims, Mae Stewart, all supplied information from their specialties. Thanks to the reference librarians in the Tulsa Public Libraries, the Huntington Library in San Marino, CA, to Special Collections at UCLA, and to the Performing Arts Research Center of the New York Public Library. Laura Bottoms, and Hildegarde Bartlau at the Oral Roberts University library were especially helpful in securing inter-library loan materials and information.

Vocal professors Elizabeth Dodd, Judith Auer, and Melody Long Anglin should be thanked for their suggestions for Chapter 18. Gratitude to James Sheldon and William Loring for translations of the French letters, and Siegfried Schatzmann for translation of the German letters. To my readers, Rachel Caldwell, Lee Cowan, Willard Williamson and Lena Wykle, my hearty thanks. My sister, Irene Small, deserves recognition for her research in St. Paul archives for Farwell materials, and another sister, Doris Emily Hendrickson, author of many Regency Romances, for her encouragement and some editing. My two older sons, Bryan and Allan Davis, also deserve thanks for their moral support. Bryan did much of the first music copy work and provided guidance and use of his computer equipment when I was wintering in Florida. Thanks also to John Parker for the loan of his laser printer to do the finishing work in Tulsa.

A very special thanks and recognition to Hallett Hullinger, my proficient computer consultant, who prepared the formatting and camera-ready copy of the book. Thanks also to his wife, Nancy, for her expertise in layout for the music examples and illustrations.

Another well-deserved thanks goes to my understanding editor, William C. Loring, for his meticulous editing and guidance. His dependable help went far beyond duty and always provided stimulus and undergirding when needed.

# Introduction

That fateful day was a warm Maryland one in 1961 when my friend, Bob McKay, delivered his surprise gift. From his loaded station wagon he carried one large file-sized box after another to my living room until eight of them stood waiting my inspection. My curiosity soared. What kind of gift was this? Bob's triumphant demeanor spoke of a successful accomplishment.

Bob saw my questioning look and explained: "I found these at Security Warehouse in Washington, D.C., and bought them for non-payment of storage fees. There is a lot of music in here and some other interesting stuff you should enjoy written by Arthur Farwell. Ever hear of him?" he asked.

I admitted singing one of Farwell's songs on a recent program, but that I knew only his vital statistics.

"The contents of these boxes should tell you more about his life", Bob replied, as together we began to explore his gift.

And what a treasure it proved to be! Our eyes popped when we spotted an inviting old diary dated 1865 written by Farwell's mother, Sara Wyer, who I later learned was a first cousin to Ralph Waldo Emerson.[1] There were two journals written by Farwell, himself, dated 1893 and 1898. We discovered files of letters from famous people such as Frank Lloyd Wright, Reynaldo Hahn, Hedwig and Engelbert Humperdinck, Leopold Stowkowski, Arthur Shepherd and twenty-five letters and cards from Roy Harris. Some of the boxes contained old published music as well as many music manuscripts signed by Farwell; also other music composed by his contemporaries.

Like mine prospectors of old, we continued our careful digging until the truth of the situation struck us. Here was indeed a rich treasure that could take years to unearth and evaluate! I little dreamed then how this gift was to change the future course of my professional career.

In later probing I found copies of lectures Farwell gave on his four transcontinental journeys to promote the cause of American music; also class lectures and copies of talks given before various clubs. There were fascinating photographs of pageant and community music productions with a special group showing scenes and leading characters for his *Pilgrimage Play* given in the

Hollywood Bowl area. There was a folio of drawings Farwell prepared from dreams or visions he had experienced, along with explanations of their meaning as used in his lecture on Intuition.

One box contained small books such as one by Alice Fletcher on *Indian Music* and Thomas Troward's *Edinburg Lectures on Mental Science*; also the manuscript for his unpublished book, "Intuition in the World-Making". The treasure hunt went on and on.

What was I to do with all of this "gold"?

As a widow with three young sons to raise, a position as music teacher to fill, and performing dates to honor, I had little time for research. But when I talked to Edward Waters at the Library of Congress Music Division, I learned that they were aware of the warehouse holdings of the Farwell boxes and had asked to be notified when these were to be auctioned. However, the Library was never notified of the selling date, so my friend had no competition for his purchase. What a miracle that Bob had been able to secure the materials for me! Now I sensed a Divine hand in receiving my gift and I welcomed a role in the future destiny of the Farwell collection. What was that to be? I decided to begin with performance combined with new information I could learn about his life.

After examining many of Farwell's songs, I prepared some groups to sing in lecture recitals that I presented in the Washington D. C. area. These were warmly received, so I continued to perform them on demand. I began studies for a PhD at Maryland University in 1964 and later taught at Oral Roberts University in Tulsa, Oklahoma, except for a Sabbatical leave to finish the degree in 1972. I studied Farwell's drawings and paintings as a basis for a term paper in a required class on "American Paintings". My dissertation[2] was based largely on my Farwell collection and I was known as "The Farwell Lady" around the music department at College Park, Maryland.

The responsibilty for caring for this valuable gift always haunted me. I discovered early that the cost of buying insurance for it was prohibitive, so I took every precaution to protect the collection wherever I moved it. When a visiting minister was my house guest in Maryland, we simply prayed God's protection over the boxes, and God honored that prayer to this day.

Fortunately, I met Jonathan Farwell, Arthur's youngest son, after seeing him perform in *The Threepenny Opera* at the Washington D.C. Arena stage. This encounter opened the door to meet other family members who were overjoyed to learn that their father's unaccounted for personal papers and manuscripts were safe in a professional musician's hands. (Farwell's widow, Betty, who was hospitalized with a disabling illness, had not told his family her warehouse account was in arrears.)

Eventually, Farwell's oldest son, Brice, came to my Maryland home from Briarcliff Manor, New York, to borrow my collection for microfilming. His efforts added permanence for my Farwell files.

As scholars became aware of my Farwell holdings, I received many inquiries for help in their related research. In later years, visitors came to my home in Tulsa, Oklahoma. Barton Cantrell, pianist, came to explore the piano works; David Hall came to examine the Roy Harris letters for his book on Harris; a graduate student came from Texas to study the music Farwell printed on his lithograph press to use for her thesis. Naima Prevots reached me in my Florida winter quarters to exchange information for her book *American Pageantry*. My Farwell materials became the source for two papers I presented at Sonneck Society conferences, as well as for an article I wrote for *American Music*[3] So the Farwell collection has had substantial exposure.

As I continued to study about Farwell through the years, I was impressed with his crusade to promote the American composer and his music. In the storm surrounding the question of American nationalism in music, I found Farwell's visionary stance to be noteworthy. In all his adventures, Farwell sense of mission was prominent. He was truly concerned about bringing good music to the masses - "the democratization of music" he called it. In following his many ventures, I came to know Farwell not only as a composer, but also as an artist, a conductor, publisher, editor, teacher, critic, community leader, organizer of music clubs, a municipal employee, writer and a lecturer. I also discovered him performing in the role of parent, husband and friend. Rarely does one find a musician who is able to accomplish as much as he did under such formidable odds.

Of his 116 *oeuvres*, Farwell may be best known for his Indian-inspired works, but he wrote music based on cowboy tunes, Negro spirituals, and Spanish-Californian tunes. He also wrote many compositions not related to folk music. He composed for orchestra, chamber groups, piano, voice, music for pageants, community singing and one opera. These range in style from his earliest ones written under Germanic influences to his twenty-three thoroughly "modern" polytonal studies for piano composed during the years 1940-1951.

The Farwell name is becoming a more familiar one thanks to warm recognition of his work and music. Historians such as Gilbert Chase and Daniel Kingman have sung his praise in their newest books. Premieres of his mature music, new recordings, and the Boosey & Hawkes publication of *Thirty-Four Songs on Poems of Emily Dickinson*, have promoted the hearing of his music. New scholarly research on Farwell's life and work continues to appear.

When the donation of my Farwell Collection and that of the Farwell family is completed, Sibley Music Library at the Eastman School of Music in Rochester, N.Y. will house the Farwell Archives and will make his "treasures" more easily obtainable both for performance and research.

Barbara Zuck sums up Farwell's Americanist efforts[4]

> Through his writings, his music, and his unceasing efforts to get a hearing for American music, Farwell emerged as the most eloquent spokesman for Americanism in the early years of this century. . . Farwell was clearly an exceptional personality. Prolifically creative in composition, he was also an effective leader and organizer. Perhaps no single composer, with the exception of Aaron Copland, embodies the spirit of Americanism as completely as Farwell, for his Americanist efforts extended to nearly every facet of his own and the nation's musical life.

Daniel Kingman adds more in his discussion of eight musical pioneers:[5]

> Arthur Farwell's music may not impress us today as being his most important contribution (though it has been

unduly neglected), but many of his ideas, as he eloquently expressed them, and the example of his accomplishments, are relevant in today's world and amply repay an acquaintance. It is thus that he looms large, and he is a fitting figure to be considered as the last of our pioneers.

Although Farwell may not have been fully understood or appreciated during his 79 years, he can now be seen in fresh perspective. Based on my Farwell Collection, plus information generously supplied by the Farwell family, other scholars, and libraries, this book is an effort to present the intimate story of Arthur Farwell's life, music and philosophy. It seeks to set forth his rightful place in the history of American music, where he should hold a more distinguished post today.

# PART ONE

## LIFE

# Chapter 1

## Arthur Farwell's Early Years

One of the "talks of the town" in fashionable New York City before the turn of the century was a highly successful Irish seer, the fabulous Cheiro. Before emigrating to America, he had read the palms of England's elite with amazing accuracy. His press releases and broadsides proclaimed that he had been advisor to Lord Charles Russell, England's Chief Justice, and that Lord Kitchener of Khartoum, as well as other distinguished members of the British nobility - including the future King Edward VII - could be counted among his patrons.

Arthur Farwell, at 20, was halfway through his electrical engineering studies at the Massachusetts Institute of Technology in Boston, but he had already determined to devote his life to music. Studying electricity with his mind on music was disruptive to both pursuits. What did the future hold for him? A visit to the city would be expensive, but it might be productive to see this palm reader, Cheiro. After all, had he not forecast the downfall of Parnell, the Irish nationalist, and the ruin of Oscar Wilde? Perhaps Cheiro could give him some guidance and good advice.

On April 8, 1895, Arthur wrote his recollections of this unusual session with the famous Cheiro. Because Cheiro's "reading" was an amazingly accurate assessment of Arthur Farwell's personality and pointed to future events with some truth, the record is quoted in full along with Farwell's comments:

> From Cheiro's attractive parlor on Fifth Avenue I was shown into his private room, a sort of den, in which the principal objects that attract one's attention are a small table covered with a cushion and just above, an incandescent lamp which threw a strong light upon my hands as I laid them on the table. Cheiro sat opposite and after examining my hand for a moment, spoke rapidly and without the slightest hesitation. I have not tried to write down the order of Cheiro's remarks nor his exact words except where I have used quotation marks. He said:

"Your hand is strongly imaginative, inventive and idealistic. You are wholly unfitted for a business life and have not the faculty of accumulating money. You do not care in the least for money and will always do your work for its own sake. You will be very unfortunate in regard to money in your early life. You cannot win at games of chance, they will always go against you. (Very true) Your life must be that of a student, you must invent and create, and your work will be original and along new lines which will make your struggle for recognition all the harder. Your will and determination are tremendous. You will carry everything through in spite of everybody; no one can influence you. To attempt to dissuade you or to change your mind when it is once made up, is pure waste of energy. You are very independent of people. 'This' he said, 'you will be less likely to believe than anything I will tell you: that in later life you will have some strange almost mysterious power over people.' (Of the exact nature of this he did not speak.)

"Your life will be a long one, you will live to be about eighty but you will not be strong or robust. However you have a powerful source of vitality and your sicknesses will be numerous but of small importance. If you look up the records you will find that some of your ancestors lived to a fine old age. Your throat is your weak point, you should take great care of that and the upper part of the lungs; there is no danger deep in the lungs. You have any amount of brain power but not enough self confidence, you can never get too much and can never be spoiled. You have not the slightest trace of vanity.

"Religion will not hold you in the least, you will be ruled entirely by principle, which is extremely strong with you. You are absolutely straightforward, faithful and constant. Those who know you will understand that your word is your bond. People will not understand you, especially relatives who may even withhold money that you would otherwise get; [Here Arthur added a note in the margin: 'True'.] These people do not know what to make of you, but that will not trouble nor affect you in the least. You will have few friends, you will 'admit them but will not let them interfere with a greater affection.'

"Principal illnesses at 27, 33, and about 37. Your tendency is strongly philosophical. You are tremendously affectionate but it is impossible for you to show it; you are wholly undemonstrative. You are even timorous with people (too true) but never before obstacles. You would face danger fearlessly."

(After obtaining my assurance that I desired him to tell me everything he saw, he went on:)

"Your hand is not a lucky one. You have the most terrible struggles to go through. Between 24 and 27 you will have the most terrible blows and disappointments. At 27 you will have a disappointment and a success. All this will not discourage you in your ultimate purpose. You will be resigned, but will work on, the same as ever. You will bear anything, even if your heart were breaking, without showing it. Your life will be a very lonely one, and stormy until 33 but you will bear up through everything and never submit although resigned. You are capable of extreme suffering and have a morbid tendency.

"At 33 you will have a great success and are bound to take a step toward fame. You will be a great traveler (this Cheiro emphasized) and the effects of your work will be felt largely in foreign countries.

"Until you are 33 you will have the greatest difficulties with money, after that you will have plenty: it will come as a natural consequence of your work.

"After 33 the fate line in your hand runs smoothly and without interruption upwards, a strong testimony of fame. I cannot tell along what lines you will direct your inventiveness and imagination, but you will be drawn to one of the engineering professions. You have a strong mystical tendency, as well.

"You will take pride in your work but you will care little about your successes excepting inasmuch as you will take satisfaction in work done. You are extremely sensitive and afraid of hurting people's feelings, but you

will give your opinion frankly when asked. You will have
few affairs of the affections early in life. Your ideas at 20
are those of most men at 50."

Cheiro evidently did not detect the musical aspects of
Farwell's career although he recognized his imaginative and
inventive qualities. It is interesting to note that young Farwell's
memo did not question the reliability of Cheiro's assessment or
predictions for his life. As the story of Arthur Farwell's life
unfolds, the alert reader will discover which of Cheiro's predictions
were true, half true, or completely false.

The leadership ability, and qualities of independence, dogged
determination, and strength of will that Cheiro identified in
Arthur Farwell could well be traits that he inherited from his
sturdy New England ancestors. His mother, Sara Wyer Farwell,
(Figure 1) was a seventh generation descendant of an old New
England family, the Wyers, who were among the first families to
immigrate to America. Sara's mother was the daughter of a first
cousin of Ralph Waldo Emerson, and Sara was very influenced by
Emerson's ideas. She had been raised in the New England area
until she was 21 years old when her father, James Ingersoll Wyer
II, decided it was time to move West and the family migrated to
Minnesota.[1]

Arthur's father, George Lyman Farwell, (Figure 2) could trace
his lineage through his grandmother, Eliza Ann Adams, to the
"old Massachusetts John Adams family".[2]     Hence it is not
surprising that Arthur and his brother, Sidney, who was two years
older, were raised in what amounted to a transplanted New
England home in St. Paul where Arthur was born on April 23,
1872.

George Farwell became successful in the hardware business.
The firm he began culminated in the incorporation of Farwell,
Ozmun, Kirk & Co. - with the trademark "Farwell OK". The
name has survived to modern times although George Farwell sold
his interest therein in 1889. (Figure 3)

The hardware business prospered under George Farwell's
leadership so he was able to provide his family with servants,
tutors, and many of the luxuries of his time. His intimate friends
included two of the 19th century's most prominent magnates,

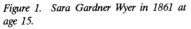

Figure 1. Sara Gardner Wyer in 1861 at age 15.

Figure 2. George Lyman Farwell in the early 1860's.

James J. Hill - railroad builder and financier, and Eugene Weyerhaeuser, one of the leaders in the lumber industry. Mr. Farwell was active in community affairs as he served on the St. Paul Board of Education in the early 1870s and was director of the St. Paul Fire and Marine Insurance Company.

Arthur's mother, who married George Lyman Farwell on February 15, 1869, proved to be an intelligent woman, dedicated to her family. She earned recognition later in life as a magazine writer and lecturer. Mrs. Farwell seemed to be ahead of her times on the subject of child rearing, but her ideas found ready acceptance in articles for The Christian Union (a Chicago paper of that era), as well as in lectures given especially from 1900 - 1913.

Her diaries indicate that she started the first kindergarten in St. Paul before her marriage to Mr. Farwell. Her sister, Elizabeth Wyer, who lived for some time in the Farwell home, developed some renown for her still-life paintings. Sara's nephew, James Ingersoll Wyer III, was well known as Director of the New York State Library School from 1909 through 1926, and thereafter as

*Figure 3. The business name still survives in this 1991 view of the building on Farwell Avenue in South St. Paul, Minnesota.*

the State Librarian of New York until 1939.    Mr. Farwell's second cousin, Abbie Farwell Brown, born in 1871, became an accomplished musician and poet.    Arthur and Abbie kept in contact over the years, but were not close friends.

Arthur (Figure 4) and Sidney grew up enjoying a particularly happy childhood. George Farwell was a devoted father who spent many evenings reading to his sons. He took them on hunting and fishing trips as well as on special summer vacations. Sunday after-noons were often the time for long rides in their "surrey with the fringe on top" into the beautiful surrounding country in warm weather, or on sleigh rides when the winter snows were ready.

Arthur showed no special interest in music until he heard another schoolboy play the violin.    It caught his attention immediately and he told his parents that he *must* have a violin at once!  Accordingly he began violin studies at age nine or ten  and "almost overnight his fine artistic nature came to light.    His appreciation came to the surface as he played with loving expression - forgetting all else around him." [3]

Soon Arthur began playing for guests and later in public as his skills progressed. Sidney took piano lessons and was able to play accompaniments for his brother. Sometimes Mrs. Farwell played the piano for her son too, so there was music-making in the Farwell household. Mrs. Farwell often entertained by giving musicals which featured other performers besides her children.

*Figure 4. Arthur George Farwell at age about two years.*

An active boy, Arthur was also drawn to the intricacies of machinery. He was called "Mr. Fix It" from his ability to repair any apparatus. He was fascinated, too, with the mysteries of electricity and at age ten he began to worry about SPACE! "Yes, but what is outside of everything? What is beyond everything in the air that we see and know?", he would ask. It was probably these early interests that later determined his choice of college to be "Boston Tech" which later became the Massachusetts Institute of Technology. However, as his parents observed Arthur's growing interest in music, they may have wondered about a more appropriate choice of colleges for him.

Arthur and his favorite friend, Robert Kirk, haunted the trash heap of the alley behind the local newspaper. There they retrieved discarded type which they used in a printing press they built in the Farwell basement. This early interest in printing was to develop significance in Arthur's adult years.

Photography was another early interest of Arthur's. He had a dark room in the basement for developing and printing the pictures he took with the camera he designed and built himself. (Figure 5) His hobby is significant when one remembers that this was pursued long before photo-developing and printing was a common practice. George Eastman founded his Kodak company in 1880, but did not market a film camera until 1888. Arthur constructed his camera sometime in 1887, at the age of fifteen!

From September 1883 to July 1885 was a time when Arthur's cousin, Ernestine Wyer, lived with the Farwells while her father arranged a move necessary for health reasons. She loved the big two story house on the corner of Olive Street and Grove which occupied a fourth of a city block. (Figure 6) Two maids kept order in the five bedroom Farwell house. Eventually two more rooms were added to accommodate Mrs. Farwell's mother and sister who later lived there for a time. Ernestine adored her Uncle George and always looked forward to the evenings when the family would gather around the fireplace and, sitting in his new Morris chair, he would read Dickens to them. He gave the children "also a great love for George MacDonald's work as he read the Scotch flawlessly," she reported.[4]

Ernestine remembered going to Frau Nolte's private school with the two boys and many of the good times they had together

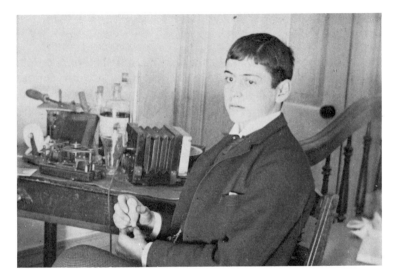

*Figure 5. Arthur Farwell at age sixteen, with camera and recording telegraph.*

*Figure 6. Birthplace and childhood home of Sidney and Arthur Farwell, at corner of Grove and Olive Streets in St. Paul.*

as children. She recalled one Fourth of July when Arthur stooped over to investigate a firecracker that had failed to go off, and it suddenly blew off in his face! What awed her most was that a doctor had to use a special brush to brush out the powder from his eyes. It seemed at the time that the injury was not serious and "Arthur's beautiful hazel eyes were not impaired", she decided.

Ernestine suspected that her Aunt Sara Farwell was a bit snobbish as she was reluctant to permit her sons to visit Ernestine's home later where six active children romped about. "Aunt Sara seemed to feel that she could do more with her time and money with just two children than her relatives could do for their large family," she wrote.[5] However, one summer when Arthur was 13, and Sidney, 15, they were finally permitted to visit their cousins' home in Red Lake Falls, Minnesota, for two weeks. This was a charming little town where two tributaries of the Red River of the North converged that supplied great times for rowing and many other summer sports.

The main attraction for those two weeks, however, was the logging work. Ernestine's father had a banking business and owned an interest in a sawmill with its mill pond and sluice-way. Each summer there were some 1000 marked logs of each log drive that had to be diverted into his channel. The logging crews moored their "wangans" (cabin boats that housed the crews during the logging season) nearby. The children were fascinated watching the log jams that were constantly forming spectacularly along the river - especially in the shallows of the millpond or the rapids below the dam. Just as in playing the game of "jackstraws", they found it exciting to see one lumberjack among several at work on the same big jam, whose skillful "peevee" (pick) loosened the key log and away went the logs down the river! Many times they saw the lucky driver have to jump on a log that went flying over the dam and among the rocky rapids. They looked breathlessly as he disappeared round the bend where sometimes he was able to jump to a rock or a safer log, but more often took a dousing.

Ernestine related the story of their ride on the wangan when they were permitted to make a trip:[6]

In the quiet waters above the dam the wangan moved slowly; then all of a sudden we went 'over the sluice' (a slope of probably 5 or 6 feet). Soon amid the falling of pots and pans, in no time at all we were anchored a mile or so down the river bank, and gladly refreshed ourselves from the avalanche of fresh doughnuts that flew all around.

After such experiences, it is no wonder that Arthur looked forward to future visits with his cousins in Red Lake Falls.

As the boys grew up and needed less of their mother's attention, Mrs. Farwell found time for more cultural pursuits and social involvement. She took German lessons, studied ancient history, and participated in study clubs where members read Shakespeare and other famous classics. She attended concerts and her diary noted especially a recital by the pianist, Josef Hoffman, in 1888, when he performed as an eleven year old prodigy. In all these activities, Mrs. Farwell tried to share what she learned with her children, seeking to instill in them an appreciation for the culture she valued.

One summer, Arthur's father took him to an Indian village on Lake Superior where he actually lived during vacation. There he witnessed Sioux Indians in strange sun dances and heard the impressive speeches of the old priests. He also experienced hunting expeditions later with his father when they often went into the deep North Woods led by Indian guides. On other occasions they saw Sitting Bull and heard of his many exploits. These early experiences provided Arthur a background and special affinity for the study of Indian music that captured his attention in 1899.

Growing up in St. Paul, Arthur had many interesting experiences. One exciting time was when he and Sidney attended the first Winter Ice Carnival in St. Paul. There are not many cities in the United States conducive to building palaces made of ice. With its sub-freezing climate and abundance of lakes, Minnesota claims it "is perfectly suited for building these natural wonders." (Figure 7) A Sioux Indian Village, skating rinks, toboggan run and ski slide were within the walls. Arthur and Sidney were fascinated by the activities within the Indian Village where they heard venerable old women spin ancient Indian tales, saw younger maidens telling fortunes for a fee, and an old chief showing off his quaintly constructed sleighs harnessed to elk.

Inside the tepees, the Indians sang their songs - "Sometimes the monotonous wail of a mourner, sometimes the plaintive, pleading strain of a lover, sometimes the harsh, strident tones of a warrior."[7] Again, Arthur's attention was focused on the Indian's music and life.

One can imagine how eagerly both boys looked forward to the second Winter Ice Carnival which Mrs. Farwell records in her diary for January 19, 1887. At that time the boys watched the Carnival Parade during the day and on the 27th must have observed with pride as their parents rode by in the elaborate evening Equipage Parade. Mrs. Farwell records how the family all gathered later on Mr. Willie Woods' rooftop and watched the storming of the Ice Palace.

A local design competition had been held for the ice palace of 1887. The winning ice palace was an elaborate 135 foot octagonal-shaped tower that was erected in Central Park. It too, was illuminated by "the recently invented electric light".[8] The palace was stormed by Fire King Coal and 25,000 cohorts who laid siege to the palace with over 20,000 Roman candles. No wonder Mrs. Farwell wrote, "It was gorgeous, particularly the fall of fire at the close."

April 24, 1887, was a special day for Sidney who was confirmed by Bishop Henry R. Whipple in St. Paul's Episcopal church. Mrs. Farwell's mind must surely have gone back to her first encounter with the Bishop on January 31, 1867, which occurred before her marriage. At that earlier time she and six friends rode a sleigh from her home in Northfield, Minnesota, to Fairbault to hear her cousin Ralph Waldo Emerson speak there. In those days Bishop Whipple conducted a school for young ladies in his house near the Episcopal College in Fairbault and was in attendance at the Emerson lecture where young Sara met him. So Bishop Whipple's officiation at Sidney's confirmation service was especially meaningful to her. Arthur was confirmed in the same church on June 17th the following year, but Bishop Gilbert officiated.

After finishing their early schooling at Frau Nolte's private school, Arthur and Sidney enrolled at Baldwin Seminary located

Figure 7. The first of St. Paul's famous annual winter carnival Ice Palaces in 1886, above, and 1887 below.  (St. Paul Winter Carnival Committee)

in a fashionable area on Summit Avenue in St. Paul. This school was considered the best preparatory school for the children of the "upper class families." Arthur's best friend, Robert Kirk, whose father was Mr. Farwell's associate in business, was in his class and one notes the names of two children from Governor William Rush Merriam's family on the rolls in 1886-87.

An advertisement for the school in the *St. Paul and Minneapolis Pioneer Press* for January 17, 1888, stated:

> Thorough preparation for our best Eastern colleges. Full courses in the classics, German, French, Music, Elocution, and Drawing. Primary, preparatory, and academic, home and day departments. For further particulars apply to Clinton J. Backus, M.A. Principal.

A brochure describing the school, substantiates the course work offered in the advertisement. Mr. Backus, Arthur's main teacher, taught Greek, Latin, and Natural Science in addition to serving as principal. His wife taught literature, history and mathematics. Eight more teachers completed the roster of instructors. The school prided itself on:

> the best mental discipline for all school exercises...Pupils should be taught to be self-controlled - to be prompt and earnest in their work as well as thoughtful and courteous in their regard for the feelings and wishes of others.

In 1886-87, when both Arthur and Sidney were enrolled in the academic department, it consisted of 45 boys and girls. The primary and preparatory department had 36 pupils so a high ratio of teacher to pupil seems evident with the staff of ten teachers. Activities enjoyed during school years included membership in a Literary Society where both boys participated in plays and read poetry in public and performed in the Boys' Gymnasium Exhibitions (Figure 8). Mrs. Farwell's diary notes that Arthur took part in the play *Stage Struck* at Unity church on February 21, 1889. It would seem that these early experiences were helpful to Arthur in later years when he was developing his community pageants.

*Figure 8.  Baldwin Seminary Senior Class outing at Shadow Falls, 1889.  Arthur Farwell has hand on his knee in foreground.*

*Figure 9.  Sidney (left) and Arthur clowning in made-up faces over a card game while on vacation in 1888.  Sidney has a big knife stuck upright into the table top, ready for anything.*

The summer vacation of 1887 was spent in Vermont at Eagle Mountain House (Figure 9). After Mr. Farwell returned to St. Paul, on August 6th, Mrs. Farwell and her sons remained there until time for Sidney to enroll in school at Andover in September. After getting Sidney settled in his new quarters, Mrs. Farwell and Arthur boarded a train for home. Mrs. Farwell wrote, "It was a very short journey, only 47 hours from Boston." This was quite a contrast to the same trip which she made as a 21 year old girl in 1865. That journey took nine days and involved several train changes and delays plus steamboat travel. What transformations had taken place in her life since then! The deep sadness which she had felt in first leaving her home and dear friends in Massachusetts to go to Northfield, Minnesota, (which to her seemed like going to a foreign land) had finally been eradicated. Married life with George Farwell had permitted many return trips to her beloved New England and now her eldest son was established there in school.

With Sidney away at school, Arthur spent more time with his mother whose influence on his life continued to grow. She took Arthur to lectures, the opera, and concerts of note that were presented in the city. As he approached his 16th birthday, he and his parents discussed where he should go to school the next year. Arthur finally decided he preferred to remain at Baldwin Seminary, rather than joining his brother at Andover.

The Farwells often entertained distinguished people of their time. On December 11, 1888, George Washington Cable arrived for a speaking engagement in the city and an overnight stay with the Farwells. He was a well-known author (1844-1925) who gained recognition for his books about old French New Orleans. Mrs. Farwell's diary for that date describes a delightful evening when Mr. Cable read from *Grande Pointe* for two hours. This was followed by an elaborate reception for him at the Farwell home. Again young Arthur had the opportunity to meet and interact with a stimulating well-known person.

# Chapter 2

## College Years

While Arthur continued his studies at Baldwin Seminary, Sidney was busy in Andover. Some illnesses had stretched out Sidney's schooling there so that by the time he was ready for Harvard, young Arthur was ready for college, too. Accordingly, in the spring of 1889 just before Sidney's graduation, Arthur joined his parents for the trip East. In Andover, they stayed at the "Stowe House" where earlier Mrs. Stowe had written "Uncle Tom's Cabin". Mrs. Farwell commented in her diary for June 6, 1889: "... Across the street is the chapel of the Divinity School, seat of all the wrangling over the new and old theology. What a strange spirit for this peaceful town."

At Andover's Commencement time, Sydney won second prize in the Draper speech contest. He also had music interests and was an admirable singer, which carried him on to the presidency of the Harvard Glee Club.[1]

On June 11, Arthur learned of his admission to the Massachusetts Institute of Technology, called familiarly "Boston Tech". This good news allowed him to enjoy his summer when the whole family vacationed with New England friends and relaxed at Mt. Moussilauke in the White Mountains.

In September, Sidney was packing for Harvard and Arthur for M.I.T. Mrs. Farwell remained in Boston until November when she returned to St. Paul to big changes. George Farwell had finally sold both his interests in the old hardware company and the family home at Grove and Olive streets. So when Mrs. Farwell returned, they reestablished their home in an apartment at the Metropolitan Hotel.

Arthur enrolled at M.I.T. for a Bachelor of Science degree with a major in electrical engineering. The Institute catalog described the program as:

> ...designed to meet the needs of young men desirous of entering upon the practice of any of the various applications of electricity, mechanical engineering and mathematics. To these are added general studies in history, literature, political economy, French and German.
> In all branches of Electrical Engineering a sound

knowledge of mechanics and motors, measurement of power and of the means of its transmission, etc., is essential.

Despite his early enthusiasm over violin study, Arthur had kept music a secondary interest. Now, this was to change. He has left two accounts, probably both true, about this radical change of his priorities. During the New England summer vacation, he was for a time at a music camp located probably in the White Mountains. There he worked by day cutting blazes for new trails, but at night he joined a musical group to play his violin. He narrates in his journal how one evening they played through a string quartet version of Schubert's *Unfinished Symphony*. This work was entirely new to him and the experience overwhelmed him. He described it in terms and tones of a religious conversion and in his ecstasy declared, "That's it! This is how I can express myself - my innermost feelings - in MUSIC! I want to be a composer!"

Reminiscing in a January 23, 1909 article for *Musical America*, Farwell spoke further about this initial experience with the great composer.

> ...The heavenly Schubert spread through my nerves like liquid fire....The mysteries of nature, of life, of creation were revealed to me. Like Tiresias of old, the heavens being opened to me, I became blind to the things of earth. I was lost - and I was saved.

Here was the beginning of his lifelong dedication and conviction. It became a firm resolve by the time of his second account, which describes how as a Freshman he first heard the Boston Symphony Orchestra. He wrote emotionally of that event in his journal: "The concert opened a whole new world for me, and I decided on the spot to become a composer". Nevertheless, firmly believing that a person must fulfill his commitments, he continued his studies in electrical engineering which still held interest for him. However, after his initial experience in hearing the Boston Symphony Orchestra, he took every new opportunity to attend concerts, going as a "standee" every Saturday and often Friday afternoon as well. He referred to his concert-going thus:[2]

> The shrine for me was the old music hall, where under Nikisch, the symphony concerts were given....There, weekly, was the vivifying Grail unveiled....Still a babe at the breast, musically, I fed on the *Liebestod*, the symphonies of Beethoven, Schubert and Haydn, the *Magic Fire* and Bach, classicals and radicals, heaped together, Pelion on Ossa, without knowing which was which, nor caring.

Arthur played in a sextet during the college years and earned money playing violin in an ensemble while also working at summer resorts.

Non-musical activities included membership in the Engineering Society, vice presidency of the Photographic Society, and service as a director of the Co-operative Society. The sole object of the latter was to advance the financial interests of the students. He was a charter member of the Sigma Tau chapter of Delta Kappa Epsilon, and reminisced about that experience in a letter to Scott Wells dated April 24, 1948.

> ...The forming and obtaining the charter of Sigma Tau was the most thrilling experience of my four years at M.I. T. I am inordinately proud of the marvelous growth of Sigma Tau, of my relation to it as Charter member, of being a Hottentot, and I have taught "The children on my knee that the alphabet begins with D K E". They can all sing the "Happy Hottentots" at table, with proper accompaniment. How we did work for that Charter!

Farwell expressed regret that he was unable to send monetary help to the fraternity due to his own pecuniary difficulties. Instead, he sent a "token dollar for what ever that's worth".

Whatever financial problems Arthur may have had in 1948, he had fared well during college years in spite of the difficult economy of that period. Too, Boston was a major center of culture and Arthur absorbed it. Phillips Brooks was the famous preacher in Trinity church while Josiah Royce, Will James, and George Santayana were notables at Harvard.  Also, Mrs. Farwell had a large circle of friends in that area including such distinguished persons as Kate Douglas Wiggin and Mrs. Ole Bull whom Arthur met too.  Hence Boston provided a stimulating environment for mental and social growth as well as musical opportunities during these impressionable years.

### June 1890 - May 28, 1893

After a full and promising freshman year, Arthur returned to St. Paul.  He spent the summer relaxing with old friends - especially  Robert Kirk - who was now also a college classmate. The two practiced their new training learned at M.I.T. in electrical engineering by winding armatures for electric motors they were building.   In the process they succeeded in burning out the expensive new electric wiring so recently installed in Mr. Kirk's shop.  No record is told however, of the punishment meted out for such experimenting.

The annual family vacation began August 4th and this time took them via steamer from Duluth on to Mackinac Island.  There they stayed at the famous John Jacob Astor House formerly owned by the American Fur Company.  Arthur practiced his old hobby of photography by taking pictures with his home-made camera of the many historic sights.

During this summer-time, Arthur invented a toy puzzle and received a patent for it on October 3, 1890.

Among the persons influencing Arthur's development must be noted his meeting in Boston through his mother's influence, with Dr. J. Heber Smith, an astrologer and mystic. (Whether or not he was also a medical doctor cannot be documented.   Mrs. Farwell's diaries always refer to him as "Dr". Smith.)

From Dr. Smith, Arthur learned to make horoscopes and earned "pin money" by creating astrological charts for his classmates.  Nearly three years later at his Class Day exercise, the class prophecy caustically referred to this hobby saying: " There is Farwell - you know him - the astrologer.  I see him using his astrology in his business and then he has to come down to earth again."  A classmate referred to these elaborate horoscopes as

*Figure 10. "The Cherubs" at M.I.T., about 1891-92. From left, J. Howland Gardner, Rob Kirk, Dick Belden, Arthur Farwell. Kirk was a son of the Kirk family of Farwell, Ozmun, Kirk business.*

*Figure 11. Corner of Farwell's room in Union Park, Boston, his Sophomore year, 1890-91, taken by him with his home-made camera. He says pictures shown include Paderewski, Nikisch, and Edison.*

*Figure 12. Prize-winning photo Farwell took with camera he made, for the Tech Photo Society competition May 1892.*

"horrorscopes" being a better word and said, "...they afforded amusements to many of his friends (Figure 10). However, we knew him to be brilliant and he was highly regarded by all of us."[3]

Another classmate who shared Arthur's hobby of photography reported an incident that suggests Arthur's interest in numerology as well as astrology. Howard R. Barton also in the Photographic Society, remembered Arthur's concern with numbers and their sequence or combination.[4] When it came time for an exhibit of their photos in May 1892 (Figures 11 and 12), Arthur asked for a certain number for his exhibit. This was given to him and he won a prize with it![5] The photo was awarded first place for general excellence and second place for artistic merit.

Mrs. Farwell felt the need to be near her sons and spent much of her time in the Boston area all during their college years. Also she was happier in the cultural milieu of her Boston upbringing than in the comparative vacuum of the Midwest of those days. Too, she was now freed from the responsibilities of the large Olive Street home. Mr. Farwell joined her whenever possible and especially enjoyed their 1890 Christmas together at the beautiful spacious home of the James Ayer family in Lowell. Mrs. Farwell records in her diary:

> Sidney left with the Harvard Glee Club on the 22nd for a concert tour of the West so was not able to stay with us. James Ayer, Jr. and his friend, Douglas Petrie, however did join us. Christmas day began with a sumptuous breakfast. Henry, the coachman, made an excellent Santa Claus and distributed the gifts. The dinner which was served at 3:30 was a beautiful affair. One of the courses was a platter of little packages done up in paper and proved to be little books for each guest....After dinner was over, the "Wonder Ball" which we had prepared earlier, was brought in on a holly trimmed tray, and the unwinding of which made a great deal of fun. In the evening, Mr. Petrie, James Ayer, and Arthur provided musical entertainment. At dinner the next night came another puzzle, a stuffed glove and its contents were to be guessed. I won that prize!. On Sunday the 28th was

much music making made by Arthur, James, and Mr.
Petrie....It was a perfect holiday as ever could be.

*Figure 13.  Arthur Farwell's violin, photographed with camera he built.*

It may have been during this Christmas vacation when Arthur
began to show interest in Beatrice Ayer, the beautiful daughter of
Mr. and Mrs. James Ayer.  She became a great love of his life
and Arthur never forgot her even though she eventually married
U.S. Gen. George S. Patton, Jr.[6]
Arthur saw Dr. J. Heber Smith frequently during the second
semester.  By May 10, 1891, Mrs. Farwell noted in her diary  that
she felt as if she had almost lost her son - "so completely is the
Dr. looking after him."
In his Junior year, Arthur began violin lessons on October
28th of 1891 (Figure 13), studying this time with a Mr. Lewis, who
praised Arthur for his progress as well as his talent and
personality.  A most significant friendship was begun during this
year when Arthur met Rudolph Rheinwald Gott (Figure 14), a
musician of unusual gifts but volatile disposition.  They developed
a unique friendship that profoundly influenced Arthur's musical
life.  Rudolph had been an "infant piano prodigy" and had played
Mozart concerti in London at age 13.  His early home life had
been an unhappy one and he frequently ran away.  After his father
died, Rudolph lived in Boston where he continued to play the
piano and compose.  After learning that Arthur played the violin,

Figure 14. *Rudolph Rheinwald Gott in 1893.*

he handed him a copy of the Kreutzer *Sonata* and said, "We will play it next week!"

Arthur tells of his frantic efforts to gain mastery  over the "divine and much - murdered Kreutzer". Brice Farwell retold his father's story of the Kreutzer performance as pieced together from Arthur's own words plus quotations from articles he had written for *Musical America*:

> The first movement left me gasping with bewilderment of delight. I had been carried as on a glowing tide of tone and rhythm. Never before had I been in such close quarters with playing like that - with the living essence and soul of music itself. And so passed this evening in the seventh  heaven. Into Liszt, Brahms, Beethoven, into the chasmy and Dantesque contours of his own concerto, my companion plunged with a mighty and transcendent passion of musical utterance less akin to the puny dealings

of man with art than to those of Nature with her
cataclysmic forces. As interpreter and creator, a "natural"
musician my friend ever declared himself.

But that night my thought was - Music, this that I
have worshiped from afar is, then, not a remote and
austere thing of dead masters and forbidding symphony
hall-it lives, it is human, it is here-here in my friend!
Like an Argonaut with the golden fleece, I sailed home
with joyous discovery.

The whole concern and passion of Arthur's life from now on
concentrated itself on these visits to his new friend. "Each was a
fresh and thrilling adventure", Arthur wrote. As a result his
engineering studies suffered, requiring summer make-up sessions.
However, he did not complain about this extra work as long as he
could also see Rudolph. He describes that relationship:

> It was music, music, and more music - until the deluge
> was unendurable, and then we would take a walk - for miles,
> sometimes, speaking scarcely a word (what was there to say
> after hours in the living presence of Beethoven, Wagner, and
> Tchaikovsky?) - and then come back and plunge in again.
> World-forgetting, we swam Auroral seas of music. So
> completely did we throw ourselves into a maelstrom of
> musical ecstasy - of adoration of the masters that there was
> room for nothing else.

Although Rudolph had unlocked the personal reality of
music's emotional nature in his friend, he could not control his
own deep feelings. Undisciplined, and impractical, his fiery
Bohemian life-style eventually took its toll in an early and sudden
death. But during Rudolph Gott's best years of 1892-1894,
Arthur's musical life was enriched immeasurably by his friendship.
Even though he recognized Rudolph's fatal weaknesses, "the
unique and dazzling gifts made Rudolph Gott an unforgettable
Zarathustran superman of music", Arthur declared.

At the end of his junior year, Arthur returned to St. Paul to
visit his father for a month. But by July 12, 1892, he was in the
East again, working and vacationing at Breezy Hill with the

Kittredge family, where his mother and other friends had preceded him.   He had daily practice sessions on his violin with Miss Fannie Stone as accompanist, and they performed frequently for the guests.   Mrs. Farwell's diary lists some music written by Rubinstein which was performed one evening, and the Grieg *Sonata* on another occasion as part of an entertainment.

The last two summers of his college years, Arthur was also busy studying harmony by himself using "Richter's awful and labyrinthine book".

In late September Arthur was back in classes at M.I.T. and Mrs. Farwell was re-established at the Thorndike Hotel.   She continued to keep a maternal eye on Arthur, and at one time spoke about her son's musical interests to Thomas Ryan, co-founder of the Mendelssohn Quintet Club.   He promised "to talk with Arthur soon and try to find out what the boy has in him."

Arthur continued to combine his musical life with college study throughout a very strenuous senior year.   There were many days when he feared he would not pass all of his courses and his eyes suffered from the long hours of strain.   Nevertheless, his musical performances continued at the Kittredge[7] mansion and elsewhere and Mrs. Farwell carefully noted the details in her diary. Arthur referred to his college studies thus:[8]

>...Not that I loved electricity less, but that I loved music more.  The demands of the course were severe; and working day and night, rising for weeks at a time at four and five in the morning, and grinding more frequently than not until after midnight, I was still not certain until the end that I should not be dropped.  But interested as I was in this work for its own sake, the lathes and engines whirred music, the dynamos buzzed music, and the imaginary quantities of zero and infinity, in the higher mathematics, whirled one off into the regions where one heard the music of the spheres.
>
>    I have often heard an innocent-looking dynamo doing the Allegretto of Brahm's *Second Symphony*, or a ponderous flywheel beating out the measures of Beethoven's *Seventh*.  I remember whistling Raff's *Lenore* to the time of a great Corliss "triple-expansion" during an

engine test, and finally bringing down upon myself the ire
of an instructor who had searched fifteen minutes to
locate the squeak in the machinery. I longed for the day
when I could throw off the restraint of the absolute and
inviolable laws which bound scientific deductions, and
unfettered, and unrestrained, drive recklessly upon the
roadways of the dawn in the phaeton-chariot of music.

In the spring before graduation time, Arthur made an
appointment with George Whitefield Chadwick and took some
compositions to show him. An entry in his journal records that
momentous occasion:

> I sat still without breathing while he looked very
> slowly over the Sonata - page by page. At length he said,
> "Have you studied form?" "No", I replied, "just read a
> little about it." "I suppose you know that this is not really
> a Sonata at all?" "Yes", I answered meekly. I should not
> really have dared to say my soul was my own. I asked
> him what he would infer and he told me it showed much
> spirit - fire - and energy - but lack of form and technical
> correctness. "It shows what you want to do and it shows
> what you can't do", he said. - I will sometime though!
> Chadwick explained that he would rather have me take
> him something original like the sonata - not having
> studied - than to take him something technically perfect
> - but resembling Mendelssohn or other composers -
> having studied their works.
>   "I suppose you know what you have got to do?"
> "Work?" I replied. "Begin at the bottom like every one
> else", he answered. I told him I expected that, but I did
> not tell him that I expected to climb on a rapid extension
> ladder. We will see! Five dollars an hour. Can I do it?
> I asked him in leaving how much of his time I had used
> up and he said, "I am glad to see any one who is
> promising." He advised me to learn the piano as fast as
> possible. "Oh - I forgot about the song," I added. He saw
> that after the Sonata and glancing at it a moment - said,
> "Well, why didn't you show me this first? This has

evidence of form about it." Then he criticized severely
and justly - the modulations which he described excellently
as "ineffective". He pointed out to me with some
amusement that I had ended it on the words 'Good night',
*pianissimo*, on high C! I felt quite encouraged though -
for he committed himself by the word "promising."

Thus encouraged by Chadwick, Arthur looked ahead to
beginning a career as a composer. His Senior thesis was entitled,
*On the Least Number of Vibrations Necessary to Determine Pitch*,
evidence enough of where his interest lay. Eagerly Arthur
anticipated graduation in May so he could be free to concentrate
on his music. As a young man of integrity, he had completed his
commitment to the Engineering degree. At the same time, he had
become more and more involved with music each passing year and
had made helpful contacts with people in the music world. Fiery
Rudolph had opened the windows of his soul to the rich
potentials of the musical life, and Chadwick was willing to help
him with composition. We can imagine his joyful relief to be able
to join other Seniors for the Baccalaureate service at Trinity
Church on May 28th and the graduation activities that followed.
Degrees were conferred the next day with ONE girl being among
the graduates as Mrs. Farwell noted in her diary.

# Chapter 3

## Serious Music Study Begins: 1893-1897

After his graduation, Arthur returned to St. Paul June 30, 1893, where conditions had changed somewhat since his visit of the previous summer. Now his parents were "house-sitting" for the Abbots family who had left town for the summer. Arthur commented,

> "The first time with a house to ourselves after four long and weary years. We have no servants yet but expect some tomorrow. - Also a piano tuner of which we are in great need for I hope to begin lessons soon. Hurrah!"

The turbulent emotional times and growing pains of the would-be composer are expressed in his journal (Book II) which begins on July 6, 1893. Here we witness his development through independent study combined with formal lessons. In it he confides his struggles to compose while nursing his heartaches over a girl named Bertha and other girl friends. Obviously, composition and girl friends were two closely related interests of his young life. That Arthur was a person of deep feelings becomes evident in this journal-confessional. Some lines are heavily scratched over while others and even some whole pages are completely torn out of the book! Although some of the entries may seem irrelevant to Arthur's life story, these shed light on his attitudes and personal development, thus helping us better understand his personality.

Arthur details an exciting day when he went on a picnic with Bertha and eleven others. After his return home he was too upset to go to sleep. He sat up until two o'clock composing a piece he named *Regrets* to which he affixed a Goethe verse in German from Schubert's song *Gretchen am Spinnard*. He wrote, "I felt like Schubert when he composed that. I feel all the sadness I felt went into that piece. I took it over this morning and left it for her [Bertha] but did not see her nor intend to." (Later he inscribed that it was his *first* composition.

To pour out his feelings about Bertha, he filled in the next nine pages of his journal. Perhaps a third of those sentences were scratched out or torn out later. In one place he wrote:

I could bear it no longer - so unbosomed myself to mother. I knew she could read my mind anyway, sooner or later.    Father never would, for we are not so sympathetic - would that we were! (Figure 15)

*Figure 15. Arthur's mother Sara Wyer Farwell, with whom he shared deep mutual devotion.*

By July 17th Arthur had something to say about "sentiment":

> How I hate the word sentimental and yet how I love
> true sentiment.  It gives us a keener sense of enjoyment
> in all that is beautiful about us and also a keener sense
> of sadness.    I   suppose   I   would   be   called   terribly
> sentimental -I do not want to be foolishly so - but people
> do not know how deeply things affect me, it is truly
> painful sometimes.   Everything is such *intense* reality to
> me.   Perhaps this is a musician's lot.

By July 19th Arthur met Atha Haydock, who became an
important love of his early life.   His journal notes the date in
bold red ink figures that stretched across the top of the page.
The same day was also eventful because he took his "first
STUDIED piano lesson to Emil Zoch - he was pleased with the
way in which I had prepared it.   At least it was not worse than
beginners in general".   Evidently Arthur's conscientious piano
practicing had produced satisfying results.

On August 1,1893, Arthur recorded: "A new epoch in my life
has begun with the events of last month - everything appears in
a new light." He describes Atha as being "a wonder - the artist,
the musician, the athlete - the conversationalist, the traveler - who
will make her own name in the world."   He describes one night of
special note:

> Bright moonlight.  Louise, Atha and I went up on the
> roof at Louise's.   I took my violin.   I played many things
> - Chopin *Nocturnes*, Schubert *Symphonies*, Schumann,
> Beethoven.   It was a weird situation...they did not know
> I was also improvising.   I will write a nocturne on the
> theme I used and send it to Atha....
>      I will never forget the effect on myself of a little
> Serenade Atha played on the piano - I do not even
> remember the composer - Atha has a beautiful soft touch
> - the kind I expect and hope to acquire.

In her diary, Mrs. Farwell wrote more details of Atha's visit and told of taking the electric cars to Lake Harriet where she, her husband, Arthur, and Atha attended a concert given by Patrick Sarsfield Gilmore's band. Another entry suggests the seriousness of the relationship developing between her son and Atha. She tells of having a heart-to heart talk with the young couple about what she considered "the highest thing - motherhood". She added, "I do not believe women are ever incarnated as men. Motherhood *is* man, for is not every man one with his mother?" A later entry refers to taking Atha for a drive during which time they had a "beautiful talk on the deep meanings of her visit." Mrs. Farwell obviously approved of her son's new girl friend.

Arthur began to feel that life was assuming a rosy aspect in everything but his finances. He referred to the Panic of 1893 as being the greatest depression ever known in our country. When George Farwell sold his interest in the hardware business, he invested the money in a foundry. Unfortunately, the foundry business foundered in that Panic, thus ending the financial independence of George Farwell and his family. Arthur had about $1500.00 saved "somewhere" which he planned to use for composition studies in the fall. He had begun his first orchestral work, "Symphonic Tone Poem - Sunset", inscribed again to Bertha. (The completion of this work under this name is unknown.) On August 14, 1893, he discussed his progress in scoring it:

> ...it provokes me beyond measure - but when I think it is my first orchestral attempt and I have never studied - then I take heart and feel more confident I am not really baffled. - when the inspiration comes - this may be the best passage of at best a rash attempt. But I am working for Bertha so will do my best.

The next day Arthur reported his progress as having completed fifteen pages and 100 bars done on this same work. "If only I knew whether it is worth anything or not. If I can finish it in time I will send it to the National Conservatory for the competition....I have thought about it many times. Perhaps I can get a criticism".

By mid-August Arthur bragged that Herr Zoch was "much pleased at my progress on the piano." However, though he practiced about two hours daily, he could not complete the long assignments, but adds "Just wait two years - and then see what I can do." Referring to his composing: "...it is such a joy to see the notes go down one after the other. The question is - will it be an equal joy to hear them played - one after the other?"... "I have not spoken of my future with father - but I must soon. I MUST go to Boston to study this winter...I want Chadwick."

Arthur noted the arrival of a stray cat that came to his home which he fed. He commented, "The arrival of a cat is a sign of good luck. I wonder which of this household will have it." The same entry told of his work in sketching a head of Rudolph Gott from a photograph and the problems involved. Drawing was a hobby he indulged in quite frequently. Other activities he described included a 30 mile bicycle trip and horse-back riding. Sailing was another outlet that Arthur hoped would prove inspirational, but the winds were so strong that all he could think about was "hanging on!"

The tendency to be blue or morbid which Cheiro discovered in Arthur shows in several of the journal entries. On August 22, 1893 he wrote:

> Sometimes I feel that the only thing I can do is to write in my journal and have no inspiration for anything else....I have just practiced the piano two hours and feel as if I could never learn it. Then the postman passed me by without stopping and that makes me wild!! For when I am feeling blue anyway, nothing consoles me like a letter. (He was expecting one from Bertha.)

Arthur recognized that he had more advantages than many - but he felt cross and irritable sometimes and he complained that little things - interruptions - annoyed him and he felt disgusted with himself for showing it. He determined to reform. Thus, he expressed a need to learn self control, a discipline he developed to use much later during his parenting years.

Arthur recorded progress in piano studies in his journal. He likes a new Kuhlau *Sonatina* and expresses relief for no more

Czerny. Unable to finish his "Symphonic Poem" in time for a national competition he says: "Well, I must make a beginning somewhere - I can rewrite it sometime...I will show it to leaders in the East."

On the difficulties of composing, Arthur writes on August 27:

> How I long for the time when I can take up the beautiful clean paper and put notes down as I am writing now knowing just how they will sound. At present I cannot do anything. Everything I attempt disgusts me for I butcher it so. One has confidence in me - Rudolph Gott - and I in him - and this gives me joy. I think I could draw and paint if I studied - Oh if one could only study everything - it seems so terrible that we must give up our whole life just to do one thing well. Then I should like to sculpture....But music, the circumstance being right, has a power that nothing else has over me except natural scenery - and I feel I have a work - in that direction. I often think all forms of art are identical in essence and are all reducible to some one natural principle - as all forms of matter are sometimes thought to be the same in essence.
>
> I am disgusted with myself. I don't know why . . I can't sing, I can't write legibly, I am accomplishing nothing these days - but wait til the winter I will shut myself up and work - no one can interrupt me then....It will not do to wait for inspiration - work all the time - then when inspiration comes - it will find you at your post. This will be my motto....It must all be pent up within me. I can dispel it all by playing the Kreutzer with all my fury, but when the Andante comes it all comes back to me and my brain reels for the moment....All this storm within me - it has lasted three months. I thought once it had subsided - but fool that I am - I was mistaken - O ye gods!

By September 3rd, Arthur's plans to go to Boston were complete. He had a long talk with his father who did not oppose his going, but explained that no family financial help would be available. By now Arthur had about $1700.00 in savings, which

he hoped to make last for two years. Settling his future plans for
the time being seemed to bring back the creative impulse. He
then wrote a song which he gave to Charlotte Hastings as a "peace
offering" for not having called on her before. He took his violin
to her house, played it on the porch, and later inside her house.
He insisted all the lights be put out, explaining that a "violin
without accompaniment is not itself in the light - especially in the
case of simple melodies such as Schubert's *Serenade* or
*Traumerei*".

Emotionally hectic days preceded his departure for Boston,
particularly in relationships with his girl friends. He complained
that he always seemed to say or do the wrong thing at the wrong
time, and to have no command of the right words when needed.
While still being upset about these matters, he wrote, "I found
some relief today in working upon that part of the *Symphonic
Poem* where the 'grief Idealized' first appears - but when I think
for a moment of her [presumably Bertha] - I cannot contain
myself..." The next page is torn again, but he does leave us a
poignant expression of his loneliness:

> Yesterday I went back to the flat - nobody was at
> home. I felt very lonely. When I am in a company and
> go off by myself, I am never lonely. But when nobody is
> to be found in a place, where somebody might be expected
> - I am. I wanted words - expanse - the walls of a room
> would kill me. So I took a scrap of paper and 'Das
> Rheingold' and boarded a car going out of town...but I
> could not write - only mused. In sorrow I can have a
> little peace in the companionship of nature. I sat there
> under the trees an hour and a half and returned much
> calmer at heart.

Bertha and Arthur had a serious confrontation before he left
St. Paul. She had suggested they get together for a very frank
discussion. In anticipating the dialogue, Arthur noted on
September 17, "I felt like a condemned criminal being led to the
scaffold". The results of that meeting were worse than he
expected and Arthur's feelings were badly crushed; Bertha had not
realized how deeply he cared for her. Her parting words had

been, "I owe my loyalty to another." He told his journal later, "O Bertha, I respect you for that loyalty; remain as loyal to him as I have been to you. My part is over."

Meantime, he had made only one mention in his journal of his growing deep feelings for Atha Haydock. (Perhaps this was true because Atha did not live in St. Paul.) He had written "If I had not met Atha this year, I might have been a misanthrope (if that's the word). She has been my salvation." In any case, Atha and her family were soon to enter his life again in New York.

By September 23rd, Arthur was Boston-bound, but stopped in Chicago to see his friend, Lawrence Dixon, who took him to visit the World's Columbian Exhibition. He wrote in his journal about seeing "so many wonderful sights, it would take volumes to describe!" He found the illumination at night to be "glorious and truly an inspiration." He spent a day at the art galleries as art was always an interest, and "enjoyed the French and Russian sections best." He was fascinated with exhibits in the Woman's Building, the White City, and the Midway Plaisance where he noted the Native American exhibit at the far end.

Continuing his eastward journey, Arthur's next stop was in Brooklyn. There, upon arrival, he went immediately to see his friend Rudolph, and discussed future plans. After an "old time lunch of black bread and coffee & cheese", Rudolph played the piano for him. "I was all ears and for the time was perfectly happy, as much so as anyone can be on this earth I believe."

Later, Arthur made arrangements for Rudolph to meet Atha, who was in New York City en route to Paris, and rented a private practice room at Chickering Hall for the meeting. His journal describes at great length the glorious time of music-making enjoyed by Mrs. Haydock, Atha, her sister Thomasa, and the two men. Arthur played his songs on the violin with Rudolph accompanying, and then Rudolph launched into one great piano work after another. When he finished, Arthur wrote on September 29, 1893 - "Words would have seemed so insignificant and out of place that scarcely anyone spoke."

By evening of that memorable music-making day, Arthur and Rudolph went to the steamer *Burgoyne* to see Atha off for Paris where she expected to continue her studies in art. Arthur carried his violin on board. They all went up to the bow, where he

serenaded Atha in the bright moonlight.   After bidding her
farewell, Arthur discovered that Rudolph had already left, so he
went down the gangplank alone.   As he started to leave the wharf,
the boat official stopped him and cross-questioned him about his
violin.   Proving that the violin was indeed his in the brouhaha
that followed, he was delayed a half hour in this trying situation.

After a few more days of exhilarating music-making with
Rudolph, Arthur left for Boston on October 22nd.   The second
day there he began his search for a room with $3.00 a week as his
determined limit for this expenditure.   After a discouraging search
- (no heat, no sunny exposure, no room for a piano) - he finally
decided it best to accept his good friend Dr. Smith's earlier
invitation to spend the winter in his pleasant attic room.   He
would enjoy the sunny exposure and superb outlook on the
Vendome and new library.   He would try not to be a burden to
the good "doctor".

Arthur reported, "The first thing I did was to write a note to
MacDowell asking when I could see him, for I wanted advice."
After receiving a courteous reply, Arthur visited MacDowell and
questioned, "Is there anything in orchestration or harmony or
kindred subject that I cannot learn alone?"   MacDowell replied,
"No, but you can learn many things quicker with a teacher.   What
do you know about form, orchestral coloring, balancing of
instruments?" he continued.   To which Arthur replied, "Only what
I know by intuition."

MacDowell said his prices were too high for Arthur's slim
resources, so he recommended another teacher.   "But", he added,
"Come up occasionally and I will look over your work and correct
it and help you out and it will not cost you anything."

> He was extremely kind to me and I felt much drawn
> to him.   His generosity is unusual for these days.   The
> result is I am studying with Homer Norris who has
> studied abroad and also studied with Mr. MacDowell.
> Also piano with Thomas P. Currier who is also a pupil of
> MacDowell.

Under the same date line for October 22, 1893, our young
composer writes that he had composed three songs without words

for violin and piano since settling in Boston. "I would rather believe they are good than to show them to my teachers" was his naive reaction. (Figure 16)

However, by November 18, 1893, Arthur expressed his discouragement thus in his journal:

> Time flies - and what have I to show for it? A few poorly done exercises in figured bass and a very faulty execution of three Kuhlau Sonatinas. Ye gods but this is slow - and I work all the time. I have not had my slippers off all day - have stuck right to my desk. Can I ever compose? My ideas will not run freely these days. Chadwick told me last Spring that when one began studying harmony in earnest - the desire or inspiration to compose left temporarily. I believe he was right. Many thoughts I have had I know have been original - and I have written down many with what little knowledge of harmony I had but now I have no thought but occasionally little fragments. But the development refuses to come. My work cannot be in vain. I must be accomplishing something. Oh if only I could see it. It is so slow - slow! Mr. Norris makes the harmony very interesting and is in nowise pedantic. I am reading Schubert's life. There is a strange magic in it for me and impresses me deeply. So obscure, yet what heavenly inspiration. No words can express my feelings for the dear Schubert. Oh if I could only write 6 songs in one day - an opera in 2 weeks. Schubert thou immortal!

Arthur continued his composition and piano studies all winter in Boston. By January 6, 1894, his mother reported that she had received a "fine letter from Arthur's music teacher, Homer Norris. He writes warmly of his talent and personality. "

Arthur studied counterpoint with Norris and occasionally sought advice from Chadwick and MacDowell. The latter composer held open sessions on Sunday mornings. Arthur spoke of exposing his work there "to the fire of MacDowell's devastating criticism."

Figure 16. Arthur Farwell, the young engineer turned student of music composition, from a visiting card image in the Boston years after college.

These visits to MacDowell are also never to be forgotten. I have never gone before an audience, even one of cowboys, Comanches or Bostonians, with more insidious qualms than those which preceded these occasions. MacDowell, while at heart the kindliest of beings, was, when I saw him always savage and breathless. I never knew at just what particular moment he would, critically speaking, carve out my heart. Restless, mobile, eager, nervous, omnivorous of notes, he seemed never to know a moment of repose. He expressed himself continuously, immediately, without reflection, without reserve. His very nature was expression. I have always been grateful for the slashings and lashings I received at his hands.[1]

In the summer of 1894, Arthur was 22 and ready for a break from his studies. He longed to see his dear friend, Atha Haydock, who was home from her European art studies. So he visited her in Cincinnati for a month, and then went on to St.Paul to be with his parents. By September 20th, he left for New York City to see Atha sail for Europe again, and then returned to Boston.

Arthur describes the two years from 1895 to 1897 in Boston as "a true Bohemia....The world still fresh and dewy, the struggle hard, but not sordid, the responsibilities of life and the meaning of the history of art not yet realized, these were Elysian years."[2]

Arthur and a friend (possibly John Marshall) whom he called "the Pauper", took a modest room together and soon were joined by a third fellow (Winslow Mallery) whom they labeled "the Prince". The Prince was "opera mad" in addition to being an authority on all matters of philosophy, psychology, literature, and art, which sagacity enabled Arthur and the Pauper to derive "many of the benefits of a classical education".

The three men took advantage of every opportunity to attend concerts and operas. Arthur describes his first experience of witnessing Walter Damrosch conducting opera at the Boston theater, where the three sat in the gallery.

There, intoxicated with tone, I first saw the fires flare up around Brünhilde's rock, and in a trance of epic gloom, watched the slain Seigfried borne off by the huntsmen. There I first went down also in the tonal maelstrom of "Tristan"...things good to know.[3]

Eventually Arthur, the "Prince", and the "Pauper", exchanged their places in the audience, for ones on stage where they secured jobs as supernumeraries. Beginning with the lowliest of spots they soon were given "the best places on the stage where we could witness the triumphs of the giants of those days, the de Reszkes, Melba, Calvé, Nordica, Eames and their colleagues."

Money was always a problem. Arthur wrote, "There was a tentative pupil or two, but they fell away....The Prince mortgaged his books, but that did not last long." Then Arthur heard of a school in an outlying town that wanted a conductor for a chorus of pupils.

> Taking what vague recommendations I could get, I went out and arranged the matter. Then, as I was not sure whether I could conduct, never having tried, I took one lesson from dear old Carl Zerrahn, and was thereafter master of $20.00 a month.[4]

Arthur's efforts at composing were also producing results since a number of his piano pieces were to be published. After receiving help from MacDowell in the preparation process, he wanted to be sure everything was in proper order for publication. Accordingly, he wrote to MacDowell on April 5, 1895, asking several questions. It is enlightening to read Arthur's defensive comments written later on the envelope of MacDowell's reply:

> Written obviously during my very callow period. I had been after him so much on his "Sunday Mornings for American Composers" that I didn't want to go again just then, so I wrote him, not realizing what a lot of unnecessary questions I was pestering him with. He himself had picked out from some 17 or 18 early pieces, the 14 or so that I put in *Tone Pictures After Pastels in Prose*, and I wanted his further guidance in seeing the work through. We hung on his every word in those days.

MacDowell's letter explains the young composer's chagrin:

> I really cannot advise you as to a proper title. You must stand a little on your own two feet. An Italian-English Dictionary would be a good thing to consult as to translation of terms. I think in my songs, I retained the usual p & f, but have forgotten. As for where your dedication should be placed - do think it over yourself and decide. How on earth can I tell? I am sorry that I cannot help you by heading your subscription list. Reasons too numerous to mention. The opus number question is a matter again for your own judgment. If you seriously think 1 per cent of your earlier compositions are quite worthy of publication it is one thing - if not it seems to me that your first thing which you consider really worthy of that honor should be op.1. - All these questions of yours have to do with more or less mechanical details which I think you ought to be able to solve by this time - something like the sharps and flats, etc. etc. in the pieces. "Ritard" is "retard" in English, "crescendo" is "increase", - for Heaven's sake man use your thinker; and I am not an "intelligence Bureau". Working hard all day makes me savage you see. All of which is meant in a kindly spirit by
> Yours truly,
> E. MacDowell

By July 27, 1895, Arthur returned to St. Paul to spend some time with his parents. Mrs. Farwell was flattered that she had received her son's FIRST copy of his *Tone Pictures After Pastels in Prose*, previous to his arrival. Composition work alternated with social affairs as usual before he left for Boston again on October 17th. His brother, Sidney, left home by December to enter the employment of Thomas Mott Osborne in Auburn, New York.[5]

Arthur's journal, book VI, beginning June 5, 1896 reveals more of the heights and dark valleys of his love affairs and always his progress in composing. Grace (Gigi) Hall is the newest Boston girl friend and Arthur spends much spare time with her.

On June 9th, 1896, he describes an unusual experience with his music:

> A novel sensation this morning. They rehearsed two of my compositions on the promenade concert orchestra, with a view to putting them on the program. One was quite successful - the other doubtful and would need changing a little. In places they sounded so differently from my expectations that they were scarcely recognizable.

The next day Arthur told Gigi of his success with Max Wilhelm Zach, (1864-1921) the conductor, who agreed to play his scores on June 19th. "Zach gave me good encouragement as to my orchestration, - his only objection that these compositions were too short." So Arthur reported working on his scores to improve them. On June 16, he described their rehearsal:

> I had a strange feeling standing there in the Old Music Hall this morning and listening to a rehearsal of my scores. I thought of the nights I had stood there seven years ago listening to the symphony concerts and dreaming that the old hall should ring with my music some day - and here was a partial - a miniature fulfillment! How life has changed since then - how sad and glorious and beautiful. There seems nothing real but the ineffable.

By June 17th, Arthur had finished writing his *Intermezzo for Grand Orchestra* and he expressed hope in gaining a rehearsal of it with Zach and his Promenade orchestra. (He does not tell of such success nor is the work under this name to be found.)

The debut of this first orchestral work took place at the Promenade "Pop" concert on June 19, 1896. The orchestra performed his *The Round Under the Bell* (also named the *Sorcerer's Dance*) and *The Sage's Dance*. His party of ten included his mother, Aunt Lizzie, the Halls, John Marshall, Winslow Mallery and other friends. Arthur called it a "singular gathering - incongruous and yet fit". He reacted to the performance saying, "the rendering was all that could be desired", but complained that his pieces "followed a composition over which the audience had been ultra - enthusiastic, so mine was not applauded over-vigorously - but well!"

Farwell's journal is confusing here as there is no record elsewhere of either of these pieces listed for orchestra. Both of them were published originally in 1895 for piano. Perhaps these are the two pieces he refers to in his June 9th entry for which he probably prepared an orchestral version, now unaccounted for.

Mr. Trombler, an old musician friend from Wyoming, Minnesota, (near St. Paul), was in the audience and went over to congratulate Arthur. Mr. Trombler's presence was of special significance, because it was he who first encouraged Arthur to study music when Arthur was about nine years old. Bliss Carman, (1861-1929) the famous Canadian poet, was seated nearby and also moved to the Farwell table to offer his congratulations.

After the concert, Arthur noted that "Grace Hall was at her best but I was at my worst - tired - but" and he has crossed out the next two lines in his journal. He reveals his inner struggling by continuing as follows:

> I wonder daily how I can let myself become so fond of anyone after all that has happened. The very recollection [of Bertha?] makes me shudder with a sense of the same black - black pain that I bore so long. I will not think of it - it will kill me yet!

Arthur put aside his inner struggles long enough to conduct the little chorus at Thayer Academy four times on their Class Day program. He was introduced to members of the Senior class and prevailed upon to dance with them. He wrote, "I rose for the time to the height of their youthful enthusiasm and played the part of 'gallant' to the best of my ability."

Shortly after this, Arthur met his brother's employer, Mr. Thomas Mott Osborn, who invited him to spend the summer at the Osborne summer home on Lake Owasco in New York. Arthur discovered that in addition to being recognized as a good business man and a specialist in prison work, Mr. Osborne was also a gifted musician and skilled pianist who could sight-read almost any music. He also organized and conducted a symphony orchestra in

Auburn.    During this particular summer, Arthur found that
Osborne "played through with technical ease all the Beethoven
sonatas, one each day, in a reading which was the first he had
given them in many years."[6]

At Lake Owasco, in the placid beauty of his surroundings,
Arthur had productive days.   His journal for August 27, 1896,
reads:

> The summer has gone.! - and not a word have I
> written to remind me of this to myself - most momentous
> summer.  Mr. Osborne's summer home here on the lake
> (Lake Owasco) is a beautiful spot where I have had
> everything that could make me happy - except _____
> Nevertheless, I have been very happy most of the time   -
> and what time I was not, I have as usual - suffered the
> torture of the damned.   Also I have done much work -
> several songs - a *Capriccio* for piano, [music missing]
> begun some piano  works, scored on the *Virginia*, [*Death
> of Virginia*] and rewritten part of the *Wilderness* [missing
> also] and most important - have sketched out a suite for
> orchestra in seven movements several of which are
> finished - and one scored. [See catalogue.]   This was a
> "task" set me by Grace Hall in the Spring.
>
> Mr. Osborne has proved himself one of my strongest
> friends and is more able to help me than any one.   He
> has promised me an introduction to Damrosch and Seidl
> and may accomplish the performance of some of my
> orchestral works by them this winter.  Of more immediate
> importance he has secured me a scholarship of $250.00 -
> Originally intended to assist someone at Harvard, but not
> finding the right person this year, he gives me the amount.
> The scholarship was founded by Osborne himself.   This
> will enable me to live in decent quarters next winter with
> perhaps some kind of a studio.

On August 29,1896, Arthur's entry refers to a letter which he
received from Atha Haydock saying: "The company in Cincinnati
has made an assignment and we have lost nearly everything!"
Arthur realized that this would mean many changes for her whole

family. Atha would not be able to go to New York to continue
her art studies as planned and the beautiful house must be rented
to tenants. He philosophized:

> One can only hope that the reason such things come
> is that one NEEDS them. The fact that I am living in
> just the state brought about by such calamity (?) does not
> hurt me - although to a certain extent it must retard my
> progress. But I am in no wise sorry for myself - for like
> Atha, I "glory in the chance" of showing in time what I
> can do.

Arthur finally exchanged his idyllic days at Lake Owasco for
a new setting in Boston on St. Botolph Street. Soon he was
established in a little suite of two rooms - bedroom and study
with a piano moved in. "Quite regal for me", he wrote on
October 4th.

Later in October Arthur traveled to Auburn, New York, for
a hearing of his *Love Song* written for orchestra. It was accepted
for performance and included in rehearsals in New York City with
Anton Seidl conducting. Arthur tells the story of how he sneaked
into the hall and hid to hear his composition rehearsed. He was
afraid it would not come up to the conductor's expectations and
he dared not face Seidl if it displeased him. However, Arthur
found the rehearsal was "most satisfactory in every respect and far
exceeded my expectations". Afterwards, he came out of his hiding
place and introduced himself to Seidl, who was very cordial. *Love
Song* made its debut as *Andante from a New Suite* on October 17th
with Seidl conducting his "Metropolitan Permanent Orchestra from
New York" at Auburn. The performance went even better than
at rehearsal. "I talked with Seidl who gave me much
encouragement."

For the above occasion, Arthur was a guest at Mr. Osborne's
beautiful palatial home in Auburn, where he was also showered
with gifts by his generous host.

> Had it not been for him I could not have written the
> Suite - for he gave me opportunity for both the
> composing and performance. Had it not been for Gigi -

I would not even have conceived the Suite - for it was her
idea - so I am doubly grateful for my friends.

On October 29th Arthur expressed some of his feelings and
also described his Boston activities:

> I have spent many happy hours at '206' [Gigi's
> address]. The happiest hours of my life. - Unless perhaps
> those unconsciously happy ones  - before pain had any
> existence for me.  Perhaps now, I am building mountains
> of woe - but I refuse to believe it . Took Gigi last night
> to see 'The Benefit of the Doubt' at the Hollis, the first
> time in my twenty four years of life that I ever took
> anyone to the theatre...This morning - a long letter from
> Atha which shows her to have been, like myself,
> undergoing a humanizing process.  The wail of humanity
> has reached her soul - only recently - though I felt that
> long ago.  Still life is much more human to me now than
> formerly, and HEART is everything!  I sometimes wish
> my head were equal to my heart - but I fear it can never
> be in this world.

On November 7, 1896, Arthur described a symphony concert
he attended where Melba was soloist.  "Such singing - I had
almost forgotten what good singing was like".  He noted that he
has sent four songs to Mr. Osborne, who promised to send them
to Breitkoff - "who is more likely than not to return them with
thanks - which are more insulting than curses - coming from a
publisher."
     While waiting results from Mr. Osborne's efforts, Arthur
joined his mother in attending the opening of the Cambridge
Conference on Religion held on November 8th in Cambridge.
During this time, Mrs. Farwell and her sister, Lizzie, were winter
guests at the spacious Cambridge home of Mrs. Ole Bull, widow
of the famous violinist.[7]  Mrs. Farwell had become much involved
with the program of the Conference due partly to having met the
Swami Saradananda earlier.  Now a speaker at the Conference, the
Swami was also a guest at the Bull home.  Mrs. Farwell had
always been drawn to the study of religions and was much

attracted to the Swami and his teachings.[8]   Hence she arranged
for a meeting between him and Arthur, who also became
interested in the Swami's ideas.

At last a day for celebration!   On November 14th Arthur
received acceptance from Ditson for his *O Ships That Sail.*   He
noted in his journal, "Here beginneth the second lesson".   The
next day Arthur obtained his contract from Ditson as well as the
permission from Roberts Brothers to use the words of Mary F.
Robinson.   He also sent his score for *Love Song* to his friend,
Winslow Mallery, (now in Chicago) who hoped to get Theodore
Thomas to play it.

That evening he attended a lecture that much impressed him
on "Man and his relation to the solar system from the standpoint
of religion and metaphysics."   One notes here Arthur's strong and
growing interest in spiritual matters as well as a continued pursuit
of the study of outer space which began in childhood.   Other
remarks in his journal for that day recount the serious health
problems of Gigi's mother which also upset him.

For the next few weeks Arthur continued to divide his time
between composing and dates with Gigi Hall.   They attended the
opera and plays (thanks to some passes) and visited the art
galleries.   He was emotionally devastated when he learned that
Mrs. Hall had died suddenly.   On January 7, 1897, he wrote:

> To record the closing events of 1896, would be to
> record a tragedy such as I never passed through before -
> for  Mrs. Hall's death is a loss which those who knew her
> will never cease to feel - and I shall never pass beyond
> the beautiful influence of that short year's acquaintance.
> If she could be to me what she was in one short year,
> what must she have been to her life long friends!   I do
> not know that real suffering itself can be greater than
> seeing those one loves best suffering - and feeling the
> inability to console them. "If it were only oneself one
> could bear it," but when it is another - it seems impossible
> to bear for that one.   The events of the past months, the
> hopes and fears from day to day - would be terrible to
> record - nothing could cause me to forget them. . . Most
> of the year 1896 - has been most prosperous for me - at

least comparatively - and has brought the greatest happiness I have ever known.

For financial reasons, by February 22, Arthur had to give up his comfortable quarters in Boston. By invitation, he moved out to Cambridge where he joined his mother, still a guest at Mrs. Bull's. He appreciated the comforts of his new residence, but it was not as convenient as his former studio. Worse yet, he was upset about the job he had taken at a bookstore in Boston:

> I must give up my time for a paltry dollar a day and work like a slave over old books and magazines. I have been at it a week and 3 days and it is not agreeable. The evenings have compensated somewhat, for week before last I went to the opera every night - saw all the *Ring* and *Meistersinger* and *Fidelio* - and last week I went to see Richard Mansfield every night. He gave Gigi a pass for his entire two weeks and we made the most of it. Friday night (repetition of Beau Brummel) I went in late and Sat. I went to the Symphony. Therese Carreno played the Rubinstein *Concerto* MAGNIFICENTLY! Farewell to composing for awhile. Except for rare moments, I wish I had never been born. It seems as if I could never drag myself out of this mire of storm and doubt.

By early spring of 1897, Arthur was in a more cheerful frame of mind for he had been able to pay off a number of small debts and was enjoying Mrs. Bull's beautiful house. Then, too, he knew that he and his mother would be moving back to town about the first of April. One real drawback: his watch was at the pawnshop. (This was probably the fine watch he received on his 21st birthday from his father.) He resented his "attachment to worldly things". Thus early did he express his attitude toward material possessions - one that he later passed on to his own children.

Arthur gave some lessons at Back Bay in addition to working at the bookstore, but his mind was more on plans for future study. Mr. Osborne had offered to finance his study in Europe, an opportunity he should have welcomed. However, he had mixed feelings about accepting that generous offer. He states:

...I think I should like to spend a year in New York, earn my living there, and get a little foothold and standing to which I could return after going to Europe at some future time. To that end I have written a number of letters to N.Y. to see what there may be for me there. If in this country, I am quite determined to be there next winter.

Evidently Arthur's letters to New York were not productive. He finally accepted Mr. Osborne's munificent offer and they made plans to sail in July. Meanwhile, Arthur felt the need for a change from his hated job at the bookstore, so he resigned three weeks prior to sailing time. He wrote, "I made a flying trip to my old haunts in the mountains, gave vent to five month's pent-up feelings in a few songs, which, returning to Boston, I sold to grudging publishers for $5.00 each."[9]

# Chapter 4

## European Travel and Study (1897-1899)

Arthur Farwell wrote a series of articles he entitled "Wanderjahre of a Revolutionist" that ran weekly in *Musical America* from January 30, 1909 through July 3, 1909. In these he described how the certainty of a European journey - "the mere anticipation of a truce in the struggle with the wolf at the door - robbed the second year of 'Bohemia' somewhat of its authentic flavor." However, his trials at the bookstore over, and the brief respite in the mountains ended, he looked forward eagerly to his first ocean crossing and his travels in Europe with his benefactor, Thomas Mott Osborne.[1]

After landing at Plymouth on about July 10, 1897, the two travelers went on to London for a time of exploration. While there, Arthur wrote that he felt as if he were in the hand of a strange fate which took him from one place to another without his own volition. His journal for this period contains passages of soaring and youthful exuberance - a Mark Twain innocence encountering the wonders of Europe's culture with unbounded idealism, and a nascent artistic discernment. Everything was revelation! In London he wrote:

> I have spent hours in the National gallery before the Raphaels and Botticellis, and Rubens, and Velasquez and Turners! and felt the spirit of the paintings as it is impossible to do from reproductions. The marvelous preservation of color impressed me.

This feeling of the superiority of original art work was carried over to Arthur's attitude in later life when he insisted that no "canned" music could ever take the place of real live performance. One wonders what he would think of today's "high tech" recordings and electronic composing! Probably distaste, but with admiration for the scientific advancement.

He reacted strongly also to an opera performance and wrote on July 27, 1897, "Last night, *Tristan*! Heavens! I never heard such a performance and cried my eyes out in the last act. I had not been feeling well and am a wreck today."

When Arthur and Mr. Osborne left England for the continent, their summer travels included stops in Sweden, Denmark, Italy, Switzerland, and many cities in Germany.  Since Mr. Osborne was on business, he was often entertained and Arthur was included in these events.  Therefore, he witnessed many of the social customs of these countries, and also developed a more sophisticated palate than could be acquired in Boston or St. Paul.

On August 11th the travelers reached Bayreuth - the Mecca of their pilgrimage.  There, they were joined by Mr. Osborne's friend, Mr. Klipfel, a German captain of artillery, who was also a fine violinist.  After taking up quarters "in a wing of the old palace", the trio spent two weeks of "golden days", with "hausmusik", bicycling about the Bavarian roads, afternoons at the festival, and evenings sitting at the cafés.

After attending the opera at Bayreuth, Arthur declared, "There is nothing in the world, in any art, equal to this marvelous production of *Parsifal*....It is like a great and wonderful dream of Heaven."  Three days later Arthur saw *Das Rheingold* and admitted that the curtain was not up five minutes before he was in tears!...."I cannot imagine why, except that it was so wondrously beautiful," he wrote.  After seeing *Die Walküre* he described that as "another lifetime experience."  He expressed fears that he would begin to take all this good fortune as a matter of course.[2]

Along with hearing such great music, he notes in his journal for August 13, 1897, that he was inspired to write a new song. He also lists some of the distinguished guests he had seen at the festival: the Prince and Princess of Wales, Balfour, Arthur Sullivan, and a "crazy Frenchman who founded the Order of the Holy Grail".

Arthur had deferred making specific plans about study in Germany until he received further counsel from Anton Seidl, who was still in Bayreuth.  Seidl recommended Engelbert Humperdinck (Figure 17) as an excellent teacher, and Arthur arranged to meet him.  He describes that occasion on August 17, 1897:

> Humperdinck received me graciously.  He is not prepossessing with his significant nose and rather scrawny beard, but he has fine sparkling eyes and a splendid forehead.  I went back to him with some of my songs and

the Willow Point Capriccio....He talks no English, so I was
obliged to fall back on the little German I know.  I think
I shall like him very much....Two days later I met him on
the street and asked if he had looked at my music.
Indeed he had and I breathed again.   I had expected
torrents of scathing criticism.   He told the captain
(Klipfel) I had talent, and understood harmony.

After Humperdinck agreed to accept Arthur as a student in
the fall, the travelers went on from Bayreuth to Nuremberg, and
then to Vienna.  They visited the house and haunts of Beethoven
and Schubert which reminded Arthur vividly of his earliest
enthusiasms.  Eight years later in reminiscing about his early love
for these composers, Arthur stated:

> Even now, I was still accepting all those things
> naively, without historical comparisons.  Music was simply
> music to me.  I had not yet apprehended the truth that
> living music today cannot be produced by imitating even
> the greatest of the masters, but only by doing something
> as alive for our day as their music was for their day.  I did
> not appreciate what startling innovators, what inventors,
> what revolutionists, these early masters were in their time.
> They not only felt music, they THOUGHT it; thought
> their way out of the old into the new.  And the vigor of
> that flaming creative thought keeps their music alive
> today, as a mere falling back upon their natural musical
> feeling - their primal emotion - would never have done.
> These things were still unknown to me - I had not yet
> learned to think.[3]

After further sight-seeing in Venice, Verona, and Interlaken,
mountain climbing in Switzerland and then on to Paris, Arthur
and his benefactor returned to London.  Mr. Osborne concluded
his business efforts and sailed back to America.  Now making his
own arrangements for his music studies, Arthur was settled by
September 24th in the pension of Frau Berg in Boppard am
Rhine and that evening was a supper guest at the Humperdinck
estate.

*Figure 17.        Herr    Engelbert
Humperdinck, from a photo Farwell
published    in    Musical    America,
February 6, 1909.*

*Figure 18. Frau Humperdinck, from a
photo Farwell preserved throughout his
life.*

Frau Humperdinck (Figure 18) took him all through their
beautifully furnished three-story house, - the tower with its "Hänsel
and Gretel" wallpaper, and then through the extensive grounds so
well laid out with fruit and vegetable gardens. She also introduced
Arthur to their three children, as well as to the goat, the rabbits,
the doves, and their little dog, Loki, whom Herr Humperdinck
called "ein Feuerhund". Thus they welcomed Arthur into the
entire Humperdinck household, where he soon felt very much at
home. He describes that first evening in his journal, Book VI:

> I had to think hard at times to realize where and with
> whom I was, and even then it seemed as if I must be
> dreaming. Herr H. gave me a Humperdinck cigar which

is a veritable brand!  The box has pictures of Hänsel and
Gretel on the cover.  He himself smoked a long pipe
which reached nearly to the floor. . . .

Back in his room at the pension, Arthur considered the
names of other guests staying there which included the Countess
Rantzan.  He noted, "I am so used to countesses by this time -
that this one does not frighten me."

In a pencilled sketch Arthur wrote probably much later about
his experiences in Boppard, he describes himself and his own
feelings, putting them into a fictional character, Clement Harris:

Clement Harris was an incomparable specimen of that
rare bird, the American born under highly respectable and
commercial middle-west circumstances, but through some
freak of heredity or reincarnation, bringing with him a
remarkable genius for musical composition and a super-
idealistic nature.   Everything he saw appeared more
wonderful and rosehued to him than it would to others.
He was a phenomenon of heightened sensitiveness and
sensibilities.  All his geese were swans.  He was often
enough in love, but he did not "make love".  The girls
that held his fancy were all goddesses, whom he
worshipped from afar.  He sowed no wild oats.  What did
he need of such rank vegetation who lived in an eternal
bower of roses?  His moral reputation was spotless.

Harris had been "discovered" by a generous patron of
music in the East, who had sent him abroad to study
musical composition.  We find him sight-seeing and
sound-hearing about Europe, in a summer of the late
nineties, before getting down to his year's work in the fall.

It was at the Wagner festival in Bayreuth that he
chanced to fall in with Jim Torrance, an old music-loving
friend who had considerable experience of the ways and
byways of the continent, and especially, could distinguish
at long range the bouquet of the product of every vineyard
of the Mosel and the Rhine.  They were seated in one of
the most frequented cafés of the quaint Bavarian town,

keeping an eye out for the celebrities certain to put in an appearance from time to time.

Then the story used quotations of a conversation concerning where and with whom "Harris" planned to study composition. When "Harris" identified Humperdinck in Boppard, Torrance derided that small town as being even worse for town-gossips than any small mid-western town that "Harris" had ever experienced. He warned, "You can't live in Boppard three months without your reputation being punctured like a porous plaster, a thief, a bigamist, a Don Juan, a murderer. - Heaven knows what they might have you!"

"You're crazy", retorted Harris. "you may have set out to paint some of those towns red; but you know I'm a quiet sort o' cuss, and only interested in my music." Harris took no pride in his deserved reputation for virtue, but he understood it. In the first place, he couldn't imagine what anyone who lived so morally unimpeachable and studious a life as he, could possibly do to occasion such disaster, and in the second, he couldn't bring himself to believe anything so terrible of a sleepy little town on the castled Rhine.

"Well, wait and see", said Torrance. I'll bet you a prime dinner, with all the trimmings, the first time we meet afterwards, that within your first three months of it you'll be the hero of a first class Boppard scandal."

"Taken", replied Harris, mentally consuming the dinner in advance. Torrance did likewise and the men went on their ways.

The narrative continues with descriptions of the charm of Boppard and its surroundings. Then it went on:

After a month of getting acclimated to so quaint an environment, Harris was getting on swimmingly. He had found a pleasant room in a pension presided over by Frau Hügel, although she resembled a mountain more than a hill [a pun]. She was a veritable Brünhilde after middle life, with red hair and a laugh that exploded like a bomb and shook the foundations of Boppard, and a capacity for sudden rage equally gargantuan. It was difficult to know which was more terrible and frightening, her laughter or her rage, both were so dynamitic of attack. Frau Hügel was also the social apex and arbiter of Boppard.

Arthur does not provide an end to his story, but it does give the reader a picture of his self-image at Boppard, written in a delightful light style that may have been done "tongue-in-cheek". It also reveals Arthur's sense of good humor. (He probably won the bet with his old friend, Jim Torrance!) Now we continue with our own narrative of Arthur's composition studies.

When he took his first lesson from Herr Humperdinck a few days after getting settled, the two spent the entire time on *Death of Virginia*. He was "pretty blue" by the end of the hour and felt utterly discouraged as he exclaimed, "I have so much to learn". But his teacher replied "Yes, but you are already far." Herr Humperdinck found *Virginia* rather "bold and risky in modulation with not enough development of the themes, but had little to criticize in the orchestration." Arthur was encouraged and determined to rewrite the composition.[4]

By October 19, 1897, Arthur could report that he was making good progress with his lessons. (Figure 19) He had written several songs and Humperdinck declared, "You have a great talent for songs." These lessons were informal and Arthur went up to Villa Humperdinck whenever he had sufficient work to show him. They would spend several hours over it, and his teacher-host usually served coffee and cigars, and sometimes a glass of yellow Marsala.

On the evenings when Arthur was also a dinner guest, they would congregate after the meal in the study, where Humperdinck usually read, smoking his long pipe while Arthur played chess with Frau Humperdinck. "Which do you like best, chess or counterpoint?" Humperdinck would tease. Sometimes Frau Humperdinck would read a letter from Frau Wagner who reported news from Bayreuth. She usually sat in her special place which was a little seat in the window near the piano.

*Figure 19. Farwell in 1898 while studying with Humperdinck.*

One day Herr Humperdinck scowled when he studied Arthur's lesson using experimental chords. He growled, "Das geht nichts!" But then he took the music to the piano and played the offending chords. After a moment's pondering over them, Humperdinck now beamed, "Aber ja, das geht!" Arthur relaxed; his teacher had first only *looked* when he said the music "would not go", then he *played* it and changed his mind, saying "but yes, it *does* go!" Sometimes the sound understood by the eye is not as telling as the one heard aloud by the ear, as Humperdinck was reminded that lesson day.

In November 1897, Arthur developed an illness of the inner ear that required his going to Bonn for several weeks of treatment. The infection had attacked the auditory nerve so that he heard continually an uneven trill on e to f#. In Bonn, Arthur was also getting treatment for his knees and was pleased when he was allowed to walk two hours a day. While recuperating, Arthur declared that he had succeeded quite well with an obstinate passage in the first movement of his *Suite*. However, the loneliness as well as the pain from his illness, colored everything with "morbid gloom". No wonder he labeled this experience as the darkest spot of the year. "...My best friend in Bonn was Beethoven's statue from which I received more sympathy than from any of the people I met."[5]

When Arthur took the train for Boppard on December 24th, he was surprised to find Herr Humperdinck, also on board, homeward bound from a month's stay in St. Petersburg. Humperdinck was very sick with what later was diagnosed as an inflammation of the lungs and he groaned with every breath. So, Arthur was relieved once they both arrived safely in Boppard, where he later joined the Humperdinck family for Christmas festivities. He wrote in his journal that he was "so touched and surprised at receiving a gorgeous writing portfolio of pressed leather" from Mrs. Humperdinck. He added that he could never find anyone in Germany who would be so kind to him as the Humperdincks. He also related that Humperdinck refused to take any money for the lessons he had received all winter. Instead he told Arthur to save his money for study in Italy the following winter. Arthur adds, "I may remain next year and go South with him!"

In his January 2, 1898 journal entry, Arthur commented on the gifts Humperdinck received in St. Petersburg: "two laurel wreaths of silver, one from a prince, and the other from an admirer in the capitol. His success in London was also great."

Humperdinck was working at this time on the overture for his opera, *Koenigskinder*, and Arthur accompanied his teacher to Heidelberg where the composer conducted his overture at a concert of the Bach-Verein. Arthur related that he heard the concert from the Green Room. "When Frau Thode spoke of three songs by Liszt, which occurred on the program as 'drei Lieder von Grosspapa', I felt near to the royal family indeed."

For several days after the concert, they were royally entertained at Villa Beausejour by the charming Frau Daniela Thode, the daughter of Hans von Bulow.[6]

On February 4th, Humperdinck took Arthur to Frankfort. There, he met Frau Thode at the studio of Hans Thoma, the artist, where they saw his finished works, and some in progress. Arthur maintained a life-long enthusiasm for painting, probably due to such early encounters. Returning to Boppard the next evening, he continued his studies there until moving to Berlin on March 5th along with Humperdinck.

Humperdinck had to be in Berlin in preparation for the first performance of his *Koenigskinder*. He introduced Arthur to a group of his personal friends - two of whom were to play important parts in Arthur's future - Hans Pfitzner, and James Grun.

The first night in Berlin they attended a "Stammtisch", which may be explained as a regular gathering of kindred spirits with varied backgrounds, around a table in a café for fellowship. There were composers, publishers, (the "lion and the lamb lying down together"), actors, sculptors, bankers, elderly ladies, architects, and dignitaries of various kinds. Siegfried Wagner was there; Max Brockhaus, the publisher; Hans Pfitzner, the composer, and James Grun, the poet. Arthur wrote that the conversation was prolonged and brilliant, and when finally the "Kellner" went around the vast table, and each guest in turn paid his own reckoning, "I first realized the meaning of a 'Dutch treat'". He continued:[7]

The owls who outsat the rest were Pfitzner, Grun, and
myself.  Grun spoke English as well as German....He was
the intimate friend of Pfitzner, and as Humperdinck had
designated the latter as my musical mentor in Berlin, I fell
at once into a closer relation with them than with any
others whom I met.  I took a room near Pfitzner's abode.

Life now became very strenuous for the young composer -
physically, socially, and intellectually.  He claimed that he lived
three lives at once: social, as he wished to learn something of the
nature of German society; operatic, for he haunted the German
opera; and the life of serious study.  He had a nice room with a
balcony, with breakfast, at 27 marks a month, and the use of his
landlady's piano free for giving her little girl piano lessons.

Grun, who was Arthur's main point of contact in this new life,
was an unusual personality. (Figure 20)  He was about one-third
through with writing the poem of *Die Rose vom Liebesgarten* for
Pfitzner's opera and had given up his job in London to come to
Berlin to devote his full time to this colossal project.

Grun had been thrown homeless upon the world early in his
life but nevertheless had managed to secure an excellent English
education.  Arthur recognized that the grim and rugged reality of
Grun's experiences had given him "a profound sympathy and a
startling directness in his relations with others which took one by
storm."[8]   Although Grun seemed rather delicate physically, this
was in strange contrast to his volcanic mentality.  One would not
guess that he had done rough work in London.  An episode in
earlier years in Mainz had brought Grun and Pfitzner together.
These two men were "artistic complimentaries in a remarkable
degree".  Their meeting eventually produced *Der Arme Heinrich*,
lifting its composer out of oblivion and bringing better times.[9]

Grun had been a prodigious student of Wagner, and of
dramatic construction in general.  In the nocturnal wanderings
with Arthur, Grun outlined the scheme of *Die Rose*, the motive
of which had been suggested to him by a painting by Hans
Thoma, *The Guardian of the Garden of Love*.  Arthur wrote:

*Figure 20. James Grun, from a sketch by Hans Thoma.*

...my association with Grun was an intellectual and spiritual shaking up, such as I have never experienced before or since. Pleasant dreaming was over forever for me. Grun was a natural disturber. Wherever he went there was a row. He challenged every conventional or outworn idea, every musty tradition or custom, every suspicious or impeachable motive that arose within the range of his watchful consciousness. Woe to the unhappy wretch who presumed to go against him with a word or a deed that did not ring true.[10]

By March 11, 1898, Humperdinck was into his last rehearsal of the *Koeni kinder* and Arthur was invited to hear it. Humperdinck lent Arthur a full score which he studied profitably to write in his journal:

It makes me feel sad for the great public - they can
never come to the full realization of the beauty of such a
work, without knowing the SCORE!  From the first to
the last bars in "Idealization" a halo seems to be thrown
about the love of the fated *Koenigskinder*, and one must
be made of something harder than mortal flesh not to
shed tears more than once in the progress of the story.

### Grun, Pfitzner, and Guilmant

For the five months Arthur lived in Berlin he was in daily
contact with James Grun.  After their separate work days (Grun
on *Die Rose*, Arthur on his composition lessons) the two men met
at some café or went on one of their nocturnal wanderings when
time ceased to exist and dialogue continued long into the night.
Under Grun's friendly but sharply critical tutelage, Arthur
discovered that music quickly lost the static quality which it
heretofore had held for him and he began to realize what music
really is - a continuous, living development.  He recognized its
flux and change in accordance with the spirit of the time, and for
the first time he saw clearly the folly of attempting to duplicate
the style or manner of any composer of the past.  In addition to
guiding him to this new point of view, Grun introduced Arthur to
Walt Whitman, whose writings were to be so influential in
Arthur's later work.  Grun also shared his ideas about folk music
that were to become cornerstones in Arthur's mature thinking.

The first time that Arthur mentioned these prolonged
nocturnal rambles to Pfitzner, he was greatly distressed and exclaimed, "The very greatest favor, the one above others, that you
can do me is not to keep Grun out nights!"  Pfitzner expected a
certain number of pages each day of the nascent *Die Rose* from
Grun and was fearful of any delays[11].

This may have cut down the night walks, but did not prevent
their feasting in Grun's quarters on a basket of delicacies sent him
by Eugene d'Albert as an advance payment for his poem *Die
Kleine Seejungfrau*.

Pfitzner was present that evening and had *Tristan* on his
mind as some friend had presented him with a full orchestral
score.  He proceeded to play through the entire first act with an

intensity and passion that Arthur had seldom seen.   Though
Pfitzner sang throughout with a "composer's voice", it was "one
vastly expressive."

Arthur spoke further of Pfitzner thus:

> It is not to be supposed that Pfitzner was averse to
> the nocturnal life of the cafés.  But the noises of the day
> were such that most of his composition had to be done at
> night.   Besides, he was not a carefree student, or a
> vagabond poet, but a highly respectable citizen with a
> position in the Stern'schen Conservatorium.   When we
> could get him out, he was the brilliant star of the
> occasion, his thought as trenchant and flashing as the
> lightning strokes of his composition.[12]

When Grun finally completed the poem of *Die Rose vom
Liebesgarten*, there was a great rejoicing by the STAMMTISCH
of which Pfitzner was a member.   They sat a long time after
dinner sending messages of the good news to D'Albert, Brockhaus
and other friends throughout Germany.   But Arthur notes that it
was a longer time before the music was finished, and still longer
before the opera had its first performance in Prague.

Arthur discovered that studying with Pfitzner was a difficult
experience.   Opinionated and intensely absorbed in his own views
of musical art, it was not easy for him to exercise the patience
needed to sympathize with persons who were less trained
musically, or who held different views.   Arthur would no sooner
put out a "poor little shoot of composition than he would lop it
off here, or there, in a trice."   While Pfitzner's expressed reasons
for doing so proved of great value to Arthur later, they were
annihilatory at the time.[13]

After he discovered that it was an art to know how to study
with Pfitzner, Arthur made the following rule for doing it:

> First Principle:  Finish a work before showing it to
> him.  To disregard this principle is to fly in the face of
> Providence and nervous prostration.  When I once showed
> him a theme upon which I intended to write a set of
> variations, he sat back as if he had been struck in the

face. When he recovered from his astonishment and was able to speak, he exclaimed, "This theme is more complicated than you could dream of making the last variation!" Needless to say I did not come far with the variations. He was certainly right, and I was wrong - not to have first finished the variations. Pfitzner's nature, his heart, is kindly and simple as a child's; but his brain is a whirlwind full of lightning strokes. He is more full of surprises than Pandora's box.[14]

Arthur's days in Berlin came quickly to an end. He had to return to Boppard in the early summer of 1898. There he enjoyed a two-week visit at Villa Humperdinck, before going to England to spend the rest of the summer.

Arthur became ill as a result, it seems, of living too strenuously in Berlin. He was able to recover in Surrey, where he also studied Italian in preparation for his anticipated work with Humperdinck in Naples the coming winter. By fall, however, when Arthur arrived in Paris en route to join his teacher, he received word that circumstances prevented the Humperdincks from carrying out their plans. So Arthur had to change his study plans also and decided to remain in Paris for the winter.

He determined that a study of strict counterpoint seemed to be his chief need. Accordingly, he applied to Alexandre Guilmant, whom he considered the master of contrapuntal technic, and began his studies. Since he had only a limited knowledge of French, he resolved to fraternize with the English-speaking population of the Latin Quarter. There the second of his two early dreams came true; the first was student life in Germany, and now, here was the life of the "Quarter".

After the *Gemüthlichkeit* of Germany, Arthur felt very lonely in Paris. He found lodgings at the Hotel Foyot, and discovered a café on the Boulevard St. Germain which served German food. There he also made new friends and gradually became accustomed to the life of Paris. His studies continued uneventfully. Twice a week he crossed the river and presented his counterpoint exercises to the critical scrutiny of Guilmant. Sunday mornings he often went up to the organ loft of La Trinité and listened to Guilmant's magnificent improvisations upon the organ. Guilmant gave Arthur his calling card with a note thereon granting him admission to the loft area. Arthur describes those experiences:

> The choir and antiphonal organ across the spaces of the church would give the stanza of a hymn - perhaps the Spanish Hymn; and between each stanza Guilmant would improvise upon the theme, treating it each time in a different manner. First he would treat it in a lyrical, and again in a dramatic way; then he would modernize it, weaving into it the tints of the modern French school. But most remarkable of all were his contrapuntal improvisations. It is no great feat to let one chord fall into another, with occasional passing notes to heighten the musical interest. But to invent and carry forward simultaneously a number of involved contrapuntal parts, to lead them safely through the troubled waters of modulation and dissonance into the calm waters of consonant harmony, all the while keeping close to the theme - this is a different matter. To watch Guilmant do this, and do it with a composure and SANG FROID that was absolute, is a musical experience to remember[15]

The matter of Arthur's studies in Paris needs clarification. He never attended classes taught by Vincent d'Indy at the Schola Cantorum, as Alan Levy incorrectly states in his *Musical Nationalism*.[16] Arthur spoke highly of French composers, but Alexandre Guilmant was his only teacher in France. Letters in the writer's Farwell Collection between Arthur Farwell and Guilmant, indicate clearly that Arthur's lessons took place in Guilmant's studio in Paris and not at any school. At that time Guilmant was living in Meudon at 10, Chemin de la Station. He often made a special trip to his Paris studio at 62 rue de Clichy for Farwell's lessons.[17]

The Schola Cantorum is never mentioned in these letters or in Farwell's later writings, although Guilmant was a founder of the school along with d'Indy and Charles Bordes. In all her research, the author has not found a reference to d'Indy as being one of Farwell's teachers, and Farwell himself, never acknowledged this relationship with d'Indy or the Schola Cantorum. It seems that

Guilmant taught organ at the Schola Cantorum, but his calling card states "Organiste de la Trinité et de la Societe des Concerts" and below that, "Professeur au Conservatoire".[18]  A date on the back of one card reads "Dec. 1898".

Another error in Levy's book is a second reference to Arthur Farwell studying at the Schola Cantorum in the years between 1910 and 1925 where he states that "particularly Farwell, Mason and Porter, were interested in developing consciously American musical styles, usually through the use of indigenous American materials.  At the Schola Cantorum they could do so without fear of derision."[19]  It is true that Farwell was interested in the use of indigenous American materials, but he did not pursue this concern at the Schola Cantorum as Levy implies.  He returned to the United States from his European studies in 1899 and never returned to Paris.  The reader will learn what he was very busy doing in the United States during 1910 to 1925 as this narrative continues.

Arthur became acquainted with a group of young Australian painters who had quarters near the Boulevard Raspail.  He especially frequented the studio of Edwin C. Officer, the poetic quality of whose landscapes appealed to him.  Officer played the violin as an amateur and another painter friend, Pshotta, from the United states, played viola.  Pshotta had one of the largest studios in the Quarter where the acoustics for string playing were superb.  With Arthur playing first violin, these men soon found a cellist to make up a string quartet.  Meetings were on Thursday afternoons and combined rehearsal with a social time.  Thus was inaugurated one of the most pleasant institutions of Arthur's Paris days.

Toward the end of the Winter of 1899, Arthur received word of an opportunity to give a musical lecture at Cornell University.  There was to be a possibility also of giving a course of lectures later.  Arthur accepted the challenge and decided on his subject - Richard Wagner.  He felt best qualified to speak about Wagner since in his association with James Grun in Berlin, he had gone very deeply into Wagner's life, art-methods and theories.  Too, he had seen the best available productions of Wagner's operas and had even met Cosima and Siegfried Wagner.

The thought of giving such a lecture was very frightening to Arthur at first as he felt ignorant of platform procedure. So to accustom himself to the expression of Wagnerian principles, he brought up the subject AD NAUSEAM at every opportunity. When his friends finally rebelled and tabooed the topic, he gave the lecture every afternoon at four o'clock to the ducks in the Luxembourg garden![20]

As the time approached in May for Arthur to leave Europe, he evaluated his two years there. He felt that not only had he learned the technical musical skills which he had come to study, but also that he had gained much more first-hand knowledge not found in text books. These were those things that come only from "contact with persons of fine nature and of deeper and wider experience than one's self." Despite the joy of all his wonderful experiences, Arthur did not regret saying good-bye to life in Europe. He longed for "familiar faces, a familiar tongue, and familiar food".[21]

Soon he was in England and spent several days in London before sailing home. The last sight he remembered was the lonely figure of James Grun waving farewell from the wharf.

# Chapter 5

## Overview of 1900

Arthur Farwell returned from Europe in 1899 to launch his professional career as a composer in the United States. At the dawn of a new century, what conditions, attitudes and social concerns of the American people did he find?

Peace, Prosperity and Progress seemed to be the business of the United States at this time. Industry was singing, and happiness was expected along with prosperity. The Reverend Newell Dwight Hillis of Brooklyn declared: "Laws are becoming more just, rulers humane; music is becoming sweeter and books wiser".[1] Similar statements set the mood for the new century and this early decade was tagged as *The Cocksure Era*, *The Age of Optimism*, *The Age of Innocence* and *The World of Confidence*. In world affairs the United States had begun to be more internationally minded after its brief war with Spain in 1898. In commerce, it was also more involved with foreign trade.

Beginning with the economic recovery of 1897 from the "Panic of 1893", the colorful years leading to the first World War were a time of social and material achievement. Although the theme of social protest dominated current literature and politics, the historic American faith in progress remained steadfast. This pre-World War I generation did not believe that the abundant life in America depended on resources of virgin lands that were disappearing. They could not accept the fact that the ever-shifting, westward moving frontier line suddenly had nowhere left to go. They did not realize the truth of Frederick Jackson Turner's thesis that described the uniqueness of the American people whose "singularity had its genesis and its flowering in the existence of the frontier." Now that frontier was gone![2] Yet the people believed "There would always be new frontiers of opportunity as long as the road to advancement was kept free of corrupt men and monopolistic schemes."[3]

This simple faith in the American dream of unlimited opportunity and the inevitability of progress pervaded American thought almost as a fundamental belief, and Arthur Farwell grew up in it. Even President McKinley's address to the Congress at this time reflected the same refrain: "At the outgoing of the old and the incoming of the new century you begin the last session of the Fifty-sixth Congress with evidences on every hand of individual and national prosperity and with proof of the growing strength and increasing power for good of Republican institutions."[4]    Senator Albert J. Beveridge of Indiana was still more eloquent when he declared a social manifesto:

> God has marked the American people as His chosen nation to finally lead in the regeneration of the world. This is the divine mission of America, and it holds for us all the profit, all the glory, all the happiness possible to man. We are trustees of the world's progress, guardians of its righteous peace.[5]

But side by side with the popular success stories of the Horatio Alger and Rover Boy series, grew the middle-class fear that the mammoth enterprises of the Rockefellers and Carnegies might choke off competition for the aspiring small businessman. Many Americans thought that these monopolistic combines stifled individual enterprise, dictated prices, and squeezed the national economy. According to the census of 1900, the average American working man earned about $12.00 a week. The great majority of workmen lived a marginal existence, while the wealth of the nation was controlled by 20 per cent of the people. Yet the working people were fascinated by the society news which was often spread across the front pages of the New York City newspapers. While ordinary folk struggled, the wealthy partied.

Lavish parties were only a portion of the glittering display fostered by the wealthy. They also built replicas of royal French palaces or imported them piece by piece from Europe. Art collections were another way of demonstrating social prestige. Works of old masters decorated homes of industrial tycoons, along with shelves of first editions of rare books and bric-a-brac gathered from the Old World. Culture became "a badge of position rather than a means of enjoyment or enlightenment."[6]

This "badge of position" continued to dominate the attitude of the "nouveau riche" toward all cultural activities and strangled the efforts of many artists, musicians, and writers who actually sought to elevate the quality of American culture. (As we shall see, this was a condition which Farwell was to fight valiantly to improve.)

In contrast to the ostentatious display of society's "400", urban and rural America found other simpler ways of using their leisure time. Rural America profited by new inventions, but was still too burdened with farm work and lack of transportation to have much leisure. Rural folk continued to find joy in church picnics, the county fair, and the mail order catalogue!

It was the city dweller who profited most by the new improvements in living - the telephone, electric lights, the electric trolley car and the elevated railroads. Trolley companies developed amusement parks at the ends of their lines that were designed to attract customers especially on weekends. These were well patronized.

The men of this era joined such popular fraternal organizations as the Elks, the Freemasons, and the Moose. Since the women benefited increasingly from the improvements in living, they too had more leisure time and many participated in one or more of the many diverse cultural clubs that sprang up during these years. Americans also took time to read. "More important than Chautauquas, libraries, or even the public school in determining the cultural level of the adult masses, were the newspapers and magazines", declared Harold Faulkner.[7] Huge news-gathering agencies met public demand for better news coverage and printed material for every member of the family. Magazines were also influenced by large-scale advertising and the desire for mass appeal. Some soon drifted easily into the muckraking of the Theodore Roosevelt period as they exposed the tyrannies and crookedness of politicians and businessmen.

The theater of this time, while enjoying unusual prosperity, declined steadily in quality. The powerful theatrical syndicate of Klaw and Erlanger controlled the organization of theaters. Stock companies rooted in the creative traditions of the guild spirit faced extinction. What guild actors feared most was the effect on talent of the grinding, long, profit-making runs confining them to a single role for years.

Aristocratic social pressures dominated the musical scene in this era, especially in the field of imported grand opera which was the most popular musical activity of "Society" in 1901. Maurice Grau, as director of the Metropolitan Opera House, launched the epoch of "great casts". While he was indifferent to matters of scenery and costuming, he provided audiences with famous singers, but the public who filled the house showed little discrimination. They went primarily to see his famous stars, or to be seen -- as wealthy boxholders. Irving Sablowsky suggests that, at both the Metropolitan Opera House and Chicago's auditorium, "opera was a tenant rather than a homeowner. The sponsoring social lions provided a house in which they themselves could occupy the boxes, then leased the stage to a manager who produced an opera season as a commercial enterprise".[8]    The manager sometimes made a profit, but smaller ventures were not so fortunate.

Despite the society-appeal of the opera in New York, instrumental music, also almost entirely imported, fared better in reaching a wide national audience. Beginning with the founding of the Boston Symphony in 1881 and the St. Louis Symphony the same year, followed by the Pittsburgh Symphony in 1895, the Cincinnati Symphony in 1896, the Los Angeles Symphony in 1897, and the Philadelphia Symphony in 1900, other orchestras soon joined the ranks to provide concerts for an ever-growing audience. While financial support was apparent - though often slow - musical discrimination continued at a low level.    Symphony orchestras had to program music of more popular appeal in order to lure audiences to the concert halls.

The musical taste of Sunday afternoon audiences who attended Victor Herbert's orchestral programs in New York City is evident in the results of a poll taken in 1905. Audiences chose the following selections for his all-request program: Suppe's *Poet and Peasant Overture*, the *March* from Raff's *Lenore Symphony*, Rubinstein's *Melody in F*, Massenet's *Neapolitan Scenes* and selections from Victor Herbert's operettas. "Not a single symphony or classical overture was chosen, nor any work by Bach, Mozart, Haydn, Brahms or Wagner!"[9]

However, music festivals, so happily a part of the late nineteenth century, continued to draw attendance in the early twentieth. The Bach festival of Bethlehem, Pennsylvania, was born in 1900. Cincinnati created a permanent festival chorus in 1873 which lasted for 25 years, and other musical organizations were developed to carry on this work. The Litchfield County Choral Union of Norfolk, Connecticut, originated in 1902 as did the

Worcester festival in Massachusetts. In tracing the development of music festivals, Rose Yont wrote that she could go on indefinitely describing these festivals, "for they have sprung up as if by magic all over the country."[10]

While music festivals drew large crowds and vaudeville always attracted an audience, concert goers did continue to increase their patronage of formal concerts. The attraction, however, was mostly other than a love for great music. A performer's unusual profile or his strange stage behavior fascinated many, rather than listening to the music itself. "A great artist, concerned only with his art, and disinterested in exploiting either himself or his personal peculiarities was not likely to have great drawing power, even if he was a master of his field."[11]  In spite of the growth of these many musical activities suggesting an appreciation of music in America, it remained true in the early years of the 1900s that, as in the preceding decades, "Americans were still as innocent as children in their tastes.... The American public was ready to buy its music culture; but it was too timid, too uncertain of itself, to cultivate a culture of its own."[12]

Faulkner summarized this period in history by stating "Certainly nothing characterized the America of the first fifteen years of the present century more than a reforming zeal, a quest for social justice that would remake the old America."[13] However, while America was growing philosophically, economically, and politically, its cultural life had not yet caught up. The gain in per capita wealth meant more money available for music and luxuries, but as already indicated, those attending concerts acquired little musical taste or discrimination. To such a world Arthur Farwell returned to seek for the fulfillment of his artistic ideals.

# Chapter 6

## Professional Career Begins

When Arthur Farwell returned to the United States on the steamer *Menominee*, May 2, 1899, he brought with him not only new scores as a result of his studies, but also a matured outlook on his chosen profession. (Figure 21) His friend, Rudolph Gott, of college days, had opened his heart to the passion of music; but James Grun had opened his mind to new dimensions of the art of music. The intellectual and spiritual shakeup young Farwell had experienced, developed into a general maturing of his vision which shaped his future career.

As Farwell prepared to touch American shores again, he felt as if this were a sort of second birth. He had known his country prior to the European stay, but now he knew her "why and wherefores" and the knowledge came, he said, as "a draught of the elixir of life." He declared further:

> We know now the burden of old - world traditions
> which the mind and soul of humankind have thrown off
> that we may breathe the air of a freer, if newer and
> cruder land. One realizes instinctively that an American
> must be a different kind of being from all others, and that
> he needs his own institutions, his own ideas, his own
> arts.[1]

After enjoying a warm reception with his family and friends, young Farwell presented his Wagner lecture to students at Cornell. They proved happily to be a more receptive audience than the Luxembourg garden ducks in Paris. Then Farwell returned to Boston for the summer, to a discovery that would affect the subsequent course of his life, - "would drive him to distant corners of the land, and would involve him in endless wars and controversies."[2]

While searching American legendary lore for literary purposes, Farwell went down to Bartlett's old Cornhill bookshop. A clerk handed him a copy of Alice Fletcher's *Indian Story and Song* which he bought and began to study carefully. The legends brought back boyhood memories of his early vacations in Minnesota when he had lived briefly in an Indian Village on Lake Superior.

They also gave meaning to many recollections of things he had
seen there, but did not understand at the time. They also told
about the spiritual life of those Indians. This confirmed some of
Farwell's own inner life of the spirit that was moved by the
reverence shown in the Indian ceremonies and songs to the Great
Spirit. Oddly, the music itself seemed unimportant at that time.
Later, he had to reverse this judgment completely; it was the
Indian music he first ignored that became a pathway for Farwell's
mission leading to the establishment of the Wa-Wan Press,
opening a vast and major development of his musical career.

In what he found in the Fletcher study, the still unimportant
Indian music must have become the key to the creative
formulation going on in Farwell's mind as he began to seek a way
to express a spirit for America in music. For him, such a spirit
was generic to the natural setting of this continent, as his love for
it grew deeper with every exploration in his later cross-country
travels.

In the fall of 1899, Farwell settled in New York City. He
spent the winter teaching and going to Ithaca from time to time
to give lectures on music history at Cornell.

An important insight came that winter from something he
gleaned from the work of a painter. Certain of the remarkable
canvases he had seen in the studio of Arthur Bowen Davies (1862-
1928) produced an effect on him similar to much of Wagner's
music. Farwell decided:

> I finally arrived at the fact that, *whether or not* they
> represented actual scenes from mythology, these particular
> pictures were mythic in expression - expressive of a feeling
> of a race, transcending mere individual thought or mood.
> This led to a discussion of the technic of the matter, and
> finally to an understanding of some hitherto baffling
> points in Wagner's music, and his means of attaining at
> times a super-personal - in short, a mythical expression.
> By this knowledge I was able to profit much in subsequent
> work with Indian music, which took me into mythical
> fields.[3]

Figure 21. Arthur Farwell in August, 1899, just after his return to America from European music studies.

While Farwell was still living in New York, he agreed to do
some work for Frau Seidl. She engaged him to prepare the scores
of Anton Seidl's concert arrangements of Wagner's music from the
parts. Seidl never used scores for his performances as he had
them all memorized. Farwell had heard Seidl conduct the Wagner
arrangements several times. It was Daniela Thode in Heidelburg
who requested Frau Seidel to have these scores made. Farwell
reported that Frau Seidl engaged him to do the work without
knowing that he and Daniela were friends. He prepared these
manuscripts in "the old St. Denis Hotel, corner of 12th Street and
Broadway in 1900."

Farwell had been asked to give a more extended course of
lectures on music history at Cornell in the fall of 1900. To
prepare for these, he accepted the invitation from Thomas
Osborne, who had given him his study in Europe, to spend
another summer on the shores of Lake Owasco among the Finger
Lakes in New York state. He pitched a tent by the water's edge,
under a clump of enormous willows, and set up a table at the
doorway so he could sit and work looking out over the twelve
miles of water. With a canoe pulled up on the beach and a few
good books he felt "like the monarch of a rich domain". His study
concentrated on the five volumes of Ambros's *History of Music*
which he read in the original German.

In September, Farwell established himself in quarters in
Ithaca. There in his leisure hours he picked up Fletcher's book
of Indian songs again. This time, however, he did not play these
melodies on the piano with the provided harmonies as he had
done earlier. Instead he *sang* them as actual songs, taking great
pains to carry out the rhythms exactly as indicated. "Here was a
revelation," he declared later. Now the melodies took on new
meaning. Primitive as these songs were, each now appeared to
Farwell as a distinct and concentrated musical idea. While the
full force of the rhythmic idea did not become evident
immediately, the material itself took a strong grip on him and he
felt impelled to develop something out of it. Its magnetic appeal
grew from his accumulated knowledge of the background for these
primitive tunes as well as from the memories he carried from his
youthful life among the scenes of these legends. Without such

understanding, Farwell believed that he would not have found these tunes so meaningful. He explained:

> Here was congenial poetic material, the substance of art, in inexhaustible quantity, and the spur of melodies twin-born with it, to set it moving in a musical direction. Nothing was more natural than to take advantage of the situation. In fact the combination fairly called out for action of some kind.[4]

As an experimental beginning, Farwell gave some of the melodies from Fletcher's book the harmonic setting that their legendary or mythical significance seemed to require. His intention was to produce some experimental sketches for piano which used the native Indian melodies in a way that expressed the legendary and mythical subject also. These early experiments were made merely for the pleasure of making them. He stated that there was "no foreshadowing, even of the interminable discussion of 'American folksongs' and their relation to American music, that was to arise later."[5]

> I had no other aim than to produce something beautiful to the modern musical sense; even the thought of doing something different never entered my head. I knew vaguely of Dvořák's reference to Indian songs, and had heard MacDowell's *Indian Suite* years before. For the latter work, as music, I have always had the greatest admiration, but have never regarded it as particularly expressive of the Indians.[6]

Farwell and MacDowell developed opposing views on the use of Indian materials. Perhaps the reason that Farwell did not find the *Indian Suite* "particularly expressive of the Indians" was that MacDowell "absorbed and refashioned the material into a valid personal expression" in which the Indian themes lost much of their cultural characteristics.[7] Farwell retained the Indian themes so they were recognizable, and developed his scores around them.

After finishing a number of sketches based on the melodies and legends in Fletcher's book, Farwell wanted to try them out on an audience. Therefore he introduced two of them into one of his morning lectures at Cornell. They were received with such interest that he was asked to play them the same afternoon at the house of one of the professors for some special guests. Listeners there found the music both enjoyable and novel, so Farwell determined to test a broader audience. To this end he invited a group to Barnes Hall on campus one evening to hear all of the pieces he had prepared, together with an explanatory talk on the subject, touching upon some interesting phases of Indian mythology. This crude but successful affair was the basis of a more complete lecture-recital he developed two years later. It became the means by which he was able to travel coast-to-coast in an interesting and profitable way.

Farwell finally chose to leave Cornell University in the spring of 1901 when he became convinced that the university was "hopelessly behind the times". The faculty had refused his petition for expansion of the music history offerings in spite of the popularity of his classes. Farwell moved to Newton Center, Massachusetts, to join his parents who had reestablished a home there a year earlier after their many years in Minnesota.

He rented a small hall in Boston and began to present a course of lectures on the *Relation of Art to the People*, but attendance was low. Farwell thought he had a "fine stock of ultra-idealistic ideas" to unburden, but he was certain that none of his listeners understood what he was talking about, except for a young art student.

Farwell was rescued from his "world-converting" lecturing by receipt of a commission to write some music for a prospective book of school choruses. This took him to New York City to meet Frederick Manley, who was literary editor of the new books. (These became known as the *Laurel Song Books*.) Manley's task was to evaluate the commissioned composers and assign to them the poems most nearly fitted to their talents. He also needed to transact business with the composer, Edgar Stillman Kelley, at his Long Island hideout. He invited Farwell to join him on what became an eventful day-long excursion. As a result, a friendship developed between Manley and Farwell and instead of the two days which Farwell had expected to be in the city, he stayed there two months.

Those two months became memorable ones. First, because Farwell led an ideal life doing paid work in his chosen art, thus providing his living; and second, because he was meeting all the composers within a reasonable radius of Manhattan. Besides Edgar Stillman Kelley, these included Henry Hadley, Harvey Worthington Loomis, Maurice Arnold, Victor Louis Saar, Horatio Parker, David Stanley Smith, Henry Holden Huss, and others with whom he was in constant contact during this time. Writing nearly nine years later for *Musical America*, Farwell declared:

There was work for us all. These were Elysian days. We lived in the cafés, a congenial group of us, and lived well. Manley's poetic fervor stimulated us all to work. He himself wrote many of the poems which he dealt out to us, and we wrote the songs, in cafés, hotel corridors - any where, with the occasional help of any friendly piano which we could press into service. It was a joyous, creative life of companionship, artistic effort and emulation and freedom from care - a veritable little Renaissance. It was nothing less than a revelation to see how greatly our productiveness increased under these ideal conditions...One does not wonder that great art works have been produced by epochs when such conditions have prevailed for years throughout whole cities and nations. As the demand rises and persists, the spirit rises to meet it.[8]

By the time the little group of composers dispersed, Farwell felt he had seen that the creative musical impulse was awake in America and ready for advancement.

# Chapter 7

# The Wa-Wan Press Story

While Farwell was associated with the group of composers involved in preparing music for the Laurel Song Books, he took time to examine other compositions by his colleagues. These composers were mostly young men whose works were not yet well known. Based on what he had seen, Farwell decided to remain in New York City for the summer (1901) for three reasons: to determine further what was going on in musical composition in the United States, to learn what influences were at work on composition, and to ascertain what trends were noticeable.

After studying the scores of many young composers, Farwell determined that new directions in composition were indeed arising. No longer were German influences so strongly dominant. These new colleagues were progressive and sensitive to developments of newer trends in other countries, especially Russia and France. He described what he had discovered:

> The nature of these compositions was such as to make me feel that we were nationally, on the eve of a signal extension of the musical imagination, into fields hitherto untrod. I felt - taking it in the broadest possible sense, and excepting a number of strong individual creators whom the country had already produced - that the epoch of national assimilation was about to close and the epoch of output, of original creation, was to begin.[1]

These discoveries weighed heavily on Farwell's mind as he pondered over his own future direction. As fall approached, he felt pressed to find constructive steps ahead. He considered the matter from every point of view. Where could he find something that would meet his personal need and desire to compose, and also promote the promising work of his new colleagues? To him, the life of teaching seemed rarely to lead to any broad fulfillment or goal of life. He had never entertained any serious concert ambition as a performer on the violin or piano. He thought that there was just one thing, "the core, the very grail of life - and that was musical composition". Nothing seemed worth undertaking to him unless it aimed directly at its accomplishment and its advancement. The problem was to find a practical occupation that would lead to this ideal end.

As he considered the situation, Farwell remembered the German domination of music he had encountered in Europe. In its own essence he had accepted the notion of musical nationalism he found there. But now he realized that his future direction could not be as another importer of German culture and musical achievement. It had to be new, innovative, and his very own direction. With due respect to the music of the great German composers, he felt that American composers should not be tied to old European models. He began to perceive how much his elder colleagues in American composition were a product of the dominant German influence in their own works as manifested in traditional forms, harmonies, and subject matter. He recognized this influence was so strong and popular that American audiences and publishers rejected any serious music not sounding like its German-inspired counterpart.

Farwell was aware of Dvořák's earlier challenge to American composers to utilize native folk melodies, and he had begun to respond with the study and use of Indian melodies. In thinking about developments in France, Russia, Norway, Bohemia, and Spain, he observed that "the countries which were gaining a national individuality of their own . . . were doing so through their own folk music." Therefore Farwell was persuaded that the future possibilities of American art music ought to lie in her folk music. Yet first, he realized that America had to throw off the yoke of German influence which was clearly the main reason publisher's doors were closed to him and his colleagues. Gilbert Chase declared later in *American Music*,[2] "A revolt against this [German] domination was an absolute historical necessity". Farwell insisted that "such a state of affairs made it intolerable for a composer in this country." He wrote to Edward N. Waters, "I was just plain mad, and I vowed I would change the United States in this respect. I was just not willing to live in a country that would not accept my calling."[3]

To "change the United States": this audacious vow would seem an impossible goal, but Farwell was determined on some course of action. What germinated in his mind took form as a unique concept for the publication of the best serious compositions of Americans whose work he had seen. What now became the Wa-Wan Press was to be but the first step of a movement that was to help change the musical scene in America in the next ten years.

Innocently, Farwell set out on an unbeaten path, unaware of the many tribulations ahead. Had he forgotten the earlier warnings from Cheiro? Maybe. However, his stubborn determination became a visionary faith firmly grounded in a cause he had formulated after months of observation and deliberation. Now he would do what his mentors, William Blake and William Morris, had done with printing. He could produce his own rejected Indian pieces along with the best of the new progressive composers he had discovered. Now his keen intellect and organizational skills would create what was to become "an undertaking that is possibly without parallel in our nation's music history - certainly so with regard to idealism and self-sacrifice."[4]

Edward Waters commented on Farwell's position:[5]

> Apparently, however, he was never to experience complacency, and one of his strongest dissatisfactions came from learning of the non-existence of the American composer in the American social scheme. It was more than a source of dissatisfaction to him; it was a situation he considered a national shame, one that cried aloud for immediate remedy, and he prepared to give battle. *It is doubtful if any other musician in our history would or could have acted similarly, but Farwell was ever an energetic fighter for artistic positivism, **and in his eyes the absence of native composers was a national weakness, the result of national neglect.*** (Culbertson's emphasis)

### Wa-Wan Press Beginnings

In the Fall, Farwell went to Yale to discuss the matter with Edgar Stillman Kelley who was presiding as chairman of the music department there. He secured the manuscripts for two of Kelley's songs, *Israfel* and *Eldorado*. While these songs had been written ten years earlier, no publisher would take them during the first five of those ten years; during the second five years Kelley refused to let the publishers have them. Because Kelley was very interested in Farwell's printing plan, he gave him permission to publish the two songs. Farwell decided to make a start with those songs and a number of his own little sketches on Indian themes.

The Farwell home in Newton Center became, in late 1901, the office for the new press (Figure 22) with Farwell's father, George Farwell, as his only assistant in the initial work. He arranged for White - Smith Co. of Boston to do the music engraving and lithography and then engaged John Temperley, printer in Newton Center, to run off announcements and stationery. The typographic cover designs in their base form, were done by D. Berkeley Updike of the Merrymount Press, Boston. Updike was a printer renowned for his typographic excellence of design.

*Wa-Wan* was chosen as the name for the press because of Farwell's work with music of the Omaha Indians. It is the name of one of their great ceremonies and means "to sing to someone", - a meaning which Farwell deemed appropriate to the aims of the publication. He lived to regret this choice of name and remarked, "Had I foreseen at that time that such a name would mislead people as to the broadly American aims of my undertaking, I would probably have chosen otherwise."[6] He selected Walt Whitman's phrase, *I hear America singing*, for the Press' motto.

Without capital, the operation began with Farwell's efforts to build up a large subscription list. He rented a small office in New York City to facilitate this matter and spent the early winter commuting between there and Newton Center. His plan was to publish two books of music each quarter - one vocal and one instrumental - at a price of eight dollars a year. (The price was reduced to $6.00 the following year.) Subsequently, the music was published separately in sheet music form.

Figure 23 is a sample of the typographic cover design used for all the single issues. The chaste severity of its style contrasts with the usual flowery style of that time. Later Farwell wrote, "So far as I have been able to find out, we were the originators of the straight typographic design for music covers, thus ending the supremacy of the awful scroll-work stuff formerly prevalent. Many publishers took up our idea."[7]

*Figure 22. Home of the Wa-Wan Press at 3 Moreland Avenue, Newton Center, Massachusetts.*

The first announcement of the Wa-Wan Press was issued December 1, 1901 in a seven page, four by seven inches brochure. The cover stated simply: " The Wa-Wan Press, Newton Center, Massachusetts.    Established for the Periodical Publication of Contemporary American Compositions.    Edited by Arthur Farwell."    The inner pages summarized the philosophical motivation behind the Wa-Wan Press.

After stating the purpose for the Press, the brochure gave descriptions of the first new works to be published.    These included the two songs by Edgar Stillman Kelley previously mentioned, plus Farwell's *American Indian Melodies*.

Shortly after Farwell mailed announcements to potential subscribers, he tried to create an advisory board for the Press. He approached Chadwick, Arthur Foote, and Charles Martin Loeffler as well as others, but only Loeffler showed special interest so the board was never formed.  However, earlier in 1902, Farwell had met Henry Gilbert, a man "of militant musical originality" who

Figure 23. *An example of the typographic cover design for single issues of the Wa-Wan Press.*

was to become his strongest ally. Here it must be made clear that
Gilbert was not a "founder" of the Press with Farwell, as Alan
Levy states in his *Musical Nationalism*[8].    Farwell founded the
Press alone, and his only associate in the beginning of the Press
work was his father, George Farwell, who helped with some of the
business details.

Not long after the press began to produce, Gilbert brought
Farwell his manuscript of *Salammbo's Invocation* for consideration.
Farwell accepted it for publication together with a *Negro Episode*.
It was **after** this meeting that the two men became close friends.
Later, Gilbert's help proved to be invaluable, because this ardent
nationalist "felt strongly the need of the movement, and had the
time and will to work for it. . . . As a revolutionist, Gilbert fairly
outdid me,." wrote Farwell.    "He opposed on principle nearly
everything in the existing order of civilization.[9]

Without Gilbert's help it is doubtful that the Press could have
existed as long as it did.  Arthur Shepherd was another composer
friend whose assistance was invaluable.  He not only contributed
his compositions for publication, but also assisted in organizational
and other professional matters related to the Press venture.

### Numbering Plan for the Press Volumes

For five years the annual volumes of the Press appeared
quarterly.  Odd numbers were assigned to vocal works and even
numbers to instrumental pieces.  Vol. VI in 1907 was changed to
a monthly basis.    Twelve numbers were published, each one
containing an instrumental and a vocal selection.  Simultaneously
with this change was an attempt to start a *Wa-Wan Press Monthly*,
one magazine issue appearing with each music issue.    Farwell
designed the *Monthly* as a means of communication with the Wa-
Wan Society music clubs he organized to promote American music
nationally.  For some strange reason the *Monthly* was numbered
to match the music it accompanied, although the two items were
separate entities.  For example, the third music release for 1907
(Ide's *Lovers of the Wild* and Beach's *Rhapsody*) is labeled Vol. VI,
No. 43.    The "Vol. VI" correctly denotes the sixth year of the
publishing venture, with "43" referring to the forty-third musical
publication (but this is NOT the 43rd piece, as several pieces

would often appear in one number). Then the copy of the *Monthly* for March 1907, is also Vol. VI, No. 43! Evidently this was to make sure the magazine and music were associated together.

Chapter nine tells the story of the National Wa-Wan Society and its related *Bulletins*. When this Society was reorganized to become the national American Music Society in 1908, the *Wa-Wan Press Monthly* was replaced by the *Bulletin of the American Music Society*. This was intended to have an independent career, but only four issues were printed before it was discontinued.

## Criteria for Selecting Music

Farwell set up definite artistic criteria for evaluating works which were submitted for publication. The emphasis on quality of the music regardless of its commercial value was unusual for that time. He described these criteria thus:

> There were two major departments of our plan. One comprised all American work showing talent or progress along any of the paths of musical tradition. The other comprised all interesting or worthwhile work done with American folk material as a basis. Salability had nothing to do with the matter whatsoever. Of course we could not keep out occasional unimportant fillers, while we were working exclusively with a periodical series. We simply wanted to show that they were making progress, whatever their tendencies.[10]

Daniel Kingman finds Farwell's stress on quality and avoidance of commercialism important and significant for today:[11]

> Like William Morris before him, whose ideals partly inspired the enterprise, he completely eschewed commercialism, being likewise aware of the extent to which it could perpetuate and surround people's lives with shabbiness and mediocrity. For this reason, Farwell's work has special meaning for today.

### Farwell Letters to Help John Parsons Beach

Farwell and Gilbert were responsible for applying these criteria to compositions submitted for publication in the Wa-Wan Press. Farwell's correspondence with the budding composer and pianist, John Parsons Beach, reveals how he handled criticism of Beach's work and is probably indicative of how he dealt with the work of others. In a letter dated June 4, 1903, Farwell responded to John Beach with these encouraging words:

> "I hear America Singing"
> Dear Singer of Songs - I am glad to have your music and letters, both of which are expressive of good things...I am impressed with the beauty and force of your music, and am ready to prophecy an important place for you among our song writers - at least - if you continue a normal development.
> I have given the Sonnets but a hasty reading - but they do not convince me as completely as do the songs - though they are full of good moments. I want to go over them more carefully. It seems to me that you have the faculty - in a pronounced degree - of *expressing* - of saying what you set out to say, with fullness and simplicity. . . .

Several of Farwell's letters to John Beach have been preserved and the reader notes Farwell's habit of decorating his letters. He liked to put a quotation at the top of the first handwritten page, or embellish it with some simple design. This trait is observed in his letters written in later years also, and Farwell's son, Brice, declared that his father always was sensitive to the quality of his writing-paper and liked to have it monogrammed or decorated in some special way. An undated letter exemplifies these traits:

> To live, - work so that others may grow
>
> Dear Beach - I am happy to say that each day renews our admiration of your songs. Especially the shorter ones, which share distinction with the others, yet have a peculiar spontaneity of their own. Gilbert - with his exceptional

faculty of distinguishing the true from the false - is also genuinely impressed with the quality of these songs. He took special delight in the *Lilac* and *Ici bas*. The former as he pointed out, sets up a definite and unusual mood in the first two bars, and sustains it to the end.

In regard to the four shorter songs, - they contain in a striking degree the qualities for which we are searching, and we shall be glad to print them if you can give them to us without encumbrances on the poetry.... [Here follows the question of securing rights to use the text and the need for a sponsor]...I haven't the means at my command for this purpose - unfortunately...meanwhile - may your work advance with sureness and power.

Several years passed before Farwell sent the following undated letter to Beach. This one tells of the pressures Farwell experienced in his efforts to promote his cause, gives evidence of his own continuing composing, and comments on Beach's compositions.

I am not dead, though I have been in bed, living on morphine and opium, dead to this world. Wisdom tooth out with severe nervous attack following it, was part of the cause. I have been going through hell fire and damnation - but thank God I am beginning to see my way out - I think. How in the devil Destiny thinks up so many ways to make a man suffer, I don't see. Or, since I am not a fatalist, how we - men - can do it for ourselves, I cannot fathom. I wish I had that much genius in composition.

Of the compositions you sent, the prelude to the *Monologue* seems by far the most wonderful - it is a dream. *The Rhapsody* is doubtful as you suggest - but is a fine effort toward something you will undoubtedly attain eventually in a more convincing form perhaps. I need more perspective on it yet. The *Intermezzo* is charming - though not having the *rare fragrance* of your best work. The *Song* has sort of laid by - through all my labors and vicissitude, and I scarcely know it yet. The *Monologue*

should be completed - is it yet?  It convinces me of the
need of print.

I am coming into some influence in Boston - having
the complete control of the programs, subject to counsel
and discussion with several others - of a series of chamber
concerts to be inaugurated here under important auspices.

Have finished a new composition, *Symbolistic Study*,
No. 2  *Ici-bas* is winning friends...Gilbert has been on a
big jamboree in Washington. . .

As this letter shows, Farwell did take some time to compose,
in spite of the heavy demands of running the Wa-Wan Press.  The
combined help of his father and Henry Gilbert enabled Farwell to
undertake other initiatives vastly important, not only to the
survival of the Press, but also to his ceaseless campaign for the
American composer and his music.  Later we will examine his
series of lecture tours and his efforts to build societies across the
land that would nurture the life of American music among the
people.

While Farwell was in Seattle on one of his Western tours, he
wrote again to Beach to arrange to see him in Minneapolis en
route to Boston.  He was eager to hear Beach play some of his
piano compositions as well as to visit with him.

I am anxious to get back home again now and *think
it over*.  My life is in for some big changes I feel - after all
this broadening experience, - but just what, I don't know.

Two ideas concerning you, seem to stay with me - that
we should be more closely associated, and that your work
should be more widely known.  Long live the American
Renaissance!  If only Gilbert and you and I  could live
near together for a year so that more things would
develop through friction - we could move the United
States several inches along the map.

Write the *Carnival* - I can't think of one who could
do it better for piano.

Eventually Beach did move to Newton Center and lived in the
Farwell home where he composed and taught piano to aspiring

students. Before that took place, however, Beach experienced a difficult time with the blues for which Farwell offered this advice:

> "O while I live to be the ruler of life, not a slave,
> To meet life as a powerful conqueror."

Dear John,

The tone of your letters, which I am very glad to get, makes me feel that you are still a little shaky about the knees. Don't forget that you are facing a great, but unwieldy opportunity, and are facing it *alone*, at present, and will have to stand like a *pyramid*. If you are bound to advance, you will be struck at enough from without: - therefore, at least put yourself in a position where you cannot be struck also from within, by the *blues!* *Curse* them, literally, - and yourself for entertaining them, - and don't give them *two seconds* lodging in your mind, or you are lost. The world which your own pain opens up within you must become a panorama which you can look at impersonally, as Dante did at the chasms of Hell, which were nothing else than his own inner evil - and pain-worlds. The whole of evil can be transmuted by self-conquest, into a source of knowledge and poetry.

Why don't you write a pianoforte composition on some such program as this: -

> Darkness and gloom. Effort to rise into the light - thwarted by darkness and pain. Exhaustion; - dim and dream-like memories of early ideals of happiness and beauty. *Sudden* determined and lofty resolve. The upward struggle - Light and the regaining of *ideal - Life*.

There, by the time you've got that put into music, there won't be much left in you for *blues* to get hold of! And you'll have cleared yourself out for bigger things, - which will then suddenly put in their appearance.

In the *Autumn Song* and *A Woman's Last Word*, you began to objectify your own experiences; in the *Kings*, to objectify experience *and ideals*; - now, why don't you carry this out to its logical conclusions, and not express such of those ideals as some one else has suggested in a poem, but be, in conceiving the *form* of a composition, the *framer* of that experience and those ideals as they actually are within *you*, in their entirety, so far as you can see them. You will then be the wielder of an artistic power as large as your own spirit, will discover the key to that musical *form* that is essentially yours, and in coloring it will achieve a greater result than by coloring a form conceived by some one else.

This is the step from the lyrist to the *Poet*. - from the genius to the *Seer*.Of course the program I have given is *my* way of seeing it, i.e. the present situation; - you should objectify from your own point of view, - not mine or any one else's. Of course too, I don't mean that you should stop writing songs (heaven forbid!) but perhaps they will be incidental to a greater work, more wholly representative of you.

From one who is sometimes in the dark ### and sometimes in Hell ###, but who never gets blue ###

In his handwritten letters to Beach, Farwell always used an old fashioned pen and black ink, heavily underlining some words twice for emphasis. In his letters, one senses Farwell functioning as editor, counselor, teacher and friend. He wanted to help people, to give support especially to young composers and provide them with the results of his own experience. The fact that Farwell took time for this kind of personal letters, not once, but repeatedly, in spite of his busy Wa-Wan Press work, shows his keen interest in helping young promising composers.

## Folk Music and American Nationalism

During this period of writing personal letters to help young composers like John Beach, Farwell was also doing more serious thinking about the condition and future of American music. He remembered the impact of sights and sounds he experienced during his visit to the World's Columbian Exhibition in

September, 1893. There he had observed American pride in its inventiveness and industrial growth, as well as the ethnic exhibits that included Native Americans. Because so many Americans attended the Exhibition and similar fairs, these activities played a significant role in fostering the growth of American nationalism, of which Farwell was aware.[12]

Then came Dvořák's challenge to American composers to use black and Native American folk music in their compositions. Farwell was convinced that *now* conditions were ripe for the development of a true American music. He took the position that "to be entitled to the name of 'national art' or 'American music', it is not sufficient that the musical art-work should be produced in America, or by an American. It must have an American flavor. It must be recognizably American, as Russian music is Russian, or French music, French." He felt that it was precisely this point upon which "hangs today the fate...of a music which shall be broadly American." In further analyzing the situation, Farwell was concerned that it be looked at "through unbiased eyes". He expressed these ideas and more in his introduction for Volume 2, part I, September 1903, of the Wa-Wan Press:

> Since our national musical education, both public and private, is almost wholly German, we inevitably, and unwittingly, see everything through German glasses. . . The result of this today is that the German quality in music, dominating our whole musical life, has made it almost impossible for any other quality to gain recognition. . . . Therefore the first correction we must bring to our musical vision is to cease to see everything through German spectacles, however wonderful, however sublime those spectacles may be in themselves. This correction is to be effected by making the thorough acquaintance of Russian and French music of the present. Thus fortified, we will no longer fear that the composer is going to the dogs when he revels in a new and unusual combination of notes; that is, one which differs from the good old German tradition. We demand an impossibility of the American composer. We ask him not to shock us by

being unGerman, but at the same time to give us American music.

Among the elements that might be used to create recognizably American compositions, Farwell broadly suggested "notably ragtime, Negro songs, Indian songs, Cowboy songs, and of the utmost importance, new and daring expressions of our own composers, sound-speech previously unheard." He concluded:

> The promise of our national musical art lies in that work of our composers which is sufficiently unGerman; that is, in which the German idiom is not the dominant factor. It will cost American culture many pangs to learn this simple fact. The German masterpieces are unapproachable, especially from another land and race. All that we do toward imitating them must necessarily be weak and apologetic, bringing honor neither to German traditions nor to American music. It is only by exalting the common inspirations of American life that we can become great musically.

Gilbert Chase wrote that "These statements were subversive because they undermined the foundations of musical composition in the United States, upon which rested the work of our most eminent composers, from Paine and MacDowell to Chadwick and Parker."[13]

No wonder Newton Center became the "storm center" as Farwell and his supporters fought to break the fierce grip of the so-called "Official Voice" on American composers. Farwell criticized those works based on certain traditional models as tending to become dry, hard and pedantic. "Yet he never stooped to the narrow chauvinism and wholesale condemnation indulged in by the lesser minds."[14] Instead, he recognized the value of our European musical heritage, but felt that given true freedom of expression, the American composer's mind would respond to beauty from any source, however unofficial.

Farwell's "subversive challenge" for composers to pursue Dvořák's folk-music approach, faced formidable opposition. When the respected critic, William Foster Apthorp, reviewed the performance of Dvořák's *New World* Symphony for the conservative *Boston Evening Transcript* on January 1, 1894, he denounced the use of folk music and added:

> To our mind, the great bane of the present Slavic and Scandinavian schools is and has been the attempt to make civilized music by civilized methods out of essentially barbaric material. The result has in general been a mere apotheosis of ugliness, distorted forms, and barbarous expression.

Apthorp reacted similarly to hearing MacDowell's *Indian Suite* saying that "most barbarous tunes, of no-matter-what origin, have so much in common that it takes an expert to recognize anything very specific in their musical character"; so he thought the whole notion of an American music based on Negro or Indian melodies was fallacious.[15]

Here then, is the chauvinism Farwell was facing. And understanding it, we can perhaps forgive what seems to us now pedantic overstatement of his cry for freedom.

Dvorák published his ideas on *Music in America* in February 1895. Before the end of that same year, Reginald de Koven, (1859-1920), had challenged Dvořák's premise in an article on *Nationality in Music, and the American Composer.* This appeared in a massive and luxurious two-volume publication edited by Anton Seidl called *Music in the Modern World.*[16]

De Koven, composer of many operettas, held that the Indians were a dying race with no influence on this nation. The Negro melodies, he said, are "imported exotics," while the Creole melodies are equally not indigenous. He held that Dr. Dvorák was in error to cite them as a possible basis of a national school of music. De Koven was not alone.

Gustav Mahler, who was in America from 1890 to 1910, said "it seems to me that the popular music of America is not American at all, but... that...which the American negro, transplanted to American soil, has chosen to adopt.... They doubtless copied and varied the models of the white people to whose households they were attached." He held that the crude themes of the red-skinned aborigines were far from representative of the great American people. Mahler felt that some day the amalgamation of Teuton, Celt, Latin, Anglo-Saxon, Czech, Slav and Greek will be more advanced, and then America may look for results.[17]

Zoltan Roman[18] quotes Oscar Sonneck as feeling "compelled to deny that the American Indian supplies us with *American* folk-songs.... The folk-songs of the Indian are American folk-songs only in a geographical sense, just as the Indian is an American only in a geographical sense."

Frédéric Louis Ritter, in his seminal 1880 history of American music, would not even mention Indian songs. Although he praised the "songs of the colored race," he found black composers of art music wanting, and he disapproved of "cultural-musical crossover."[19]

Louis C. Elson dismissed American Indian music contemptuously in 1900 as being the "lower savage plane" and so without any direct influence.[20]

Dvořák actually was as sensitive as Mahler to the idea that in the commingling of all the ethnic components of America would be hidden the germs of the best music yet to come from this great country.

De Koven held further that the dominant race in America was Anglo-Saxon and that they were unmusical as a rule. "No great music," he declared, "has ever been written by people living under a republican form of government." He cited Switzerland for an example. Moreover, he pointed out that America was just beginning to develop a leisure class and, "as a *sui generis* democracy, is too young to have any tradition or precedent deep enough to build a great music." American composers must get their education from the background culture (the European establishment) and begin from there.[21]

That is exactly what Farwell had done. He was aware of such ideas and knew his battle ground. From the spirit we find in his statements, he clearly was saying - "Well, let's all try our best and see what we can do!" And that's quite American for a start.

In 1903 Farwell wrote *A Letter to American Composers* in which he addressed himself to "all composers who feel the pulse of new life that marks the beginning of an era in American music."[22] He refers to the movement as one which will lead to

"the untrammelled growth of a genuine Art of Music." He
explained his idea further:

> Such an art will not be a mere echo of other lands
> and times, but shall have a meaning vital for us, in our
> circumstances, here and now.  While it will take the
> worthier traditions of the past as its point of departure,
> it will derive its convincing qualities of color, form, and
> spirit from our nature-world and our humanity.... In fact,
> because of the distinctive qualities which are moulding
> themselves about us, American music, as its true nature
> develops, must necessarily have the utmost native
> distinction, however broad and all-embracing that
> distinction may be.

But in 1904 the popular view still was that all folklore was
"ephemeral and exotic", which prompted one writer to declare "the
commercial spirit of the age, and our conventional mode of
existence, have so far effaced original types of character and
romantic phases of life that the folk-song seems already a thing
of the past."[23]
By 1909, Farwell was still facing the existing struggle of using
folk music and its relationship to American nationalism.  In an
article for *The New Music Review*, for July of that year, entitled
*National Work vs. Nationalism*, he wrote:

> I am engaged in national work, work for the nation,
> in its development, and not in injecting "nationalism" into
> its music....  I see before me the ideal musical
> circumstances in which I should like to live in my own
> country, and I shall work to the end, to create those
> circumstances about me.  I am for *national work* in the
> cultivation of a creative musical art, and in the bringing
> about of better conditions for composers, - and not for
> *nationalism*.
> ...Folk-songs are worth while for their sake; they do
> not need their nationality to recommend them, - their
> intrinsic beauty is sufficient...I spend part of my time
> studying and developing them because they appeal to me

strongly and intimately; and to do this is not a propaganda for nationalism, but a part of the *national* work.

The entire matter of the folk-songs is now distinctly a side issue, a personal matter for each composer to work out for himself.... The battle that has been waged about them has served to call attention to their existence, and that is perhaps the greatest good that has come out of the matter. The composer is to settle this question in his private workshop.

### Supporters for the Press

Undaunted in the earlier years, however, by all such controversy, Farwell plunged ahead with his efforts to promote American music by means of the Wa-Wan Press and continued to use folk-songs in some of his own compositions. People rallied to his side. Lawrence Gilman was an eloquent spokesman for the cause as were many of the Wa-Wan composers. In his article "The New American Music" for the December 1904 issue of *The North American Review*, wherein Gilman also reviewed music in the earliest Wa-Wan Press volume, he stressed that the movement inspired by the Press was "in the way of liberation, an extension and enlargement of the expressive medium." He believed that the traditional restrictions on key relationships, harmonic consistency and melodic structure are now unhesitatingly "cast aside for free expression in an adventurous spirit".

A Russian reviewer's reaction to these early Wa-Wan Press publications is revealed in two documents in the author's Farwell collection. The editors of the *Journal of the St. Petersburg Society of Musical Assemblies* asked Mr. A. Davidoff to study the volumes they had acquired and to prepare a report for the Journal if he found them interesting. Davidoff's letter to Farwell, dated March 31, 1903, sheds light on a Russian's attitude toward American music and on Farwell's work in particular. He writes in part (translated from the French original):[24]

I must confess that in all the music from overseas that I have known up to the present time, I have found nothing to appeal to me. Consequently, I approached the study of your editions while already prejudiced. But I take a true pleasure in being obliged to change my opinion of American music, which is evidently too little known here. I can no longer content myself with a simple review of a few lines.

I will be happy to interest the musicians and Russian public in your music...Accept, Monsieur, my thanks...as well as expression of my most distinguished sentiments.

The second document is an English translation of the very lengthy report prepared by Davidoff. Dated July, August, September 1903, this includes the following observations:

I have before me certain books of music ...magnificently produced. They...belong to the series of the Wa-Wan Press, at the head of which stands Arthur Farwell...whose object is to create a national musical art in America. Young musical Radicals are grouped around him, declaring war against the Conservative school brought up on German music.

Davidoff proceeds to refer enthusiastically to the essays written by Farwell, and he presents his opinion of the culture of his time. These statements seem to summarize the Russian point of view:

We are used to consider Americans an unmusical people and it would be impossible to say whether they will ever create anything like the Symphonies of Beethoven, and the operas of Wagner and Glinka. Yet the music I see before me has overturned forever our attitude towards their musical creation.

Servants of music, let us all join together. Whatever degree of glory should be decreed to us in after years of history, let us join in unanimous work, and shake hands with our Transatlantic brethren, answering the appeal of the Wa-Wan Press. Art has but one fatherland and this fatherland is the world...And once more I greet the Wa-Wan Press, wishing it all possible success.

Obviously, Farwell's publications had found a warm reception in far-off Russia, and he must have been encouraged by such recognition. (Remember Cheiro's prediction that the effect of his work would be felt in foreign countries?)

Farwell evidently also sent promotional copies of his first Press issues to the French composer, Reynaldo Hahn, whom he may have met in Paris. Hahn reviewed them and responded in French with typical native politeness expressing his congratulations for the excellent work. A rough translation of his hand-written letter adds:

> You have good reason to encourage a renewed music in your free and proud country. In that branch of art, the Anglo-Saxons have until now been inferior to other people and that without any other reason seems due to a lack of vigorous impulse.
>
> You have been well-inspired personally, sir, in drawing actively on the old Indian chants, so relishable and so poetique, a source of ideas and of musical riches, and permit me in passing to say to you how I have found your harmonies happily chosen and just right as to character and as to feeling.

Hahn was referring to Farwell's *American Indian Melodies* which were published in this first issue. Hahn's letter went on to give his reactions to the music of other composers represented in the early volumes:

> Mr. Harvey Worthington Loomis, whose talent I enjoy particularly, was not unknown to me.... He is a poet and at the same time a clever and solid artist whose writing is remarkably pure. He is rare to be equally gifted with imagination and with surety in technical judgment .
>
> Mr. Arthur Reginald Little, by the elegance and the simplicity of his form remind me a little of our dear and regretted Benjamin Godard [1849-1895], whose best works

you probably do not know! As to Mr. Henry Gilbert, you have in him a solid pioneer: I sense in him, across his music, energy and a love of sharp colors, he is a painter whose genre offers a sensible contrast with that of Mr. Stillman Kelley, all literary and intellectual, with, however, an exceptional melodic tone; the front to last pages of *Israfel* is absolutely delicious in its clarity, singing and caressing....Now I have said enough, I think to prove to you that it is with my very sympathetic attention that I have read all that you have done me the honor to send me. I will always be very happy to praise to others the merits of the young phalanx that you lead to the way of glory.

For more than a decade, Farwell led his "young phalanx" of composers while the Wa-Wan Press issued new American music by thirty-seven composers, nine of them women. (Let women composers note well!) Both Farwell and the Press enterprise had adventurous encounters during this idealistic mission. However, once underway, Farwell began further initiatives in related, but new directions, towards his ultimate goal. These took him finally beyond Wa-Wan and out of publishing for another quarter of a century. These activities were a development of the "Grand Design" of the Wa-Wan movement that began with the Press and spread nationwide to the founding of new organizations for promoting American music. So fruitful and productive were these new ventures that they require separate consideration, even though he kept Wa-Wan going throughout their demanding efforts.

Ultimately, because he was based increasingly in New York City, Farwell found his commuting to Newton Center for Wa-Wan work becoming more and more difficult. So in 1912, he turned the Wa-Wan catalog and stock over to G. Schirmer "on a pure royalty basis". He spoke modestly when he wrote, "This is a pretty long record for an idealistic enterprise of its kind."

Lawrence Gilman was more complimentary when he extolled the Wa-Wan Press as "probably the most determined, courageous, and enlightened endeavor to assist the cause of American music that has ever been made."[25] In commenting on the quality of the music issued, Gilman declared:

Let there be no misconception in the matter: this
music professes, through its appreciators, no virtue merely
for being of American origin: they are not of those who
in the caustic phrase of Mr. Philip Hale, would "cover
mediocrity with a cloak of patriotism". The music which
Mr. Farwell presents to our attention is, as it happens,
American, and it is abundantly characteristic; but, first and
above all, it is excellent and moving art.

### Press Evaluations in 1932 and 1935

Farwell reminisced about Wa-Wan Press days when he
answered a series of questions put to him in a letter by Juliet
Danziger who sought information about the Press and especially
his Indian works, for an impending magazine article.[26]
In his reply to Danziger on September 29, 1932, Farwell
emphasized that:

the Press was based on all progressive works, ...and
that the primitive American music element was only one
factor. An examination of the files will show that only
a small proportion of the output was devoted to this
aspect. My contention from the beginning was that Indian
music was merely one of many factors capable of
development in America, as my writings of the time will
show, and it is others who attributed to me the idea of
Indian music being the foundation of American music. .
. But it was talked out of all proportion. . . and not
enough was said about other types of work appearing in
the Press by Gilbert, Kelley, Oldberg, etc.

Farwell wrote of his financial struggles with the Press venture,
but added that there was also a brighter side:

...and so we got along: it was mostly hand to mouth the
whole way.... The Wa-Wan Press (Figure 24) never paid
us anything except as we could draw upon it a little. I
called it "my wife", as I had mostly to support it which I

*Figure 24. Chief Eagle Plume examines Indian music from the Wa-Wan Press with Farwell.*

did with my lectures.

...as to its "measure of success", I found such a vital interest in it everywhere, that alone constituted the success I sought - - it was winning its point, of commanding attention to American composers, that was all I cared for. I would never have gone on all those years if I had not found myself in a highly vital current in it all. When we began, the national attitude was "We haven't any American composers"

and when we left off the general question was, "Who are
the best composers?"   With that I was satisfied. ...While
I would not claim that this change was wholly due to the
Wa-Wan Press, I do believe that with our ceaseless
stirring up of the national question it was the major factor
in this change.

The reaction to the enterprise was vital and active
everywhere. The reception I got all over the country on
the basis of it was wonderful, and those years of glorious
adventure and effort I look back to as the most glowing
and inspiring of my life.   I have two huge volumes of
press clippings which I sent back from my travels which
will easily attest the vigor with which these ideas were
taken hold of.

In replying to the question of his own ideas regarding
enterprises of this sort, Farwell answered Danziger thus:

I regard such adventures in artistic progress as one of
the finest uses to which life can be put, second only to
the act of artistic creation itself.  It is moreover, a form
of creation, for it creates new conditions in the nation or
the world in the sphere of the arts.   Discouragements
must be as nothing to those who engage in such ventures.
...It is extremely interesting to me to see the Wa-Wan
Press, which I inaugurated with such naivete, is continually
more and more spoken of in histories.

Also related to his Press work is a letter in the author's
Farwell Collection replying to Quaintance Eaton who was seeking
information about Farwell's Indian work for a magazine article she
was preparing.[27]  His letter, dated June 12, 1935, gives new insight
(which Eaton ignored) into certain aspects of that work.   He
wrote in part:

There have been some misconceptions concerning my
work and ideas which have dragged out an interminable
existence, and I am hoping that you will be so good as to
be sure that your article does not perpetuate them.

Perhaps the chief one is that I am supposed to have held earlier that Indian music is or should be the basis of American music. I have never given out such an idea.... Another is that I am sort of a follower of my good friend, Charlie Cadman. I had been composing Indian music, playing it and lecturing on it two years at Cornell (1899-1900), and publishing it several years before Cadman began sending me his compositions, and those were not Indian music at all. I advised him to tackle the Indian music or other American folk music sometime about 1902 to 1904. This is what started him on it.

One point has never been brought forward plainly; I mention it only as it might be of use to you, but I am not making any point of your using it if it doesn't serve you. This is that I am the first composer in America to take up Dvořák's challenge (1903) in a serious and whole-hearted way and make a dead set on developing the musical folk sources of this country. In a way Dvorak's challenge brought forth a response in the Wa-Wan Press. (MacDowell's use of Indian themes was of course only sporadic, one or two essays in the matter.) What I told above about Cadman's beginnings is of course not to be published. That is, not unless it should come from Cadman himself. I give you the facts merely so that no error in dates or chronology will slip into your article in this respect.

Obviously the Indian question was still haunting Farwell and he hoped Eaton's article would put that matter to rest.

The value of pioneering in altruistic publishing was demonstrated in the republication by Arno Press of the entire Wa - Wan Press issues in five handsome volumes in 1970 under the editing initiative of Vera Brodsky Lawrence. Only a sense of its historic significance could have motivated the undertaking of such a project. The definitive introductory essay by Gilbert Chase recalls Farwell's spirited artistic patriotism and makes generous assessment of his unselfish labors.

Much earlier, in 1911, George Foster Peabody also recognized the pioneering value of the Press when he sent Farwell the twelve notes totaling $1200, each marked "Cancelled". Peabody had sent $100.000 a month for a year in the early struggle, but this represented the only outside money Farwell had borrowed. The Press never had sufficient funds to repay that debt, and as of February 16, 1911, it was erased.

Of course the Farwell family had made personal sacrifices all during those eleven years. Sidney resented the assistance which his parents had given his brother in those financially difficult times because he needed money personally too. Sidney was left with the problem of helping to support his parents, a situation which tended to make him bitter about his brother's activities.

Present writers have had more to say about Farwell's work. In summing up his views on the Wa-Wan Press endeavor, Daniel Kingman declared:[28]

> It was more than just a publishing venture; it was the embodiment of an ideal - an ideal held with tenacity and vision by one man above all in his time. Arthur Farwell sounded for American music the same note that Emerson, two generations earlier, had sounded for American literature: first, find your own voice, cultivate your own field; second, do not divorce art from life.
>
> It should not disillusion us to realize that the actual music published by the Wa-Wan Press, including that of Farwell, is in general less impressive than Farwell's optimistic and inspiring pronouncements. His ideals *were* in time fulfilled, but it took another generation. The age and the people that perceived the need were not capable, at the same time, of substantially filling that need. Like Moses, they could show the way prophetically to the promised land, but they were not destined (or equipped) to enter it.

The recognition Farwell was gaining in American musical circles during the years with his Wa-Wan venture, led him into new avenues in his tireless endeavors for the American composer and American music. Some of these must now be examined.

# Chapter 8

## "Westward Ho!" (1903-1907)

Even in the early years of the Wa-Wan Press, Farwell was inspired to embark on new ventures. Some were extracurricular, but others profoundly affected Farwell's fortunes and his Wa-Wan Press.

In the fall of 1902, for instance, he and Henry Gilbert organized a *Stammtisch* (designed after the fashion of his experiences in Germany) which met on Saturday nights in a Boston café. Among the members were John Marshall - then music chairman at Boston University; Alfred de Voto; Felix Fox; Arthur Hadley, 'cellist and brother of Henry Hadley, the composer; Alvah G. Salmon, alias "Uncle Rimsky", because of his Russian affiliations; and Percy Atherton. Architecture, romance languages, and other professions were represented as well as music. The weekly meetings were a pleasant source of relaxation and exchange of views that gave them all fresh inspiration to battle the creative and intellectual challenges of the coming week.

After a very busy winter, a consuming *Wanderlust* hit Farwell in the spring of 1903. He felt that he had valid reasons for wanting to travel to the unseen West far beyond his native Minnesota. First, he was eager to gain first-hand knowledge of the musical conditions of the whole country, to investigate the trends and learn what future promises of national development existed. Secondly, he had by now completed a number of compositions based on Indian themes and was anxious to test them on a large variety of audiences. Thirdly, he yearned to get out into the Indian country and *hear the Indians sing*. Beyond all this, he now had a means of making the journey - namely , the Indian music. He had discovered that recitals of his Indian compositions, accompanied by explanations of related Indian myths and legends, were a saleable commodity. Furthermore, now Henry Gilbert was available and could be depended upon to handle the Press in his absence.

### First Western Trip, 1903

Accordingly, Farwell spent much of the summer of 1903 in bombarding the West with letters announcing a lecture-recital, *Music and Myth of the American Indians.* (See figure 25 for brochure cover.) The response was "prompt and vigorous" so by fall he had arranged a series of engagements taking him from Boston to San Francisco.

Starting in September, Farwell visited first the haunts of his old home in Minnesota. The majestic stretches of nature had always appealed to his sensitivity to beauty and now, standing on a high bluff overlooking the Mississippi River, he exclaimed, "What scenes these are to make one breathe deep - to invite the soul to expand and rejoice! What great unwritten music lingers about these dreaming lands!"[1]

In Chicago, Farwell met Louis Campbell-Tipton and discovered his *Sonata Heroic* which he promptly sent back to the Press for publication. In St. Louis, Farwell stayed with Ernest R. Kroeger whose work he also admired. Other stops included Kansas City, Denver, Albuquerque, and the nearby pueblo of Isleta where he first heard the native Indians sing some of their songs informally. Then "wide-eyed", he went on to see the Grand Canyon, describing it as "an incredible other-world, ...the indescribable - the ineffable". On Christmas morning, he set up a station on a remote spot of the rim where he built a fire to melt the surrounding snow and to keep himself warm. Later he wrote, "All day long, until nightfall, I sat there watching the lights and shadows play and change over the strange distances and depths of this wonderworld, and heard the unwritten symphonies of the ages past and the ages to come."[2] These impressions stored in Farwell's heart and mind, were to serve him well in writing future compositions.

Farwell spent a week at the Canyon going on horseback along the rim, or on muleback, or afoot threading down into its "Dantesque depths". Only the anticipation of California's beauty could lure him away from such stirring local colors. After traveling thus from coast-to-coast, experiencing the great contrasts of our land, Farwell was deeply impressed with the grandeur of this country. He wrote later:[3]

And greater than this is the thought that comes to one of the race of men and women inhabiting and increasing in this land, and weaving out a racial and national destiny - to what end who knows! Pioneers have conquered the soil and captains of industry have established a material civilization. It is unthinkable that upon this magnificent foundation there should not arise from these inspiring scenes and these active, curious throngs a development of the arts, of painting, music, literature, drama representative of the realities of American life and the ideals of our nation as they take shape.

It is leaders that we need - persons of initiative, who see that this vast national material, people and art-media alike is plastic, mouldable - persons who have the vision, the will and the courage to create new and definite shapes, whether in the forms and methods of our civilization or the forms and methods of our art. We need the spirit which impels us to act, and to act at once, and should be forever discontented with a spirit which waits for others to act.

Clearly, Farwell was himself a man who took initiative and active risks for his ideals. His lecture tour not only led him to meet more of the country's composers, but also led into further adventures in the development of his vision.

In January 1904 when Farwell gave his first lecture-recital in Los Angeles, he was honored by the presence of the distinguished authority on Indians of the Southwest, Charles F. Lummis[4], who subsequently invited Farwell to be his house guest. There, in an unusual massive dwelling which Mr. Lummis himself had designed and hand-built with stone in modified Spanish style, Farwell experienced native music, food, and what seemed to be revealed as the very heart of the Spanish life of the old Southwest itself. Farwell reported that he not only heard many of these native songs, he "swam in the musical atmosphere of them - the suave or vivacious songs of the Spanish settlers and the weird, somber, and mysterious songs of the dwellers of the desert."[5]

On January 17, 1904, Farwell signed the now-famous Lummis "House Book" by writing the opening phrase for his harmonized score of *The Old Man's Love Song*. Below the music he added, "With the Dawn I Seek Thee" (words from that song) and "Comerado, I give you my hand." This first visit to the Lummis home was followed by others. For another entry on December 11, 1919, Farwell wrote: "After fifteen years, I found much (including the constancy of the warm friendship of C. F. L.) - but am still seeking." The music notation this time was a treble clef melody in the key of E flat with the words "Up with the break of day, Out in the trackless way." The key thought in the two entries was "seeking". The friendship with Lummis, begun in 1904, continued over the years as they worked together in preparing the *Spanish Songs of Old California*, published in 1923.[6]

Before Farwell left Los Angeles, he met the noted singer and choral director, Harry Barnhart, who later was to become a close friend and vital part of Farwell's community music activities. Hence, when Farwell continued on his scheduled journey, he took with him not only very vivid impressions of this colorful folk music of the Southwest, but also memories of people he had met who were to be helpful in his future career.

Going on to the San Francisco area, Arthur Farwell met the composers William J. McCoy, H.G. Stewart, Edward Schneider, and Joseph Redding. These men had contributed their talents to the building up of the great midsummer *High Jinks* of the Bohemian Club that was held on the Russian River in their grove of giant redwoods.[7] The *High Jinks* Farwell witnessed here was a music drama that was to be the inspiration later for his growing mission of bringing music and the people actively together.

Before leaving San Francisco, he met another composer, Carlos Troyer, whose work based on Zuni Indian tunes was sent back to Newton Center for publication, along with some pieces written by McCoy and Schneider.

Other rewarding contacts included the morning spent in the studio of William Keith, a painter who specialized in scenes of the Sierras, and a time with another artist, Maynard Dixon, whose scenes of Indian and cowboy life impressed Farwell.

More western stops also included visits with outstanding local artists. In Portland, Farwell was pleased to view a Mr. Ladd's "magnificent collection of Barbizon paintings", in addition to meeting many local musicians. In Seattle, Farwell met a Mr. Curtis whose life-work had been spent in making a series of photographs of the Indians of North America. Farwell recognized the significance of this ethnological endeavor and was equally impressed by the remarkable collection of Alaskan objects he viewed in Tacoma. Thus we note Farwell's keen interest in the visual arts was broadened during his western visit.

Then followed some difficult traveling through the blinding blizzards of Montana and the Bad Lands before returning to his home base in Massachusetts. Once home, Farwell pondered over what he had seen and experienced. He considered the stirring visual arts he had witnessed which were a vital part of the western life, but he concluded that it was the *people* who seemed so wonderful to him. "...all so busy building, building, a great civilization - and to what end?" This question was one that perplexed Farwell as he continued seeking the answer.

Farwell's stay at home was short-lived as Lummis wrote proposing that he return to Los Angeles to help in completing a study of the Spanish Californian and Indian music for the Archaeological Institute of America. However, much to his dismay, Farwell learned that the Archaeological Institute could not provide the necessary funds. His heart was in the project by this time, but he could not make the trip without financial assistance. What should he do? Finally he hiked out to a secluded spot in the woods where he often retired for solitude in order to deliberate on this problem. He tells the story of what happened there:[8]

> As I stood thinking it over - a peculiar stone, almost buried in the earth at my foot, attracted my attention and I stooped to pick it up. What was my astonishment to find that it was a magnificent flint arrowhead! As a student of science and a graduate of the Massachusetts Institute of Technology, I am not a superstitious person, but this little piece of flint, I must confess, sent a strange tingling up my spine to the roots of my hair. Flint is not found in this neighborhood, and one no longer expects to pick up Indian relics about Newton Center. It was a

question of centuries - when the last Indian battle could
have been fought upon this spot.  Perhaps this timely and
eloquent arrowhead helped me decide - perhaps not.

As a result of this experience, Farwell acted on an inner
"hunch" and carried the point to see Dr. Seymour, president of the
Archeological Institute, in New Haven.  In a subsequent meeting,
it was settled that Farwell should receive compensation to go to
the Southwest and work for the organization as originally planned.

### Second Western Trip, 1904

So, early in the summer of 1904, Farwell started on another
trip to the Southwest.  His first stop was in Chicago to see his
old friend, Arne Oldberg, whose music he admired.  Then on to
St. Louis where he attended the Louisiana Purchase Exposition
and was joined by the "Prince" (Winslow Mallery) of old Boston
days.  Eventually Farwell went on alone to Los Angeles where he
was soon settled in the exotic Lummis home, El Alisal. (Figure
25)  This was more like a Spanish castle with its towers, its walls
of boulders, the patio with its great round wall and spreading
sycamore, plus all the treasures within.  He felt to work there was
"more like a romantic holiday than a labor"[9].
     While working under such ideal conditions, Farwell transcribed
from the phonograph and from actual singing, several hundred
songs which were prepared as a report for the Southwest Society
of the Archeological Institute.  He considered a good number to
be of high quality and "some are remarkable finds, nuggets of
folksong of the greatest rarity and beauty."
     Lawrence Gilman recognized the value of this work also while
it was on-going and wrote: "This valuable collection will be an
acquisition which the Archeological Institute is anxiously awaiting,
and when finished is a work Southern California may be proud
of."[10]  (These songs are still in print and may be had at the
Southwest Museum, which Lummis founded.)
     After completing his assignment, Farwell left one "dream-
world" for another - attendance at the Bohemian Club's *High Jinks*
presentation of the *Hamadryads* near San Francisco.

Figure 25.  Arthur Farwell, photographed by Charles F. Lummis at his home,
El Alisal, in California in 1904.

Following that inspiring experience, Farwell returned to Los Angeles and spent four more months transcribing additional Indian and Spanish songs from the phonograph. Then he made business stops in Kansas City and St. Louis before settling down in Chicago to engage in some musical work for several months. Back finally in Newton Center, he was asked to speak at Boston's Twentieth Century Club about his experiences in the West. In this talk he described at length the many composers he had met in his travels whose works were relatively unknown in the East. His audience was curious to hear some of this new music and proposed that a Society be organized for that purpose. Farwell thought this an excellent idea and took prompt action on it, as will be seen in Chapter 9.

### Third Western Trip, 1905

When Farwell went West for the third time in July, 1905, he took his mother with him. Both of them had passes on the Atchinson, Topeka, and Santa Fe Railroad to help with their expenses.[11] After enjoying the glories of the Grand Canyon, they journeyed on to Los Angeles where Farwell continued the work of transcribing songs for the Southwest Institute of Archaeology. Interest in music by American composers was also planted in a group of sympathetic people for what four years later became a strong Los Angeles Center of the American Music Society. After completing his assignment, Farwell and his mother returned to Newton Center in October.

One spring day of 1906, Farwell received a telegram urgently requesting his presence in New York City on an important matter connected with American music. With nothing to lose, and perchance something to gain for his cause, Farwell decided to accept the invitation. He soon met at the old Arts Club with a group of enthusiastic young men who wished to organize a series of orchestral concerts of American compositions in cooperation with the Russian Symphony Society, Modest Altschuler, conductor. The result of that meeting was the formation of the *New Music Society of America*. In a preliminary announcement its goal was stated as being "the production of interesting and important novelties by native composers. . . by the Russian Symphony

Orchestra."    The new organization recognized that there "exists already a large and increasing fund of American compositions of a high order of merit which are condemned to remain unheard unless some organized effort be made to bring them before the public." American composers were invited to send in their scores for performance consideration.  Selections from those works were to be made by a Score Committee consisting of Modest Altschuler, Rupert Hughes, N. Clifford Page and Lawrence Gilman.  The organization  went so far as to give two orchestral concerts during the following season and then faded out of existence.[12]

The fundamental and fatal weakness of the New Music Society as Farwell saw it was that it was based on rather vague hopes of assistance from "certain wealthy persons which animated one of its founders." These wealthy persons regarded the importation of an expensive foreign conductor as a first requisite, but did not promise funds to import one.  This proposition unquestionably did not support a distinctly American enterprise and "led to the resignation of the founder in question" and hence to the "death of even those vague hopes of assistance which had been cherished." Thus the New Music Society as such passed into history.[13]

### Fourth Western Trip, 1906

By the fall of 1906, Farwell was ready for a next step, a further new initiative.  His special work in the Southwest for the Institute of Archeology was over.  On his three western trips, he had given many lecture-recitals on Indian music, playing his own developments of Indian themes and using the occasion to also say a few timely things on American music in general.   Now he decided it was time to prepare a completely new lecture-recital, *A National American Music* in which he aimed to "synthesize the whole matter."

Accordingly, he prepared a brochure which included the outline for his Indian lecture-recital as well as the format for the new lecture. (Figure 26)  Farwell listed the following questions and provided musical illustrations as part of each answer:

I.   Is a National Musical Art desirable?
II.  What is "American Spirit" in Music?
III. Have We Any American Folksongs?
IV.  Shall Folksongs Enter into a National Art?
V.   What Shall We Do?

Armed with his new discourse, Farwell started on his fourth
trip West with a different objective. This time he was concerned
about "looking more closely into American conditions, particularly
with regard to the publication situation, and the matter of
American willingness to give a hearing to American works. The
result of this quest was, if depressing, also illuminating in its effect
upon action to be taken."[14]

In planning his schedule for this western trip, Farwell had
considerable correspondence with his composer friend, Arthur
Shepherd, in Salt Lake City, who urged Farwell to include his city
in the tour. Farwell already had planned to end his tour in
Denver and estimated it would require at least $75.00 to travel
from there to Salt Lake City and back for "R. R, Pullman, meals,
fees, carriages, baggage, transfers, etc. not to mention time". His
railroad pass did not include travel to Salt Lake City which was
part of the problem and money was extremely scarce. He wrote:

> I am having hell financially, and this trip has not only
> got to *be made*, but its got to be made to *pull me out*...i.e.
> I shall have to earn money beyond expenses as the
> pressure here at home is fierce, and Variations, Sonatas,
> etc. sell about one in two months.
>
> In justice to my family and the difficult situation here
> it doesn't seem fair to make so extensive a show, a
> pleasure trip. Do you see any way to make it earn
> something? I'm mighty anxious to go over. It seems to
> me that if I could be certain to take in $100.00, I could
> do it. Then if I could get some more dates, Provo (where
> my name is at least known to school authorities), Ogden,
> etc...it would be so much more towards the butcher, the
> baker, at Newton Center, and new Mss. in print for the
> glory of American music, (and I've got some good ones.)

# LECTURE RECITALS
### Presenting Original Pianoforte Compositions

By
## ARTHUR FARWELL

President of the National
American Music Society

President of the Boston Center
of the American Music Society

Founder and Editor of
The Wa-Wan Press, Newton Center, Mass

*Figure 26.  Cover for one of the brochures Farwell used for his lecture recital tours, from 1904 through 1907.*

Shepherd finally made arrangements using two agents to book lectures in his city and others nearby. Farwell settled for a guaranteed fee of $200.00 for presenting five lecture-recitals involving two different topics.[15] At that low price he did not feel he should stand the expense of advertising; but he did offer for a fee, to furnish window cards which had his photograph on them and blanks for adding the local dates. These he would make available, delivered, for $4.00 per 100, and circulars for distribution at $1.25 per hundred.

As the February lecture-recital dates approached, Farwell was concerned that not enough interest was being mustered in the Salt Lake City area and wrote thus to Shepherd:

> The enclosed postal from Graham [an agent] today. He's getting cold feet. Can't you put a little dynamite under him! Brace him up. Tell him to tell his people that I'm the only man in the country wholly devoted to the development of American music - that now's their chance to hear me. Make him get busy! And he must think my itinerary is made of putty. I've been sticking to those first 8 (or 9 or 10 days) in Salt Lake City from the first and can't make such easy business of changing them. Thanks for the offer to put me up. I shall enjoy and appreciate it.

When Farwell finally began this trip west, he stopped first in Detroit. After visiting other cities on his itinerary, he went to Colorado Springs. There for the first time, he met Frederic Ayres, composer for Wa-Wan, who became a staunch supporter and friend. After he spoke in Denver, Farwell's schedule embraced the planned-for stay in Salt Lake City where Arthur Shepherd entertained him royally. Although Shepherd was extremely busy with conducting the symphony orchestra, the theater orchestra, teaching, filling a church position and composing, he managed to join Farwell for a side trip to Logan. There Farwell presented his lecture-recital on American music and later did likewise in Provo where he enjoyed his largest audience in four years.

Farwell's Scrapbook contains many undated press clippings praising his lecture-recitals given over these years. A sampling follows:

### *Auburn Daily Advertiser*
As a composer Mr. Farwell has undoubtedly a brilliant future, both because of his musical genius and of his courage to open new roads. As a lecturer, Mr. Farwell is convincing and delightfully interesting; his work at the piano, while having none of the elements of the virtuoso, is always musical and satisfying.

### *The Violinist*
The man who says "I hear America singing" is Arthur Farwell, known to fame before Wa-Wan went to press. We like to say "Wa-Wan", it sounds so musical - just like Farwell.

### *Ohio State Journal*
Perhaps the most significant event in the musical life of Columbus in the past several years was the lecture-recital given Monday evening by Arthur Farwell.... His work is sincere, mature, burdenless, singularly free from the trammels of convention, and evidently has no boundaries. Music should not have boundaries and the new American music will be as revolutionary as were the Americans' opinion on "tea drinking in 1776".... He knows what to say and says it.

Describing Farwell to a reporter, C. Maurice Dietrich stated, "His thought seemed utterly isolated from self, a pervading purpose, underlying, issued from his words with strength and power. He came here to interest music lovers in American music. This fact was displayed in every word he uttered." (This presumably took place at a Wa-Wan Society meeting held in the Dietrich home.)

*The Cleveland Leader* declared:

> Mr. Farwell presented his subject with enthusiasm,
> and a deep and sincere knowledge of his subject, that is
> almost thrilling when illustrated with the musical themes
> of these aboriginal people.... It was a fascinating subject,
> and Mr. Farwell's method of giving it added to the charm
> of enthusiasm and conviction for the subject.... He is a
> composer of marked ability.

### National Federation of Music Club Activities

In addition to his Wa-Wan Press and lecturing activities,
Farwell participated in another significant event. He was named
an official delegate to the fifth biennial convention of the National
Federation of Music Clubs held in Memphis, Tennessee, in May
1907. By now this organization numbered about 90 clubs and
needed some special goal that would unite them in a common
interest. Mrs. Jason Walker proposed that the Federation offer
$2,000.00 in prizes for works by American composers. Farwell was
appointed on the committee making the plans to carry out her
motion. Farwell's connection with the Federation was established
through the Detroit center of the Wa-Wan Society, which joined
the Federation at this time. (See discussion in chapter nine.)
Later he wrote enthusiastically about this endeavor:[16]

> We can know what this competition meant
> historically, and in relation to American ideals, only when
> we realize that the prize fund was raised by thousands of
> persons scattered over the length and breadth of the
> United States. History must regard this competition as
> the first nationally wide-spread democratic recognition of
> a musical art in America.

Farwell addressed the convention on *Democracy in Music* and
was warmly received. In other business it was moved by Farwell
and carried that "as complete a list of American composers as
possible be prepared, a complete list of their works, and a
bibliography of existing literature upon the subject, the whole to

be published in pamphlet form". This, which would be useful to all the Clubs as a general source of information, Farwell was appointed to prepare.

Later this pamphlet became the source for a more pretentious study which he authored for the Federation in 1912. For that work he wrote Section VIII on American Music as part of the club's *Sixth Year Plan of Study of Musical History.* Therein he outlined a calendar of study topics for nine months of the club year and presented thought-provoking questions with detailed answers for club leader usage. His material covered American music from the Colonial period to the Civil War. He also listed books and music in an extensive bibliography for reference use in discussion and recitals. Furthermore, he was one of the main speakers at the sixth biennial convention when he outlined a plan of cooperation between the Federation and the American Music Society of which he was still president. Hence we note Farwell made considerable impact on the National Federation of Music Clubs as an educator for American music, beginning with the fifth biennial convention.

Farwell's lecture tours and conference appearances spanned the years 1903 to 1907, and brought increased recognition for the cause of American music. In addition to his successful crusading during those years, Farwell also acquired a better knowledge of the musical scene throughout the United States.

When traveling, he always carried a small music-paper notebook in his pocket in which he jotted down themes and musical ideas as inspiration came to him. Some were developed into major compositions decades later. Meanwhile, he devoted much time and energy on these travels to club developments which grew to become the American Music Society. Now we return to the spring of 1905 for the story of this complicated but important struggle.

# Chapter 9

# The American Music Society Story

April 20, 1905 was an auspicious occasion in Boston when Arthur Farwell met with interested friends to plan a new music organization. Earlier that spring, as we noted, he had presented a talk at the Twentieth Century Club describing the excellent "new" music by American composers he had discovered during his western travels. At that time his information had aroused the curiosity and concern of many persons in the Club's audience who proposed a society be organized to study and perform this new music. The present meeting was the result.

Accordingly, under Farwell's leadership the American Music Society came into being. Its stated purpose was "to advance the interests of American music in its broadest aspects by the study and performance of the works of American composers and the study of all folk-music touching American musical developments." The plan was essentially democratic with 32 charter members. William Cole was elected president, John P. Marshall, secretary, with Henry Gilbert, Clarence Birchard, Walter R. Spaulding, Helen A. Clarke, Sophie Hart named to the council. Farwell remained as musical director.

Plans were made for seven monthly meetings, one of which was to be a fall concert and a "big" concert in the spring. Different phases of American music were taken up at the members meetings, representative works presented, and papers read or discussions held on subjects related to American music.

This organization was a good beginning, but it was localized in Boston, and did not satisfy Farwell's vision of American music being made known all over the nation. Various ideas on how to bring his vision to life were in his mind as he began his fourth transcontinental tour in the fall of 1906, the last trip described in chapter eight. But as yet he had no ready solution to the problem.

Going West, Farwell's first stop was in Detroit. While there, some friends proposed that an association be formed based on the Wa-Wan Press idea which would carry out plans for both publication and performance of American compositions. Farwell promised to consider the same and return to Detroit in the Spring with a working plan for such an organization.

After Farwell finished his work with the Southwestern folk songs, he was able to concentrate on the problem he needed to face in Detroit on his return trip home. As he reviewed our national musical life he realized afresh that there were two chief notions that every American must understand:

(1) America set up and had in operation a great definite machinery for the performance and propagation of European music, when that was all there was to have, and before the American composer, in sufficient numbers and force to count, had come on the scene, and that

(2) The whole American people for generations has thus been educated and trained to the idea that the only real music is European music[1].

Farwell felt that to realize these things was the only way to get away from the "sentimental cant and twaddle about the neglect of the American composer." As society made a recognized place for the American composer, he knew there would have to be adjustments. He was sensitive to the problems of orchestra conductors who needed to question: "Can I risk this new work by an unknown American with my audience? Will it be sufficiently accepted to warrant the support of the backers of the orchestra who are watchdogs of its finances? Is this really a good work?"

Farwell was aware that singers and players had a similar problem in presenting new American pieces, although they were less restricted by their managers. Even when an artist wants to perform a new American work, he must consider if his audience will accept it and pay him in the long run for doing so. Artists know it takes time to prepare new works which might more profitably be spent on music that would guarantee a crowd. Farwell quoted a noted songstress who was heard highly praising some new American songs.

"Why don't you sing them?" she was asked.

"Oh, it would hurt my reputation," was her quick reply.[2] After mulling over all these accumulated ideas, he was ready for his Detroit friends when he returned to that city in the spring of

1907.  Now he had a plan in mind for organizing a national music society which he presented to the people who had challenged him on his previous visit.  The outcome, after much discussion, was the birth of the National Wa-Wan Society in March 1907.

The organization was the result of Farwell's investigation, inquiry and observation during these four years of wandering up and down across the nation.  Everywhere he had found hampering conditions surrounding the performance of American compositions and their publication.  He felt that "artistically and commercially there was pathmaking to be done."  The influence of society must be brought in a broad way to bear on gaining "adequate performance" of American works.    Too, artists needed to be encouraged by audiences everywhere to perform American works.  Farwell sought now to build audiences.[3]

The National Wa-Wan Society of America, founded by Farwell and his close associates had for its stated purpose, "...the advancement of the work of American composers, and the interests of the musical life of the American people, through the Wa-Wan Press...in association with the Centers and members of the Society throughout the United States."    With Farwell as president, the new executive board included these distinguished men: George W. Chadwick, Charles Martin Loeffler, Ernest Kroeger, Arthur Foote, Frank Damrosch and Lawrence Gilman.  In the organizing process, about six centers were developed in cities widely scattered across the nation for the propagation and study of American music.   The *Wa-Wan Press Monthly* was published as an editorial platform for disseminating the policies and purposes of the Wa-Wan Society.   It was distributed to members, together with the monthly musical volumes of the Press from March 1907 through 1908.

The following excerpt from a letter Farwell wrote to Arthur Shepherd July 18, 1907 gives a little picture of the strain he was suffering in his efforts to promote the new organization nationally:

> Well -- I've had a pretty bad illness - a breakdown - and now after a week at Saratoga with friends who have a private place there, I feel a lot better than for a long time.  But the Western trip must be postponed til later in the winter. - this must be - I must organize the society

more firmly in the East, first, not to speak of producing returns which will support the work this Fall and enable me to go West with no financial strain at this end.

I hope, however, that you may be able to make a start with a Wa-Wan Center in the Fall. I'm bound to win - and make this thing a big success - and lift this work above the stinking financial struggle in which it has thus far been involved. And this is the time to do it - with the organization of the Society...

In a later letter to Shepherd, Farwell commented: "Thanks for your encouraging words - I am going to hang on like a bulldog for I don't believe that the whole crew of us are duffers!"

By September 17, 1907, Farwell gave Shepherd strong step-by-step instructions for organizing the new Center in Salt Lake City:

Forgive me for not writing sooner - the stress of my life has been terrific - some large matters to carry, upon which much has depended, and I simply had to let my letters lie there and rebuke me.

As to the center - just get a necessary number of members pledged, by getting them together and talking to them, or approach them singly. Then organize and elect officers, a leader, a musical director (yourself), a librarian, and a secretary and a treasurer, and one, three, or five others as desired, to make up a council, odd in numbers, for voting reasons.

Then have a council meeting and decide what will be undertaken. Probably a monthly meeting of some kind in which compositions should be tried out and the principles of musical compositions discussed, and their relations to the work studied. At such member meetings, the giving of a mere casual program should be avoided. If members don't know enough to discuss the works - then the basis of knowledge of such discussion has got to be got into them, til they have some comparative sense of harmony, melody, rhythm, and form. I intend to invent a means of voting on composers by centers - for they have got to be made to express themselves.

Essays - the reading of them should form a part of such meetings.

After determining upon monthly meetings, then the best thing by far is to have one especially important social meeting, with something more in the nature of a program given, though informally enough.

At this meeting should be as many invited guests as possible, chosen from among those who are most likely to become members. (A little something ought to be said at this meeting.)

It is my experience that as soon as the center forms, others may wish to get in, i. e. others not previously interested. In this way a greater social stability is given to the center and its influence extended.

We need as members not only persons of very particular musical interest, but as well, persons interested in art advance generally, who want to see our native art life go ahead. The Wa-Wan Society has the sociological and economic situation to face as well as the purely artistic, and the persons must be impressed with that fact.

Use all means of appeal possible, the purely musical, the altruistic, the need of much better conditions in which for American music to advance, and the helping to build those conditions, the patriotic, ... any way to rally individuals to the work - but broad - ... not too specific and technical to appeal. These centers must become enlightened as to the whole status of American music and the American composer.

In its present stage of growth - the work must be carried on with as little local expense as possible, each giving what is possible in the way of place to meet, exhibitions and the use of musical talents, etc.

The need ... must be made plain - to test the work of our own composers.

As a leader, Farwell was basically always the teacher, too, and here he was passing on to Shepherd the results of his own organizational experience. It was a very full directive, but Farwell got Shepherd and numerous other men to follow it. In another letter to Shepherd written October 2, 1907, Farwell gave more instructions for educating the members of the new center.

>As to making the center work and actively attractive, show people what a lot there is to do in sifting down American music and getting at the good. And especially get hearings of the best things constantly, til they see their good. ...*The Moon Shower* (Loomis) and my *Dawn* made especial headway in Detroit. Get a peg of interest in certain works and then hang other things onto it.
>
>Remember how different people's minds are - and keep ready all means of appeal as I suggested yesterday.

While Shepherd was busy trying out Farwell's recommendations to stimulate the membership of the newly organized center in Salt Lake City, Farwell prepared the publication of the Wa-Wan Press Monthly. The first issue was devoted primarily to expressing the aim and ideals of the Wa-Wan Society with a challenge to its members to promote the cause of American music. In explaining the work ahead for the Society, he emphasized we must "labor unremittingly to place American musical life generally upon a basis of American principle." He continued succinctly:

>It means to give the American composer adequate and fair trial at the hands of the American people everywhere, not merely to be willing to, but to actually do it; it means to deny that "musical art" or "musical life" is a special expensive or fashionable luxury for a few - it means to affirm that in its truest form musical art should be a simple and available pleasure for all, ... and it means to give the American artist, whether composer or performer, an equal earning power with the European. This means for every American city, town and community to set up and to respect its own musical standards, which it is now capable of doing, and to cease in its blind allegiance to current metropolitan fashions.

The composer who creates, the general and special musical life which distributes, the individual musical consciousness which receives, - these are the three fundamental concerns of the Wa-Wan Society.... The work of the whole, is to create a true Democracy of Music.

Here we see Farwell not only as an ardent and articulate champion of the American composer, but also we note him expressing a particular conception of American music and its place in American society that was revolutionary for its time. His ideal was to create a musical expression that would have a meaningful relation to local culture everywhere and thereby to a national culture. His demand that the American composer be given "an adequate and fair trial" continues to be a problem today, even as it was in Farwell's day and others - such as when Edward Bowman led a similar struggle in the Music Teachers National Association beginning about 1884.

In the second issue of the *Monthly*, Farwell included some specific ideas for the study of American music and suggested lesson plans for this purpose. A column entitled *American Music Study* later became a regular feature whose goal was to present "lists of thoroughly representative works by American composers."[4]

The January 1908 issue of the *Monthly* announced a change in its focus from the previous appeal to "the professional and highly developed amateur" to "an appeal to the general music lover and amateur of no great technical attainment." Because Farwell felt the need for a grass-roots movement in music, he stated that "the Society must represent popular power. This change has nothing to do with the question of quality and taste. Simplicity and beauty will be the aim in the music of the monthly issues", he concluded. He explained further how the base of all simple beauty in music is the folksong. Hence, he planned to publish "American" folksongs of various kinds as well as "composed" songs.

Farwell believed that this new general program would serve the "greatly desired end of bringing American composers into much closer touch with the people, who, in the end, will be their strongest allies." Here again, one notes Farwell's concern to relate music to the people.

In addition to the change of focus in the monthly issues of the Press, Farwell announced that occasionally there would be issued compositions outside of the monthly series. These works would carry out the special purpose of the original Wa-Wan Press series, but now could be even better since they were freed from the need to have a broad audience appeal and could be technically more difficult to perform. Provisions for student memberships were also announced at this time.

An important aspect of the work done in each of the Centers was the distribution of music through its "libraries". Club members had the privilege of exchanging any composition in the monthly series for any piece in sheet-music form in the library. It seems that a member functioned as a Librarian who was in charge of more than 100 compositions of widely differing styles and degrees of difficulty, as well as "works in 'book' form i.e. in heavy colored paper covers, for reference and occasional use."[5]

Farwell frequently visited the Centers to help club members in various ways. He suggested the formation of special extension committees whose function was to "secure, through the cooperation of orchestras, choruses, and artists, the performances of works impossible within the centers themselves." His aim was that the "whole mass of the best work of American composers be sifted through the American consciousness."[6]

In May of 1907, we found Farwell active at the Biennial convention of the National Federation of Music Clubs in Memphis. When that work was finished, he traveled to St. Louis where he formed a Center for the Wa-Wan Society assisted by Ernest R. Kroeger and other friends of the new movement. About the same time, two more Centers were created: one in Salt Lake City by Arthur Shepherd, the other in Colorado Springs, by Frederic Ayres.

Worn out from his strenuous schedule, Farwell slipped away to Saratoga, New York, as noted earlier in his letter of July 18th to Shepherd. After recuperation, he began his fall campaign for the extension of the Wa-Wan Society in New York state. He made his headquarters alternately in Rochester, Geneva, Syracuse, and Auburn with Centers being established in the first three cities.[7]

Farwell obviously had found the work of developing an organization to be an exhausting challenge. He expounded on the subject fervently:[8]

> Let him who contemplates it consider long and well before engaging in this phase of human endeavor. Once embarked, he must eat trouble as a fireman entering a burning house "eats smoke." He must even cultivate a relish for it. To be responsible to one's self is hard, but to be responsible to an organization of other selves, which one's self has launched, is another thing beginning with the same letter. For this reason the organizer must be a zealot, a prophet, a crusader. His eye should ever be on the great end to be gained. The most complex and discouraging obstacles, difficulties, intrigues, should be to him nothing more than momentary annoying details, undergrowth to brush aside as he goes his determined way. It should be to him so absorbing and life-giving joy to be approaching, however gradually, the goal of his dreams, that no accident or unbeautiful circumstance can prevail against it. He who would lead must lose his self in his purpose. Taunts, insults, slurs, must pass through the eternal etheric purposefulness of his nature as storm winds pass through the yielding and elastic network of treetops. He must not care where he lives, nor how, as long as he can serve the cause to which he has given loyalty and life.

Farwell's words actually describe himself as a leader and organizer. He had learned through hard experience what has to be done in creating an organization of small substance, even more so a nation-wide organization. Do we see here an affirmation of Cheiro's analysis of Farwell's tenacious temperament? It is doubtful whether a person of less determination could have accomplished so much nationally as Farwell was able to do.

Farwell reflected on his success with the Wa-Wan Society in another letter to Shepherd dated November 20, 1907. In it he speaks strongly and warmly toward building a team of like-minded leaders to expand the cause, yet he protests that the demands of this work, however vital to it, do greatly limit his time and energy for composing. Here are excerpts of his thinking:

> You have written me that a change is necessary in your life - that you will leave Salt Lake City, and that you want to go East.
>
> The need of a big change lies before me too - can we not find a resolution of it all in helping each other?
>
> The Wa-Wan Society is working out well - is the realest thing I have undertaken yet because the most immediately human - and is the only pathway being cleared for the broad national systematic hearing of American composer's works. There are now six centers since Buffalo and Rochester are added, and others are to follow. Here is a little grip - little enough in extent but big with significance. Let this work be pushed further ... and... we will have a great force in motion - a force that must be reckoned with in the development of American music - a force second to no other... as it reaches out and unites the best elements in the community.
>
> There will be fallings away - shifting, disloyalties - as are always the case - but the dead may bury their dead, and we soon discover the faithful, and find our normal and rightful following.
>
> As you well know, it is no whim, but deep need, that has driven me into this work - need of a place in American life for an American composer - as a composer - not only as a teacher or a player. And need of a practical work which should also satisfy this need. It has all led, little as I foresaw it, to the Wa-Wan Society - there is the creating of the necessary conditions for advance as a composer - and there is a practical work, by means of which we can step to that condition.
>
> This need that I speak of I do not feel to be a personal thing. I believe that I am the first one to feel it with sufficient intensity to act upon it, and that in doing so, I am responding to a need arising in many others... as composers begin to realize fully that they are American after all, living in America, and that Europe is going to

give them nothing but traditions of artistic heroism, and occasional contemporary inspirations. Our life, our home, is here! Therefore we must, in our need, make it acceptable, desirable to us, as composers.

The Wa-Wan Society, aiming directly at the satisfying of this need, will be a power in our hands exactly in proportion as we extend the organization. And if I can do as much as I can alone, burdened also with other tasks - how rapidly and strongly we could bring it forward, did but several of us write and act concertedly....

In regard to the latter - this month I have done work in organizing which will bring about $500, one half of which is profit.... The field - the country - is enormous and many people are eager and willing to take hold....

This following constitutes a power... in another and very important way. It gives us our organ reaching and influencing people all over the country, who are going East and sending sons and daughters East to study.

It has long been my hope and expectation of building up a kind of center... where some of us could live and have a center of operations - where possibly a few persons could be associated who would be wishing to spend more or less time in or about Boston... where they could receive musical instruction, where they would be drawn by the reputation of our work, where they could find an attractive musical rendezvous. From such a center, we could make trips for organizations, or recitals...as occasion demanded.... Little by little we would bring about the necessary adjustments... but meanwhile cooperating at the start...for the maintenance of ourselves and those dependent upon us. My mother is eager for... such an attractive center for artistic and intellectual people.

Now it comes to me that the solution of your problems may find itself in just such a step. It would require work and fight - but you are a worker and a fighter clear through, but it would mean the building of a substantial future....

My great need today - and for these years - is helpers - helpers to organize.

I have had to learn the path I mapped out for myself... for this absolute necessity for organization. But I have had to carry on the literary and artistic work at the same time - which is too much - and to go on being both... would be a menace to my health altogether too great to be contemplated. And it is particularly the organization work that I must recede from, because the literary work and the general direction of the movement devolves directly upon me, and others can organize exactly as well as I.

Also the organization work must go on, for in that lies the realization of everything.

What I have learned ... is, how to organize, and that I can teach to others.... Tomorrow, you will now have had the beginnings of experience in that direction. It is not more difficult to organize in a place where you are not previously known than in your own place - in fact, I think it easier - one carries a certain glamour coming from elsewhere.... And the Wa-Wan is getting better and better known more and more credited.

It comes over me overwhelmingly that now is the moment of opportunity... to make a great reality of this work - which requires only that we make a common cause of it. I could not, at the present stage, pay you a living salary,... but if we could all combine in some way at Newton Center, say, and work in the common cause of mutual maintenance - at least until we could bring it further along, there is no reason why it could not be done.... What such living arrangements might be - would have to be determined - a large house might have to be taken....with some plan for a common table.

John Beach has broken away from New Orleans, and is living at our house now - and has a few pupils. I think of him as a teacher rather than an organizer, though he will probably begin to work for recitals about the east....

I have been working too hard - but it is through the success of my method that my eyes are opened to its possibilities as a practical way forward and now simply, I want others to join in carrying it out - where it can be of mutual helpfulness.

I must stop doing more than one man's work - and as quickly as possible. I've done it for years - and it is jolly. Only through others taking hold can I come into my own best and special powers or gain the respite I must have if I am not to suffer from overestimating my strength....

Well, think it over - and write me... your impressions why shouldn't we unite forces and do something?

Kreider is loyal to the core - and Goldberg, and both will help in their spheres. Kreider is free and devoted to me and my work, and I think may not be far from a step in the direction I am suggesting to you.

Write me - at Newton Center.

While Shepherd contemplated the implications of Farwell's letter, Farwell pushed on with other plans. His efforts in upper New York had produced good results, so he began planning for a start in New York City.

Meanwhile, he made a short trip at the end of December 1907 to join Noble Kreider, a composer and excellent pianist, in Goshen, Indiana. Together they made a recital trip to Evanston, Illinois, where they were hosted by Arne Oldberg of the School of Music at Northwestern University. With Oldberg assisting, the three men presented a concert, each performing his own compositions. From Evanston, Kreider and Farwell visited Kansas City and St. Joseph where their performances were warmly received.[9]

Back in his home in Newton Center, Farwell reviewed his original goal of bringing "the whole mass of the best work of American composers to the American consciousness". Because of developments which he had observed in his recent travels, he sensed the need for some drastic changes in the present organizational plan of the National Wa-Wan Society.

Originally, the publication of a periodical series of music by American composers was a definite part of the plan, but this is what was creating a problem for Farwell. In trying to maintain high standards of music for the Wa-Wan Press, he had disregarded technical simplicity and included difficult pieces as well as rather simple folk songs.   The plan led to some unevenness in the monthly series that upset some subscribers.   Since the Society aimed at "the betterment of both the artistic and the economic situation of the composer," carrying out these aims became a great strain on him.   However, he never once thought of abandoning this arrangement.   "It would have been like cutting off my right hand," he said.[10]

Moreover, the needed change in the organizational structure of the national Wa-Wan Society was precipitated in the spring of 1908, by the presentation by concerned friends in New York City, of two major concerts devoted exclusively to music by American composers.[11]  These programs served as a catalyst to awaken new interest in promoting the cause of American music through some newly organized means there.    But what to name it? Sophisticated New Yorkers turned up their noses at the Indian name of Wa-Wan.  They thought it might prove misleading as to the broad aims of the society and insisted on a more proper name for it.

This situation created a dilemma for Farwell.  He already had an existing American Music Society in Boston which was totally detached from the Wa-Wan Press.  Then there existed at this time about six centers of the National Wa-Wan Society which were definitely related to the Wa-Wan Press publications.  The music issued monthly for its members had been an extension of the series issued quarterly for five years previously for independent subscribers.  As that organization grew, so did the performance capabilities of its members change.  While a few well trained members had the technical skill to play the more difficult compositions published, more did not.  The latter could accept these compositions when rendered by an artist on the concert stage, but they had not the technical prowess to get its meaning from the printed page.

This problem could have been met by a total change of the nature of the music published, but this would have defeated the very purpose for which the Wa-Wan Press was established - "the publication of works of artistic distinction by American composers, irrespective of other considerations."  Farwell felt that there was an "incredible superfluity" of simple American compositions of the conventional style already being published - "one of the horrors of the time".[12]

Even if the nature of music being published could have been changed to meet the demands of the growing Wa-Wan Society, a still more serious difficulty had begun to appear - the prospect that the organization in any case could not be promoted at a sufficiently rapid rate to meet the increasing publishing expenses.

As Farwell analyzed the complexity of the situation, he finally determined that the National Wa-Wan Society, in spite of his high hopes for it, would have to be abandoned. The publication aspect, as an integral part of the plan at that stage of development was clogging the growth of the organized movement as a whole. He realized above all else, the organizational movement must move forward if the needed forces were to be marshalled to promote a hearing of American musical works on a large scale. He concluded that "the Wa-Wan Press must be thrown out of the organization [Wa-Wan Society], as ballast is thrown out of a balloon struggling to rise."[13]  Farwell's decision was four-pronged; he would:

> 1. let the Wa-Wan Press go on as a wholly independent personal enterprise, "preserving and even accentuating its ideal artistic purpose";
> 2. organize the New York Society as a center of the American Music Society;
> 3. invite the centers of the Wa-Wan Society to become centers of the American Music Society and discontinue all publication of music as far as the Society was concerned.  Members would be offered a liberal selection of the existing publications of the Wa-Wan Press for the unfulfilled portions of the series to which they were entitled;
> 4. ask the American Music Society of Boston to accept the new arrangement for a national organization under a governing board and itself become the Boston center of the new American Music Society being formed.

For once, everything happened as Farwell had planned!  After the Boston Society concurred with the new plan, he returned to New

York City where the New York Center of the American Music Society was consummated in May 1908 with the distinguished concert singer, David Bispham, as president. (See Figure 27) After the other local organizational matters were

*Figure 27.   David Bispham, prominent baritone and first president of the New York City Center of the American Music Society, 1908.*

completed, the formation of the new national American Music Society followed in which each local organization was to be known as a "Center". Farwell was elected the national president, and Walter Damrosch, its musical director. The presidents of the different Centers became vice presidents of the national society. Thomas Tryon was elected secretary, and Joseph L. Lilienthal, treasurer. The Board of managers consisted of the president, musical director, secretary, three honorary members chosen for life, and the musical directors of the several Centers. Honorary members on the board were George W. Chadwick, Charles Martin Loeffler and Frank Damrosch.

When this reorganization of the National Wa-Wan Society took place, the following cities joined the new American Music Society: St. Louis, Colorado Springs, Salt Lake City, Rochester, San Diego and eventually Detroit. The shock of some fundamental changes was too much for the existence of four of the newer Centers who could not face the throes of reorganization so soon after what had been a difficult task of original organization. However, the Centers continued to grow in number and influence.

This change also precipitated the disappearance of the *Wa-Wan Press Monthly* which was replaced by the new *Bulletin of the American Music Society*. This was intended to have an independent career but only four issues were printed - for June, October, and December 1908, and March 1909 - before it, too, ceased to exist.

After effecting the new organization in New York City, Farwell decided he could accomplish more by staying home in Newton Center. He needed to determine what means were available for developing the different phases of work and organizations already underway. In addition to his Wa-Wan Press and the national American Music Society, he had an educational plan for a music school at his residence which had been developed during the summer with Arthur Shepherd's help.[14] Shepherd had responded to Farwell's long challenging letter by moving East where he became a faculty member of the New England Conservatory of Music. He was vitally interested in this project.

Too, Farwell concluded that he had accomplished a measure of the goals he had set for his travels. These he listed as: 1) to learn the land; 2) to determine how musical art had developed in America, both imported and native; 3) to study aboriginal forms of music in the United States at their source; 4) to meet musicians and audiences and to encourage them to study American composers and their music; and 5) to engage in the active organizational work for the advancement of American musical art.[15]

Furthermore, Farwell realized the only thing lacking now was a *national* medium of communication whereby the events and ideas relating to the American music movement could be announced. (*The Bulletin of the American Music Society* only reached its own members.) What better means of doing this than via *Musical*

*America* which had national coverage?   Little realizing where his next step was to lead, Farwell made arrangements in the fall of 1908 to send regular correspondence to the paper's Boston office. It is interesting to read a letter in Farwell's scrapbook from Paul M. Kempf, managing editor of *Musical America*, dated November 13, 1908.

> ...I am disposed to give you a free hand in the subject matter and treatment of your material, providing you keep in mind the fact that we do not want genuine sharp and serious criticisms of musical performances.

Mr. Kempf's remarks suggest that his readers were still not very discriminating.   But his goal may have been to reach a broad readership that included the non-trained musician as well as the professional.   Then too, *Musical America* sold much advertising space to performing artists and Kempf may have been concerned about offending a large source of the magazine's revenue.

By late December of 1908, Farwell visited New York City again to attend the first concert to be presented by the American Music Society in Mendelssohn Hall.  He took this opportunity to visit also the office of *Musical America* to discuss his work.  As a result, he was offered an editorial position as chief music critic with the magazine.   Later when Farwell reviewed his own situation, he accepted the position because he realized that the Wa-Wan Press could go on perfectly well in his father's care, and the school could be guided effectively by Arthur Shepherd and his mother.  Thus he could free himself to accomplish more for the American Music Society and other interests by being in New York City rather than Boston.

Progress with the national American Music Society from now on moved swiftly.  The New York City Center presented a series of all-American concerts beginning with the one on December 30th and concluding with an orchestral concert at Carnegie Hall on April 18, 1909.   George Chadwick, who had conducted his work, *Lochinvar*, at the third concert, returned to Boston and aided in giving the largest concert yet undertaken by the Boston Center at Jordan Hall on May 18th.

Meanwhile, Eugene Nowland, with strong local support, succeeded in organizing a large Center of the society in Los Angeles which became second in size to that in New York City. Mary Carr Moore organized a very active center in Seattle in the Spring of 1909 and became its first president. This new group put together three concerts for American Music Day at the Alaska-Yukon-Pacific Exposition on September 25th. The following December they produced a concert honoring the American composer, Dudley Buck. In 1910 and 1911, the Seattle center sponsored composition contests, the winning compositions being performed on a special program. Dean Skilton of the University of Kansas, organized another Center in Lawrence, Kansas, and other Centers followed in San Francisco and elsewhere until perhaps about twenty Centers finally were active across the country.[16]

Farwell, himself, wrote the story of the American Music Society as he knew it in 1910 for the New England Conservatory's yearbook called *The Neume*.[17](Pages 111-115). Excerpts follow:

The conditions were entirely ripe for the coming to birth of such a movement as the American Music Society. Nothing could have proved this more conclusively than the rapidity with which it was accepted in all quarters. Since the organization of the Society in Boston [in 1905], some fourteen or fifteen Centers have come into existence. . .

The one difference between the American music Society and other organizations which have existed in the interest of American music is that the American Music Society is absolutely national in its scope, sympathy, and knowledge....In the making of programs, therefore, it is the purpose of the society to make them representative of the best work which American composers have produced from coast to coast, so that the work of one center, while giving fair representation to its local group, shall represent in the main the very choicest of all American music, and thus stand, in each of its centers, for the national idea.

When Arthur Shepherd was questioned in 1956 about his memories of the American Music Society, he responded on May 4th:

...To the best of my recollection it centered in and about New York City. I recall participating in one or two concerts in N. Y. under its auspices. I recall playing the first American performance of Edgar Stillman Kelley's *Quintet for Piano and Strings*; it is possible too, that I played my *First Piano Sonata* on the same program.

Various musicians of prominence were either members or interested parties to this Society. Lawrence Gilman was a very active participant and in his editorial post on *Harper's Weekly* he became a warm champion of American music and the various persons involved in the Wa-Wan and American Music Society.

I attended various meetings of the Society, held usually after working hours and sometimes running into the wee hours of the morning. These meeting took place in Eugene Heffley's studio (at one time the studio of Edward MacDowell) on the 7th floor (I believe) of Carnegie Hall. Heffley was a prominent piano teacher and a personal friend of MacDowell's. I believe also that the late Marion Bauer was a participant in these activities. I recall also the participation of Modest Altschuler and his brother, Jacob. Modest was at that time conductor of the Russian Symphony Orchestra. I recall too, a performance of a composition of Lawrence Gilman himself in which a viola part was played by Jacob Altschuler.

Shepherd obviously spoke only about the history of the Center in New York City and more research is needed to determine the course of other Centers scattered about the United States.

In July 1909, Farwell quoted a writer on the Pacific Coast who reported on the importance of these Centers: "With such influences as these, the cause of music will be furthered in ten years beyond the measure of a century's unaided progress.[18]

Whatever their life-span, these Centers met a need in each area at that time and helped to pave the way for more recognition of the American composer and his music. Additionally, these

Centers served as models for new music clubs that were spawned in later years to encourage the American composer and promote his music.

The American Music Society was an outgrowth and vital part of the Wa-Wan Press movement. When Farwell first envisioned the Press as a way forward that could provide him with ample time for musical composition, he had not imagined the additional time and energy his lecture-recitals would take. Nor could he have dreamed of the enormous and almost endless challenges he must meet in organizing societies for American music across the land.

Farwell's highly public activities of developing the Press and organizing the American Music Societies must surely have contributed to the recognition of his name in the nation's musical circles. But none of these efforts would have enjoyed any success or fulfillment at all if Farwell had not found common cause among fellow composers, to which he refers in letters to Shepherd. Cheiro was accurate in his prediction of Farwell's extensive travels in this cause. The palmist's perception of a "mysterious power" over people may have contributed to Farwell's dogged determination, but there may also have been an inspired awareness by Farwell himself of the timeliness of these rare and highly innovative endeavors. In one way or another, the American composer has benefited ever since!

# Chapter 10

## New York City, 1909-1918

### Chief Critic for *Musical America*

The burgeoning efforts of the American Music Society in New York City were only a small part of the bustling artistic scene when Farwell moved to the city in 1909 to serve as chief music critic for *Musical America*. Changes in the fine arts world, represented dramatically by the 1904 Armory Show, were still very much in the air. Farwell's pen responded boldly to what he discovered around him, both in his writings and in his music. In his new position as essayist and reviewer, he made significant new professional friendships. He contributed frequently to an anonymous weekly column of insights and comment called, *Mephisto's Musings*. He took advantage of his position to espouse the causes dear to his heart, finding the magazine a prime platform for continuing his crusade for American music. As Farwell became active in community music, he focused his writings more on the needs of the people and widened his mission. (See list of his writings in Appendix I.) Farwell's work for *Musical America* brought his name regularly before the public eye and added to his growing prestige.

Farwell's correspondence in 1910 indicates a further concern, although a small one. In letters to the renowned Berkeley Updike of the Merrymount Press in Boston, who prepared work for the Wa-Wan Press, Farwell sought help of a different kind. At *Musical America*, Farwell observed with disgust the conditions of musical advertising from a typographical standpoint, and wanted to see more distinction in the professional cards of his friends who advertised in *Musical America*.

He complained that the general aim among musicians competing for attention, was to get their names as big as possible, as different as possible from others, and the uglier the type, the better. Farwell asked Updike for help with an experiment to make a very small advertisement as distinguished as possible. He considered it absurd that a person whose life stood for art should not be represented in a way that was completely artistic.

Farwell hoped that his experiment would lead to a redemption of musical advertising and encourage others to do better. Even though this venture in aesthetic concern was but a sidelight to Farwell's assignments, this trial may have helped, as eventually other clients negotiated for similar work.

## Supervisor of Municipal Concerts

New York's Mayor William J. Gaynor (1910 - 1913) offered Farwell another avenue to bring music to the people during his reform administration. Gaynor appointed him in 1910 as Supervisor of Municipal Concerts in the city parks and recreational piers. While fulfilling this position, Farwell continued to write for *Musical America*, composed music for several pageants, and directed some activities of the *Wa-Wan Press*.

The condition of graft that existed in the municipal concerts for many years preceding Farwell's appointment was incredible. Previously, a park band consisting of twenty-four men included eight or ten "dummies" who were saloon keepers or laborers, for example, rather than real performers. These men, holding instruments to their mouths without playing a note, sat in the band as regular members and received the same salary. This graft had become a matter of open scandal by the spring of 1910. Farwell, with the help of the Park and Dock commissioners and a citizen's committee, eliminated this graft. The concerts were systematized and their quality raised. With the cooperation of Charles B. Stover, the park commissioner, Farwell presented symphony concerts, instead of band concerts in the chief center - the mall in Central Park. These became very popular at once and were given every weekday evening and on Saturday and Sunday afternoons.

Farwell reported that in the concert system of New York City, in Manhattan and Richmond alone, about eighty band and orchestra concerts were performed each week at an approximate cost of $100,000 each summer. He stressed the importance of the Central Park orchestral concerts for the audiences of 8,000 to 15,000 people. Many who had no previous familiarity with any but the cheapest kinds of street music, now were exposed to the world's masterpieces. He noted:

The same faces were often seen in the same seats day after day, week after week and year after year - many coming often as much as three hours early to get their favorite seats. For the recreation pier concerts, the people of the poorer districts will often send their children alone at three and four in the afternoon to hold seats for them until the concert in the evening.[1]

Farwell attended many of these concerts to observe audience reactions and noted the therapeutic effect the music had on them. As a result of his observations, he developed the idea that "mass-appreciation" was something which large audiences developed in a short time from emotional contagion rather than as a result of education or growth in listening skills. He declared:

> While it would probably have been difficult or impossible to interest individuals of this mass intellectually in a single page of Beethoven or Wagner, here in the mass, and under the proper conditions, there became evident a *mass-spirit* or *oversoul*, capable of receiving and eager to receive, all of reality that the music contained....Under these conditions the emotion of the composer is communicated in its fullness directly to the spirit of the mass and its real meaning conveyed to them without any reference to an appreciation of the construction or other technical factors which went into the making of the music....Furthermore, I am convinced that in this phenomenon, the *educational process is short-circuited by a spiritual process*. (Farwell emphasis)

This observation was based on the fact that he saw this "mass-appreciation" at the Central Park concerts not as a matter of education or growth during the four years, but found it as reality within the first week.[2]

These conclusions became an important basis for Farwell's later work in community music. He explained his theory:

> In giving music to the people there exists this heretofore little understood principle which is in direct

communication of that which was in the soul of the composer to the masses. Through this fact there arises a new musical gospel, which is that music at its highest is not for a few, but for all; not some time, but now. It can be received by all and it is to be given to all.[3]

Farwell trumpeted his "new musical gospel" in frequent grandiloquent essays as he also strove to put into practice the principles he espoused.

Rose Yont also recognized Farwell's theory of "mass appreciation" which she named "a spontaneous psychic element." Writing in 1916, she made these observations which coincided with those of Farwell's:[4]

...Four years before, most of the same people had never heard a symphony concert. This was an experiment at first, and proved that love for the best music is not an educative process. The people were as attentive the first year as the fifth. Most of the audiences were "East Siders".

Farwell continued to fight for more free music in the parks. He wanted to present opera as well as concerts since he believed everything dramatic appeals more strongly to the people than even the best purely symphonic music. So, in addition to the band and orchestra concerts, "opera nights" eventually were made a regular attraction.

On three afternoons a week, from three o'clock to five, music for folk dancing was added for children. The carefully supervised sessions were held at the East 37th Street, East 24th Street, East 112th Street, and West 50th Street Recreation Piers. The East 24th Street Pier was the center of folk dancing activity. It was also the largest and most accessible pier. A Mr. Somerset, who led the band there for the entire ten week season in 1911, was able to develop a good knowledge of what music was required for the dancing. The band leaders for the other piers were appointed for only two weeks at a time.

Folk dancing activities were an effort to draw the various ethnic groups together to promote a democratic spirit using music and dance. These activities culminated in an impressive "Children's Folk Dance Festival" which Farwell rehearsed and staged. The ghetto children included Jews, Italians, and Hungarians who were taught to perform the dances in costumes of their various ethnic groups. Farwell thought that these experiences would educate ethnic Americans who were unfamiliar with their own culture, and give them a sense of pride in it. He believed that other Americans would come to appreciate the contributions each ethnic group had given to American culture. Here we find Farwell functioning again with an educator's heart in his concern for children.

The performances were not only a valuable experience for the children, but also they drew the attention of music and dance educators to these new ethnic sounds. This successful Festival inspired many annual cultural fairs in large cities with big immigrant populations, sponsored later by the International Institute. These fairs have continued to the present since first organized in 1920.

Another feature of the Parks and Piers program was the regular performance of new American orchestral works. Underlying this special attraction, as with all other activities, was Farwell's dream to promote good American music and to use music as a "tool to raise mankind to a higher plane of love and brotherhood". He envisioned a revitalized musical life in America that would be brought about only as part of a larger cultural evolution resulting from a new spiritual consciousness.

However, not everyone favored Farwell's efforts. Gertrude Farwell shared a family story told by her husband of his early experiences as Supervisor.[5] One day when he was on the East Side trying to make arrangements for an outdoor concert, some ruffians pelted him with stones, swore at him and shrieked, "Get out! We're tough, and we want to stay tough. Take your dang long-haired music out of here!"

Farwell visited three or four concerts every night. He maintained two offices in the city, one being at Number 10 West 40th Street. His work, in addition to hiring musicians, included correcting proofs of programs sent to him from all the conductors and bandmasters in the city. He made suggestions for the programs and had to approve every one given by his staff.

Farwell held this post from 1910 to 1913, a long time for an idealist to survive in what had been such a political mess.

One special service which Farwell rendered during his term was designing the centenary program commemorating the first use of the City Hall, as well as the 135th anniversary of the signing of the Declaration of Independence. His assignment to this task may have come about through the recommendation of Farwell's old friend, Thomas Mott Osborne. Ever since their European travels together, the two men had kept in contact. Osborne's letter to Mayor Gaynor on April 18, 1911, speaks for itself :

> Allow me to introduce to you my friend of many years standing, Mr. Arthur Farwell. I have known Mr. Farwell long and intimately and am greatly interested in his development as a musician and one who is endeavoring to bring the American people into close touch and loving reverence for the great art of Music. I have known of his ability as a composer and the thorough training he has received, not only as a musician but in general education...
>
> As well as I could I have kept in touch with him in his work as Supervisor of Municipal Concerts in New York City last summer and have been much interested in the many new and popular needs which he introduced in that work, and the many new American musical works in which he aroused public interest. In fact, his devotion to the cause of American Music and his enthusiasm for our National work in the line of his art has been one of the most important factors in arousing attention and interest in the works of American composers, and his services in that field have been very great.
>
> I have also talked with him about his ideas for a musical celebration of the Fourth of July and the making of that holiday something besides a mere noisy and dangerous display of firearms and fireworks. Mr. Farwell is a man whose good judgment and common sense you can trust as well as his musical ability, and I take great pleasure in recommending him to you.

Osborne's letter may have prompted Mayor Gaynor to confer with Farwell. The celebration, with Farwell devising and supervising, took place on July 4, 1911, at New York's City Hall. Realizing the need for an appropriate hymn for such an impressive event, Farwell composed the words and music for *Hymn To Liberty*. This was sung by a selected mixed chorus from the United German Singers. The program began on the steps of City Hall followed by the escorting of the mayor and guests to the stand of honor by a uniformed guard of patriotic societies. Frank Stretz's military band was featured in addition to the United German Singers. Distinguished speakers and soloists lent further dignity and prestige to the day.

Arthur Farwell's parents received a hand written invitation, signed by George F. Kuntz, chairman of the City Hall Celebration Committee, to attend the exercises and hear the performance of their son's patriotic hymn.

Later, Farwell wrote about his ideas for similar celebrations for the Division of Recreation of the Russell Sage Foundation who published in 1912, a little book, *The Celebration of the Fourth of July by Means of Pageantry*. In addition to Farwell's article, it featured one by William Chauncy Langdon on pageantry.

### Third Street Music School Settlement

By 1915 Farwell entered still another arena - that of director of the Third Street Music School Settlement, then in its 21st year, where he succeeded David Mannes. This school was a famous institution on the lower East side of New York where poor children were able to receive excellent instruction in all branches of music at prices ranging from ten to sixty-five cents a lesson. It had a staff of one hundred teachers and a student enrollment of one thousand pupils. The school had four orchestras, two of which Farwell conducted. He held this position until June 1918.

Farwell first made sure that the institution was running properly as a conservatory with competent heads of departments. Eventually he massed the pupils into a great chorus of eight hundred with a combined orchestra of two hundred and presented them at Carnegie Hall. He claimed that he surprised the board of managers of the school by showing them that such a "community concert" could be successfully given and crowds attracted to it without the necessity of engaging a famous soloist to draw the audience.

The result of the concert was a substantial financial gain for the school and an improved reputation in the city that it had not previously held. "For the first time the city was brought to realize what a tremendous work was going on which it had scarcely suspected."[6]

A torn newspaper account from Farwell's files dated March 7, 1918, also describes this concert which included works by Grieg, Tchaikovsky, Beethoven, Saint-Saens, Haydn, Schumann and Mendelssohn's *Rondo Capriccioso* played by a twelve year old boy. It points out that this was "perhaps the first time, certainly not more than the second, in twenty years' existence of this unique institution that it had appeared in its entirety." The reporter was impressed with the necessity for doubling the size of the Carnegie Hall stage, as well as with the beauty of its lighting effects. These had been prepared by Farwell's friend, the architect Claude Bragdon, who was the famous designer for the "Song and Light" festivals. The reporter added:

> An interesting feature of the program was the community singing in which the audience joined in "The Star Spangled Banner" as the opening number, under the leadership of Harry Barnhart. The carols from the *Evergreen Tree*, arranged by Farwell, which had a semi-private hearing at the MacDowell Club this winter, were heard for the first time in public, the composer conducting... Many children traveled far to do their part.

Here is evidence of Farwell's skill as an educator and organizer. Not only was he concerned about providing good musical training for children of little means, but also he anticipated that the new prestige following the concerts would contribute to the children's pride and an upgraded self-image. Though Farwell maintained earlier in his life that he did not want to become a teacher, nevertheless, he functioned as an educator in nearly every phase of his career.

Even President Theodore Roosevelt was aware of the wholesome social values of music for these children.    After attending a concert at the Third Street Music School Settlement, (very possibly the large one Farwell presented), he spoke to a group of those youngsters saying:

> Boys and girls, do not envy your neighbors who have many automobiles in their garages, while you have your piano, your violin, or your cello.  Prepare yourself to earn a living wage, but do not forget to leave the casement open to let in the "light that never was on sea or land." Let the love for literature, painting, sculpture, and above all, music enter into your lives."[7]

### Special Friends

During these New York years, Farwell made many new friends and reestablished old friendships.  Several of these persons played important roles for many years in his personal life, or were even a vital part of his professional career.  As a handsome bachelor who was frequently in the public eye, Farwell could have been a "social lion" if he had so chosen.  At one point he reports that he had acquired a "new toy" - a horse - that he enjoyed riding about town.  However, in the main he preferred the company of people in the arts, science and literature.

One unusual relationship was that with Kahlil Gibran (1883-1931), the Lebanese painter and author of the widely read book *The Prophet*.  Farwell met Gibran through Alice Haskell, a composer, who had brought her work to Farwell for possible publication in the Wa-Wan Press about 1904.  Her sister, Mary Haskell, and Gibran were devoted friends for years, and Mary introduced him to Farwell in New York.

Gibran was trying to find some ways of earning money through his drawings.  He decided to make portraits of some of the leading people of that time and then sell them as a collection. In his letter to Farwell dated May 2, 1911, Gibran explained his idea further:

...My series of drawings of the big men who represent the art and knowledge of today will be published eventually in a folio. If you will give me the privilege of drawing you, I will not take more than forty minutes of your valuable time. And should you care to see the heads which I have already drawn, I will gladly bring them to you.

Farwell recognized Gibran's talent and monetary need and helped Mary by providing introductions to persons he thought likely candidates for Gibran's work. Farwell was an unselfish person and always willing to help a fellow artist. Eventually Gibran drew Farwell's portrait. Gibran related his reaction to that picture in a letter written to Mary Haskell from his one room Greenwich Village studio on May 5, 1911:

Beloved Mary. At nine o'clock this morning I was down town planning things with a Syrian editor, and at half past two I reached Mr. Arthur Farwell's studio. The drawing I made of Mr. Farwell is among the very best. He said it expresses his whole inner being, and he *must* have a photograph taken from it. Afterward Mr. Farwell and I went to an exhibition of paintings by some of the New York artists. Mr. Farwell introduced me to Mr. Macbeth, the art dealer.[8]

Comparing a photograph of Farwell (figure 28) taken about the same year as the portrait sketched by Gilbran (figure 29), shows the strong resemblance.

Correspondence with Mrs. Charles Kelsey gives evidence of another special friendship. It is probable that Farwell met her in Berlin while he was studying there with Pfitzner. The Kelseys were wealthy people with homes both abroad and in the United States in which they often gave musicals.

At one such program on January 13, 1912, in their large Berlin apartment, Hiram Tuttle sang Farwell's song *The Farewell*. Mrs. Kelsey sent Farwell a copy of the printed program and noted that "All were enthusiastic" about his music. Her accompanying letter added: "The guests numbered 86. They included - Counsel General Thackera and family - Count & Countess Montgelas (in the immediate circle of the Kaiser), the Berlin correspondents of [Musical] Courier, Musical America & Chicago Musical Leader. Also the sister of William Sherwood (Mrs. Watson) and her husband." Obviously, Mrs. Kelsey had assembled a distinguished and discerning group of people and was concerned at that time about promoting music by American composers. The program included works by Sidney Homer, MacDowell, and Mrs. H.H.A. Beach in addition to the song by Farwell.

Mrs. Kelsey's letter was followed by a thoughtful gift to Farwell. It was an attractive monogrammed seal of his initials she had ordered from Tiffany's to be used on his personal stationery. She knew that he liked to personalize his correspondence, which was a fairly common practice at that time. Farwell treasured that seal and later included it on the cover designs of four compositions he printed on his lithographed editions during the 1930s. (Figure 30)

The friendship begun in Berlin continued though the New York years, and was strengthened later by their mutual work in the National Federation of Music Clubs for which Mrs. Kelsey was president for two terms. She kept in contact with Farwell, believed in him, and encouraged him whenever possible.

Another woman friend was the distinguished choral composer, Gena Branscombe. Farwell became acquainted with her while publishing three of her songs in the Wa-Wan Press in the years 1905 - 1906. He may have first met her in Chicago where he stayed several months on the return from his second western tour. The friendship was renewed in New York City, where Branscombe settled after her marriage to John F. Tanney in 1910. Like Farwell, she had studied with Humperdinck in Germany, and they held other common interests. Her passionate belief in the power of music as a great healing and regenerative force was similar to Farwell's ideas. In her long career as a choral conductor, she always sent Farwell tickets to her concerts in the city. His files include copies of the Branscombe Chorale programs which he attended after resettling in the city in 1939.

Farwell's life-long friendship with Harry Barnhart began on one of his western trips when they first met in California. It was strongly rekindled in New York City after Barnhart moved East. Becoming a close friend and colleague, Barnhart served not only

*Figure 28. Photograph of Arthur Farwell made in the Wa-Wan years. Compare with the artist's sketch, facing.*

*Figure 29. Photograph of a sketch of Arthur Farwell made by Kahlil Gibran in New York, in May 1911.*

# Land of Luthany

Poem

*for*

Violoncello and Piano

After "The Mistress of
Vision," by Francis Thompson

$1.25 net

Composed
Printed
and
Published
by
ARTHUR FARWELL
East Lansing - Michigan

*Figure 30. Music cover showing Farwell's use of Tiffany AF monogram design given him by Mrs. Charles B. Kelsey.*

as director of Farwell's community chorus, but later also as the best man at his wedding.

Originally, Barnhart did a one-man vaudeville act under the name of Horner Barnet before he found his place as a song leader. He was mistaken both for William Jennings Bryan and Clarence Darrow, and was likened to Abraham Lincoln in spirit. It was said that a composite portrait of these three men might resemble Barnhart's personality because he had "the showmanship of Bryan, the doggedness of Darrow, and the dedication to a cause like Lincoln".[9]    (Figure 31)

*Figure 31. Harry Barnhart, enthusiastic community singing leader and lifelong friend of Arthur Farwell.*

The success Barnhart secured with his choral groups, was the result of his two-fold aim: to awaken in participants the strong desire to sing, and then to develop the power to do so. For this he found that three things were necessary: encouragement, direction, and the overcoming of self-consciousness. The first two he provided by excellent leadership and a natural enthusiasm and aptitude. The last came about by the mass and group singing in which the strong and confident singers sustained the weak ones and covered up their blunders, until they gained the needed strength and confidence.[10]

Claude Bragdon (1866-1946) was an architect and artist in light designing who engaged Barnhart to provide singing at an elaborate social affair he and his wife gave in Rochester. This occasion gave birth to the first "Song and Light" program there, that was developed further for the New York concerts in 1916. It was probably Barnhart who introduced Bragdon to Farwell. These three men became close friends as well as professional colleagues.

Farwell's friendship with Sergei Rachmaninoff, pianist and composer, (1873-1943) began when Farwell reviewed his performances in New York City for *Musical America*. Farwell's enthusiastic and favorable reviews helped to popularize Rachmaninoff's work nationwide. In a February 22, 1910, review, Farwell commented on Rachmaninoff, the man, and the performance of his *Third Piano Concerto* with the Philharmonic Society of New York at Carnegie Hall:

> Rachmaninoff again demonstrated the tremendous popularity which he has gained since coming to America. There is something about the man so simple and human, and at the same time so powerful, so artistically mighty, that his appeal is a dual one - the appeal of strength as well as of quality.... This Rachmaninoff is a mighty fellow.

What began as a critic's interview in the "Green Room", became a lasting friendship. In the years that followed his American debut, Rachmaninoff visited Farwell whenever his concert schedule brought them together. (Figure 32)

Charles Tomlinson Griffes (1884-1920) visited Farwell quite frequently after his return from studying abroad. He and Farwell shared happy memories of their experiences with Humperdinck, as Griffes had studied briefly with him. Farwell's files include autographed copies of three songs from Griffes dated 1912, followed by a group of piano pieces dated October 1915, "In remembrance of 10 West 40th". Farwell befriended Griffes and encouraged him in composition. It may have been Farwell's interest in Indian music that influenced Griffes to compose his

*Figure 32. Sergei Rachmaninoff and his daughter with Gertrude and Arthur Farwell in Menlo Park, California, about 1919.*

*Two Sketches Based on Indian Themes* for string quartet in 1916-1918. Whether Farwell provided the themes for these compositions is not documented, but the likelihood of his doing so, is very strong.

Noble Kreider was a Wa-Wan composer with whom Farwell developed a life-long friendship. It was he who rescued Farwell after he collapsed from overwork on a Broadway play, *Garden of Paradise*. Kreider took Farwell to Bermuda to recuperate where his loving care helped to restore Farwell's former energies. (See Figure 51 in Chapter 16.) In the 1930s when Kreider lived in Goshen, Indiana, and Farwell was in East Lansing, Michigan, the two men continued to meet often and Farwell's files hold many letters they wrote during those years. Kreider was a virtuoso pianist and piano teacher as well as a composer, and a highly cultured world-traveler. He was probably too delicate in health for the rugged demands of the New York concert world. The Farwell children remember the beautiful flowers "Uncle Noble" sent after their father's death that were given the place of honor on his grand piano.

Farwell developed many other loyal friendships during his years on the East coast, and he was a frequent guest at gatherings of distinguished persons. One such affair was a dinner honoring Walter Damrosch where the long guest list included musicians of international reputation. Farwell's personal charisma as well as his reputation in music circles attracted a wide range of noted friends, from the rough-hewn Carl Sandburg to the prima donna, Rosa Ponselle, whom Farwell reportedly "spanked" at her birthday party! These friendships once made, were seldom lost.

Farwell enjoyed his social contacts with these special people and many others less known in the city, and dated several admiring ladies. Nevertheless, he maintained his hectic schedule as music critic for *Musical America*, as supervisor of municipal concerts in the city parks and piers, and later as director for the Third Street Music School Settlement. Concurrently, he was active in the growing pageant and community music movement until he left New York in 1918. The next several sections of this chapter focus on Farwell's important work in these exciting new endeavors. Therein he found further opportunity to fulfill his vision of bringing uplifting music to the people through ways in which they could participate and enjoy - another phase of his crusade for the "democratization of music".

## Community Music and Pageant Work in the East

During the early years of the twentieth century up until World War I, America was struggling with problems created by the industrial revolution, a surge of foreign immigrants, and the migration from farms to the cities. Many leaders wanted to do something to improve national conditions. The resulting spirit of reform was expressed in various ways during the "Progressive Era".

The use of pageants as a means for social change and as a teaching tool became a popular vehicle beginning in 1905 when the first American pageant was produced in Cornish, New Hampshire, by Augustus and Augusta Saint-Gaudens. Farwell played a major role in making music an integral part of the pageant movement, which had for its original goal to produce "theatre of the people, by the people, and for the people." This goal was one close to Farwell's heart and one he enthusiastically promoted.

Farwell's work with the Park and Pier concerts, together with his contact with childrens' potentials at the Settlement were joined with other burgeoning forces to nourish his aspirations for a growing musical life of the American people. Among leaders and members of the American Music Society, ground had been gained in bringing more concert activity to life in a number of metropolitan centers. Both the growth and the conceived purposes of the new pageant movement sang to Farwell of participation by Everyman in the street. He was conscious of the spirited unifying power of large groups singing together.

During Farwell's years of varied work in New York, he became familiar with the various elements going into the makeup of the musical side of pageantry. Later he remarked that he saw it required only the imaginative faculty of the poet to bring all of these elements into the form of a great communal music drama. "These are all the qualities and elements that went to the making of the Greek drama. Here is the whole thing, and all you have to do is bring it together and you have something for the people that will be tremendous", he concluded.[11]

The inspiration for Farwell's pageants and masques, which became such a large part of the Community Music movement, really began in 1904 during his second trip to the West coast. It was then that he visited the Bohemian Club's *Midsummer High Jinks* and watched the production of one of the Club's great annual Grove Plays, *The Hamadryads* by Will Irwin and William J. McCoy. (Figure 33) This experience, which he claimed marked a turning point in his life, exerted a profound personal influence. He found it astonishing to learn that without the presence of a genius like Wagner, the people of an American city could assemble their talents and produce a music drama capable of giving an uplift and inspiration comparable in many ways with that he had received from the great music dramas at Bayreuth. He stated later that he realized:

> If an American community by reliance on its own resources and by disinterested cooperation, could produce so wonderful a "community drama" with music, it was only a matter of time before there must arise in America a new form of people's drama, a new great type of democratic art-work, characteristic of the new world.[12]

It was about four years after Farwell first experienced a Grove Play that the pageant movement began to find its way into America. It was guided by the influence of Louis N. Parker, the English play and pageant writer whose work in England had gained him international recognition. Several Americans were deeply interested in the movement, including Percy MacKaye, William Chauncy Langdon, and Thomas Wood Stevens, playwrights; Virginia Tanner and Mary Porter Beegle, dancers; and Frank Chouteau Brown, architect and scenery designer. Farwell worked with this group to form what eventually became the American Pageant Association in 1913. Meanwhile he "planned to develop the musical aspect of the pageant to its fullest possibilities."

Farwell renewed his excitement for the Bohemian Club's Grove Plays by a return visit on August 7, 1910, to see *St. Patrick at Tara* composed by William A. Sabin, a personal friend. By August 18th, Mr. Sabin and Mr. McCoy had honored Farwell with

*Figure 33.   Scene from a Bohemian Club Grove Play in woods on Club grounds on the Russian River, California.*

his election to non-resident membership in the Club.  (In 1937 he was transferred to the Club's Professional List.)[13]

In 1912, while he was still supervising music in New York, Farwell wrote the music for Louis N. Parker's Broadway play, *Joseph and His Brethren*, which was based on the Biblical story. While this was an indoor theater production, it primed Farwell for some true pageant writing.   Early the next year he wrote the music for the *Pageant of Meriden*, (New Hampshire) and the *Pageant of Darien*, (Connecticut).   The latter two were authentic community pageants.   Not only did Farwell compose the music for these three productions within an eight-month period, but also he assisted with the direction of each.  (See figures 54, 55 in chapter 21.)

By now, Farwell was relieved of the pressures of former work for his Wa-Wan Press which he had turned over to G. Schirmer. This freed him for directing his seemingly endless energy to other creativity and to the promotion of the pageant movement.  Also,

he had given up the reviewing of concerts for *Musical America.*
Instead, this outspoken advocate, blasted its readers with more
writings to awaken them to the possibilities of a new era that
would bring music to the masses.

## The American Pageant Association

Although the APA was not fully organized until 1913, Farwell
was involved with earlier attempts to bring goals and guidelines
together, and worked with its leaders.  From 1908 through 1911,
three pageant leaders tried to form some kind of association for
sharing ideas: William Chauncy Langdon, Lotta Clark, and George
Pierce Baker.  Each brought a different perspective to what finally
became the American Pageant Association.   Langdon saw
pageantry as a "Civic force";  Clark viewed it as an educator;
Baker thought as a Harvard professor who was actively involved
with experimental dramatic forms combining music, drama, speech
and "symbolic visual effects."   With their combined talents and
philosophy, these leaders viewed pageantry as an agent for
changing society politically and artistically, to meet both local and
national needs.  Their ideas were in tune with the times and they
led the way for other reformers to use pageants as an agent for
change all during the "Progressive Era."

In 1910, Langdon found a sympathetic ear in Luther Gulick
who headed the Department of Child Hygiene for the Russell Sage
Foundation.  Langdon worked under him.[14]  Gulick's philosophy
was that "Democracy rests on the most firm basis when a
community has formed the habit of playing together".[15]  Since
pageants could be viewed as an extension of creative play, Gulick
concurred with Langdon that they should have a vital part in
dealing with social reform problems of the day.

Langdon proposed a Bureau of Pageantry and invited Baker
to help.  When John Glenn, director of the Sage Foundation,
refused to give Langdon money for starting the Bureau, Langdon
then talked the Foundation into a donation of $2,500.00 to create
a pageant at Thetford, Vermont.   Langdon promised to
demonstrate in a pilot project that the pageant was as great a civic
force as he claimed it to be.  Langdon brought together six small
towns in Vermont and appointed an advisory committee of twelve

specialists which included Farwell, the only composer. Thus began Farwell's official pageantry involvement.

With Farwell's approval, Langdon had commissioned James T. Sleeper, a local composer, to prepare the music, while Virginia Tanner was engaged for the dance. Langdon himself, wrote the script and directed. These were the professionals working with the committee - the rest were residents of the towns. In addition to his own original pieces, Sleeper used some music by Bach, Dvořák, Tchaikovsky and Farwell's *Hymn to Liberty*. Mr. Sleeper also mustered people for a chorus and an orchestra, a process in which Farwell probably assisted.

The Thetford Pageant took place August 12, 14, and 15, 1911. Farwell was impressed, finding that the homespun quality of the pageant did not detract from the performance's emotional impact on audience and participants alike. Moreover, there were practical results in the community life. One old farmer exclaimed, "Huh! that's the first time the town of Thetford ever did anything all together!"[16]

Langdon's work had justified his theory of using pageants for social change so he could report positively to the Russell Sage Foundation. Some of these changes were:[17]

1. The Masters of the two Granges in town met to unite their granges in order to secure government help for a soil survey, and expertise for a forest survey.

2. Three villages promoted the Boy Scouts with plans to have every boy enrolled in the organization, and to have it centered at the Academy. The Corn Growing contest sponsored by the Department of Agriculture would be one of the honors in which the Boy Scouts would be working.

3. Similar plans were made to arrange for the girls to have a Camp Fire Girls organization started. The Corn Growing contest would be open to these girls too.

4. A Choral Union composed of choirs from a number of towns of the upper Connecticut River Valley created to sing in the pageant, was to continue as a center for musical culture.

5. An orchestra formed for the pageant continued after its conclusion and planned to function with the Choral Union.

6. The ministers of the six towns united to observe a day of town-wide religious celebration.

It was to be two more years before the APA was established at a two day event in Boston, January 31 - February 1, 1913, with 800 Pageant Masters assembled. The Twentieth Century Club was the host.    By now, thousands of people had been involved, whether as performers, seamstresses, prop-builders, or ticket-sellers.    The year 1908 saw five pageants produced; 1909 had six. The following years found a dramatic increase in the number of productions.    By 1913, there were 46 pageants planned in fifteen states.    Hence, interest in forming a unifying organization to help the leaders was strong at this time.    There was also a deep concern that unless this powerful tool had some professional control and means for exchange of information, that the artistic quality  and social values of the pageants would deteriorate.

At the Boston meeting, a basic organization was initiated: William Chauncy Langdon was elected president, Lotta Clark, secretary, and  Farwell became a charter member of the Board of Directors with a four year term, renewed in 1917.   He remained active in the eastern organization until he left for California in 1918.   It was early in this period that Farwell's growing awareness of the pageant's potential led him to compose the music for his Meriden and Darien pageants, already noted.

## St. Louis Pageant and Masque

With the APA now functioning, thanks to the vision of these leaders and the many enthusiastic members, the pageants improved, and guest performers and speakers were often invited to participate in its meetings. We find Farwell in his next pageant activity visiting St. Louis.   This was when a Conference of Cities was held beginning May 31, 1914, in conjunction with the large *Pageant of St. Louis*.   He was invited to speak there on *Municipal Concerts, Music and the Pageant*.   Other speakers included Luther Gulick, Frank Damrosch, F. X. Arens, Charlotte Rumbold and Henry Bruere.    Bruere, speaking on *City Government*, spoke strongly for pageantry and the arts claiming that it is impossible to win the people to an active interest in government until you begin to dramatize and humanize government acts.

The pageant and masque ran from May 21st to June 1st, with its goal purporting to show how art could facilitate and encourage democracy. It also was a celebration of the one hundred fiftieth anniversary and founding of St. Louis. (Figure 34) Pageant leaders claimed that the whole city was involved and that the pageant broke down barriers, as we saw in Thetford. But it remained true that blacks were not involved, nor is it clear how many of the poorer labor classes were included. Farwell wrote with his usual positivism in the August issue of *Review of Reviews*.[18]   He found the production to be:

> ...an ideal cooperative enterprise of the most stupendous nature, and from the artistic [standpoint] a world-event in the history of drama....The production of community dramas of this nature provide for the mass of the people an access to the arts of music and dance, and of drama, realistic and imaginative, which has been denied them in the narrower, traditional, and financially forbidding art-world. Such community drama presents a form which may well be considered as the most complete flowering of the present wide-spread movement to bring to the whole people the refreshment and inspiration of the arts.
>
> It is with this aspect of the pageant that the writer has been particularly concerned, and through which both experience and observation have shown him the possibility not merely of community drama, but of a veritable community *music-drama*, capable of realizing for our American democracy a public art-life the possibility of which has been unsuspected, or doubted, and even denied....Richard Wagner conceived his music-drama as a national and democratic function. But it has been shut away in opera houses...and claimed by the very restricted "musical world".

Percy MacKaye shared Farwell's vision for the future of the community drama. Their collaboration was to be a long and close one. MacKaye claimed it is frequently asserted that the ideas of art and democracy are irreconcilable; that art differentiates and uplifts, whereas democracy assimilates and levels. To this he disagreed, declaring that in such an assertion the ideals of democracy and commercialism are confused. "Commercialism always levels; true democracy never!" Like Farwell, MacKaye

*Figure 34. Scenes from Percy MacKaye's Masque of St. Louis, a drama symbolizing the spirit and meaning of the early life and growth of the city.*

believed that American pageantry had the potential to become an art form that could remain fresh and vital as long as it remained close to the people and was controlled by creative artists. "For true democracy is vitally concerned with beauty, and true art is vitally concerned with citizenship."[19]

## Pageant Music

Initially there was confusion about what kind of music was appropriate for pageants. Since the problem needed focusing, Farwell addressed it in an article for the American Pageant Association's *Bulletin*, No. 43, December 1916. He expressed the Association's definition of the pageant itself, that it was meant to be an original statement in celebration of an occasion or a person important to a particular community; and it must not be a commercial, profit-making affair. It was to be a formal, scripted work presented to a paying, seated audience often in an outdoor setting. Its structure involved a series of Episodes - usually three to seven. These were self-contained and if any were eliminated, it would usually mean not a loss of continuity, but that one facet of the plot would not be explored.

It was easier to find agreement on definitions for the basic pageant, than on what kind of music should be used for it. Farwell's *Bulletin* article declared that the subject of pageant music was still a very chaotic one in 1916. He stated that it was wrong to try to force one's own ideals upon the huge national community where pageant activities were going on in so many widely separated places, all with different interests at stake. He gave advice to composers and declared further:

> ...A few principles of fundamental nature, however, seem to have asserted themselves. The foremost is that pageant music should be created for the pageant and not adapted. If the pageant movement is not creative, it is nothing, and everything in its artistic constitution should be created....Aside from the creative process involved, it is distracting to hear familiar music, laden with other associations, used with a pageant which should direct attention wholly upon itself...

The chorus should be more and more developed in pageant music. Community singing is the order of the day and is developing in many sections. The pageant movement should both use and inspire this development. The people need and want new songs, and there is a great field for such work in making the melodies as simple and broad as those of Stephen Foster, though with harmonies somewhat more modern and rich.

It is important that author and composer should stand in close relationship. Literary men are notoriously unmusical, and apt to conceive scenes and texts in a form which does not admit of the full and true expression of the power of music. The musical aspect of a pageant or masque can be killed, even by a text exceptionally fine from the literary standpoint. The musical aspect of the pageant has to go into its very conception and that conception comes from the author. Hence the great importance of mutual understanding, from the outset, between author and composer. For one thing, musical climaxes develop more slowly than literary climaxes, and the author will often fail to give an opportunity for the music to develop with anything like its full power. In general, the rate of progress of musical ideas is less rapid than literary ideas, and this should be understood where musical effect is required.

We are to look at pageant music not as an offshoot from the world of music in general, but as something more vital and creative than most of that which arises otherwise. For it marks a departure from the artificialities and decadent importations which constitute much the greater part of the affairs of our musical world, and fills a distinct need of the people for something which is appropriate and belongs to them.

Here in Farwell's writing we see his persistent crusading for music for the people as well as his concern that script and music be planned together. Percy MacKaye echoed Farwell's thoughts about "Decadent importations" when he pointed out that "The

American Drama still lies fallow for we have listened too long to the courtly muses of Europe".[20]

## Song and Light Festival

In his pageant productions Farwell recognized the community role and value of the chorus work, but none of these choruses had developed into independent and permanent organizations.  As early as 1912, Farwell had conferred with Harry Barnhart about creating such a group and they wrote out the democratic principles for a Community Chorus, the name being used for the first time.[21]  "If you could only bring the people together, wholly democratically, and without any consideration of voice trials or previous musical training," said Barnhart, "great things would come of it; the spirit of song would unite and lead them."  Barnhart went on to Rochester, New York, to put into practice the principles upon which the two men had agreed, and organized a very successful community chorus there.

However, it was January 1916 before Farwell could act on the ideas he and Barnhart had discussed.  Then he and John Collier of the People's Institute, called a meeting of interested singers who became the nucleus for the Community Chorus in New York City.  Harry Barnhart was invited to direct the Chorus, and Farwell was elected its first president.  Rehearsals were attended by several hundred people "to whom the movement came as a great inspiration".[22]

In the spring of 1916 the Community Chorus held Sunday afternoon meetings, preceding the regular orchestral concerts in the Mall in Central Park.  Even the onlookers were invited to sing, and word-sheets of many well-known songs were distributed among them.  Regular rehearsals were held elsewhere during the week and the Sunday meetings were called "sings".  Recruits were drawn for the Chorus from the Central Park crowd so the movement grew rapidly.  People who were shy about auditioning for a singing group were attracted to the community chorus because no auditions were required for membership.  When Farwell was criticized for the quality of his singers, he stoutly declared with typical idealism that the primary goal of the community chorus was not a musical one, but rather for the "emotional, intellectual, spiritual unification" of a community, and that "the art of music" was only the vehicle for this higher purpose. This purpose was similar to his conception of how an audience could be united mystically by "mass-appreciation", as he discovered in the earlier municipal park concerts. Farwell tried to provide quality music that still met the needs of his singers, but their performance was more than ordinary "crowd singing". Nevertheless, it seems that the social benefits the members derived from singing were more important to him at first, than the artistic values. However, his desire for the highest quality of musical performance gradually became a priority as the chorus grew in confidence and ability.

A special festival called *Song and Light* was developed to close the first season of the Chorus on September 13th. This was made possible by Mayor John Purroy Mitchel, Commissioner of Parks Cabot Ward, the officers' advisory board, executive committee, and the members of the Community Chorus.

For the performance, the Chorus, now numbering over 800 members, was placed on the north shore of the lake at the head of the Mall in Central Park. The orchestra consisting of 65 members chosen from three of the best orchestras available, was located on a special platform built over the water. This was covered with vines, and at each end was one of the tall special lights made by Claude Bragdon. Over the orchestra platform a great luminous and colorful proscenium of Bragdon's screens was arranged, and lanterns of his design were hung in the largest trees. Every visible white light in the Park was transformed into a spectrum of vivid colors as the light shone through his geometrically designed screens. The particular date was chosen because a full moon overhead was due to add its light to the scene.

Outdoor night performances require extensive illumination so that the musicians can see their music and the listeners may have visual pleasures as well as auditory ones. Bragdon had worked three years on the highly imaginative panels and huge globes used for the concert. No two panels were alike. Some of these were ones he had prepared for his own gala affair in Rochester. Mr. Bragdon rightly earned the title of "Master of Light" listed on the program! (Figure 35)

*Figure 35. View across Central Park Lagoon of New York City's "Song and Light" Festival, September 13, 1916.*

The *New York Telegraph* reported that one half million candle power of electricity was used by the engineers of the New York Edison Company in the lighting scheme. "The effect was soft, fanciful and delicate." In addition to the lights in the proscenium area, thousands of lanterns were hung along the shore of the lake where every boat and skiff was pressed into service and "was packed with rapt listeners." A special launch was docked at the east end of the lake for the representatives of the press, who wrote glowing reports for their newspapers the next day.

The *New York Times* gave insight into a problem that arose because of the current street car strike. A squad of Boy Scouts was recruited to assist the police who had been drafted from strike duty to handle the large crowds. One of the police precautions was to have a half dozen patrolmen in rowboats provided with ropes and life preservers, who patrolled the borders of the lake, ready for accidents. It seems that none occurred.

The musical program featured Mme. Alma Simpson, soprano soloist, Frederic Watson, pianist, and Harry Barnhart, conductor. The chorus sang ten numbers with orchestral accompaniment, and the orchestra performed four works alone. Farwell conducted the first public performance of his specially composed *March! March!* and *Joy! Brothers, Joy!* which involved audience participation. One *Sun* reporter pointed out that many of the musical selections were suggestive of the watery surroundings of the park lake. The *Barcarolle* from *The Tales of Hoffman* was especially appropriate, *Siegfried's Rhine Journey* from *Götterdämmerung*, and *The Beautiful Blue Danube* waltz were the other water-related numbers.

Sixty thousand people who assembled on the south shore for two evenings, enjoyed this free spectacular concert. This was accomplished in spite of the street car strike. The concert on September 12, 1916, was described as the "first music and light show in the United States" according to one source[23] - but the real first effort at combining "Song and Light" had been in Rochester on September, 30, 1915.[24]

One feature of the New York City Festival program left an indelible impression on observers. It was the audience's participation in singing Stephen Foster's *Old Black Joe*. When the refrain was reached of "I'm coming", one section of the community chorus sang it softly and was echoed as whispered song by the other chorus section. This line repeated, and then the whole chorus rolled out "For my head is bending low."

> Immediately Mr. Barnhart hushed both his chorus and orchestra, and from across the lantern-lighted shadows across the lake there came the sound of another chorus - an unformed one - singing: "I hear those gentle voices calling, 'Old Black Joe.'"
>
> Never in concert hall or opera house have I heard music that thrilled me as did this simple melody of Stephen C. Foster, as it came across the water from a shadowy mass of people - "neighbors," at last, in a mighty metropolis - who were singing for the very joy of it. *If ever Walt Whitman's "I Hear America Singing" is to be*

> *realized, it is to be in just such a welding of America's racial*
> *units in a community gathering.*[25]    (Culbertson emphasis)

Kenneth S. Clark's above review of the festival appeared on the first page of *Musical America*. "New York Carried on Tidal Wave of Community Music," shouted the headlines. His enthusiastic article concluded: "That the 'Song and Light' Festival was able to crystallize this community feeling in spite of the inherent resistance of a great cosmopolis is perhaps the greatest triumph in America's community music movement."

Clark berated the city officials for not providing funds for the Community Chorus and adjured the Board of Estimate to make a significant appropriation for music for next year. He stated that it was private enterprise which initiated the festival and private generosity which made possible the repetition of the event which had been originally announced for one night only. "Gift from a millionaire? No; it was a prominent concert artist, who gave the chorus a check for an amount covering the salaries for the orchestra for the second night's work."[26]

Cabot Ward, Commissioner of Parks, was quoted by a reviewer for the *New York Herald* on September 14th as saying of the event:

> I have been interested in the work of the Community Chorus from its beginning, as I have believed that here existed an opportunity to bring together and to unify many citizen movements. Each Sunday thousands have flocked into the park to unite and participate in a form of recreation new to New York - the expression in song of a real community spirit. The influence has been a helpful one. The Song and Light Festival has been a worthy celebration.

As president of the Chorus, Farwell had done more than direct the group's activities. He had sung bass in the Chorus and acted as assistant director in addition to composing the two new works for the Chorus. Here one sees Farwell mingling closely with those he served and being sensitive to their growing needs and interests. Yes, "he heard America singing!"

Some time later as Farwell looked back to his successful Song and Light Festival, he lauded the promising potentials of the community music movement:

> When groups and crowds of people throughout the country come together regularly to voice themselves in song, it is beyond human power to estimate the extent of the force which has been launched....The song of the nation is powerful beyond all knowing or dreaming... when that song is truly the voice of the nation, ...the meaning of community music in America today is that America is seeking and beginning to find that voice.

As Farwell reflected on what had happened during the Festival concert, he predicted "It is impossible to know what this movement will lead to in its next stage."[27]

Farwell's files include an essay written by a member of this Chorus who expressed his feelings after a rehearsal held September 4, in preparation for the Song and Light Festival. It gives an intimate and hearty picture of one person's memories of that event as follows:

> The rehearsal is over. - *Pilgrims Chorus - Hail Bright Abode -Heavens Are Telling - Hallelujah* and all the music for the great Song and Light Festival. Two hours of the greatest activity and intense strain, but Mr. Barnhart finishes in fine form. There is a rush to the platform by those who want to get next to the throne.
>
> Fred Watson looks up with a smile. He knows he has done a good job and running the piano for such a rehearsal is no snap. He has to be a mind reader and know what Mr. Barnhart is going to do before he speaks. Now he can go out and walk the streets for an hour to quiet down before he can sleep.
>
> There is the woman who brought a tub of lemonade. She is looking for Mr. Brice, the treasurer; she has money for him.
>
> Mr. Plumb, the Newark real estate man, stops me to

note Kitty Cheatham's beautiful and artistic rendering of "Swing Low" that she has just sung for us - a long sustained nasal resonance tone. We agree that we have never heard anything like it.

Mrs. Fox is off near the door selling cartoons of Mr. Barnhart at 10 cents each, makes them herself and turns the money into the treasury.

Among the basses I see a little old Italian with a sprawling plaid necktie, music in hand and a red book and a cotton umbrella under his arm. He says to Mr. Barnhart, "You maka me feel lika younger. Wisha you mucha success. I lika make you present. I bring you nica big buncha flowers."

And there is the Countess. She was a Wagner opera singer in Berlin. Now she likes to sing "My Bonnie" with the Community Chorus. Now she is eager to share and tell of that wonderful spiritual life, that has come out of suffering on her Polish estate and her miraculous deliverance from that war swept spot.

Walking down the aisle is the big broken spectator. He speaks to no one but he did tell Mr. Barnhart that he had saved his life. "It was hearing those old songs that we used to sing on the back step that did it."

The soul is dead that is not quickened by the experiences of such a rehearsal. Good will abounds. Smiles are all around. The people are loathe to go. They delay, linger and wait - all but Arthur Farwell, the president of the Community Chorus. He is pleased with his *March, March* and his *Joy! Brothers*, but he is ill at ease. Speak to him and he says, "Yes, yes" to anything. His head is teeming with musical ideas, and he longs for a lodge in a wilderness, where he can write and write.

After Farwell attended Barnhart's second presentation of his Song and Light Festival in Rochester on August 1, 1916, he wrote a review for *Musical America* identifying the program as a "new art form". Farwell stated that such a beautiful event is one of the many unexpected things which arise from a true "community" movement. He believed that "it is not difficult to foresee the entrance of *motion* into the 'Song and Light' festival, and eventually the dramatic form." These ideas came to life later in Farwell's use of light to dramatize music and movement at the Theater of the Stars in California.

At the Christmas season another special program was presented by the Community Chorus, when Farwell offered a *Tree of Light* in conjunction with the performance of Handel's *Messiah*. The Chorus of 1,000 singers sang in Madison Square Garden with an orchestra of 90 players. Farwell said that when he began rehearsals for the *Messiah*, 80 percent of the singers had not previously heard the music.

The Community Chorus performed portions of *The Messiah* again the following year, Mr. Barnhart conducting, assisted by the Senior orchestra of the Third Street Music School Settlement with added wind players and Farwell, conductor. This concert had a more serious setting due to America's April entrance into World War I. Program notes written by Farwell described the mood:

> It is not in a traditional sense that we present portions of this masterwork of Handel, but rather, in these days of terrific stress, when we are all drawn hour by hour into closer realization, and touched with the crisis that hangs over us, it seems fitting that we all, in every part of our great nation, heroically proclaim in a loud and joyful voice our faith in the victory of the true God, bringing forth a love and brotherhood, such as never has reigned upon earth among men.
>
> The text is taken from all portions of the Bible and has a direct meaning for every human being, without interfering with any religious belief or sectarian doctrine, but rather strengthening our unified faith that we shall have a brotherhood of man, that slavery and murder shall be driven from the face of the earth, and the reign shall be for ever and ever.
>
> Come let us sing and work together to this end!

Some community singing took place at this concert before the oratorio was performed, and a written prayer in the program prefaced the singing of two hymns at the close.    It was an impressive evening.

## Caliban

Farwell rarely had only one project in progress at a time. While he was developing his Community Chorus, he had already composed much of the music for what became his greatest effort in New York City in the field of community music and pageantry. This was to write and conduct the music for Percy MacKaye's masque *Caliban by the Yellow Sands*, produced in May 1916, to celebrate the Tercentenary of Shakespeare's death. This was only one of the many pageants produced across America memorializing Shakespeare's death, but it must have been the most spectacular and imposing one. The pageant used a cast of 5,000, a chorus of 500, and an orchestra of 80 musicians. This huge work was produced fourteen times in Lewisohn Stadium. A Boston version of *Caliban* using Farwell's music, was produced in Harvard Stadium beginning July 2, 1917. One writer referred to it as "a feast of color and music, acting and dancing, of pageantry and light, such as New York had never witnessed; it set a new mark for community music drama for the country." [28]

Gertrude Everts Brice, a cousin of Kirk Brice - the Treasurer of the New York Community Chorus, had witnessed nearly every performance of *Caliban* in 1916. (She would, the following year, become Mrs. Arthur Farwell.) In June 1965, she reminisced in an interview with the author, about the excitement of *Caliban*. She declared she had never forgotten the thrill of it all - its dramatic opening as four trumpeters blared the introductory notes from four corners of the stadium - its Roman orgy scene where men rode flashing chariots around the arena, and the Shakespearean excerpts which took place on a separate stage at the far end of the stadium. Since public address systems were unknown, actors had difficulty in presenting their lines. "How do you project Romeo and Juliet across two city blocks?" she queried. People complained that they could not hear, but they could see and the visual splendor made up for other inadequacies.

Mrs. Farwell stressed the unifying influence of the work. A large number of ethnic groups which existed as separate entities were incorporated in the *Caliban* cast. Many of the scenes were planned by Shakespearean scholars, so details were authentic as well as impressive. Thousands of people participated in some way by raising funds, sewing costumes, and selling advertising, if not dancing, acting, or singing. Percy MacKaye called this "Community Engineering". Mrs. Farwell emphasized, "Everyone who performed felt the excitement and wondered when they could do it again." She quoted John Collier as saying, "I am dedicated to seeing this whole great metropolis being turned into a Town Meeting - into what used to happen in small communities when American Might was acting on the Boston Common, for example."

Farwell's work was a tremendous success. Its production was an expression of his goal for Community Music, which Mrs. Farwell pointed out was "the education of a human being through the magic of art - such as was accomplished in *Caliban*."

In spite of the obvious success of *Caliban*, its producers were dissatisfied with the work. The huge cast made production difficult and some people expressed a desire for a less pretentious work. Accordingly, Farwell wrote the music for *The Evergreen Tree*, a Christmas masque for community singing and acting with script by Percy MacKaye, which had more modest requirements. This was performed successfully by the New York City Community Chorus and later met with popularity in many communities. Farwell reported that it became known as "the Modern Messiah".[29]

### Farwell's War-Time Music Activities

The advent of America's entry into World War I terminated further commissions for Farwell to compose music for pageants until 1920. Hence he concentrated his energies on community chorus work.

America's entrance into World War I changed the direction of most community music efforts. Because of American patriotic activities and the accompanying enthusiasm aroused, the community singing movement was lifted from its localized sphere and carried quickly across the nation.

One catalyst was the War Department Commission on Training Camp Activities, known as the Fosdick Commission, which was organized in Washington, D. C. at this time. Lee Hanmer, in charge of recreational activities for the Commission, went to the officers of the New York Community Chorus for help in instituting singing in the army training camps. This plea coincided with the National Conference on Community Music assembled by Farwell and his associates. A flyer inviting citizens to the Conference described the power of the community music movement in "bringing to the people of the nation a new message of unity, of patriotism, of brotherhood in song, and of universal expression in beauty and joy".[30] It further identified the movement with:

> ... a new current of social consciousness....The movement recognizes fully the place and value of a high development of artistic refinement, but in its present stage it exists primarily to liberate the spirit of the people through free participation in great forms of self-expression. In it the people of the nation free themselves from dependence upon traditions of the past and create their own traditions. Enfolded and fortified in a new unity, through music, they create a new nation by the utterance of the deepest in the national soul, and a new art by the perfecting of that utterance.

The lofty tone of Farwell's writing is typical of his thought-life. His idealized perception of the unifying power of music among the people was not new. It has shown some dynamic vitality in other ways before Farwell's time and since. The singing of great Christian hymns in the vernacular was a unifying and inspiring force in Luther's Reformation. Joan Baez and other singers-for-causes have exploited this unifying power, which clearly is related to the drawing power of rock singers and gospel groups as well. It is this power which moves immense assemblies of young people to identify with the performer and the music. What Farwell was trying to do was not as "far-out" as some might think. Rather, it may have been his often pompous and Victorian means of expression that were unusual. Here Farwell's social leadership is another expression of his mission - to make music a vital, uplifting part of the everyday lives of the people.

Distinguished persons, who were heads of other large organizations, gave their support to this endeavor in Community Music.[31]    Many people from all over the country accepted the invitation to attend this conference in New York City to exchange ideas on what had now come to be a definite movement and national concern. The Conference culminated in the organization of the National League for Community Music; Farwell was elected its president. When Mr. Hanmer was invited to address a session of the Conference, he succeeded in arousing great enthusiasm for the development of Army singing.    As a result, the Fosdick Commission appointed Farwell to attend the Officer's Training Camp at Plattsburg, New York, to study the possibilities for developing army group singing. He was the first person to be sent to an army camp for this purpose.

### Farwell's Marriage to Gertrude Brice

Probably as a result of this appointment, Farwell was financially able to marry Gertrude Everts Brice, a twenty-five year old aspiring actress who was twenty years younger than he. Farwell was attracted to her ethereal beauty. Tall, slim and poised, her large, intelligent brown eyes dominated her delicate face, framed softly by dark waved hair. She wore it banded across her forehead, caught into a rather Grecian-looking knot in back. She and Farwell shared a love of the arts and she also sang in the Community Chorus which he had organized. (Figure 36) Prior to meeting Farwell, Gertrude Brice had trained for a career in the theater and lived in New York City at the Three Arts Club. This was a residence for young ladies from good families who were beginning their careers in the arts.

As their friendship developed, Farwell learned more about Gertrude's background. She had grown up in a large comfortable house in Lima, Ohio, with maids to do the cleaning. Gertrude's mother, Carolyn Everts Brice, had founded the Shakespeare Society in town, and Shakespeare was considered the family "patron saint".    Unfortunately she died prematurely in 1908. Gertrude was sixteen years old when she was left with the care of her younger sister, Betty, and a brother, William, as well as supervision of the housework. Her father, Jonathan Brice, a civil

*Figure 36.  Gertrude Everts Brice, 1916, in New York before her marriage to Arthur Farwell.  (Photo by Underwood and Underwood)*

engineer, lived until 1932, but was in declining health after his
wife died.   When circumstances permitted, Gertrude was finally
allowed to attend a Cleveland drama school where she was warmly
encouraged by the director, Tyrone Power, Sr.   Eventually
Gertrude left for New York to seek work in the theater.

Among Gertrude's personal papers is a description of her
introduction to Arthur Farwell.  She wrote:

> I met Arthur Farwell in the Spring of 1916 at my
> cousin Kirk Brice's estate near Huntington, Long Island.
> Arthur had just finished conducting the music which he
> had written for the Shakespeare Tercentenary Masque,
> *Caliban by the Yellow Sands*.   As I had witnessed a
> performance of this great civic festival, produced in the
> Stadium of the City College, I was quite excited and
> thrilled at the prospect of actually meeting the musician
> who had composed and conducted the music.  To me, the
> music held together the many arts of architecture, light,
> movement, color, spoken and sung words in a synthetic
> whole that, without the music, would have been impossible
> to create.
>
> It was May now, and very warm, and my attempts to
> find a job in the magic world of theater had all but met
> with disappointment and frustration.   This, in spite of
> fantastic predictions of teachers and press during my
> student days.   Kirk thought a week-end in the country
> would help restore my drooping spirits.  "Arthur Farwell
> is down here resting after the labours with *Caliban*," Brice
> said, "but you won't mind meeting him, I suppose?"
>
> We met on the farmhouse porch.  Arthur stood at the
> top of the steps, a slim man of average stature with
> almost white hair framing his face, salt and pepper gray
> at the back of his head.   But this I noticed later on, I
> think, for at the moment of greeting, all that I saw were
> the sapphire irises circling the large black pupils of his
> eyes in a face both youthfully eager and mellowed with
> experience.   He wore a white Burmuda suit that could
> have been improved by pressing, and a blue tie.   Of

course I did not realize it at the time, but in that instant, my life with Arthur Farwell had begun.

The marriage took place at the "Little Church Around the Corner" in New York City June 5, 1917.  Harry Barnhart, who was to serve as best man at the wedding, took Farwell to the service in his carriage.  En route, he hollered out the window to some attractive ladies, "Take your last look at the most eligible bachelor in New York, now no longer available!"  Kirk Brice gave a new Mason and Hamlin grand piano and a set of Wedgewood china to the couple as wedding gifts.

Gertrude brought to her marriage a lineage as distinguished as her new husband's.  She maintained she could trace her paternal roots to Robert the Bruce of Scotland, the name change to Brice taking place among that part of the family who migrated to Ireland.  The Everts maternal side claimed Miles Standish as an ancestor, and the Standish coat of arms hung on cousin Kathryn Everts' bedroom wall at Camp Arden.  (A place that was to figure in the future life of the Farwells.)

After a brief honeymoon at Lake Carmel, New York, Farwell took his bride with him to Plattsburg where the first Farwell home was on Lake Champlain.  Farwell was the logical choice for the Army assignment due to his broad range of experience with community music and his prestige as the new president of the National League of Community Music.

When Farwell studied the conditions for camp singing, he found many unfavorable ones.  However, he did conduct a number of "sings" in the Y.M.C.A. hut and the newly constructed large amphitheater.  Later he made an exhaustive report to the Fosdick Commission, also proposing principles and methods for community singing in the army camps.

Walter R. Spaulding, a member of the National Committee on Army and Navy Camp Music, reported, "The whole movement of singing among soldiers was the direct result of the work done in Community Choruses in large Eastern cities."[32]  He also commented on the contest to gain good new songs for camp-singing saying that hundreds of new songs were submitted and many actually tried in camps.  However, those which proved to be of real significance were few.  So the committee was "proud to include on their merits *March! March*! by Arthur Farwell, *Under the Stars and Stripes* by F. S. Converse, and *The Road Home* by John A. Carpenter" in the second edition of the Army Song Book.

What had begun as local expressions of community music in cities here and there, grew to be a nationwide movement in 1917. When the United States entered World War I, "We became for the time at least, a singing nation welded together by the unifying power of music," declared Edward B. Birge.[33]  David Ewen called the World War "the most important factor up to that time, in converting America into a musical country".[34]  This conversion was brought about by means of the community music movement that swept the United States at this time.

However, the whole pageant era and this wartime conversion were but temporary steps along the way in Farwell's conception for the "democratization of music". Perhaps they were the biggest steps ever taken, and the path of Farwell's dream is still untrod. But Arthur Farwell had been ready with his dream when the opportunities arose and he met the challenges which often resulted in personal triumphs. There were disappointments in the movement, but Farwell never despaired over them. He chose to press on in spite of discouragements, even as Cheiro had predicted.

Farwell continued to do some writing for *Musical America* and functioned as Director of the Third Street Music School Settlement until 1918. By the spring of that year he was ready for a change from the city's pressures. He later told his eldest son, Brice, he realized the toll that was taken on his creative energies by the socially exhilarating, yet publicly demanding stresses of his life. These stretched from the beginning of his western tours, through the American Music Society work, and the whole spectrum of his community music activities in New York. Also he was concerned now about having a more normal married life to share with his new beginning family. (Figure 37)

In making a change, he knew he would come to miss the stimulus of that past life. What he now wanted was a life away from those outward distractions, in order to quietly and inwardly cultivate his own musical directions. Hence, he welcomed an invitation to lecture at the University of California at Los Angeles for a six weeks session. So, after preparing for departure, Farwell

*Figure 37.   Gertrude Brice Farwell, shortly after she was married.*

carried his infant son, Brice, in his arms, and with Gertrude at his side, they boarded a train for Los Angeles. Little did he realize then how much the challenges of community music would pursue him in California, or how many years would pass before his return to New York, or the emotional travail and difficulties that lay ahead in his marriage to the beautiful young Gertrude.

# Chapter 11

## California, 1918 - 1927

Arthur Farwell was 46 years old when he accepted the invitation to lecture at the University of California at Los Angeles for a six week's summer session in 1918. This western trip was different from his previous travels because by now he had acquired his new family. Gertrude was 26 years old and young Brice had just arrived in April. Different arrangements were necessary to include them, but Farwell had no plans for a stay beyond the summer.

However, because he enjoyed being closer to his beloved mountains and away from the hectic pace of New York City, he gladly accepted a new contract to stay in California for another year. This proposal was to serve as lecturer and acting head of the music department of the University of California at Berkeley. Evidently the administration had been impressed with Farwell's ability. He was to be appointed Associate Professor of Music in the University for the period July 1, 1918 to June 30, 1919 at a salary of $3,000.00.

At Berkeley, in addition to directing the affairs of his department, Farwell presented 130 newly prepared lectures. He also took time to write and compose an original masque, *California*, which was produced at the Greek Theater in April of 1919 by members of the music department. (Figures 56, 57 in chapter 22)

Farwell saved his initial lecture which he prepared for a course in History and Appreciation of Music. The lecture entitled, *Introduction to the Study of Musical History* was completely handwritten in pencil, covered 59 pages, and included added remarks on the margins as well as corrections or changes within the text. He began with a consideration of *why* we should study musical history. His words are valid also today:

First, simply to know more about this art and...to know how it came to be what it is. Without this knowledge we can have no sound judgment in contemporary musical matters, and it is with contemporary musical matters that we shall be more and more concerned, as we become active in the affairs and the world of music.  The person who does not study the history of music is, in the musical world, like a person who grows up in some remote spot getting only such fragments of knowledge of life as happen to come his way, without completing or coordinating them.  Such a person has opinions and prejudices but no authority or capacity for leadership.  He knows what he likes, but as Whistler said to the old lady, "So do the beasts of the field!"

Farwell went on to point out that, on the other hand:

The person who studies the history of music is, in the musical world, like the man who travels, observes, reads, and thinks.  He knows men and their motives and ideals, and he is familiar with the great historical and political movements.  Such a man has laid the foundations of authority and leadership.  He knows what he likes and why he likes it, for he has formed broad ideals for himself, based on a knowledge of all that men have done and are doing, and he can form worthy judgments - and is able to assume the position of an authority and a leader.

Farwell declared his belief that the reason for much of the confusion of taste and ideals of his day, and the "blind leading the blind" was due to the lack of a study of history.  "People who have studied history carefully, do not repeat famous historical blunders; they go forward."

"To know how to go forward is one of the great purposes of all historical study", he continued.  After giving examples of the laws used by mathematicians and astronomers, he suggested:

If, then, we study the history of music, we should not seek merely to amass a knowledge of consecutive facts and events, but should ultimately seek to direct it to a full comprehension of the present, and to the end of acquiring the power to direct present events forward along lines of natural and artistic law.  We must learn to compute the true law of the curve.

As he conceived this goal, Farwell felt that this was the "great end" to be gained in the study of the history of music. "If our knowledge does not increase our power of immediate service, it is worthless and vain."

Farwell added that he did not wish to belittle the other things that an intelligent study of musical history accomplishes for us, such as the improvement of our taste, the heightening of our capacity for enjoying (and also for suffering), the familiarizing us with interesting epochs and personalities of the music world. These he considered but by-products of such study, and valuable only insofar as they "increased one's capacity for *Service*."

> The history of music is the history of the human spirit. If we are to get the most out of it, it is therefore necessary for us to start with some conception of what the human spirit is, what is its nature and constitution. This is of the most fundamental importance, for there is no advance possible today other than an advance along spiritual lines.

Farwell was convinced that whether in life or art, there is but one course open to us. "That is a course that will lead us closer to the establishment of the Kingdom of God on earth and to true human Brotherhood. If our application of music to life does not bear in that direction", he declared, "it was vain."

"When the issues of today are wrought out, we and all our works will be swept out of existence if we are not found to have advanced toward the goal for which the deepest heart of mankind is longing, waiting, and working," he predicted.

Farwell launched next into a discussion of the nature of the human spirit, and its relation to musical art. He tried to determine some sure ground from which to reason and deduce ideals and conclusions. He pointed out the primary principle as being "Universal Law" from which we conceive one God, the universal spirit, who is the source and foundation of all that is. Coexistent with Law is a second principle he called "Personality". This he identified as the active plastic principle of life acting through and in the law which gives rise to personality in man. These two principles of Law and Personality, which he stressed as coexisting in the cosmic order, may also be conceived as reflected in the spirit of individual man, who is made in the image of God.

In relating these philosophical ideas to music, Farwell pointed out that form in music derives from Law also, and musical quality derives from Personality. He declared that composers do not establish the law on which musical form rests; it is inherent in the nature of things as gravitation does, or the human form. He stated that while two composers will equally respect the one law of form, and each compose a work in strictest accordance with some one manifestation of the law of form, the two works will be entirely different in quality, or "personality". He noted that there had been nothing to conflict in the obedience to one law, on the one hand, and utter freedom of personal expression on the other. "The musician who understands this properly . . . will not only begin to get a true conception of the relation of form to matter, and what is due each, but he will also get a glimpse of the profound depth in which these musical principles are implanted in the universal order." (Here Farwell may have borrowed or developed his concepts of Law and Personality from Thomas Troward's writings.)

Farwell next elaborated on these ideas in an effort to impress on his students the importance of form and its relationship to the universe. "We may profitably explore...in our endeavor to learn what manner of spirit this is that seeks to reconstruct life ideally through art, and what may be its goal. To do this it is possible to draw illustrations wholly from musical processes and to explain them in musical terms. In general, such a course will be followed this semester."

He then presented his ideas on the four distinct planes or worlds of the human soul: (1) the Archetypal, (2) the Creative, (3) the Formative, and (4) the Material. "The first and highest plane rests on the conception of unity, the second on duality, while the third and fourth involve multiplicity", he said.

From this discussion, Farwell made several deductions concerning music. He noted that there are four planes or worlds making up the complete man. He called attention to parallels in music using four parts, such as the symphony having four movements; the sonata form, which consists fundamentally of four elements: a first theme, a second theme, a development section, and a recapitulation. He also mentioned the fugue which usually had four voices. Also the harmony of the human voice naturally falls into four parts, - soprano, alto, tenor, and bass. The musical scale of the octave is composed of two tetrachords or series of four notes exactly alike in pattern. These examples and others led Farwell to propose that some principle of importance must be active here. He further suggested that many fundamental elements go in threes, and gave more philosophical deductions, too detailed to repeat here. He summarized these ideas to find a four-fold nature in musical form, a four-fold nature in man, and a four-fold nature in the universal creative mind - three levels making a span of two octaves. He concluded thus:

> Our chief purpose thus far in bringing these matters forward is to indicate that underlying music and its relation to man there is a great universal and unchangeable plan of law and order, and that only in accordance with that plan can musical art rise to the realization of its highest possibilities. Until this truth becomes plain to us, we will not have the reverence necessary for the study or practice of musical art with any true sense of its past heights or its future possibilities of achievement.

Farwell referred to the history of music as being identical with the spiritual history of the human race. He suggested that every insight gained of the true nature of great art works, was an added light of understanding on the meaning of musical history. He spoke of the flowerings in the history of music as being identified with the greater issues of the human spirit. "Those great musical creators through whom these higher growths occurred, were keenly sensible of the divine import of the messages of which they were hearers." Summing up his lecture, he concluded:

> If then, we ask how shall musical history be studied, the answer is that it will be studied in the light of the spiritual attitudes of the greatest figures and in the light of the spiritual movements of mankind, to the present day. Due attention will be given to what are regarded as purely

artistic considerations, but we should not be deceived by
those who attempt to conceal poverty of the heart and
spirit as well as cynicism and irreverence, by a dazzling
intellectual display that too universally today passes for
artistic worth.

Detailed consideration is given to Farwell's first lecture
because it reveals the flavor of his subsequent lectures and also
shows his approach to the teaching of music history.    The
textbooks on the History of Music available in 1919 did not satisfy
Farwell who was concerned that his students gain insights beyond
mere factual knowledge.    Hence he used the lecture method of
teaching this course.
        In addition to teaching his classes, Farwell was interested in
student activities that had any relationship to music.    One such
work at the University was in connection  with the Student Army
Training Corps.    As part of that curriculum, students  were to
have experience in group singing.    Of course this appealed to
Farwell's zeal for community singing and he contributed to the
singing program.    However, the war was over before the program
could be well established.
        Farwell presented extension lectures beginning March 15,
1919.  The newspaper announcement read:

> Mr. Farwell, now acting head of the Department of
> Music at the University, is widely known not only as a
> composer but as the leading spirit in a number of
> progressive musical movements in America.  Mr. Farwell
> is peculiarly qualified to speak on American musical
> problems as he has for years been solving these in an
> artistic and a practical manner.  . . . Each lecture will be
> followed by question and discussion time with the
> audience.  Admission will be twenty-five cents per person.
> Following is the schedule of lectures:
> 1.   America's New Musical Vision and Task - March 12
> 2.   Musical Government by the People - March 19
> 3.   The Vehicle of the New Movement - The
>       Community Chorus - March 26
> 4.   The People's Music Drama - April 2

5.   Shaping America's Soul Through Song - April 19

George Boosinger Edwards, a newspaper critic, reported on
Farwell's extension lecture given April 2, 1919 thus:[1]

> Surely it was Arthur Farwell that Yeats was thinking
> of when he wrote, "We who care deeply about the art find
> ourselves the priesthood of a forgotten faith; and we must,
> I think, if we would win the people again, take upon
> ourselves the method and manner of a priesthood." For
> it was only the Spirit of priesthood that could have
> sustained Mr. Farwell's enthusiasm for Community Music
> through four of the five lectures in the face of the small
> audience...But it was as apostles of this newest (and
> oldest) faith that his listeners received his message.

Although Edwards may have found Farwell's presentations to
be priestly, Farwell himself, would not have acknowledged such a
role as a conscious attitude.  He tried to objectify and assess the
import of his visionary insight into national problems as well as
musical ones.   Edwards must have sensed Farwell's complete
selfless dedication to a cause for which he witnessed the natural
outpouring from an idealist's heart.   It was Farwell's tenacious
dedication to music for the people that carried him through later
difficult situations in California.  (What a strong echo of Cheiro's
early predictions!)
In addition to these extension lectures, Farwell was involved
with community music activities again.  Less than six months after
he assumed his duties at the University in Berkeley, he was
elected president of the Music Teachers Association of San
Francisco.
The announcement of Farwell's election brought favorable
comment in the December 14, 1918, issue of the Pacific Coast
Musical Review which reported that it was especially pleased
about the fact for:

> ...it considers Arthur Farwell one of the most
> distinguished American musicians and feels that his
> presidency will not only prove of inestimable value to the

San Francisco Music Teachers Association from the standpoint of added prestige, but it knows Mr. Farwell will leave nothing undone to bring the Association to that dignified and useful position which its membership and the city of its home justifies.

...It is perhaps not indelicate for us to say that we believe Mr. Farwell's election is the first milestone in the eventual attainment of a big and influential Pacific Coast Music Teachers Association which in cooperation with the California Federation of Music Clubs will prove of tremendous influence in the rapid growth of musical endeavors in the far West.

Later the M.T.A. honored Farwell with an elaborate banquet which Alfred Metzger reported:[2]

...More than 100 members of the profession and their friends were in attendance to pay their respects and express their gratification over the fact that a musician of national reputation had been broad minded enough to accept the post of presiding officer and add prestige and fame to the organization. It was one of the largest gatherings in the history of the organization and proved one of the most successful ones both from a social and artistic standpoint. The guests included some of the most prominent critics of the coast - Frank Patterson of the *Musical Courier*, Mrs. Beals of *Musical America*, and Ray C. B. Brown of *The Examiner* being among those present.

Arthur Farwell received an ovation that came from the heart, and he spoke at length concerning his principle ambition - the democratization of music in America.

These reviews suggest the national stature of Farwell as a musician. Unfortunately, such recognition was not to be long lasting.

By March of 1919 Farwell had organized the Berkeley Municipal Community Chorus with the University supplying financial aid. The comptroller was requested by the Deans to give him $200.00 to be used for the purchase of music for the chorus.

The money was to be repaid by selling the music to its members, which seems a rather unusual procedure. The *Musical Review* reacted to the new organization with this report:

> Mayor Irving has lent his assistance to the movement, and upon his invitation a large committee of sponsors has been formed from a great variety of occupations and from all quarters of Berkeley. Mr. Farwell has been loaned by the University of California for this service...Mr. Farwell and his associates in New York were the founders of the community chorus movement, a movement very different from so-called community singing, for it permits the people to organize and mobilize their song power, and by regular rehearsing to produce great festival events. Mr. Farwell regards the community chorus as a great free club for the people, a social movement welded together by song, rather than a purely musical organization. "Music", he says, "reaches only 3 percent of the American people. Only through the community chorus can we have a musical nation and a creative musical democracy."

If Farwell's words sound somewhat naive to us today, we should remember that in 1919 movies were in their infancy, and the recording industry was still years off. Neither involves the audience or community participation Farwell advocated.

Using this new organization and assisted by two readers and a solo singer, Farwell produced *The Chant of Victory*, a municipal Fourth of July ceremony, for Berkeley. This new work which he composed especially to celebrate the end of the war, included national songs as well as a number of his own choral compositions. The performance was repeated on July 6th at the Exposition Auditorium in San Francisco as the chief event of the State Convention of the California Music Teachers Association, for which he was still president.

Farwell showed his public spirit in another way. By the fall of 1919 he was leading four-minute singing in the movie theaters of Berkeley. Another activity resulted from receiving the mayor's appointment to serve as chairman for vocal music on the Music Committee for the Fleet Reception.

Farwell did not renew his contract with the University at the end of the academic year.   We can surmise a disagreement and a break, or simply accept his statement that he wished to concentrate his energies on directing community music.   As a result, the community profited by his selfless endeavors.

### Life in Santa Barbara

The next two years when the Farwells lived in and near Santa Barbara, were very difficult ones.   In addition to young Brice, two more children - Arthur Bragdon, born May 7, 1919, in Oakland, and Beatrice, born October 9, 1920, in Santa Barbara, were added to the growing family during this period.   Mrs. Farwell told of the hard times;   they lived a day-to-day existence in donated living space and with donated clothes.   To make matters even more demanding, Farwell's father, almost destitute since his wife's death in 1913, joined the family in California.   There, he helped with the housework, cooked all the meals and baked bread for the family.   Edgar Kirk reports, "So bereft of funds was the family at this time that Rev. Leon Mears went to his church to procure money to buy clothes for the elder Farwell."   What a sad situation for a man who once had been a wealthy and successful businessman.[3]

In the midst of this trying situation, Farwell seemed to live in a world of his own making, almost oblivious to the household problems.   Perhaps the sorrow he experienced earlier at his mother's death, was renewed when his father came alone to join the family.   Nevertheless, he seemed to be driven to fulfill what he felt was a predestined mission - to bring music to the people - the democratization of music in America.   Egocentric maybe, but his idealism reached out in an honest humanitarian desire to improve the life and spirit of the common man.   He railed against materialism all of his life.

Throughout the California years, he refused offers from Hollywood film makers to compose music for the movies.   He considered the first music written for movies as "hack writing", and to write for commercial purposes was "crass materialism".   He would have none of their "tainted money"!   He told producers that he would compose on his own terms or not at all.[4]

Instead, Farwell busied himself with organizing the Santa Barbara Community Chorus. *Musical America* took note of its Christmas concert with Farwell conducting both chorus and orchestra. The report spoke of "the brilliant consummation of Arthur Farwell's efforts in behalf of community music" in the presentation of this concert.[5]   (See Figures 38 and 39.)

> Fully 3,000 persons raised their voices in Spanish songs (a novel feature), Christmas carols, and works of Handel, Haydn, Wagner and Gounod. The Spanish songs, of which five were sung, were scored by Arthur Farwell. Original numbers by Mr. Farwell were his *Prelude and Chorale*, *Joy! Brothers, Joy!*, and the *Entrance and Processional of Country Folk* from his *First Pageant Suite*. ....Mr. Farwell's original numbers were received with hearty favor.   The concert indicated that Santa Barbara is embracing warmly the idea for which Mr. Farwell is working.

The Spanish songs referred to, were from the large collection of folk songs which Charles Lummis had gathered in Southern California. Farwell arranged some of these appealing tunes for his community chorus work.   Lummis claimed that "these Spanish songs have, in Mr. Farwell's splendid Community Choruses, become fully as great favorites as their Saxon kindred, *Swanee River* and *Old Kentucky Home*."[6]   Farwell himself noted:[7]

> Their (Spanish songs) power to animate and thrill the people in community singing is remarkable.  The present need of the community song movement is to enlarge its scope, to escape from the old ruts and to find new songs of the right kind which the people will take delight in singing.

The Spring of 1920, this organization undertook a more ambitious performance when it presented an original pageant, *La Primavera*, "The Coming of Spring", which Farwell composed especially for the Chorus.  For photographs taken at the daytime dress rehearsal see figure 58 in chapter 21.

*Figure 38. Public rehearsal for Christmas concert of Santa Barbara Community Chorus, 1919. Farwell, by flagpole, is conducting.*

*Figure 39. Christmas Concert of Santa Barbara Community Chorus, at Plaza del Mar, 1919.*

Someone asked Farwell how he managed to get his large crowds and choruses of untrained voices to sing in tune. Here is a response, from his files, that relates partly to the problem:

New Teaching
1. You have heard that people cannot sing without vocal training. I tell you that the most wonderful trained voice in the world is not as beautiful as the voice of any crowd of the people.
2. You have heard that many persons cannot sing in tune, and so how can the singing of a crowd be musical. I tell you that you never heard a great crowd sing off the key, and you never will.
3. You have heard that people cannot sing in parts without a knowledge of sight reading. I tell you that people sang in parts before notes and staff were ever invented.
4. You have heard that true art is only for the cultivated few. I tell you that the joy and beauty of musical art is for all, here and now, and that he who holds true beauty in any form away from the people is a thief and a robber.
5. You have heard that the symphony orchestra is the highest type of musical art. I say to you that the symphony orchestra is the servant of the voice of the people.
6. You have heard that your real musical life must consist of concerts and recitals given in the usual way. I say to you that a musical system that serves but three per cent of the people of our nation, is weighed in the balance and found wanting.
7. You have heard that opera, which sets the rich in the boxes off against the poor in the gallery, is art. I say to you that is Belshazzar's feast, that has seen the handwriting on the wall.

Somehow Farwell was able to make the people in his choruses sing together in tune as singing off-key was not noted by critics.

The value Farwell placed on community music-drama was intensified as time passed.  He continued to be engaged as a speaker on the subject.  Speaking before the convention of the California Federation of Women's Clubs on May 24, 1921, he reiterated many of the ideas expressed years earlier.  The occasion included the presentation by the club of a pageant-drama, *California, the Land of Dreams* in a beautiful Yosemite Valley setting.  There Farwell challenged the women to make this production the first of a series of community music-dramas and to establish a *People's Periodic Festival* to be held on a regular annual or biennial basis.  Regarding its form he explained:

> Every great flowering of an art has been preceded by a development of the form of the vehicle....Before opera there were the *Maggi* or May festivals and various forms of popular semi-religious drama.  Before Wagner could evoke the stupendous soul of his "music drama", a body had to be prepared previously through opera.  Evolution both in life and art, shows us everywhere the soul striving upward to the preparation of the perfect body or vehicle, through which it shall finally shine forth in unbelievable wonder and glory.
>
> Such a striving is the pageant drama in America today, a striving toward the great drama of the ideals of our people...The men and women working seriously in the field of pageant-drama in America today are as surely paving the way for those who are to do for the world from our standpoint, what the Greek dramatists and what Shakespeare and Wagner did for theirs.
>
> ...We need to be less concerned about the theme of our drama than with calling upon the dramatic poet to express himself, and providing the conditions in which his vision can come to objective realization upon an actual stage.   God has given the poet his calling and is with him to guide him in the practice of it.  The great themes are few and are not missed or mistaken.

In such passionate rhetoric, Farwell painted a picture of the possibilities for inaugurating a periodic festival drama of the people, "utterly uncommercial", (important to him) which would demonstrate the high ideals of these club women who could "light a torch to brighten the new civilization of the West!"

A Thanksgiving Song Rally was sponsored by the Santa Barbara Chorus in November 1921. A reporter for the *Pacific Coast Musical Review* again complimented Farwell for his "good work" and believed that his "brilliant success in Santa Barbara will form a nucleus for other community chorus concerts in California."

In these various activities Farwell may have had some financial backing, possibly as an employee of the park department.[8] He also may have received honoraria from his speech presentations. Otherwise there is no record of his having any other paid position in Santa Barbara during this time.

Mrs. Farwell was caught up in her husband's vision, and some few remaining pictures of her show her performing in the pageants, draped in shimmering Greek tunics, or robes, playing "The Spirit of Woman" or some such role. "Never mind whether there was food on the table!" she reportedly said.

### Santa Barbara School of the Arts

Farwell was instrumental in founding the Santa Barbara School of the Arts. In a letter to Bernard Hoffman of Santa Barbara dated January 9, 1933, Farwell describes his part in its establishment. He claimed that it grew out of a need for training in the arts which members of the Santa Barbara Community chorus came to realize. After the presentation of *La Primavera*, he addressed the audience and performers asking how many would like to have the opportunity to study music, dramatics, and dancing with the view to participating in further events of a similar nature. Over 100 persons registered their names and choice of study at the library the next day. Next Farwell told how he deposited $500.00 on an old adobe building and later secured more funds to buy it. At this point in his letter, he wrote of his encounter with a painter, Mr. Lundgren:

I told Mr. Lundgren what I was doing; it was a chance conversation rather than any intention to get him interested. I had thought him a sort of recluse. At that time he expressed a somewhat tragic sense of having always wanted to reach the people - the common heart - through his work, but that he had never been able to.

Mr. Lundgren told me that he had some years before an idea of creating some such school for the people there, and that...it would take $40,000.00. The $40.000.00 was not forthcoming so nothing was done.

Farwell then stressed the power of the Community Chorus. "It centers the desire and enthusiasm of the people - it *creates*. And this is the way the Santa Barbara Community Chorus created the School of the Arts. Money will always come in following such a popular desire and enthusiasm."

Farwell was elected chairman of the Board of Directors for the first year of the school's existence, but his hopes for making a permanent place for himself there were not realized. Mr. Lundgren took matters in his own hands and influenced the local people to replace Farwell. Others claimed that it was Lundgren who started the school in spite of Farwell's insistence that it was his idea and work.

Mrs. Farwell reported that her husband's quality of creativity was very dictatorial and that it overrode his sense of personal relationships. This quality may have been an outgrowth of Farwell's inner conviction of the rightness and truth of his mission.[9] During these particular years, Farwell seems to have tolerated no opinions other than his own and some associates wearied of this characteristic.

However, in the fall of 1920, Farwell received a new challenge to demonstrate his creative abilities. His success as a composer and leader of community music brought him to the attention of the sponsors of a major outdoor drama, *The Pilgrimage Play*, and he was invited to work with its production.

### The Pilgrimage Play and the Hollywood Bowl

*The Pilgrimage Play* was an elaborate pageant based on the life of Christ that for some time was a yearly presentation in the Los Angeles area. Dane Rudhyar, a French composer who had emigrated to California, composed the music for the first production, but some of the sponsors found it unsatisfactory.

Christine Wetherill Stevenson had agreed to underwrite the project and offered Farwell a contract to compose a new score and conduct the chorus which he was to select and train for the second production. In order to do the latter, Farwell staged a production of his work, *The Evergreen Tree*, during the Christmas festivities of 1920. He told the people he hand-picked for the chorus that if they would attend rehearsals faithfully, they would be paid professional wages for singing in the *Pilgrimage Play*. By the summer of 1921, Farwell began choral rehearsals accompanied by a small orchestra, with Walter A. Allen playing an organ. However, due to lack of funds, the orchestra was soon dismissed and rehearsals continued using only organ accompaniment.

While these rehearsals were underway, Mrs. Stevenson took a trip to Palestine for special study. When she returned, she brought back the idea that the only historically appropriate music for the pageant should be that played by flutes and cymbals. This move toward authenticity of Biblical times would also be an obvious economy for the producer.

Farwell objected to her ideas as he had already spent more than a year on the score and he refused to follow her demands. Besides, under his contract, Farwell had already contracted with his musicians for their compensation. More arguments followed, but Farwell's contract held. Since she had previously signed a contract to support the project, she could not withhold funds and the production proceeded.

Farwell's correspondence of this time reveals another kind of problem that had developed. He was very concerned about the spiritual aspect of the play. It troubled him when he sensed a lack of dedication or seriousness on the part of management or players. A letter to Mrs. Stevenson dated July 31, 1921 began:

> Never in my life have I entered upon any work and engagement with such joy, such uplifted heart and desire to serve as I have had in the thought and fact of my connection with the *Pilgrimage Play*, because in it I had found a way in which at last my art and profession could be brought to direct service of Christ and his teaching,

which for many years has been the chief study and concern of my life.

I have already expressed my admiration for your beautiful and courageous undertaking in the *Pilgrimage Play*. None but a great soul would have conceived and executed it - would have been called to do it. My desire from the beginning has been to be of assistance in the carrying out of this undertaking. That desire is no less now than at any time. Indeed, seeing so clearly the danger threatening it, and the disaster toward which it is hurrying, that desire is greater than ever before, and is the cause of my writing this letter. I pray that I may even yet be able to be of service.

Farwell's penciled draft copy continues for over six pages in which he stresses that "The foundation of the message of Christ is love" and love must be the foundation for all relationships of those involved in the *Pilgrimage Play* as stated in the contracts. He pointed out that the growth of an un-Christian spirit on the part of some people in the management was hurting the general spirit of the production. His lengthy letter was his effort to alert Mrs. Stevenson of trouble ahead if not corrected. He was deeply concerned about the management's failure to create a condition of unity and mutual devotion throughout the organization.

More protest letters from Farwell that followed must have resulted in improved relationships between management and cast as the production continued to be given at El Camino Real Theatre commencing July 11, 1921. The Theatre provided a beautiful setting high in the hills across from the present Hollywood Bowl and was established before the latter. The play was directed by Garnet Holme and Henry Herbert, both of them English Stratford-on-Avon Players. The cast included four principal characters, eighty lesser roles and many groups of people for the mob scenes. Costumes were imported from Jerusalem. The chorus numbered twenty singers and was supported by an instrumental ensemble and an organ as Farwell planned. The many photographs available indicate this was an impressive production that gave great care to authentic details. (See scenes depicted in figures 60 and 61 in Chapter 21.) Farwell's successful efforts must be seen as a significant career achievement in California in his dedication to community music.

H. Russell Stimmel, who was stage manager for the production the first four years, wrote that Farwell's music was the best that was done for the play. However, he noted that after Mrs. Stevenson's death, those who took charge had other music and Farwell's music was not used much.[10]

Mr. Stimmel also recalled that they had an organ especially built to be used out doors for the production along with the twenty member orchestra. He also was impressed with the "good job" Farwell did and that he was "well liked". One particular remembrance was Farwell's reaction to reading some publicity about himself when he said, "I will be known as a composer, or know the reason why..."[11] Here we note Farwell's wish to be known primarily as a composer above everything else, a desire he reiterated to John Kirkpatrick in 1944.

Edwyn Hunt, who sang bass in the chorus, gave tribute to Farwell's memory by telling of his rather unique ability to hear a symphony for the first time and then "go back to his room and write out the complete score from memory. He did this for amusement! Since knowing him, I have known other conductors, and found that such an exact memory is not uncommon." [12] Uncommon or not, this skill is still noteworthy.

When the Farwells moved to Pasadena from Santa Barbara, they rented a big house with lovely gardens on Fair Oaks Avenue, lined with magnificent old pepper trees. Here Farwell also had more room for his aging father who continued to live with them there until his death. In 1923, Sara Emerson Farwell was born, the fourth in a still growing family. The next year, Farwell was approached for private composition study by a lanky young man from Oklahoma who was giving up a try at professional baseball to learn to write music. His name was Roy Harris, of whom we will hear more in this narrative.

### Pasadena Composer's Fellowship

In the four years following the Pilgrimage Play effort, Farwell's work centered around Pasadena where he was awarded the first Composer's Fellowship of the Pasadena Music and Arts

Association. This organization was founded in 1913 to promote the arts and provide scholarships to persons chosen by a selection committee. An active member of the organization, Mrs. Earnest A. Batchelder, was an admirer of Farwell, and recommended him for the fellowship in June of 1921. George Ellery Hale, distinguished astronomer at the Mt. Wilson Observatory, also used his influence to secure the fellowship for Farwell. (Notice Farwell's continued interest and friendships in science.) The award was for two thousand dollars per year, and with it went a stipulation that Farwell must live in Pasadena and must spend at least half of his time on composition. It was renewed three times.

Edgar Kirk claims that "Among those who remember Farwell from this period there seems to be complete agreement that one of the reasons for granting the fellowship initially was that Farwell was in desperate straits."[13] If that were true, one would expect Farwell to show some gratitude for his award by doing the expected amount of composing. However, while Farwell did spend time composing, which was the work he usually preferred, the number of compositions from this four year period did not come up to the expectations of the committee and the Fellowship was withdrawn in 1925.

Obviously, Farwell's growing family added to the terrible financial strain he faced at this time. Some of his children believe that marital conflicts began during these years, though Gertrude denied it. She was so much in love with her husband that he could do no wrong.

Whatever the problem, it is interesting to observe that when the same Fellowship was awarded to Farwell's student, Roy Harris in 1931 and renewed in 1932, there were no stipulations for him to compose as there had been for Farwell. Ernest Batchelder stated that the Association recognized that "Roy needed money to get started in some study he planned in New York."[14] Evidently, attitudes regarding the award had changed in the intervening years.

If Farwell did not compose the minimum amount of expected work, what was he doing during these Pasadena years? The answer is that he was busy with efforts in community music. His work first on the *Pilgrimage Play* drained much of his usual energies. Beyond that he organized and directed the Pasadena Community Chorus and planned their scheduled weekly Music

Meetings. He may have earned a small salary as director. He wrote the rationale for that organization, published in a four page pamphlet. A briefer expression appeared on one of the programs:

> The Pasadena Community Music Meetings are a new way of the participation of the people in the expression and administration of music for and by themselves. These meetings create a means whereby all the people can share equally in bringing about the growth of a musical life free from artificiality, and appropriate to American democratic conditions and ideals. They bring the Truth of Music, its beauty and inspiration, directly and simply to all. The meetings are held at the Pasadena High School every Tuesday evening at 7:30 o'clock, and include community singing and the hearing of the best in music. Every one is invited. There are no voice trials and no dues. Support is by voluntary contribution, and is invited from all.

Here we see an organization reminiscent of the American Music Society, but the difference is the emphasis on member participation in a community chorus. Programs list groups of songs sung by the "Community Music Meeting" (probably in unison) and other special songs sung by the "Four-Part Section of Community Music Meeting". Evidently there was a special group of singers within the whole organization who performed separately. In his usual lofty language, Farwell stressed the issues of Service and Music Reform and prepared several pamphlets belaboring his ideas.

The Pasadena Community Music Meetings sponsored special programs in keeping with its purpose. A Community Festival Concert was given with the cooperation of the Pasadena Community Orchestra on May 20, 1923 at the Open Air Theater in Brookside Park (Figure 40) Will Rounds conducted the orchestra, Farwell the chorus, and the assisting artist was the dramatic contralto, Viola Ellis. Other special programs featured the Pasadena Band and a Community Sing.

The *Twice 55 Community Songs* book was the basic text for the chorus, along with the special song sheets prepared by Farwell.

*Figure 40. Community Chorus programs were popular with both singers and audience at Pasadena's Brookside Park in the early twenties.*

For this use, Farwell translated the words into English and made four part arrangements from masterworks such as a chorale from Bach's *St. Matthew Passion*; Schubert's *To Music, My Abode*, and *By the Sea*; and Grieg's *With a Violet*. Song sheets also included original songs by Farwell and folk songs that he arranged for the chorus. (See example 29 in chapter 18 for the *Pasadena Community Music Meeting Song Sheet, number one*.) Some song sheets carried the motto: "To unite us through song, and to bring to ourselves the message and the truth of the Soul of Music."

In addition to these efforts, Farwell also taught a course in the summer session of the Pasadena Community Summer Art Colony from June 27, to August 6 in 1921. This course was entitled *Community Music and Music Drama*. It dealt with: the origin and evolution of the movement, its historic significance, aims and ideals, principles and methods, national accomplishment, and analysis and construction of pageant and masques. The course presentation coincided with the time when the 1921 Fellowship was first awarded to Farwell.  It was not a requirement for the Fellowship, but Farwell agreed to do the extra work which probably took time away from his composing.

*Song Flight* for violin and piano was composed in 1922, followed in the same year by several choruses for school texts.  A tribute to his home-town was put in a *Sonnet to a City* for soprano based on the poem *Pasadena* by Celeste Turner, also composed in 1922.

Moreover, he wrote his *Symphonic Song on Old BLack Joe* with a revised orchestral score which he used effectively in Community Music concerts.  Another work used on such occasions was his *Symphonic Hymn on March! March*! written in 1921.  About this same time he also wrote much of *The Coming of Song*, a music-drama, but there is no record of its completion or performance.  Songs and incidental music for *Sister Beatrice* (Figure 41), a Pasadena Community Playhouse production, were composed in 1922 plus *Petal Lips* for medium voice.  The year 1923 saw the composition of two excellent songs set to Emily Dickinson texts.  (See Catalogue) The major composition of this period was *The Hako*, composed in 1922 for string quartet, a really outstanding work.  It won honorable mention at the Ojai Valley Chamber Music   Festival Prize Competition in 1926.   For discussion and analysis of this work see Chapter 17.

Three more songs were written in 1924.  These are beautiful art songs set to poems by the Indian poet, Charles Roos, discussed in Chapter 18.  *Grail Song*, a masque for community singing, acting and dancing, was composed during the last year of Farwell's Fellowship.  This he prepared for full orchestra, as well as a score with parts for small ensemble of flute, piano and strings.  What other compositions Farwell may have been working on during this period of 1921 to 1925 is unknown as he only dated a composition when he completed it.

Brice Farwell senses a mystery here regarding his father's compositional output.  He thinks the bigger works dated as finished from 1927 or 1928 through 1932 seem in great contrast

*Figure 41.   Gertrude Farwell in Maeterlink's* Sister Beatrice *at the Pasadena Community Playhouse in 1922.*

to those finished in this Pasadena period. Farwell was probably busier in those later years preparing college courses when he completed these works, than he was during the Pasadena period. So it seems credible that in this Pasadena period, Farwell may well have been developing some of the themes he had collected in his theme-notebook on earlier travels. (Late in life, he said to Sara, "Remember in your age the themes of your youth".) Farwell did not like to present unfinished works, or discuss them, and may have done more compositional work during this period than the Fellowship Board realized or would recognize.

A letter to Farwell from George Ellery Hale in Santa Barbara, dated September 21, 1921, gives further insight into Farwell's thoughts after he received the Pasadena Fellowship:

> After very careful thought to your welcome letter, I advise you not to accept the Institute's offer (Carnegie Institute of Washington). It is true that I suggested it, and had hoped that it might be feasible for you to accept. But I now see that to do so would seriously interfere with the very important work of composition for which the Fellowship was founded, and with the other activities you are already committed to.
>
> Moreover, I fear it would be impossible to accomplish your object with the students of a technical school, who are invariably impatient with any duties not strictly pertaining to their professional work. Finally, it would be impossible, I believe, to give you adequate compensation for such work from the available funds, which are more restricted than I expected them to be.
>
> I hope, however, that you can arrange to give us (probably through the Music & Art Association) a few public lectures on the history of music, to which we will also try to attract the students.
>
> It is a great pleasure to think of you at work in Pasadena, where we hope to see you early in October.

It seems Farwell had been offered a position of some kind at the Carnegie Institute. The reasons for his refusal, suggested in the letter, imply that he really was concerned about living up to the terms of the Fellowship award and did not choose to jeopardize the use of his time. Farwell did arrange to present some of his works at the auditorium annex of the California Institute of Technology. His files contain two programs. One was given March 13, 1922, when the Pasadena Music and Art Association introduced Farwell as the "first American composer to hold the Composer Fellowship". The all-Farwell program included three trios for piano, violin and 'cello, *Dawn* for piano, and three songs. There was also an exhibit of paintings by Pasadena artists. Farwell played piano accompaniments for George Shkultetsky, basso-cantante, on another program sponsored by the same association on April 25, 1924. It is likely that Farwell appeared on other concerts there as well.

The letter from Mr. Hale also indicates the range of Farwell's friends that included the famous physicist, Robert Andrews Millikan, who joined the Institute in 1921. Brice Farwell told the author that when his father first visited Millikan, he carried a prepared list of questions on physics which he wished to discuss. "Dad had not outgrown or forgotten his early training in electrical engineering and pursued vigorous conversations with both Millikan and Hale whenever time permitted," Brice concluded.

Another major endeavor of Farwell's was in promoting the cause of the Hollywood Bowl. Isabel Morse Jones in her book on the Hollywood Bowl states that "it was Farwell's community music work which inspired the financing and building of the Hollywood Bowl".[15]   Farwell made friends with Mrs. Artie Mason Carter, who became known as the "Mother of the Bowl". Both believed music to be essentially a democratic art, and they dreamed of a place in which music would be given to every man "according to his ability to receive" at low cost. Farwell's successful community music activities, in which Mrs. Carter also participated, created the obvious need for a permanent outdoor amphitheater. Farwell assisted Mrs. Carter in gaining public support for this idea and in raising funds. Jones claims that the Hollywood Community Chorus was directly inspired by Farwell and calls him the "foremost among leaders of community singing." She credits him with being the "father" of the idea in America.[16]

Farwell conducted the first community choral concert in what was to become the Bowl on July 4, 1919, when he also spoke of its future possibilities. About three years later Farwell and Will Rounds were guest conductors at the Bowl for the first orchestra concert to be dedicated to outside communities. Farwell also served on a committee that planned programs for the Bowl and was a member of the Hollywood Musician's Club, where composers met to hear each other's music and talk about the Bowl.

It was also during this period that Farwell made his last big effort in folk music. Working together with his old friend Charles Lummis and Henry Edmund Earle, he compiled and harmonized *Spanish Songs of Old California*. These songs were based on melodies Farwell had collected when working with Lummis (1905-06) and Lummis had been pushing Farwell to complete them. Farwell and Lummis continued their friendship as noted in The *House Book* at the Lummis home. This shows an entry for both Arthur Farwell and his wife, Gertrude, on February 26, 1922, when they were present to celebrate Charles Russell's return visit. Hence it would seem that Farwell was not idle during these Pasadena years as some critics claimed. In spite of many pressures, he contributed meaningfully to the musical life of the Pasadena area, and may have been unfairly criticized for not fulfilling his Fellowship obligations.

### Theater of the Stars

A new undertaking for which Farwell held high hopes took place at Fawnskin on Big Bear Lake, 7,500 feet above sea level, in the San Bernardino Mountains. There Farwell had his first practical opportunity to work out a long-cherished dream - to establish an outdoor theater for the best of music and drama.

*Fawnskin* was an area that a group of realtors, headed by J. S. Waybright and H. G. Thompson, were endeavoring to establish as a year-round resort spot. Fannie Charles Dillon, a composer - pianist friend of Farwell's, (Figure 42) visited the beautiful area and was impressed with the possibilities for creating a large outdoor theater in a natural amphitheater there. Waybright and Thompson agreed her idea was a good one and offered to help in such a project. They probably hoped the theater would increase their business by taking advantage of the general fad for culture

*Figure 42. Composers Fannie Charles Dillon and Arthur Farwell in the Theater of the Stars at Big Bear Lake, California 1925.*

so popular in the Los Angeles area at that time.  After Farwell
inspected the area, he too caught Dillon's vision  and was soon
named director of the enterprise, which began in May 1925.
Whole-heartedly, and so characteristically of everything he
undertook, he threw all of his energies into the work.

"Great things are done when men and mountain meet",
(William Blake) became his motto for the project which was aptly
named *The Theater of the Stars*.  As usual, Farwell found a
platform to promote his ideas and  wrote articles for *Fawnskin
Folks*[17] detailing the progress of the work.  He prepared a flyer
to announce the first season of the Theater in which he promised
a series of concerts by prominent orchestras, ensembles, soloists of
the "highest order", on Saturday evenings throughout the summer
season.   During the opening Gala Week there were to be
performances every night.   "Incidental dramatic features of an
unusual nature" were promised.  Theatrical lighting equipment was
a source of pride, as well as "other striking and picturesque
features." (See photos 62 and 63 in Chapter 21.)  Performances
lasted one and a half hours.  Admission charge was fifty cents for
adults and twenty five cents for children.   Among Farwell's
personal papers pertaining to the *Theater of the Stars*, is the
following handwritten note:

> As the responsibility for the conception and institution
> of this theater rests with myself, as the first musical
> dramatic works to be presented are of my own authorship
> and composition, and as I have very definite ideas as to
> the purpose of such a theater at the present stage of the
> world's development, I feel that I can scarcely shirk the
> imminent task, imperative as it is difficult, of orienting
> this enterprise in the world of modern thought.  Especially
> is this the case in view of the forthcoming presentation of
> my music drama, *Eden*, which presents aspects at once
> unorthodox and unfamiliar, and at the same time stirs
> every related issue which in my opinion demands initiative
> and challenge.

The Theater project was well met by the public and Farwell
could be justly proud of his success.  As usual he thought in even

broader terms than ordinary theater as his planning raced ahead
to future summers.  He always sought for something deeper to
happen spiritually to the people in his audience.  In another
article in *Fawnskin Folks* he stated his hopes that this would be
the beginning of a movement.

> *The Theater of the Stars* is a challenge and a call to
> all who would build on the mountain tops a new and
> redeeming order of existence worthy of the best in our
> national life and character.  It is a theater and more than
> a theater.  It is the inauguration of a new movement, the
> pointing of a new way.

Letters in Farwell's files describe some of his plans for an
impressive Spanish-American Song Festival for the Spring of 1926
at the *Theater of the Stars*.  He arranged to have as patrons the
Ambassador from Mexico, Manuel Tellez, and the Spanish
Ambassador, Juan Riano.   The latter wrote his acceptance on
January 8, 1926, saying in part, "...Trusting that your enterprise,
which cannot fail to draw closer the bonds of friendship existing
between the United States and my country, will meet every
possible success."
The Mexican Ambassador, Manuel Tellez, was equally pleased
to be a patron and replied on March 5, 1926:

> You request my permission to use my name as a
> patron of said Fiesta, which you have also placed under
> the patronage of His Excellency Don Riano Y Gayangos,
> Ambassador of Spain.
> I have the pleasure to inform you that it is very
> pleasing to me to patronize such a festivity, which, besides
> its historical interest, will have that of evidently showing
> the Spanish civilization in California.
> I take pleasure in presenting you the assurance of my
> high consideration.

Along with these efforts for the Theater of the Stars, Farwell
participated in the Sesqui-Centennial Celebration of Independence
Day in the Los Angeles area.  His hard work for the *Pageant of*

*Liberty* was recognized by its Director General, Frank Lloyd, who wrote to Farwell on July 10, 1926:

> The reaction from the effort that went into the *Pageant of Liberty* at the Coliseum last Monday night prohibited my telling you personally how deeply I appreciate the many hours of hard work that you gave this program.
>
> To do such work as you did is a thankless task at best, but I know that you must feel as I do, that although some people never will grasp our unselfish intent, that we do enjoy the feeling of having served a splendid cause conscientiously and well and so far as I am concerned, I want you to know that I am most grateful to you for your interest and encouragement and magnificent results. If I can reciprocate your kindness in any way, it will be a pleasure for me to do so.

Whether or not this *Pageant of Liberty* was similar to the celebration of Independence which Farwell directed in New York City on July 4, 1911, is unknown. The earlier event had been very successful. Lloyd's letter raises some speculation as to the complete success of the 1926 presentation. Nevertheless, Farwell's efforts to promote a patriotic spirit are noteworthy at this particular time.

In spite of Farwell's success with the Spring Fiesta, and other excellent programs, *The Theater of the Stars* was doomed! What a crushing blow to Farwell it must have been when the backers of the project withdrew their financial support for the coming year.

Earlier, Farwell had realized that the management was more interested in making money than in supporting a cultural cause for the community. This cut across his idealistic approach to the project and made him even consider leaving it. However, Farwell's family had again been enlarged by the arrival of a fifth child, Emerson, on January 14, 1926, so he had stayed as Director until the project was closed. Now without his income from the *Theater of the Stars*, plus the financial demands of his large growing family, Farwell was ready to consider a move anywhere that offered him a steady salary. With this frustrating end to an undertaking for which he had such high hopes, Farwell's influence in California drew to a close.

In the difficult period after he lost financial support for the *Theater of the Stars*, Farwell decided to digest the essence of his idealistic endeavors for *The Pilgrimage Play* by sketching out the composition of a *Prelude to a Spiritual Drama*, Op. 76, for orchestra. This was not completed however, until 1935. He also renewed efforts to develop compositions from folk music themes. From a group that he called *Americana*, Op. 78, one piece for piano entitled *Sourwood Mountain* was published by G. Schirmer and has maintained some recognition and performance.

The closing of the *Theater of the Stars* largely ended Farwell's major efforts in community music. Times were changing and by 1927 the cultural interests of America had changed also. Radio had come into its own with the first nationwide hookup on January of that year, so more and more people were spending idle hours before their loud speakers. Many others used their time and money at the motion picture theaters which were thriving. Community music events lost the magnetic attraction they had held earlier for people because movies became the more popular mass entertainment. Now Farwell would have to channel his energies to the classroom for the next twelve years, but he was also to have a very productive time in composition and other creative work.

Farwell continued in his conviction that the development of community music was the best path toward creating a new musical life. Unfortunately, in spite of progress made, he was not able to secure the backing he needed, nor was he able to reach the superior artistic level for which he so longed. He wrote many essays expressing his ideas. In one of his last articles dealing with his hopes for the future of community music, he wrote in March of 1927:

> Its present crudeness does not recommend it to the fastidious, but the principles upon which it stands are of prime importance. It is chaotic, amorphous, lacking in definite purpose, but a movement which is capable of immense and unforeseen developments if grappled with by the creative artists capable of molding and giving direction

to its forces.   In its greater moments it has evinced
something of the spiritual temper of America, but it
cannot be said that it has yet identified with the deeper
spiritual currents of American life.[18]

Thomas Stoner points out that Farwell's ideals may appear
"too utopian, too much grounded in the high-minded progressive
thought of the years before World War I, or too antagonistic to
the musical establishment to have ever created a viable art."
Stoner continues his analysis:[19]

> In light of his goals for democratic music, Farwell's
> was indeed a small and, in the long run, ineffectual voice
> in a nation whose musical life was just coming into its
> own.  If in retrospect it seems that Farwell's efforts were
> misplaced and exacted at the expense of his composing in
> a more traditional vein (which he pursued more actively
> after 1925), the writings show his philosophical devotion
> to such a cause which, as he was well aware, set him apart
> from the musical mainstream.  For those, however, who
> would believe that the vitality of America's musical life
> depends on composers creating music which involves
> emotionally a fair portion of the nation's public, *the basic
> issue which elicited Farwell's vision is still very much alive
> today*. (Culbertson emphasis)

In spite of all the good Farwell had accomplished, it seems he
could not adapt easily to so severe a change in the scene he now
had to face.  This changing scene in the twenties noted above,
witnessed a general disillusionment from the ideals that had
flourished in society until World War I.  However, Farwell's ideals
were built into his character and he would not yield to the world
around him, which from his own view, had seemed to respond
positively until now.  Furthermore, Farwell's stubborn idealism
tended to alienate the very persons who had sponsored him
financially.

He tried to adjust to the natural enjoyments of a growing
family, but his worries of family responsibilities must have affected
his energies and other relationships.  His much younger wife,

Gertrude, was busy enough caring for their five children. She, too, had unfulfilled aspirations and ambitions to nurse. With these preoccupations she had little energy to provide the depth of wifely understanding and support he needed at this critical period.

During these experiences did Farwell ever think about Cheiro's predictions? Maybe. He never complained, but stoically set his thoughts to a better day which he felt was sure to come! Such was his nature and indeed, better days were on their way!

Although Farwell left pageants and community music efforts behind him, the legacy of the movement has continued. Today, evidence of the spirit of pageantry can be observed in cultural and community values as it is expressed in various forms, locally and nationally. We remember the American bicentennial celebrations of 1978, and the centennial observances for the Statue of Liberty in 1986. Many states annually celebrate historical events in summer outdoor theaters such as *The Trail of Tears* in Oklahoma. These attest to the values of a pageant's story as 1) an educational presentation, 2) the concept of community involvement with its accompanying spirit of volunteerism, and 3) the role potential for social change. Because audiences continue to patronize these events with paid admissions, is proof of their general appeal today. Farwell's original enthusiasm for these activities was therefore not misplaced.

# Chapter 12

## Michigan, 1927 - 1939

On a summer day in 1927 Lewis Richards called at the Farwell home in Sherman Oaks, California, to discuss a business matter. Mr. Richards, a noted harpsichordist, had been given *carte blanche* to recruit a faculty for the music department being newly organized at Michigan Agricultural College in East Lansing, Michigan. He wanted Farwell as head of the theory-composition section, a choice he considered ideal. Mrs. Farwell remembered that day as an exciting one. Mr. Richard was gracious and friendly as he painted a glowing picture of the potential for the new department. Farwell accepted Richard's terms with little ado, and the family began to plan for the move. Here at least was a regular salary, and though far from munificent, Farwell was thankful for a new promising opportunity.

Farwell decided he would move to East Lansing alone in the fall, leaving his family to join him the following year. He felt it wiser to become established at the college unencumbered by a wife and five children. He also needed time to build up a financial reserve for the anticipated expensive train trip, and the assurance that the new position would live up to its expected promises before asking his family to join him.

Farwell was aware that Michigan Agricultural College was the oldest college of agriculture and the first of the Land Grant Colleges established by the Morrell Act. It also served as model for other land-grant colleges founded later in the United States. However, it was not until after he arrived on the Michigan campus that he heard about the dissatisfaction caused by the creation of the new music department. Some opposition to the development of the music department had come about because of the college's strong commitment to agriculture, and music seemed far afield from its original goal. Nevertheless, President Kenyon L. Butterfield, moved ahead with plans for expansion.

Lewis Richards accomplished his goal admirably creating a music department with a conservatory caliber of excellent faculty. (Figure 43) In addition to Farwell, he secured Michael Press,

*Figure 43. Some faculty of the Michigan State Institute of Music and Allied Arts. From left: Arthur Farwell, Michael Press, Fred Killeen, Lewis Richards, director, and Zinery Kozan.*

eminent Russian violinist and teacher, to head the string section, and Louis Gravieure, a well known opera singer, for the voice department.   He also hired a group of artist teachers from the Detroit Symphony to teach their respective instruments.   Other distinguished recruits included Leonard Falcone, band and brass; Alexander Schuster, 'cellist; James Stagliano, formerly first hornist of the Boston Symphony; John Wummer, formerly first flutist of the New York Philharmonic; and Vincent Pezzi, bassoonist from the Eastman School of Music and first bassoonist of the Rochester Philharmonic.   In another department, the college boasted of "Sleepy Jim" Crowley, one of the famous "Four Horsemen of Notre Dame," as the football coach at this time.

Lewis Richards brought together the musical forces of the college with those of the Lansing Conservatory of Music to create the Michigan State Institute of Music and Allied Arts.  When the union was completed in February 1928 at Lansing, the state capitol, Theresa Shier reported in *Musical America* that this is "one of the strongest evidences that Michigan is taking an increasing interest in music."[1]

A group of prominent business men who had directed the affairs of the Conservatory, served also as directors of the new Institute, and its faculty was retained.  In an unusual move, they determined that students regularly enrolled at the State College who could pass the entrance exams in any phase of musical art would receive their instructions free of charge.

On November 27th, the Detroit Symphony Orchestra with Ossip Gabrilowitsch, conductor, presented a concert to introduce Farwell to the community.  Farwell was featured on the program conducting his tone poem, *The Domain of Hurakan*, and was "warmly received."

As the winter semester of his first year at the college moved along, Farwell's correspondence  with his wife indicated a new problem had developed.   While Gertrude initially had been enthusiastic about the prospect of moving to Michigan, now she had discovered a new freedom as a result of her husband's stable income.  Also, she had more time to take on new interests such as her involvement with the teachings of the spiritual leader, J. Krishnamurti.   This led her to believe that she had a "calling" in life which should keep her and the children in California.  By

March of 1928, Farwell tried to make his wife face up to her
responsibilities and wrote:

> I have been expecting you all winter to say what you
> did, but this does not lessen the blow when it comes. I
> do not believe you have any idea of the profound
> seriousness of what you have done or propose or its
> inevitable consequences; . . . I want to put myself on
> record at once as not agreeing at all to the family
> remaining apart from me after this one year. . . . It seems
> to me that you are losing your balance over religion, and
> that it is warping your understanding of *Life*!

Further correspondence between husband and wife finally
brought matters to a head and on April 5th Farwell wrote to
Gertrude his analysis of the situation thus:

> Our family separated in this way, for more than an
> emergency period, is a house divided against itself, both
> spiritually and materially, and could not long stand as a
> unit. The two divisions would necessarily grow fixed into
> divergent grooves.
>     While the spiritual reasons are the greatest, they are
> inextricably bound up with the material, and a continuance
> of the present division is economically untenable.
>     Any home for our family will necessarily have to be
> where my work is; and for the present that is here - and
> more advantageous and entrenched next year than this;
> with new paths opening out in important directions
> impossible in California. You have seen amply how
> impossible California is to me - except perhaps to go out
> and carry out some commission or special work.
>     For yourself - I understand well your freedom of this
> year [1927-28] (as I appreciate a sort of bachelor freedom)
> but neither of these things can weigh against a home for
> the family in direct association with the work that makes
> a family possible. Such a home will have to be made.
> Then, if you have a "mission" in California nothing can
> keep you from it. . . . . A [real] mission is a call - out and

from the basis of one's life - which one must not resist; - not an experimental living around in a place under strained conditions of separation, expecting that such a call will arise there.

After establishing our home (however true that it may be for a limited period - we can not know that) - if you have a call to any special mission in any place, it will be made possible for you to accept it. Again, if you wanted a life different from what that home would be, - and wanted to go away from it in search of a different life - I would never lift a finger to hold you.

Farwell gave arguments to answer other reasons which Gertrude presented for remaining in California. She was worried about the cold Michigan weather as being a health hazard for the children. She was concerned about the kind of friends the children would make. (Farwell replied to that with the fact that the children in East Lansing were those of cultured parents, and not "the rough-necks we had to put up with" in California.)

Farwell's reasoning finally persuaded his wife to move with the children to their new home as originally planned. But tensions between the two continued to grow and cooled the marriage. Perhaps the twenty-year age difference between husband and wife accounted for some of their difficulties, plus the fact that Gertrude was not good at handling the family finances. However, she did her best to adjust to her new home and her husband's college obligations, and plunged wholeheartedly into community activities.

Farwell quickly fitted into the cultural life of the East Lansing area and was much in demand as speaker, conductor and adjudicator for school music contests around the state. He also wrote reviews for the Lansing State Journal that reflected the breadth of his cultural background.

Farwell proved to be a very successful teacher in spite of his disdain for the profession. He later confided to his wife, "I spend my time trying to teach young people to be teachers of music to teach other people to be teachers of music and none of them know anything about it." (Many of his students were from the School of Education.) Farwell wanted people to create music -

compose, perform, or participate in it. He objected to teaching students in music theory who would go out and teach theory to others without ever being creative in music themselves. Brice Farwell reports thus on his father as a teacher:

> Students dreaded his exams; he flunked many of them. But his music history courses were very popular. Even though he used the same outlines and material each year, dad put new life into each class. Consequently many students enrolled in the course two or three times because they enjoyed it so much and learned something new each time. The classes were popular with adults who often came from town to take them. His classroom manner was highly individual. He was able to color his lecture material and his musical examples with his rich experiences of the music world. In introducing musical works, he often brought in and played the music itself. Thus he was able to bring to his students the role of the music, its musical spirit, and the satisfaction from it, much more vividly than if they just heard recordings.

Experiences described by several of Farwell's students themselves are found in Chapter 13. Farwell's personal magnetism and enthusiasm for music made his classes memorable to many who studied under him.

However, like many creative artists, Farwell found the paper work of teaching to be a dreaded chore. Edgar Kirk reports that the files of the music department contained many memos from the registrar's office to Farwell requesting that he keep accurate attendance records. He also disliked giving tests as much as his students dreaded taking them. It seems that he would prepare essay type exams and then whenever possible, have an advanced student correct them. "This practice was frowned upon by the administration, and he was in fact, given specific orders to take care of this himself."[2]

When Farwell confronted a faculty meeting with the passionate question, "How do you manage to get them all done?", dead silence was the answer. Horticulture professor John Crist, a special friend and "crony", confided in him later that none of the other teachers dared to expose their own breach of this policy as they were guilty of the same practice.3

Farwell may have had legitimate reasons for complaining about his course load as it seems to have increased in size every year, while his salary dwindled in depression cuts. In a letter of October 4, 1930, Farwell wrote to a lawyer friend, Joseph S. Clark, Jr. of Philadelphia,[4] about the developments in his teaching situation at that time:

> . . . things have come to  something of a crisis, and there has got to be some kind of a change take place in my life before long. . . I told you that I had carried 8 courses right along. They tried to put 10 of them on me this fall . . . , and to make me take on two new courses, fourth year Appreciation, and Aesthetics, and still continue for a time the 2 harmony courses I have been told I would be relieved of if it proved that the new ones were to be given, as it did. My back went up in a hurry, and they backed down in an equal hurry, getting the president to override the State Board as to an appropriation to have the harmony courses given by someone else.
>
> Richards never saw me mad clear down before; I was absolutely on the point of handing in my resignation, although it would have put me in a terrible situation to have done so. . . . Richards has never appreciated before that I have right along been pushed up against the greatest load that I could carry. He is a splendid fellow, and we are very good friends but nevertheless this condition exists. (He is a good friend of Stokowski, by the way, and played with him last year in Washington and I believe elsewhere.)

Although Farwell had been hired to head the theory and composition section, it seems that his creative abilities were more challenged by these new courses in Music Appreciation and Aesthetics. Even though the standard courses in harmony were closer to his own field as a composer, he seemed to look upon them as consumers of time better spent on his own creative endeavors. This attitude was also true of Farwell's first teaching experience at Cornell.

By April 19, 1931, Farwell took time to thank his friend, John Tasker Howard, for the gift of his new book on American Music.

> You'll think the book killed me off, but not so. A trip to New York, illness, examinations and getting a new term started, are the reasons of my delay in writing you.
>
> You have certainly contributed a mighty book to the subject of American Music, and I said it would be, one which will be a standard for a long time. . . . I haven't read the book through, but I have read enough of it to realize its immense value, both as to information and comment. It has already helped me much in one of my courses, touching on American music.
>
> I wish to thank you particularly for what you have done for me in it. This gets my bearing on the matter very much straighter and more complete than anything that has appeared, and I am very much pleased and gratified by what you have said and the way you have said it.

Heavy course-load pressure which left no time for his own composition work finally did result in Farwell's decision to resign. In his files is a ten-page, penciled letter to Mr. Richards labeled "never sent". In discussing his heavy course load, Farwell explained that six of the eight courses he taught required separate preparation for each lecture. There were three different courses in Appreciation of Music, two in History of Music, and one in Aesthetics. He complained:

> These are all subjects intimately bound up with my own artistic and intellectual growth, and which I can never give twice alike, but must constantly revise and develop. I do not and cannot give my students a cut and dry academic presentation with repetitions of the same. I give them *myself,* my life creatively, which is the reason why I have had such remarkable expression (reflected from others) concerning the character of my work given me by

President Shaw, Secretary Halliday and yourself. Except for what others in the department may do incidentally in connection with their teaching of voice and instruments, I have thus carried for the college and the Institute [of Music and Allied Arts] the whole burden of the musicological-cultural aspects of music.

The letter continued citing many of the concerns commonly held by college professors: heavy course load, insufficient salary to support his large family, advancement in rank, and other problems. Farwell probably spent his pent-up feelings on these penciled pages, but thought it advisable to write much less in his actual letter of resignation to Mr. Richards dated July 18, 1932:

I am compelled to realize that the things I intend to do and the plans I have made for myself along practical lines in the immediate future make it impossible for me to retain my connection with the Michigan State College and the Michigan State Institute of Music and Allied Arts. I am accordingly, therefore, herewith regretfully tendering my resignation from both of these institutions, to take effect at the end of the present month.
     In so doing I wish to express the pleasure I have had in my association with you these five years, and to thank you for the numerous kindnesses I have received at your hands during my connection with this work.

P.S.   I am transmitting a copy of this letter to Mr. Halliday.

Farwell's resignation was not accepted. It is conjecture that his attempt to resign had some effect on improving his teaching load. Correspondence after 1931 shows that he was involved in doing more composing, orchestrating, and other writing even though he still complained about his "busy college schedule".
     Some of Farwell's extra-curricular activities adding to his "busy schedule" are revealed in a letter dated December 29, 1933, addressed to Witter Bynner, poet and friend. Farwell gives details of a feature in the special Armistice Day ceremony he introduced in 1927 when he first came to the college. The verses of Bynner's

*Canticle of Praise* were incorporated as a basic feature in this ceremony in the immense auditorium of Demonstration Hall, the college military armory.

"The whole thing made such a hit that it was repeated every year since then and became a tradition of the college," Farwell wrote. He enclosed seven programs for Bynner, one for each year, to give him an idea of the production's set-up. Farwell indicated that he had served in various capacities - musical director, producer, and cantor. This kind of activity must have added to an already burdened schedule, but Farwell never complained about his work that involved music or pageant productions. For him, these were more than entertainment. He considered active participation in music as a highly desirable educational experience for cultural and spiritual growth, for himself as well as for the participating students and other faculty.

Michigan State College (named Michigan State University of Agriculture and Applied Science since 1955 ) was the subject of several investigations during the years of the Great Depression, in 1932 and 1933 especially, which must have added to the strain of his heavy teaching load. The Agriculture Division was apparently jealous of the fame of the music department and still resented the monies appropriated for it. Despite the pressure on the state budget caused by economic conditions, the growing prestige of the music department was a matter of pride and concern to state legislators, and the necessary funds were ultimately provided in the July 1933 budget. Hence, Farwell was able to remain at his teaching post.

While the last investigation was on-going, Farwell wrote to another lawyer friend from his Los Angeles days, James Sheridan[4], about the current situation as of February 7, 1933:

> Well, you see they're fighting back - as you predicted. The ousted gang have got the ear of our erstwhile friend, Senator McKenna, and now we're to be investigated again for the fourth time. What a world!
>
> I have it by underground that the ousted gang are nowise after *my* scalp, that they consider me pure as unwashed, or is it unborn, lamb, amidst all this saturnalia of crime. This is very consoling. A lady from Ann Arbor

who has been visiting around, there and here, told me today that she was sure I had nothing to fear whatever happened. She seemed to think that I had made a very secure place for myself, and that it was very likely they would want me over there if the Music Department is blown off the map here -i.e. if our (your) cow chorus doesn't rout the investigating committee. If there are any long-horned steers left, I think I'll get a battalion of them up from Texas - they ought to do the job all right, even if their *voices* fail them.

Farwell must have found comfort in the reassuring gossip given him by the lady from Ann Arbor, and in the possibility that the University there would welcome him as a teacher. Such information encouraged him during those trying months. In July, 1933, Mr. Sheridan wrote to Farwell questioning him about the outcome of the investigation :

How did that East Lansing war ever terminate? Now that everyone is working up his own little war, why not East Lansing? Maybe some of those boys could land a job on Hitler's staff, or with Mussolini. But I suppose it's all ancient history now.

And so it was! With University battles and gossip set aside, Farwell had more time to attend to requests of various kinds that arrived in his mail. After receipt of a new book, *History of Music* by Paul Charles Rene Landormy, Farwell responded with the requested evaluation by writing thus to Mr. E. J. B. Walsh of Scribner's Sons on March 6, 1936:

Now this book is a gift-horse, and therefore is not supposed to have its teeth examined. But I cannot figure that there is any reason why I should jump on the historical and educational band-wagon just because it is moving at the moment, when I would not trust myself very far with either the vehicle or the horse.
You ask for my reaction to this book, and I will give it to you honestly.

Precluding, I may say that on the outside of Ambros (in German only), Perry, and the *Oxford History*, I do not know where to look for any important work on the history of music.  I find only hasty, superficial and imitative books, repeating most of the old legends, errors and omissions.  They all seem to be written by inconsequential professors, on the hope of making some money.  While the Landormy work does not  fall wholly under this description, it approached it sufficiently to give me a similar reaction.

First, I deplore the book's implication (though not stated explicitly in words, except for the word "ancient") of the old arbitrary division of history into "ancient, medieval and modern," which is now smashed flatter than a horned toad.   I do not think this idea of the morphology of history should be perpetuated any longer.

Second, I deplore the limiting of the "Music of Antiquity" to the Greeks, as well as doing some little for that.  In this relation I greatly deplore the omission of all consideration, especially deep and serious consideration, of Egyptian, Chinese, Hindu, Hebraic and Arabian music history, (especially under the title of *A History of Music*), and especially when d'Olivet, Ambros and Fox-Strangway have so admirably led the way.

Third, is it not time that we had an adequate, balanced, well-judged and correct presentation of American music, instead of the usual and casual cataloguing, such as we have here?

The chapter on American music is really pitiful, with its disproportionate space given to the earliest American musicians (seeing so little space is available), its lumping together of a host of later names without any sense of their relative or their historical values, the mentioning of dozens of nonentities - without even mentioning a number of our important men, a total omission of the historical import of the successive phases of American music.

What then about good points?

In the book's treatment of the matters of strictly European music history, as unrelated to musical world-history, I think it is very sound and good, and one of the most compact presentations I have seen. In this respect it should prove both popular and useful. As I told you, I do not use text-books in my courses, but in the respect indicated, I shall have much occasion to assign reading from it in the college library, to my students. The book undoubtedly meets very satisfactorily the current educational demands in this subject, but with these demands I am not much in sympathy, feeling them to be far below the standard of scholarship which I require. I am certain the book will make money.

I pray for the day - if I must remain in the educational field - when a work on music history will appear to which I can send students without reservations or warnings.

Farwell's attitude towards teaching music history and his scholarly regard for accurate information is seen in his above reply. That he would take time from his full schedule to read, evaluate, and express his views is indicative of an educator's concern for books that would improve the dissemination of knowledge in his field.

A different kind of request came to Farwell from Louise Homer. The famous singer maintained a summer home near Bolton, New York, where she was training young singers. She sent Farwell an excerpt from the *Lake George Mirror* issue for August 14, 1936, which described in detail her teaching procedure and situation. It also included the announcement that she was offering "a free scholarship for Fall study" and listed the requirements:

We must have real beauty in the voice. I am looking for rare beauty, to tell the truth, and we must also have a noble character, ability to work hard, patience, and all that goes with it, and some natural musical talent. It need not necessarily be musical education, though that helps. An artistic temperament, imagination and youth, all this we must have.

Madame Homer asked Farwell, "Help me to find the voice." Obviously she respected Farwell's musical judgment and knew something of his concern that talented students should receive the kind of superior training which she would give the chosen candidate.

The Farwell home was a frequent "port-of-call" after special events in town or at the college. Roy Harris, Carl Sandburg, Arthur Shepherd and Noble Kreider were only a few of the guests he entertained. Some, like Harris and Kreider, made prolonged stays. Sandburg visited when he needed Farwell's help in preparing his famous *American Songbag*. After one such visit in July 1933, Sandburg wrote to his host:

> . . . you are easily one of the best talkers in the U. S. A. and that ain't no lie neither. I rode away from Lansing feeling as though I had read a row of vital books and heard the contemplations of a rarely fine human struggle.
>
> . . . again, the Blake song is worth having and I am going to learn to sing it. And I shall pray for the Rudolph Gott Symphony and never forget the lyric depth of its background.

### Frank Lloyd Wright and Taliesen

Emerson Farwell told the author the story of how Farwell met Frank Lloyd Wright, the architect. Sometime in the early part of 1933, Farwell delivered a public lecture on Music Theory at the college. Unknown to Farwell, Wright was in the audience. After the lecture, Wright went forward and introduced himself. He immediately voiced his thoughts on what he had just heard (Music Theory): "That was one of the best talks on *Architecture* I've ever heard." Needless to say, they "hit it off famously right away", according to the family report.

It is not surprising that Wright found in Farwell a kindred spirit. Wright recognized Farwell's creative powers and pioneering in music and later invited Farwell to join him in the Taliesen Fellowship at Spring Green, Wisconsin. This was to be a community of leaders in the Fine Arts who, through mutual efforts, would seek to foster high standards in the Arts as they shared inspiration and daily life. Wright's invitation was followed by a letter to Farwell on May 16, 1933:

> Your good letter has awaited an answer because I've been thinking hard over my responsibilities as offsets to my joys.
> Your "Vision" is in itself music, and it is here.
> I wish you were able to come soon. I went over a cottage we are remodeling when I received your letter and enlarged it to make it comfortable for man, wife and six.
> But I must not let you come without some warnings that finances are meager while hopes are high. There is not money at all to do more than house and feed you the first year - and that is going to require management if we are to get into the fighting quarters we have under way. I believe that if you were to join me, we would be just that much stronger and the issue easier for us both.
> But this Fellowship is an idea in the making and the makers must share responsibilities to the common cause so far as they are able.
> Work there is, good life and enough to keep us living. More must depend upon the quality of our Fellowship and the necessary time for growth.
> Needless to say I find in you not only a brother of the spirit, but a veteran in armor whose weapons and purpose "click" with my own - and whose personality I like. But perhaps you would better come along for a time to get more intimately into the "pros and cons" of the fact before you finally decide to stake a measurable share of your future on the success of our Fellowship.
> My faith in it is complete. But I should not ask you to share it on any other evidence than that of your own senses and sensibilities.

Farwell visited the Wrights to investigate the possibilities of the Taliesin Fellowship, and found that he agreed with its philosophy and basic principles. Evidently he must have been convinced that he could join the Fellowship in due time. He replied in June citing some college uncertainties, but he was eager to launch out on this new adventure. However, a month later he was forced to change his mind. After much soul-searching and agonizing over his situation, he wrote the following letter to Mr. Wright, dated July 19, 1933:

It becomes hard to write this letter, both for your sake and mine, but there is no evading it. I have been hoping until now that the situation would clear up one way or another, and that the way for my contemplated move would show itself wholly reasonable and right. This is unfortunately not the case. My Summer School salary, upon which I was largely depending, has been cut severely, and a cut has been announced in our regular salary at the college, and I cannot know yet of what additional amount this will deprive me. And when I subtract further the expense of moving all I would have to move, it is only too evident that in view of the understood conditions I would after a few months' time be placing the family in a situation of serious financial discomfort and embarrassment.

. . . With my desire in this direction as great as it has been, it is only with much wrestling of the spirit that I have been compelled to realize . . . that conditions are not ripe for this move.

I want you to know that in this I have not been influenced from any outward sources whatever, that nothing has occurred to prejudice me, and that it is the result only of my own judgment in analyzing and realizing the existing conditions.

. . . If I were *alone* this contingency would not seriously present itself to me; a fellow alone can always look out for himself. But I feel that I would have no right, by a premature move, to carry the family into a risk of that kind, which I would so readily assume for myself alone.

This aspect of the matter forces itself on me from what I see on every hand as the result of the uncertain and turbulent time in which we find ourselves. Even with the smallness of fees in the college, the enrollment has fallen off badly, and this appears to be the case all over the country. Students cannot get the money to attend. The hitherto well-established dramatic summer school in the East which my Sara is now attending, is maintained at present almost wholly by the giving of scholarships, with the patrons of the institution actually paying the railroad fares of the students who attend.

I have had a growing feeling that the load of the family would be a burden upon you disproportionate to what could be accomplished by my association with the Fellowship at so early a stage of its existence. I feel that you would be paying too great a price for what I could accomplish at this stage. If the money which you would have to spend filling these clamorous bellies could be applied directly toward the procuring of good musical productions at the Fellowship, in the coming year, I believe it would put you further ahead just now.

Then later on, in an advisory capacity I could be helpful by assisting with the plans and suggestions if you wish it, leaving future relations to accord with the growth of the enterprise. This would probably tally with Georgia O'Keefe's present relation to the Fellowship, as you described it to me.

For any inconvenience or trouble I may have caused you I am very regretful, but as I wrote you early last month I would want every reasonable assurance up to the last moment that I could do my part properly in carrying out such an undertaking as we outlined, and unfortunately my circumstances very positively do not give me that assurance.

I want to say that I have been very strongly drawn to you in admiration and affection, and it would mean much to me to count you as a friend. I can speak similarly of Mrs. Wright, with whom I would feel it a great privilege to become better acquainted.

Farwell's large family of wife and now six children with the addition of baby Jonathan, made it nearly impossible for him to join the Taliesin Fellowship at Spring Green under his existing financial conditions. Moreover, when Farwell's pioneering efforts in California and the East coast are recalled, one must appreciate the inner battle he waged before writing the above letter.

Farwell's files contain architectural drawings by Wright for the proposed Farwell home at the Fellowship. It featured a spacious studio on the main floor with vaulted ceiling and separate outside entrance. The downstairs study even included a piano sketched in on the plans with a figure at the keyboard. How Farwell must have identified with these plans and longed for their realization!

### Lithographic Press

It was early in 1930 that Farwell expressed renewed concern for the publication of his music. In the letter to his friend, Joseph Clark, dated October 4, 1930, he had discussed these worries and wrote about his hopes to have a shop and a press. He complained that the music publishers would print for him, but the product often just remained on their shelves. Hence, he decided that if he were to come into some real relation with the country on the basis of his music, that it must be done in a more personal, intimate and interesting way. He declared that he wanted to get the bulk of his work out into the world in his lifetime and get the reactions to it as well as any material returns which it might bring. "I am full of all these things, and expect to *burst* if I can't get into action before too long," he wrote, then added:

> I do not at all mind holding a university position, and giving a certain amount of lectures, but I do object to holding one which destroys the possibility of my completing my life-work. I intend to break through this condition.

Again he decided to take the matter into his own hands as he had done with the Wa-Wan Press in 1901. But the ideas he pursued in 1930 took much longer this time for resolution because his college position limited his time and efforts. As usual he found a workable plan. Having received a small legacy, he purchased a lithographic hand press which he set up in his basement. He found books on the subject and learned the necessary process for reproducing his music. Not only did he draw the finished music entirely by hand, but also the cover designs. His own description of this project best portrays the ingenuity and resoluteness with which he approached this new adventure. His announcement brochure is dated April 1936:

> I am announcing the establishment of my own lithographic hand press, for the publication of my own compositions, at East Lansing, Michigan, after several years of experimentation with the process.
>
> . . . I am doing this because it is my way of having the fun of adventure, in a world made all too drab by the tyranny of conformity, prudence, and fear. Naturally the enterprise directs itself upon issues with which I am vitally concerned, as, for example the difficulty which confronts a composer, in America, in making his work nationally known in a sufficiently personal and effective manner to those who might be interested in it. Also my love of practical handcraft demands satisfaction, and where it can find it in the service of my own art, so much the better.
>
> The present is, generally, a time of mass-thought and mass-action. However desirable or necessary this may be in certain fields, it is nevertheless directly against the spirit of art, which must remain a matter peculiarly individual. [Still true in the 1990's.]
>
> The field of music, music education, musical publication, in this machine-age, is not exempt from the disease of mass-idealism and mass-production. The composer, as an individual, must therefore find his way through this circumstance, and create a special channel between himself and those persons who may be receptive to his work. It would be absurd to suppose that in the matter of musical art the same method of communication and distribution can serve both the cultivated musician and the myriad devotees of the trivial and ephemeral.
>
> The publishers have been very hospitable to the works of American composers in the last few decades, and many

others, as well as myself, have been grateful for this circumstance, and have shared its benefits.    But the existing condition is, nevertheless, such that American artists, amateurs, and music-lovers are left with the most fragmentary knowledge, and almost without any possibility of obtaining direct knowledge, of what American composers have done.    In fact, without undue inconvenience, they can scarcely find and examine a representative quantity and variety of any composer's work.  I, for one, as a composer who desires to live with his people through his work, and renew his spirit by contact with them, do not propose to remain a ghost in a vacuum, when a little thought and action can remedy the situation.

It is my hope that in my pursuance of this venture, I will in some way and measure have overcome these difficulties, not for myself alone, but in pointing the way which in time, and with wider development, may prove to be of benefit to composers and music-lovers alike, and thus to the general cause of American music.

## Plan of Operation

In each city there shall be an authorized agency, a leading dealer in sheet music, for the handling of the output of my press.

Each agency will maintain a *single folio* containing a copy of *each of the works* which I print, these copies being *not for sale*, but for inspection only.  Thus the complete output of the press may be seen at any of the agencies *at all times*.

The dealer will have other copies of these compositions for sale, or if they are momentarily not in stock, will order them as desired.

In any locality where such an agency does not already exist, any interested person is invited to communicate with me (address, Arthur Farwell, East Lansing, Michigan) giving the name and address of the leading sheet music dealer in that city, and measures will be taken to have an agency established there immediately.

These publications may also be had by communicating directly with me at East Lansing. Music will be sent on approval if desired, though it would be preferable to have an agency established in any new locality where the music is not readily available for inspection.

## The Editions

Having first examined the possible methods of music reproduction, I finally adopted the process of standard modern lithography, the offset process, with zinc plates.

The music has been drawn by myself on tracing paper, by a combination of freehand and mechanical drawing processes, to resemble as accurately as possible a regular "engraved" music page.

A Kodalith paper negative is made from this drawing by direct contact with a printing frame, and the sensitized zinc plate is then printed by arc-light, in direct contact with the negative.

The finished music is finally printed from the plate on a small offset hand lithographic press of the sort commonly used as a proof press in large plants. The covers are designed by the composer, and are printed in various colors.

Farwell needed money for promotional purposes. Accordingly, he contacted Mr. Logan Fox in Philadelphia, explaining his project and his need for $1500.00. He itemized his anticipated expenses and remarked that without some financial help it would take much longer to make known what he planned to do. He added:

With a fair start I am certain that I can make it lead on to larger things. One way or another I *must* partially release myself from so enslaving a task at the college, which as it is, is too much for anybody, whether he has any other ambitions or not.

There is just one thing that should be made plain: this is not a "going into business", with a certain percentage of returns expected in a certain time. I shall remain an artist, and this is in a sense an avocation,

though one necessary to my program as an artist, which
I shall foster as assiduously as I can, without being over-
expectant with regards to quick returns. I am doing
serious work, and this, in music, spreads slowly. My
published works are gradually finding wider following, and
I do not expect the growth of what I shall now do to be
much more rapid, only there will be *much more* put out,
and attention will be called to it by the uniqueness of my
undertaking.

Do not worry about my being over-sanguine. I am,
however, very determined, and shall push ahead inch by
inch. If you can find it possible to help, by finding me a
patron, it will be wonderful.

. . . I intend to enter the lists again as a musical
publicist (as in my *Musical America* days) and take up the
issues of national musical development, with announcements and communications through my own channels, and
in articles in musical journals. With this will probably go
a certain amount of lectures in cities not too far distant
and occasional productions of my orchestral works.

Farwell did not acquire the hoped-for patron nor is there
evidence that he secured any loan. His work on the lithographic
press proceeded slowly, but was a joy for his "leisure" hours.
(Figure 44) Beatrice Farwell, like Sara, remembered the pleasant
times when she was permitted to watch her father working at his
press. He would go to his basement shop whistling a happy tune
and return upstairs smiling when a given task was completed. His
"adventure" became a source of great solace and satisfaction.

Farwell contacted old friends in various cities to find agencies
for his new publications. One such letter was to Mr. Sabin, an
acquaintance from Bohemian Club days. On March 31, 1936,
Farwell wrote asking him for the name of the leading sheet music
dealer in San Francisco, - "the one to whom cultivated musicians
and music-lovers would naturally go for sheet music of a serious
order." After explaining his new enterprise, he continued:

So you see I am reaching out to the country again as
I did in earlier days, only, in a new manner that I feel to

be more appropriate to the present time. I may in this enterprise be helpful in finding a way forward for other composers. I have such a mass of compositions unpublished (which I have been mostly saving up with this venture in mind) that I can not at present do anything with the works of others, and besides, I believe that by developing this manner of a more personal approach, with my own works, I can do more good for those who may wish to follow by similar methods later.

Farwell enclosed a copy of one of his newly printed works as a sample and then reminisced about "what an immense part the Club has played in my life!."

Farwell's files include a list of thirty-four names and addresses of music dealers in widely scattered cities across the country which he had developed from personal contacts and letter-writing. Ten names were encircled in red and may have been the music companies who showed the greatest amount of interest. His notes indicate that he had sent a letter and a folio of music to each of these dealers. Harold Flammer in New York was the only company that had refused to carry his folio under his outlined plan for distribution, but Galaxy did agree to handle it.

In addition to the list of music dealers, Farwell had prepared a three page list of individuals who were either president of a large music club or musically prominent in some other way. Evidently these were persons he had contacted about his new project. According to his indicated code, he had underlined in blue the names of those from whom he had received a reply. Twenty-six persons out of the list of forty-one had answered his letters.

Another person whom Farwell contacted for help in his new endeavor was Mrs. Artie Mason Carter, a dear friend from Community Music and Hollywood Bowl days in California. After describing his enterprise, he went on to say, "So I am merely setting a personal example of how it may be done, by which I hope other composers may profit in the course of time." This letter was dated February 6, 1934, which suggests how much time Farwell had devoted to making his early dream of 1930 a reality.

*Figure 44. Farwell enjoys printing some of his music for publication on his home made lithographic press.*

Farwell received national recognition in a story carried by the *New York Times*, May 16, 1937. It described his work with his lithographic press and included an action photo of him. Farwell sent a copy of this publicity to Mr. C. L. Brody, Chairman of the State Board of Agriculture, which was appointed by the Senate and directed the affairs of the Michigan State College. Mr. Brody replied with the following lines of appreciation for Farwell's work:

> I have always felt that there was considerable reluctance on the part of some of the eastern publications to mention a man from the middle west. At any rate it is surely a fine thing to know that members of our faculty are being nationally recognized by the highest authorities, and I am very happy that this fitting recognition has come to you in reward for the hard and faithful work you have done through the years.

It was shortly after the appearance of this publicity in the *New York Times* that Farwell began to search for a new teaching position and wrote to Dean Butler at Syracuse University for his assistance in this matter. While it seems obvious that Farwell had remained in his position as a teacher primarily for financial security, it also seems that he was not reluctant to continue teaching. He felt drawn to the East where he could be in closer touch with musical affairs and publishers in New York, and he thought Dean Butler might be aware of openings in his New York area. However, no new openings seemed available as Farwell stayed on at Michigan State College until 1939 when a retirement policy went into effect. This called for the termination of all college professors over the age of 65 years. By this time Farwell was 67 years old, so was forced to retire after having served on the music faculty for twelve busy years.

During this period, Farwell had established strong friendships with people in the area. One such friendship was with John W. Crist, another faculty member. When Crist was contacted in 1956 to express his memories of Farwell, he was high in his praises:[5]

> Our association together continued over a period of several years, and was one of constant and intimate

friendship. Before me, as I write, hanging from a wall of
the room, is an enlarged and framed photograph of this
extraordinary man and companion - given by him to me
at the time when fate decreed our separation.   The
inscription thereon reads: "To my friend, John Crist, in
memory of many pleasant hours." These hours were
pleasant, highly so, and my memories of them and from
them are many in number and precious above price and
beyond words.

. . . He was, and immortally is, worthy of recognition.
. . and deserves elevation and being set forth in the high
place he merited, and merits, in the advancement and the
history of American music. I knew him, and I know his
music, and I know his desert in the value of his art.

What were some of Farwell's accomplishments during the
years in Michigan? Beyond what he called a burdensome teaching
load, Farwell did manage a summer of composition in the Teton
Mountains of Wyoming, and wrote or completed a number of his
largest musical compositions.   Meanwhile, he was busy learning
the art and craft of lithography for his new publishing venture.
He also began intensive work for his treatise on *Intuition*, both
drafting and hand illustrating the work.   These things were done
in spite of the stresses of the family economy during the Great
Depression of the thirties and the devastating breakdown of his
marriage.

Farwell orchestrated two of his *Symbolistic Studies - Number
3* for performance by the Philadelphia Orchestra in 1928 under
Pierre Monteux - and *Number 6* which won a national prize
broadcast in 1939 by the Columbia Orchestra under Howard
Barlow.   He developed his *Gods of the Mountain* from trio form
to orchestra for its premiere in 1929.

He composed two violin sonatas, one for solo violin, and the
*Quintet in E minor for Piano and Strings*, a major work recorded
by the Musical Heritage Society.   Notes in his pocket-theme-books
show that he built this quintet from themes he had generated and
recorded during his Wa-Wan lecture tours decades before.

Beyond these large works, Farwell completed his only formal
symphony, the *Rudolph Gott Symphony*.   One work he considered

his magnum opus is the large symphonic song for orchestra and chorus, *Mountain Song*, finished in 1931.

Meanwhile, between or during these major works, Farwell wrote a dozen or so songs and piano works on a lesser scale. He also made a big beginning in a large group of songs based on Emily Dickinson's poems that he perhaps would later consider the jewels of his musical purpose and expression.

No matter how heavy his teaching schedule, or how preoccupied he was in the press room reproducing his compositions, or building equipment for his production of offset musical editions, Farwell was never through composing. Indeed, in spite of disturbing marital problems, the Michigan years were very fruitful ones in composition.

# Chapter 13

## Farwell's Composition Students

### Roy Harris

Arthur Farwell's influence as a teacher touched the lives of many students, several of whom became distinguished composers. Bernard Rogers, Dika Newlin, and Roy Harris were among those studying under Farwell who have gained national recognition. During Farwell's work as chief music critic for Musical America, (1909-1915), is the period when he gave some lessons to Bernard Rogers. Dika Newlin studied composition with Farwell one summer in East Lansing, Michigan, before she entered college there. The composer most closely associated with Farwell however, was Roy Harris (Figure 45).

Roy Harris was 26 years old when he first approached Farwell in 1924 about studying composition with him. Initially, Farwell was reluctant to accept a student with so meager a background in music, but after he had talked further with Harris, he discovered a common bond of creative purpose. Perhaps he remembered his own late start as a composer which gave him empathy with this young man. What began then as a simple teacher-student relationship became a fruitful friendship that lasted for many years in spite of the differences in age. (Farwell was 52 years old at this time).

A study of the correspondence found in the author's Farwell Collection suggests that Farwell had more influence on Harris's work than Harris acknowledged publicly - as much ideological and philosophical as musical. These areas of influence become apparent in reviewing their letters. In those early days, in addition to giving Harris a more solid foundation in harmony, one of the first practical things that Farwell did for his student, was to find paying jobs for him, thus freeing his pupil from having to drive a butter-and-egg truck route, that had been his immediately previous way of earning a living. One new position was as a music critic for the *Los Angeles Illustrated News* and the other as a harmony teacher at the old Hollywood Conservatory.

*Figure 45.   Roy Harris.   Courtesy, Johana Harris-Heggie.*

Mrs. Farwell recounted the times when Roy Harris brought his first wife, Charlotte, (known also as Davida) to the Farwell home for the lessons.[1]   Mrs. Harris brought their baby girl, "Bonnie," along and the two women often compared family notes as the Farwells had a baby girl, Sara, of similar age.   Mrs. Farwell described one particular lesson when Harris came out of the study gleefully rubbing his hands together while also blowing big puffs on his pipe.  She observed, "You must have had a good session!" to which he replied, "Oh boy!"  After this " the music began to come", she noted.

These early lessons in harmony included also much discussion on other topics.  Farwell's broad cultural background and visionary idealism made a strong impact on young Harris.  In addition to encouraging his student, and opening his mind to new ideas, perhaps the most important thing Farwell did was to introduce Harris to the works of Walt Whitman.  These provided something of a philosophical focus for Harris's efforts in large forms and expanse of expression.

It was Farwell who guided Harris in writing his first orchestral work, an *Andante*, that had been originally planned as part of a much larger composition, but never completed.  Harris decided to send the *Andante* to Howard Hanson, who conducted it on a spring festival of American works on April 23, 1926. It was also Farwell who used his influence with Mrs. Artie Mason Carter to make possible the *Andante* performance at the Hollywood Bowl. Mrs. Carter was so impressed with Harris's music that she encouraged him to show the work to Elly Ney, wife of Willem van Hoogstraten, the conductor of the New York Philharmonic summer season.  Ney also liked the work and sent it on to her husband who, after being quite heavily pressured by his wife, included the *Andante* on a July 1926 concert at Lewisohn Stadium. Harris was on hand to hear it.  In 1925 Farwell had given Harris letters of introduction to people in the East who might help him get established there.  However, it was the New York performance of *Andante* that marked the start of his public career as a composer.

Harris met Aaron Copland in June 1925 during a brief stay at the MacDowell Colony in Peterborough, New Hampshire. Copland recognized the young man's talent and recommended study abroad with Nadia Boulanger with whom he had also studied. Eventually financial arrangements were made through the generosity of Alma Wertheim, a patroness of the arts, and later the Guggenheim Fellowships, which provided the necessary means to study. By 1926, Harris was divorced from Charlotte and left for Paris with his new wife, Sylvia Feningsten, - a marriage also destined to be short-lived.

Harris wrote several letters to Farwell while he was in France describing his new life and lessons. One undated letter was sent from Juziers where Harris was living in a country home with a large garden. He tells of his successful experiences raising fruit and vegetables which have given him a fresh outlook on life:

> This existence is making me realize once more that . . . the modern artist's biggest problem is that of simplification. . . . I knew that simplification was our big problem when I was in L.A. but this [simple life style] has forced the idea home. I see . . . modern artists completely snowed under the storm of diversion which modern society urges on one. . . There is never any growth, any sinking of roots into a constant soil. . . . Ridiculous as it is - It is quite natural that composers should run around the world like decapitated chickens trying to trim every new sail that manages to raise a breeze - quite natural because they have no God. By this I mean they never have a set of values in the world. . . .

Harris then goes into detail of what he hopes to do about this situation. "Between me and you" he sets forth impressive goals for eight years of research: two years studying melodic contours, two years for harmonic research, two years for a contrapuntal substitution of harmonic research, and two years for form and orchestration. All this he hoped to accomplish while also undertaking the writing of eight compositions. After completing his goal, Harris dreamed of teaching other composers. "I shall somehow get a small ranch in California, and live on and work this soil, and insist that my pupils do the same, part of the time." Harris concluded his long letter of shared hopes:

Dear Arthur, if this letter seems youthful or braggadocio,
please know in your heart that I am not a bluffer - that
I know whereof I speak.  I would never write you, my
dearest friend, in such a vein.

While his studies in France continued, Harris shared other
ideas with Farwell until he suffered a fall in early autumn of 1929
that severely injured his spine.  As a result, he had to return to
the United States for special surgery and a lengthy recuperation.
It was probably during this period that Harris had more time to
think and analyze his place in the American musical scene.  Hilda
Hemingway, a young woman to whom Boulanger had introduced
Harris in Paris, joined him in the United States and eventually
married him.  The couple were living on $15.00 a week up in the
San Gabriel mountains of California, near Glendora, when Harris
sought advice from his former teacher in a soul-searching letter
written sometime in December 1930.  Most of this long handwritten letter is quoted, as it reveals the agony and profound
depths of Harris's intellectual and spiritual struggle.  Since it was
written for private eyes only, there was no attempt to impress the
reading public as were some of his later writings.  The letter
commands an expected reply with answers from the man Harris
respected and admired who would be honest with him.

Dear Arthur - friend - brother.

How indeed I wish you were here now.  I am going
through a most terrible crisis - an intellectual and spiritual
crisis - I suppose that no one can help another in these
matters but at least one can speak out his heart.  As I get
deeper and deeper into music I become more and more
convinced of my talent and my flare for the medium.
Melodies    and    harmonic    juxtapositions,    rhythms,
orchestration boldness are beginning to flow without effort
from me with as effective decisiveness as I can guide a car
thru traffic.
I feel sure and know how to govern the psychologic
laws of periodicy [sic] etc.--  In fact my tecnique (sic) is

becoming very simple and clear and direct and my support is fine.

Everything is propitious except my faith in music itself. The concert world is so badly rotten - (as rotten as the Church politic) - the very craftsmanship of the art itself is so disintegrated - standards are so muddled - I feel like a stranger from Mars - everything is so governed by commercial standards that I have only the great music of Bach and Beethoven and Palestrina and Mozart to fall back on. And were I convinced that music as a separate art must go on then I would be willing or rather spiritually able to have the faith to make me a great worker - to become a master in every sense of the word in order that the craftsmanship - the classic form - the idealism - the clarity of purpose, beauty, force and dignity of music might be preserved. But will mankind's economic and political situation ever again produce a Church and Court life supporting absolute music? Was Bach to Beethoven an exotic flowering of special social conditions which will never reoccur?

If this is true, then Bach and Beethoven mark the peak of the Occidental co-ordination of mind and spirit in my opinion. And if this is true one can imagine the unimaginative fibre of the Ravels and Respighis who obscure all standards by coloring up great mixtures of styles and ideas - (it is as though bill boards were displayed in art galleries). One can understand also the poor understanding and taste of our audiences. But what of me? - (and there must be hundreds like me) who see Bach, Mozart, and Beethoven for what they are and yet crave and are capable of a new classicism which would be just as austere - just as plastic - just as solid - just as soaring as the old. In a sense serving the same tenets of homogenuity [sic] and continuity but speaking a less redundant language - a more plastic rhythm - a more colorful harmony - a less four square melodic contour.

If there is to be such a new classicism, who is to savor it - for whom shall it be concieved [sic] - certainly not the concert hall audience of today. Will it come through

educational institutions as part of psychological training?
Will it come to take the place of literature which I think
is on its last legs?

These are the questions which harass me and which
must be answered to my own mind before I can go forth
with that Faith which makes genius out of common clay
and irresistable [sic] force out of tired men.

I suppose the trouble lies in the fact that I was born
socially minded, that I am a Democrat feeling that Art for
Art's sake is merely a plume for the filthy rich - and that
real Art must be socially functional.

This question was raised the other day:  How could
music have been extant since the dawning of man and
then suddenly become dead - (as Latin or Greek became
dead.)?  This question must be answered first by defining
the difference between music and sound - i.e. Music as a
separate art - (self enunciating and complete) and music
as an accoutrement to literary and dance ideas.  Music as
a separate art has a spiritual end to fulfill - or rather to
be explicit, a psychological end.  In this capacity it releases
and gives form to subconscious impulses - it formulates
and becomes the sense counterpart of our subconscious
selves.  In such a capacity music becomes the language of
priests and seers.

In its sound capacity i.e. as an accoutrement to
literature and dance it merely aids and emotionally vivifies
the program it serves.  In the former capacity it must have
form and clarity and continuity - it must definitely
impress an authentic mood and at the same time assume
the form of a separate entity.  Thus classic or absolute
music must evolve with the evolution of man's
subconscious impulses, or die as an art.

But on the other hand program music best serves its
purpose when it employs the formulae which are most
obviously recognized - (especially form and melodic
formulas - orchestration can always cover up and color old
ideas to make them then sound new or appear new.)
(Consider Wagner - Strauss - Rimsky K -- and Stravinsky
in this Light.)  See articles accompanying letter.

The point I wish to make is that there has been enough music already written to go on with if music is no longer to continue as a separate art. By a zealous industrialism such as is now being used by movie compilers the various formulae can be juxtaposed *ad infinitum.* - We would continue to have commercial music - but no art of music - just as we continue to have furniture and shoes but no art of cabinet makers or boot makers. We could have musical factories such as the musical departments of the movies represent and if this will satisfy the demands of people's musical appetite that is what we will have.

Faith, dear friend Arthur is the prerequisite of all action and that is my great prayer. I propose to myself this line of action: To assume that I have one of 2 courses to pursue according to my innate capacities (1). To conclude that music is a dying art and to forsake it for the study of psychology in relation to education (and even then this would lead one back to the auditory sense because I believe that the relativity of words has held back the growth of man to a great extent whereas the development of the auditory and visual sense will aid his growth by releasing his subconscious). (2). To conclude that music will go on as a separate art and will eventually grow towards the modern or new classicism which I am groping towards now and certainly contain within me. In this case I should go on and become a master and teach classic standards of craftsmanship assuming that I am writing for an ever growing educational movement which embraces music as an ethical study as well as a psychological exercise in releasing the subconscious.

The latter course is healthiest for me and if music goes on I might be a step - a beginning towards something great in the evolution of man- if it turns back i. e. dies as a separate art - I might be one more favor of a race's worn out passion and as such lived in vain.

What do you think Arthur? Sit down and tell me *typewritten so I can read it,* a long letter.

You see I can intellectualize about it but that does not give me the emotional drive which only Faith can fire.

News

Am married a 3rd and last time to a wonderful Irish-English-Scotch girl - comes from old old families. - The Townshends in Ireland and the McGregors in Scotland. She is as near like a man as a woman can be and still arouse a virile man's passions. Related to Bernard Shaw and the Huxleys all of which she takes no cognizance of. She is in love with ME. The first woman who ever has been - I realize that now. Very brilliant mind - fine robust physique - very unusual capacities. Is helping me do copy work - we are copying the parts for the Symphony which will be played here by the L.A. Philharmonic in February.. . . The 2nd movement contains your old "Johnny" favorite. Will send sample of Hilda's copying. . . . Am starting to prepare a *History of Musical Formulae*. . . It will take years & will be part of my life work if I go on in music. Answer soon.

Farwell's equally extensive reply, reflects something of the discussions the two men must have experienced earlier and reveals also much of the intensity of Farwell's convictions about his world and his hopes for music in it. It was dated January 9, 1931, and gave advice to Harris as well as his reactions to Harris's soul-baring letter:

Gosh! I was glad to hear from you, especially as you gave me a good bit of your inner life. And I take it that you are well from your terrible time with that accident.

If there is anyone in the world who can understand your letter and all that it implies, I am the one. You are going through exactly what I went through beginning at Highland Park in 1925-6. Only we arrived at it somewhat differently: You have come to it by getting about the world and seeing evidences of the present horrible condition; I was seeing it piecemeal from my seclusion in California, but had the whole story brought forcibly to my attention in concentrated form by Spengler. I positively couldn't sleep those days, I was so shaken up. The reasons for Faith in music (i.e. under present conditions of western civilization) seemed to vanish. And that is the thing you have come upon.

. . . Every artist in America ought to go through this struggle today; if he doesn't, there is something the matter with him. And on the issue rests the future. This is only for great souls.

I am of course, now, not Spengler, or Schopenhauer or Wagner or anybody else but *myself.* Consequently if I use Spengler, or anybody, in talking to you, to bring out points, it is only from what I have digested and assimilated to myself, and is part of the self that I now am.

I am glad you see the rottenness of the concert world. It has gone to hell. And I am glad you ask "who will savor it?" if you do produce what you want to. That corresponds with what I have been saying a long time, that a great spiritual prophetic soul in music cannot today speak his message through the concert hall and concert world, for it can not be to that de-spiritualized audience - they are far, far from it. The needed message cannot be spoken there.

You and I, and a good many others in this are born out of the soul of America, out of the proto-soul of a new race - a race worthy of a new continent - - how then can we help feeling like a "Stranger from Mars" in this decadent Western (European) civilization that has been driven at last upon this confusion and directionlessness. If we were really a part of it we would be heart and soul *with* it, doing *Ballet Mechaniques*, *Sacres* and all the rest, and feeling that we were IT. The fact is we can't. We are forerunners of another breed that bears within it a spiritual germ worthy of generating one day a new *Great Culture* of the World. The discovery of America, the pouring in of the races of the world, a new and broader nature world, a new absorption of the primitive (negro and Indian) - in short a new continent - - - all this would be a travesty without the outlook which I am presenting.

It is unthinkable that such a new continent and a new race as this can remain and be a mere tail to an old-world world-view that has had its day.

It is nothing to me that a horde of young Europeans arise to strive to carry on in the arts, in European civilization. Of course they will, and they will be part and parcel of what that civilization has become, and will be equally chaotic, muddled, trivial and directionless. Who of them are saying what you or I, in our deepest souls, want to hear? Or even hinting at it? Stravinsky? Honegger? Ravel? Hindemith? And what is to become of this young American (???) crew that is playing up a shallow "modern idiom" to tickle the critics and modern concert audiences in the metropolitan centers? They are going to be wiped off the slate.

I have been wondering lately if you were going to come back from Europe as one of this latter crew, or whether you were going to see through the hollowness and shallowness of it all, and preserve to yourself the saving doubts, questions, dissatisfactions.

Isn't the publishing world a fine reflex of this commercialized and rotten condition you have so well described? The big electric companies (with the movies) have bought up all the publishers, whose immediate directors are now minions of the electrical-movie overlords. They don't dare now to venture in any genuine artistic direction. Schirmer alone has held, and their "prestige fund" is all that is left to advance any and all serious effort in America. And this overcrowds them fatally. Where they once published the bulk of their composers, they will, and can, now publish only perhaps one in ten or twenty of the works he submits.

Your letter makes me feel that you have not *really read your Spengler*. From first to last your letter is the most corroboration of the most vital part of his observations, only arrived at through your own observations and struggle. You recognize "Bach to Beethoven" as the high point of culture, and find only these to fall back on (except Palestrina, the high point of the *Gothic* period of the culture, space-searching vocal polyphony.) Quite so. You are precisely repeating Spengler when you say, "If this is true then Bach and Beethoven mark the peak of the Occidental co-ordination of mind and spirit." Only you mistake in speaking of this as an *exotic* flowering, for it is flesh and bone of the Occidental culture at its maturest and healthiest.: I guess you meant merely *passing*, a period occurring once in the culture and then going by forever. That I think to be true. I have become reconciled to that. The most we can do in that sense and spirit, I believe, is to furnish forth an afterglow, a warm homage (if we are capable), that is, *still within the scope of the Western culture.* This follows necessarily from something that you yourself have recognized when you wrote "In the former capacity (music as a separate art - self enunciating and complete) it must have form," etc. Precisely. And today the Western culture has not one single form that is prophetic - that we feel is yet to be carried on for years or generations, to a height felt but unperceived, as Europe of the 17th and 18th centuries carried on the sonata. Their whole stock of forms is now broken up: and at the end of the Romantic epoch there was not one left that has a future. There was nothing but *styles* left to work with, rehashing all the old forms with impressionism, jazz, expressionism, etc., etc., *ad infinitum and ad naseum.* The *symphonic form* created Beethoven. He rose with it, through it, upon it. Without it, *or its equivalent*, there would be no Beethoven. (Of course that is bound up, too, with the Time-Spirit.) Whoso will rise now, or anytime, must do so upon a form which belongs to the Time-Spirit and offers a vast growth ahead, looking toward its fulfillment and perfection.

The symphony concert came into existence to provide for the people hearing symphonies. When that form has said its say, symphony concerts go on as institutions, by momentum, but become spiritually hollow. The world will not be served afresh through this medium.

What then, you ask, is to be done with these powers you have acquired - this capacity you feel to provide the

new classicism - 'solid, austere', etc.? Except for sporadic
hearings, I believe your concert world of today, and what
there is left of it for tomorrow - with the de-spiritualized
social bearing which it has fallen to - will not want or
accept this new classicism, or any other real spiritual
message.  I think that hope is gone forever.  I once
naively thought - in a number of years, when Americans
have learned to become conductors, they will give the
composer in America his opportunity, and we can then
move forward rapidly.  Not one bit.  It is a tighter
European clamp today than ever.  Wealthy 'society', which
alone can support symphonies (your 'filthy rich') will have
no other than a foreign conductor, and he will play to
them.  This is a vicious circle that will scarcely be broken.
The system will go down with the flag of this scheme still
flying.

Then I think you are quite afield with regard to
'educational institutions and psychological training.' These
things will 'do their bit', though rather indirectly,
contributing this or that factor to the forthcoming
American life.  It is not education and psychological
training that is needed, it is *spiritual vision.*

Western civilization will not overcome itself.  It is
defeating itself at a terrific pace.  A new spirit in the
world will have to defeat it.  And that spirit  will not
arise on the depleted soil of the senescent Occidental
culture in its original European home.  It will appear
somewhere else. One of the types of the new is likely to
come from Russia (which is not Europe).  But the
American soul will not fall in with this.

I can see our task only, only as the search for the
*true Spiritual America.*  I think we must go deep into
ourselves, see what people and the world we were born to,
open our deepest intuitions, perceive what lies and waits
at the deepest center of the American soul, and wherever
we find any crumb, even of that true spiritual America,
use our powers to express it, and find an appropriate *form*
in which to express it.  It may well be that the forms *to
be* will seem to have  no place in our immediate scheme

of things.  Any forms that fit our immediate scheme of things can scarcely contain what ought to come forth from us.  Our deep need is not for 'successful composers', but for daring prophets willing to be martyrs.  Deems Taylor will not create the future.  Nor Carpenter with his *Krazy Kat*.  Nor Copland with his *Cat and Mouse*.

I believe we were true and right to absorb our primitives - Indian and Negro- as part of the immense blend of the future race here.  Then, in the midst of this chaos and confusion, *I* have felt strongly that the next thing to do is to go to our own greatest American aspects of Nature, and put down what it gives us.  This marvelous Nature world of America will certainly be a powerful factor to the spiritual quality of future America.  This Faith lies back of my *Mountain Song*, which has become a tremendous work during these seven years.  (This is what I got out of the High Sierras.)  Song is in it, but there is also full scope for symphonic composition.  This work doesn't belong to any department of our present scheme of things, and may have to wait a good while for presentation.  Attendance upon this might become one day almost like a Nature Ceremony - something quite apart from the life of the symphony hall. And I believe it will feed the American soul when it is properly presented.

But beyond this Nature approach to the American musical problem - which I feel to be very important - there remains the purely spiritual approach, which demands the seer - the prophet of the new Great Culture of the American continent, with its own world-view.  A *Symphonic ceremonial* (from which Song, in one form or another, is not likely to be absent) organized as a festival performance for the people of any American community, wholly apart from the symphony concert world, might be a germ-thought of a way forward, of a new form embodying a new spirit, with a history of development before it, that would demand all the powers which we have acquired.  (and more).

Well, you are entering into the sphere of the terrific questions which have nearly driven me to despair these

last years, having mercifully been preserved from them
during the time you needed to acquire command of your
*metier*. I have given you some hint of my position on the
matter, and I can assure you it has been ground out these
years, with agonizing grinding. But I am finding myself in
my own right at last.

This may throw some light on your two final
alternatives. As to the first, I may say that it is possible
to conclude that music is a 'dying art' in one Culture and
a *borning art* in another at the same time. Which makes
it unnecessary to forsake it for any damn psychology.
When spiritual insight is there, psychology takes care of
itself.

As to your other possible conclusion, to go on toward
your own vision of a new classicism, I look at this as good
with the terrific *IF* - if it has no smug hope of nicely and
smoothly continuing the Occidental culture, but seeks the
vision of a fundamentally new human spirit in this new
continent. Your assumption that you would be working
for an 'ever growing educational movement' of any kind
I think to be in error. I would say rather that you should
assume that you were working to terminate every ethical
and psychological movement that conforms to Western
civilization  today, and to storm the human spirit with a
new vision of life and the meaning of life. *Then* you
might be "a step - a beginning towards something great in
the evolution of man".

You are letting your "classic standards of
craftsmanship" (which are all right in their place) eclipse
somewhat the spiritual vision to which they should be
applied. *That* is the prior consideration.

I already had your Freeman articles, and made
numerous marginal notes. It is getting too late to go into
that now, and I guess I have probably covered and
superseded everything I wrote there.

I was certainly interested to hear of your marriage.
Tell Mrs. Harris, from me, to realize that she is married
to a composer which will give her sufficient experience
and training (if she can stand it) to last her for several

incarnations. I know because my wife is married to one. The best of wishes and felicitations to you both.

Perhaps I can get the college to get your sonata records.

Well, my *vita nuova* began day before yesterday, when I installed in my room a beautiful lithographic hand press which I purchased for five hundred dollars, upon which I shall from now on print all my own compositions, and the publishers can go to the devil. Before I can use it I have to learn the process of preparing the zinc plates which are necessary to use with it. With this I shall defy and outstrip the *circumstance* which now restricts me, and contact a larger world.

Bye-bye. Write very soon, and tell me what a lunatic you think I am. I love you, as always; you are a great part of my life: we touch vitally somewhere.     Arthur

Harris obviously listened to his old teacher's advice and continued a career in music rather than in psychology. Moreover, the author's Farwell Collection holds further correspondence that shows Harris's desire to share news or ask further advice. However, the only letter available relating to any response to Farwell's January missive was penned early in the summer of 1931:

Dear Old Arthur - Father Confessor and Co-birthdayist of Will Shakespeare: [April 23rd]

It has indeed been a long time since I wrote (I have dunned myself a hundred times and read your last letter half as many). But at last I take pen in hand to write portentous news. I am East bound on July 1st. . . . When and where can I see you for a few prescious (sic) days. We have so much to say & I want to show you all my work and see all your new music.

Harris went on to describe some future plans and included a copy of the theme for the fugue he used in his recently composed Toccata which he says he is "crazy to show you and other things". This letter is typical of other letters wherein Harris sought help of one kind or another during these early years of his career. The

refreshing style of writing between these two men has a warm
feeling of spontaneity regarding whatever is going on in their lives.
Some selected excerpts from these exchanges are revealing of both
men and are worth sharing.

When Harris arrived in Washington D.C. after one such visit
in the summer of 1931, he wrote to express his thanks for
Farwell's hospitality and added:

> . . . Please look around and see if you can find Hilda's
> appetite - She seems to have left it with a blue eyed
> gentleman of repute. The cuff links will follow tomorrow.
> . . Don't forget the data and names of books dealing with
> Gregorian Chant. . . .
>
> Dear Brother Arthur - You made me have a heavy
> feeling in my stomach leaving you thusly - - We ought to
> see more of each other. Life is so short and precarious.

Evidently Farwell was too busy to answer Harris's letter, so
by early September of 1931, Harris dashed off another handwritten letter reprimanding his old teacher:

> I see that neither God, man, nor the devil can wring
> a letter from your merry bones - not even a pair of cuff
> links - so I shall write you again.
>
> What about a note this time? . . . We did not go to
> Peterboro after all - have stayed right on here   and
> worked liked a horse.  Have learned very much -   Ye
> Gods what a lot of bunk historians write when you have
> the music beside you. The English for the English - the
> French for the French etc. etc. The case for the French
> is the strongest of all nations as far as inventive genius is
> concerned. I become convinced that Nationalism in art is
> not a very live issue.  What is important is that music
> should be a live issue. . . .   The important thing seems
> that  musical  creative  genius  thrives  in  congenial
> environment. Arthur, what did you decide to do about an
> article concerning your friend and pupil - having kept his
> string quartet and symphonic reduction - lo these many
> moons?

I leave N.Y. the 20th so please send everything to the above address at once so I'll get it. The Toccata will be done in Rochester instead of the Symphony in October. Plan to come back by your way  - Miss Shire thinks she can ring me in on a lecture.

More letters deal with various compositions which Harris was writing. He sent copies of some of these to Farwell for his criticism and approval. By September 28, 1931, Harris wrote again from New York City asking Farwell to forward his string quartet and a sextet which Farwell had been examining as it was going to be published. Harris also shared news of a catastrophe that had just happened. "Some racketeer broke into our car last night . . . and stole all the parts of the Toccata and the whole score of my Symphony". A subsequent letter rejoiced in the "return of the Symphony and Toccata but not the Toccata parts." Harris was also excited about the prospect of sharing a program to be conducted by Howard Hanson on which Farwell's *Gods of the Mountain* was to be performed and Harris's *Toccata*. However, plans for Harris's part on the program did not materialize at that time. Instead Harris tried to make plans to be in Rochester to hear Farwell's work performed:

I want so much to hear your work but I have had so many mishaps in N.Y. that we are broke - and having to get out a new set of parts to boot - . . . But please write me when the concert exactly is - and if I can borrow the money I will come up *if* you will be there. *Will you be there?*
Now then - Please send on your quartet and violin sonata & any small chamber music -  Arranging for 'intime' musicales at publisher's house - *No good without parts.*

In late 1931 Farwell prepared an article for the Musical Quarterly about Roy Harris and his music[2], an assignment which Harris himself, had a hand in arranging. Harris supplied Farwell with quotations about himself and gave Farwell suggestions for the content of the article. Since these letters reflect a personal

analysis of what Harris valued in his own writing and indirectly
also reflect Farwell's earlier teachings, consideration is given to
key paragraphs. (Because Harris did not date many of his letters,
the dates have been determined by internal evidence.)

[Early October, 1931]
Dear Arthur,

Again I am sending coals to Newcastle but it was
agreed that what you don't want would go in the
wastebasket.

I especially hope that you will stress the Western
influence as opposed to the Eastern European influence -
and that I am classic in my approach as opposed to the
"Neo-Classic" - i.e. every element related and subsidiary to
the whole. That melody and form are the two things I
am strongest in and most insistent on . . .

Our people have accepted the appraisals of past
generations concerning masters.    Unconsciously they
approach the old masters on the "ecstatic plane".    But
they look at our own people on the cold rational plane
and are suspicious of authority and creative fervor . .   .
The Democratic ideal needs leaders but is very prone to
level all creative activity . . . Our people are suspicious
of leaders . . . Of course I want you to stick to your guns
. . . but I must in loyalty tell you that many people will
be shocked to hear from your pen that I am of the caliber
which you find me.

It might be well for us both if you state in the
beginning that you judge my works on the same
craftsmanship grounds that you learned as a student to
understand the classics - length and quality of melodic
line, rhythmic vitality - continuity and unity of form -
consistency of harmonic texture and style and above all
the creative drive behind it - variation of expression,
gamut of mood.

Again I think it well to say that the form is so lacking
in repetition , so constantly reconstituted in melodic line,
rhythm etc. that the casual observer will not hear or feel

its organic continuity - especially these who have been trained to think of form as a series of sequential mosaics - a pattern of easily discernible characteristics turned inside out and upside down.

In another 1931 letter to Farwell, (no specific date), Harris included musical examples from his compositions each of which showed specific traits which he considered typical of his work. This letter also suggested that Farwell point up the fact that Harris had "eschewed Programmatic tendencies from the first at a time out West when all the rage was Programmatic - Debussy, Strauss and early Stravinsky."

Harris also discussed the matter of classicism and said his was not the "neo" classicism of the Stravinsky school which he felt really attempts to give the feeling of classicism by using the materials of the past masters. Instead his classicism "has to do with the study of the nature of the material itself and relating each element (harmony, melody, orchestration, firm rhythm) as a subsidiary to the whole. . . "

In a later letter, Harris criticized the "new academicians" who had sprung into being since 1922:

. . . Not to be completely out of the picture they have taken to their bosoms the 'accepted' moderns - a close scouting of these moderns will show that the only thing which is modern about them is their harmonic and orchestral garments - take these off and here are all the old Gods with false faces. Stravinsky's *Petrouchka* with its obvious quotations from folk tunes - little snatches sequentially treated - color - harmonically and rhythmically (in spots) orchestrally. No melodic line - no form - no attempt to organic growth - Ravel - Respighi - the same old bag of shabby tricks - . Debussy saw the farce of this and began to break thru it but succumbed to programmatic effects because of the preoccupation of his generation with such effects. But the lurking Academician has sensed the old wine in new bottles business and goes around proving how modern he is by supporting these old melodies and old forms and even old moods jazzed up -

so they can point a disparaging finger at the spontaneous fresh work - which they cannot follow.   Their only conception of form being the mosaic carpentry of the most obvious characteristics of the so called first theme. This practice which is so hard to get out of our blood is strangling music.   The eternal sequence a password for mediocrity. [Yes, it is in Bach and Beethoven - but their work is great in spite of it not because of it and moreover at the crucial point they used it as a springboard to take off into new regions.]*    Damn the sequence.    The principle of balance is all important. (* Bracketed sentence was scratched out lightly in the original letter)

Harris went on to suggest that Farwell should emphasize that form was his strong point.  To the critics who might say, "Yes, but it is cerebral form - not spontaneous form," Harris retorted that this was not true.  "I swear. . . that I never begin a piece until the dynamic form, the long form line is complete in my mind.  That is always my first great struggle.  To rule out modern life - to gain tranquility long enough to see and feel the form - and I think my work shows it."  Harris also discussed the problem a real creator has in knowing where intuition ends and technique begins:

A creative technique means a definite genius for organic formulations which is just as important as the original idea and just as authentically intuitive.

I have been seeing things the last few days about my music which I never knew were there.   The intuitive creative process is always a jump ahead of the mind.  The mind is a miser and a scheming nit wit - when he rules the throne - the Kingdom soon declines with over taxation and underproduction.

Harris's last letter in this 1931 series designed to help Farwell with writing the article about himself, suggested quotations to fortify some of Farwell's statements.  Harris listed John Tasker Howard's comments in *Our American Music*: "In some respects Roy Harris is the white hope of the nationalists, for this raw boned Oklahoman has the Southwest in his blood. And he puts it into his music. In Harris we have a trained musician who has his reason for writing as he does."

Another quotation Harris suggested was from Paul Rosenfeld: "This young Oklahoman constitutes one of the chief potentialities of American music if not modern music altogether."

Farwell had not been writing for publication as often as in earlier years, and his article on Harris made a notable stir. More than forty years later, Brice Farwell heard Gilbert Chase quote its opening line from memory - "Gentlemen, a genius! But keep your hats on." Farwell's belief in his student was strong enough for him to accept and honor some of Harris' suggested treatments in the article, which Farwell would never have done if they were contrary to his own convictions. It was a deep and enduring friendship, based on profound and mutual respect.

After Farwell completed his article which was published in the *Musical Quarterly* for January 1932, Harris reacted to his reading of it by writing to Farwell, "The article was very fine - and something extremely hard to live up to. . . "

When Farwell realized that he might not be able to join Frank Lloyd Wright as he hoped at the artist's retreat Wright was developing at Taliesen in Wisconsin, (see chapter 12) he wrote a lengthy very confidential letter to Harris. In this, Farwell enthusiastically described the beauties of the retreat and recommended that he be allowed to suggest to Wright that Harris take his place. Regarding this invitation, Harris wrote to Farwell:

I would be interested to do work out there. It *exactly* fits into my ideas. Art related to humanity who are close to the soil. But I am scheduled to give 12 lectures at the New School of Social Research beginning Jan. 13th I think. Please extend my warmest greetings to Fk. Ld. Wright. I have met him and liked him very much. Believe in him. He is one of 'ours'. Please if you can let him know that next year I would be able to put my shoulder to the wheel. Tell him I was spoiled before I ever began - I committed the crime of believing in myself. Thanks deeply to you!

By January 26, 1933, Farwell was arranging for Harris to
present a lecture at Michigan State College at Harris's request.
He also responded to topics Harris had suggested for lecture
subject possibilities:

> Sure; I will get the $50.00 fee. I've sounded out the
> students and am assured of a fair proportion of it already
> -their small mites enthusiastically offered even in these
> hard times. . .
>
> Subject: - It will be a young crowd; they are eager to
> know what's going on, and why, and what's in the wind in
> all this modernism. And where does America come in.
> Therefore the Gregorian is cut out. Melodic contours is
> too *special* for our present need. Too much history,
> review of the Culture, would not be too good -as they are
> getting that pretty thoroughly from me and my assistant.
> Your hearers will come to see and hear a *new man in the
> field, a much heralded man, and in the American field,*and
> they will want to know what you are about, what it is you
> are doing, where it is taking us, whether you agree with
> other modernisms, what is the outlook for America and
> the world in music.
>
> Certain adductions from the past would be O.K.
> where they help you to explain something in the present,
> but don't take up too much time on history interpre -
> tations.
>
> I think, as I write, that *American Music* would be by
> far your best topic here. That's what they know you for,
> and want. Or a qualified title, as *Progress in American
> Music.* (Then you can put in what you want, but make
> that your basis.)
>
> Richards wants dates right away. Several. . .Certainly
> I insist on your staying a week - longer if you can. Bring
> works, I want to go over them, and show you new stuff.
> I've developed a lot since we thrashed it out in N.Y.
>
> Love to Hilda and yourself. I hope she will be with
> you - let me know.    Arthur

Harris replied on Feb. 10, 1933, from Glendora, "Land of Sunshine, Fruit and Flowers" with a whimsical note that was addressed to "Professor Nero H. Farwell, Cow College, Revered Doctor Farwell", on the inside salutation. He indicated that Hilda would be coming along and added, "Would like to stay a while and write a work for String Quartet." Harris followed this by another as he tried to consolidate plans that included the giving of a lecture in Cleveland first before driving on to East Lansing. This time Harris reiterated his eagerness to see Farwell and wrote: "Much to tell you when I arrive - about March 5 - for a week - or maybe even two if you can put me up - Always broke, undercapitalized."

After Harris's visit and subsequent return to Washington D.C., he wrote again the early part of June 1933:

> Good Lord it seems ages since we said goodbye in your office. What are your plans for the summer? How did things turn out? I have asked Mills College to release me, and am staying on for the summer; and next Fall. Making arrangements for recordings of chamber music. Finished quartet. The last movement is a 'hum dinger'.
>
> Business:
>
> Please send your string quartet. I have spoken to Copland about it - and wish to submit it for Yaddo Festival - *with parts*. Send as soon as possible.
>
> Also please write a letter of *praise* about my lectures - stating that you heard me both at Michigan & M.S.C. - on official stationery. I am getting out a circular in which I wish to quote you - for lectures.
>
> Koussevitsky asked me to write him a new work for next season - out of a clear sky. He had his mind made up. Isn't that a merry dish to set before the *Roi*!

Now Harris evidently planned to do more lecturing and needed Farwell's recommendation for promotional purposes. Farwell promptly obliged with a formal but enthusiastic letter.

Harris wanted Farwell to hear the broadcast of his Symphony over N.B.C. scheduled for January 27, 1934 and wrote to tell him some details. He also asked Farwell "If you like work please send

warm letter to Koussevitzky (& including friends if possible.)
These conductors want to know that their hard work is attended
and appreciated - This is their only check up." Harris also
asked Farwell to contact any of his friends at Ann Arbor who
might "do likewise - O.K." Harris hoped that the occasion might
be a "conflab of your literary friends".

Farwell responded to his friend's request with a rather lengthy
letter on February 6, 1934:

> The radio reception was not good anywhere
> hereabouts, but nevertheless I got a pretty good idea of
> the work, especially as I know your music as well as I do.
> The second movement came through best, and gave a very
> pathetic impression, even one of despair - I presume
> reflecting the despair of the year 1923. The kettle drums
> and cellos were too loud, the latter sounding like
> trombones most of the time. But the remarkable clarity
> of orchestration was not lost on me, especially, what I
> have noted in all your other works, the maintenance of
> this clarity *together with* the poly-harmonic scheme. The
> intellectual energy of the first and third movement is
> terrific, but I was able to follow a good deal of the
> thematic development, especially in the last, for this came
> through much better than the first.
>
> I can say scarcely anything of the first movement, the
> reception was so bad. The second is of wonderful beauty
> and depth of mood, and the last splendidly brilliant, with
> some especially memorable places of clarity and light. I
> thought your poly-tonality in general somewhat moderate,
> and not of a nature to prevent a pretty general
> understanding - *if* one knows something of the matter. A
> pretty big if.
>
> The whole effect was to me immensely vital and
> prophetic. I said to Crist I expected they would be
> writing books on you a hundred years or so from now. I
> wrote Koussevitsky that I thought the presentation to be
> an epochal event.
>
> But my chief desire was that I could have heard it in
> person. I wonder if you felt a slap on the back when you

began speaking in the Mike! It was just as if you were in the room, and it made me mad that I couldn't talk back. The speech came through a lot better than the music.

Dear old Press couldn't make much of it, and said that if you kept on he bet that in ten years you would go back to the classics! I tried to make him understand that you had gone there at the beginning, but he didn't get it. Richards was away, but heard it from some other place. He said he was unable to find that this music means anything to him. Dr. Crist sees what you are driving at. He is about the only one around here who does, apparently. I'm telling you, what I have told you before, that you are asking people to grasp a new harmonic, melodic and rhythmic scheme *all at the same time*, and not many can do it, at least in a hurry. Give them time.

I would never have believed the Stravinsky on the program was Stravinsky at all, if I had not been told so on authority. If this is going back to the classics, God preserve us from it. He was going back to *Vienna* all right, but not to the house of Beethoven. He got on the wrong street, and landed at Johann Strauss' place. . .

I heard from Dashiell, saying my article was all right, and would appear in May. Many thanks for your very important part in this. . .

I am working hard on the score of the symphony all the time I can get and it is going fine. I have international copyright on the *Land of Luthany* and it is now on sale in London. Schuster gave a copy to Zimbalist here last night, hoping he would arrange it for violin and play it. And I am printing my *Vale of Enitharmon* for piano, revised and much better. . . .

The article to which Farwell refers in his letter is one he wrote for Scribner's magazine entitled, *Let Us Play*. This resulted from a recommendation Harris made to Mr. Dashiell in August 1933. Farwell's files include considerable correspondence related to its planning and final printing. Harris had told his friend that "Scribner pays well" when he encouraged Farwell to take time for writing the essay. " I think you could do a swell job on it," Harris

declared and added, "If you can't write it, I'll do the job myself."
Here one notes again a reciprocal camaraderie that opens doors
for one another and is pleased to do so.

In a letter revealing more of Farwell's influence, sent from
New York City sometime during the first half of 1934, Harris
wrote to him in part:

> . . . Thanks for your fine encouraging letter. I still
> have the first letter you wrote me in which you said my
> letter had the 'stuff of which great music is made'. How
> I hugged that letter to my heart and told the confirmation
> to the great mountains which had watched over me since
> my childhood - They knew it too -and gave me many a
> mood to store away for tired days and sleepless nights.
>
> They, and you, dear friend, made me go on clinging
> to ideals, which the concert halls sneered at. Now those
> same halls are anxious to cooperate not because they
> believe in me but because they have not exploited me and
> are desperate for *something* real.

Better times had come to Harris and he also reported in the
same letter how his compositions were being accepted for
publication, performance and recording. He referred to
completing his *Song for Occupations* for the Westminster Choir
and added, "Wish we could go over it together." So it seems that
Harris still valued Farwell's musical judgment. He continues:

> (**Grand Secret**) not to be divulged even to Johnny -
> I am making a transcription for String Quartet of the *Art
> of the Fugue* and Roth Quartet will record it all for
> Columbia discs. What an achievement for America to
> walk away with!
>
> What did you think of my little piece for string
> quartet and flute on the 8th side of the Symphony
> records? Wrote it to order for recording - 2 1/2 days
> limit to finish it. Am coming to the viewpoint that if a
> composer is a natural one and has his language in hand,
> he ought to be able to turn out to order like Bach and
> Palestrina etc., did. The late 19th century Romantics

became too concerned with their own subjective feelings - not enough with the nature of their materials and the medium of their art. Am composing (in that attitude) stronger works and at a real practical speed.

. . . So we will certainly make the grade. Just must keep clear head. Go on studying and growing and working for a great mastery of every detail of melodic writing, harmonic color - orchestral resource  - firm expansion - dynamics. It is all a grand never ending world to contemplate and absorb.

Soon it was Harris's turn to encourage his friend when he heard of the trouble brewing in Farwell's life. Harris had been aware of marital difficulties when he and Hilda had visited the Farwells frequently beginning in the early 1930s. He probably was also aware of the political battle which was being waged especially in the years 1932 - 1933 at the college. In one undated latter written at Squire's Hill in Glendora, California, Harris wrote consolingly:

Thanks for your quick response to my note - I am a lopped eared hound dog not to write more often. My God I must learn to type - I get so weary holding a pen in my hand.

Concerning your shakeup - I do not worry over you because I know that you have touched such great and hallowed mystic faces that you will not harm anything or person in the process of growth - Your reverence for life is one of your most endearing qualities.

I am always so far behind that it seems the Gods are vicious to demand their pound of sleep every night. - New works coming up. More anon.

Love and Courage to You,
'Le Diable est mort'

Farwell's domestic and financial difficulties continued for several years as he tried valiantly to overcome them. He received another encouraging letter from Harris written in New York City on July 17, 1933:

I have owed you a letter for a long time. And now where shall I begin? You know I am with you in your troubles. Would that I had money. I feel that you are a rare spirit and a gentleman so that I would tend to feel that anything you do is justifiable.

The important thing seem to me that you have much to give to young formative minds and that you must keep your white hot love of beauty alive at all costs. You must not let bitterness worm his way into your well nigh impregnable self. - I suppose this can only be done by embracing the immediate positive elements which present themselves in our environment from day to day. If our todays are creative - our tomorrows will certainly be so.

I would be unhappy to see you separated from Arthur and the two girls. They lean on you quite heavily I feel. As for Lansing - perhaps it is as good a place as any - if one can get away sometimes. How have things turned out? There is youth - time - day - night - shelter - the never ending ebb and flow of conflicting impulses working within each personality - each trying to trick the mind onto bringing its broad guns of rationalization on their side. - A grand cosmic tragedy - wherever we go - unless we have the authority of soul and command of will to mould these actors into a plot of our own design. New York would not lend itself to your tomorrow because she is convinced that only youth has tomorrows. She only understands thrice worn platitudes. I shall have a whirl with her next winter.

Have been given a house in Wilton, Conn. [to use] We're dreadfully broke, living in some ones else's apartment while they are in Europe. . . . Did not go West. . . .What are you working on? Are you healthy? Can you still eat like a horse? Has beer come in? I am going vegetarian non-alcoholic - non-tobacco again. Too much to do - can't stand the grind without a more vigorous dietetic regime . . .

One notes here Harris's appreciation of Farwell as a teacher who still has "much to give to young formative minds". Perhaps he remembered his own student days with pleasure and recognized Farwell's skill in that capacity, while also trying to give him some much-needed encouragement.

What conclusions can be drawn from Farwell's influence on Harris, based on reading the given correspondence between these two men, and considering the kind of relationship begun in early teacher-student days?

Farwell gave more than guidance in traditional harmony in those early lessons. Dan Stehman reports Harris as saying that some of the foundation for his mature harmonic vocabulary was laid during this period. Harris also told Stehman "First thing he [Farwell] let me do was to develop new ideas in harmony. He encouraged me 100 per cent. As a matter of fact, some of the harmony I've been teaching . . . was developed way back there, because they're basic principles."[3]

Farwell exposed Harris to many kinds of scores which they studied together. He also encouraged Harris to study the orchestral scores of Tchaikovsky and Beethoven especially, from which Harris learned what he called "dynamic orchestration", - one "which grows out of the acoustic properties and the idiomatic techniques of the instruments themselves."[4]

Perhaps even more important than these lessons was the introduction to the works of Walt Whitman that Farwell provided Harris. Both men found inspiration from this kindred spirit, and critics often speak of the "Whitmanian sweep" of Harris's writing. The titles and subject matter of many of his compositions also reveal Whitman's influence.

Closely related to the Whitman influence was Farwell's strong spirit of patriotism and national pride. He loved America, its people, its scenic grandeur and nobility. He was proud to be an American. His patriotism was not the flag-waving kind that developed during World War I, but more of an organic kind that sought the best for his country and its people. It was based on the convictions that had prompted him to crusade for the American composer at the turn of the century and determined the course of some of his best years. Undoubtedly these feelings were shared frequently with young Harris whose awareness of his own pioneer roots were strengthened by his teacher. These feelings Harris echoed in later works that critics claimed to be "Truly American".

Farwell introduced Harris to important people on the west coast such as Mrs. Artie Mason Carter who proved to be a life-long friend and a boon financially. The contacts Farwell provided Harris in the East also proved valuable.

Farwell's enthusiasm and efforts in Community Music were later paralleled by Harris when he organized such groups as the First Cumberland Festival in 1951, the Pittsburgh International Festival of Contemporary Music in 1952, and the International Congress of Strings at Greenleaf Lake in his home state of Oklahoma in 1959. Even more notable is Harris's community music "mind-set" which shows in certain of his works: the *Folk Song Symphony* (1940-42) written for high school choruses and *Folk Fantasy for Festivals* written for the Juilliard School in 1956. Also to be noted are his later works (1975) *America, We Love Your People* for chorus and band, plus his *Bicentennial Symphony*. All of these efforts have the community - populist touch close to Farwell's heart. The seeds planted by Farwell in 1924 and 1925 may well have taken root, years later, thus revealing another Farwell influence in these compositions and projects.

One may speculate what would have happened to Harris's career had he not studied with Farwell at that critical period of his life. Surely his native talent and personal drive would have been productive eventually, without Farwell. But one might postulate a career with different direction and results and even compositions of a different nature. Farwell's visionary idealism, breadth of culture and intellectual acumen plus his encouragement in practical ways were important factors that started young Harris toward his goals. It was a "mind-set" and a point-of-view Farwell gave him that remained through the years as well as the influencing exposure to Whitman.

Harris referred to Farwell as his "Father Confessor and Mentor". In this role Farwell guided and responded effectively to the emotional, intellectual, and spiritual struggles of the young composer. All through the 1930's Harris found a haven at Farwell's home in East Lansing. (It was there he wrote the first movement of the Quartet No. 2 - Three Variations on a Theme.)

When he needed material comforts of food and lodging, he found them at the Farwells. When he needed help with research and study materials, Farwell cooperated. Sometimes Harris needed just a listening ear or sympathetic heart; these too he found in Farwell. One cannot ignore the value of a loyal and wise teacher who encouraged and nurtured his student as Farwell helped Harris. From Nadia Boulanger, Harris received needed discipline and the "nuts and bolts" of composing. But Harris's visionary aspect was established by Farwell in a warm, friendly relationship.

The main point to be made here is that Farwell obviously played a larger part in helping Harris's early career than is generally understood for which he should be given due credit!

## Other Students

Of the many students who sat in Farwell's classes and graduated from Michigan State College, three of them have been located: Carlton Eldridge, Marjorie Affeldt Ziprick, and Lewis Garner. These students had less fame than Roy Harris, but each has had a successful career. One of these - Carlton Eldridge, a blind musician, wrote an impressive testimonial on April 1972, telling how much his former teacher meant to him.

> For four years, from 1929 through 1933, I sat in classes of one of the most remarkable men I have ever met - Arthur Farwell. He told me one time, that if he had three students in a life-time who knew what he was talking about he would consider himself a success. I would like to think that I am one of those three - or, at least close behind. I have all my notes taken in his classes in my library, and I refer to them often. (In Braille.) . . . Over my piano I have his picture with his signature, calling himself my friend. This is one of my prized possessions.
> I left East Lansing in 1949 and have been teaching in Springfield College in Illinois since that time. Beside voice, and choir work, I teach an in-depth, ala-Farwell course in music literature. His theories on the meanings, and the aesthetics of music go on, as best I can impart

them. He taught us that there is much more to music than the pure mechanics of harmony and sound. That there is much more than the sensory or intellectual plane in music. That there is a third and higher plane of music - being the intuitive, as spelled out by D'Olivet. In fact, in recent years I have been doing considerable research relative to the force of music upon the mind and soul of man, and upon the consciousness of the entire social fabric. I have prepared a lecture - given over a wide area on *Music in War and Peace*. In this I have plagiarized on Arthur Farwell's ideas and knowledge.

I have forgotten very little that was imparted to us in those approximately 528 hours of lectures and countless personal sessions. He seldom repeated himself. I had four years of what was called at that time *Music Appreciation*, two years of music history, one of Aesthetics, one of church music, plus sessions in harmony and counterpoint under him and his assistant.

In another letter to the writer, dated June 1, 1972, Mr. Eldridge noted Farwell's dedication to the cause of American music:

. . . My course in American music with Farwell, was so important to me as he was *Mr. American Music* himself. Little details which never have been known were given in his class.

Farwell set out to find an American idiom. He said that we were handicapped because we had no true American forms which had evolved within ourselves. . . . But when I knew Farwell, he had come to realize that there could be no National idiom, that America was too diverse. But there could be many idioms.

One thing that he constantly decried was that American composers must be clever or trivial to be recognized. Nothing deep or great could be understood or taken seriously by the American public. But he had boundless faith in our people and land. He was content to wait. He realized that he, as well as any great figure, would not be understood until after death. He was not seeking acclaim, but wished to contribute.

Both Mr. Eldridge and Mrs. Ziprick stated that they have preserved all their class notes taken during Farwell's courses, thus attesting to their high regard for Farwell's teaching. Mrs. Ziprick, also a college teacher, was on the faculty of the music department at La Sierra College, La Sierra, California, when she gladly shared her thoughts on August 12, 1971, about Farwell as a teacher:

> Arthur Farwell was an interesting, quiet-spoken, but dynamic teacher in the classroom. He strode back and forth across the front of the classroom intent on his thoughts, thinking creatively even as he spoke. He was intent on material and truth. He was inspirational and with me, personally, his inspiration has never left me. He was popular with his students in a quiet, deep way. I never felt that he was trying to develop a following, but he was so deeply involved in his own thinking of composition and this he just had to share with students who were concerned and who cared. He was also aware of the individual accomplishments of students and quick to express his appreciation of their accomplishments.
>
> He made no special effort to be challenging in the modern sense of the word, but as he carefully weighed his words during a lecture, one was forced to think deeply too. He was so close to the truth that you felt you must try to dig for truth also. It was a real privilege to study with him for so many years.

These remarks are high praise from college professors who retain such sharp memories of a teacher under whom they studied many years previously. The same kind of admiration was also expressed by another former student, Lewis Garner, now deceased. A lawyer for 24 years, he was practicing law in Washington D.C. when the author interviewed him in August 1971. He recounted:

> I was just a kid from the farm as far as background goes and knew little about the Arts. I was not a music

student but interested in playing French Horn. I took
courses in History of Music and Music Appreciation from
Arthur Farwell and his teaching was different. He was
full of what was going on in the world, and he had such
great enthusiasm. He kind of awakened me to the
Cultural Life. Farwell fitted the History of Music into
history in general. He had phenomenal knowledge it
seemed - talked about Wagner's prose works which
covered ten volumes. Also about Spengler. Farwell
brought the History of Music to life. He was not
concerned about having students memorize exact dates; we
just had to have them down close to a quarter of a
century

  It was not an easy course. Farwell talked about Cause
and Effects. He was very deep and had great intellectual
energy and vitality. In speaking, his ideas just poured out
of him.

Mr. Garner's enthusiasm for his former teacher was contagious
as he reminisced about Farwell during the interview. His
memories were also remarkably detailed and clear in spite of the
lapse of 35 years. Only master teachers can so stimulate their
students that their teaching is still vividly recalled more than three
decades later. Several former Farwell students whom Edgar Lee
Kirk interviewed described his classes with the same fervor.[5]

  Considering that he [Farwell] left Michigan State in 1939,
these recollections are a compliment of a kind not often
given to a teacher. . . . His classes in music literature
seem to have made the most lasting impression. He had
a wide knowledge of styles and periods. This knowledge,
combined with his personal magnetism and enthusiasm for
music, made his lectures memorable to many of his
students . . . As a teacher, he was, despite his aversion to
teaching, most successful.

These quoted remarks confirm what Roy Harris's letters have
implied, that Farwell was an excellent, caring teacher.

# Chapter 14

## "Life With Father"

Farwell's life in Michigan required him to balance composing, teaching, and managing a large family all at once. We may gain some welcome insights to his mature character (as well as relief from the serious crusader) by examining his home life and domestic relations in some detail. Fortunately most of his children have been available to share memories and letters from their "life with father" in this vivid period of their lives.[1]

Brice, the eldest, was ten years old when the family moved to East Lansing in 1928. Jonathan, was not yet on the scene (to be born in 1932 when Farwell was almost sixty). The rest had come in between: Arthur Bragdon, Beatrice, Sara and Emerson, the latter child only two years at the time of the move.

They describe their father as about five feet eleven inches tall, of medium build with a shock of hair that had turned white before he was married. His blue-grey eyes were unusual. When serious, they were at once warm, wise and intense in the sense that he seemed to see deeply, engagingly, and penetrate to a person's innermost being, a trait noted by several of his students. There was no nervous darting about or tic, or chronic squint or strain. Even if under stress, his eyes did not reveal it, though they could take on a far-away, distant look when his thinking was equally far away from the immediate scene. However, they had a special twinkle and sparkle especially noticeable whenever he laughed or told one of his many stories from college or Minnesota days.

His skin was fair and fine-veined, his face well-proportioned with a generous mouth and firm jaw. He had a serious but gentle demeanor, a jaunty carriage and made a strong presence in any room. Something of youth clung to him even in advancing years. He now no longer dressed in the handsome high-style of his younger years, which had impressed the ladies, but preferred old and comfortable clothes. However, he carefully brushed his old grey Fedora and just as carefully checked it for proper angle when donned, and remained always concerned with cleanliness and being what he called "presentable".

One eccentricity was the wearing of Tom McMann boot shoes with hooks and laces all the way up which he frequently shined with black polish. He found these more comfortable than ordinary shoes and wore them until they were no longer obtainable. On camping or wilderness outings, he added leggings.

He objected to many new things. He considered the "new-fangled gadgets" to be too mechanical and related to a material culture which he disliked. Instead, for writing, he used a dip pen and bottled ink; for shaving, his old straight razor and razor strop. He hated cellophane and plastic, calling them inventions of the devil. He once dashed off a poem called Hymn of Hate about the horrors of getting into cellophane packaging. He probably never thought of setting it to music - though he would have enjoyed the irony of it. He might have subtitled it Hymn of Crackle!

Family as well as friends knew him for a good raconteur with a lively sense of humor. Never rough or crude, he could be romantic and dreamy one moment (perhaps singing *Juanita* to the girls), wry and witty the next, or roaring with laughter over *Popeye* and other favorite comics in the evening paper. Claiming to be spiritually descended from Tom Sawyer, he loved a prank, but was not a real practical joker.

As a father at home, Farwell charged at every household task with high-wire energy as if it were a game to be done with grace and dispatch. The children were expected to follow suit. Except for specific times for relaxation, or at his desk, he was a man in a hurry. He was not "uncareful", but he got things done. He kept his desk in perfect order, as well as his basement tools, and he couldn't understand why his wife couldn't be as neat as he. Gertrude preferred writing poetry to dusting and cleaning, and the children were roused more than once to battle the dirt and restore household order, with father in the lead. Gertrude was absent at such times, and if there was a marital argument about it later, which is probable, it was kept behind closed doors. Tearful scenes and arguments were not proper for children's eyes and ears.

Here it is well to remember that Farwell had a strict Victorian, but protected upbringing, and that he was twenty years older than his wife. Gertrude had had to take over the care of her father and siblings from the age of sixteen, and perhaps had expected to find in marriage a more leisurely existence than Farwell's salary and the rearing of six children could give her.

Whatever the strain and stresses that were building in the marriage during the 'thirties, both parents held primary concerns for the welfare of their children. All of them interviewed agree parental affection and gentility prevailed, making their childhood in some ways ideal, a good balance between structure and traditional American freedom. Although real emotional expression was difficult between parents and children, individual interests were encouraged. More childish fun and noise were allowed than might be expected where the father's needs for privacy and quiet were great. Indeed, so great were these needs that Farwell moved his work and sleeping quarters to the attic in the Evergreen Avenue house, leaving the second floor master bedroom to Gertrude, and the grand piano, as always, in the living room. With the lithographic press soon to be set up in the basement, it was a busy household, and provided many of the children's happiest memories. (Figure 46)

A typical day at the Farwell's had to be run like clockwork to accommodate everyone's schedule, and Mr. Farwell saw that it was. In winter, he was the first one up to feed the coal furnace and "rassle" the fire to life. Mrs. Farwell was usually busy in the kitchen by six thirty. Meanwhile, the children scrambled into their clothes and washed up in the single bathroom, often able to see their breath in the cold morning air. Mrs. Farwell's health suffered unduly from the harsh Michigan winters, especially from a painful sinus problem, usually worse in the mornings, but she rarely pampered herself by staying in bed. A full hot breakfast was on the linen-covered table by seven or shortly after, with all present but dawdlers and babies.

However, on Sundays Mr. Farwell often prepared the meal himself as Mrs. Farwell had church obligations. When feeling festive, he made flapjacks, learned from Maine lumberjacks, and served these with butter and sugar between the thin layers.

On weekdays, Mr. Farwell was the first out of the house, to tramp through the snow to an eight o'clock class. Winter or summer he always walked to the campus, even for a brief period when he owned a car. The children followed, going their several ways to school, also on foot in a day before school buses or "Snow

*Figure 46. The Farwell children in East Lansing, 1936. From left: Jonathan Kirkpatrick, Emerson, Sara Emerson, Beatrice, Arthur Bragdon, and Brice.*

days". When the snow was piled high at the door, they tunneled their way to the sidewalk with father's help. Later they made snow forts of the drifts for snowball fights and snow angels on the untouched pure white lawn. Schools were near enough for the children to return home for lunch, a regular sit-down meal which their mother had ready for them. Mr. Farwell ate his lunch in town nearer the campus. He always returned home between three and three thirty to spend the rest of the afternoon composing in his attic study or working with the press in the basement.

Little Sara would often meet him afternoons at the nearest corner. She recalls how he always had a spring to his walk, how they would swing hands together while she tried to match his stride, how they chatted of this or that, or sang together *In the Good Old Summertime* or some such old song. "Everything he did in physical motion had a rhythm and a 'rightness' to it", she said, "except when he was upset or too much in a hurry. Then his movements would become abrupt and sudden, and his normally musical voice, gruff or even howling." The children knew not to bother him during his afternoon work. The oldest were busy anyway with their own outside affairs, though Beatrice was often called on to help with shopping and dinner preparations.

Dinner was promptly at six o'clock, with father presiding in genial mood over the vegetarian meal, (meat was served only on Sundays, a concession to Gertrude's Theosophical predilections), and mother fussing over proper table manners, shocked at signs of slang or other linguistic deviations from the King's English in her brood. These were mostly pleasant family gatherings, with latitude for teasing and general fun, and even parental arguments over politics or word pronunciations. Mrs. Farwell was a staunch Democrat and committed Socialist, and considered Eleanor Roosevelt a heroine. Mr. Farwell objected to the president - "didn't like the cut of his jib". Both parents were sticklers on words. If a new or strange word was mentioned, the adjacent encyclopedia might become the source for a lecture on science or history.

If tensions arose, or a fight between any of the children, Farwell's solution was to call a halt, change the subject, and begin one of the tales from his rich store of memories. He told of ice palaces in St. Paul, tramps in the Rockies, fishing for fresh trout, lumberjacking in Maine, Navajo and Sioux Indians who had been his friends; and there were Parisian pastry orgies - sitting all night on the steps of Notre Dame with a friend to eat them, meetings with great people in Europe, Boston or New York. He had known a much larger world than this small provincial Midwest town and this "cow college" where he was pinned down, and he wanted his children to know something of it - something of a vaster cultural heritage, and a vaster, marvelous America.

Gertrude would eventually recover her sense of humor and wonder at the angel-beasts her family presented. Then she would offer an apt quote in comic dialect from some poet or playwright before rising to bring on her latest dessert - a pie or pudding made from her mother's old *Boston Cook Book*. Dessert was a necessity to the Farwell palate (he also added sugar to such things as grapefruit and tomatoes) so they were well made and remain memorable to the children.

After-dinner cleanup was done by three of the children on a rotation basis. Farwell settled in his easy chair while Gertrude put the youngest to bed. In a fairly regular ritual, Sara would get her father's slippers, pipe and the newspaper, then climb onto his lap when he had finished reading. They would have a hand-game session lasting a short time which involved a lot of gentle hand slapping and catching. "He had beautiful large square hands, and he smelled so clean and good." Once he examined Sara's palms and told her about his experience having the "great Cheiro" read his palms. He declared that nearly everything the palmist had predicted had come true except that his compositions would become well known in Europe. (This is happening more and more, with a compact disc just made in Italy, for instance, but recorded long after Farwell's death.)

Sometimes he and the children would play telepathy games. These called for hard concentration and were perhaps, in Farwell's mind, preparation for adult meditation. Other more relaxed group games were Anagrams and Monopoly. Farwell enjoyed playing chess to relax and was an accomplished player. Some evenings he spent playing with Brice who always lost until he tired of this. He finally went to the library and got a book on how to improve his game. Thereafter, he often beat his father. But neither of them could beat Roy Harris when he visited, Harris being a formidable chess-player. But Harris's wife, Johana, his fourth and enduring one, preferred to play the piano when she came with her husband. Brice said he consoled himself with wide-eyed adolescent dreaming of Johana and thought she played piano as beautifully as she looked. (Johana Harris remarried after Roy's death and continued to concertize, receiving rave reviews for her performances.)

Young Arthur ("Art") sometimes played chess with his father, but he preferred manipulating his electric trains set up in the basement. Or he could be found in his room, scanning the world with his ham radio equipment. Sara called him a "genius" with mechanical things. In later years, he became a skilled draftsman and tool designer, sometimes inventing and creating his own new tools.

Beatrice, the family scholar, often did her homework in the evenings, or practiced piano unsupervised if she wasn't off with her friends. When Mrs. Farwell was finished with evening "chores", she might read a "wonderful Irish story", a Dickens novel, or King Arthur legend to Sara and Emerson in some quiet corner.

Noisiness and rough-housing were kept to outdoor play as much as possible, and physical affectionate hugging was rare. Farwell would tote the little ones around the house on his shoulders, or swing one of them from the floor by gripping them by hands and feet, but by and large it is suspected that "he thought children were little savages that needed to be brought to an age of civilized speech before anything can be done with them." (Sara reported that he said this once, but it was probably in jest when he no longer could tolerate the decibel level.)

There were no musical times around the piano with everyone joining in. Instead, Sara and Beatrice often sang familiar songs as duets from the old *I Hear America Singing* book and Beatrice sometimes played the piano. Serious musical evenings or Sunday afternoons occurred too, but only when music students from the college came, or some out-of-town performing visitor. Then, all was real music, and the children could listen, but were not expected to participate. Sometimes a chamber group would play a new Farwell piece and excitement would fill the air. Michael Press would exclaim, "Farwell! Why do you write such DIFFICULT music? Or, when they played something of Farwell's that he could hear performed correctly for the first time, he would cry out a delighted "Caramba!" This was intellectual hugging, the kind that made him happiest.

Beatrice and Jonathan became proficient at the piano, but neither became musicians. Farwell felt the pressure of time for his own work too heavily to take on teaching them himself. Hence he provided students from the college in the Michigan years for them. Only Beatrice continued her studies. Jonathan learned from other teachers later in life.

Eight-thirty was the children's bedtime and Mrs. Farwell gathered them in her room for songs and prayers before seeing them into their beds with often a motherly and comforting backrub. Best remembered of all times were the Irish and Scottish ballads she taught them using perfect accents that they still sing. Also they remember the hilarious sailor songs she had learned from her Annapolis father and brother Bill: *Nancy Lee, Will Jones,* and *Barnacle Bill, the Sailor Man* among them. "Her voice would go from a sweet soprano to a deep bass rumble. We would try to join in and end up laughing and tumbling all over the bed, and beg her to sing it again", Sara reported. When Farwell was left to put them to bed, their mother being away for the evening, he would see them through the Lord's Prayer, or sometimes not. But they were told they could say their own silent prayer in bed just as well, and then given a good night pat to send them off.

So ended a day of "Life with Father", and there is much in both his behavior and letters to show that he truly loved his children, however difficult fathering was for him.

Evenings gave Mrs. Farwell some free time from her family to exercise her outside interests. She regularly attended meetings of the downtown Theosophical Society, which on one occasion was visited by the national president, Annie Besant, herself. (Sara tells of going with her mother and remembering a buxom lady in white.) Gertrude was an active member of the Lansing Civic Players Guild. She directed Shakespeare plays and "all kinds of things" for this active community theater, and acted in many plays from O'Neill to Molière. Mr. Farwell would sometimes attend these, and give her his considered critique. She was gifted with a wide range dramatically, and had a beautiful speaking voice, deep and rich that Sara inherited and developed.

The children also have fond memories of theatrical afternoons at home, when their mother put sheets over their heads and they acted out the witches' scene from *Macbeth*. Near Christmas time there were pageants to be readied, and costumes to be made. Most of the children cut their theatrical teeth on some short version of *The Evergreen Tree*, playing a wolf or elf. More formally, there was her "Intimate Theatre" at home for which she rented rows of chairs and potted plants and gave readings of whole plays, acting all the parts. "She could make your hair stand on end with Lady Macbeth". (Sara played Fleance when her mother directed the play down town). "Or she could make you laugh til the tears came down your face as Sir Toby Belch or Malvolio in *Twelfth Night*." The latter she read through  - with cuts - on actual *Twelfth Night* for several winters at St. Paul's Church in Lansing. Gertrude used her dramatic skills as therapy from the pressures of perpetual sock-darnings, cooking, canning, and cleaning. She had many friends in the community, but only a few close ones. When she changed from her old house dress into a formal, to entertain or to attend a musical or theatrical affair, she was truly beautiful. Beatrice remembers a blue velvet long gown that shimmered. The rest of the time she was just "mother", quite ordinary and often over-tired.

Farwell taught the boys how to use a cane properly as gentlemen of "breeding" and all the children were warned never to swear. "Do not take the name of the Lord in vain. People who do, go down, down, down," he declared in descending tones. "Don't go down," he admonished. He also advised, "Keep eye contact when speaking to a person."

"Dad was a remote father in the sense that he was usually so busy and involved with his musical affairs," said Brice. "But when he was home and 'free', he was a conscientious parent. He was interested in our work at school and expected us to get good grades. When we were naughty, he spanked us with a hair brush. Arthur seemed to get more of this than the rest of us." Sara's memory is different. She grew up thinking that neither parent believed in corporal punishment and said none was used on her.

Farwell loved the outdoors and especially the mountains. While other Michigan families went hunting or just driving, he took the children on hikes or family outings and taught them the beauty of nature and the wonder of the universe. In the summer of 1932 when a solar eclipse was due, he gathered them and explained what was about to happen and why. Then he helped them smoke a piece of glass for viewing, and shared the excitement of watching the moon's shadow "eat up" the sun.

Farwell took the children to concerts with him, usually just one at a time, and again he was teaching. Sara recalled one such experience attending an orchestral concert. The Tchaikovsky *Fourth Symphony* was to be played and Farwell wanted Sara to be able to recognize the main theme. He leaned over and whispered, "Sing to yourself, 'See the little boy with his hat on'. The rhythm of the words will help you." After the concerts, if Farwell knew the performers, he would take the children to meet the guest artist in the "Green Room". Some years later, he introduced Sara to Rachmaninoff backstage at Carnegie Hall. So the children had this kind of cultural experience as they grew up.

Farwell was inclined to formalize situations with high-sounding phrases that characterized the situation in symbolic language. He enjoyed rituals when he could bring them to life. Brice said that this was evident at the Senior recitals at Michigan State. When he introduced a student performer, his words seemed to elevate the young musician as if Farwell were holding up a beautiful piece of crystal in the light, rotating and admiring the uniqueness of its points.

Christmas was a very special time for the whole family and a good example of the rituals which Farwell planned. Christmas Eve was the time for reading aloud of "Twas the Night Before Christmas" with everyone trying to keep up with all the names of the reindeer. They always had a live tree with real candles placed in holders that clipped onto the branches. These special holders were imported from Germany and difficult to purchase. They were carefully placed so they would not catch any of the trimmings or needles on fire. Mr. and Mrs. Farwell decorated the tree on Christmas Eve after all the children were asleep. Early Christmas morning after breakfast was over, each child was given a lighted candle to carry and all paraded in single file, - singing the four verses of *Silent Night* as they marched toward the parlor. What a thrill for them when the parlor door was thrown open and the tree, now resplendent with every candle lit, met their expectant eyes! No other lights were used in that room so the candles seemed to shed a magic glow of their own while the children took turns distributing the simple gifts found under the tree. Even during the Depression years, Brice remembered one Christmas when there were two bicycles under the tree. He realized years later how his parents must have sacrificed all year in order to be able to buy these expensive but dearly prized gifts.

On relaxed or more intimate occasions, Brice recalls seeing his father perform an unusual balance act which always impressed the guests. Mr. Farwell would lie down on the floor and put a half-full glass of water on his forehead. This he would balance while rising to a standing position without spilling a drop!

While the Farwells did not do much entertaining as such, guests from the music world frequently dropped in at their East Lansing home after giving a local performance.

Visits by Noble Kreider, who came from Goshen, Indiana, were frequent. He was an excellent pianist as well as a good composer and a close friend of Farwell's. Brice declared that "When Noble came, it was as if Chopin were there!"

On one occasion Farwell brought Shaw Desmond, an Irish poet and author, (1877-1960) home for dinner. Gertrude remembers him questioning her husband, "When was the last time you brought your wife any flowers?" His quick reply was, "I don't know. I haven't paid the ice bill yet."

Mrs. Farwell reported that the two men had an in-depth conversation later as they had much in common. Desmond had founded the short-lived International Institute for Psychical Research in his fervor to learn more about psychic phenomena, his all-pervading concern. Of his more than 60 books, many reflect this psychic interest, one which Farwell also shared. Farwell's experiences with induced intuition and his symbolic dreams were a matter of earnest discussion.

Carl Sandburg's visits were especially enjoyed by all the children. He autographed their copy of *The Rutabaga Stories* and wrote, "May the Zizzies be good to you".

The children were also excited when Frank Lloyd Wright came and talked about the prospect of moving the family to Taliesin in Wisconsin. They were impressed with him as a person as well as with his ideas. Hence the entire family shared the disappointment when financial circumstances prevented their joining him.

Rarely did the children ever see their father angry or evincing lack of self-control. One incident deeply etched in their memories occurred at the supper table. The kitchen was in the process of being painted. So all of the best china had been removed from the cupboards and stacked on top of an old pool table with folding legs, set up in the utility room nearby. Little Jonathan had been left to play around in the kitchen where he eventually got near the pool table and bumped into one of the legs which happened to have a loose brace. The leg gave way and down came all of the lovely wedding Wedgewood. The loud crash of breaking china was followed by a stunned silence at the supper table. "Dad's face turned white and he just sat there a few moments to regain his composure. He said nothing but finally got up from the table, silently grabbed Jonathan and took him upstairs to his study," Brice reported. He also remembered that his mother jumped up from the table and ran after her husband shouting, "If you hurt Jonathan, I'll hurt you!"

One of the rare times Brice recalls his father ever swearing took place one Sunday morning, sometime earlier, when Brice was about eleven years old. Mrs. Farwell was trying to herd the children to church. Mr. Farwell did not attend, but he wanted the children to do so and he expected them to be there "On Time!" Brice had mislaid his cap somewhere and had looked in vain for it. Finally as the clock warned of the passing time, Farwell's patience ran out and he hollered in exasperation, "Damn it - get out of here - cap or no cap! You're going to be late for church!."

Emerson started studying the violin on a three quarter sized instrument with Morris Hochberg, a graduate student teaching at the college. He had perfect hands for the violin and showed considerable promise, but had to give it up when he outgrew the small one as there was no money for a larger instrument.[2]

Beatrice and the other children took piano lessons from Cecil Pollack, their father's student, for three or four years. Sara was a tomboy and had trouble sitting still long enough to practice the piano, so her studies were short-lived. Beatrice thought Miss Pollack a strange and unattractive lady, but very nice. She was impressed with her sight-reading ability and remembers one evening when Miss Pollack was playing through some of her father's new scores. Mr. Farwell was standing nearby listening, and finally suggested, "Take that a little faster," which Miss Pollack did and never missed a note! Beatrice finally got tired of the lessons and wanted to stop, but she did not dare tell her father. She eventually told her piano teacher first, who then helped her break the news to him.

Beatrice reported that they had certain rules about entertainment. Saturdays were allowance days and amounts were graded according to age of the children. One year, Brice, the eldest, got fifty cents, while Sara received fifteen. Furthermore, the children were allowed to see only two movies per month. "Father had a horror of us getting addicted to a culture which presented an entertainment. He preferred audience participation. The other reason was a financial one, I am sure."

Brice remembers the only car that his father ever owned. It was a used Hupmobile with a rumble seat that he bought after a car became necessary for the many trips he made about the state. He nicknamed it *Pegasus*. These trips were in response to invitations to speak at special gatherings or to judge school music contests. Mr. Farwell was in demand for these purposes, and he found a car the most convenient mode of transportation. However, none of the children were old enough for a driver's license so none of them had the opportunity to take a turn at the wheel before the car either wore out or was sold.

Sara was only five years old when the family moved to Michigan. She developed a special closeness with her father which the author noted from reading her adult correspondence with him as well as from interviewing her. Sara recalled how she used to watch her father at work when he returned home from classes:

If he went to his attic studio to compose, I could not usually go there, but if he went to the basement to his Press, then I could tag along and I loved that time with him. I enjoyed the smells of the chemicals and just watching him work - the doing of it. He would take such gratification in every little phase of the work. Everything was done in a kind of "rhythmic dance" as he moved methodically from one phase of the printing process to another. It was remarkable, watching him do it. Sometimes he would let me "help" him. He loved the whole procedure and never seemed discouraged if a problem arose. He delighted in all the materials, the sense of power of making a thing of beauty with his own hands. He had a strong sense of craftsmanship. I would see how he would take a box with all the little notes in it and print these with meticulous care. He had great joy in all these accomplishments and I am sure it was a good escape valve from his college pressures. However, dad was careful to protect me from the downbeat of life - the negative side of things - as I grew up. These and other times with the family were tremendously happy times. I have wonderful memories of the East Lansing days.

Sara reminisced about a more serious time when her father took her alone up to his study for a talk.

> It was my last year in junior high school. Dad explained that he and mother were getting a divorce and why. I was closer to dad than to mother and I felt at that time that dad was justified in divorcing mother though I had a little different opinion later. Dad said mother didn't know how to keep house or manage money and she went on religious tangents. Dad was often embarrassed at the sight of mother's careless housekeeping, when he brought guests home.

Mrs. Farwell did have difficulty in managing money. Her husband had to keep the budget money for household expenses in separate envelopes - one for groceries - another one for utilities, etc. A large part of the stress that developed in their marriage - especially during the Depression years - was related to finances. She felt that there always seemed to be money for what the master of the house needed. She questioned the fairness of him having a car when she and the children lacked proper clothes. "Hand-me-downs" were the rule of the day. Sadly, in her frustration over the lack of money for things she saw as needs, she would mishandle the budget, and then have to borrow from friends to try to make it up.

Mrs. Farwell never resolved her housekeeping frustrations, but she did her best to make an enjoyable home. The fact that she had been raised as a "lady" with servants for the hard work was a handicap. She had hoped for a more gracious life with the handsome Arthur Farwell when they were married. Sara reported:

> Mother just never knew what a fire she had burning within her, what a Medea was there! How could she turn the grand lady she envisioned herself to be, and that she had seen in reality and read about among the Theosophists, into an ordinary hum-drum mother hen? She couldn't, but she would try as motherhood was holy. She would hold up as long as the children needed her, as long as Arthur needed his meals on time, as long as unwitting rebellion

didn't set in. It was a gentle gamble she lost, but she made a most valiant try.

One of the things that came to Mrs. Farwell's rescue in the Michigan years was her gift of laughter and a pixie, self-mocking sense of humor which her husband enjoyed. She could go from tears to laughter in seconds and could make jokes out of her perceived shortcomings, often using quotes from her store of literature to make some rueful or funny point. She knew the poets, the Bible, Dickens and Shakespeare as well as Mr. Farwell did. These she used often with gaiety and to her purpose of the moment. Burns was used for "O wud some power the giftie gie us to see our sels as ithers see us" - rolling all the r's. When the children made a scene or fought with each other, she quoted Whitman for ". . . give me violent children!" "Barkus is willin'" was a quote from Dickens and appropriate for many occasions.

Mrs. Farwell expressed concern that their children have cultural advantages and wrote letters making good contacts for that purpose. She arranged for the two girls to attend Camp Arden in Brattleboro, Vermont, and Sara was there for several summers. This was a camp that emphasized the arts and drama in particular. Gertrude's cousin, Katherine Jewell Everts, was director. Her partner, Elizabeth Fay Whitney, provided the funds for the camp and they awarded scholarships for the girls. These two women were often referred to in the family as "the Arden Aunts".

Sara recalled her first trip as a young child going alone to Camp on the train when her father drove her in his *Pegasus* to catch it at another city. En route, Sara served as navigator and proudly read the map for him because his peripheral vision was poor. After arriving in Jackson, Michigan, they had an hour to spare. Farwell's admonition to Sara was, "Go to the public library if you ever have time to spare." So they did just that. Sara remembered her father picked out a book of William Blakes's poetry and read *Tyger* to her, and then commented on the work. "It was thus that I got bits and pieces of his inner life."

Farwell handled all the logistics of the train travel for Sara with utmost care. He sought out the porter and tipped him so he would be sure to watch out for his little girl on the long train ride East. He slipped eight dollars into Sara's hand - more money than she had ever seen before. She was not afraid to travel alone. She also had the comfort of knowing that someone would meet her at the station in Massachusetts to take her the remaining distance to Camp.

In 1931 Mrs. Farwell also went to Camp Arden as a counsellor of one of the cabins and served all summer even though she was in early pregnancy with Jonathan. Sara and Beatrice took their turn as did other girls with helping in the camp kitchen. Somewhat later, because they recognized Sara's dramatic talent, the "Arden Aunts" and some of their friends arranged for her to attend Skywood Hall, a private arts high school for girls in Mt. Kisco, New York.

Brice recalled one afternoon of his father looking at his file of old Bohemian Club programs and announcements. He pointed out various ones to Brice and said, "See. Here are wonderful examples of style, the creative arts and graphic arts which have been exploited to develop the theme of something, or spirit of it, in the promotional literature sent out to members." The choice of papers, colors, old fashioned type, engraving, - all used to promote the Club's programs and events - Farwell found to be an "eloquent expression of taste in making fun worthwhile in the life of these people." These things were important to Farwell.

The differences in personality and philosophy between Arthur Farwell and his brother, Sidney, become obvious in a letter that Sidney wrote to Brice upon his graduation from high school in East Lansing in 1936. Although the two brothers had grown up together in the same environment, both loved by their parents, both well educated, they left college for divergent worlds. Sidney's practical nature led him to become a horticulturist, and he owned a large apple orchard business in Hudson, Massachusetts. How remote from Arthur's artistic and creative activities! Brice saved his uncle's letter and shared it with the author. Written on September 16, 1936, a portion follows:

This is rather a tardy acknowledgement of your invitation to your school commencement. My only excuse is having so many things to do. You see, a farmer's business has its greatest activity just when most people are thinking of vacation. In the winter, when the snow is deep, he is better able to sit down for a quiet moment, & smoke his pipe, or write his nephew a letter. But beginning with the frost coming out of the ground in the spring, he is almost at his wit's end for one reason or another, and so until the snow flies.

I suppose you had a great time at commencement. It is a wonderful time in a boy's life. Many things that at that time are considered as of great importance, fade out entirely as life goes on. I have not forgotten how I felt at your age. . . . With all its ups and downs and bitter disappointments, it is just about the happiest time in the lives of most boys. I suspect your Daddy might not agree with me, for you see he had a very scientific and artistic mind, which was occupied with the deeper and really important things of life. But I guess I would say  that he also got a lot of fun, out that period of his life too, on the side of fun and his association with the boys and girls, games, and sports, etc.

You will carry memories of these school days all your life. The pleasure from them will never die, and no matter how dignified and sedate you may become as a man, you will always treasure them in your secret heart, even if you have no one to talk to about them.   . . .

I am going to tell you one or two things. If I were to try to help any boy to an understanding of our everyday business life, & tell him of the things that have many times pushed me ahead, I should first tell him that when he goes after a job, especially if it is his first, to disregard his own wishes, take anything he can get - in a good concern. And when he does, let him remember that no matter what he may think, the man running the business can run it without any help from him. Some man in the concern will soon find out what kind of a feller you are - whether you've got anything useful to him or the concern - he'll find it out in ONE WEEK!

Once in, you've got to sell yourself to somebody above, and it is up to you entirely how high you sell yourself. Keep your own counsel, don't tell all you know, and keep your eyes open, til you see where there is a hole in the line that you might get through with the ball.

Don't offer your opinion till you are absolutely sure you
know what you are talking about. . . never criticize
ANYBODY, in or out of the concern, as long as you stay
with it.  Men running concerns are looking for boys who
can take it & like it, and you need no self-advertising, for
in a week or two, they'll know what you've got better than
you know yourself.

Sidney's letter continued with more advice in the same vein.
He told Brice not to be too concerned about the pay or ask about
advancement possibilities at first.   His conclusion stated that he
hoped someday this letter of advice would prove useful to Brice.

For Uncle Sidney, or any "uncle" not knowing his nephew well,
to write in such tones is not so remarkable.  What is remarkable
is how rightly Sidney observes that his own values and those of his
brother, Arthur, are so disparate.

Brice believed that his father never had his focus set in the
directions of his uncle's wise counsel when his children needed
some advice for the future.  Instead, he said:

Father would try to probe with us what it might be that
each of us wanted most to do with our lives, to express and
give to life and the world of our inner aspirations.  Oh, dad
would observe to us some perception he might have of a
strength or weakness in talent, interest or direction we may
have shown, and perhaps encourage what looked potentially
viable.   But his center was in what each of us is, in
ourselves, rather than in how to manage career progress out
in the world.

Is this kind of thinking egocentric?  Is it essential to being an
artist?  When one reviews the life-paths these two men took, one
sees the contrast between them more vividly:  Sidney going on to
a quiet, moderate success in the apple business after his
graduation from Harvard, and Arthur leaving his technical training
at M.I.T. for a passionate mission in music.   Arthur's career
became a stirring life of one stress after another, in pursuit of
values found in the soul but not in the bank.   He left to the

world a documented heritage of artistic endeavor and expression that has found some lasting merit. Sidney left very little.

One of their father's traits on which the entire family agreed, was his sense of mission that was very important to him. It was "bringing music to the people, and the people to a greater love of music." This had been top priority in his years on the East coast and in California. Early in his career he was working with fellow musicians, but later it was with the people themselves in the Community Music activities where he found the most satisfaction. He wanted people to be involved with music as participants - not as spectators.

Farwell envisioned a new society ennobled by the uplifting power of great music. He despaired of music as an art for only the wealthy and those who could afford the price of admission to concerts. These ideas so central to his thinking all of his life, were expressed in a pamphlet, *When Thou Makest a Feast*[3]. He shared the goals of his mission with his family; they talked about it and they grew to have some understanding of what he meant by the Democratization of Music in America. The family too, like Walt Whitman, *"Heard America Singing!"*

# Chapter 15

# The Last Years, 1937 - 1952

Farwell's marriage to Gertrude suffered turbulent times. In California as the children began to grow up and demanded less hour-to-hour care, Gertrude ventured out into involvement with Theosophical Society meetings that ultimately affected their marriage. Ironically, Farwell had introduced her to the teachings of Theosophy in New York days where he had known people close to the movement, if not in it, such as Claude Bragdon and William Butler Yeats, and later he regretted doing so. He considered Theosophy a "Mishmash of ideas. It was too theatrical, and was caught up in sensationalism and phenomenalism". Though he admired some of the people involved in it, he looked on such groups as something that frustrated women got involved with instead of playing bridge or canasta.

Farwell largely abandoned Theosophy in favor of a more Emersonian and individual road to self-realization through self-reliance and inner questioning. But Gertrude constantly sought spiritual guidance through her church and a series of ministers, through mediums occasionally, and through her vast Theosophical readings. She often kept an alcove shrine with altar, candles, and a picture of the Virgin Mary for her quiet meditations. On her dresser was a picture of Jinarajadasa, who was a tutor of Krishnamurti, and she would travel far to hear the latter speak.

Farwell tried to be tolerant of other people's religious and philosophical views, but when his wife grew so zealous about Krishnamurti's teachings that she wanted to find a place in his organization in California, rather than join her husband in East Lansing, Farwell was understandably upset. After he persuaded Gertrude to come and bring the children, she did her best in establishing their new home. The marital relationship continued with more than the usual "ups and downs", but Farwell's indomitable spirit prevailed for a time.

Farwell's attitude to Theosophy must have been one of the problems that made Gertrude's relationship with her husband more difficult since he had been the person who introduced the study to her. She accepted and was stimulated by the teachings of Madame H. P. Blavatsky, founder of the Theosophical Society, whose eclectic philosophical ideas were based largely on Brahmanic and Buddhistic teachings. In Michigan, Gertrude did not stand up to her husband, or claim her own experiences as valid and quite as spiritual as his. Instead, she frequently retreated to silence or tears. Perhaps the anger cropped out in laissez-faire housekeeping, or in more disciplined fashion in her marvelous theatrical performances downtown at the Players Guild.

However, after six more years of struggling through serious marital problems, Farwell was convinced that Gertrude had not been either a proper wife or mother to their children. In September 1934, he wrote a letter to Gertrude while she was visiting her sister in Ohio, notifying her his attorney would take up the matter of a divorce. He stated that he had come to the realization "the inevitable parting of the ways has now come."

Some of their differences were ironed out during the next two years and the idea of divorce was deferred. However, by August 10, 1936, Farwell had reached the limit of his endurance and wrote this revealing letter to his friend, James Sheridan:

> I am well, and what happiness I can have comes from the exercise of my energies rather than from circumstances, which latter are heavily encumbered at present.
>
> Gertrude has simply gone off the handle; runs me horribly into debt with secret bills (I had to sell my life insurance last summer to pay them); July 17 she went to Europe, having made plans for six weeks or more without having let me know anything about it, and I found out by accident only two days before she sailed. She intended to go to the Theosophical conferences in Holland and Geneva, and the children told me that she had money from friends for passage both ways and trip from here to New York and back. She knew I hadn't the money for her trip, and that I was up against it because of the heavy summer expenses of the children; nevertheless on top of her duplicity in concealing her project from me, she tried to make me borrow $200.00 for it. After she went, I learned, in a forcible manner, that she had, two days

before going, bought a coat at a dress shop down town, for $44.00, giving a bad check for $50.00 and taking the change. A felony, of course.

I at once got a lawyer and instituted divorce proceedings. The bill was filed last Friday. She has been making life progressively more and more terrible these last nine years, and this last was too much - I can't stand it any longer.

I learned yesterday that she has applied to almost everyone of my friends she thought might let her have money. Exactly as I expected, she is now trying to extract money from me through the European consulates by cable. There may be deep waters ahead in the next few months, but my life has got to be wholly differently arranged.

[Family news]. Brice probably goes (I have to say "probably" to everything nowadays) to Boston Tech in the fall. He still holds a little legacy that will carry his first year - though Gertrude tried hard to get it. (I am his legal guardian, you know.) Arthur is visiting the Beckmans in Oakland, Calif., and will stay there for his last high school year, and maybe for his whole college course. Beatrice is home, tall and handsome. Sara, the most darling child imaginable, is at a dramatic school in Vermont, her fifth summer there. Emerson and Jonathan are just kids . . . Noble Kreider, of Goshen, Ind. is visiting me.

Mr. Sheridan promptly replied to Farwell's heart-to-heart letter on August 12th with support and encouragement:

> I suppose it would be in order to condole with you and say soothing words, and that I hoped for the best, etc. etc. But I won't. I'll tell you - now that it can be told - that I congratulate you from the bottom of my heart, for that is my sentiment. For years past Edna and I have felt the same way about it; but, of course, we could not allow ourselves to say anything that might break up a man's home, particularly where small children were involved.

Now, however, that the breaking point has been reached, for God's sake *stick to your guns*, and free yourself from the hell you have been living in for so many years past. A man of your brain, gifts, and honest attitude toward life and the world, should not allow yourself to be ground into the dust of failure through a sickening mess of that sort. *You have stood it too long already.* And if you shortly hear a roar like thunder coming from all directions it will be the approving "AMEN" of your countless friends who have thought as Edna and I do for years past. *And don't forget this*: You should go through with it for the *children's sake*. They are entitled to *normal* surroundings. See to it that they have this environment from now on.

Other friends wrote similar letters to Farwell urging him to carry out his plans for the divorce.

The older children had begun to sense the strain since their mother returned from her sister's home in Ohio, but it was not until she embarked for Europe that Farwell bared his heart to them, asking for their understanding and support. All were well aware of how hard it was for the family to make ends meet in those Depression times, and it was inconceivable to them that she could have found any way to afford passage. The practical issues were thus very visible to them. But since their mother never defended herself to them, they could only imagine at the time that their father was the suffering party over the whole relationship.

More maturely, later, some of them felt that their mother's ideas and her acting out of unconscious rebellion were not completely wrong. They came to realize that their mother too, had suffered, often silently, with her loss of personhood under Farwell's demanding Victorian ways. Their limited financial resources denied her natural longing for such things as a touch of beauty in new clothes or maybe new wall-paper to brighten a dull room. But at the time, the children understood that their father had no good alternative.

Arbitration was suggested as a temporary solution, but a divorce was ultimately finalized on January 14, 1937. Mr. Farwell moved out of their rented house into an apartment near the campus, taking his piano and lithographic press with him as well as other personal belongings, and leaving Gertrude with the children.

Mrs. Farwell strongly and emotionally asserted many times that Arthur Farwell was the only man she ever loved and that she would always love him. The divorce made no difference to her, and, painful as it was to her personally, she could understand his need for freedom. She never expressed jealousy about Arthur's eventual second marriage, whatever she may have felt. She proved to be good at sublimation, and bearing a sense of martyrdom. Her high and dramatic sense of purpose made her give over her conscious life to the role of motherhood with a capital *M*. She made herself believe that it was a glorious one, destined by the high gods to produce spiritual children of the New Age, of which she and Arthur were the forerunners. She was as high-minded as Arthur Farwell, but her temperament was devotional, religious and spontaneous; whereas his was intellectual and ruled by will power, with emotions strictly under control and more subtly expressed. Perhaps his development as a composer, whose music was full of emotion, required this, as well as the exigencies of an active public career.

By the time the divorce was settled, Brice had been graduated from the East Lansing High School and completed a year at Michigan State College. Attendance at M.I.T. was no longer realistic. He traveled Europe on a bicycle in the summer of 1937. In 1939 he resettled in Minneapolis where he later enrolled at the University of Minnesota. The divorce situation brought young Arthur, age 18, home from California after a year's stay with old family friends. Just graduated from high school, he became the eldest at home, with Beatrice 17 years, Sara just 13, Emerson 11, and little Jonathan only five. Farwell arranged to pay the house rent and a monthly check to Gertrude. He continued to teach at Michigan State College until a new retirement law went into effect in 1939.

After finishing high school, Beatrice went to live with her aunt, Elizabeth Brice Wilson, (Gertrude's sister) in Galesburg, Illinois, and earned her A.B. degree in art history at Knox College there. She graduated Phi Beta Kappa in 1942.

Sara was at Skywood Hall, a boarding "prep" school in Mt. Kisco, New York. Her "Camp Arden Aunts" made this possible, by securing scholarships and helping with other expenses until she graduated in 1941. She had a serious spleen problem which kept her out of school for a year and delayed her graduation. This illness became a great concern to her father.

Mr. Farwell made several trips back to New York City, in part because of Sara's spleen condition, before he finally made it his permanent residence. When he did so in the fall of 1939, he left his lithographic press for disposal with his son, Arthur, who remained in East Lansing for a time with the family. Except for what inventory of music he still had on hand, this move to New York marked an unduly early end to Farwell's refreshing try at making some of his music available with his own press and designs. His press runs of these hand-made editions were only about 200 of each work. There was no way he could find to afford space in New York to house and operate even his small press. As much as he regretted giving up his press, he would always remember the daily joys he experienced in building, developing and using it. Also, he had the great satisfaction of proving to himself what he had been able to accomplish with it.

However, his finished music masters, done on tracing paper, made elegant originals for the recently developed diazo or "white print" copying process. Over the remaining years of his life, he converted by hand a large proportion of his later manuscript music onto these tracing paper masters. In a way, his selections may give an indication as to which unpublished works amenable to this process he considered initially worthy of such preparation.

In spite of his many domestic problems, Farwell composed continuously during the 1930's. The year of his divorce, he wrote the *Piano Quintet in E Minor* (which was recorded in 1978 and met with very favorable reviewing by Irving Lowens.) Other successful compositions written during this period have already been mentioned at the close of Chapter 12.

## Second Marriage

While Farwell was indeed looking forward to renewing life in New York after almost a quarter of a century, the timing of his move was governed as much by domestic and family matters as by his retirement from Michigan State College, or his hope for his music. First, there was a big surprise to everyone, including his family, when he suddenly announced his second marriage, this time to a former student, Betty Richardson, a graduate of Michigan State College, who was forty years younger than he. She moved to New York City before he did, and their marriage took place September 28th, after Farwell also moved there in the late summer of 1939.

This news came two years after his divorce from Gertrude. Somehow there had been some tongue-wagging over the possibility that Farwell had further motives for the divorce than just the problems he had recited to his old friend James Sheridan, which were about the same as he told his children and a few others. In fact, one gossip columnist in Lansing had alluded in print to such an intrigue even before the divorce was finalized.

Farwell had been single until 46, and far too devoted to the work and ideals of his cause to have had much time or interest to devote to "affairs" - after his youthful yearnings and disappointments. We cannot forget that he grew up with all the Victorian prohibitions and inhibitions. His marriage with Gertrude lasted 20 years and was productively fertile, if not too supportive or fulfilling otherwise.

He told Brice he believed that energies sublimated from bodily passions were part of the source of his intuitive sensitivities and powers. But he wrote that he had decided on the emotionally vivid world of music, requiring human warmth, as a means of expressing his spiritual aspirations. Accordingly, his human existence and needs could not be denied or forever repressed.

Now Farwell was past 65. He had had 20 years of some household sharing and companionship, and had found pleasure in much of it, however unsatisfying the marriage. So it is not surprising that he looked for another companion.

For his last years in Michigan, however, Farwell did live alone, relieved by the freedom from the former domestic stress. He busied himself with his press, some private teaching[1], some productive composing, and frequent visits from his children, who enjoyed helping him with his housework and watching him cook. If he initiated or entertained new close personal friendships with any women before or during this period, even including his new bride-to-be, it was done too discreetly for any of his children to perceive it at the time.

The timing of Farwell's move east was also affected by Sara's persisting spleen problem, as noted. This accounted for Farwell's back and forth trips from Michigan, which surely must have included visits to Betty before their marriage.

He deeply hoped to avoid Sara's need for surgical intervention. The doctors gave her a 50/50 chance of surviving an operation to remove her spleen at that time. Farwell was much concerned about her until he learned, through his friend, Harry Barnhart, of a Health Spa at a Clarkstown Country Club that might be able to obviate the surgery. Barnhart made the necessary arrangements for Sara to move there in the summer of 1939.

The health prospects for Sara at this unusual spa remained rather nebulous. When her drama mentors, the "Arden Aunts" learned of this situation, they exerted their benefactress' authority, and intervened. Farwell himself was uneasy about the rather exotic Clarkstown environment for Sara, once he had experienced it, so he cooperated.

The "Arden Aunts" - Kathryn Everts and Elizabeth Fay Whitney - (both Anthroposophists[2]), contacted their Dr. Linder, a homeopathic physician, and arranged for him to treat Sara. Dr. Linder was also an Anthroposophist and was connected with the Rudolph Steiner School in New York City's East Side.[3] His treatment did not bring the desired results either, so the surgery to remove Sara's spleen was performed successfully in 1941. The first words she heard on awakening from the finally ordered operation were her father's at her bedside: "Sal! We're at war!"

Sara recalled the time when her dad first informed her about his recent marriage:

> Dad told me about Betty when he took me back to Skywood for school in the Fall. It was the first time I ever saw dad blush. He had tears in his eyes in explaining all this to me. It was beautiful - this China doll that he had a special feeling for. She was small and fragile-looking - so different from mother who was tall and

rather strong.  He talked a lot about his book and about
how much help Betty was in doing the typing for it.  Betty
was very supportive of dad's work.

Later, Sara reminisced also about her own visits to see her
father after he had settled with his new bride in New York:

> These visits were always happy times.  He had a lovely
> apartment on the second floor at East 12th Street.  Once,
> after I had been to see the opera *Tristan* with some of my
> school girl chums, I went to call on dad.  He sat down at
> his piano and played a whole act - from Memory!  He
> knew all the music.  Of course I was impressed.

Sara's Aunt Betty Wilson secured a scholarship for her studies
at Knox College where Beatrice had also attended.  Swarthmore
College had offered Sara a good scholarship, but her parents
wanted Sara under the watchful eyes of some family member,
which Gertrude's sister provided.  However, Knox College did not
have a drama department for Freshmen, so Sara left there at the
end of her first year.  Too, she was having to follow her illustrious
sister, Beatrice, who had gained recognition during her Knox
College years, and Sara preferred to be recognized for herself.
Accordingly, at 19 years of age she went to New York City for
drama study and experience.  After she was gainfully employed,
Sara sent money to her father as often as possible, and regularly
to her mother.  She was very aware of her father's meager pension
from the college.  It was only about $60.00 a month, even after
the authorized amount was doubled, in recognition of his stature.
Into the domestic affairs of Farwell and his family during
these years came a psychic from Eastern Europe, Agnes M.
Stanko, who now lived in New York.  She introduced herself to
Farwell at a social affair by saying, "I was told in India to look for
a family in America whose members have extra toes and I believe
you are that person".  Indeed she had met such a man.  Arthur
Farwell himself had been born with extra digital growths on each
hand and foot, and all of the Farwell boys had extra digital
growths on feet, hands, or both, when they were born.  But all of
them had these appendages removed in early childhood except

Jonathan. He had six good toes on each foot and persuaded his
parents to let him keep them.

This unusual introduction to Madame Stanko must have
startled Farwell and a lasting friendship ensued. He found a
kindred interest in exchanging his intuitive experiences with her
psychic, spiritual and moral disciplines. She felt that she was
destined to act as a protector of the family with her disciplines,
but sometimes her presence seemed overpowering. Farwell was
mature enough to adopt a balanced attitude to her intense and
persuasive teachings, but he welcomed her aid with young Arthur,
who had received an army medical discharge and was having some
difficulty adapting to a disturbing disability. He, and especially
Emerson, strongly accepted her guidance. They and Betty Farwell
called her "angel", while Brice, Beatrice and Sara learned to stay
out of her way.

Farwell himself thought her highly genuine and helpful. He
set five of her poems, written in her limited English, to music, in
the years 1943-48. Emerson recalled an occasion when Madame
Stanko was visiting :

> Dad had a lot of pictures of personal friends laid out
> on the table. These were all vital-looking people and
> every one of them had committed suicide. Mme. Stanko
> studied the photos and warned me, "No matter what
> happens, don't you ever do a thing like that!" We were
> astonished at the number of them! Dad and she both
> believed in reincarnation. He remarked to her, "What I
> don't do in this life, I'll pick up and carry on when I
> come back."

Young Jonathan received the most buffeting from the divorce
and the moves east. Gertrude had only Emerson and Jonathan
with her when she left East Lansing in 1939. Young Arthur had
preceded them to Newark, New Jersey, where he had a job and an
apartment. Gertrude joined him there briefly with her two
youngest boys. Before Arthur went into military service in 1942,
Jonathan's well-being had become a concern.

During this period Gertrude had to secure employment and
went from one poor-paying job to another, but was ill prepared to

handle her new role as mother and wage-earner. After young Arthur left, she and Jonathan lived in boarding houses, cheap apartments, or furnished rooms. She was unable to provide a stable environment for the boy. By the spring of 1941, Jonathan had been placed in a foster home with a family named Williams, in Englewood, New Jersey, and went to the Steiner School in New York City with their son, Roger. The Anthroposophists doled out some funds to help Gertrude, and Jonathan was sent to one of their camps that summer. After a brief try at living with his father in the fall, the Farwells decided that Jonathan needed more consistency, care, and discipline than either of his parents could provide in balance. He was then put in the foster care of Hans and Friedl Just in New York City for two school years. By high school age, he was fortunately awarded a scholarship to Wooster School, a private boarding school in Danbury, Connecticut, that his mother's contacts had managed to secure for him.

Emerson also went to New York City after high school graduation, as a hopeful actor. (Figure 47) He did appear in a few plays among the extras, but then he too, went into the army for his World War II duty.

With his family thus dispersed, and more or less launched on their own, Farwell was absorbed with his own new life. Rebuilding his old status in the New York musical world seemed disastrous at first. The chief reason he had moved back to New York City was that he wanted to be in the main-stream of the music world again where he would be known and recognized as a composer. However, when he visited the offices of G. Schirmer at that time, he was chagrined to discover he was no longer known there. This must have been a devastating blow for Farwell, but his belief in his creative powers remained unshaken. His indomitable spirit refused to be discouraged by circumstances and he determined to demonstrate that he was a composer worth hearing. As a result, he wrote some of his best compositions in his last ten years.

Farwell's correspondence with Carl Engel, editor at Schirmer's, is revealing. On May 20, 1941, Farwell wrote to him about getting some of his compositions published and sent this rhyme with a concluding line of music:

The wolf's at the door
The dub's in the mesh
Loud is the bell
The bills are unfurled.

The claw's on the floor,
The thorn's in the flesh'
The devil's in hell' - - -
All's wrong with the world. [Notated with the last phrase of
    H.H.A. Beach's *The Year's at the Spring*]
    Apologies to the two Bs - Browning and Beach.

Carl Engel replied nine days later with a rhyme and also
borrowed a last line of music for his own text:

What is a publisher to do
If wages rise, materials too,
And if composers will submit
Their costly scores, but ne'er a hit?

Why don't you write some ripping song
Or piano piece? - you can't go wrong.
That is the thing that brings a check
For ev'ry hour thus spent, by heck! [Notated with opening
    phrase from Ethelbert Nevin's *The Rosary*]
    Apologies to E.N.

Fortunately, Farwell still had friends in the city who respected
him and his music and wanted to help. John Kirkpatrick, a
pianist who specialized in playing music by American composers,
was especially encouraging. In his concerts, he included two of
Farwell's Indian pieces, - *Navajo War Dance, No.2* and *Dawn*,
which he first edited with Farwell. He was also instrumental in
having these published by Music Press, Inc. When Kirkpatrick
performed the *Navajo War Dance* and *Pawnee Horses* in 1942 at
Town Hall, the performance was well received, though the music
critics were not in agreement about Farwell's compositions. The
*Herald Tribune* critic described them by writing, ". . . they made no
pretense of modernism." *The Times* critic stated, ". . . they had

*Figure 47.  Emerson Farwell with his father in New York in the late forties.*

obviously been wrecked by ultra-modern trimmings." No wonder Farwell was cynical about New York music critics!

At home with his new wife, Betty, Farwell was not worried about critics. Betty tried to comfort him with love and understanding. She was well educated, having earned her undergraduate degree with majors in music and English and a master's degree as a librarian. She held a position at the Rudolph Steiner School and for a time at the Columbia Library to supplement her husband's small college pension.

However, she became quite possessive of her husband's love. On one visit to the Farwells, Brice recalls that Betty slapped him for showing some filial affection toward her - something he could never forget. Brice thought her mores "pretty stern. She was dad's and to her I had acted 'fresh'!" Her attitude towards the other Farwell children, especially Jonathan, created some difficulties too, until he went off to Danbury to school.

Farwell was ill a large part of the year 1941. His eyes were a serious problem and required the removal of cataracts. Respiratory illnesses also haunted him. (Didn't Cheiro warn him about a weakness in his upper lungs?) As if these disturbances were not enough, he was forced to move from his attractive apartment on East Twelfth Street. However, before this occurred, there was a bright spot in the year, the birth of his daughter, Cynthia Torrance, in November. Now Farwell became a father again at 69 years of age!

They found their new abode up on 684 Riverside Drive. While the neighborhood was becoming transitional, their apartment was ample, with good space for the piano in the living room, which looked out over the Hudson River and the Palisades from a large picture window. Here he lived and worked the rest of his life.

## "Retirement" Activities

In time, Farwell became involved with meetings of various musical groups, attended concerts, and renewed other friendships with former acquaintances. He was always extending invitations to friends to "come up and see us" and many visitors obliged. He finally joined ASCAP and served on some of its committees. His

chief concerns however, outside of his family, were his composing
and the writing of his book, which he finally titled *Intuition in the
World-Making*. The book had been started years before, along
with the drawings of his symbolic dreams[4] which formed a
significant part of the book.

Betty acted as booking agent for her husband's lecture on
intuition (Figure 48). Entitled *The Science of Intuition*, it dealt
with: 1) Its laws, use and control; 2) Its power to solve personal
problems; 3) Its part in shaping our changing world. Farwell
illustrated his lecture with screen projections of original drawings
and paintings he had drawn from his experiences with intuition
and visions.

Farwell invited about forty persons to his home for a "trial
run" of his lecture presentation about July 30, 1940. These guests
included, in addition to a few friends, several distinguished
teachers, a few musicians, but mostly strangers. He admitted this
was an experiment and he wanted to have an impartial audience.
A review of the affair reported that "from the careful attention
to all that Mr. Farwell said, and to the lantern-slide illustrations
on the screen, and from questioning that lasted twice as long as
the lecture, it is clear that the experiment was a success."[5]
Following this "trial run", Farwell presented the Intuition lecture
at the Psychic Forum the last week of November 1940. He
continued to give his lecture in the New York City area where
later it became part of a six-week's series entitled *Intuitive Power*
that concluded on November 12, 1945.

Farwell always had a wide variety of acquaintances, who were
stimulated by his keen mind and broad cultural background. His
good friend, "Kitty" (Katherine) Heyman, a concert pianist and
Wa-Wan composer, (Figure 49) introduced him to Scriabin's music
through her concert performances. It is not surprising that the
man, as well as his music, fascinated Farwell. When he discovered
that Scriabin had embarked on experiments with esoteric
harmonies connected with Theosophical ideas, Farwell was
interested. Farwell's early studies of Theosophy made him curious
about these musical expressions by Scriabin. As a result, he
attended some of the Scriabin circle meetings where he also met
another devotee of this music, Faubion Bowers.

# THE SCIENCE OF INTUITION

Its Laws, Use and Control

Its Power to Solve Personal Problems

Its Part in Shaping Our Changing World

## ILLUSTRATED BY PICTURES

A LECTURE

by

# ARTHUR FARWELL

With screen projections of original
drawings and paintings of
his experiences with
intuition and vision.

*Figure 48. Cover of Farwell's Intuition lecture announcement.*

*Figure 49.   Katherine Ruth Heyman, Wa-Wan
composer, concert pianist and life-long friend of
Arthur Farwell.*

A well-trained pianist, musicologist, and author of a book on
Scriabin, Bowers proved to be another stimulating friend for
Farwell.  Bowers also played a part in Sara's life during the post-
war occupation of Japan when she was engaged by the USO as a
Civilian Actress Technician to entertain the troops there.  At that
time Bowers was aide to General Douglas MacArthur and had
access to the Kabuki Theater where he frequently took Sara.
Farwell sent letters to Bowers via Sara for delivery during those
years, as he could not keep up with his friend's address changes.

While Sara was working in Japan, she wrote to her father as
often as possible.  Sara was probably her father's favorite child.
She tried to show her love for him in tangible ways even though
they were separated by many miles.  She mailed a large box from
Japan for his Christmas in 1946 which contained numerous
thoughtful gifts.  Farwell's letters in response to receiving the

package reveal his delight and appreciation as well as his living conditions. His December 3rd letter noted:

> An overstuffed Christmas box has arrived here from you - a prodigious affair much exciting our curiosity. From its size, I am sure it contains things for all in the family - and I will see that they are properly distributed.
>
> Charles Ladd gave all the cousins he could dig up a gorgeous Thanksgiving dinner in his apartment. Betty, Cynthia, & I, your mother, Brice & Helen, Art, Em and Jon were all there and various other relatives.
>
> Noble [Kreider] will be with us for Christmas bringing with him Charles Burkhardt, a pupil in piano and composition, very gifted, whom we met last summer, indeed saw a lot of.
>
> Dr. Williamson of the Westminster Choir tells me they will present my new Indian choruses in a public concert in New York before starting on a tour Jan. 13. I am getting very curious to hear them, and may go over to Princeton to do so in a short time.
>
> My Christmasing will undoubtedly have to be extremely modest this year. . . .
>
> Lots of love from us all - with special heaps from
> Dad

After the excitement of Christmas was over, Farwell finally had time to write again to Sara on January 19, 1947, to express warmly and at newsy length his gratitude for her many gifts:

> Here I am again, an unmitigated sinner in respect to writing you. *I* am chiefly to blame, but the aftermath of the holidays has played a large part. Almost for the whole holiday season and for a time afterward we were a hospital here, even while Noble and his protege, Charles Burkhardt were visiting us, til Jan. 6. What with taking care of family and visitors my hands were full, and then it all proved too much for me, and *I* busted up a bit. So even the Christmas season aftermath was much delayed. I am just feeling like myself again.

So! - You certainly outdid yourself in thinking and doing for us all for Christmas! And the effect of it all in doing was augmented by the uniqueness and charm of the things you sent. A thousands thanks! The kimonos were (are) gorgeous, and made us look like Oriental lords and ladies (and children!) We had a lot of fun keeping Noble from seeing them at first, after he came, and then all donning them one evening and appearing before him in them.[6] With my none-too-careful attention to clothes, I am almost afraid to wear mine, for fear some harm may come to it. It ought to be spread out and hung on the wall like a tapestry!

The tea service was a godsend as well as Sara-send. We had one cup left in the house with a handle to it. Cups and saucers are about unobtainable in New York now, without buying very expensive complete dinner sets. The china you sent is very attractive and has served us beautifully for a lot of occasions since.

All who received gifts have been immensely pleased and I expect you have heard from them all before now. I don't think Bet has written you, but I know how delighted she has been with her gifts. She has been pretty well worn to a frazzle with a bad sinus attack - they always lay her very low, - and taking care of Cynty whose condition hasn't been too good and has kept her out of school a good deal. - and now work (at which Bet is a demon) on top of that.

Your picture of that wonderful Christmas telephone event (one of the nicest presents of all) was quite accurate, all of us crowding about the phone in the hall waiting our turn for a few words. Your voice, which came very clearly, brought you right into our midst - making it seem as if you were here! That was an inspiration! (as well as an expense!) Thanks for letting us know about the *timing* of the call. . . . The enchanting surprise of the money order of Nov. 29 was surely a lifesaver, just at that date, when it seemed almost impossible to do anything for anybody for Christmas. Again - many thanks. . . .

My two commissioned 8-part a cappella Indian choruses written last summer for the Westminster Choir, have made a great success on their recent Southern tour. Now they're off again, but will perform them here at Town Hall March 20th. I haven't heard them yet myself (except as a composer hears his unperformed stuff!)

I am much isolated in my work - just now working like mad making a complete piano-vocal score of the opera. The *sketch* was complete a good while ago, but there is considerable compositional reviewing to do in making a valid piano-vocal score and one little newly introduced scene yet to compose. . . .

Now heaps of love from us all, and extra ones from myself, who is your very-proud-of-you     Dad

Some insight into Farwell's daily life and limited finances are revealed in a thank-you letter he wrote to Sara later on July 6th:

Your gifts were wonderful!  The money order, and such a generous one, saved the day in a wonderful manner.  While we do get on, even if we have to get through some squeaky places.  A providential circumstance of this kind is one of those squeaks, and we're figuring so close that one Saturday we were hanging onto a nickel here (after B's dime to get to work and back Monday was provided for), so that Monday I could get down town and borrow something to hold us til B got a payday.  But that meant no food in the house for our noon dinner Monday. So we would have been dinnerless after B got home at 1:00, until I got down town and back probably about 3:00 P.M.

Well, Monday morning your money order came! When B got home, she found a leg of lamb!  You can imagine her surprise!  I'm not trying to give you the impression that we are frequently in awful need - we squeak through pretty well except sometimes for a day or so at the end of the month, - but only to let you know what a special providence you happened to be on this occasion.

Your writing [?] box[7] is charming and decorative. Friedlander explained all the workings of it to us. He's been up a couple of times and we all have had interesting conversations. He has a most high opinion of you - and why shouldn't he!

I'm writing some articles which I hope to sell to help out our income, and working hard on the piano-vocal score of the opera.

Here I copy a bit from an article, *The Art of Meditation* by Marie Pontz, whoever she is. But it is an interesting article. This statement may interest you.

Then followed a lengthy quotation to which Farwell added his own reactions. He often discussed philosophical concepts with Sara whom he found to be very receptive to his ideas. Father and daughter had much in common, which may have been one reason for their close relationship. She treasured her father's letters and saved many of them to reread in later life.

One letter to Sara in which Farwell explained the laws for meditation and gave detailed instructions for applying them, carried a challenging conclusion:

If you had not written me as you did, and if I did not love you as I do, I would not have written you all this, some of which most people apparently do not know. I have so much faith in you, that you will rise to real heights (whether they make an outward show or not is of little importance.) I pray that you hold yourself high and true, and find the right laws by which you are to live, so that you will maintain always your shining self and increase it, and be well worthy of bearing your grandmother's name as well as your middle name from her cousin. [Sara Emerson Farwell].

In addition to caring for family responsibilities, Farwell continued to compose and do a limited amount of teaching. On one occasion he responded to a plea for help from his pianist friend, Jeanne Behrend, to teach one of her classes in American Music at the Juilliard School of Music. In a letter to her, dated

December 8, 1949, he thanked her for the check she sent to pay for his services and commented on that experience:

> *I* enjoyed the hour and half very much, and am interested to hear reports of it from the other side! Will you let me know what they thought of it, please.
>
> An hour and a half was *desperately* short for filling out the outline you gave me. I wanted to leave them with a fairly rounded picture of the epoch I was so deeply mixed up with - its personalities and the inter-relations of individuals and tendencies, that the time for records was greatly curtailed. I could not have rounded out the matter if I had played more of my records than I did. All I could get time for, for records, was two movements of the MacDowell "Indian Suite" and the final part of the 3rd and all the fourth movements of my Quintet. I realized that you, scarcely being around at the period I was to cover (or make a stab at covering) couldn't have told what I had to tell but that if you wanted to have more of my records played, you could do that if you wish. . . .
>
> I'm glad things went well on your trip.

Farwell listed the recordings of his works that he had available for her to borrow which included besides the Quintet, *Land of Luthany* for cello and piano, two movements of his unaccompanied violin sonata, *Symbolistic Study No. 6*, and *Prelude to a Spiritual Drama*. He felt that these recordings left much to be desired, "but still give some idea of my work, and in part and at places, come out well."[8]   Farwell's concern for his teaching stint is obvious and shows his basic interest in teaching was still very much a part of him even at 77 years of age!

Jeanne Behrend recorded Farwell's *Sourwood Mountain* and *Navajo War Dance, No. 1* and played these compositions on her tours to South America and Europe. Farwell had considerable correspondence with her regarding her performances and promised to write something especially for her. At one time he questioned her to learn if she had any idea how many copies of the Victor recording had been sold. He was endeavoring to ascertain if Schirmer's reports to him were accurate. He complained about the vagueness of the reports he received from them and commented on his "microscopic stipend through them, as composer, of the two cents a side prescribed by law"!

On May 17, 1950, Farwell wrote to Jeanne to apologize for not congratulating her sooner on her recent marriage. One excuse was that he had been hospitalized for a minor operation which put him out of circulation for awhile, and "the stitches haven't been taken out yet. Anyway I am now beginning to live again." His special news was that "with seven children, I became a grandfather for the first time last week! But I never did feel old enough for that and don't now!"

Farwell may not have felt like a new grandfather at 78 years and his energy belied that category. Having first married at 45 years of age, and being twenty years older than his first wife, he often presented more of a "grandfather image" than a younger father might have given. This image must have been true in his second marriage with his youngest child, Cynthia too. But age had little to do with family loyalties and love for their father which all of the children generously gave him.

Whenever possible, the older Farwell children visited their father in New York, at least on the special occasions of his birthday and Christmas. In one of his last available letters written on December 30, 1951, Farwell described his Christmas (which proved to be his very last one) to a friend, Mrs. Stickle:

> . . . all but one of the seven children up for the tree, with a couple of their husbands and wives, some cousins, etc. We still use *candles* on the tree, as I have all my life, but one has to go over to the German part of New York, on north 3rd Av. to get them, and the little holders used to put them on the tree.
>
> I am just pulling out of the tiredness following the weeks of Christmas shopping and preparations. Much as I enjoy it from one angle, it's always a drag from another. But I'm anxious to get back to composition, which was going swimmingly when the Christmas cyclone struck.

Farwell's handwriting in the above letter is not written with his usual clarity or vigor, but one notes his progress in composition is strong. His health continued to decline until, after another short illness, he died quietly at Lexington Hospital on January 20, 1952. It was such a mild and seemingly routine illness that no one even in the family, beyond his immediate household, Betty and Cynthia, knew that Arthur Farwell had been hospitalized, until it was over. He would have been eighty years old in April. (Was not this Cheiro's prediction ?)

Gertrude Farwell attended her former husband's funeral as did their children. Sara reported:

> If mother had any mourning to do, she did it privately, which was kind, as it must have been deep. At the service she held us each in her arms to comfort *us*. Then she stood at her full height, dignified and flushing to a radiance I had never seen, her eyes looking young again and not tired. Something must have come full circle for her then and she seemed, for that moment, completed. It had been a long haul to become a grand lady she had always been inside, but for that moment she could reveal her wholeness to her children and the world. It was not anything I ever saw again.

Except for the written scores of his life-work in musical composition, Farwell had nothing to leave his family but the grand piano, his books, and a few personal effects. Each of his children was handed a big envelope in which their father had saved over their lifetimes, the childhood letters, cards, a few drawings and things they had given him in their own creative scrawl. In this way, too, he had loved them.

Looking back over his father's years with Betty, Brice feels that Arthur genuinely loved and respected Betty, and gave himself to the new marriage as strongly as he could, and still, at the same time, conserve his time and energies for his musical work.

> Dad had a number of little daily routines that he performed almost ritually, to save his time, such as the way he heated the milk for his regular shredded wheat breakfast, how he made his cup of coffee, the way he scoured the milk pan, the manner in which he cleaned up

the kitchen.  Because Betty went out to work, he shared
the household in these patterned ways.

Having welcomed Betty's strengths, support and comfort
throughout the years they lived together, Farwell did  recognize
with increasing concern some weaknesses in her stability as time
passed.   Nevertheless, he left his musical life-work in Betty's
hands.  He was hopeful that her musical and library training, plus
her devoted help for these last ten years, would enable her to
preserve his music by finding an institutional home of national
and enduring stature where it could be safe and available for
posterity.   He also counted on her to find a publisher for his
treatise on *Intuition in the World-Making.*

Not too long after Farwell's death, Betty sold his piano and
eventually moved to Washington, D.C.  There, for lack of space
in her little apartment, she stored her husband's files of music
and memorabilia in a large storage warehouse in the city.  It was
about nine years after Farwell died that this author acquired these
files.  In 1978, she received a letter from Betty inquiring about
how the manuscripts were being cared for.  Betty wrote in part:

> I hope you will understand my interest in knowing
> more of the condition of the MS and its care.  I have
> been a librarian for a great many years of our short lives,
> of the Collection. . . .
>      I am not the kind of person to pressure matters, but
> to be frank, one of the reasons I married Mr. Farwell was
> that I had faith (very much so) in what he had done and
> planned to do for the remainder of his years.  He worked
> consistently each day after our marriage, and succeeded in
> rounding out his plans for the completion of the work he
> believed in. . . .

Betty suffered a nervous breakdown due to her frail health
and had to spend considerable time in an institution, but she is
still alive and under special care at this writing.  Their daughter,
Cynthia, died October 26, 1983.  The children from Farwell's first
marriage are still alive and active in their respective careers with
the exception of young Arthur who died March 26, 1986.

Gertrude Farwell carried on to the best of her ability too. Eventually her children rallied to support her financially so she could live in a modest yet comfortable apartment in New York. She got involved in theater again, acting in off-Broadway plays as a character woman. She went to theater parties with the casts, met Marilyn Monroe who delighted her, also met Tennessee Williams. She read for Elia Kazan (but didn't get cast), played the chorus leader in Sara's production of *Electra* - even though she broke her hip at the first reading and had to be rushed to the hospital. She continued to write poetry as she had done all through the years and wrote letters to presidents and poets as if she knew them - sometimes she even got answers. All this is quite a lot for a lady "cast off into the cruel world" in her middle age - pre-World War II. As she grew older, she spent more time visiting in the homes of her married children, and lived with Brice's family in Briarcliff Manor, New York, until her death in November 1971. When the author interviewed her in 1965, Gertrude was mentally sharp and still holding high her blazing torch for Arthur Farwell.

Arthur Farwell, in the many facets of his creative and challenging career, worked unceasingly until the end as a serious composer. He crusaded vigorously for his idealistic aims of a recognized place for the composer in American life, and for a vibrant life of good music for the American people.

Early in his life, Farwell had said that what he was writing would have to wait for more opened eyes and ears beyond his own time. Recent examination has led to gratifying discoveries in his music. What it holds of enduring musical value may exceed the scope of this study. Part II gives here one musician's exploration of Arthur Farwell's musical legacy, together with some available observations of other critics.

# PART TWO

# MUSICAL WORKS

# Chapter 16

## The Composer at Work

*Today . . . I have not an idea in my head and it exasperates me, - the creative merely does not exist and it is torture. At times this creative element in my nature overwhelms me and I am happy. But when it is lacking, it is torture.*

So wrote Arthur Farwell in August of 1893 before he began his formal studies in composition. That story has already been told, but the created results of his study remain to be viewed.

Many influences contributed to the development of Farwell's compositional style and thought-life. We saw him struggling with the study of harmony on his own during college days. From the time he first began to compose, Farwell's devotion to it was emerging from urges deep within his own nature that he had to express. Those early expressions were frustrated due to lack of adequate training. After asking MacDowell how far he might hope to develop with continued self-teaching, Farwell accepted MacDowell's advice to take formal lessons. These included the studies under Homer Norris, Chadwick, some input from MacDowell, and finally the full plunge in Europe with Humperdinck, Pfitzner and Guilmant.

In addition to the influence of formal studies, we should remember the impact of opera on young Farwell. In Boston he learned much from witnessing Walter Damrosch conduct all of the *Ring*, and Anton Seidl and Mancinell conduct another opera season. Furthermore, he later experienced opera first hand from the stage. As an extra in the midst of the action, he absorbed the excitement and reality of the medium. Whether "drinking air from tin cups in *Carmen*, parading as a noble of Brabant, carrying Russitano in on a palanquin, or even Melba in a sedan chair," Farwell lived the roles; they became a part of his young life. These, and his European experiences with seeing opera, especially at Bayreuth, gave Farwell a rich understanding of music's relationship to drama. He could tell a story in music (*Gods of the Mountain* e.g.) and one suspects he preferred images for inspiration more than abstraction. He made full use of this bent in producing his early pageants and masques as well as in writing his own opera.

For the five months that Farwell lived in Berlin, his daily contacts with James Grun, the poet, made a lasting impression on his way of thinking. Farwell claimed that he learned much from Grun who made him think and "think hard". He continued:

> If I presented a thought to him [Grun] which was not alive - fairly wriggling with life - I became conscious of it at once by a sharp crack on the head, so to speak, from his mental shillalah. And these rude awakenings had much to do, later on, with my attitude toward work and toward developments and controversies in the field of American music.

> Grun insisted on a knowledge of musical history, that we should be alive to the point which we have reached in musical development, and to the process of getting there. He insisted on form - not any existing conventional or crystallized form, but the **idea** of form - that a musical work should have recognizable internal proportions making it a logical organism. He insisted on the value of folksongs, those melodies sifted and tested by time, which are the "old wine" of melody, deceptive in their simplicity and not to be equaled today. He urged Parry's great dictum, that whenever the musical art of a country becomes weakened through over-refinement, it derives new strength from the simple melodies of the people. And he particularly insisted upon dramatic truth in the musical setting of a given text. If the text says dark or deep, the music must be convincingly dark or deep - the music must tell no lies.[1]

When we examine Farwell's songs, we find a strong relationship between text and music showing Grun's well-absorbed influence. Farwell carried home Grun's ideas on folksongs to bring them to life again when he began his Wa-Wan Press.

Furthermore, Farwell's travels and study in Europe had opened his eyes to distinct national trends there that included the use of folk music. This experience culminated later in an eagerness to see his own country develop a distinctive character in music as well.

Walt Whitman became another important influence after Grun introduced Farwell to his works. Whitman's ideas not only affected Farwell's own philosophy and ideology, but also in due time, that of his pupil, Roy Harris.

Although Farwell's thinking was greatly influenced by Grun, his philosophy was perhaps most deeply imprinted with his New England heritage that surrounded him all during his formative years. Born into a family of culture in which books and high ideals were an integral part of daily living, Farwell developed an outlook on life much shaped by the Emersonian transcendentalism of his kinsman. Emerson's thought so pervaded Farwell's youth that as an adult his speech reflected the phrases and philosophy of the Transcendentalists. One sees this reflection throughout his essays.

Sara Wyer Farwell, Arthur's mother, was a particularly strong influence on her son all of her life. She introduced him to the study of astrology and to the Eastern mysticism of the Vedanta Movement through Swami Saradananda. (The Theosophical Society begun in New York in 1880, also caught his interest for a time in the New York years.) These teachings opened Farwell's mind to the writings of other Eastern mystics whose ideas confirmed much of his own spiritual experiences. Remember that Cheiro told young Farwell he had strong mystical tendencies? His respect and reverence for Christ also became visible in his work for the *Pilgrimage Play*.

In time, he studied intently the writings of Oswald Spengler, Fabre D'Olivet, and Judge Thomas Troward, as well as Wagner's prose writings. All of these contributed ideas that were formative to Farwell's own philosophy and world-view. Farwell was an avid reader and a deep thinker who spoke out against the growing American materialism and institutionalism. Here we see the paradox of the all-American rugged individualist, pioneer and lover of freedom - seen from Europe as "barbarian" - seeking for

Truth and Beauty in a life-long quest, attempting to express them
freshly in the most unmaterial of the arts - music.

In a reply to David Ewen giving his principles and beliefs as
a composer, Farwell wrote the following in September 1945:

> My aim in composition is for truth and beauty - truth
> to what I honestly feel, and the highest beauty I can sense
> and capture. Truth and beauty are qualities divine and
> sacred. When they are applied to music, music must be
> held equally divine and sacred. In proportion as music
> becomes a revelation of the spirit of truth and beauty, its
> worth is greater to man. Music born of the intellect is
> not enough. Its matter should spring from the intuition,
> to be molded into shape by intellect and emotion.
> Intuition is awakened by asking of the Spirit within.

Another influence, perhaps less important, but nevertheless
having impact, came with the Irish literary revival, instigated and
developed by William Butler Yeats. Yeats' poetry and essays were
coming out thick and fast in the first years of the new century,
and Farwell bought and read them all. Yeats gathered around
him the best writers and artists in Ireland, and recorded the
movement's development in detail. He revived interest in Gaelic
and pre-Christian legends, started the Abbey theater, encouraged
every young talent, and wrote (significantly for Farwell) of his
magical and mystical experiences and his association with the
Theosophical Society in London.

Obviously these activities were similar to Farwell's early work
for music in America, which also was a push for a national stamp.
The sense of a kindred spirit must have encouraged him. While
there is no evidence of correspondence, there was a happy meeting
between the two men years later, after a Yeats lecture in
California. Gertrude Farwell was present at this visit and found
their talk so inspiring that she wrote a sonnet about gods who
"could speak through speech of man/ In little rooms filled with the
pipe-smoke blur:/ I looked from Pisgah on the Promised Land".

As for the Germanic and Wagnerian influences in his music, so often criticized in early works, he defended himself late in life to his children by saying: "Every artist stands on the shoulders of those who have gone before him. What other models were there, and who greater than Wagner for me to stand upon?"

That Farwell knew he must free himself to be his own man in composition, we have seen; his constant experimenting with American themes, plus his development toward wholly original expression, shows how far he went to do so.

Farwell became very interested in cultivating the conscious use of the intuitive faculty and wrote a serious treatise on this subject, which he named *Intuition in the World-Making*. His interest in applying this practice to his compositional work was the result of heavy demands on his time and skills. Farwell explained how he first resorted deliberately to the application of intuition to his musical problems:

In 1913, I received commissions for the compositions of music for a series of pageant dramas. I knew that to do this extensive work against a time schedule I should have to operate in a very different way from my usual one, which at that time, was not free from the occasional necessity of waiting about, or straining for musical ideas. And most of the ideas required for these pageants were a sort quite different from those to which I would ordinarily apply myself.

In thinking about the task before me I conceived, in a half-fanciful way, that the universe must contain somewhere or somehow all the musical ideas which had never yet been thought of or written down. I believed that if I could find the right means of access to this universal store, I could put my hand at once on any musical themes I needed. To attempt this I thought of a "place of music", where the universe concentrated all these ideas, and where they could be had on application. I imagined a great assemblage of all possible means of producing music, a universal orchestra, including all instruments, and a chorus. Thus I gave the "universe" the chance to produce and play for me any theme I needed, on any instrument or instruments. Then I set this musical mass equipment, in my mind, in a semi-distant, misty dream-spot, far enough away to be free of any interference from myself. As definitely as possible, I then thought of a particular kind of theme I needed for a certain scene in the drama on which I was working - a Roman march, a pastoral motive, or whatever it might be. I watched the musical equipment of the universal store I had created, intently out of a dreamy state of my own, with closed eyes, keeping out of my mind every thought except the one on which I had concentrated. It required only a moment before the appropriate theme spoke out from the appropriate instrument or instruments, apparently wholly by its own volition, and absolutely without any effort of composition on my part. At once I found myself spontaneously released from the dream-state, and went to work in the ordinary way, developing the theme which the "universe" had given me. This process I repeated for months, obtaining immediately, and in rapid succession, the themes I required, which always fitted precisely my expressed need.

Farwell had psychic experiences throughout life which he interpreted as spiritual guidance. They were always in answer to a question, and came as visions or dream-like episodes in vivid images which he never forgot. He painstakingly sketched or painted them years later for his treatise on *Symbolic Dreams*. One such drawing (Figure 50) pictures the technique just described. Farwell referred to this drawing as an answer to his question, "How can a musician think of God?" He tells how, in the intuitive response, the three tones sung by the singer rose as a shaft of light toward the sky, changing its angle with each change in pitch. On its touching the dark cloud, the heavens burst at once into brilliant light and music, which had to be the beginning of the song the singer had just ended, but an octave higher.

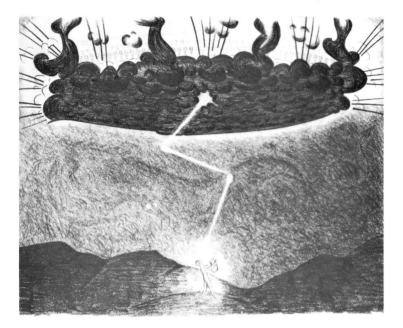

*Figure 50. Farwell's drawing of the visual aspect of the response he received to a meditative question, "How can a musician think of God?"*

The meaning he received from his question was, "Where man's song ends, God's song begins.

The drawings and paintings in water-color (showing William Blake's influence), were eventually reproduced on slides and used in his lecture, *The Science of Intuition* discussed in chapter 15, and also were included in his unpublished treatise. In that study, Farwell develops what he intended as an objective discipline whereby others may cultivate this latent faculty. He narrates his first spontaneous symbolic dreams, then takes us through similar occurrences in his musical work, and at last to the "Place of Music" he described in the excerpt quoted above. In studying the nature of these phenomena, he eventually read widely in Jung, read and eschewed Freud, and explored other artists' experiences with the creative process. Finally, he proposed ten "laws" for this superconscious process, a kind of "spiritual psychology" or, as he named it later, the *Science of Intuition*.

Despite Farwell's success in employing intuitive methods to meet deadlines, one project was almost too much for him. The daily changes made in the script for the Broadway play, *Garden of Paradise*, made such frequent demands on his time and energies that he became seriously ill. His friend, Noble Kreider, (Figure 51) took him to Bermuda for recovery as told in chapter 21.

*Figure 51. Farwell with composer, Noble Kreider, a close life-long friend, under a banana tree in Bermuda, 1915.*

Once again at work, back in New York City, Farwell began composing with more freedom. His health now restored, he was able to concentrate on new avenues of musical expression. He practiced his use of intuition in many works all his later life.

After Farwell moved to Michigan, his daily life was more scheduled so he could do some composing every day. According to family reports[2], he utilized his "Place of Music" practice whenever necessary as he had done previously. Farwell preferred to get up early and do his composing in the morning. Coming home from afternoon classes, he went directly to his attic study, and composed at his desk until six o'clock dinner time. His daughter, Beatrice, describes the exceptions when he needed to hear something:

I remember how dad would come dashing downstairs to the piano and play with a kind of chord stuttering, sort of singing along as he composed. He always kept a battery of sharpened pencils handy which he used as he played chords, over and over again, erasing and making changes. He was very intense at the piano. You could almost hear the intensity. Because of his eye trouble, he would lean forward to write[3].

A former student, Carlton Eldridge, reported how Farwell sometimes arrived at the college music building at five in the morning. His loud singing, foot stamping, and growling at the keyboard could be heard from a block away. No one dared to disturb him while he was intent on developing a new composition.

Farwell occasionally relaxed from this intensity by improvising at the keyboard for a younger daughter, Sara. She remembers how she would dance in Isadoraesque fashion around the living room to her father's playing as they both were caught up in the joy of improvisation.

Gertrude Farwell told how she would sometimes be helpful with her husband's composing problems. "He would say, 'Something is wrong with this. Listen and tell me.' Sometimes I was able to tell him and he'd say, 'That's it! That's it!'".

In a letter dated November 5, 1936 to a favorite cousin, Mabel Torrance, Farwell described his efforts with composition thus:

> Your good letter deserved a prompter answer than this, especially as you may have been wondering about my going down to New York. Would that I could! Truth is - I have been composing, and when I am *really* composing I am as oblivious of the regular affairs of life as the "ordinary drunk" of the night courts. Four songs (Emily Dickinson) and the first movement of a piano quintet (piano and strings).
>
> I have managed to squirm over to the college for my lectures, and don't think I have missed any, and back to composing, working till two or three in the morning. It is really dreadful how seemingly impossible it is for me to pull away, once ideas start flowing. I take it with me to meals, to bed, on the street, anywhere I am. Poor Beatrice knows it puts a stop to my doings if she plays the piano, but occasionally she comes and asks furtively if I am composing. I usually tell her "no", and either try to turn to something else, or go out for a walk. If she knew that when I am at it, it's a going on *all* the time, she would never dare to go to the piano, and I don't want to discourage her in that.
>
> I have a New York representative at last for my publications: it is the "Galaxy Music Corporation", 17 West 46th Street. So now . . . you can tell people they can see and obtain everything I put out on my [lithographic] press. My old friend A. Walter Kramer (long the editor of Musical America) is publications manager, and I have just learned that another good acquaintance of former days, Marshall Kernochan, is President. So you see I have friends at court.
>
> Forgive my silence and be glad that I got some good work done!

This intensity which Farwell experienced when composing, he also felt as a young student when responding to the performance of beautiful music. He confided to his journals how he wept openly or even became ill as a result of some great artistic experience that took him to "another world". In Germany, he often was so affected emotionally by the concerts he attended that afterwards he would wander aimlessly in the streets for hours. Frau Berg, his pension-keeper, frequently had to unlock the front door for him at wee hours in the morning. He would enter still dazed, but sober and dishevelled.[4]

This overpowering, often exaggerated, emotional/physical reaction to great art has been called the "Stendahl Syndrome"[5] This definition well describes Farwell's youthful experiences with music by the masters.

Farwell's letter to his cousin Mabel indicates that he suffered similarly when he was deeply engrossed in composing; i.e. like "the ordinary drunk of the night court". This inner compulsion to compose was so strong that it indeed obliterated everything else. When ideas began to flow, Farwell wrote that he felt he would "burst" if he could not express himself musically.

### Farwell's Ideas on Sonata Form

Farwell's *Symphony*, the *Sonata in G Minor* and the *Quintet* were some of the abstract works he composed using sonata form. This form held a significant place in his work during his lifetime and he had much to say on the subject. As early as 1912 Farwell wrote an article for *Musical America* entitled "Sonata - Only Possible Form".[6] Therein he states his belief that the sonata form constitutes the perfect or "ultimate" form because it observes certain natural "universal laws." These laws reflect the balance in the cycle of life. The first and second thematic ideas reflect the dualism of life as found in male and female; the first two ideas create the development section and according to Farwell, they represent life's procreative capacity. The recapitulations reconsider the original ideas.

By 1915, Farwell expanded his ideas on the sonata by writing another article for *Musical America*, "Musical Form Under New Human Conditions."[7]   This time he suggested that "form comes from the spiritual within" and declared "true artists will not try to continue a form that has already been perfected." Instead, he insisted that they will attempt to develop, alter, or rejuvenate a form. "Artists of true creative impulse and purpose will be seen to spend their lives in finding the fullest perfection for some one such characteristic form or group of forms." Although Farwell meant to challenge other composers to this kind of writing, he warned them against creating such complicated forms that people could not understand the music. He was very concerned that music should communicate with the listener.

A much later article on the sonata form was published in the January 1941 issue of *Musical Quarterly* under the name "Sonata Form and the Cabbala."[8]

Here Farwell still adheres to his earlier ideas on the importance of sonata form, but he makes an interesting comparison of it with the ancient oral tradition of the Hebrews, the *Cabbala*. Through what becomes ponderous reading, he explains how the letters IHVH that represent Yahweh or Jehovah, the sacred name, are related to the universal "primal creative process" which he believed corresponds closely to the sonata form and its universal laws.

Farwell finds the exposition section of the sonata form, with its masculine and feminine principles, to be the "IH" of the Sacred Name. The development section with its free exercise of formative principles, is the "V", and the recapitulation, with its reflection of the whole, is the final "H", or to put it concisely: exposition, development and recapitulation = IH-V-H.

Farwell stated that his study of C. Hubert H. Parry's article on the Sonata in *Grove's Dictionary of Music and Musicians* proved to be "highly provocative of inquiry" and led him to ponder what Parry meant when he refers to the "inner self" of man's nature from which he declares the form of the sonata has sprung. This led Farwell to consider psychological and philosophical possibilities of influence which finally brought his own thinking to the *Cabbala* and the Sacred Name.

After developing his arguments on eleven pages in his article, Farwell concludes:

> If the Cabbala's exposition of the Sacred Name, IHVH, reveals the ultimate formative principle of the sonata, the "psyche" which it reflects, and the universe which the psyche reflects, in a more complete and vivid presentation than can readily be found elsewhere, it may well be thought to be worth our attention. . . If he [Parry] had been a Cabbalist, he would very likely not have been so puzzled as to the form of the "inner self" on which man first gropingly, and at last triumphantly, patterned the sonata.

Such philosophical thoughts were behind Farwell's understanding of the sonata form.

### Harmonic Explorations

Farwell did impressive in-depth preparation before starting certain compositions. His files contain a folio of harmonic studies which he labeled "Harmonic explorations with given scales." These included studies in "Oriental Tetrachord", "Discussion of Oriental Chromatic Scale", "Two similar tetrachords", "Two dissimilar tetrachords", and "Inverted Oriental Chromatic C major scale". He analyzed the characteristics of each and listed facts which he expected to find useful in his writing. On another page in the folio he worked out resolutions of various kinds of cadences that could be used in Oriental chromatic scales - both major and minor; also modulating chords from minor to relative major keys. He devoted another page of music paper to examples of scales in each of seven modes with some given chords. He used 24 large music sheets to explore every possible chordal motion based on the chosen variety of scales. The style of writing and age of paper suggest that he did these studies early in his career, possibly in preparation for *Gods of the Mountain* that utilizes unusual scales.

He obviously wrote the series of work sheets for his *Polytonal Studies* in the late 1930s as preparation for the 46 studies which he conceived. He finished only 23 of these. The results of the studies however, are available as composed for piano solos. Some are remarkably beautiful.

Although Farwell began his composing career later than many, he made up for his tardy start by continuing to compose over a long life-span. His catalogue lists 116 opus numbers. Whereas some composers hit a peak in composing and then write music of little consequence, Farwell's output seems generally to have improved in quality with his age.

## Musical Characteristics

In examining Farwell's early compositions, one finds that he worked with traditional methods even while he experimented with different instrumental combinations, or transcribed from one medium to another. His use of Indian and other folk-related themes was based on his strong conviction that they were an important part of the quest for America's musical future. However, as pointed out elsewhere, they were only a small part of his total output. He was tagged all his life as an "Indianist", which caused him much grief, as well as neglect by later conductors and performers, continuing even to the present writing.

In his compositions written from 1920-1950, Farwell intensified the use of destabilizing elements in his harmonies. The tonal ambiguity resulting from his expansion of classical tonality, reflects the wide-spread experimentation that developed during the late nineteenth and early twentieth centuries. Many composers at this time were exploring and expanding their definition of tonality. A number of developments caused this expansion of classical tonality in the nineteenth century. Some important ones included the increasing scope of classical functions, less dependence structurally upon tonal centers, and the growing use of more chromaticism.

Arnold Schoenberg suggested that extended tonality refers to any far-reaching relationships or transformations that exist within a single tonal region.[9] Therefore, one might say that extended tonality refers to those works still providing a central tonal focus or point of reference regardless of how weak or ambiguous that focus may become in the course of a work.[10]

The resulting tonal ambiguity and weakening of the centrality of the tonic was handled technically in different ways by composers. In the early 1930s, Farwell was already exploring new ways of expanding tonality while other colleagues remained in the traditional-school style. In this respect, he served as a bridge between the traditional school and those composers who were moving to atonality.

Farwell's approach to expanding tonality included new kinds of chord progressions as well as a larger chord vocabulary, increased chromaticism, and new experimental tonal plans for his works. His later approach to chord progression deemphasized the usual tonic and dominant functions. In long works, he used them to frame large sections while permitting the inner parts to wander far from the tonal focus.[11]

Farwell's chord vocabulary relies strongly on seventh and extended tertian chords, with strings of seemingly unrelated seventh chords being common. Frequent diminished triads or augmented sixth chords occur in unexpected places. Sometimes Farwell moves to polytonality or bitonality as in his *Piano Quintet*.

Another characteristic found in some compositions is that the overall tonal plan of a work may be clouded by an unclear tonal focus at the beginning, but is subsequently clarified. He also avoids the traditional movement to the dominant or relative major or minor in later works. Sometimes he moves a half or whole step away from the opening tonal setting.

Many new techniques became popular during Farwell's career such as atonality, serialism, and pantonality, but he felt that these failed to communicate with people. His letters to Harris expressed his contempt for "*Ballet Mechaniques* and *Sacres* and all the rest". He complained, "Who of them [the young European composers] are saying what you and I, in our deepest souls, want to hear?" So Farwell continued his search for ways to express himself in music that were as acceptably "modern" as he liked, and remained in his extended tonality school of expression throughout his lifetime.

Farwell has been criticized for being a romanticist[12], but Gilbert Chase finds romanticism to be a worthy attitude. In his comparison of "traditionalists" who were also romanticists, he discusses how individual talents are affected by their position in the temporal sequence of history. As an example he points out in 1966 how "chromatic dissonance is characteristic of the music of our time, no matter what formal tendency it follows". He concludes: "Yet, throughout all its assimilation of dissonance, chromaticism, serialism - what you will - the essential romantic attitude persists, both by what it rejects and by what it affirms, as a reminder that beyond the stylistic and technical transformations of art, a flame is handed down and endures.[13]" Farwell tried to keep that flame alive!

In a letter to the author at Christmas 1988, Emerson Farwell wrote about his father's attitude towards "modern music":

> I know that dad suffered professionally for not following the (then) avant garde trend toward dissonant, atonal composition, but he remained true to his own inner ear and voice. Although he admired the intellectually challenging complexity of some of his contemporaries' works, as I heard him state a number of times, such compositions were devoid of all heart and soul, in his view. It seemed to him that for the sake of novelty, shock, innovation for its own sake, and/or intellectual bravura, the followers of this mode had "sold their inheritance for a mess of pottage." They would never find it possible, in that school, to express the kind of spiritual beauty, or emotional enhancement of human life that he felt was vital to works of lasting value.

Ned Rorem (1923 --) voiced similar views about modern music in his "ferocious condemnation" of serialism: "A modernistic brand of ugliness that everyone hated without admitting it is not longer being manufactured with the hope of being unpopular."[14]

Furthermore, Farwell would have echoed Rorem's own resentment when he asked himself: "How do you feel, after lonely years of treading a diatonic row, when atonal philanderers now garner publicity by skulking home to weigh themselves on a C major scale?" Farwell probably suffered more neglect than Rorem has.

But Farwell has his enthusiastic admirers. After Barton Cantrell, gifted pianist, read through some of Farwell's music at the author's home in the fall of 1970, he later wrote to her his reactions: "The searing inspiration of just those few Farwell pieces I played, is burned within me. I believe when his finest things are finally performed and recorded widely, and lived with as standard music is now, his highest inspiration will be found to be "loftier" than others have claimed. . . . I have played the violin Melody Op. 77 you gave me, and find it lovely - small, of course, but I like the way he thinks in his music."

After Cantrell had studied and played more of Farwell's music, he wrote to the author again on May 20, 1971:

> The more I get into Farwell's style, particularly his harmony, I find him to be one of the greatest creative natures. His harmonic world puts him with a half-dozen of the most magical and evocative American composers. Not because they are American, but happen to be, and I happen to be. I borrowed the piano arrangement of the Rudolph Gott Symphony and was overwhelmed when I played it. Very, very great to me, especially the finale, which is not always true with symphonies.

From 1893 to 1952, Arthur Farwell was pioneering for composers in America, constantly composing amid other efforts. He had a clear idea of what his music should be, and a dauntless vision that a native born America composer must be able to find a living and a recognized place in the world of American musical art. His use of Indian music in his drumming for a national musical art of American idioms is well known. However, his own musical ideas, and even his visions of an American musical art did not rest with the Wa-Wan ceremony or the peace pipe!

*Figure 52.   Farwell composing at Joseph Clark's Double Diamond Ranch in the Tetons, 1930.*

As he moved from east to west, and then back east again after a productive dozen years in the mid-west, all along the way Farwell developed original ideas of his own. His frequent strong inspirations came from the rugged American mountains as symbols of the country's grandeur and greatness (Figure 52). A number of his titles support this vision as he developed it in his music. He stuck to his own aesthetic convictions even when his compatriots went off in other musical directions that captured the fancy of the avant garde, as Emerson Farwell wrote. He would not play business games with his art or compromise his values for commissions or hearings.

In his last years, Farwell reiterated his belief that he would come to be more widely known and heard after his death than during his life, or at least his later life. Accordingly, he preserved much of his notes and materials for posterity to evaluate. Now the challenge remains to delve, hear, and assess his prolific legacy. We begin the delving in the next chapter.

# Chapter 17

## Farwell's Use of Folk Music

### Indian

The American fascination and interest in genealogy has sent many a family scurrying to locate its roots. There has also been an accompanying surge of interest in our American Indian heritage and their tribal life as expressed in music and dance. Gilbert Chase vividly describes the Indians' story and the work of ethnologists who have researched the music of the many native tribes. He asserts that "Concerned observers have generally agreed on the importance of music in American Indian tribal cultures."[1] He concludes that "Historically and ethnically, the vast continental impact of Indian tribal music and dance, with its related rituals and myths, will continue to be an enduring and distinctive cultural heritage of the United States of America."[2]

President Theodore Roosevelt showed interest in the music of the American Indian. When the Indian Bureau in Washington was told to destroy everything relating to the civilization of the Indian people, Roosevelt did all he could to preserve Indian music and art. "It fits in with all my policies of conservation", he said. "I don't know anything about Indian music, but the translation of Indian song poems shows them to be of rare value."

In her book, *Music at the White House*, Elise Kirk writes further about action taken by the president. When Roosevelt learned that government agents were punishing Indians who used their native tongue to sing or speak, he had all such legislation revoked. She states: "He even arranged to have a Cheyenne victory song performed during a Cabinet luncheon during which the Indian question was being discussed. 'These songs,' he said, 'cast a wholly new light on the depth and dignity of Indian thought - the strange charm, the charm of a vanished elder world of Indian poetry.'"

Farwell had already discovered the importance of music to the native Americans when, as a young boy, he experienced living with a tribe of Indians in Minnesota for a short time one summer.

This piqued his curiosity to learn more about these people in later years. So when Dvořák challenged American composers to utilize native folk melodies in their compositions, Farwell's first choice of Indian music was a logical response as he began delving into native folk music at the turn of the century. His discovery of Alice Fletcher's book, *Indian Story and Song from North America*, became the catalyst for further research and composition. [3]

Farwell did far more than adopt Indian themes in his compositions. He made a thorough study of the myths and functions of the Indians' music and pointed out the strong relationship between their music and religion. "Song, an invisible agent, is to the Indian the direct means of communicating with his invisible god," he wrote. Accordingly, Farwell sought to create music that used the Indians' tune in an appropriate setting related to the special occasion in which it was used.

An unpublished essay written by Farwell about 1936 expresses more of his thoughts on Indian music:

> American Indian music is a much bigger and more important matter than most people are aware of. In the first place it is the gateway to the entire Indian mythology, and thus to the deepest understanding of the Indian. And in the second place, it holds much greater possibilities for one department of American musical development than have yet been realized.
>
> As to its unearthing through ethnological research the first honors must go to Alice C. Fletcher, one of America's greatest and noblest women, who gave practically her whole active life to the Plains Indians, and who is, perhaps, the first American to make her way to a genuinely deep understanding of the Indian.
>
> The absorption of Indian song in American musical composition is another matter. I am well aware that the strong nationalistic movement in American music in the first decade of the century has, temporarily, I believe, been overshadowed and virtually abandoned by the newer generations of American composers. As their earlier

forbears in the 19th Century were dominated by the European classic and romantic eras, these newer men have been similarly dominated by the later European schools and fads, impressionism, expressionism, atonalism, "pure dissonance", and what not. A greater technic has unquestionably been gained, and reputations have been made by composers who could prove to local critics that they were "in" on the latest European isms, but meanwhile, for the most part, America has been betrayed. The only national expression during this period has been jazz.

However, Emerson's words are as true now as when they were written - "One day we shall cast out the passion for Europe with the passion for America." And in this inevitable deed we shall absorb the characteristic contributions of the Indian as certainly as the Roman culture absorbed the expression of the Etruscan, as the Arabian absorbed the Persian, the English in India the Hindu, and so on. Naturally our general cultural foundation is European, but we are gradually choosing and absorbing the cultural elements which give us our own characteristic national quality.

I am only saying this as regards our music, what I have always said since the first days of my *Wa-Wan Press* in 1901, that the Indian song is *one* of these elements. I am willing to add that, for two important reasons, it is one of the most promising. We have no folksong in America of such immense dignity as that of Indian song. This is a quality too great for either the popular or the artistic mood of the United States in the last twenty five years. But its day will come. In the second place Indian song is the golden thread which, in following it, will lead us to innumerable legendary and especially mythical concepts of great variety and beauty, scenes, pictures and ideas limitlessly inspiring to the composer.

I may add that this is simply one of the pathways which, since 1899, I have sought to open up for American music. Compositions on an Indian basis represent only eleven of my one hundred works bearing an opus number, though several of these eleven include several compositions, and I have used Indian thematic material in various other connections, especially dramas and pageants. It is somewhat strikingly significant that my little book of harmonized *American Indian Melodies* has maintained a steady sale for thirty five years, far outstripping all my other works in this respect.

### American Indian Melodies

These *American Indian Melodies* were harmonized for piano and became Farwell's first compositions using Indian tunes to be published in the *Wa-Wan Press* in 1901. His seven page introduction explains the background for the music and emphasizes "It must be understood that these songs are entirely dependent upon mythical or legendary occurrences, which they qualify or interpret, or upon religious ceremonies of which they form a part." Alice Fletcher's research was the source for these songs and most of the melodies can be found in her book *Indian Story and Song from North America*. Farwell's suggestions for performance warn:

> It is quite possible, in fact dangerously easy, to render these melodies in such a way as to make them appear quite meaningless; and, on the other hand, it is possible, and dangerously difficult, to so render them that they shall carry certain conviction. Each is a problem, to be worked out by itself, and the surest method of procedure is to study the spirit and temper of the American Indians.

Farwell sent a copy of *American Indian Melodies* to Humperdinck, his former teacher. Reacting to the music on February 23, 1902, he expressed his approval thus from Berlin:

> Dear Arthur, So glad to have news of you. I have
> played your "Indian songs" on the piano. They are very
> interesting, well harmonized, and for European ears are
> not too badly sounding.
> I hope will you soon publish the songs of the Eskimos
> as well? . . . E.H.[4]

Farwell also sent a copy of these Indian melodies to Andrew
Carnegie who acknowledged his gift on May 2, 1908. He endorsed
the long-lasting value of American folk songs as a most precious
heritage any nation can possess, saying they will "furnish the
foundation for the grand works we may in later days expect."

The first composition in this piano collection is *Approach of
the Thunder God*. The tune is sung by the leader as he blackens
his face and awaits the command of the God of War.   Farwell
suggests that it should proceed "not too rapidly, in deliberate
rhythm, and should carry with it the feeling of a dark and terrible,
but thoroughly controlled force.  It is not a thunder storm in
progress, but the ominous and muttering promise of one."

*The Old Man's Love Song* is a flowing contrast with its serene
and appealing melody (Ex. 1).  One can understand why Farwell
used this beautiful melody in other later works. He claimed that
it is "not inferior, in its idyllic quality, to the music which Wagner
conceived for the "Flower-maidens" in *Parsifal*."   This is the
background for the *Old Man's Love Song*:

> In the old Omaha tribal life, dawn was the hour for
> the singing of love songs; for it was then that the girls
> went out to fetch water from the springs, and the young
> men lay in wait for them.  But old Non-ba-non-zhin, who
> had lived his life to the full, was seen to go to the brow
> of the hill each morning at dawn and sing his love-song,
> "With the dawn I seek thee".   His secret was never
> disclosed, but it is presumable that he was seeking his
> final union with the "Great Mystery".

The next piece, *The Song of the Deathless Voice*, tells the story of a war party which traces down a voice calling in the night, only to discover that it is a disembodied spirit of a warrior singing over a spot where he fearlessly met death. Farwell describes this music as a "concentration of related, but utterly different emotions, in an extremely short space." Furthermore:

> The first call, with its long attendant pause, is sufficiently objective, but the phrase which follows is legato and dreamy, the expression of a spirit patiently waiting until some brave, still in mortal life, should come to claim its latent courage for his own, to use again in mortal deeds of valor. The third phrase is a mere echo reverberating over the hills. The following phrase in F# minor is again a bolder note, but still fraught with the patience of a vigil that may last forever. This dies away, and dissolves in darkness and night. What follows is, in spirit, and almost in note, a repetition of all that has preceded. The call is different in form, but still pauses, like the first, as if waiting for the long desired but never returned answer, and is followed by the same subjective expression of a spirit eternally waiting the movements of a mysterious destiny that shall bring it again into earth life. . . . An understanding of the meaning of each pregnant phrase must be gained, before the song will yield forth its spirit in the playing.

*Ichibuzzhi* is an entirely different kind of music. Marked "Presto, light and spirited", it is a vivacious call to action to a respected leader who is expected to bring victory in the forthcoming battle. Farwell feels that the music is totally devoid of savagery, in spite of its aboriginal method of accompaniment - beating upon drums, or with sticks. He also finds an element of humor in the soft repetition of the last half of each phrase, which is enhanced by the abrupt ending.

*The Mother's Vow* expresses a deep personal sorrow and breathes a haunting pathos which Farwell claims "worthy of

Tchaikovsky". Here he suggests that the leap of an octave upon E is a blended wail and sigh, and should be dwelt upon. The Indians use only sighing vocables for much of this song. The melody proper begins at the double bar and the pianist needs to make this sing. A climax should be developed at the fifth bar of the melody, which, with the remainder of the phrase, "should be rendered with despair, mingling with pleading, that dies in the immensity of its own gloom." Farwell suggests this program:

> The mother may be pictured standing out on the wind-swept plains, addressing her plaint to the approaching Thunder Bird, Wa-gi-un, and the pathos of the song may be heightened, if at certain moments the hearer is made to feel that the wind carries away portions of the melody, making them suddenly more faint and distant. This is notably possible in the sixth and eighth bars from the beginning of the melody proper, where the bass moves from D# to E, and then from A to G, but requires the most delicate treatment, free from all exaggeration. Despite the rubato quality, the melody should proceed flowingly, without halting, the harmonies dissolving one into the other in an unbroken flow. A deep feeling for the underlying idea will contribute more than anything to the effective expression of the song.

*Inketunga's Thunder Song* is a tune which Farwell took directly from a phonograph cylinder in Miss Fletcher's possession and is not recorded in her book. This belongs to the class known as *Songs of Personal Expression* and tells the spiritual experience of a man who goes to a secluded spot to fast and commune with Wakonda, the Great Spirit. The powers that send down the rain speak to him, and he frames his song accordingly. First, is a deep ominous note typifying the thunder, and then the tremulous call, born of his impression of the lightning. This response repeats. Then on a single note the mood changes, and the singer feels that the gods have spoken to him. This strain finally sinks to the mysterious note, with the lightning motive repeated, followed by the proclamation of divine communication. The import of this special song for the Indian cannot be overestimated as this is his very special song that he will hold sacred all his life.

The next piece, *The Song of the Ghost Dance*, is one which Farwell considers "the most deeply and broadly pathetic of any of the following songs." It cuts deeply into the very heart of the Indian's life - his love of his hereditary surroundings and racial traditions, and broadly, as it pertains to the entire Indian race. Farwell feels that this song reveals the pitiful consciousness of a lost cause and a doomed race because the "extremely gradual extinction of Indian life and rights, is something more deeply tragic than the sudden annihilation of a nation as in the case of Poland."

Steeped in gloom from beginning to end, the song tells the story. Farwell considered that only a vast chorus, or the orchestra would better express the soul of this song instead of the piano because it stands for the entire Indian race, not for an individual.

*The Song to the Spirit* is a funeral song despite its freedom from any tragic feeling. The Indians use no words to sing this gentle song as the departing spirit must hear no sound of lamentation. Only sighing vocables are sung so the dead will be "softly wafted to the invisible spirit as it departs." The music is "tenuous and seems to hover in the air as if ready to move in whatsoever direction the parting spirit may take". The Indians accompany this song by beating two willow sticks together.

*Song of the Leader* is a strong martial-type song and requires "only boldness" in its rendering. Farwell claims that it has none of the difficulties of subjective expression that occur in the other songs.

The concluding *Chorale* is self-evident in meaning as a broad expression of religious faith. Farwell points out that it is unusual because it ends in a different key from the one in which it began, and it has a continuous onward flow without mathematical divisions of phrases. He suggests that the organ would be a better instrument for this song than the piano.

These melodies do not require technical skill, but the pianist needs a real understanding of the place each song has in the

Indian's daily life.  The author played these pieces first *without* reading Farwell's introductions and then played them again *after* studying his explanations.  The results were somewhat transformed by the new insights gained.  Adults with limited technical skills, but with interpretive ability, should enjoy recreating these simple yet interesting Indian melodies as Farwell has harmonized them for piano solos.

The manual that Farwell prepared for C.C. Birchard's *Laurel Song Book* for school choruses includes suggestions for performance of the many songs in the text including three of his own.  Here one discovers that he used two of the Indian melodies from this collection:  *Old Man's Love Song* appeared as *Song of Greeting* with a text written by Frederick Manley, who also prepared verses for the second tune, *Song of the Ghost Dance.*[5] Farwell was pleased that Manley maintained the meaning of the original texts for his new verses in both songs.

Farwell writes for four parts, but uses simple vocal lines. *Song of Greeting* in the *Laurel Song Book* has soprano and alto singing the melody an octave apart in the first five bars.  The tenor part is in unison with the alto, but the bass has a nice separate line that sustains the text on longer notes to anchor the melody above.  After a held whole measure rest, the opening melody begins again, this time in a different rhythm in the soprano, followed by new part-writing for the other voices.  The result is an attractive song for young voices.  The accompaniment is basically the same as the piano arrangement for both songs.

*The Song of the Ghost Dance* has all voices singing in unison which would be effective for this music.  Manley's new verses are very singable for children.

Farwell adds more information in the manual for these songs than he gives in the introduction to his *American Indian Melodies.* He comments on how remarkable the *Song of the Ghost Dance* is in two aspects: First, it exhibits the depth of feeling to which an Indian can attain, and secondly, it shows in how perfect a melodic form he may express that feeling.[6]

In the Ghost Dance, the Indian dreams of earlier days, before the violation of his hereditary rights, days when he enjoyed the freedom of field and forest, and in the song, prays that Wakonda, the Great Spirit, shall look down upon him and pity the hopeless wretchedness of his present condition. It is thus the cry of a lost people, conscious of the piteous impossibility of regaining its lost estate. So great was the pitch of frenzy to which the Indian was sometimes wrought by the ceremony of the Ghost Dance, that it incited him to uprisings which were repeatedly suppressed by military force, and finally the singing of this song was forbidden in certain tribes by the United States government. The ceremony is, however, essentially peaceful and deeply pathetic in nature, it being merely the Indian's reflection upon circumstances that incited him to strike a blow for his natural rights.

The form of this song is particularly interesting. . . It consists of three contrasted pairs of phrases, the members of each pair being similar. The antiphonal effect of the repetition of each phrase is peculiarly impressive and appealingly pathetic. The first dual group of phrases is to be attacked strongly, and rhythmically well rounded. There is somewhat of the heroic in the feeling of this first passage. The second group is quite different in feeling, being softer and more *legato*. It exhibits a certain dreamy sadness not present in the first group. The third group is perhaps most representative of the spirit of the song, the simple human quality of its pathos needing no special characterization. The song closes with a repetition of the second group. It is essentially a dirge, and no solemnity in the rendering can overbalance the native solemnity. . .

The melodic peculiarity of this song should deter no chorus from an attempt to render it. The effect which, as it stands, it is capable of producing, is its own justification, and it must be realized that it can be undertaken only in a spirit of deep seriousness, if its Indian significance is to be preserved.

Here we note Farwell in the role of educator who wants to
expose young singers to experiences with American folk music, and
he provides helpful instructions for the choral director.[7]

## Vocal Solos Arranged from Piano Solos

Farwell rewrote three of these Indian melodies as solos for
low voice which were published by Schirmer in 1908 as opus 32.
An amplified version of the story behind the *Song of the Deathless
Voice* is included with the solo. The music has been changed
from the key of A major to G major with an introduction and
interlude added. The time signature has gone from 3/8 to 6/8
which suggests a longer phrase line for the singer. Parallel fifths,
some fourths and octaves predominate in the accompaniment.
The second verse opens with a dramatic call based on an
ascending fifth for the singer. The rest of the verse is similar to
the first in both voice and piano with only slight changes in the
latter. Repetition serves to emphasize the Indian characteristics
of the song as well as the quality of mystery surrounding the text:
"Behold, here a warrior fighting fell, A warrior's death, died.
Hear, O hear, There was joy in his voice as he fell."

In *Inketunga's Thunder Song*, Farwell has taken the few notes
of this melody and created an impressive song that dramatically
presents the Indian's experience in seeking his god, Wakonda.
Again Farwell has changed the key and moves from A major used
in the piano solo version to the key of D major. The thunder is
aptly described with forte chords and octave tremolos in the
accompaniment while simple harmonies lend dignity to the text:
"Wakonda! Deep rolls thy thunder! Wakonda! They speak to
me, my friend; the Weeping Ones, Hark! In deep rolling thunder
calling."

The third song in this group of vocal solos is *The Old Man's
Love Song*. As pointed out before, Farwell used this melody in
several other compositions. (See example 1.) It appears in *Dawn*,
Op. 12, as a fantasy for piano. He also arranged this melody,
fittingly, for an eight-part mixed chorus publication. The Omaha

melody uses vocables plus some text: "Daylight, Dawnlight, wakes on the hills;   Singing, I seek thee when young is the morn." Performers of this work should remember the underlying story as previously related, which is printed with the song.

### *Dawn*

*Dawn* is a six page work for piano published in 1902 by the Wa-Wan Press in single issue as well as in the bound volume. (Example 2.)   Farwell uses two Indian themes: the first is the same hauntingly lovely tune from *The Old Man's Love Song* and the second, an Otoe melody.   The author's copy is especially interesting as Farwell marked it in creating his arrangement for orchestra and he indicates planned instrumentation.   Roy Harris also made an arrangement of *Dawn* for strings and piano which the Tuesday Musicale in Pasadena performed on May 20, 1924. (This was a period when Harris was studying with Farwell.)

Farwell elaborated on his conception for this work when he introduced it in the *Wa-Wan Press*.  He refers to the problem of the composer "who seeks to develop the unconscious musical folk-expression about him into consciously organized forms, which shall intensify the poetic content of the original expression."  *Dawn* is a result of such a study.

Farwell's   orchestral   version   of   *Dawn*   has   had   frequent performances.   For the program notes, Farwell wrote that he "treats the song as an invocation of the spirit of life at dawn," and uses the second theme as "the response of the dawn to the invocation."

Farwell's friend, John Kirkpatrick, was interested in playing *Dawn* on his piano concerts.  To that end he received Farwell's blessing to edit the work.   On August 27, 1944, Farwell acknowledged the receipt of Kirkpatrick's efforts, and wrote to thank him:

> . . . the copies are beautiful!  And it delights me that you
> have taken hold of this work - dating from 1902, I believe
> - for I have always felt that it had a quality which would

remain in people's affection a good while if they could get
familiar with it. I played it all over the U.S. in the early
lecture tours of mine and it always went strong. But I
didn't play it as well as you do, unfortunately. I have
made the little corrections in the copy.

I was pleased to see your picture so prominently
displayed in the Trib. Sunday - & very happy to discover
that you are playing a bunch of my things at the library
Saturday. I shall certainly be there. . . It gives me more
happiness than you can imagine, that I did not work in
vain those early promising days. Many are disposed to
give me credit for encouraging American composition and
composers in that period - much fewer to admit that I did
anything in composition myself. You are helping to
rectify that matter, a deed of which I am thoroughly
appreciative.

Although it is still true that Farwell's efforts on behalf of the
American composer are readily acknowledged, unfortunately his
own excellent work as a representative composer of his times is
only recently being recognized.

### The Domain of Hurakan

*The Domain of Hurakan*, Op. 15, published in 1902, is another
early work for piano based on Indian melodies, (Ex. 3a). Farwell
states that this is not to be understood strictly as a tone painting
of the storm. Rather it is a "rhapsodic treatment of certain Indian
melodies for their own sake". This time Farwell uses three themes
of widely divergent origin. The first theme, in a broad swinging
rhythm and with irregularly alternating bars of 3/4 and 4/4 time is
a Vancouver game song. In this game the rhythm accompanies
motions of the arms and hands in passing a small piece of wood
from one hand to another. The opponent must guess in which
hand the stick is hidden, and often heavy stakes are won or lost
through the choice. It is written in A major.

The second theme, more sprightly in D major, is a game song of the Pawnees. The third theme is a Navajo fragment, the "Night Chant", which occurs near the end of the middle or "nocturne" section of the work. The first four bars of the melody of the "nocturne" section consist of a previously unused portion of the first theme of the work, but treated in a different mood, and transposed in key.

The title page includes a quotation: "Over the waters passed Hurakan, the mighty wind, and called forth the earth." Farwell further describes the background for this music:

> These game songs are mere songs of exuberant spirits, without legendary significance. But it is the same spontaneous exuberance exhibited by nature, in the play of the winds and waves and has therefore, been developed in that spirit, which is no other than the spirit of Indian creation myths. The Central American mythological character, Hurakan, has been taken as symbolical of these cosmic and elemental feelings and impulses. It is interesting to know that our word hurricane, which came into use only in the latter part of the 16th century, was borrowed from this name. It will amply repay anyone to . . . read the records of these early American myths.

In this thirteen page composition, Farwell has succeeded in developing the exuberant spirit of the game songs. The initial theme has a sturdy buoyancy featuring a strong rhythmic pattern that Farwell uses effectively throughout. The music suggests the fun the children were having as they played the games. In two instances he uses three staves in order to write an F# octave bass pedal effect which is to be sustained for five full measures while the right and left hands are busy elsewhere above it. (Example 3b. This same music is repeated at bars 124-131.) Farwell interjects quotations at various points in this work. "Proud music of the storm, blast that careers so free," is the first one. A change of key and mood is marked, "I am he that walks with the tender and growing night!" (Ex. 3c) Here Farwell has created a beautiful melodic B major section. The flowing left hand suggests the quiet steadiness of the Indian walking proudly with the night as if he belonged there and is a natural part of it. Eight bars later he adds, "Up from the mystic play of shadows". The music ends impressively (Ex. 3d) with chords starting slowly in the bass and rising in pitch "with intensity" to conclude triumphantly FFF. Surely this work deserves the accolades given in the following reviews.

The reviewer for the Ohio State Journal wrote enthusiastically on December 1, 1903:

> *The Domain of Hurakan* is really a great work, noble in its conception, broad in its architectural plan, rich in its imaginative color, deep in its poetic meanings and it will stand as a great work long after Arthur Farwell has been gathered in.

By January 24, 1904, a critic for *Musical Courier* examined the same score and proclaimed:

> While it embraces the ternary form it is in no way conventional in treatment, containing varied moods in abundance and an atmosphere of romanticism peculiarly its own. The composer has aimed for orchestral effects, and has secured some excellent ones, although the middle section lies somewhat unpianistically for the left hand. [With which this author agrees.] Even this portion is far from impossible, however, and it is compensated for by the beautiful harmonic background effected by it to the exquisite middle theme, which is full of poetic beauty. Farwell is to be especially commended for his understanding of the value of rhythmic contrasts, this being, in the writer's opinion, not only one of the most valuable requisites of musical composition, but one in which it would seem that the national characteristics of America are peculiarly reflected, and which it remains for the "newer school" to develop. One may remark, finally,

that *The Domain of Hurakan* is a work well worthy of gracing any artist's program by the side of those masters whose merit is established.

In his article "The New American Music" for *The North American Review,* Lawrence Gilman also wrote enthusiastically about *The Domain of the Hurakan.* After lauding Henry Gilbert's *The Isle of Fay,* Gilman went on to say :

> Farwell's *Domain of Hurakan,* a study in elemental symbolism, is an equally remarkable piece of writing in a wholly different kind. It is a fantasy conceived in the spirit of the Indian creation-myths, a finely vigorous and notable achievement. There are few more masterly passages in any music of American composition than the superb climax with which the work ends, (Ex. 3d) and the insinuatingly lovely episode in B major, with its eloquent intimation of nocturnal moods. (Ex. 3c)

Farwell sent a copy of *Domain of Hurakan* to Humperdinck, his former teacher, for criticism. On February 17, 1903, Humperdinck wrote "I like your *Hurakan* composition very much. I find it original and well constructed - appealing. The music would be a delight to the piano player. This one copy according to your wishes I have passed on to Mr. R. Stonuss. Have you also sent one to Pfitzner?"[8]

*The Domain of Hurakan* was also arranged for orchestra and impressed one critic with its brilliant color.[9] Program notes for the orchestral version are given in chapter 22.

Alice Fletcher, whose research of Indian music had provided Farwell with themes as well as inspiration, was an occasional visitor in the Farwell home in Newton Center. After hearing Farwell's *Domain of Hurakan* performed in some concert, she wrote thus to Farwell's mother on September 13, 1903:

It has been quite a disappointment to me that my recent visits to Boston and Cambridge have been too short as to preclude the pleasure of calling upon you. I regret it particularly at this time because I should like to tell you how impressed I am with the progress your son is making.

Not only are his gifts becoming more and more apparent in his composition, but his grasp of the opportunity to develop Musical Art in America is beginning to [be] better appreciated and will soon be fully acknowledged.

Yesterday was a noteworthy day. I had the rare pleasure of listening to your son's composition "Hurakan". It is large and masterly. American in scope and feeling. How he grows in power of expression. I could not but exclaim to myself - and I thought of you, and was glad in my heart for you.

His trip this Autumn will surely do him and the country good. How I wish it were in my power to further his plans more effectively than I am permitted to do. But what lies in my power to give, you may be sure he will receive.

I remember with so much pleasure my afternoon in your charming home. I shall hope to see it again some day, and if you ever come to Washington you will be most welcome in my little dwelling place.

Warm greetings to your husband and sister.

### *Impressions of the Wa-Wan Ceremony, Op. 21*

Farwell's popular *From Mesa and Plain* Op. 20, for piano, published in 1905, included *Navajo War Dance, No. 1, Prairie Miniature, Plantation Melody, Wa-Wan Choral,* and *Pawnee Horses*. These were followed by another piano work, his *Impressions of the Wa-Wan Ceremony of the Omahas,* Op. 21. also in 1905. This Wa-Wan ceremony, which held deep significance for its participants, was also very meaningful to Farwell who wrote a lengthy detailed introduction to the work. In view of what ethnologists are saying today about Indian music and mythology, his remarks in 1906 deserve consideration:[10]

> When all is said, when all is done that can be done to-day to crush or to obliterate the race that dwelt in this land before me, there still remains a dignity, a vastness, a freedom, in our memory of the Indian of the Plains, an investiture of heroic circumstance, which seems destined to haunt us until at last it shall be accorded a full and adequate measure of artistic expression. . . . Now that the organic unity of Indian mythology is beginning to record itself through the labors of devoted investigators and students, and the larger motives of the Indian's customs and deeds appear, there is all the more reason to think that the appropriate time and place shall give birth to art of large proportions arising from our memory and knowledge of the race.
>
> However, as it may, the present affords the opportunity for a distant glimpse, at least, of scenes and actions which may one day draw nearer. . . . The ceremony [Wa-Wan Ceremony] known under this name by the Omahas was common to all tribes of plains and Mississippi valley Indians, and may have had a much wider application. Many tribes revered the feathered stem or *calumet*, the emblem of peace and of divine will, by means of which Marquette was enabled to make his voyage down the Mississippi in 1672, in safety. The knowledge of this ceremony is one of the few existing circumstances by which we may differentiate the cosmic scheme, the true mythology of Indian life, from its tangled masses of legend and superstition.
>
> At the base of the ceremony lies the idea of peace among the tribes, or among different gentes of one tribe, as well as an implication of human increase, the blessing of children. The ceremony consists in the formal presentation of the sacred pipes by a man of one tribe or

egens, designated as the father, to a man of another, designated as the son, and is characterized throughout by the dignity and order of the divine powers and relations which are symbolized by the pipes.

In this introduction, Farwell continues describing in great detail the procedure for the ceremony. A shorter version goes on:

To do this, the "father" has to rally about him a considerable party of his family and friends, carefully rehearse many songs traditional in the ceremony, and burdened with many gifts and ceremonial objects, journey to the village of the "Son", where the rites are performed.

The preparation of the journey requires many weeks. Gifts of all kinds must be assembled - the particular products of the tribe - and the songs must be perfectly learned, as it is a point of honor to have them go without a flaw, and moreover their power with the gods is vitiated if they are not sung correctly. The chief ceremonial objects are two feathered stems, the *Calumets*, or symbolic pipes, which have no bore for smoking, but to which are affixed objects representative of cosmic or natural powers which the Indian must regard in carrying out the ceremony.

The journey requires sometimes a number of days. The calumets compel peace, and any war party which is met must give up its expedition and return home. When the village is approached, a runner is sent ahead with a tobacco pouch. If the man designated as Son feels he can honorably accept the ceremony, which depends on how many horses he and his family and friends can give in return for the gifts brought by the Father's party, he accepts the pouch. If he feels that he cannot do so, the Wa-Wan party is hospitably received and sent home after a feast is held.

The ceremony is held in the great "earth-lodge" and lasts four days and nights. Whenever one of the Son's party calls for a song, by this he pledges a horse. The songs are sung four times as the singers circle the lodge, while the calumets are lifted from the wildcat skin on which they have been lain, and waved with symbolic motions. The different days of the ceremony have different significance. One of the features is the descent of the visions, which are beings from a higher sphere who have brought revelation and enlightenment to men. The "ceremony of the dawn" is of particular interest and beauty. The young men of the Son's party are often reticent about calling for songs, because of the necessity of giving a horse in each case; and they are rallied by the old men, who recount historic and traditional instances of generosity.

On the fifth day all the gifts are exchanged, this being done at the hand of a little child, who holds a symbolic place in the ceremony. Then follows a joyous general dance, after which the Wa-Wan party returns home. The return journey is often fraught with danger, as the calumets have been given up, and there is therefore no protection against war parties.

This great ceremony . . . constitutes practically a complete presentation of the mythology of the Plains Indians.

It is important to remember that the entire significance of the Wa-Wan ceremony was expressed through special songs. Space has been given to Farwell's description of the ceremony because a knowledge of it is vital for understanding the music he has written. Secondly, the name given to his Press gains new meaning when viewed in the light of the Wa-Wan ceremony, the term Wa-Wan meaning "to sing to someone". Any pianist wishing to perform these rather simple pieces is urged to study the remaining details printed in Farwell's introduction to the collection.

In preparing these piano pieces, Farwell realized a long-time ambition to give "modern expression" to the spirit and events of the Wa-Wan ceremony. He felt that he pushed the Indian atmosphere and idiom about as far as it will go in modern music, and because of their "experimental psychology", he named the suite *Impressions of the Wa-Wan Ceremony*. He calls these piano pieces *Impressions* because they aim to reflect the peaceful nature of the ceremony, the breadth of the prairie, and serve as an introductory insight into lesser known phases of Indian life. "Peace, fellowship, song, - these gifts of the Great Spirit shall not pass with the Indian, and may long remind us of the efforts and deeds through which he sought to attain them," Farwell concluded.

Included in the *Impressions* are: 1. *Receiving the Messenger*. 2. *Nearing the Village*. 3. *Song of Approach*    4. *Laying Down the Pipes*. 5. *Raising the Pipes*. 6. *Invocation*. 7. *Song of Peace*. 8. *Chorale*. These compositions present more problems for the pianist than the earlier *American Indian Melodies*. The Indian tunes are not so obvious here because Farwell weaves extraneous materials around them which threaten to obliterate the Indian melodies for the unwary player in several instances.

One writer found "interesting and effective treatment of the Indian color" in these pages. He thought that the set of pieces "contains some very atmospheric pages in which the strange monotony that marks the Indian song is obtained by novel uses of diatonic material at once bold and beautiful."[11]

In *Nearing the Village*, Farwell uses 3/8 meter in the treble clef, with 2/8 in the bass where a repeated "A" is played under a sustained "D" for almost the entire first page. Then it drops to play a fifth under a sustained "D" an octave lower.

*Laying Down the Pipes* has two technical difficulties - both in the bass. First is an awkward tremolo pattern for much of the first page followed by a "tremolo with one finger, in imitation of a drum". This instruction is tiresome to execute as given for ten and a half bars. The pianist can of course secure the desired effect by alternating fingers in the usual technic for repeated notes of this kind of pattern.

*Invocation* has a sturdy quality that seems more characteristically "Indian" in its melodic line and rhythm. The music for the *Song of Peace* fulfills the promise of its title. The mixed meters of alternating 2/4 and 3/4 do not interrupt the melodic flow and should not be a problem for a young student. The concluding *Chorale* has a broad religious feeling which is expressed in chords and octaves. Boys studying piano whose hands are large enough to play octaves easily, should enjoy playing most of these Indian pieces.

Farwell continued his correspondence with Humperdinck who was still interested in his former student's work. On January 22 1907 Humperdinck wrote: "Now I have American students more frequently who also study Indian music and it seems therefore that your example has been followed by other students."[12]  That Farwell's  study and use of Indian themes should encourage fledgling composers to do likewise and travel to Germany  with their results is indeed surprising.

### *The Hako String Quartet*

*The Hako* String Quartet, Op. 65, was composed in 1922 and is the only new significant work using Indian themes which Farwell composed after his *Wa-Wan Press* days.  *The Hako* won honorable mention at the Ojai Valley Chamber Music  Festival Prize Competition  which was held in 1926.  In a Pasadena newspaper report by Carolyn Pearson Keszthelyi, we read:

> It is fitting that Arthur Farwell of this city should be honored by the Ojai Valley Chamber Music Festival Prize Competition by conferring honorable mention upon his Indian string quartet, *The Hako* and the performing of it at the festival this month.
>
> The judges, Alfred Hertz, Frederic Jacobi and the members of the San Francisco Chamber Music Society, knew nothing of whose work they were judging.
>
> The fact that Mr. Farwell was the only American  to receive an award in this competition, open to the whole world, and in so difficult and distinguished a field as string quartet writing, is a sufficient indication of his status in the sphere of American music.

The work was produced during the composer's four-year incumbency of the composers' fellowship of the Pasadena Music and Art Society, and is the first particularly notable recognition he has received for any of the great amount of work he did during that period.

Mrs. Elizabeth Coolidge, leading national patroness of chamber music, who foregoes her famous Berkshire festival this year to combine with Frank J. Frost for one in the Ojai, has asked Mr. Farwell for his quartet for performances which she plans to arrange with string quartet organizations in the East.

Mr. Frank J. Frost sent Farwell a congratulatory letter on March 22, 1926, announcing the decision in the contest:

. . . Please accept my congratulations for the distinction attained by your work, and allow me to tell you that I am particularly pleased that from about seventy manuscripts submitted from the whole world, that a composition by an American composer was one of the very best!

In discussing the program for the last concert of the Festival, Mrs. Coolidge and I would like to know how you feel about having your quartet, *The Hako,* performed. The program would be as follows:

Farwell - String Quartet in A major (The Hako)
Mozart - Quartet for Flute, viola and violincello in D Major
    Ojai Valley Prize-winning Quartet of 1926.
Concert to be played by The Chamber Music Society of
    San Francisco.
It gives me great pleasure to enclose an invitation to you for the Festival.  Congratulations again, and many thanks for submitting your work for our Festival.

Evidently Farwell was unable to accept Mr. Frost's invitation to attend the Festival as he wrote to Arthur Cohen on October

17, 1935, that he had not heard the *Hako* performed in public. In replying to Cohen's request to borrow the *Hako* score, Farwell also discussed its music:

> . . . and I do not know whether it will stand up or not. The Pro Arte read it through for me here, marvelous reading of the notes but with no conception of the nature and content of the work, or the Indian spirit. Under Mrs. Coolidge's aegis it was played by the Letz Quartet in Boston, but I could never get any account of the performance or its reception. McKay produced it at the U. of Washington, Seattle, in his very interesting course of chamber music there. It was received with much interest, but I felt that either it was not played convincingly, or is not convincing in itself, - I don't know which. I told you that it was "Honorable mention" at the Ojai Coolidge Festival, California. I was informed that it was a toss-up whether the *Hako* or the Huybrechts work should have the prize - only one being offered. Eighty works were sent in, and these two were regarded as at the top.
>
> But despite this recognition, I am myself not convinced about the work, not having heard it played under my own rehearsing or by anyone who understands the spirit of Indian rhythms and Indian mythology. I am very anxious to find out whether to hang onto this work, or throw it in the wastebasket. I have thought of making an orchestral work of it.
>
> Certain things must be brought to its interpretation before it has even a chance of proving itself, e.g. the immensely reverential spirit of the Indian in general, and his immense dignity, and the unction with which each syllable is taken in his singing. Specifically, I might speak of the reverential attitude of the chanted prayer of the priest which forms the greater part of the introduction; the manifest anger of the woodpecker passage (bottom of p.4 et seq. The rising of the woodpecker's crest in anger

is one of the symbols employed in the ceremony); the
dignity of the processional at J, p.9, where the held note
of 1st vl. indicates the flatness of the plains, the 2nd vl.
the swaying of the feathered stems, viola the inevitable
drum, cello the priests' chant, - each in its own character,
yet making a whole in a certain formal ceremonial spirit;
the mystery in the "place of visions" p.11; the gradual
growth from this point, M, night, with the owl, darkness,
mystery, leading to the "ceremony of the dawn" here
simply the gradual effect of increasing light and
excitement, into the recapitulation, at N, with the main
theme now in a new treatment. (Where this theme first
appears, p. 3, at the beginning of the exposition, it is
supposed to be in a *dream*, the dream which the "son" has
of the coming of the Hako party.) Now at N, it is *fait
accompli*, and in the open, the very opposite of its first
use. The rest is in the spirit of the concluding joyous
dances of the ceremony.

In short, the work has to be dramatized, and
dramatized with an intelligent and sympathetic
understanding. The hearer should feel - "here is
something real, purposeful, expressive, going on, even if
I do not yet understand the full meaning behind it."

I realize that the work is thus hedged about by a
somewhat unusual set of conditions, and am still
wondering whether it can be pulled through by a vigorous
and convincing performance, whether with time and
understanding of its Indian implications, it will at last
carry the day - or simply, whether I have set out to do
too much with a string quartet. Perhaps you can help
me to settle all this. . . .

It was unusual for Farwell to doubt his work. Perhaps his
doubts arose for *The Hako* because it was his first string quartet,
or perhaps he questioned his returning to the use of Indian
themes again after a long absence. Farwell's early training on the
violin had given him a sensitivity for strings so the medium should

not have been a problem. Most likely, the problem with the *Hako* may have been Farwell's difficulty in using traditional notation to indicate all the subtle inflections related to the spirit of the Indian ceremony he was trying to express musically.

He went on in his letter to Mr. Cohen deploring the fact that the Pro Arte quartet still had the original score "somewhere in Belgium or France". Hence, he would have to send photostat copies - white notes on black paper - in answer for Cohen's request to borrow the music.

Further correspondence with Mr. Cohen seems to indicate that his Stringart Quartet of Philadelphia did perform *The Hako* which was well received. Mr. Cohen was very enthusiastic about American music in general and about Farwell's music in particular.

The composition of the *Hako* was undertaken at the suggestion of Joseph Zoellner and dedicated to the Zoellner Quartet. As implied in Farwell's letter to Mr. Cohen, the music is based on the Pawnee ceremony called *The Hako*. The term *Hako* means "breathing mouth of wood" in reference to the drum which was carried by the Hako party to accompany the songs. The Hako ceremony involved the priests, the benediction of Tirawa, Father of All; the "place of visions" and the "place of the powers" - the thunder, lightning, winds, etc. Farwell's letter also gives suggestions for interpreting the music.

Although the Hako ceremony inspired the program for this work, there are other elements that indicate Indian influences. The melodic lines, often pentatonic, include many repeated notes or chant-like effects. The high-to-low melodic contour and irregular phrasing are Indian characteristics. Meters change quickly and short sections contain polymeters. Where irregular meters are used, many syncopated and heavily accented rhythms appear. The monodic character of Indian music is reflected in the frequent unisons; harmonies include some open fifths or fourths.

The well-proportioned sonata form includes an introduction, exposition, development, recapitulation, and coda. Three melodic themes or motives make up the introduction - all within the bounds of a pedal on E, the dominant of the whole. A chant-like pentatonic melody provides the opening theme in several sections, and precedes a short declaratory theme in 5/4 meter. The last theme always appearing in unison, is a fast moving chromatic sequence of sixteenth notes.

The exposition features a flowing pentatonic first group theme in A major in triple meter and appears in four varied ways. A more chant-like second group theme is in compound duple meter. Farwell combines motives and themes from the introduction in the development and uses only short snatches of the first and second exposition themes.

The recapitulation includes the first exposition theme and some of its variations plus the second theme which now is combined with the first melody. The coda includes two of the introductory themes and both of the exposition themes. Both the coda and recapitulation sections feature unusual combinations and artful treatment of themes which summarize a work worthy of winning a prize!

### *Pawnee Horses*

The two piano compositions by Farwell most performed today are *The Navajo War Dance, Number 2* and *Pawnee Horses*.

David Ewen quotes Charles Martin Loeffler as claiming that *"Pawnee Horses* is the best composition yet written by an American".[13]   It was successfully revived in 1944 by John Kirkpatrick who also prepared and performed his edited version of the *Navajo War Dance, No 2*. Both of these works have been performed and recorded by Grant Johannesen who used them as two of his "Russian Encores". Robert Goldsand also featured these Indian-based compositions on many of his piano concerts. Ramon Salvatore currently has been using both of these Indian pieces on his concerts featuring works by American composers.

After reading the newspaper reviews following one of Kirkpatrick's recitals in New York City, Farwell commented thus to the pianist on January 23, 1942:

You certainly did a magnificent job with both of them [Navajo War Dance and Pawnee Horses] extremely difficult works, and I am exceedingly grateful to you. I haven't a word to say in criticism - I couldn't ask for an interpretation in both, any closer to my intentions and desires.

I was glad the papers were unanimous as to your artistry, but wished they might have been a little (!) more intelligent as to the program. One instance as to my pieces - *Herald Tribune* said they "Made no pretense at modernism". *The Times*, "They had obviously been wrecked by ultra-modern trimmings"!! This goes by the name of criticism. Undoubtedly you found just as many jokes *in re* other works on the program.

Farwell gives some background for his *Pawnee Horses*. During one summer when he had been experimenting with some of the materials he had gathered in the Southwest, he was especially drawn to a melody which was an Omaha song. This he described as being so complex and difficult in its rhythm as to render it virtually impossible to be sung by "any known singer except an Indian". Hence he decided it would be best developed as an instrumental number. *Pawnee Horses* was originally sung by an Omaha who had evidently taken so many of the horses of his enemies - the Pawnees - that he was "superiorly indifferent to any further conquests." Upon seeing a number of horses galloping in the distance, he sang, "There go the Pawnee horses; I do not want them. I have taken enough." Farwell claimed, "the melody carries the rhythm of the gallop and spirit of the scene as only an Indian would have conceived it."

The three introductory measures are unusual in structure - especially when one considers that they date from Farwell's Wa-Wan period. (Ex. 4) If the reader will follow the notes connected by dashes, he will discover two uses of the whole-tone scale sounding one eighth note apart, one scale in the right hand and the other in the upper part of the left. Whether it was the special intent of the composer to use whole-tone scales here, or it was instead just a by-product  of the harmonic writing, is a question.  These three measures also serve as melodic relief from the vigorous rhythm of the Omaha melody which Farwell writes for the left hand thumb in the opening section.  The primitive melody proceeds downward as is typical in many Indian melodies. After it reaches its resting point, the three measures used as an introduction slip in again and lead to the repetition of the theme, played forte this time by the right hand in octaves for a climax. This, too, dies down to be followed by the same introductory measures in pianissimo with an extension that fades away in the high treble - possibly to suggest the horses disappearing in the distance.

Farwell responded to public comments about the nature of Indian music by saying:

> Too many people think of the American Indian only as a "savage".  I had in my Indian music depicted many phases of Indian life that were far from savage, but true to its quaint, poetic and picturesque aspects, as well as to its mythological conceptions.  Being criticized because of these matters, as being untrue to this "savage" Indian nature, I wrote the *Navajo War Dance* in 1905, in the hope of gratifying my critics in this respect. . . . I have employed bare 4ths in the work, as I have heard the Navajos sing this dance in 4ths.

### Navajo War Dance, No. 2

The *Navajo War Dance No. 2* is one of the last compositions from the *Wa-Wan Press* era and Edgar Lee Kirk thinks this is one of the very best compositions that Farwell ever wrote.[14]   Another critic commented that "The barbaric crudity is still further implied in the *Navajo War Dance* where Farwell has renounced almost all defined harmony, preserving only the vigorous rhythm of the dance in the bold intervals of the Indian melody."[15]   John Kirkpatrick's edited version  was published in 1947 by Music Press. Inc.

The dance is built on two simple contrasting melodies noted in Example 5a. From these Farwell created a three-part form, the first and third parts being built around example 5a and the middle section on the theme as shown in example 5b. The sections are approximately the same in length. Both melodies are strongly centered on E, but Farwell did not fight this tendency. Instead, he builds up tension by utilizing the lack of any key. Edgar Kirk compares this work with Ravel's *Bolero* and points out that Farwell "did the same thing that Ravel did", but Farwell completed his dance in 1904 - long before Ravel wrote his famous *Bolero* in 1928.[16]

In order to make use of tension created by the lack of modulation, Farwell manipulated the dynamics. Kirk noted that because Farwell was writing for a single instrument, he could not develop a long sustained crescendo of the kind Ravel did with orchestral instruments in his *Bolero*. However, Farwell found his solution in the fact that the dance utilized two contrasting sections and he made each one rise to its own climax. The leanness of texture and dynamic marks at the beginning of the two sections help the performer in keeping the volume level down. From these measures, both dynamics and texture build up, increasing in sound, and are reinforced by an ostinato in the first section to give the dance an awesome power and vitality. (See Example 5c for the concluding page.) The technical demands on the pianist here are considerably more than what was required in piano pieces written only a few years earlier. The challenge in this dance is to execute the dynamics in such a way that one sustains the increase in volume and tension to the very end! The results when well performed are exciting indeed.

In May 1947, Farwell sent a copy of the revised *Navajo War Dance No. 2*, to Rudolph Ganz, president of Chicago Musical College. Ganz, also a concertizing pianist, didn't have time to acknowledge the music until August 12, 1948, when he apologized profusely for his delay in writing, and expressed his enthusiasm for the music saying, "I think it is an excellent piece, and I am adding it to the collection of recently written American works to be presented to the student body in the library of our college in September."

One of Farwell's friends was the Indian poet, Charles O. Roos, who gave Farwell a special edition of his book of poems. From this book Farwell selected four poems to set to music: *The Ravens are Singing, A Dawn Song, Dark Her Lodge Door*, and *Invocation to the Sun God*. The first two songs were published eventually by G. Schirmer in 1929, but Ditson published *Dark Her Lodge Door* earlier in 1927. The *Invocation to the Sun God* has never been published. Because these songs are not based on real Indian themes, *The Ravens are Singing* and *A Dawn Song* are reviewed in the discussion of Farwell's art songs in chapter 18. (See example 20.)

Earlier in January 25, 1926, Mr. Roos, who had been concerned about publication of *A Dawn Song*, wrote to Farwell reporting that Forster Music Co. of Chicago had turned it down. He tried to console Farwell about the matter by writing that the new editor "turned down some of Grunn's, Lieurance, and others. . . . He is very partial to modern stuff - jazz etc." He urged Farwell to try John Church or Carl Fischer instead. Roos's comments about Cadman are worth noting:

> Last week I got an order from Cadman for another Operetta. I do not believe Cadman will write many more songs, as he is of the opinion that it will be better to devote all of his time to the writing of Opera and Operettas. Maybe he is right, but I do not like to see him give up the song writing, for this is his best field.

Farwell had other Indian contacts. The Indian baritone, Os-ke-non-ton, a Mohawk chieftain who sang Farwell's Indian songs, wrote to him February 9, 1926, using stationery designed to look like birchbark, to report his successful concerts. He enclosed a recital program to be given April 5th at Town Hall in New York along with some of the many complimentary press reviews he had received. He noted that he was singing Farwell's *Inketunga's Thunder Song* and asked for more songs to add to his future programs. He was sailing for Germany April 10th and requested letters of introduction to Farwell's acquaintances over there who might be helpful to his career. He signed his letter "from your old friend". Farwell cooperated willingly as he often did.

An unusual calling card in Farwell's collection, is one with an original autograph by the famous Indian Apache chief, Geronimo. It was generally known that the man could not read or write, but he had learned how to print his name in big capital letters. While Geronimo was "in captivity" at Ft. Sill, Oklahoma, he became something of a commercial property.[17]  During this period, Geronimo made extra money by selling photographs and other items, possibly his autograph as well.  A note by Farwell accompanying the autograph states that "This autograph is authentic and has been in my possession for many years."  Since the notation is from Farwell's Los Angeles address, we can date these remarks to the early 1920's, and assume that he acquired the autograph much earlier.  It is very possible that Farwell attended the Pan-American exhibition at Buffalo in the summer of 1901, or the Louisiana Exposition at St. Louis in 1904 where Geronimo made public appearances.  Farwell's interest in Indians during these years could have prompted his curiosity to investigate Geronimo's exhibition at which time he secured the autograph.

### Choral Arrangements for the Westminster Choir

John Finley Williamson, conductor of the Westminster Choir, (Princeton, New Jersey), commissioned Farwell to arrange some Indian songs for his choir. By March 10, 1937, Williamson had received the *Navajo War Dance* and *The Old Man's Love Song*, and wrote that he liked them both and wanted to use them. "You are an artist in that you do not mix a white man's knowledge of harmony with Indian music. It will give us great joy to sing these numbers." He concluded:

Do you wish to publish them before we use them or shall we use them from manuscript? My hope is that you will publish them so when we use them the people over the country may purchase them as I know they will be very popular.

Farwell decided to have his choruses published and arranged two more Indian songs for an eight-part a cappella choir of mixed voices for Dr. Williamson: *Pawnee Horses,* and *The Mother's Vow.* Farwell used Indian vocables in all of the songs and added some English phrases to create stunning effects. In *The Old Man's Love Song,* Farwell works bits of the melody into an introduction of the choral version using only vocables for the first 13 bars. A tenor solo then carries the tender love song melody on more vocables for five bars when it changes to words. He develops the original melody into a nine page concert piece.

In arranging *Pawnee Horses* (example 4) for choir, Farwell held close to the piano score. This is true for *The Navajo War Dance* as well. These Indian choruses should be just as popular with choral groups today, if not more so, as when the Westminster Choir performed them.

These works were published by Schirmer in 1937. Farwell was hard pressed to complete the arrangements and do the proof reading on the scores before his deadline. By May 13th, he had completed the last song in the group and sent Carl Engel at Schirmers the necessary corrections, program notes, and pronunciations for the Indian vocables. He reminded Engel that the unusual character of these songs made certain explanations very important to their proper rendering. He insisted that each song should have its proper program notes printed along with the music, "presumably inside the front cover".    (This was done.) Writing further to Engel, Farwell stated:

> You did not say anything about a piano part, *for rehearsal only,* in the songs. I wrote one in the *Mother's Vow,* which you can use or not, as you please. It doesn't make any difference to me. The Westminster Choir got along without such a rehearsal piano part, and no one ever mentioned its absence. I imagine that *a cappella* choir members are mostly all good readers, and don't have

to have their ears whanged at to know how printed music ought to sound. If such piano parts are required, I can of course make them; it is practically nothing but a matter of literal transcription, with occasional concessions to the number of fingers on the hand.

Of course the 28th, when the students at the school disperse, is painfully close at hand, but I know Dr. Williamson will be willing to mail copies out to the students at their homes, if it is the only possible way to get them into their hands. They have to memorize them perfectly during the summer, to give them the following season.

Farwell reported his recent publication success to his old friend, A. Walter Kramer at Galaxy Music Corporation, on May 23, 1937:

Engel ate up the a cappella Indian scores, took all four of them without looking at them. You see they had copyrights on some of the same titles, as they appeared as piano works, and it would have made complications to have them appear anywhere else. That is why I did not plan to publish them myself in the first place, but Schirmers were sore on me, and I wanted to give you first whack if it had worked out that way. Anyway, if you want something from me on your catalogue any time, you can have it . I can't possibly draw and print all the compositions I have finished.

I certainly had one great time in New York and Princeton. Saw about everybody I wanted to except Downes and Gilman. They were both away at festivals. But I left Downes some data, and he gave me a dandy story in the Times, with a photo, [about Farwell's lithograph press venture] last Sunday, the 16th.

By May 5, 1946, Farwell had reason to bring his daughter, Sara, up to date on his work with Indian-related compositions:

And now I am to be commissioned to compose some
more Indian choruses for the Westminster Choir, when I
go to Princeton next Thursday. They have had such
tremendous success with the ones I did for them before,
that they want new ones for their tours. Toscanini heard
them do my *Navajo War Dance* and said something to the
effect that it was the best American composition he had
heard. He wanted to orchestrate it, but found that as
written for the voices it won't transcribe rightly for
orchestra! I guess I'll make an independent orchestration
(i.e. independent of the vocal treatment) and show it to
him.

Then in the summer I am to go down to Roanoke
Island, N. Carolina, and witness the drama of the *Lost
Colony*, a revival again, now that the war is over, and get
a commission to compose a new opening Indian scene for
it. The existing one doesn't satisfy them.

These can not be very large commissions financially -
but they will help out, and will give me again the strange
feeling of *being wanted* as a composer.

At 74 years of age, Farwell had reason to reflect on his
creative output and the lack of its performance. How he must
have longed for the recognition he felt his compositions deserved.
What comfort he derived from feeling wanted again!

The four Indian songs listed earlier that Farwell arranged
became a vital part of the Westminster Choir repertoire and
fulfilled Dr. Williamson's prediction for their popularity. He
eventually approached Farwell for more Indian music and Farwell
responded with *The Indian Scene* and *Navajo War Dance, No. 2*
in 1946. However, Farwell had many problems with their
publication and his files show a contract with Carl Fischer which
he turned down. Among other things, it seems that the publisher
required him to surrender his regular 10% royalty fees for the
editorial services which they had asked Dr. Williamson to provide.
Farwell realized that Fischer intended to capitalize on the

Williamson name to promote the music and hence had asked him to be the editor of the new "series". Farwell had no objection to Dr. Williamson being paid, as long as the money did not come from his own royalties. Considerable correspondence followed until an angry Farwell finally balked at dealing with Fischer and refused to sign any contract.

By May 4, 1947 Farwell was able to report to Sara on the performance of these Indian works:

> The performance of my choruses by the Westminster Choir came off quite sensationally I think, and Dr. Williamson made some nice remarks about me from the platform.

> Yesterday my *Navajo War Dance No. 2* came off the press - the original *piano* piece - after waiting just forty years for publication. This from "Music Press", Richard Dana's enterprise. It comes out as one of a series of American piano works under the editorship of John Kirkpatrick. I'm hoping more of my works will come out by the year 2000.

> The a cappella choruses were to come out as part of a series under Dr. Williamson's editorship - but Fischer presented me with such an outrageous contract that I withdrew them. Williamson is extremely anxious for me to do a lot more works of the same or general sort - Says I'm the only person in existence who can do the Indian things the way I do. So I shall make the two performed . . . the nucleus of a series of similar works. . . .

Farwell wrote Sara further about the progress of his works on July 6, 1947:

> My *Navajo War Dance No. 2*, is out now, from Music Press, a young going institution. Jeanne Behrend (who made the records of my No. 1, and *Sourwood Mountain* for Victor) was in from South America where she has been playing my things with great success, and now wants

more of them. Also John Kirkpatrick was here for lunch, Saturday, and has taken up my concerto *Mountain Vision* (prize work) to look over. So little things move along - but only to remind me how much I've got that hasn't been moved along yet! . . .

Even a casual look at Farwell's list of works should convince one of the wealth of untried music that "hasn't been moved along yet!"

In Farwell's letter to Arnold Schwab on February 3, 1951, giving him some of his memories of James Huneker, the critic, he writes of their disagreement on the importance of Indian music:

> I had no piano at this time, and Miss Porter kindly let me work with hers during her absence from the apartment. On one occasion I was working on a composition on an American Indian theme. Huneker, [who lived in the adjoining apartment] chancing to meet Miss Porter next day in the elevator, asked her if it was not an Indian composition on which I was working. She told him it was, whereupon he said, "You know, don't you, that there is nothing in it?" - meaning in developments of Indian music generally. Miss Porter said to me afterwards, "Who is he, to make decisions of that sort?" There for once, I caught him wrong as a critic, or perhaps rather as a theorist, for as I was no pianist, he could have heard only my fumblings with the instrument, in details of the composition, and not the work as a whole, adequately rendered. For my Indian works have been among my most successful compositions, in piano, choral and orchestral forms, both in the United States and abroad, and now after fifty years, are increasing in number of performances and acceptance. (It was only Nov. 17th last that my *Navajo War Dance No. 2* had a most successful performance in Paris, at "Le Centre de Premieres Auditions," which means that it will be performed in a number of the principal European cities. The

Westminster Chorus has given four of my Indian *a cappella* choruses very widely through several seasons. My *Domain of Hurakan* for orchestra has had many hearings, and various pianists . . . are programming my Indian works. It is in fact a matter of regret to me that my Indian works are being brought to performance more widely than my very greatly numerous other works, not based on folk themes of any kind. The element of novelty coupled with a wave of Americanism probably accounts for this.)

I am mentioning this, in parenthesis, not with any idea of publication, but only that you will see that Huneker was wrong in his supposition concerning the possibilities of developing Indian themes. I think he was influenced by Krehbiel, [critic for the N.Y. Tribune, 1880-1923] who kept incessantly howling, particularly against me, that Indian music was "only ritual, and had no relation to art." I never held the matter against Huneker in the slightest, as I liked him very much as a man and a mind, and honored him for his achievements. I just know he was mistaken in this particular matter, and never argued it with him. I think he would have changed his mind completely if he could have heard my Indian works well performed.

Farwell's concluding sentence is the key to his Indian works. "Well performed" means that they must be performed with sensitivity to the background from which the original themes were taken. Farwell has provided all these details in the introductions to his Indian-based compositions to aid the performer. A careful study of the information supplied should lead to a better performance of these impressive compositions.

Because Farwell's Indian-based compositions played a significant role in his life and work, all of the Indian works, including varying forms of some melodies, are listed in a separate section of the Farwell catalog, as well as in the sections on their respective musical genre.

## Other Folk Music

Farwell set out to prove that America does have distinctive and beautiful folk-song, "born of a life amidst our own forests, prairies, and mountains, which may form a basis for musical art-works worthy of larger dimensions." He pointed out in a *Wa-Wan Press* introduction of 1902 that "in all times and all places great musical art works have almost invariably been but more highly organized forms developed from simpler modes of folk-expression." He gave examples of how the great composers of all nations such as Josquin, Bach, Beethoven, Dvořák, Grieg, Tchaikovsky, and especially Wagner, in their native lands, "drew their diverse qualities, in many cases the arrangements of the notes of their themes, from the simple songs of the people."

However, Farwell often expressed his disappointment that his reputation as a composer rested primarily on his Indian inspired compositions. When the nation was embroiled in the discussion of Nationalism in music, he staunchly insisted that *all* kinds of indigenous musics should serve American composers in opening new avenues for expression. To that end, Farwell did extensive studies in music of the negroes, the cowboys, and tunes of Spanish - Californian origin. His files reveal a collection of cowboy songs in particular. In most instances, he had only the words, but these had caught his fancy and pencil sketches suggest how he planned to use some of them.

### Cowboy Songs

*The Lone Prairee*, a cowboy song recorded by Henry Gilbert, was harmonized by Farwell and published in 1905 by the *Wa-Wan Press*. Farwell considers this to be probably the first cowboy song to be printed. It is in the minor mode with a rhythmic snap which one writer says is:

> . . . peculiar to negro music, though it is in triple rhythm,
> and acquires a certain exotic flavor by the constant use of
> the minor seventh instead of the leading tone.    Its

outstanding ethnic character, if it has any, is, however, Irish. It is not improbable that the cowboy song should have acquired a certain tone from the Indian, though a generous admixture of the Celtic idiom is most certainly to be expected from the racial character of the cast.[18]

Farwell said that he had a great deal of difficulty in writing the accompaniment for this song.[19] He wanted to provide for the necessary rhythmic license of the melody so that the free and easy way in which it needed to be sung would preserve its original mood. To do this without interrupting an accompanying effect which he felt should suggest "the continuity, the unbroken loneliness of the plains," was a challenging problem. After throwing away several accompaniments entirely, over which he had spent much time and effort, he solved the problem by "the use of a species of compound tremolo which alone could represent the constant limitless plain, while the melody could move along in its own characteristic way." (Example 6) Accordingly, he used chords in tremolo to support the tune through two verses with the introductory bars being repeated between them.

A ballad specialist, Phillips Barry of Newbury, Vermont, wrote to Farwell on October 29, 1905, complimenting him on the accompaniment of *Lone Prairee* which he liked very much. "It seems to me to be exactly what the melody requires, a sort of background, over which it passes, like the wind of the Lone Prairee". Mr. Barry supplied Farwell with the words for four verses for *The Lone Prairee* as well as texts for *The Ocean Burial* and *On Springfield Mountain*. The latter he said originated in West Massachusetts in the 18th century and "has since passed into oral tradition".

Farwell's files hold a considerable number of texts for cowboy songs. He had obviously spent many hours researching tunes and variations of the same text, but did not have the time to develop his ideas. In a letter to Mr. J. L. Hubbell on August 18, 1908, he wrote for help in "making a complete collection of cowboy songs." He enclosed a list showing what he had collected from his sojourn in the West and asked for assistance in completing certain fragments of the songs. He declared, "It is becoming more and more difficult to get these songs, which ought to be saved before it is too late; and I shall very greatly appreciate any help you may be able to give me. . . . "

Farwell discovered that very few of the cowboy melodies were in permanent form, and the texts even less so. It became evident that cowboy songs were rarely sung twice in the same way and in many cases the melody varied with each verse. True, they all displayed the essential characteristics of folk music which Anne H. Master lists: "oral transmission, simplicity, a direct point of view, and a primary concern with the fundamentals of the life they depicted."[20]

John A. Lomax (1867-1948) shared Farwell's concern for preserving the cowboy's ballads from extinction.[21] When Lomax was gathering cowboy songs for his collection *Cowboy Songs and Other Frontier Ballads*, he discovered, as Farwell did before 1908, the same problems of varying verse fragments and changing tunes for each verse. In preparing his book, Lomax solved this difficulty by selecting and putting together in one song, what he deemed to be the best lines from different versions, all telling the same story. He sought to produce a book that would be popular and was not concerned about scholarship. Published first in 1910, Lomax's book met with tremendous success. While there is no evidence that he and Farwell ever met, their common interest in cowboy songs indicates the nation's growing interest in American folk music and the need to find and preserve it.

Farwell's list of cowboy songs for which he had complete words and music was as follows (notes are Farwell's):

1. *Cowboy's Lament, Wunct in my saddle*
2. *It was a long and tiresome go.*
3. *Up on the Trail. I was up on the trail on the 20th of June*
4. *I'll drink and I'll gamble (I know only one stanza to this)*
5. *O come now my fair maidens.*
6. *A bunch of jolly cowboys discussing plans of ease.*
7. *The Cowboy's sweet by and bye. (Air: My Bonnie)*

8. *Jane, O Jane, My red headed Jane.*
9. *Good ol'a Tige is a good ol'a hound.* (Evidently negro origin)
10. *My wife has a fever.*
11. *Dying Cowboy.* (Have complete words but music of refrain only.)
12. *Fanny Moore. (Old Irish Tune.)*
13. *The Zebra Don.*

Farwell stated that he had the words complete for the following, but *wanted the music*:

14. *The Cattle King's Prayer*
15. *Sam Bass*
16. *The Texas Ranger* (Music would be the same as *The Texas Cowboy*)
17. *The Texas Cowboy.*
18. *The Change is Great, You See. No more the herd of long horns.*
19. *Ramon de Campoamor.* (Spanish)
20. *The Texas Bomer.* (Bummer or Boomer?) A widely different version of *Texas Cowboy* apparently.
21. *Bonnie Black Bess.*
22. *The Lone Star Cow-Trail.*
23. *Roll yer tails and roll'em high,*
    *We'll all be angels by and bye.*
24. *Arkansas Traveler*

Some friend supplied Farwell with seven verses for another cowboy song not on his list called *The Cowpunchers*. No evidence of music for the words is in the files.

However, these cowboy songs are found among his manuscripts: *It was a Long and a Tiresome Go*, which he had first recorded and then harmonized; *Up on the Trail*, also recorded and harmonized, but the text is missing; and *Wunct in my Saddle*, which is a variation of *Streets of Laredo*. The latter he recorded to be harmonized, but prepared only the melody and the words.

In reviewing the evidence Farwell found on cowboy songs, one can agree with Anne Masters' quotation from Sarah D. Lowrie who wrote about the subject matter for cowboy songs in the *Philadelphia Ledger*.[22]   She found that there was one joke - a fall from a bronco; one sorrow - a lonely grave; one temptation - cutting loose in a prairie town; and one business - getting the little dogies back and forth to new lands.  The purpose for singing also tended to fall into two groups:  a) day-herding songs when the goal was to keep the cattle moving.   These have a loud refrain.   2) Night-herding songs with the purpose of lulling the cattle to sleep and preventing a stampede.   These were always softly sung songs.   Masters claimed that the rhythms of the cowboy songs are unique, approximating the rhythm of the Western horse; "The cowboy had to sing in time to his horse or not at all."[23]

### Folk Songs of the West and South

Other folk music Farwell used includes the Negro spiritual *Moanin' Dove* which is number one in his collection *Folk Songs of the West and South*, published in the *Wa-Wan Press* in 1905.  *The Lone Prairee* is number three in this collection.  Also included is a Negro melody, *De Rocks a-Renderin'*, two Spanish inspired pieces - *The Hours of Grief (Las Horas de Luto)* and *The Black Face (La Cara Negra)* - and *Bird Dance Song* from the Cahuilla tribe of Indians.

*Moanin' Dove* is a tune better known as *Sometimes I Feel Like a Motherless Child*.  Farwell's version is based on a Negro "spiritual" collected and recorded by Alice Haskell.  He has prepared the notation with careful attention to the rhythmic patterns and supplied a piano accompaniment featuring simple chordal movement to create a slow rocking effect.  The bass frequently uses a fifth alternating with a sixth in pairs.  This accompaniment remains the same for all four verses, but Farwell changes the rhythmic patterns in the first verse to fit the words and uses another rhythmic pattern consistently for the last three verses.  A commentator noted Farwell's "remarkable utilization of the Negro element in *Moanin' Dove*, . . . beautiful in its atmosphere of crooning sadness."[24]

The author's Farwell Collection contains an orchestral version of *Moanin' Dove* which is scored in his handwriting, but not signed. Another orchestration is also available with an added note stating, "Orchestrated by Benjamin Lambord." He was another Wa-Wan composer (1879-1915) who evidently found an interest in this song. His orchestration is based on Farwell's melodic notation and harmonization. It covers nine pages of music paper and seems to have been planned with variations, because the piano enters as soloist on an unfinished version.

In his preface to *De Rocks A-Renderin'*, Farwell writes that the pure Negro "spiritual" is not found where the Negro lives in contact with whites. "The origin of the melodies is unknown, but the words are often improvised anew at the religious meetings where the spirituals are sung." *De Rocks A-Renderin'* is from the islands off the South Carolina coast, "where the Negroes do not see a white man oftener than once a month." Farwell has derived his harmony for the accompaniment from "a consideration of the dramatic or poetic content, and not from the harmony book."

In the accompaniment, Farwell uses the right hand to undergird the melody with chords that outline it. (See complete song in Example 7.) The left hand plays tremolo octaves in rising half steps for the verse section. The chorus has sustained chords that again carry the melody.

The *Bird Dance Song*, although Indian-based, is discussed here because it is included in this particular collection of folk tunes. It has an unusual setting. (See complete song in Example 8.) The text is made up of meaningless syllables used by the Cahuilla tribe to imitate various birds. Farwell suggests that the song be sung "low and tremulous, flute-like and in obvious imitation of low weird bird-tones". Where triplets occur in the melody, he recommends "a mere quaver of the voice, not a distinct triplet". He uses whimsical touches in the harmonization and ends the score with an adventuresome unresolved dissonance, thus creating in 1905 what might be called Farwell's first "radical" Indian setting.

The two Spanish Californian folk-songs in the collection especially interested Lambord:

> Their Spanish character is unmistakable, though the tone is a little more plaintive than we are wont to expect from their original Southern habitat. *The Hours of Grief* and *The Black Face* are both set in the minor, and the 2/4 (quasi 6/8) measure, with the characteristic dotted rhythm, only accentuates the sombreness of the sentiment. Syncopation is used sparingly, at the end of a phrase only. The subject of the latter song - the lament of a dusky youth over his unhappy love for a white beauty, would bespeak negro origin too, and the general character of the piece is certainly reminiscent of the Creole dance songs with their Habanera rhythm.[25]

Perhaps Farwell's most popular work based on a non-Indian folk tune is his *Sourwood Mountain* as discussed in Chapter 19 with Farwell's piano music. A piano piece using cowboy tunes is *Prairie Miniature* also discussed in the same chapter.

### Spanish Songs of Old California

Farwell spent many months collecting old tunes of Spanish origin. One result of his collaboration with Charles Lummis is the collection *Spanish Songs of Old California* which was published in 1923. Of the more than 450 unrecorded Spanish folk songs of the Southwest that Lummis gathered, Farwell selected fourteen to harmonize for the collection. In general, he reverted to a simple equivalent of the native guitar for the accompaniments in order to preserve the "essential character and primitive power of the songs". In the introduction to the collection, Lummis wrote:

> For 38 years I have been collecting the old, old songs of the Southwest. . . . It was barely in time; the very people who taught them to me have mostly forgotten them, or died, and few of their children know them. My

versions are authentic, both in music and text; and Mr. Farwell's pianoforte accompaniments are of his unsurpassed sympathy and skill.

Here are 14 Songs of 14 kinds - songs that Fremont the Pathfinder heard and loved; and ahead of him, Dana, of "Two Years Before the Mast." They range from the unfeigned Mother Goose of "Quelele" and "Zapatero", through the magic pertness of "Pepa", the shrewd "Primavera", the passion of "Magica Mujer", and "Adios Amores", the wistful "Pena Hueca", the Heine-like "Barquillera", the whimsical "Charro". Spanish lends itself notably to the onomatopoeic. . . . Two admirable examples here are the sway of the hammock in "La Hamaca" and the pelt of the rain in "Capotin". One cannot help but love these songs - the homely quaintness of some, the sheer beauty of others, and the charm of them all.

These songs "belong to be sung in Spanish"; but I have written an English version which will sing, and still preserve the sense very closely - the most difficult form of literary gymnastics I have ever found. . . . At any rate, we shall have saved a heritage of lasting beauty, to which abler poets may do better justice.

Plans to produce a second volume were mentioned in Lummis's letter to Farwell dated January 31, 1926. Lummis included a summary of the song book's business status for the previous twenty six and a half months. At that time he expressed hope that they could "get at the Second book within mebbe 10 days." He also probed the idea of getting sheet publications of the songs. However, preparation of the second book was delayed because of Lummis's poor health.

On November 20, 1926, he responded to Farwell again who had asked him for a reckoning of his share of the royalties:

. . . I enclose $20. This makes $70 you've had in royalties in 1926. Under our agreement I should have had $140; but I haven't drawn a cent of royalty for myself this year. Sales are so slow that even our very modest "overhead" keeps our balance low.

I've been having a wonderful time with my Indian and other friends as it were [sic] the Harvest Home of 40 years. It is unspeakably beautiful the way they treat me. And this week I have been able to "Do the Impossible" - & to bind the Pueblo Indians and the Indian Bureau to a plan of cooperation.

I am asking Skeath to take 500 1st Bk - & if he will I'll put on 500 more. Our stock is down to almost zero. As soon as I have the mentality to do it, I'll turn out the translations for 2nd Bk.

While sales of the collection may not have been large during those years, the book has had a valuable place in the California schools and elsewhere. Farwell used some of these songs in his Community chorus work where they were especially well received. They are still recommended for their appropriate settings with English translations where folk songs of this origin are desired. The Southwest Museum in Los Angeles, founded by Lummis, still keeps these fourteen songs in print and available for purchase.

Gustav Reese[26] wrote to Farwell on September 1, 1936, that Schirmer's had received application for permission to include *Hammock* (Ex. 9) from his *Spanish Songs of Old California* for a book intended for use in public schools in Texas. Farwell was happy to agree to a new contract for its use and pleased to know this music would be learned by school children.

The results of Farwell's successful use of folk materials proved its inspirational value, and other colleagues such as Henry F. Gilbert, Harvey Worthington Loomis, and Charles Wakefield Cadman, accepted the challenge to use indigenous materials in their compositions. Such use was all part of the movement for a national music that developed at the turn of the 20th century and enriched the musical life of our country. Here Farwell's role in awakening composers and American audiences to the potentials of our native musical assets is commendable. New studies on the music of American Indians continue to appear.[27]

**Example 1.** *The Old Man's Love Song*

# The Old Man's Love Song.

Harmonized by
ARTHUR FARWELL.

**Example 2.   *Dawn***

**Example 3a.** *The Domain of Hurakan*

# THE DOMAIN OF HURAKAN.

"Over the waters passed Hurakan, the mighty wind, and called forth the earth."

ARTHUR FARWELL Op.15.

Exultingly, with accent and motion.

NOTE: *The management of the pedal, except in a few instances, is left to the player.*
Copyright 1902, by The Wa-Wan Press.

**Example 3b.** *The Domain of Hurakan*, **measures 20-27.**

**Example 3c.** *The Domain of Hurakan*, **measures 77-79.**

**Example 3d.** *The Domain of Hurakan,* **measures 182-194.**

**Example 4.** *Pawnee Horses*

**Example 5a.** *Navajo War Dance No. 2.* **First theme, 7 bars.**

**Example 5b.  Second theme, measures 53-66.**

**Example 5c.** *Navajo War Dance, No. 2*

M.P.-P.1-8

**Example 6.** *The Lone Prairee*

**Example 7.** *De Rocks A-Renderin'*

# DE ROCKS A-RENDERIN.'

Negro "spiritual" recorded by
ALICE HASKELL.

Harmonized by
ARTHUR FARWELL.

Broadly, impressively.

When yo' see de rocks a-ren-der-in,' In dat day, In dat day,
When yo' see de moon a-bleed - in,' In dat day, In dat day,
When yo' hear de trump a-call - in,' In dat day, In dat day,

O —— sin - nah, —— Why will yo' die in dat day?

**Example 8.**  *Bird Dance Song*

BIRD DANCE SONG.
CAHUILLA TRIBE.

Recorded by
CHAS. F. LUMMIS.

Harmonized by
ARTHUR FARWELL.

Moderately, with motion.

**Example 9.** *La Hamaca* (The Hammock)

La Hamaca
(The Hammock)

# Chapter 18

# Farwell's Vocal Music

## Art Songs

Farwell idolized Franz Schubert and greatly admired his songs which he had carefully studied. So when Humperdinck told Farwell, "You have a great talent for writing songs," he was encouraged to continue his efforts in song-writing. Farwell recorded this compliment in his journal and added "I wish I could write even one song as good as the immortal Schubert's."

Farwell found song-writing a meaningful outlet for expressing his inner feelings. His early journals revealed this as he reacted to youthful love affairs by composing a song for his current girl friend. As his skills matured, so did his songs. They often reflect stylistically some of the trends in the development of the American Art Song from 1895 through 1949.

Farwell's choice of poetry for his songs was usually excellent. His files contained a folder of poems that appealed to him, written by little known poets, but his personal library included volumes by the major poets whose works he sought more often for inspiration.

In his early songs, Farwell turned to the German writers Johanna Ambrosius and Heinrich Heine. He also composed settings for three poems by A. Mary F. Robinson. He dedicated several songs to a girl friend, Gertrude Hall, who wrote the words for his song *To Be A Child Once More*.

Farwell himself, wrote poetry which he used quite successfully for some songs. Beatrice Ayer, a love who eventually became Mrs. George Patton, Jr., was Farwell's inspiration for both words and music in *Transfiguration*. The song was never published.

Although Farwell's early songs were sometimes related to his love affairs, other songs were the result of times when he was strongly moved by nature. The grandeur of western mountains especially stirred him and we see evidence of his ardor in *Mountain Song*. This was a later major orchestral effort containing several chorales, for which he also wrote the words.

Farwell was intensely loyal to his country and created original lines for two patriotic ballads that were prompted by World War I. Later, he composed both words and music for more patriotic songs during World War II.

"... A song exposes the composer's craft of melody, harmony, and rhythm, above all his gift to limn a poem's quality,"[1] said Ernest Bacon. Farwell's gift to do just that is evident in most of his songs. Indeed his choice songs may well be among his best work and their accessibility should promote their performance. The author has derived much pleasure in singing many of them and we now consider a sampling.

The system to designate pitch is as follows: capital letters are used for pitches within the octave below middle c (CDEFGAB); lower case letters designate pitches from middle c to b above (cdefgab); thereafter a number 1 is added for the next seven pitches (c1, d1, e1, f1, g1, a1, b1). High c becomes c2 but this pitch is not found in the Farwell songs.

### The Early Art Songs 1895-1907

Farwell's first songs, published without opus numbers, show the influence of his early training under Chadwick. These reflect the Victorian parlor song in the choice of sentimental texts so popular at that time, as well as in the settings. Farwell used the pseudonym John Francis for two songs: *Blow, Golden Trumpets* and *The Message of the Lilies*, published in 1897. For other songs published in the years 1895 through 1898, Farwell used his own name, but still listed no opus number. Of these, *Strow Poppy Buds* is a song noteworthy for its haunting melody which flows fluently through the two verses written by A. Mary F. Robinson. (See example 10.)    Set in modified - strophic style the second verse builds to a climax by repeating in sequence a half step higher, for the line "But do not mock the heart that starv'd to death". This work was dedicated to Gertrude Hall in Boston.. The music already reveals Farwell's potential as a gifted song-writer.

During these early years of composing, Farwell translated into English two German poems by Johanna Ambrosius and set them to music. The songs reflect his Germanic training and may have been an attempt to prove his capability to compose "serious songs". German texts were often used by other American composers such as MacDowell and Chadwick at this time. Farwell composed eight songs to German texts which he set impeccably. The first effort, *Silenced are my Songs*, (*Dahin*), published in 1898, has a Brahms-like rhythm in the piano part, but the total effect is weak. *Meeting*, (*Drücke Mich An Deine Brüst*) published in 1902, is more successful. The rhythmic pattern of dotted quarter, eighth, and two quarters, lends unity, while the changing accompaniment adds support to the text.

*Invocation* is another short song, published in 1898, written in a different mood that suggests some Richard Strauss influence in its accompaniment. Its text by W. E. Henley, appeals to the "good and kind western wind" to bring his loved one back again "over the western sea" so that at least he may know she is near. Written in 6/8 meter, the flowing accompaniment of sixteenth notes captures the motion of the waves and wind as it undergirds the refreshing melody, still reminiscent of the current parlor songs. Example 11 shows the wistfulness expressed as the climax concludes a pleasant song.

In *Wenlock Town*, published in 1902, Farwell has captured the quiet reflective mood of A. E. Hausman's poem, *'Tis Time, I Think, by Wenlock Town*, which describes some of the seasonal changes made by nature. The music also shows Farwell's early Germanic training.

*O Ships That Sail* belongs to this early period and contains clichés typical of the salon songs of that time. The text is another poem by A. Mary F. Robinson. However, *Thou'rt Like Unto A Tender Flower*, (*Du Bist Wie Eine Blüme*) set to a poem by Heinrich Heine which Farwell translated from the German, fares much better.

*Mädchenlieder*, Op. 2, composed in 1897, are the first songs to have an opus number. Farwell had asked MacDowell's advice about using opus numbers when he was preparing his first piano pieces for publication. MacDowell had advised him "your first thing which you consider really worthy of that honor should be Opus one." Farwell then gave that honor to his collection of piano pieces *Tone Pictures After Pastels in Prose*. But the *Mädchenlieder* he considered good enough to label Opus 2. Here he has succeeded in writing songs worthy of an opus number. Written in simple folk song style, the texts for these four songs are from Ambrosius again, but Farwell does not claim authorship of the translations. All the songs are attractive, and because of the contrasts in style, they make a gratifying performance group.

Especially appealing are numbers III and IV where he develops the sadness and pathos of the texts. Number II is more dramatic. (See example 12.)

The eminent critic, James Huneker, wrote of these songs January 24, 1900 in his column "The Raconteur" for *Musical Courier*. In comparing these with Farwell's *Ballade* for violin and piano, he believed these to be "far better" and found the folksongs "Charming".

*A Ruined Garden*, Op. 14, No. 1, published in the Wa-Wan Press in 1902, is an early work which is worthy of performance today. Using a nine verse poem by Philip Bourke Marston, (1850-1887), Farwell has captured the dramatic essence of the lyrics. Here we see his growth as a song-writer in terms of craftsmanship and length. Most of the earlier songs were only two or three pages long; now Farwell meets the challenge of a longer poem.

Marston laments that all of his roses in the garden are dead due to heavy winds that came and also destroyed his song-birds. He decides he must leave his garden for the winds to plunder and go to a land where there are no roses or birds or spring - only poppies blowing "row on row". There he will be "made whole of sorrow" and forget the past. The text refers to more than an experience with nature. It encompasses some personal tragedy from which healing is necessary.

Farwell wrote an orchestral accompaniment for the song which was used with a featured singer on an N.B.C. broadcast early in 1934. In a letter to Dana Merriman at N.B.C. dated January 11, 1934, Farwell gave suggestions for its performance:

> The song should take just five minutes or a little under if the first part is taken fast enough: the last part can't be hurried as its essence is utter repose. . . . It is the vocal work I would rather have done than any other. It will make great demands both on the lyric and dramatic quality of the singer.

> Because of the tempo and mood changes of this song (which is a sort of little "song-cycle" in itself) it will be very necessary for Mr. Littau and the singer to have a good understanding of it together before it goes to orchestra rehearsal.

It was sung in N.Y. by Maggie Teyte with this same orchestration, and as she never looked at it until the day before the performance, she and the conductor had an awful time of it. . . . Florence Hinkle made a great success with this song in many places about 1907-8.

Unfortunately the orchestral accompaniment he refers to in the above letter is missing and one wonders if it might be still shelved somewhere in the old N.B.C. files.

Farwell begins the song in the key of C minor with a scale-wise melody shown in example 13a. The piano accompaniment is sparse and follows the melodic line first in octaves, then with full chords. The mood grows more agitated in verse five which is reflected in groups of 16th notes in the piano until the melody builds up to a climax on "I will leave my garden for winds to harry" where the piano plays descending octaves in the bass while full chords support the singer's high $f^1$'s, $g^1$'s and $a^1$ flat. An effective piano interlude moves on to a different key and calmer mood for the closing verses where "I shall be made whole of sorrow". The concluding page is given in example 13b.

Benjamin Lambord approved only part of this song. In reviewing Farwell's vocal compositions for *Music in America*[2], he criticized first the melody of Farwell's *Sea Vision* Opus 34:

. . . A score of rich color and poetic descriptions in which the voice has little of what has heretofore been known as melody, but performs a more modern function of sounding the salient notes of harmonies that are woven in an ultra-modern profusion of color. The same is true of several other large songs such as *A Ruined Garden* (Opus 14), *Drake's Drum* (Opus 22), and *The Farewell* (Opus 33).

Then Lambord went on to point out in the second section of *A Ruined Garden* that "there is a clearer line of melody over a harmonic scheme of haunting loveliness." Evidently Lambord's ears considered Farwell's other melodies too "modern" to please him except for the second section of *A Ruined Garden!*

## The Emily Dickinson Settings

The songs for which Farwell may be most recognized are his impressive settings of poems by Emily Dickinson. Since the publication in 1983 of his *Thirty-Four Songs on Poems of Emily Dickinson*[3] has made some of his best songs now available, these are being listed with increasing frequency on recital programs.

Farwell sent eight of the songs he considered his best settings of Emily Dickinson's poems to G. Schirmer sometime early in 1950. These included the now popular *I'm Nobody, The Grass So Little Has To Do,* and *Wild Nights! Wild Nights!* Nathan Broder[4] returned all eight of the manuscripts with a note dated April 19, 1950, expressing regrets that their Reader's Committee did not recommend acceptance of any of them.

It took a concert singer, Paul Sperry, to discover the value of these Dickinson settings which he examined in manuscript while searching for new repertoire. Later he relates thus in the introduction to the 1983 editions:

> In 1975 I began to prepare three concerts of unknown American songs to perform in New York City as my contribution to the Bicentennial celebration. I must have sight-read close to 2,000 songs that year. A lot of them deserve the obscurity into which they had fallen, but when I started looking at Farwell, whom I had not heard of before, I knew I had made a major discovery. When I put the programs in final shape, I chose eleven of his Dickinson songs - more by him than by any other composer. I have performed that group of eleven many times since then, and the audiences' enthusiasm has reinforced my conviction that these are among the very finest American songs.

Paul Sperry has recorded these eleven songs as listed in the discography. These and many of the songs written in Farwell's maturity are highly recommended for study and performance.

Emily Dickinson (1830-1886) was Farwell's favorite poet, and he set 40 of her poems to music in 39 songs.[5] Dickinson's gifts as a poet are well described by H. H. Waggoner: "If one were forced to choose just one poet to illumine the nature and quality of American poetry as a whole, to define its ... preoccupations, its characteristic themes and images, its diction and style ... one ought to choose Dickinson."[6]

Born in Amherst, Massachusetts, (1830-1886), the daughter of a prominent lawyer, Emily Dickinson attended Amherst Academy for six years and then one year at Mount Holyoke Seminary. She also studied the piano and became an accomplished pianist as well as a good singer. She especially liked to improvise on the keyboard, but poetry was her real form of music. Until she was about 30 years old, she was frequently called on to sing or play for guests who came to the Dickinson home. She had her first encounter with the piano at age two and a half years, but did not secure her own piano until about age fourteen. Her knowledge of music and sensitivity to it is apparent in her poetry. Daniel Pinkham stated, "Her ear must have been extraordinarily good!"[7]

Many books have been written in an effort to understand the complex personality and work of Emily Dickinson. One popular view is that she suffered the trauma of disappointment in love, "put on virginal white, withdrew from 'the world', and sang out her sorrow."[8] But, in her book about Dickinson, Elizabeth Phillips does not agree with this idea. Rather she points out Dickinson's daily involvement with her family household tasks and related problems plus her failing eyesight as being the more relevant background for her behavior and poetry.

Dickinson had few appropriate ways to express her excess emotional energy during the times in which she lived. Hence she found release in the body of work she created which has brought her recognition as a great lyrical poet of nature, love, death and immortality. Richard B. Sewell predicted in 1963:[9]

> Emily Dickinson will grow stronger with the years as we continue to outdistance the sentimentalities that still cling to her. Her eccentricities will fall into perspective. We will become increasingly aware of the toughness and sinew of her poetry, its range and versatility, its challenge to our understanding. We will test our knowledge of humanity against hers and find that we can learn on every front. Far from the little figure of frustrations and

renunciations and regrets, we will come to see her as a poet of great strength, courage, and singleness of purpose.

By 1985 Harold Bloom could write in his introduction to *Modern Critical Views: Emily Dickinson*, (N.Y. Chelsea House )

Of all poets writing in English in the nineteenth and twentieth centuries, I judge Emily Dickinson to present us with the most authentic cognitive difficulties. Vast and subtle intellect cannot in itself make a poet; the essential qualities are inventiveness, mastery of trope and craft, and that weird flair for intuiting significance through rhythm to which we can give no proper name. Dickinson has all these, as well as a mind so original and powerful that we scarcely have begun, even now, to catch up with her.

Contemporary composers have discovered the possibilities of Dickinson's poetry. David Leisner, a New York composer, explained why he used her poems for some of his recent songs: "Her poetry is lyrical and has a densely packed power and emotional urgency - the kind of attributes that make a song composer's mouth water."[10]

Etta Parker set one of Dickinson's poems in 1896, followed by Clarence Dickinson in 1897, who set six of them. These seem to be the first composers to put any of her poems to music. Clarence Dickinson may have been drawn to them because Emily was his cousin. Most settings have been made since 1945 onward.

Farwell was among the earliest American composers to be attracted to Dickinson's poetry. He first recognized its potential qualities as early as 1907 when he composed *Sea of Sunset*. He continued to be inspired by her poetry all through his career and created his last setting in 1949. He seems to have had a special affinity for Dickinson's work - a special kinship to her spiritual roots and mysticism. This is not surprising when one recalls Farwell's New England heritage and exposure to Transcendentalism and Emersonian thought. He had been reared in what amounted to a transplanted New England home in St. Paul. His college years in Boston plus some ten more years of living in Newton Center, gave him further roots in Massachusetts.

Thus he could relate personally to the Amherst area and its traditions and felt strong socio-cultural bonds with Dickinson.

Moreover, Farwell's thoughts often dwelt on the same subjects which prompted Dickinson's poetry. He stoically objected to institutionalism - especially in the church - and echoed such ideas as she expressed in *The Sabbath*. Farwell enjoyed being close to nature and found solace and inspiration in the outdoors, even as Dickinson did. Because his own prose writings were often peppered with references to Greek mythology and other symbolic terms or names which reflected the scope of his wide reading, he appreciated Dickinson's use of symbols and metaphors. He also revered the Bible and was sensitive to her many Biblical allusions.

He was impressed with Dickinson's daring *use* of unusual expressions. "This [use] is, to reveal to us in new colors and new relations the beauty of the visible universe, and then, by this exhaustless and compounded symbolism, to bring us home to the awe and wonder of the boundless universe, which our spiritual selves inhabit."[11]

Farwell suffered bitterly from unrequited love during college days; consequently he greatly admired how Dickinson met what he understood to be a similar problem.[12]

These are a few of the reasons why Farwell responded to Dickinson's poetry. Beyond these was his admiration for Dickinson's extraordinary power to express profound thoughts in terse and simple style. He probably would agree with Dan Beaty, a contempory Texas composer, who also set poems of Dickinson to music. Beaty believed: "The poetry of Emily Dickinson is, beyond its beauty of symbol and meaning, perfectly musical in sound and rhythmic syllabication. The poems' compactness and singular subjects are, along with the above traits, models of the lyrical foundation on which any good and effective song must be based." From about 124 solo art songs Farwell composed, he set 39 of them to Dickinson's poems as already mentioned. No other poet's works were favored as much as hers. At the most, (not counting the early translations from Ambrosius) he set only five poems by Percy Bysshe Shelley, five by William Blake and four by Charles Roos.

The Dickinson settings could be broadly classified in various ways: by subject matter of the text, (Nature, Death, Love, etc.) by style of accompaniment, or chronologically. The latter method of study has been chosen in order to show Farwell's development as a song-writer, and will be divided into three time periods. Songs composed to the verses by other poets during these same periods will be considered later under "Non-Dickinson Settings", also in chronological order of composition.

### The Early Dickinson Settings, 1907-1926

Emily Dickinson did not title her poems, so Farwell devised his own titles usually from her first lines.

The title, *The Sea of Sunset* Op. 26, pictures in music the subject matter of Dickinson's poem. Although the song was composed in 1907, it was not copyrighted until 1917 and then published in 1928. The colorful lines describing the land that the "sunset washes" are aptly enhanced musically by lush rolled chords. These are often followed by thirds in a pattern of three sixteenth notes, adding to the effect of water washing onto the shore. The opening two measures are repeated often in the accompaniment throughout to provide unity. (Ex. 14.) Edgar Kirk found that this sequence is used in eighteen measures of non-functional harmony in the song. He also noted that this pattern lacked root movement which is "not readily apparent to the ear as the bass line suggests a chord change in each instance."[13]

Farwell uses a four measure piano postlude which does not end the song on a tonic, but surprisingly leaves the music up in the air with a pianissimo unresolved A flat seventh chord. Perhaps he intended it to refer to the lands of "the western mystery" in the text.

William Treat Upton describes this song as "painted with broad brush, though of a languorous movement which well interprets 'the western mystery'."[14] The romantic setting for this attractive music reflects Farwell's European training, but hardly shows the craftsmanship he used in his later Dickinson songs.

For nearly sixteen years, Farwell was preoccupied with developing folk-based songs and other kinds of composing, so it was not until 1923 that he used another Dickinson text. First he chose *I Shall Know Why* (Op. 66, No. 1). In this poem Dickinson states that she will no longer need to ask why "when time is over" as Christ will explain answers to her questions in that "fair schoolroom of the sky". There she can forget her present anguish.

Farwell's writing has matured and already shows a deeper sensitivity to Dickinson's text than his first effort. Without introduction he begins a sustained melody in the key of D flat. The piano part flows between both hands initially until the left hand joins the right in the treble clef for the second verse which features syncopation and some imitative writing. The eight measure interlude brings the singer back to a mood similar to that of the first verse, but the melody embraces wider skips. The song then moves to a fortissimo climax on "anguish that scalds me now". This climax is then repeated with a "greater retard" for emphasis. Farwell uses considerable chromaticism as well as a change of key before he concludes this inspired song.

*Resurgam* (Op. 66. No.2) was Farwell's next Dickinson setting, composed also in 1923, but publication of the two songs had to wait until 1926. This is one of Dickinson's so-called "love poems" in which she feels that at last she has been "identified" in a love experience. Farwell sets this poem in a rapid tempo to capture the exultant mood of the text. He writes a four bar introduction built on a figure pattern of dotted eighth, sixteenth, eighth, which repeats throughout the entire song in the piano part. The upper voice of these figures rises with each repetition in the piano, to produce a driving momentum. The opening melody features octave skips on each "At last" which sustains "last" for emphasis and moves quickly forward in frequent wide skips. The surging accompaniment undergirds the vocal line as it climbs higher with each phrase to end on a sustained high A flat in the stirring climax.

Farwell obviously felt encouraged by the successful Schirmer publication of his Dickinson songs and turned again to her poetry for two more songs in 1926: *Summer Shower* and *Mine*.

William Treat Upton refers to these Opus 73 songs as examples of those "setting forth some phase of modernist treatment."[15] In his *Supplement to Art Song in America 1930-1938*, he discusses two schools of composition: the Traditionalists and the Modernists. Here we note one critic who takes Farwell out of the conservative class where his age should logically have placed him. Instead, Upton includes him with those composers all a generation or more younger, such as Copland, Barber and Ives, who show a more decided "modernistic" trend!   In the same discussion, he also points out the artistic upheaval and revolt against romanticism following World War I as a time given to intensive experimentation when composers sought to find some mode of expression different from that of the previous hundred years.   Farwell was among those listed who continued to seek for more ways to expand tonality as he searched for a new personal idiom.   An analysis of his songs only foreshadows changes to come.

However, when Farwell wrote to William Treat Upton to congratulate him on his *Art Song in America*, he questioned Upton's use of "modernity" to describe his own songs.   A letter dated February 6, 1930, comments thus:

> . . . I haven't had time to do more than skim through it [Upton's book].   It certainly fills up a big gap in the literature upon our own music (a literature that is mostly gaps!).   I thought you treated me very well, though I fear the modernity with which you credit me would scarcely be recognized as such by the expressionist crew. . . Also I wonder if I shall ever write any more songs; who ever sings serious American songs, anyway?   Graveure here, wouldn't touch one with a ten foot pole.   Oley Speak's *Sylvia* is apparently as far as he gets.   I never see a song of Ayres, or of mine, on a program anywhere.   Does anybody sing any of them?   If not for the present, do they have any meaning for the future? ? ?   After all, I have faith in the future.   We're in a curious  state, strained, artificial, divorced from the true soul of music.   But the next generation has another revolt in store.

*Summer Shower*, Op. 73, No. 1 was one of the songs which Upton favorably reviewed.   It has a picturesque text singers should enjoy adding to their repertoire.   Dickinson describes the summer shower from the onset of the first drop falling on the apple tree to the coming of the sunshine that "threw his hat away".   Farwell develops the feeling for a summer shower by starting with just two notes, c - B, in the piano, suggesting a "drop" of rain, that is reiterated by the voice on f - a. (Ex. 15)  The accompaniment adds another "drop" of c - A to the pattern, until these three notes (c B A) are developed to become a steady figure in the bass suggesting the "patter" of the shower.  This "patter" continues with varying notation of seconds and thirds until tension is built for the climax on "The East put out a single flag".  Here the piano flourishes a rolled E major chord followed by the continued "pattering" in the left hand to the softer, slower close  on "And signed the fête away".  Farwell makes effective use of rests throughout the song which underscores the text and strengthens its melodic appeal.

Ernst Bacon sets the same text as an *Air for Soprano and Chorus*.  In his version, the piano establishes the mood with a light staccato music-box type of pattern that continues in the bass through most of the accompaniment.  The vocal lines are pleasing, but do little to reflect the meaning of the words.  The soloist alternates phrases with the chorus that consists of soprano and alto voices.  Farwell's setting is more imaginative.

Farwell's *Mine* (Op. 73, No. 2) is a two page song featuring a non-tonal melody.  Here we find more of the "modern qualities" to which William Treat Upton refers.  A look at the text explains a great part of the rationale for the melody.  Richard B. Sewall compares this poem with another one in which Dickinson claims the "Title divine is mine!"  He finds ambiguities in explaining the meaning of both poems and adds that "Mine" is "often looked upon as a love poem only.[16]  Here Farwell sets the great exultant mood of the text by reflecting its ever-mounting emotional movement with eloquent harmonic color and intensity. (See complete song in examples 16a and 16b.)

The melody has a complex chromatic structure, but the opening phrases are basically scale-wise and the leaps not difficult to sing.  One observes how Farwell builds intensity by raising the pitch in four sequential patterns thus putting the stress on each succeeding "Mine."  When he reaches "Mine" on $e^1$ natural he keeps this pitch for the opening note of the three following phrases, thus further emphasizing each "Mine".  This makes the jump to the final "Mine" on high $a^1$  even more dramatic.  Preceding that is an unusual measure where he uses a sixth skip down (from $e^1$ to g) on the word "Titled," and repeats the interval in reverse on the word "confirmed" as if to confirm the text in music too. The same skip of $e^1$ to g finishes that measure and prepares for the exciting climax. Here the melody makes a dramatic leap to high a flat sustained over thick chords in fortissimo for three measures. The closing five bars for "while the ages steal!" feature another sustained $f^1$ flat in the voice. The piano reminisces with some of the sequential melody which pictures the movement of "the ages" and brings the dynamics to a soft ending more appropriate to "stealing away".

Although written with the key signature of A flat, the tonic triad is used only once in the first measure of the song, and does not reappear until the final cadence. Furthermore, nowhere else in the song is the A flat triad even implied as a tonal center, nor are the centers that are evident, with few exceptions, even closely related to A flat.

Harmonically, one sees that the final cadence is built on a V/13 chord which is used here as a release of tension. The last two measures before the tonic chord, (which go from an altered ninth chord to a chord of the augmented eleventh, and then to a chord of the thirteenth) build up a large amount of impulse toward the tonal center. Farwell cleverly refrains from complete cessation of tension by inserting an altered sub-dominant seventh chord over the tonic pedal as if to "steal" away, before resolving it to the final tonic. This construction serves to heighten the mood.

### The Middle Period of Dickinson Settings, 1936-1944

It was ten more years before Farwell turned to Dickinson's poetry again. The discouragement he felt when writing to Upton in 1931 - about nobody singing serious American songs - finally gave way to his yearning to express himself musically through her provocative lines. Then followed the productive period from 1936 until 1949 when he composed the 34 songs which Paul Sperry guided to publication with Boosey and Hawkes in 1983. Volume one includes songs from Opus 101 through Opus 105. Volume two features songs from Opus 107 through Opus 112. Looking now at the beauty found in these songs, it is hard to believe that G. Schirmer was deaf to them in 1950.

Farwell's continuing growth as a song-writer is evident in the new songs and one notes certain characteristics. Many are still short in length with regular phrases usually four bars long. Harmonies remain vertical with little use of counterpoint though more imitation is used, and the tonal centers shift more quickly. Chromaticism increases in the melodies and especially in the accompaniments which become more difficult. Melodies reflect the text charged with deeper emotion. His goal "to put musical flesh on the poet's word-frame" often results in the use of "word-painting."

As long ago as 1625, Joachim Thuringus classified words in his *Opusculum Bipartitum* that could be "expressed and painted" into three types: "(1) *verba affectuum* (words of affection), such as rejoicing, weeping, laughing, as well as words that suggest sound, such as bird; (2) *verba motus et locorum* (words of motion and place), such as to stand, to run, to jump, heaven, hell, mountain; and (3) *adverba temporis, numeri* (adverbs of time and number) such as quick, slow, twice, often, rarely".[17]

Farwell's songs reflect his use of all three types of word-painting in his repertory of expressive devices. His skill in employing metaphoric musical language improved with the years, making touches more subtle and effective. While some composers reject such efforts for suggestive reality as poor writing, others favor their use. More recently, Ruth C. Friedberg claimed:[18]

> . . . This metaphoric musical language not only has a very definite existence, but also figures strongly in what we have come to be familiar with as the art song style of word setting, no matter what the language of the poetry. It is, in fact, a very important factor in our perception of the composer's choices as appropriate or inappropriate and thereby in our judgment of the song as a success or failure. The only area of art song in which this would perhaps not be true are some contemporary examples in which the words are used purely as sound elements without associative meaning.

The author tends to agree with Friedberg's position.

One of the products of these later years is Farwell's unusual setting for Dickinson's *Unto Me*, Op. 101, No. 2. This poem seems to be a dialogue in which Jesus Christ invites a sinner to come to Him. The sinner's response reflects his concern for acceptance because he is "spotted" and "small". Jesus reassures him that "the least" is esteemed in Heaven as the "chiefest".

The music is so written that it could be sung as a duet between a low voice and a higher one. (Ex. 17) Again we find a close relationship between text and melody. Farwell gives the words of Jesus to a higher vocal line and sets the sinner's reply within a low minor sixth. Starting on middle c the sinner's first response stays on c and only moves up a half step once. His next response starts on e flat and hangs on d flat as a center. Farwell's able use of rests emphasizes the weakness of the "sinner" whose halting melodic line runs mostly in minor seconds and stays in a low tessitura. He builds up to the fortissimo climax on "Occupy my house" by separating previous phrases with rests and rich chords in the short piano interludes. This song is especially effective when the singer can project the distinction between the two characters.

Ernst Bacon recognized this idea of duality when he set the same poem as a duet for soprano and contralto with an added verse for chorus. Bacon has the sinner's role sung by a soprano, and Jesus' response by the contralto, with the tessituras for each being the reverse of Farwell's.

In the text for *Good Morning, Midnight!* Opus 101, No. 4, Dickinson laments that she must stay in Midnight's realm because Day rejected her. She really prefers the Day with its inviting pleasures, but since that is not possible, she begs Midnight to "please take a little girl He turned away!"

Farwell creates a quiet setting. He uses E flat minor to imply the poet's sadness in being rejected by Day. The second verse changes to a bright major key depicting the sweetness of the Day's sunshine. His third verse returns to the E flat minor measures used in the beginning. Short broken-up phrases bring out the poet's conversational mood with Midnight. Farwell's piano accompaniment is based on half note chordal movement for all the verses except the second one. He makes the poet's favored choice of "Day" the climax on $g^1$ for a broadened five counts. He puts the imploring, "Please take a little girl", in strict time, but the last line he stretches out slower and slower to underline the poet's sadness for being rejected by Day. To add further emphasis to her rejection, Farwell imitates the voice for "He turned away!" in the concluding accompaniment which ends triple piano.

*Safe in Their Alabaster Chambers* (Op. 105, No. 2) was written in Farwell's 1938-41 period when he continued to expand tonality in varied ways. Dickinson depicts three scenes in this text. The first verse describes the buried dead, lying in satin lined coffins, who wait through the passing years for their resurrection. Verse two is the scene above the graves where the "laughing breeze", "babbling bees", and piping "sweet birds" delight in the bright sunshine. Verse three spins out to a broader view of the universe where she notes the fall of kings and leaders over a long expanse of time.

Farwell sets this poem in E minor and 6/8 meter. He begins the song slowly without introduction. (Ex. 18a) His melody stays on the opening b flat for the first measure suggesting the prone position of the dead. The darkness of the first phrase is slightly relieved by a brief skip up to $e^1$ flat, but it returns to b flat and continues in what is basically a descending line for the first verse. The piano part is written in the treble clef for both hands. The left hand plays a hypnotic e flat ostinato on a pattern of dotted eighth, sixteenth, eighth, followed by two eighths in duple rhythm. These occur under simple chords to emphasize the buried dead. The right hand plays only two chords per measure, the second one always being lower and nearby. This creates a rocking effect as if the silent dead were being rocked in their timeless slumber.

A brief interlude using imitation from the last vocal phrase leads to a bright E major key and a complete change of melody and mood with an accompaniment which reflects the happy scene above the graves for verse two. (Ex. 18b) The vocal line uses skips and varied rhythms including syncopation. The accompaniment flows with sixteenth notes and does some word-painting for "Pipe the sweet birds".

The music for the third verse returns to the opening measures and E minor key. Here Dickinson pictures Time as it "passes in a world of successive, but living generations." "Crescent" refers to the small moon as it goes from month to month until the

Resurrection. The fall of dynasties represents the passing of many years. Then the word "*snow*" completes the cycle of ideas. Not like the hardness of *alabaster* in the first verse, *snow* is velvety soft like a blanket. (Ex. 18c)

For this verse, Farwell supports the voice with full chords in both clefs without the ostinato. The pattern of movement is the same as before, but the second chord in each measure is farther away from its predecessor than in the first verse. This wider expanse of space depicts "Grand go the years" and the movement of time in the cosmos. The forte chords for "Doges surrender" drop to a soft reminiscence with thinner texture. Here the rhythmic ostinato slips in again and is repeated until it fades away in the closing cadence. The same haunting ostinato figure throughout emphasizes the waiting of the dead that stretches out to eternity, and repeats the gentle rocking effect used in the first verse. The swinging rhythm of the lines again suggest a cosmic Mother Nature rocking her dear ones to sleep.[19] The total effect is a profound one.

An engaging song in a totally different mood is Farwell's *The Sabbath*, Op. 105, No. 3. Farwell was dissatisfied with the institutional church and rarely attended services as an adult. Instead, he often worshiped outdoors where he felt the presence of God in the beauty of His handiwork. Thus the text of this poem held a special interest for him. Here we also find evidence of Farwell's sense of humor in his sympathetic rapport with the poet's lines.

Farwell sets a quiet mood as he begins without introduction with simple statements in the piano, while the voice "goes to church" seriously singing repeated notes on different rhythms. (Ex. 19a) The piano has inner weaving melodies that move diatonically and stabilize the key of E flat. He likes to use bird calls to echo a text and does so here for the bobolink. He puts the tolling of the bell in bass octaves, then returns to the treble clef with both hands and gives the bobolink another song. (Ex. 19b) The music becomes more somber and stately for "God preaches". "The sermon is never long" acquires a full measure for "long". For the next phrase - "So instead of getting to heav'n at last" - Farwell writes "arduously", using pressed out chords that move by half steps. The voice rests and a fermata builds up suspension for the final line, "I'm going all along!" Here the piano zips away in sixteenth note bass figures with more bird chirping in the treble clef. Thus concludes this sprightly moving song in which Farwell deftly demonstrates his use of pictorialism.

Daniel Pinkham included this poem as part of an impressive commissioned work *Getting to Heaven* performed on October 24, 1987.[20] His work is based on six Dickinson poems and written for soprano solo, chorus, and small ensemble of brass and harp. His approach to *Keeping the Sabbath* (number four in the group) is far different from Farwell's. Pinkham makes little effort to mirror the text in his music. In fact he told the author that he disliked efforts to do any "Mickey-Mouse" word-painting. Instead, he preferred to use other ways for expressing the poem's mood.[21]

In this instance, Pinkham sets a playful mood with seventeen measures of introduction in waltz time that might have seemed irreverent in Dickinson's day when associated with going to church. Pinkham uses the same waltz accompaniment for the first two verses with some changes of the melody in verse two to accommodate the words. Four measures preface the third verse where the music is more concerned with text. The waltz accompaniment shakes its earlier syncopation and moves in more sedate 3/4 time for "God preaches". Pinkham handles the climax lines as Farwell does by climbing in half steps on "getting to heaven at last". Farwell stresses these in the piano part, while Pinkham emphasizes the voice supported by single chords in the accompaniment. Pinkham continues with the singer sliding up to $g^1$ on "I'm going", to conclude triumphantly "all along" on five measures of a sustained $e^1$. He undergirds this with five punched out fortissimo chords that echo the previous syncopation. The prevailing mood of the rhythmic waltz takes the listener by surprise, but one can almost see Dickinson dancing happily around in her garden on a Sabbath morning as the text unfolds in its unique way. However, one doubts that she would feel comfortable with Pinkham's dissonances and disjunct melody even if she approved of his light-hearted reflection and commentary on her lines. This is a fascinating comparison with Farwell's convincing song written in more traditional style.

A haunting melody characterizes Farwell's setting for Dickinson's *These Saw Vision*, Op. 105, No. 4. In the poem,

Dickinson addresses a dead young girl whom she has loved and
cared for, and now Paradise is the "only palace fit for her
reception." Beginning in the key of C major, the melody threads
its way downward within a small range for eight measures via
some minor and seventh chords in phrases that relate sequentially.
Then it gradually moves upward with much repetition of rhythmic
patterns and similarity in tonal phrases. By keeping the tessitura
in the low and middle range, the singer's $e^1$ on "Paradise" which
is the high point of the poem, stands out in greater contrast. The
piano accompaniment consists of two chords per measure that
sustain the meditative mood all through the song and it only
changes to a moving broken chord bass line in the climax. This
song is particularly suited for a mezzo soprano who has a real
sensitivity for the text.

Farwell enjoyed Dickinson's nature poems and responded with
*The Little Tippler*, Op. 105, No. 6, which begins "I taste a liquor
never brewed". His sense of humor seems to delight in the
thought of Dickinson's "inebriate" bee weaving happily among the
flowers. Farwell puts it to music with "drunken" moving figures
in the right hand of the accompaniment. (Ex. 20) The left hand
chords support the melody. Written in the key of D flat major,
the score uses considerable chromaticism that creates tonal
instability for the reeling bee. Farwell shifts the rhythm patterns
to accommodate the text thus producing a kind of staggering effect
in the melody. As is rather typical, he builds up to a sweeping
climax for the last verse. There he changes the right hand eighth
notes to sixteenths that broaden triumphantly to show the "little
tippler leaning against the sun" on a sustained $f^1$ climax. Then
the eighths scurry to conclusion on a fortissimo chord. The total
effect is one of emotional exhilaration for the "little tippler."

Clarence Dickinson, included a setting of this poem in his
group of six songs for Mrs. Proctor, mentioned earlier. He used
the first line, *I Taste a Liquor Never Brewed*, as the title for his
song. The "scherzando" marking sets the mood for a melody that
swings jauntily along in a style of that time. Mr. Dickinson uses
the same tune to start the second verse and the fourth, but writes
a change for the third verse, suggesting a ternary form. The
structure is divided into two sections separated by a four-measure

interlude.    The voice line is usually duplicated in the piano accompaniment.

A descending chromatic six note motive repeated for four measures depicts the drunken bee in the bass accompaniment of the B section.    Here the composer handles the rhythmic irregularities by beginning these lines on the downbeat instead of the usual eighth pickup notes of the other phrases.    Another attempt to do word-painting is found in the last phrase where he writes the "drunken bee" motive again in unison in the voice and piano right hand, for "see the little tippler".    Like Farwell, Dickinson creates an effective pitch climax on the word "sun". The time span of some forty years between Dickinson's writing and Farwell's, accounts for much of the difference in style. Farwell's rendition also shows how much of his early training he has left behind him.    Had he set these same lines in 1897, would they have resembled Clarence Dickinson's style?    Possibly.

Farwell's longest setting of a Dickinson poem, is one he named *Summer's Armies* (Op. 105, No. 9).    In colorful language she describes nature's activity in her summer garden, beginning with "Some rainbow coming from the fair".    This outstanding song is one Paul Sperry has featured so effectively on his recitals and is recorded.    The imaginative text deserves the ravishing harmonic treatment which Farwell bestows on it.    The song gains its title from the military mood suggested by the words "baronial bees march, one by one," and later from the reference to "the regiments of wood and hill In bright detachment stand."    Farwell uses horn-like patterns and later some "trumpet-call" figures   woven into what becomes a fast-paced tonal tapestry for Dickinson's poetry.

Many of Farwell's songs have difficult accompaniments and require a good pianist to play them up to tempo.  *Tie the Strings to My Life*, Op. 107, No. 2, composed in his 1941-44 period, is an example of such a song.    The galloping figures in the accompaniment (Ex. 21), and quickly moving intervals of sixteenth notes in unexpected skips, all must be played fast "with agitation", and there are no resting spots for the pianist until the final chord.

Thomas W. Ford considers this poem to be one of the most overtly religious poems ever written by Dickinson.[22]    He claims that here she is openly announcing her desire to seek a religious life and renouncing her former ways. "She uses the image of a

coach and horses to indicate her departure from the life she used
to live." Recognizing also that her choice is not easy, she
requests to be put "on the firmest side" so she "will never fall" in
her journey to the Judgment. The piano plays a rhythmic gallop
pattern that moves with the vocal line as it "rides to the
Judgment" for eight bars. After a measure of rest for the singer,
the piano moves on to set a quieter mood for the poet's
affirmation of faith in God's care. The voice now has a four-bar
melody over a flowing accompaniment that suggests her peace. It
is followed by a sweeping melody that broadens and increases in
volume to say "Goodby to the life I used to live." After the
phrase "And kiss the hills for me," Farwell uses an eighth rest for
emphasis, and drops the melody from the sustained high tessitura
to write a skip from g up to $e^1$ flat, that emphasizes "just once".
The piano moves down pitch-wise through modulations, while the
singer rests - only to reenter without piano to produce the climax
on "Now", followed by a determined chord in the piano. Then
comes the convincing declaration, "I am ready to go!" Insistent
chords in the right hand of the accompaniment move against the
now galloping left hand rhythm pattern first used in the beginning,
as the music rushes boldly in Rachmaninoff style, to a stunning
triumphant end. *Tie the Strings to My Life* is a song that grows on
the singer and audience alike and one that the author found to be
especially effective as the closing number on her recitals.

*On This Wondrous Sea*, Op. 107, No. 3, was written during
the years 1941-44. In the text Dickinson deals with the concept
of Eternity using nautical terms as if she were sailing in a ship.
She asks the pilot (God) if he knows their destination (Heaven).
The pilot assures her that indeed he does know where he is
piloting her and soon she will join others already there. She cries
"land, ho! eternity" and asks "at last?" (Another version of the
poem uses an exclamation point instead of a question mark at the
end of the sentence.)

Farwell writes a key signature of D flat, but rarely stays in the
key. After a one measure introduction that ends with a hold, he
moves slowly and quietly in 6/8 meter. The melody sits placidly
on repeated f's for the first measure. The piano has six
arpeggiated sixteenth notes followed by two eighths in duple
rhythm or a dotted quarter chord, in a rippling pattern that

suggests the quiet movement of the waves. "Ho! pilot, ho!" is declaimed on $e^1$ flat, dropping an octave to e for "pilot" before returning to $e^1$ for another "Ho!" Farwell undergirds these pitches with sturdy chords that follow the voice.

In the second verse, the flowing sixteenths in the piano are exchanged for very slow pianissimo dotted quarter note chords. These depict the silent coast where earlier ships have anchored in the harbor. Then Farwell builds up a tremendous climax for the closing lines alternating the sweeping sixteenth note runs with full chords all of which also climb pitch-wise in each succeeding phrase to the fortissimo finale on high A for the singer. (Ex. 22) Truly this is a fitting setting for Dickinson's compelling words.

Daniel Pinkham uses the same text to conclude his work, *Getting to Heaven*, which also included *Keeping the Sabbath*. In discussing his writing of *On this Wondrous Sea* on a radio broadcast,[23] Pinkham declared his big problem was to begin in an "extraordinarily tranquil way and develop an almost motionless quality to a full fortissimo climax in three minutes." To accomplish this, he wrote the opening lines for solo voice with harp accompaniment that provide the tranquil effect he sought. He spins out the word "silently " over seven pitches. The chorus enters for the second verse which he also keeps pianissimo as Farwell did. Then the brass pick up the concluding lines and supplement the chorus for "Land Ho!". Pinkham repeats "Ashore at last!" three times, each phrase climbing in pitch to develop the stirring climax.

In setting these same words, Farwell uses phrases rising softly in sequence to anticipate the climax; but instead of phrase repetition, Farwell sustains "Ashore" for eleven beats on $a^1$ and "at last" for seven beats on $f^1$ for his climax that ends with daring flourishes in the piano. The two settings make another engrossing comparison, Farwell's song having been composed about forty seven years earlier than Pinkham's.

*Heart, We Will Forget Him!* expresses Dickinson's struggle to forget a man she has loved. This poem was probably written in the years between 1858 and 1865, a time of great emotional upheaval in her life. She addresses her heart, suggesting it should forget the warmth he gave, and she will endeavor to forget the light he brought into her life. She urges her heart to hasten and not lag in the forgetting process or she may remember him.

Farwell composed his moving setting (Op. 108, No. 1) for this poem in 1944, not too long after he had written *On This Wondrous Sea*. He begins in the somber key of E flat minor and without introduction, plunges directly into the text. The word "Heart" is set off in apposition by a rest that follows the opening note. (Ex. 23) The plaintive slow-moving melody is confined within the octave of e flat to $e^1$ flat as if to suggest how the poet is hugging the problem close to her breast, not really wanting to let go of her love. It features repeated notes, diatonic movement, and only a few large intervals. A quiet accompaniment of four contemplative chords per measure sustains the serious mood of the text. The second verse changes key to provide contrast. A forte "Haste!" on $e^1$ flat is urgently set off by a short rest (Ex. 14), followed by an octave drop on soft pitches that emphasize "lagging", with two more rests and a retard that do likewise. The last two measures move slower and wistfully to an E flat major chord as if to suggest happy memories of the beloved.

Aaron Copland set *Heart, We Will Forget Him!* in 1951 as number five of a monumental song cycle, *Twelve Poems of Emily Dickinson*. These he intended to be a musical counterpart of Dickinson's personality. He uses two pages for his setting to provide in his inimical style what Farwell does in just one. Copland's interpretation of the text is similar to Farwell's. His tempo marking is "very slowly - (dragging)" suggesting that she is really not wanting to "forget him", but is trying to do so as the tempo continues "moving forward". Copland writes a two measure introduction and the rather sparse accompaniment covers wider and more moving horizontal lines than Farwell's, as if to imply the depth and breadth of the poet's suffering. Copland changes key for the second verse as Farwell did, and builds up to an impassioned climax with a fortissimo on "That I" followed by a faster tempo for the remainder of the phrase "my thoughts may dim". Then the musical motion slows and softens as if swept by memories that bring the melody to a halt by the caesura. The concluding "him" ends in the key of E flat as it began.

John Duke's setting of the same Dickinson text in 1978 is an entirely different approach from these already described. His is not a nostalgic remembering, but music full of anguish and agitation. Duke writes "Passionato" in a fast tempo and starts with a single fortissimo treble clef chord as the only introduction. "Heart" is sung on $g^1$ punctuated by rests for emphasis as the melodic line drops an octave portraying the pain felt by the poet as she tries in vain to forget her loved one. The right hand piano part has sixteenth note figures that hold a counter melody over quarter notes in the bass. Duke uses an interlude between verses which Farwell does not. Duke sets off "Haste" as Farwell does, but Duke goes on to build a fortissimo climax on $a^1$ for the first note of the concluding phrase, "I remember him!" This implies a different interpretation of the poem that has inspired settings by at least nine composers.[24] Each of the described songs has its own special appealing beauty, and there is no obvious "right" or "wrong" use of the poem here.

Farwell wrote a number of one page settings for the short Dickinson poems. *Ample Make This Bed*, Op. 108, No.7 is an example. Written in E flat minor as is *Safe in Their Alabaster Chambers*, the two songs bear a strong resemblance to each other. *Ample Make This Bed*, written in 12/8 meter for the voice, and 4/4 for the accompaniment, moves ponderously with chords set on each beat in a kind of rocking movement that weaves back and forth reminiscent of the aforementioned song. On the last words, "interrupt this ground", Farwell writes an E flat major chord on "ground" which does "interrupt" the tonal sound briefly before he resolves it to close on the original E flat minor key. The total result is a memorable impressive setting for a solemn text.

Another setting for a short poem in an entirely different mood is the winsome song, *I'm Nobody! Who Are You?*, Op. 108, No. 8, written also sometime in 1944. Here Farwell has sought to capture the duality of two "nobodies" who are self-satisfied and do not wish to be publicly proclaimed "Somebody". The poem is written essentially in common meter (8, 6, 8, 6), but Dickinson has manipulated the syllabic count and stresses of the first stanza lines to create an intimate chatty effect. However, she writes with regular meter for stanza two which stresses the tediousness and boredom of being "Somebody".

As is typical of many of Farwell's songs, this one too, begins promptly without introduction. The sparse accompaniment suggests the emptiness of being "nobody", and the delicate four note arpeggio used on the first beat of several measures gives the music a whimsical quality. The opening arpeggio is not in the tonic which does not enter until the fourth beat. Again there is a close relationship between music and words. Farwell carries out the conversational quality of the poem by the frequent use of rests between phrases. He uses a descending perfect fifth interval as a motive to emphasize an open empty feeling. We find it used for the first declared "I'm nobody" and echoed on the second question, "Are you nobody, too?" Repeated notes underline the "pair of us" and more rests surround "don't tell!" which is echoed in the piano to emphasize the need for secrecy. "Banish us" drops down on another perfect fifth interval - a to d, followed by repeated d's that continue the idea of duality.

Farwell sets "How dreary to be somebody" to phrases in the piano that seem to sigh "ho-hum" with the singer, (Ex. 24). He creates an amusing bass figure featuring triplets on minor seconds to resemble the frog's croaking for "Like a frog". This "croak" continues after "To tell your name the live-long day", to imply the endless boasting until it fades away on a bored "bog". The pert sauciness of this song makes it one that singers should find useful where a light touch is needed. However, the song is more than just a "clever" work because the text has something contemporary to say to audiences and the convincing music matches that spirit.

Carlton Lowenberg located at least fourteen settings for *I'm Nobody*, indicating its popularity among composers.[25] Some brief comparisons follow:

Sergius Kagen composed a setting in 1950 which is somewhat similar to Farwell's. He changes time signatures in nearly every measure, develops the idea of duality, and does some word-painting in the end for the croaking frog.

Ernest Bacon's setting made in 1932 is more contemporary in sound with bitonal implications to suggest two 'Nobodies'. He uses skips of a seventh in the bass which may suggest the frog skipping along.

Although Farwell, Kagen and Bacon made use of word-painting, Vincent Persichetti did not. However, like them, he writes his 1958 setting in a light-hearted vein with frequent rests to separate vocal statements and questions. His three pages do not seem as appropriate for Dickinson's terse verse as Farwell's score does on two pages.

Another song showing Farwell's ability to deal with humor is *Papa Above!*, Op. 108, No. 9. Here he writes scampering runs in the piano to suggest the mouse's movements at "Regard a mouse!" in the first phrase. The cat is recognized with a flippant staccato chord. He builds up the climax beginning with "While unsuspecting cycles", leading to fortissimo chords and octaves that exclaim "Pompously " in repetition. Then after more "scampering" the music "steals softly" for five and a half beats on "away".

### The Last Dickinson Settings, 1949

Gilbert Chase recognized Farwell's spiritual and philosophical ties to Dickinson when he referred to the three Emily Dickinson Songs of 1949 by claiming that Farwell "was evidently experiencing and expressing an ever-deeper identification with the mystical-symbolic message of poems such as *Wild Nights! Wild Nights!*, *The Grass So Little Has To Do*, and *An Awful Tempest Mashed the Air*".[26]

Brice Farwell agrees with Chase and told the author that the reason his father especially liked Dickinson's poetry was because:

> . . . her way of expressing her convictions about life, here and hereafter, were of a kindred spirit to his life. To extend to the music-listening world the union of her thoughts, poetically, and his own through music - this creation of song around her thoughts - was, he felt , as close as he had come to expressing, by his art, the mission that drove his own spirit in his life effort. Thus his sense of mission and calling are meaningfully expressed - an integrated combination of his music with his philosophic or spiritual aspiration.

The three songs of Op. 112 were written three years before Farwell's death in January 1952. In *Wild Nights! Wild Nights!*, number one of this opus, Dickinson expresses her deep longing to be with someone. Some critics interpret this as a romantic love poem.[27] Another suggestion is that she is addressing Jesus Christ with her need to be "moored" in His safe port (Heaven) where she would no longer need to worry about directions for her life.[28] Because Farwell had suffered many struggles - both inner and outer ones, he could identify with the poet's turmoil. The subject of eternal verities was also one close to his heart.

He plunges immediately into the intoxicating exuberance of *Wild Nights! Wild Nights!* without any introduction as the melody emphatically declares the title on repeated figures of two notes dropping half steps - $c^1$ flat to b flat. (Ex. 25a)  This interval of a second occurs frequently in the melody and is a unifying element along with the rhythmic figure of an eighth followed by a quarter note used on the first beat of six scattered measures.   These rhythmic patterns do not agree with the poet's accents.   Here Farwell purposely distorts the normal accents to add restlessness to the score.  However, in two measures this rhythm throws the emphasis significantly on the pronoun "I".

The piano accompaniment sets the tumultuous mood with a triplet figure of widely spaced notes in contrary motion in both hands for the first four bars.   Then the left hand stretches to eighth notes against the triplets in the right hand as the accompaniment expands to play opulent harmonies that surge forward in a mounting wave of chromatic color.  The left hand adds rippling sixteenth note patterns leading to the climax on "the sea".  When the voice exclaims "moor to-night in thee!" and ends on high g, the closing measures for piano pick up the triplet figures - again in contrary motion - and conclude exultingly on what the author thinks Farwell intended to be a bright E major chord. (Ex. 25b).  (Was the c flat meant to be b flat?  Farwell had serious eye problems and this could be an error in the MS.)

*Wild Nights! Wild Nights!* is another poem which has inspired at least nine American composers according to Lowenberg's count.

In *The Grass So Little Has to Do*, Dickinson seems to wish her life were as simple as a blade of grass where "only butterflies brood and bees are entertained".  Later she concludes that the ultimate end of grass is to dream away in "sovereign barns" and she longs to be "a hay".  This poem could well have been written after a day when the tediousness of housework had overwhelmed her spirits.

Farwell set this text as Op. 112, No. 2, sometime in 1949. His music suggests the carefree, contented life of the grass. (Ex. 26a) He begins after a single measure of introduction. Here he almost buries the frolicsome melody line in the treble clef's accompaniment where both hands scamper lightly above it in broken triadic figures as if to agree with the poet that indeed the grass really "so little has to do." Farwell uses a high degree of chromaticism and nonharmonic tones. Forward harmonic movement is produced by chains of seventh, ninth, and secondary chords, plus avoided cadences that blur tonal definition until measure 18 where a cadence in E flat settles the tonality.

The vocal line is written in 4/4 meter while the piano is in 6/8 throughout the song. Over the even eighth note figures in the piano, the melody moves rhythmically in a pattern of dotted eighths followed by a sixteenth and its reverse form to create a kind of skipping movement. The ends of seven phrases are characterized by another pattern - a quarter note tied to an eighth on the third beat. These rhythms also serve a unifying purpose. The murmuring motion of the treble clef piano accompaniment provides a quiet moving undercurrent for the dotted rhythms in the voice until the last verse. (Ex. 26b) Then the left hand jumps to the bass clef and fairly shouts for joy in lavish arpeggiated harmonies to express the pleasure of harvest in "sovereign barns" which the melody also emphasizes. The voice rests for a measure while the piano whisks a quick arpeggiated "whoosh" and then complete silence prepares the listener for the bold concluding line, "I wish I were a hay!" This is set to two simple chords followed by a measure which sums up the left hand material.

Earlier, the use of minor seconds is prominent throughout the melody, but these do not occur in the piano until the final measure on "Hay" where the right hand repeats minor seconds three times in accelerando - as if to emphasize hurriedly again, but politely, how little the grass has to do. A high soft E flat major chord strikes an "Amen" to this sparkling setting of Dickinson's poem. Paul Sperry sings a sensitive interpretation of this song on his recording of Farwell songs.

Ernst Bacon composed a cheerful setting to the same poem in 1944. His version uses minimal piano accompaniment and he instructs the pianist to play "glassy" on certain pianissimo notes, and adds "with a little preening", "dreamily" and with "exquisite warmth" at other points as he develops the "littleness" of the grass's activity.

Another well-set version of the same poem is Persichetti's *The Grass*, published in 1958. His song bears more resemblance to Bacon's setting than to Farwell"s. His music is very relaxed and seems to suggest the on-going easy life of the summer grass.

Jo Ann Sims has analyzed carefully the Farwell and Persichetti settings of *The Grass so Little Has to Do* in her doctoral thesis.[29] Her admirable comparative study is more detailed than space permits here, and gives further insight into these compositions.

*An Awful Tempest Mashed the Air,* (Op. 112, No. 3) is from Dickinson's 1860 period of writing. In this poem she sees her beloved Nature blackened as with a "spectre's cloak" and inhabited by demonic "creatures" who "chuckled from the roofs", . . . "whistled", . . . "shook their fists" . . . and "swung their frenzied hair." The tempest Dickinson describes may well be symbolic of an inner storm which she so often suffered. However, by the last verse, she says morning has "lit", and the "monster's faded eyes" have turned slowly away. This is followed by peace "like Paradise" which has returned to her inner being as well as to the outer atmosphere.

Farwell has written a volcanic setting appropriate to that vivid text, where his music is closely wedded to the words. (Ex. 27a) Beginning in the treble clef with a single sforzando staccato chord - like a clap of thunder - the accompaniment drops both hands to the bass clef for an agitato "stormy" introduction of three measures. The piano continues to mirror the text and vocal line with stunning, imaginative writing. One hears the "creatures chuckle", and feels the shaking of their fists as the tempest is met with music that furiously skips widely over the keyboard. (Ex. 27b) The initial tumult subsides with a two measure piano interlude that prepares the way for the quiet of morning's arrival. Farwell can't resist using some trill-like treble figures for the "birds arose" that provide relief from the earlier heavy harmonic texture. "Peace" returns with rolled chords and thinner texture as the music softly changes to D major for a sunny and serene ending.

John Duke also used this text in his *Six Poems by Emily Dickinson* which were published in 1978. *An Awful Tempest Mashed the Air* is the most exciting of the group. Like Farwell, Duke strives to present the fury of the storm and uses the meter of 5/8 4/8 to suggest its uneven gusts, and perhaps the inner ambivalence of the poet's problems. Duke, like Farwell, begins with a smashing single fortissimo chord and quickly drops the dynamics to a softer but agitated introduction. The agitation and volume pick up with the entrance of the voice and build to a long fortissimo climax on "frenzied hair". A nine measure interlude leads into a slower tranquil mood for the last verse beginning with "The morning lit." Then the music slips from A minor into A major for the concluding "Paradise", a change similar to Farwell's.

Duke uses seven pages to develop his ideas for this poem. Farwell condenses his ideas into three stormy pages and moves swiftly through frequent chromatic changes in order to create the biting awfulness of the tempest he presents.

In reviewing these songs, we have seen how the universality of Dickinson's thoughts expressed so deeply and skillfully in her own cryptic fashion, has challenged the depths of many composers.

The more one analyzes and compares the structure and mood of Farwell's Dickinson settings with those by other composers, the more one is impressed with the admirable craftsmanship of Farwell's songs. He captures the quintessence of each poem in a warm and understanding manner that makes the songs a pleasure for singer and listener alike. The remaining settings for which space did not permit a discussion, are of the same high quality and source of enjoyment. Although they were composed between 1907 and 1949, they are as fresh and original as settings written more recently by other composers.

Farwell was concerned about the fate of his songs. In a letter to his composer friend, Noble Kreider, written May 26, 1948, he stated:

> Meanwhile I am the forgotten man about here. [New York City]. None of the current generation of artists ever heard of me, especially as the leading orchestra conductors will no longer play anything of my generation. And now Schirmer is going to destroy the bulk of the plates of my songs which they publish, unless I will buy them from

them, (which I can't do), and the few remaining copies.
You see, I haven't gotten around to going after singers to
sing them - so they just lie on Schirmer's shelves. Yet I
feel that they represent a lot of my finest work, and in the
long run would prove a real contribution to American
song literature.   It's rather tragic to me and I am
pondering how I can turn defeat into victory.

There was no way that Farwell could turn "defeat into victory"
during his lifetime.

### Other Settings, 1912-1935

Even though Farwell considered his settings of the Dickinson
poems to be among his best works, he composed songs for poems
by other poets that certainly deserve examination.

An earlier and longer song than the Dickinson settings is *Sea
Vision* Op. 36, composed in 1912.   This is set to a poem from
*Duandon* by George Sterling.  Its twelve pages are another good
example of Farwell's sensitivity to text as he has carefully done
more than put music to words.  Here one is reminded of what he
wrote in 1902 in the Wa-Wan Press about the relationship
between words and music.  He believed that the poem should:

> serve the composer as a point of departure and not. . . a
> mere desire to tally the text with a melody in appropriate
> rhythm. . . . A point of view is necessary which shall
> carefully balance the matter expressed with the manner of
> expression. . . . Devotion to a point of view invariably
> characterizes a higher degree of art appreciation.[30].

*Sea Vision* is a song where the scope of the poetry must be
grasped in order to appreciate Farwell's sensitive setting.   The
poet envisions the bottom of the sea into which he has thrown his
"pearls" or precious dreams, and longingly waits for his beloved.
He sees "All dreams that Hope has promised Love" and "All joy
held once and lost again".  "These and the mystery thereof", he is
guarding under "the sundering main."

The music begins (Ex. 28a) in G flat major with a repeated arpeggiated bass in the piano that undulates to set the mood in the brief introduction for "Far down, where virgin silence reigns". The melody, too, has a downward cast. The key changes on page three where the waving bass line is exchanged for repeated octaves on B during the seven bar interlude. The octaves under the flowing melody also serve as a unifying element in the succeeding measures. A slow section beginning on page eight (Ex. 28b) uses alternating chords to build up to a broad climax on "vain". This is one of several climaxes in the song with a notable one on $b^1$ flat on the word "joy", page nine. An interlude of 21 measures sustains the mood and prepares for the closing verse in another key and time signature: "These and the mystery thereof I guard beneath the sundering main". Here the melody settles down on middle c# after which the accompaniment returns to the same arpeggiated bass figure used in the introduction, but in a higher pattern and different key. Simple chords in the right hand stay in the bass clef until it moves quietly to parallel the left hand as it continues higher to a concluding pianissimo chord. The total effect of this song is stunning when well performed.

*The Ravens Are Singing* Op. 69, No. 1 is an entirely different song and exciting to perform. This is a setting of a poem by the Indian poet, Charles O. Roos, a friend of Farwell's. He describes the scene for the Indian warriors' return to camp with one of their dead. "The ravens are singing; the red moon walks in the sky. The night falls and a black cloud walks in the sky." The warriors come through "ghost dawn pale", so "silence the drummers" and "Sound loud the deathwail".

William Treat Upton declared in 1930, "It is doubtful if Farwell ever wrote a more powerful song than *The Ravens are Singing.*" Here a somber melody is sung "against a dirge-like accompaniment with its unceasing, sinister drum-beats" which Farwell has handled "with great skill". Upton points out further "The dark color of the whole, yet with no monotony of effect, indicates interpretative and technical craftsmanship of a high order. All of Farwell's recent songs show fine command of harmonization."[31] Upton considered this song another example of Farwell's "modern" writing.

In this song, (Ex. 29a) Farwell's use of parallel thirds in a frequently repeated right hand figure serves as relief from the persistent repeated bass notes. The chords are often minus the third which emphasizes the Indian quality of the accompaniment. The climax comes (Ex. 29b) after three bars of rest for the singer who then proclaims without piano, "Sound loud" followed by a crashing forte chord in the piano while he wails "the Death wail" portamento on a descending octave.    Farwell's use of the portamento here is a striking realistic "modern" touch which Upton probably observed.

*A Dawn Song* Op. 69, No. 2 uses another poem written by Charles Roos. This captivating song has an airy, buoyant quality, contrasting sharply with *The Ravens are Singing*. The text speaks of the gray wood-dove who "flute-calls his tale of forest love across the vale" at the break of dawn. The piano accompaniment provides the perfect delicate setting for the moving melody. The song is noteworthy especially because it is rather impressionistic. The time signature moves frequently from 3/4 to 4/4 and 5/4. The piano accompaniment often changes in style and differs from Farwell's usual writing. It features a flute-like motive in measures appropriate to the text as well as some sweeping thirty-second groups and other contrasting triplet patterns.    Because of its frequent changes, the song is not as easy to sing as other Farwell songs of this period, but well worth the effort required.

*Wishing*, Op. 59, No. 2, is a short gratifying solo for medium voice, set to a whimsical poem by Thomas Hood.    Farwell has captured the fanciful imagery of the text using a light-hearted approach. (Ex. 30a) He writes a lilting melody with a barcarolle-style accompaniment for verses one and two.    In verse three, (Ex. 30b) he moves briefly from the original key of E flat to B major with sparkling sixteenth notes in the treble clef and the same barcarolle rhythm added to the bass.  This exquisite song deserves to be heard today.

## The Blake Settings

William Blake (1757-1827) was an English poet, engraver and painter as well as a writer and visionary. Blake's vivid imagination and visionary experiences infused all of his work. Farwell went deeply into Blake's life and poetry where he found confirmation of his own intuitive experiences that he described in his book, *Intuition in the World-Making*.

Brice Farwell's excellent thought-provoking article on his father's settings of William Blake's poems is noteworthy.[32] These Blake-inspired songs include: *Love's Secret* published in the Wa-Wan Press in 1903, *The Wild Flower's Song* published by Church in 1920, *The Tyger* composed in 1934 and unpublished, and two songs written in 1930 and published on Farwell's lithographic press in 1935 - *The Lamb* and *A Cradle Song*.

Upton calls attention to the attractive simplicity of style Farwell used for *The Wild Flower's Song* which he claims "exactly fitting the William Blake text." Upton further notes that "This simplicity is retained throughout the song, in spite of the fact that the harmonies are rich and novel. In this combination of simple feeling and rich harmonic color it is a notable song."[33]

*The Lamb*, Op. 88, No. 1, also has an appealing simplicity so appropriate to the text which is drawn from Blake's *Songs of Innocence*. (Complete setting in Ex. 31.) It is in strophic style with a melody based on triadic or scale movement with little of the chromaticism that colored much of his other writing.[33] Since this was the first composition Farwell published on his own press, he sensibly chose an uncomplicated work to print.

This song is an excellent example of Farwell's preference for phrases of regular length being only twenty measures long with four-measure phrases. Its musical continuity is secured by elided cadences which hide the phrase regularity. An examination of the concluding two measures shows especially well how Farwell camouflaged his cadences. (Further examinations of other scores reveal that his cadences rarely imply an immediate release of tension. Usually this release is gradual with the cadence extended by the use of non-harmonic material.) In *The Lamb*, complete repose is not achieved until the very last beat of the song.

Blake's *The Lamb* has been a very popular text for composers. In the research for his bibliography, *Blake Set to Music*, Donald Fitch found 225 different settings for it.[34] In about 1928 Arthur Somervell set *The Lamb* with a more somber mood than Farwell did. It is found reprinted in the same collection, *New Songs for New Voices*, as Farwell's *Afternoon on a Hill*. Somervell adds seriousness to the words by doubling the melody in an inner voice an octave below the melody line in the piano.. Both hands play in the bass clef for the first three phrases where the lowest bass notes run in parallel thirds to that octave doubling. The accompaniment follows the melody line as it does also in Farwell's setting. Both composers use the strophic form. Farwell's music has more appeal because of its simplicity that seems more appropriate than Somervell's heavier setting.

*The Cradle Song* Op. 88, No. 2, is a longer composition than *The Lamb* having a total of six pages. This was the second piece which Farwell prepared on his lithograph press. It illustrates Blake's contrasting topics and is taken from his *Songs of Experience.* (Ex. 32) Farwell uses a gentle rocking bass throughout the first four pages. The melody often moves in four dotted eighth notes per bar against two dotted quarters in the treble clef piano accompaniment. A change of mood takes place on "When thy little heart does wake, then the dreadful lightnings break." Here Farwell quickens the tempo and creates an agitated accompaniment that climbs gradually in pitch to a fortissimo climax as if to suggest how naughty even a baby can be!. (He had enough experience with his own children to know!) The last page repeats the eight bars from the beginning to which he adds a concluding phrase that incorporates very softly two bars of the agitato section before it fades away on a rocking "Sleep, sleep".

*The Tyger*, Op. 98, reflects the maturity of Farwell's craftsmanship. This is his most elaborate setting of all the Blake poems. The very nature of the text demands it and the powerful imagery is the kind to challenge Farwell's imagination. According to Fitch's findings, this Blake poem also stimulated 78 other composers to create settings.

Writing in 4/4 meter and in the key of A flat, Farwell uses alternating A flats an octave apart in triplets for his bass line accompaniment. Treble clef chords in half notes frequent the treble clef writing. The words, "Tyger! Tyger!" are set in declamatory style on dropped octaves $c^1$ to c, for the voice. Thereafter, the melody winds chromatically from one phrase to another. As the text grows more exciting, so does the music. Farwell moves the triplets from the bass to the treble clef. Rests punctuate the melody line for "What the hammer? What the chain?" and the vocal figures are imitated by the piano. Farwell uses nearly a full page to unravel and conclude the momentum he has developed earlier. One notes a relationship to Blake's poem, *The Lamb* here in the line "Did he who made the Lamb make thee?" Farwell instructs the singer to perform the words "make thee" as "semi-spoken with wonderment." This reflects his own respect and wonder for God's creation.

Farwell has lightly crossed out eight bars on the last page of the manuscript which suggests they might be omitted. They are followed by the same text in a different setting, thus giving the singer a choice of renditions. Singers should explore the powerful *Tyger! Tyger!* for its potential program use today.

### The Shelley Settings

Farwell composed five songs to poems by Percy Bysshe Shelley (1792-1822), the great English lyric poet who believed that poetry turned all things to loveliness. Farwell's setting of Shelley's poem *On a Faded Violet* Op. 43, No. 2, composed in 1914, won recognition by William Treat Upton who, this early, recognized Farwell's "modern" traits when he wrote: "Although this later song abounds in the most modern harmonic effects, it nevertheless is able to maintain a studied simplicity, which but adds to the effectiveness of its subtle characterization." Upton also liked Farwell's *Daughter of Ocean*, No. 3 from the same set of Shelley poems declaring it "shows fine vigor and sweep.[35]

Benjamin Lambord also liked the Shelley settings and wrote: "In *Daughter of Ocean* and *Bridal Song* (Op. 43, No.1), the composer has applied in a more modern and highly colored scheme some of the experiments with secondary seventh chords that lend such interest to his later Indian studies." His comments are of special interest considering they were written not long after the music was published in 1914.[36]

*Song of Proserpine*, Op. 72, No. 1 was the fourth of five poems penned by Shelly that Farwell set to music. One should understand the myth on which the poem is based to appreciate Shelley's text and Farwell's music.

Proserpine (or Persephone) was the daughter of Zeus and Demeter, the latter being goddess of agriculture, productive soil, fruitfulness of mankind and guardian of marriage.

Mythology says that Proserpine was abducted by Pluto, while she was gathering flowers in Sicily. Demeter sought everywhere for her daughter and threatened destruction for all mankind by withdrawing fertility from the earth if she could not find Proserpine. Zeus promised to bring their daughter back from Hades providing she had not eaten anything while she was there. The problem was that she had eaten some pomegranate seeds. As a result she was compelled to divide the year, spending six months with her parents and the other six with Pluto in Hades.[37]

In Shelley's *Song of Proserpine*, Proserpine addresses her mother as Sacred Goddess, Mother Earth, and pleads for rescue: "Breathe thine influence most divine on thine own child" even as "Thou dost nourish these young flowers . . . "

In Farwell's setting of this poem, he deviates from his usual practice of setting one syllable per note. Instead he writes a flowing melody characterized by the frequent use of two notes per syllable and even three and four notes per syllable in the last verse. The opening "Sacred Goddess" rises three notes to $c\#^1$ and drops an octave in a kind of opening bow. Most phrases that follow have an ascending line that feature a large intervalic drop at the end. The first opening $c\#^1$ to $c\#$ octave drop is used three more times.

The introductory cadence and following four measures of voice and piano accompaniment are repeated identically for the beginning of the second verse. However, thereafter, Farwell uses a more florid melody on "Fairest children of the Hours". (Ex. 33) After the second verse ends, a one bar interlude is followed by the repetition of "Breathe thine influence most divine on thine own child, Proserpine" as written at the end of the first verse. These repetitions and the rhythmic patterns which match Shelley's trochaic feet, serve to unify the whole. The result is a distinctive product that differs from many earlier songs by Farwell. It was published by G. Schirmer in 1943 although composed in 1926.

*To Night* Op. 76, No. 2, was Farwell's fifth setting of a Shelley poem. This was a revision in 1926 of an earlier "student version" according to Farwell's notes. It has not been published.

### Hound of Heaven

*The Hound of Heaven* Op. 100, set to the famous poem by Francis Thompson, was written for baritone and orchestra in 1935. Farwell had correspondence with the singer, Roland Hayes, who had suggested the poem to Farwell. Letters indicate that the 40 page length of the work became a problem and prevented Hayes from performing it. The score is impressive and deserves consideration as to how it might be cut, making it more usable. Farwell himself planned to rewrite it and thought about dividing the text between a chorus and soloist, but never completed it.

### Characteristics of Arthur Farwell's Art Songs

Performing or listening to a sensitive performance of Farwell's songs is the best way to evaluate them. What might look questionable on paper, becomes beautiful when properly performed, as Humperdinck discovered in evaluating one of Farwell's lesson efforts. We might question whether Farwell's songs arouse emotion that is compatible with that aroused by the poetry - thus synthesizing the images to make a complete expressive experience as Donald Ivey suggests in his *Song, Anatomy, Imagery and Styles.*[38] The answer is "Yes, many of Farwell's songs do arouse that kind of emotion."

Farwell's choice of poetry was of higher quality than that used by many of his contemporaries. In composing a song, he first sought to interpret faithfully the essential significance of the poem. He would agree with Francis Poulenc who believed that he must "translate into music not merely the literal meaning of the words, but also everything that is written between the lines."[39] What was the poet trying to express? As Farwell stated in the Wa-Wan Press, he believed that the meaning and feeling of the poem should serve the composer as "a point of departure", a goal Farwell realized in most of his art songs.

He believed also that the purpose of collaboration is the creation of a mood, which he found to be the generative source of the poem and music alike. He was concerned with bonding them to create a richer whole. His later songs are exemplary in this respect; he gave "wings to the words" and created music that

also had a life of its own.    He would agree with Robert Franz
who wrote:    "The word... forms the skeleton which the sound
clothes as its flesh."[40]

Farwell's gift for melodies is obvious and singers find them
very singable though some melodies seem difficult to master at
first due to many chromatics and changes in tonality.    Also
apparent is Farwell's ability to limn the essence of the lines of a
poem with appropriate music.    The vocal range is usually an
octave and a fourth with most notes occurring on the staff.
Climaxes often have a $g^1$ or $a^1$, but not higher than $b^1$ flat.

In reviewing the piano accompaniments one observes
characteristics common to many of the songs.    The piano part may
be quite difficult, but Farwell often uses enharmonic changes to
facilitate easier reading for the pianist.    Usually the lowest notes
form the harmonic foundation and there are pedal points in many
of the fast-moving songs.    Notes from the melody line may be
found buried in the upper-most part of the piano part, or
sometimes in the bass clef.    Though obscured, this writing
undergirds the singer with pitch-security.    This "voice doubling"
often occurs on the strong beat; then the lines go independently.
Sometimes these notes from the vocal line may be found an
octave higher in the piano.

When Farwell writes piano solo passages between phrases or
verses, he often anticipates the singer's next pitch at the end of
the interlude.    Not only does this help the singer during the
learning process, but also this prepares the listener for what is
coming musically.

The "middle" or "inner" notes of the accompaniment are the
most active ones.    These serve to complete the harmony implied
by the bass line and melody.    Vernon Mueller discovered that
these voices are "carefully planned to provide melody lines that
rival the vocal melody and emphasize brief melodic motives."
Moreover, he found that these inner voices usually establish and
continue the rhythmic and harmonic movement by using chromatic
passages within the given harmony.[41]

In examining Farwell's harmonic practices, Moeller believes
that Farwell's use of triads and extended tertial harmony give
evidence of the changing times in which he lived.    He noted that
certain sounds in Farwell's music reflected equally upon late

Romanticism, Impressionism and the more contemporary sounds of the period in which he wrote.[42] This is especially true of the songs set to Dickinson texts.

Further study of Farwell's harmonic practices reveals how vividly he exploits the freedom of harmony in both vertical and horizontal senses. His linearly-inspired harmony begins quite simply, but becomes more complicated until it reaches the climax. After that it is simplified to the end. The closing bars often contain a harmonic or melodic excerpt taken from the beginning of the song which serve to reestablish the initial mood and unify the whole.

In examining Farwell's rhythmic practices, one sees that he usually follows the meter found in the poem, but not rigidly so. In order to avoid a "sing-song" effect, he used rests to separate the metric feet or he held notes long enough so that important words would fall on the strong beats of measures for emphasis. Sometimes he distorted the natural rhythm of the text by mixing rhythm patterns for the same reason. Another technique was to use a "Scotch snap" so that the entire word of more than one syllable would be sung on one beat.

One finds some bimetric meters in the songs, such as 12/8 with 4/4; also the consecutive use of different meters such as 3/2 and 5/4. The reasons for metric change within the songs stem from situations involving augmentation or diminution of a measure to satisfy poetic accents. Or it may be to provide a piano interlude between verses where he wants to accentuate a poetic idea.

A survey of his songs indicate his preference for poems written in iambic feet having also a regular construction. His songs also show a preponderance of two or four measure phrases. He was careful about syllabification and rarely wrote more than two notes to a syllable.

Farwell depended upon the form of the poem to a large extent in organizing his musical settings and most of them are "through-composed". Much of Dickinson's poetry is divided into stanzas of four lines each. In setting her poetry, he followed her metric scheme and used short rests in the vocal part, between stanzas, or longer vocal rests with piano interludes which prepare the listener for what is to follow. Sometimes he reiterates an earlier musical idea to shape the song. The later practice is quite common and tends to suggest a ternary form. However, the restatements of earlier ideas are usually just repetitions of the basic motive or theme with only minor variations rather than actual developments of the original ideas. In a number of the Dickinson settings, Moeller discovered that it is more common to find the accompaniment restating motives which occurred originally in the voice part; some are melodic, but often the motives are purely rhythmic in nature.[43]

Farwell's indications for interpretation are marked in the beginning with suggestions like, "Slowly, with breadth and majesty", "Buoyant and elastic", "With dash and sweep". In *On This Long Storm* he was more specific in the effect he wants. He wrote "half whispered", stressed, with "very slight retard" for the end of the phrase "The quiet nonchalance of death".

In checking the variety of tempo markings at the beginning of his songs, one sees that twenty of the thirty-four Dickinson songs are marked "Slowly" or "Very slowly". It seems that these particular poems which caught Farwell's interest were of such serious nature that they required a more solemn or dignified setting. However, Farwell's songs also show his delightful sense of humor as exemplified in *Papa Above!*, *The Sabbath*, *I'm Nobody* and others which move quickly.

Farwell often ends a song in a key different from the one in which he begins. He uses imitation, sequences, motivic interplay between voice and piano, and frequently avoids traditional chord progressions to create more colorful, lush chromatic harmonies in the accompaniments. Rhythms are dictated by the texts which he studied carefully. He keeps a balanced relationship between voice and piano. Neither has excessive importance, but they become a united whole so that the music intensifies the mood of the poet without overwhelming the text.

In discussing poetry and music, Susanne K. Langer uses the term "assimilation" to mean "a song conceived poetically which sounds not as the poem sounds, but as the poem feels."[44] This quality will be found in a number of Farwell's mature songs.

In reviewing the list of Farwell's art songs it is difficult to find a stopping place as he has written so many gems. Even as Paul Sperry expressed excitement when he discovered the settings of the

Emily Dickinson poems, so the singer should delight in exploring Farwell's treasury of art songs.

## Patriotic Songs and Community Music

Farwell's first musical expression of patriotism was his *Hymn to Liberty* composed in 1910 for a special celebration in New York City.[45] Before the song was published, he sent a copy to his former teacher in Germany for criticism. Humperdinck approved most of the music, but suggested some changes for chords in two phrases resulting in a different melody line. Farwell rejected Humperdinck's suggestions in favor of his own ideas, and the published form retained Farwell's original version. (34a, b) Evidently, Farwell's decade of experience in composition had already given him a secure basis for his own judgement. Or was he too stubborn to consider the changes? More likely, Farwell may have decided that his own particular melody and harmonic progressions better suited the text which he had also written. He also prepared an orchestral accompaniment for this song.

World War I inspired Farwell to write the words and music for a dramatic ballad *Soldier, Soldier* published by John Church, which he dedicated to his infant son, Brice. A study of the text shows it to be a series of questions and answers between the soldier and an onlooker.[46] Farwell often tried his hand at writing poetry, especially when he could not find a poem that expressed some ideas he wished to put into music. MacDowell contended that often a song was better when the composer also wrote the words. Other writers disagree. Michael Tippett believes that "The moment the composer begins to create the musical verses of his song, he destroys our appreciation of the poem as poetry, and substitutes an appreciation of his music as song." He also felt that when we hear a good song we are rarely disturbed "by the quite possible fact that the poetry is poor."[47]

We will not evaluate Farwell's poetry as such, but rather consider the song itself. (Ex. 35a) The music moves in a steady march rhythm and melody in strophic style for three verses. Originating in D major, the key drops to A flat minor for the verse beginning "Drummer, drummer." (Ex. 35b) Here Farwell uses a drum roll figure in the bass on each first and third beat for two pages. Then he moves to C major and uses triplets with repeated notes to develop an agitated, ominous mood for "Soldier, soldier, why does the air grow chill?" The music builds in both tempo and tension for several pages until the climax is reached with a return to the refrain. There Farwell suggests "the soloist may be joined by a chorus, or the audience familiar with the refrain." The total effect could be impressive.

*Our Country's Prayer* with text by Carl Roppel was another product of this war period. This was published by John Church as a solo and later for four-part chorus which became popular with Farwell's community choruses.

World War II prompted Farwell to write both words and music for three more solos: *We Want Straight Talk*, *Lend a Hand*, and *Let's Go*. These were also in keeping with the spirit of the times. Using a poem by H. I. Phillips, *A Soldier's Explanation*, Farwell composed another narrative solo that asks the soldier "What-cha fightin' for?" and gives the soldier's reasons.

In 1943, Farwell also composed a song *God of Battles* based on a poem of the same name, written by Lt. Gen. George S. Patton, Jr.

During this period Farwell was drawn to writing a new national anthem and experimented with several studies, again supplying his own texts. *One World* and *America's Vow* were the results which he prepared for unison and piano, and for four voices with piano.

The psychic, Agnes Stanko, who influenced the lives of the Farwells (Chapter 15), wrote several poems relating to the war which Farwell set to music. He prepared her *Millions of Souls* for unison singing and for four voices with piano. Stanko wrote the melody for her *Soldiers are Calling* and Farwell supplied the harmony. The verses are weak for both songs and Farwell's settings do little to improve them. However, the fact that Farwell did set these texts and two others suggests his loyalty to friends and his patriotic spirit.

Farwell's songs for community singing written during World War I were widely used at that time. One of them, *March! March!* for unison singing, was published by Schirmer in 1916. It was written for piano in D flat, also for trumpets and trombones and finally for orchestra. Brice Farwell said that his father was always disappointed and perhaps a little bitter or jealous that this song never gained the popularity of George M. Cohan's *Over There* and Farwell could not understand why. This is an instance where his idealism failed to communicate. Farwell wrote the text in which he tried to put the challenges of war on a spiritual level. "Love to hate shall never yield/ While the sword of God we wield/ On to Armageddon's field: March, comrades, march!" Such lofty phrases hardly had strong public appeal even when set to sturdy martial rhythms. Another problem was his melody that lacked the snappy bounce of Cohen's song.

Other vocal scores written for community chorus during 1916 include *Joy! Brothers, Joy!*, and *After the Battle*, published by G. Schirmer.

As Farwell's performing community choruses grew in musicianship, they needed greater musical challenges. So he went beyond unison writing to writing in four parts for them. In 1918 John Church published four more choral works: *Our Country's Prayer*; *Breathe on Us, Breath of God*; *Watchword*; and *Hosanna*. The latter work was dedicated to the pupils of the Third Street Music School Settlement in New York.

Church also published Farwell's *O Captain! My Captain!* written for four part men's voices. In this setting of Walt Whitman's famous poem, Farwell tries to capture the dramatic essence and mood of the poem. (Ex. 36a & 36b) He uses tempo changes and frequent tremolos in the accompaniment to emphasize key words. This 17-page song should have been appealing to large male choruses of that day. All of these songs were intended to be more demanding vocally than earlier choruses had been.

In 1920 when Farwell became active with community singing in California, he wrote six more songs for this purpose: *We Will Be Free* - (Ex. 37), *On a Summer Morning*, *Sing Brother Sing*, *Any Time for Singing*, and *Sing Awhile Longer*. *Defenders* was written for, and dedicated to, the Berkeley Defense Corps, Berkeley, California.

In 1922, Farwell prepared song sheets for the Pasadena Community Music Meetings which he directed. Song sheet number one (Ex. 38) includes *We Will Be Free*. One notes here that he has set *De Rocks A'Renderin'* in a lower key than the original solo to make it easier for Community Music singing. We also see two Spanish-Californian folk songs and an Indian folk song. Another song sheet for community singing included his translations of songs by Schubert, Dvořák, Kjerulf, Hugo Wolf, and a Bach chorale. Farwell tried to provide music of high quality and interest for his groups.

*Sister Beatrice* saw production in 1922 with the Pasadena Community Playhouse. The only music available from that effort is one vocal solo which deserves mention. It is *Song of the Holy Virgin* based on a poem of the same name by Maurice Maeterlinck. Farwell uses the Dorian mode to create a simple haunting melody that is used strophically. Farwell suggests that in the dramatic production the song should be sung "as if singing to oneself". This is one of the few solos Farwell composed using a religious text.

In 1912 Farwell wrote *Symphonic Hymn on March! March!* for orchestra that could be performed with or without chorus. His *Symphonic Song on Old Black Joe*, Op. 67 was composed probably about 1923. (See Ex. 69 in chapter 22.) This work proved to be a very popular one on his community music programs as did the Spanish-Californian folk songs which he arranged. These two works for orchestra were the most elaborate works he wrote primarily for community programs.

Although most of Farwell's choral writing was for a specific purpose as in pageants or for community music programs, he also composed octavo music. *Keramos* (The Potter's Wheel) is a likeable setting of Henry W. Longfellow's poem in this category.

*Keramos* was written in 1907 for four part mixed voices with soprano and tenor solos. It was published by Remick Music Corporation as Opus 28. Farwell also wrote a male quartet version which was not published. Farwell was intrigued with the word "turn" for which he wrote "turning" figures in the women's voices over the bass melody for the first verse covering four pages. He changes keys from A flat, to A, to A flat again, then E flat and finally returns to the mood and movement of the original A flat. This is a challenging early work that might appeal to high school choirs if its nineteen pages and traditional styling are not deterrents. The music offers varieties of tonal color and rhythmic movement supported by an appropriate piano accompaniment.

Farwell's major work *Mountain Song* written in 1931, is basically for orchestra, but it features several chorales which are worth investigating. *Depth of Pines*, (Ex. 39) is one of the simpler ones. In this "symphonic song ceremony" Farwell was striving again for a new musical form of expression. The music is discussed further in chapter 22.

The tender *Old Man's Love Song* for mixed chorus is discussed in chapter 17 with Indian music, as are five more Indian a cappella choruses written especially for the Westminster Choir. The latter were published by G. Schirmer in 1937. Other Indian based solos are also found in this chapter.

The Reverend Sidney T. Cooke[48] approached Farwell with his text for a United Nations anthem and persuaded him to set it to music. Much correspondence followed before the task was completed in 1946. (See examples 40a and 40b for complete vocal score) Farwell also prepared an orchestral score for the anthem. Cooke's reaction to Farwell's score for his text is shown in his letter to Farwell dated November 27, 1946. "I regard your composition as *Powerful*, the very thing needed here. I am glad to have it for the hoped for negotiations. . . . I am ever so pleased at the cooperation between the two of us."

### Songs for School Children

In addition to writing choruses for adults, Farwell also wrote choruses for school children's song books. The first four part songs composed for Silver Burdett in 1914, were followed in 1922 by three choruses for Ginn and two for Hinds. Farwell also composed some very attractive solo songs based on verses for children. His *Afternoon on a Hill*, first published in *New Songs for New Voices*, is appealing.[49] This song was composed at the request of David Mannes who, with Louis Untermeyer, edited the collection. Mannes sent Farwell several children's verses from which to choose for his setting. (March 7, 1927) His choice was a poem by Edna St. Vincent Millay.

In reviewing Farwell's vocal compositions, one finds a wide spectrum ranging from simple art songs to include music for children, patriotic songs, community choruses and on to the complex settings of the Emily Dickinson poems.

The music written for community choruses may be out-dated today, but it met a real need for that time. Farwell was concerned about providing simple, yet challenging music that appealed to the amateur singers in his groups, and he was frustrated in not finding many appropriate scores available. He seems to be one of the few major composers of that period who wrote music for the specific purpose of community singing. His goal in so doing was to "uplift" people and enhance their love of music and singing - a challenge to this "practical idealist."

Further analysis of Farwell's work in other genres will point out excellent compositions worthy of performance today. However, since his art songs are more accessible than some of his other works, and are of such high quality, these are especially recommended for study and performance. Moreover, not only his Dickinson settings, but also his earlier composed songs and the Indian-inspired ones merit consideration. The author is excited about the innate beauty of Farwell's art songs. She hopes her sampling and discussion of them will stimulate other singers and teachers to investigate more of these riches. Surely at least his best songs deserve a welcome in the singer's repertoire today and his other vocal works should not be overlooked.

# Example 10.    *Strow Poppy Buds*

**Example 11.**    *Invocation*, measures 9-20.

**Example 12.** *Mädchenlieder, No. IV*

# IV.

**Example 13a.** *A Ruined Garden*

Poem by
PHILIP BOURKE MARSTON

ARTHUR FARWELL, Op. 14

VOICE

All my ros - es are dead in the gar - den, What shall I do!

PIANO

Winds in the night with-out pit - y or par - don Came there and slew;

All my song-birds are dead in their bush - es, Woe for such things!

23799 C

**Example 13b.** *A Ruined Garden*, **measures 54-63.**

**Example 14.** *The Sea of Sunset*

# The Sea of Sunset

Poem by
Emily Dickinson*

Music by
Arthur Farwell. Op. 26

\* Reprinted with the kind permission of Little, Brown & Company, copyright owners.

33536 C

**Example 15.** *Summer Shower*

# Summer Shower

Poem by
Emily Dickinson*

Music by
Arthur Farwell. Op. 73, No. 1

* Reprinted with the kind permission of Little, Brown & Company, copyright owners.

**Example 16a.** *Mine* (First page)

**Example 16b.** *Mine* (second page.)

**Example 17.**    *Unto Me*

**Example 18a.**    *Safe in Their Alabaster Chambers*, measures 1-5.

**Example 18b.** *Safe in Their Alabaster Chambers*, measures 12-17.

**Example 18c.** *Safe in Their Alabaster Chambers*, measures 25-30.

**Example 19a.** *The Sabbath,* measures 1-5.

**Example 19b.** *The Sabbath,* measures 12-17.

**Example 20.** *The Little Tippler*

**Example 21.** *Tie the Strings to My Life*

**Example 22.** *On This Wondrous Sea*

**Example 23.** *Heart, We Will Forget Him!*

**Example 24.**   *I'm Nobody! Who Are You?*

**Example 25a.  *Wild Nights! Wild Nights!*, measures 1-4.**

**Example 25b.  *Wild Nights! Wild Nights!*, measures 22-27.**

**Example 26a.** *The Grass so Little Has to Do,* measures 1-2.

**Example 26b.** *The Grass so Little Has To Do,* measures 17-24.

**Example 27a.** *An Awful Tempest Mashed the Air*, measures 1-3

**Example 27b.** *An Awful Tempest Mashed the Air*, measures 9-12.

**Example 28a.** *Sea Vision*, measures 1-9.

**Example 28b.** *Sea Vision*, **page 8.**

**Example 29a.** *The Ravens Are Singing,* **measures 1-9.**

**Example 29b.** *The Ravens are Singing,* **last 13 measures.**

**Example 30a.** *Wishing*

**Example 30b.** *Wishing*, **concluded**

**Example 31a.**   *The Lamb*

**Example 31b.** *The Lamb,* concluded.

**Example 32.**    *A Cradle Song*

**Example 33.** *Song of Proserpine,* **measures 21-30.**

**Example 34a.**   *Hymn To Liberty.*

# HYMN TO LIBERTY

Words and Music by ARTHUR FARWELL

Rise, ye na-tions! Man is free! Hail to dawn-crowned Lib - er - ty!
Hew the rock and fell the tree, Build for home and Lib - er - ty!
On - ward, dauntless, glo - rying, free, Hurl the tides of Lib - er - ty!

Armed, on the hills of morn, See, a val - iant host as - sem - bles,
Faith guid - ing hand and heart, Strike in Freedom's deep foun - da - tion
Stay not while time shall stand, Break the na - tions' bars a - sun - der,

*For marching, the variations in tempo may be disregarded*

**Example 34b.** *Hymn To Liberty.* concluded.

**Example 35a.**   *Soldier, Soldier,* **measures 1-6.**

**Example 35b.**   *Soldier, Soldier*, measures 80-89.

**Example 36a.**   *O Captain! My Captain!* **Page 18.**

**Example 36b.** *O Captain! My Captain!* **Page 19, conclusion.**

**Example 37.**    *We Will Be Free!*

**Example 38.** *Pasadena Community Music Song Sheet, No. 1*

PASADENA COMMUNITY MUSIC MEETING
Sheet 1

Poem by
JAMES THOMPSON

**1. WE WILL BE FREE**

Music by
ARTHUR FARWELL

With great breadth

**2. PENA HUECA**

Moderately

Spanish Californian Folk Song

Recorded and translated by C. F. Lummis

**8. LA GOLONDRINA**

Spanish Californian Folk Song

Slowly

Translation by A. F.

**4. DE ROCKS A'RENDERIN'**

With immense breadth

Negro Spiritual

**5. OMAHA GAME SONG**

With motion and accent

Indian Folk Song
Recorded by Alice C. Fletcher

Copyright, 1922, by Arthur Farwell

**Example 39.**   *Depth of Pines* from *Mountain Song*

DEPTH OF PINES.

**Example 40a.** *The United Nations Anthem.*

**Example 40b.**   *The United Nations Anthem,* **conclusion.**

# Chapter 19

# Farwell's Piano Music

When Farwell visited Chadwick for advice about his music studies shortly before graduation in May 1893, Chadwick encouraged him by calling his work "promising". But Chadwick also admonished him to "learn how to play the piano as fast as possible". Accordingly, after Farwell arrived home in St. Paul later that summer, he made arrangements to take lessons from a piano teacher referred to only as Herr Zoch. The lessons continued until Farwell left for Boston the last of September. By that time he had learned to play Clementi and Kuhlau Sonatinas, and had "finished Czerny" (whose exercises he disliked). Piano study and practicing continued during the years in Boston and Newton Center. Hence Farwell developed adequate skill and the self-confidence necessary to perform his own Indian compositions for his four transcontinental lecture-recital tours and Eastern engagements.

An Auburn, New York, newspaper reporting on his lecture - recital there, referred to his work at the piano, "while having none of the elements of the virtuoso, [Farwell's playing] is always musical and satisfying." Another report in the *Cleveland Town Topics* stated: "He handles the piano in a musicianly manner though he evidently lays no claim to technical ability". The obvious implication from these comments is that Farwell had studied piano long enough to make a musically effective presentation of his own compositions. This indicates what background Farwell brought to writing music for the piano, which forms about twenty three percent of his total works. His preoccupation with Indian and folk music is evident in a large portion of his earlier piano compositions. However, this is not true of his best late works such as the *Polytonal Studies* and the great *Piano Sonata* which were totally abstract works.

## Early Piano Works, 1895 - 1923

Farwell's first published work, *Tone Pictures After Pastels in Prose*, Op. 7, contains a collection of nine short pieces for piano. These are simple and almost in the nature of study pieces for the young pianist. They are the compositions which MacDowell helped the fledgling composer select for the collection and bear something of his approval. The difference in technical demands should be noted for these early pieces as compared with the greater requirements for the pianist in the *Navajo War Dance* composed scarcely a decade later in 1904. Farwell not only had matured as a composer, but also had probably improved his own piano technical skills by this time.

Farwell relates some background for the writing of his *Tone Pictures After Pastels in Prose* in a letter to Arnold Schwab dated February 3, 1951. Mr. Schwab was gathering information for a biography on James Huneker and asked Farwell to supply any recollections he had of this famous critic. Farwell had known the man and made this reply:

> The beginning was way back in 1896 or '97, before I sailed, in the latter year, for European study. It was presumably in 1896 that my teacher, Homer Norris, wanted to have me bring some of my work to publication before going abroad. So we decided on a collection of little piano pieces after sketches by Gautier, Baudelaire, Bertrand, etc. published in a little volume called "Pastels in Prose". This collection was privately printed. From Boston we sent to New York to have a cover design made by Louise Cox (wife of Kenyon Cox), who had an indirect connection with Huneker, and suggested that through this connection my collection, when published, could be handed to him. Huneker was then writing a column called "The Raconteur", in the *Musical Courier*. The title of my book of pieces was entitled *Tone Pictures after Pastels in Prose*.
>
> It was just at this time that Max Nordau's sensational and notorious book, *Degeneration,* was published, in which he decried as degenerate the mixing of the different arts and their terminologies. So Huneker began his encouraging and fairly long review of my work (the first serious review I ever had) with the words *Pictures in Tone, Pastels in Prose*, a title that would drive old Daddy Nordau wild!

The review written by Huneker to which Farwell refers, was published in the *Musical Courier*, July 31, 1895, and went on:

> *Pictures in Tone, Pastels in Prose!*   Surely this is decadentism gone mad. You remember, of course, Stuart Merrill's charming little volume made up of translations from the French.
>
> And how admirably they are done! Much of the color and music of the originals lurks in the pages of the book, for which Mr. Howells wrote an introduction.. . . He prints the prose poem, and then gives you the music evoked by it.
>
> He has taste, much feeling and a genuinely graceful talent.   Graceful rather than profound.   Echoes of Schumann and Chopin there are, but fancy reigns.   I especially liked *The Red Flower*. [Here Huneker quotes the entire prose]
>
> To this Heine-like poem Mr. Farwell has made a very pretty tone picture. The simple story is told simply in a few phrases throbbing with emotion. The episode of the horse's hoofs is suggested, and the return of the theme in the minor very neatly put.
>
> *The Stranger*, after Beaudelaire, is redolent of Chopin's second study in C sharp minor, Op. 25.   The most elaborate piece is *The Round Under the Bell*, by Louis Bertrand.   It has an eerie atmosphere.   Altogether this seventh opus of Mr. Farwell's is promising.   The volume privately printed is got up in an attractive and bizarre style. . . . The volume is really something quite unique.

The collection includes the following compositions each prefaced by a prose quotation of the same title: *Roses and Lilies, The Sages' Dance, The Stranger, Indifference to the Lures of Spring, The Red Flower, Anywhere out of the World, Evening on the Water, A Poet Gazes on the Moon,* and *The Round Under the Bell*.  The last piece is a very descriptive one and also the inspiration for Cox's unusual cover design.

In *The Round Under the Bell,* Louis Bertrand's prose describes twelve sorcerers who were dancing under the big bell at Saint

John's where they invoked the storms that awaken a sleeping man
living nearby.  A sudden crash of thunder kills the sorcerers and
he sees their books of magic burning like a torch in the black
belfry.  The frightful conflagration painted the walls of the Gothic
church "with the red flames of purgatory and hell, and prolonged
upon the neighboring houses the shadow of the gigantic statue of
Saint John."  It is this later scene which is depicted on the cover
design.  The prose is certainly the kind to stimulate a composer's
imagination and Farwell has responded accordingly.  The music is
marked "with wild fury" (Ex. 41a) and well suits the prose as
Farwell builds up a furious musical storm. (Ex. 41b)    He
concludes his piece quietly suggesting that the storm is over.

Farwell listed two numbers from this collection as having been
premiered for his first orchestral appearance, but no orchestral
version of them is known.  (These were *The Round Under the Bell*
and *The Sages' Dance*.)

*Northern Song* and *Romance* are two piano solos published by
Ditson in 1897, before Farwell left for his European studies.
These are rather typical salon pieces reflecting his early training
and carry no opus number.

*Owasco Memories*, Op. 8, a suite for piano of five numbers,
was written in 1899 but not published until 1907 in the Wa-Wan
Press.  This collection includes: *Spring Moods*, *By Moonlight*, *By
Quiet Waters*, *The Casino Across the Lake*, and *Autumn Comes*.
The suite was also arranged for piano, violin and cello in 1901,
but not published in that form.

### Works Based on Folk-Tunes

About 1900 Farwell began writing music based on Indian
themes and some of his most successful piano music is in that
category.  His very popular *Navajo War Dances* and *Pawnee Horses*
are discussed in chapter 17 along with *Dawn* and his turbulent *The
Domain of Hurakan*, because they are based on actual Indian
melodies.

Some of Farwell's short pieces make excellent recital numbers
for the piano student.  A young male student who can play
octaves should delight in Farwell's *Prairie Miniature*, Op. 20, based
on two cowboy folk songs.  It was published in the Wa-Wan Press

in 1905 as part of the group named *From Mesa and Plain*. Although this is one of Farwell's early works, it shows marks of the mature composer to come. The complete score is given in examples 42a and 42b.

The first cowboy tune begins in the right hand with a catchy triplet figure as part A of an ABA form. The B melody is given a lower setting as the left hand plays a "duet" a sixth below it. Then the melody is repeated an octave higher as the upper tone of a series of chords which are supported by bass triplets suggesting a soft gallop. Part A returns after sixteen measures with its melody played in octaves above the original theme for an eight measured close. Farwell does not include fingerings for his music, so a teacher may need to make recommendations for them. In fact, a good project for some doctoral candidate in piano pedagogy would be to prepare a series of Farwell's piano works to include fingerings and some editing.

*Ichibuzzhi* is another solo that also should have appeal especially for the male student. It was originally published in the Wa-Wan Press in 1902 and offers a greater challenge to the performer than *Prairie Miniature*. Here Farwell has used Indian material from his piano solo of the same name, published in *American Indian Melodies* a year earlier. (See Chapter 17 for further description) The later version is elaborated to cover six pages as compared with only one page in the original. A comparative study of the two solos would be an intriguing one for students in a composition class.

**Symbolistic Studies, 1900 - 1914**

Farwell became interested in the literary movement of the Symbolists who exalted the metaphysical and intangible with symbolic meaning and aimed to unify the arts. As early as 1901, he wrote his first composition reflecting this vein of thought, *Symbolistic Study No. 1, Toward the Dream*. This was followed by a more complicated solo in 1904 - *Symbolistic Study No. 2, "Perhelion"*, Opus 17. The title (from perihelion) refers to the position of a planet or comet when it is closest to the sun. In the Northern Hemisphere, the earth is at perihelion at midwinter when the sun shows a larger diameter, but this is not visible to the naked eye. Farwell does not explain the reason for his title here but rather leaves it to the performer's imagination. (He crosses out the first "i" in *Perihelion* on page one of his score, but omits it on the outside cover.) The music has sweeping melodic lines kept in the right hand, played often in octaves. These build up to a section which is played another octave above its original theme in the treble clef. Perhaps Farwell was symbolizing being close to the sun in writing notes that go to the top of the keyboard. It is surprising to find so much chromatic change throughout. He gradually lowers the melodic contours from their lofty treble position to settle down in the bass clef ending. Writing in the key of E major, Farwell has another surprise in the final cadence where he uses what should be an E major tonic chord to conclude the work. It occurs after a long rest in the right hand and the score looks as if he forgot to add the treble clef sign after writing a measure in the bass clef. If he really intended the last chord to remain in the bass clef too, then it becomes an unresolved E seventh which would be unusual for him. However, Farwell concluded his arrangement of the Indian *Bird Dance Song* with an unresolved dissonance that was published in the Wa-Wan Press in 1905. Perhaps the ending of the *Symbolistic Study, No. 2*, "*Perhelion*", was an adventurous step away from traditional ones. Farwell began to score this solo for orchestra, but never completed it.

*Symbolistic Study No. 3*, "Once I Passed Through a Populous City" was sketched originally for piano, but was later completely scored for orchestra. It is discussed in Chapter 22. Two more efforts for orchestra dealing with Symbolistic Studies, Numbers 4 and 5 were begun in the years 1905 and 1906, but never completed. No further symbolistic studies were attempted until 1912. Then he composed his *Symbolistic Study No. 6*, "*Mountain Vision*" originally for piano solo which he arranged much later with instruments as also discussed in Chapter 22.

Farwell's studies dealing with Symbolism might also include his *Domain of Hurakan* written in 1902, although it does not carry the label as a Symbolistic Study, and might rather be considered "program music". Lawrence Gilman identified it as a "study in elemental symbolism" which is an apt description of Farwell's depiction of the elements of nature. Another work which might be included as an example of this approach to composition, is Farwell's *Impressions of the Wa-Wan Ceremony*. Here Farwell stressed that these pieces were meant to be "Impressions" not program music and hence might qualify as being also symbolistic. However, after writing his *Symbolistic Study No. 6*, in 1912, Farwell's interest in Symbolism as a composing technique seems to have drawn to a close.

After selling the Wa-Wan Press to G. Schirmer in 1912, Farwell wrote no piano music for several years except for a short work done in 1914 that he revised much later in 1940. He called it *Laughing Piece*. Perhaps he was too involved with writing music for pageants and community music affairs to concentrate on writing for the piano.

**Earliest Examples of Impressionism, 1923**

After moving to Pasadena in 1921, Farwell began composing again for the piano. A few of his compositions from this time show traces of impressionism. He was well acquainted with the music of Debussy and was a personal friend of Griffes and Loeffler, both American impressionists. Farwell's files contain autographed copies of five of Griffes' works. Farwell was an early supporter of Griffes and should be credited with helping him gain an entry to the performing and publishing world. While he did not actually teach Griffes, "he was a strong influence on his development".[1]

Two of the Griffes songs were inscribed in 1912 and the three piano pieces were gifts in 1915. All of these copies look well-worn and *The Lake at Evening* bears the inscription, "In remembrance of 10 West 40th, To Arthur Farwell". This was an address in New York for Farwell at that time and was probably the site of stimulating dialogue and fellowship. Perhaps Farwell spent considerable time studying these and other similar compositions and was stirred to experiment with some of the methods used by these impressionists. However, he should not be considered as a part of this movement. Only one 1930 work shows any trace of impressionism.

Two piano pieces composed during the year 1923 show some of this impressionistic influence. The first is *Treasured Deeps*,

Opus 43, No. 1 which is built on the idea of an accompanied melody. At the bottom of the last page Farwell has placed a postscript quoted from *The Gardener*, by Rabindranath Tagore: "I long to speak the deepest words I have to say to you; But I dare not, for fear you should laugh." This may be intended as a clue to what Farwell was trying to express as *Treasured Deeps*. Technically, this is not as difficult to play as it looks, as the tempo is slow. Nevertheless, the pianist must have good control to play pianissimo throughout most of the piece and still articulate the melody against the complex arpeggiated chords.

In *Flame Voiced Night*, Op. 43, No. 2 page 14, measures five and six, one finds the use of sustained arpeggios that slightly suggest impressionism. Otherwise its sound and appearance are a little Chopinesque.

## The Michigan Period, 1927-1939

It was 1927 before Farwell wrote another piano composition and it was not published until 1930. This was *Sourwood Mountain*, the third of a group he named *Americana*. Number one of that Opus 78 was entitled *Rarin' to Go*; number two was *Plantation Plaint* which was a revision of number one and finally published by Schirmer in 1944.

*Sourwood Mountain* has enjoyed great popularity over the years since its composition in 1927. Perhaps this is due to the familiarity of the folk song used as the main theme. The original Tennessee Mountain *Cracker* tune contained only eight measures, but Farwell added an equal number to make a sixteen-measure melody. The composition is a mixture of rondo and variation forms. The melody of the F major section, after its four bar prelude, is built on the rhythmic pattern of the main sixteen measure theme, but taken exactly backwards. This music is rather typical of Farwell's music in the use of chromaticism, regular phrase structure, complex vertical sonorities, and is quite regular rhythmically.

The work begins with an easy vamp pattern in the introduction. The first version of the theme has his characteristic French sixth sound and cross-relations occurring throughout. The other three versions of the theme are similar except that the texture grows thicker in each one. This composition is another work which has been recorded.

Jeanne Behrend, pianist, sent Christmas greetings to Farwell sometime in the 1940's from Amsterdam where she was concertizing and declared, "They think *Sourwood Mountain* is swell!" And so do American audiences!

*Dream - Flower*, Opus 79, followed in 1928 and is a solo that should be an effective "recital piece" for students. In ABA form, the opening melody is a tender lyrical one of no special difficulty. The middle section is more of a challenge because the pianist must bring out the melody found in the upper notes of the right hand intervals. The texture thickens when the three bar theme is repeated in fuller chords that use more chromatics as it weaves along to the climax before thinning to a single line. Seen through the eyes and ears of a good teacher, this solo offers many opportunities for teaching basic artistic playing while the student is also experiencing music written by a distinguished composer.

*What's In An Octave?* Op. 84, written in 1930, is an example of Farwell's experimental journeys. The music all takes place between two Fs beginnning slowly and softly with both Fs acting as drones throughout the entire A section. The inner voices develop the melody that is carefully interwoven between both hands. (Ex. 43a) It gradually builds up several times to a final forte climax featuring a trill in the tenor voice, but then diminishes to pianissimo in conclusion. The B section offers more contrast without the drones in a four voice fughetta (Ex. 43b). This develops over four pages, followed by a repeated section A that changes in the concluding nine measures, thus completing the adventuresome ten page study. Farwell evidently was meeting the challenge given by Pythagoras -"All the knowledge of music is to be found within the octave," - a quote which he wrote on his manuscript. Grant Johannesen has used *What's in an Octave?* as a study work in his Master Classes at the Cleveland Institute.

*In the Tetons*, Op. 86, written in 1930, is an attractive suite of five numbers. These pieces reflect Farwell's love of the mountains and his affinity for the Tetons where he spent a vacation one summer. The first piece, *Granite and Ice* is bold and rugged with loud, full, smashing chords involving many chromatic changes. The second number, *Lonely Camp Fire* is a quiet contrast and reflective in nature. *Arduous Trail*, number three, (Ex. 44) is a brisk humoresque with a catchy bouncing rhythm. Farwell has added some suggestions for interpretation: in bar 17, he notes "Leaning against a tree, breathing, and listening to the birds." At this point, the rollicking rhythm changes to quiet sixths which culminate in a soft whole note chord, and a bird-like "twittering" occurs high in the treble clef. The "On the trail" tune resumes for twelve more measures when another suggestion is given. This occurs in a quiet pattern similar to the earlier one, but in chords this time: "Leaning against a tree, breathing, and listening to the brook." Appropriate music follows until the return to the original tune which is now in full sumptuous chords to give the piece a vigorous conclusion.

The simplicity of the harmonic structure in *Wild Flower*, number four in the suite, serves as a refreshing change from the thick harmonic writing of some of the previous numbers. Farwell acknowledges his debt to MacDowell by stating "Homage to MacDowell" under the title. This piece was published in another version as *Purple Lupine*, Op. 86, in 1941 by G. Schirmer who changed the title. It features an appealing melodic line. However, the music has less contrast than *Dream - Flower*, Op. 79. Technically simple, it seems similar to Farwell's early works, but the harmonic structure is richer. Sara Farwell told the author that "Schirmer would take only dad's little easy pieces (like *Purple Lupine*) which made him 'hopping mad'! He did not apologize for these smaller compositions, but felt they did not represent his best work. G. Schirmer was more concerned about what would readily sell." *Purple Lupine* should be a good addition to a student's repertoire.

Farwell had originally planned to write two suites of five numbers each, but never finished more than seven numbers. A marginal note on *Wind Play* states: "If second book of *In the Tetons* is not completed, *Wind Play* should go in the first book as #5 and *The Peaks at Night* as #6."

*Wind Play* lives up to its name and is an octave study for right hand with a running bass line. No metronome marking is given; he indicates "moderately fast, well nuanced". Some fingering is given for this piece, probably the work of Noble Kreider, an excellent pianist, composer and teacher who wrote thus on December 9, 1931 to Farwell:

> I haven't worked on your Wind or anyone else's wind;  I will do so and finish the fingering.  You will be surprised some day to hear a work that was suggested by *your* Wind, and yet there is no resemblance.  Somehow after playing your work, the idea came to me.

The suite concludes with *The Peaks at Night*.  This work starts very softly in a slow tempo with a motive marked "mysteriously".  A triplet figure is prominent in the writing which never rises above "piano", but yet develops a sustaining interest with the use of abundant harmonic changes.  The piece concludes with the original theme now in the bass in octaves and overlaid with light high staccato 16th notes in the treble clef.

Each number in the suite can stand alone or be used in combinations differing from the order which Farwell planned and still be effective on a program.  This suite is now being performed publicly by pianists who have discovered its inherent beauty.  Farwell's manuscripts are carefully prepared and worth the necessary challenging study.

### 1930, A Harmonic Turning Point

The *Vale of Enitharmon*, Opus 91, composed in 1930, was a work composed especially for reproduction on the lithographic press which Farwell was now planning and developing.  The beautiful figure on the cover is from a sketch by "A. E." (George Russell, the Irish poet) which Farwell prepared from the original that hung on his studio wall.  In explaining the title of this piano work, Farwell stated, "*Enitharmon* in the unique mythology of William Blake, has been interpreted, in one phase, as *Spiritual Beauty*".  In composing *Enitharmon*, Farwell sought to express this special kind of beauty as he felt it.  The work went through several revisions before he was ready to prepare it on his lithographic press.

*The Vale of Enitharmon* marks a turning point in Farwell's harmonic originality.  It is tonal in most sections, but is extremely

chromatic and includes two heavily pedaled monophonic passages
to create chords that seem to eliminate the presence of a key
center.   "The middle section is as unpredictable as any music
composed primarily of triads can be."[2]

Some influence of impressionism is also found starting on the
third page of music (numbered as page 6). (See examples 45a and
45b)   Beginning with a new section marked "Moderately with
motion", Farwell uses the mixolydian mode on D flat consisting
generally of three-note, close position common triads.   These
eighth note chords move in both hands, usually stepwise in
contrary motion, which Farwell states are all of equal duration
although he groups some eighths in a triplet pattern.  The use of
a mode and the chordal movement both suggest impressionism.

Noble Kreider was very impressed with this particular piano
work and wrote for a copy in 1934.  "I have longed to play it
more times than even you have fingers and toes - indeed have. I
know I can do it, for you have written something there that
satisfies my soul emotionally and pianistically."  After Mr. Kreider
had received the music, he wrote again:

> You know the joy I have in at last having a copy of
> *Enitharmon*, which I find just as beautiful as I did when
> I played it from your ms. with its flats and naturals that
> resemble each other so much.  I shall learn it.  I feel that
> no one can play it better than I.  I have a feeling that the
> triad part may be a bit too long.  What do you think?
> This work of yours appeals to me greatly for its poetical
> qualities, the veiled atmosphere of the entire work.

Farwell also shared this piano work with another of his old
Wa-Wan composer friends, Arthur Shepherd, who responded on
January 13, 1936, just as enthusiastically as Kreider had earlier:

> True to form I am weeks late in acknowledging your
> Christmas greetings.   The particularly interesting form
> which they took this year is added reason for a more
> prompt response on my part.  I never cease to wonder at
> your unfaltering pursuit of idealistic expression.  Your
> charming Christmas chorale and your highly effective

piano composition *Enitharmon* bring renewed evidence of the authenticity of your creative impulse. But that was of course- never in doubt.

The personal touch is there in every measure and that is the feature - I presume, that communicates most from friend to friend. The same qualities, are likewise in evidence in your "hand made" publication with the very charming cover design. Once more - I am simply "flabbergasted" at your energy - talent - artistic integrity!

Farwell's *Prelude and Fugue*, Opus 94, is a rewarding piece to play. The fugue was composed first in 1931, the prelude in 1936. The *Prelude* is written in the key of C major and 4/4 meter. Farwell wants it played "with motion, lightly" (Ex. 46a). The right hand bears the burden in most of the writing that features a beautiful melody built on a sixteenth note figure of three thirds and a sixth tied to another four note figure in sixths. This melody is extended for three measures before it moves an octave higher and is developed. The left hand is simpler and focuses initially on middle C in repeated notes and gives support with eighth note harmonic intervals throughout.

The four-voice *Fugue* stays in the same key and meter as the *Prelude* with the theme appearing first in the alto voice. (See example of opening page, Ex. 46b). It moves next to the tenor, then the bass, and finally to the soprano voice in measure 10. Farwell uses motives derived from the theme to create a well balanced work. It builds up to an exhilarating climax when the bass plays the theme "forte" on the third page and sustains the interest through extended imitation to the sturdy concluding measures. This composition is one of the few works Farwell wrote in contrapuntal style.

Farwell's *Indian Fugue-Fantasia*, written eight years later, is another work in contrapuntal style. Although it has a strong Indian theme, it is related in techniques to his *Prelude and Fugue* just discussed and makes an interesting comparison.

Farwell wrote this music originally for string quartet in 1914, but revised it for piano in 1938, numbering it Opus 44. More *Fantasia* than *Fugue*, the stirring music follows a four-voice fugal-style and opens with the vigorous Omaha theme announced in G major. This moves "moderately fast" with forceful 6/8 rhythms in the bass clef for nine and a half measures and features repeated staccato notes along with slurred notes and octave skips. (Ex. 47) Next the alto voice picks up the theme in measure 10 while the bass provides a quiet countermelody. The main theme easily provides potential material for imitation between entries of other voices until the soprano enters over the same countermelody in measure 21. Soon Farwell uses octaves in the treble clef to emphasize the theme which later is also played in octaves in the bass clef. The score quickly develops a rousing fortissimo section that eventually settles down to a serene sustained mood featuring the soft countermelody in the upper voice. The score continues with a series of contrasts and features some parts of the original Indian theme in imitation, augmentation, and inversion. He often passes fragments of the theme from one voice to another while building a new climax.

The theme abounds in octaves for the final climax which Farwell reaches with forte chords. Starting high in the treble clef, he uses parallel octaves of theme fragments that descend crashingly to the bass clef and land on a pedal ocatve G. Over this, the melody climbs up again in an accelerated fortissimo passage of triadic and chromatic figures terminating in two full chords. Farwell's vigorous Omaha Indian theme is one that lends itself to much manipulation and development, providing a challenge to the pianist as well as it did earlier to the composer. While some might criticize this nine page score as being over-extended, the author finds Farwell's use of the catchy, robust Omaha theme a notable achievement in fantasia style, a delight to the ear, and fun to play.

Farwell composed a number of tone poems for piano during these Michigan years that are worth learning. *Lyric Tide*, Op. 82, No. 1 is a slow moving melodic piece, while *Thwarted Current*, Op. 82, No. 2, is in stark contrast, full of motion, "wild and tumultuous." The music lives up to its name, is fragmented, and never seems to "go" anywhere. *Emanation* and *Fire Principle* are Opus 93, composed in 1932. The latter piece bears Farwell's cryptic comment on the score: "If anyone wants to understand this, he may get some help from Jacob Boehme's 'Three Principles of the Divine Essence'. - But I didn't get it out of any book!"

These tone poems were followed in 1934 by *Four Meditations* as Opus 97. The latter four are all written in slow tempo and a meditative mood as the title suggests.

*Two Tone Pictures* - Number 1, *Pastel*, and Number 2, *Marine*, were finished in 1936 as Opus 104. *Happy Moment* was composed in the 1939-1940 period. The latter solo deserves more than a passing remark. Farwell had a good sense of humor and tried to express this quality in several compositions. An earlier effort to be humorous was a solo titled *Laughing Piece*, written in 1914, and revised in 1940.

*Happy Moment* is a perky three page work written in a humoresque rhythm and an ABACA rondo form. (See example 48 for page one.) In the key of A major, it opens with what sounds like an A minor triad that quickly leads away to the A major chord. Embellishing notes introduce the opening theme and add to its whimsical quality. The short B section has a contemplative melody undergirded with some chromatic writing that provides contrast to the rhythmic A section. The C section changes to the key of D, is a little slower, and its melody is supported by chords in half notes. Farwell repeats this melody with slight variations in the bass before returning to the original "skipping" A section. The concluding four bars are built on the B section theme using imitation to make an effective ending.

The revised *Laughing Piece*, written predominately with staccato notes, is to be played "light and jocularly". It features clumps of sixteenth notes that jump in sequences to produce a jaunty melody. Scalar passages made up of small intervals, scamper in ascending lines. The total effect is appealing and should be worth the effort needed to create the "jocular" mood intended. These two examples of Farwell's attempt to put humor into music would make an admirable illustrative performance group on this subject. They balance what might otherwise picture Farwell as a long-faced serious idealist, but Sara Farwell remembers how jovial he could be.

## The New York Period, 1940 - 1951

### Tone Poems

Farwell began to compose for piano again not long after he moved to New York and married Betty Richardson. The birth of his daughter, Cynthia, in November 1941, probably inspired him to write these tone poems. During the next year Farwell composed two little poems for piano, Op. 106: *1. Girl Singing* and *2. Strange Dream*. These were followed later the same year by *To Cynthia*, a piece dedicated to his adored little daughter, which is reminiscent of *Girl Singing*.

### The *Polytonal Piano Studies*

In 1940 Farwell began writing a series of polytonal piano studies based on complicated charts which were intended to systematize his harmonic ideas for the project. Originally he planned to compose 46 studies, but completed only 23 of them during the next twelve years. Neely Bruce thinks they all deserve attention, although some are more successful than others. He declares that "the finest are among his most original and beautiful works".[2]  Bruce continues:

> The abstract compositional process frequently results in surprisingly poetic music, and the piano writing is idiomatic and often brilliant. The polytonal studies clearly served as a harmonic source for Farwell's last piano piece, the Piano Sonata Op. 113 (1949), which is probably his masterpiece.[3]

Farwell first prepared a work sheet for each *Polytonal Study* before beginning to compose. Several of these sheets contain information as well as chordal structures. The work sheet for *Study Number Two* includes statements about chordal relationships. It is possible that he intended the given progressions to be used by students for practice prior to learning the study as he wrote: "All the progressions should be played in all possible positions and inversions, and backwards as well as forwards, to accustom the student to their effects."

The first eleven polytonal studies deal with major keys; the numbers 12 - 21 are written in minor keys; numbers 26 and 34 use a major key combined with a minor one. Farwell has given specific dates of composition for only a few of them and these were not composed in numerical order. For example, *Study Number 2* was composed in May 1940, *Number 3* was completed on April 28, 1945, *Number 8* on May 30, 1940 and *Number 4* just a day later in the same year. He finished *Number 5* on March 19 also in 1940 and *Number 11* in 1942, but *Number 26* was completed earlier on June 10, 1940.

Space does not permit a detailed discussion of each of the studies since structures are complicated, but characteristics of a few will be given. Much could be said of each one in an analysis. These pieces reveal the maturity of Farwell's craftsmanship in his carefully planned details.

In playing through these studies, the author was impressed with the variety of pieces created. Farwell uses contrapuntal techniques freely in many of them, while in others he designs vertically in colorful homophonic style. The writing is lean and every note is important. The lush chromaticism characteristic of earlier works does not appear here except as it occurs naturally in the combination of keys. True, he does wander about in an accumulation of accidentals, but the declared tonalities are maintained. Although some studies are musically more satisfying than others, the total results are impressive.

*Polytonal Study No. 1* is perhaps the simplest study of the collection. (Ex. 49) Farwell writes a two bar introductory treble clef theme in the key of G major that the bass clef echoes in the key of C major just one measure later. He uses the theme in sequences and inversion.

A new theme in the middle section has full quarter note chords played forte against an arpeggiated eighth note bass until the first theme returns quietly. Now, however, there is a constant pushing forward to a sforzando A flat octave in the bass held for four bars by the sustenuto pedal. Soft thirds in the upper treble clef move diatonically above the pedal point for an ethereal effect that gently sinks down by sixths and thirds to a relaxed broken C major chord in the left hand. This is succeeded by another G major chord in the right hand to conclude the study.

*Polytonal Study No. 4* features sixteenth note treble figures running in thirds in C major against the bass eighth notes in A flat. The rather simple bass line allows the pianist to concentrate on the fast moving consecutive thirds in the right hand. The results are very effective.

*Polytonal Study No. 5* (Ex. 50) is contrapuntal in style with the sturdy main theme becoming forte octaves when introduced in the bass and echoed in the treble clef. A second climax uses a bass sustained G flat octave for four measures while the treble clef unwinds sequentially. In the closing measures Farwell moves both clefs to the key of A flat, then continues without preparation to the concluding measure of both clefs in G flat, a progression that catches the listener's ear off-guard.

*Polytonal Study No. 6* is one of the few studies that has a title, *Sea Picture*, (Ex. 51). Farwell's use of slow triplets in different patterns suggesting the roll of ocean waves, may be the basis for his title. This beautiful six page study is one of his longest.

*Polytonal Study No. 8* uses the key of E flat against C major. Written in 6/8 meter, the right hand plays a slow melody of dotted quarters over a broken triadic bass line of eighth notes. The left hand has busy scale passages to support the rapid octave melody in the second section that is really a variation of the main theme played nearly twice as fast. The original theme returns for an extended "A" section. This time the melody is held over a sixteenth note pattern while the triadic bass is the same as in the beginning. Farwell inverts his melody and substitutes scale passages for the broken triads before he unwinds this study which is structurally appealing, but maybe less satisfying musically than some of the other studies.

*Polytonal Study No. 10* (Ex. 52 ), written in D major against B flat major, is a waltz that Farwell develops into a sparkling salon piece. Its four pages dance delightfully to a boisterous conclusion of sumptuous forte chords.

*Polytonal Study No. 13* (Ex. 53a) in 3/2 meter uses F minor in the treble clef and C minor in the bass. The whole study is ingeniously built with variations on the opening four measures that feature closed triads in the treble clef played by alternating hands. The first variation stays in the treble clef and simply breaks the triads into two eighths with the melody being held on a quarter note. Both hands move to the bass clef for variation two and play the chord theme simultaneously.

In variation three, each theme triad is echoed by an enriched chord an octave below. In variation four, the right hand plays the melody while the left hand - also in the treble clef - plays the chordal theme on broken triadic patterns of triplets just under the melody line.

In variation five (Ex. 53b) the melody is extended downward in disjunct lines over sixteenth note bass figures. The treble clef melody in variation six is now extended upwards over the sixteenth note bass figures that change to new triplet figures. The rhythms which have been building up in momentum and intensity move to make a fitting climax.

In variation seven the right hand fifth finger sustains the melody while the other fingers play sixteenth note figures, and the left hand plays pungent chords in a style similar to the bass in variation three. The melody line accelerates in complicated writing and sweeps to a broken B flat triad (Ex. 53c). This is held in the bass by the sostenuto pedal, while both hands move rapidly in the upper treble clef. After a significant retard, peace returns with the original theme, modified, in simpler form. The chords are gradually reduced to three that weave in and out of both clefs and finally drop to a concluding F minor triad. Not only has Farwell demonstrated his skill in the use of his theme material here, but also he has composed a spirited "winner".

*Polytonal Study No. 15* combines C minor with E flat minor in a ravishing sweep of harmonic color and intricate tonal passages that foreshadow things to come in Farwell's magnificent *Piano Sonata*. The five page *Study* features a sensuous melody that interweaves "impassioned" with chordal measures. In an ABA form, the B part has soft sustained right hand chords to be played "mysteriously" with staccato bass octaves that skip softly up a fourth making a pattern with a half note. The chordal work moves remorselessly to a fortissimo climax, then suddenly drops softly to more sustained chords. These are punctuated only by a single staccato note per measure in the bass until the section closes. The A section returns exactly as it was initially, but is developed into another "impassioned" climax - more rapturous than the first one before the extended themes settle down to a closing E flat minor chord in the treble followed by a C minor chord in the bass. *Study No. 15* is an exciting one to play.

*Polytonal Study No. 17* uses F minor with E Minor in a mixture of styles. The five bar opening melody contains the motives that Farwell develops later. An arpeggiated bass line supports the wide-spread melody throughout most of the study. Rhythmic changes and chordal passages add luster to this work.

*Polytonal Study No. 19* (Ex. 54) combines G minor with B minor in a Chopinesque nocturne style. Its slow moving melody sings out over a bass that uses repeated thirds and fourths. In its brief one and a half pages, Farwell weaves a tonal tapestry of exquisite beauty.

*Polytonal Study No. 20* is a stunning dramatic study written in loose ABA form. Farwell announces the main theme in the opening four bars (Ex. 55a). Much of the later material has its origins here. Eloquent melodies sweep rapidly in succession as the theme is developed, sometimes occuring in both keys in parallel fourths. The B section introduces a new theme in eighths featuring repeated staccato notes. This is tossed back and forth between hands until it is combined with the first theme in octaves. These culminate in thick right hand chords over thematic material in the bass. The rapid pace (Ex. 55b) is slowed temporarily with a short chordal passage that leads to the return of the original A section. However, now the theme is extended, imitated and sequenced. Germ motives are reversed or accentuated in ever mounting excitement to the bombastic closing chords. This tempestuous solo has an impressive beauty that goes beyond its challenging theoretical analysis. Farwell's craftsmanship has created a study that demands only superlatives in its description.

### Piano Sonata, 1949

Neely Bruce gave the premiere radio performance of Farwell's *Piano Sonata* over WQXR on Robert Sherman's *Listening Room* program of the *Music of Arthur Farwell* on April 16, 1975 and has performed it on concerts in various cities since that time. He found that some of the passages were awkward to play and said that "Farwell has pushed beyond what the piano can do - like Beethoven in his late sonatas - he really pushed the piano to its limits." Gilbert Chase, who also was a guest on the program, commented:

> This Sonata bears no resemblance, certainly no emulative resemblance, to any of the contemporary currents of that time. It seems to me that it took a man of great character and great individuality to do that. When you think of how different it is from his early works, you realized that here was a man who had a tremendous capacity for development and growth in every way - not only in spiritual ways but also creatively.

The *Sonata* (Ex. 56a ) has only one movement which is based on a small collection of motives that are subjected to extreme manipulation. The *Sonata* makes an opening statement with a forte descending fifth - a to d played slowly, which sets the mood. After the held d, followed by several rests, the main short theme of "me, fa, sol, la" enters undergirded with pleasant harmonies. After one repetition of the four theme notes, the melodious first page is soon replaced by turbulent and chromatic writing that grows more complicated as the music progresses. (Ex. 56b) The development builds hauntingly and powerfully, through compelling quiet spots and torrential cascades, unexpected transitions and new rhythms that build both inward and upward into incredible force. After much development, (Ex. 56c) too complicated to discuss here in detail, the last page (Ex. 56d) utilizes the same opening fifth, now in octaves plus chords and rapid sixteenth note passages incorporating earlier motives, to build the last climax. Now it rushes headlong into a whirlwind fortissimo finish of overwhelming force and passion. Then it concludes, abruptly, on the same first two notes, a to d, used in the beginning, as if to say, "That's it!" Bruce felt that it has a "technical ruthlessness surprising in a composer known chiefly as an arranger of Indian melodies". (A "fame" that Farwell fought all his life.)

This one movement work lasts about 13 minutes. Bruce remarks further that "The harmonic idiom is unlike that of any other composer, and the sonata's emotional intensity and dramatic impact are rare in American composers of Farwell's generation."[4]

Although the technical challenges in the Sonata are formidable for the performer, (a real "knuckle-buster"[5]) the music provides an exciting experience with Farwell's skill in composition. This work well deserves a place on present day piano concerts.

Brice Farwell attended the world premiere of the *Piano Sonata* on March 29, 1974, performed by Neely Bruce at a seminar at S.U.N.Y. on the Buffalo campus. He described his reactions to his father's music to his family who could not attend the concert:

> I regret I am not colorful artist enough to convey the moving and stunning feeling or what to me is the musical richness and powerful tapestry of this sonata. The demands on the pianist are stupendous. One hears it without quite realizing this because he is so compelled, carried relentlessly through it, caught in its moving tone and feeling. I think its exposure to the ear of the musical world will most surely mark a turning point from the archival indifference to Farwell's creative work. Bruce's enthusiasm has been undimmed by the challenge of doing it.
>
> Neely Bruce said yesterday that reactions at a preliminary hearing in Illinois, like those today and yesterday, were uniformly positive. . . . I returned home to find an unsolicited letter from an Illinois colleague of Bruce's, saying he was astounded both by the work Neely had done on the Sonata and by the composition itself!

**Late Short Pieces**

Two short works that make an interesting contrast to the *Sonata* were both composed in the 1940's. *Strange Dream* Op. 106, No. 2, could well be program music depicting an unusual dream of his child's imagination. From a placid beginning, its ABA form uses changes in key, harmony, and tempo to build up a contrasting middle section, and then returns to part A in modified and amplified form. Only two pages long, and written in a kind of improvisational style, the piece has a certain charm and is not difficult to play, once the chromatics are mastered.

*Melody in D Minor*, written in 1948, is also only two pages long and features an eight bar bass melody against soft chords in the treble clef. One can easily imagine a cello playing this melody. Aside from reading the chromatics which abound, the pianist has no real technical difficulty to surmount. Like Grieg, Farwell handles these short forms effectively.

Two piano works unclassified by opus should be mentioned because they represent a departure in style. *Palm Tree Daughters* is Oriental in its basic rhythm and mood. Oddly, Farwell has written two versions of the same music - different only in the keys he chose. In what seems to be the original version, Farwell writes A flat and D flat for the key signature. Under the title he has penciled "Actually [Palm Tree] *dates*, a poem in Mark Van Doren's *World Anthology*." This poem evidently had been the inspiration for his music. The second version omits the two flats and has no key signature. Instead, Farwell has used A flat and D flat as accidentals where needed, which makes the reading much simpler. The manuscript includes several phrases to use as possible alternative measures for different sections.

Another solo in an Oriental mood is his *Fantasie on a Turkish Air*. In both this and *Palm Tree Daughters*, the right hand melodies predominate over bass parts that step out the rhythms. Since no date can be determined for these two works, the author wonders if they might have been conceived while Farwell was working on *Caliban* which did have some Oriental scenes.

Chapter 16 discusses Farwell's folio of harmonic studies which includes special studies in Oriental tetrachords, the Oriental chromatic scale, and inverted Oriental chromatic C major scale as well as examples of many kinds of related progressions. The two piano solos referred to above may have been a result of these exercises.

\* \* \*

The catalog lists more piano music written by Farwell where pianists will discover notable music of varying degrees of difficulty. Farwell often used some of the same material over and over again as do other composers, yet his treatment reveals fresh insight in

its management.  Farwell's love for vertical writing is obvious in
his use of lush chords and frequent modulations.   Lavish
chromaticism characterizes many of his compositions, but there
was a tendency towards leaner writing in his later years especially
as shown in his remarkable *Polytonal Studies*.

The pianist looking for a concerto is referred to the discussion
of Farwell's prize-winning Opus 37, *Symbolistic Study No. 6,
Mountain Vision* in chapter 22.  This is written for two pianos and
string orchestra.

Farwell's piano compositions represent a broad variety of
styles, moods and difficulty.  From the earliest simple salon-styled
*Tone Pictures* to the rugged *Sonata*, the pianist finds many
interesting challenges.  Whether Indian inspired or otherwise, the
titles of Farwell's piano pieces suggest a wide range of emotions.
*Dawn, Domain of Hurakan, Treasured Deeps, Flame Voiced Night,
Emanation, Strange Dream, Fire Principle, Happy Moment, Pastel*
and *Vale of Enithharmon* are just a few titles to stir the
imagination.

Farwell's performing skills at the piano may never have
reached beyond academic and lecture levels.  But it is clear that
among both his Indian treatments for piano discussed in Chapter
17, as well as piano works examined here, that he generated an
impressive variety of highly expressive pianistic experiences for the
eager scholar or performer, and even more for the willing listener.
Many of these works should appear on today's piano concerts.

**Example 41a.** *The Round Under the Bell* **from** *Tone Pictures After Pastels in Prose*, **measures 1-9.**

# The Round under the Bell

**Example 41b.** *The Round under the Bell,* **measures 27-43.**

**Example 42a.** *Prairie Miniature.*

# PRAIRIE MINIATURE.

**Example 42b.**   *Prairie Miniature,* **conclusion.**

*Prairie Miniature, 2*

**Example 43a.** *What's in an Octave?*, measures 1-21.

# WHAT'S IN AN OCTAVE ?

**Example 43b.** *What's in an Octave?*, measures 54-70

**Example 44.**   *Arduous Trail* from *In the Tetons Suite*

**Example 45a.** *The Vale of Enitharmon*, measures 26-34.

**Example 45b.** *The Vale of Enitharmon,* measures 35-43.

**Example 46a.** *Prelude*, measures 1-10.

**Example 46b.** *Fugue*, measures 1-15.

**Example 47.**      *Indian Fugue-Fantasie*

**Example 48.**   *Happy Moment*

**Example 49.**    *Polytonal Study, No. 1*

**Example 50.**    *Polytonal Study, No. 5*

**Example 51.**    *Polytonal Study, No. 6, Sea Picture*

**Example 52.**     *Polytonal Study, No. 10*

## Example 53a.  *Polytonal Study, No. 13*

**Example 53b.** *Polytonal Study, No. 13*, page 2.

**Example 53c.**    *Polytonal Study, No. 13,* **page 3.**

**Example 54.** *Polytonal Study, No. 19.*

# Example 55a.   *Polytonal Study, No. 20.*

**Example 55b.** *Polytonal Study, No. 20,* **page 4.**

**Example 56a.** *Sonata for Piano*, **measures 1-24.**

SONATA
for Piano.

Arthur Farwell
Op. 113.

**Example 56b.** *Sonata for Piano*, measures 25-41

**Example 56c.**  *Sonata for Piano*, **measures 272-297.**

**Example 56c.** *Sonata for Piano*, measures 298-314, conclusion.

# Chapter 20

## Chamber Music

Farwell's training in violin is responsible for much of his interest in writing for strings. Outside of solos for oboe, a woodwind quintet, and a suite for flute and piano, his other chamber works are all for combinations of strings or strings and piano. Many of these have strong audience appeal and should be performed today.

### Early Works, 1898 - 1917

Farwell's first chamber works written in this period reflect his Wa-Wan Press activities as well as his experimentation with instrumental color and unusual scales. These compositions include: solo works for violin and oboe with piano accompaniments; a woodwind quintet; a trio for harp, violin and cello; and the same trio arranged for piano, violin and cello; as well as an unfinished string quartet.

The *Ballade* for violin and piano was published in 1898 as Opus One although a set of piano pieces was published earlier in 1895. Since his early music training was on the violin, Farwell felt at home writing for his own instrument. (Ex. 57) The pleasant melody moves through several keys and meter changes, but shows little evidence of his rich chromaticism appearing in later works.

Writing January 24, 1900, for the *Musical Courier* in his column "The Raconteur", James Huneker reviewed this early work, saying: "He has talent, but at present is straining a bit. His Op.1, a very ambitiously written *Ballade* for piano and violin, shows this. It is not simple in feeling or in its technical expression."

*Owasco Memories*, a suite for string trio, *Choral-Around the Lodge*, for violin and piano, and *Prairie Miniature* for woodwind quintet, are arrangements of works originally published by the Wa-Wan Press as piano solos. In these, Farwell uses traditional methods while experimenting with different instrumental combinations.

Farwell spent the summer of 1896 at Thomas Osborne's summer home on the shore of Lake Owasco in New York state. Among other compositions begun at that time were several piano works. Some of the string trio for *Owasco Memories* could well have been sketched then and completed after his return from Europe, during his second summer stay in 1901.[1]   Obviously inspired by the beauty of his surroundings, Farwell chose descriptive titles for the five movements: 1. *Spring Moods*, 2. *By Moonlight*, 3. *By Quiet Waters*, 4. *The Casino Across the Lake*, and 5. *Autumn Comes.*

The trio begins very traditionally with a diatonic introduction, but has chromatically altered pitches decorating the diatonic theme in later movements.  Farwell uses pentatonic lines in the second movement.  Then in the fifth movement he builds freely on the introductory themes of the first movement.  This string trio possesses melodic charm and offers no real technical difficulties.

*Prairie Miniature* arranged for woodwind quintet is number two from the piano collection *From Mesa and Plain* and is a lively work based on two cowboy tunes. (See chapter 19, example 42, for the piano score.)  The coloring created by the five instruments is very appealing and this music should be welcome on programs today.  When *Prairie Miniature* was performed by the Oklahoma University Faculty Quintet in a recent concert, it received enthusiastic applause!

*Choral-Around the Lodge* for violin and piano was number four *From Mesa and Plain* and is a part of the Wa-Wan ceremony of the Omaha Indians and implies a program.  In harmonizing the original Omaha melody, Farwell uses characteristics which are common to all of his Indianist compositions:  the pentatonic scale, changing meters, syncopation, parallel open fourths and fifths, extended unison passages, and irregular phrases.

*To Morfydd* for oboe and piano published in the Wa-Wan Press in 1903, possibly was stimulated in part by his friendship with Rudolph Gott, who became an accomplished oboist. However, Farwell claims that the music was inspired by an Arthur B. Davies painting whose work he greatly admired.  Morfydd was a Welsh maiden who was betrothed to the outlaw bard, Davydd ab Gwilym, a prominent name in the poetry of Wales.  Davies has Morfydd represented at a woodland trysting-place, seated upon a mossy bank, and dreamily plaiting her flowing hair, while a youth by her side strikes the strings of a small harp.

The music is characterized by three bar phrasing which follows a consistent pattern of changing meters. The first two measures of each phrase are in triple meter, followed by one in common meter. The interesting melody makes this an attractive solo work for oboe. Farwell noted that *To Morfydd* can be performed by other instruments, either string or wind, "though written originally with the peculiar quality of the oboe in mind."

### *The Gods of the Mountain* Trio, 1917

*The Gods of the Mountain* trio Opus 52, leans heavily upon its programmatic origins. The original trio was scored for harp, violin, and cello, (see excerpts in examples 58a, 58b, and 58c); then revised for piano, violin and cello. Each of the four movements was planned as a prelude to one of the four acts of a play by Lord Dunsany, which Stuart Walker produced in 1917. The nature of this imaginative play required the intimacy of a small ensemble rather than a large orchestra. Later, Farwell prepared an orchestral version of the trio. The story of the play is detailed in chapter 22 where his orchestral music is discussed.

Briefly, the plot involves some beggars outside the city gates who decide to pass as the stone gods feared by the city-dwellers. They cleverly gain acceptance and worship by the people, but are quickly turned to stone when the angry true gods from the mountain arrive to punish the impostors.

The atmosphere for each act is skillfully set by each movement. The "tread" motive and the "fear" motives return intrusively and disturbingly in the third movement, while the last movement utilizes both of these cyclic ideas in a very dramatic way. Farwell builds each of the four movements on a different experimental scale or mode. He created his own scales for the first two movements, used a Dorian mode for the third movement, and the Phrygian mode for the last one. (Ex. 58d) Evidently Farwell especially liked his second scale as he used the principal theme of this second movement in the second movement of his violin sonata (1928) in a varied form. In 1949 he used it again in the first movement of the *Suite for Flute and Piano*, (Ex. 58e).

The chief feature of the trio is the exotic quality it possesses as the result of being written on unusual scales. The harmony of each movement is built exclusively on the particular scale employed, to the exclusion of all other notes, thus creating a special color for the music. (Compare these remarks with those in chapter 22 where the orchestral version of the suite is detailed.)

The third movement, *Pinnacle of Pleasure*, is an oriental dance of somewhat orgiastic nature. It builds up to a whirling finish, interrupted only by the momentary appearance, dramatically introduced, of the "fear" motive. This movement could be performed alone, but the four movements have such strong audience appeal that a performing group should enjoy presenting the entire work. It takes only about 17 minutes to play. The version substituting piano for harp develops a little different color, but is also effective. The orchestral version has been the most frequently performed of Farwell's orchestral works.

The *Fugue Fantasy* for string quartet was written in 1914, but never finished in that medium. Instead, Farwell completed a stunning piece for piano using the same Indian themes, described in chapter 19 as *Indian Fugue-Fantasia*.

### The Late Chamber Music, 1922 - 1950

In this period, the works that are most traditional and similar to Farwell's early works are *Song Flight* and *Melody in E Minor*, both for violin and piano, and the *Suite for Flute and Piano* in two movements. In these, the "A" sections use melodies written in traditional style with little chromaticism. The "B" sections are more tonally unfocused due to added chromatics, but often use pedal tones to define the tonic.

*Song Flight*, published by Fischer in 1923, was written in rondo form (ABCBA). It presents a rather calm "A" section in traditional style in D flat. The second section, however, has a chromatic melody that seems to focus on F, but a pedal in the accompaniment claims B flat as the tonic. Key-wise this part offers an ambiguous tonal contrast to the quiet "A" section and adds interest to the work. We see here a Farwell tendency to write a melody an octave higher than its original appearance when it is repeated in the "A" section.

*Melody in E Minor* is in ABA form and stays in E minor in spite of phrases or sections that wander to distant keys. Because of this secure tonal focus, Farwell can experiment liberally with chromatic alterations in the "B" section. This was the fifth work which Farwell prepared and printed for his lithographic hand press in 1936. The "A" section employs a predictable rhythmic pattern of a quarter note followed by two eighths. He uses sequences and repetition at the octave in the "A" section and its return. The "B" section contains a more flowing melody expressed in longer phrases. The average violinist should encounter no technical problems in this very playable solo. Farwell sent a copy of this solo to his good friend, Arthur Shepherd, who replied warmly on April 24, 1936.

> It is positively "low down" of me to be so apparently casual about acknowledging your last letter and the violin piece. The latter, avowedly in the salon class, seems to me entirely effective, spontaneous, and - what is much more to me - it shows an *impressive mastery in harmonization*. I could almost swear that you had been poking your nose into Fauré, for the chromatic element is - in this piece - much more in his vein than in the Wagnerian manner. What I mean is that in this little piece, there is suppleness and charm - and firm control of tonality; all of which commands respect & admiration. . .

Although written in 1949, the *Suite for Flute and Piano* relates more closely to *Song Flight* and *Melody in E minor* because of its traditional formal characteristics, even though it includes more tonal instability than the two earlier works just discussed. The *Suite* has two movements entitled *Woodland Colloquy* and *Nocturn*. These are printed in readable reduced size in *A Guide to the Music of Arthur Farwell* (pp. 119-125).

In the first movement one notes Farwell's heavy reliance on the motive from his own created scale used in the second movement of *The Gods of the Mountain* already discussed. The "B" section employs more interplay of phrases between flute and piano with added cadenza-like passages for the flute over a sustained piano part.

The *Nocturn* movement (Ex. 59) features a chromatic six-note ostinato in the piano for the first two and a half pages, followed by contrasting material. Then it returns for the last ten bars and concludes on the tonic. This writing is unique for Farwell and it forms the basis for a beautiful moving flute melody. This *Suite* should be a welcome addition to the flute player's repertoire. It has been carefully edited by Patricia Harper and is available from her. (See catalog)

*The Hako String Quartet*, composed in 1922, is the earliest and most significant of Farwell's large-scale chamber works. It is an exciting unique prize-winning composition that string quartet players should welcome. Because of its strong Indian program and characteristics, it is discussed in detail in Chapter 17 with other Indian-inspired works.

The *Land of Luthany*, Op. 87, for 'cello and piano, was published by Farwell himself. It was issued as No. 3, of a series drawn and printed by hand on his lithographic press in East Lansing, Michigan. The title is derived from a line in the allegorical poem *The Mistress of Vision* by Francis Thompson. There the poet speaks of:

> The lady of fair weeping,
> at the garden's cove
> sang a song of sweet and sore
> and the after-sleeping:
> In the land of Luthany
> and the tracts of Elenore.

Here again we find evidence in the title, of Farwell's predilection for references to literature. The work is a mood piece, filled with "dark colors and intense, chromatic harmonies." Douglas Moore has recorded this work for Musical Heritage Society, as well as Farwell's *Sonata for Violoncello and Piano*.

In analyzing *Land of Luthany* and *Eothen* for violin and piano, both composed in 1931, one discovers that harmonic instability and the resulting tonal ambiguity take on new meaning. This reflects the turning point we noted in his harmonic writing a year earlier in *Vale of Enitharmon*. Farwell explores his themes in greater depth within the restriction of the ABA forms which produce more variety and even some contrapuntal lines.

The overall harmonic plan for the *Land of Luthany* is to move to distant tonalities. The beginning part is in F, (Ex. 60a) then it goes to C# for the "B" section. The "A" section returns first in the key of B flat, then moves to F, its starting place. This harmonic plan permits Farwell to develop his themes in new ways. There is some canonic writing between 'cello and piano in the return of the "A" section followed by a short developmental section which introduces two new themes. These both grow out of the initial melody. Farwell explores further in this section and uses his original melody in F in canon. This is the first time that Farwell uses this kind of thematic development in his one movement-compositions and it represents a change in his style.

In reviewing the piano accompaniment of *Land of Luthany*, one observes in the opening "A" the repeated eighth note chords are continually changing to supply a rich undergirding to the beautiful reflective 'cello melody. The bass chords are characterized by frequent half step movement which occurs in aborted chromatic scale passages found alternately in the outer voices of the chords or hidden in an inner voice.

Before returning to "A", the piano part changes to a dramatic rhapsodic style, appropriate to the 'cello activity which flourishes in two cadenzas before settling down. (Ex. 60b) Then the piano plays triadic arpeggios in the bass, until the 'cello returns to the original theme.

The last page features a haunting melody line in the right hand for the pianist which ends in an F minor chord, while the 'cello echoes and extends it to the close.

Douglas Moore, who recorded this music for Musical Heritage Society, told the writer that he found *Land of Luthany* to be "a very playable solo for the 'cello".

*Eothen* Op. 92 for violin and piano contains many of the same characteristics as *Land of Luthany*. Beginning on A flat below middle C, the melody moves only gradually to higher pitches. The piano harmonies outline the key of F minor, but the violin does not play the tonic pitch until bar five - then Farwell repeats bars five and six as if to strengthen the key note in the melody. At measure 13, he uses his initial theme a third higher before moving on to the second theme which is a more flowing melody. These scalar passages are a good contrast to the wide skips of the first theme of part "A" and both themes are extremely chromatic. These may present some challenges to the violinist.

The B or second section is in E flat minor - just one step below the main tonality of the first part.   There are many unfocused progressions until midway of this section when B flat finally has a dominant function.   This middle part shows some experimenting with polytonality.   In her analysis of some of Farwell's chamber music, Linda Richer uses the term "quasi bitonality as most aptly defining the harmonic style of this section".[2]

In the return to "A", Farwell uses the second theme in an extension to present an effective short coda.  The violin and piano score for *Eothen* covers eleven pages and presents a beautiful work of considerable substance which should find a place in the mature violinist's repertoire today.

Richer concludes that 1931, which was a year of experimentation for Farwell, served as a "turning point" for him as a composer, a fact we have already noted.  She states:

> . . . the severe weakening of tonality through melodic chromaticism, the avoidance of dominant to tonic attractions, the construction of unorthodox chordal progressions, the use of semi-tonal movement in harmonies, and the experimentation with bitonality all point to changes in Farwell style.[3]

Some of Farwell's exploration of the simple ABA forms just discussed showed his use of thematic development and some brief contrapuntal sections, a style which he exploited further in his multi-movement works.

### Sonata for Violin and Piano

Farwell's *Sonata for Violin and Piano*, op. 80, was begun in December 1927, and revised in 1935.  It embraces the familiar fast-slow-fast three movement form.

The first movement in standard sonata form, uses two theme groups.  The first one is a restless triadic figure in E minor.  The second theme is more lyrical and centers on F.  A short development manipulates the themes from the exposition. Then the recapitulation reiterates the exposition in almost the same form as first written. After emphasizing the first theme group, the coda ends firmly on the tonic.

The slow second movement begins with a rhythmic introduction of Farwell's own scale first used in the second movement of *The Gods of the Mountains* (Ex. 58e). Analysis reveals that his scale, with a few alterations, supplies the basis for both melodies used in the first section, with a G major tonal focus. The second section in C minor includes new short melodic fragments before the "A" section returns in G major with several combinations of themes from both sections. Richer felt that "both the "B" section and the final "A" section seem quite fragmented and lack a firm melodic core." However, she noted that the short coda at the end brings cohesion by "presenting Farwell's scale over a G pedal to balance the beginning of the movement."[4]

However, when Stanley Butler, violinist and university professor, returned the borrowed Sonata score to Farwell, he wrote that he was especially fond of the second movement, but enjoyed playing the whole score.

The final movement also in simple sonata form begins in E minor. The second theme is in contrasting F# major. As in the second movement, Farwell writes a short development and then repeats material in the recapitulation that is identical to the exposition. However, this time the second theme returns in D major, not in the expected E minor. Farwell handles this unusual movement by writing a long closing section to return the theme to its base. The coda stresses the first theme in E minor before ending on an E major chord.

Morris Hochberg[5] gave a special private performance of the Sonata for Violin and Piano in New York City during the summer of 1937. Roy Harris was in the audience and expressed his opinion of the work to Farwell who was also present. Harris declared he was "amazed at the irony of this work being buried in East Lansing, when it was just the sort of work people are listening to everywhere."

Hochberg and his wife, Sylvia, specialized in performing Farwell's work and presented the *Sonata* again in Bay City,

Michigan, on April 28, 1938, as well as on many other later programs. It proved to be a popular and welcome composition.

## Sonata for Solo Violin

In his *Sonata for Solo Violin* Op. 96, written in 1927-1934, Farwell, unhampered by preparing an accompaniment, unleashes his ideas for what the violin can express alone. On twelve and a half pages, he writes four movements in basically traditional sonata form. The first movement starts in G minor with an energetic fast moving 4/4 theme. He uses four-note chords on the first and third beats of bars one and two, the upper notes of all intervals carrying the melody. Where the second theme enters, he wrote, "Emphasize the melody and suppress the accompanying figuration". There is much development of themes with rhythmic changes and constant chromaticism; a work sheet gives a second "trial ending"!

The second movement is a slow 4/4 and features a sustained theme with a key signature of E flat, but the chromatic movement presents a vague tonality. Farwell writes the main theme in half notes with a lower voice that moves in quarters and eighths in a subordinate melody. A middle section contains more motion albeit still in a slow tempo. Four bars of the first theme return played an octave higher until new material is added to bring the movement to a close.

The third movement is an exciting well written one in D major and 6/8 meter. It is marked "conveniently fast" and is in strong contrast to both preceding movements. Farwell uses pizzicato and repeated rhythmic figures, punctuated by rests. This frolicking music could stand alone very effectively as it offers much variety in style and thematic development and it takes only 2 1/2 minutes to play. It may be the best music he has written for violin - at least as far as audience-appeal is concerned.

The fourth movement is slow again, and in 2/4 meter with a key signature of B flat, a tonality which is established immediately and actually adhered to for several measures before the wandering to other keys begins to occur. The first theme uses figurations that combine a wide skip with a minor second in a flowing melody. These disjunct phrases are replaced by a new section using quarter notes in various single intervals and a tender melody undergirded with triplets.  There is much development of material with a hint of the third movement theme and others before the florid writing ends with a grand flourish on two chords in G minor, thus concluding in the same key in which it began.  The complete *Sonata* requires about fourteen minutes to play.

Farwell has carefully marked the critical bowings and fingerings all through the *Sonata*.  Ronald Erickson, who plays the violin on the Musical Heritage Society recording of Farwell's *Piano Quintet*, has also performed this *Sonata for Solo Violin*.  The writer was much impressed with the beauty of a taped recording she heard of one such performance.

The *Sonata for Solo Violin* is a difficult and challenging work that deserves a place on concert programs today.  The third movement especially should be rescued and used in solo performance (a personal favorite).

On December 27, 1940, Morris Hochberg played the premiere performance of the *Sonata for Solo Violin* in Detroit, Michigan, at a recital featuring violin and piano music by contemporary American composers.  In a note Hochberg wrote to Farwell reviewing this occasion he stated:

> "...Unfortunately, I wasn't able to get in the last movement but that was only because we were limited to one hour [for the entire program] and yours was the only work that can stand on three legs!  However, I played it all for Callaghan the critic at a private performance and he was very much taken by it.  I really play every note of it with two simplifications in which nothing is lost.  Sylvia [Mrs. Hochberg] tells me that she plays your violin-piano sonata just as you have it written.

Clark Eastham, who helped with preparations for the Festival of American Music, heard Hochberg's performance there and commented briefly in a letter to Farwell later.  Eastham considered the unaccompanied violin sonata to be "Really a *great* work and one devil to do!"

*Piano Quintet in E Minor*

Farwell wrote his *Piano Quintet in E Minor*, Op. 103, during the winter of 1936-1937 while he was still teaching at Michigan State College. When one recalls that this was a tempestuous time in his personal life with his divorce finalized in January 1937, and disturbing political rumblings at the college going on that might affect his job, - it seems remarkable that Farwell was emotionally capable of composing a work exhibiting such skillful craftsmanship. Perhaps it was this very act of composing that put him into a different world where he could escape from his troubles. There his spiritual nature that always sought for Truth and Beauty could express itself now in a more mature way.

The *Piano Quintet* has not been published, but has been performed and recorded. The Roth String Quartet with Johana Harris, pianist, premiered the work during a Contemporary American Music Festival held on May 24, 1938, at the Westminster Choir School in Princeton, New Jersey. The Pacifica Chamber Players recorded it for Musical Heritage Society and the recording was enthusiastically reviewed by the eminent music critic, Irving Lowens. In *High Fidelity* magazine for November 1978, he says Farwell deserves more attention than he has had and pointed out the interest and individuality of this work. Commenting further about the quintet, Lowens wrote:[6]

... Although composed some four decades after his European studies, it is redolent of late romanticism. Occasionally, Farwell ventures into polytonality and polyrhythm, but the work as a whole is essentially tonal and uses the harmonic vocabulary of Richard Strauss or early Schoenberg. The most interesting movement is perhaps the second, which "was suggested by listening to a large Chinese gong struck softly but continuously, and noting the musical effects arising from the overtones". The continuous reiteration of the lowest C on the piano throughout the movement is almost hypnotic in effect. The performers ... bring sympathy and sensitivity to their reading, and do full justice to Farwell's score.

The recording was a result in part, by Ronald Erickson's research in the American chamber music repertory. In his notes for the record jacket he concludes thus about Farwell's style:

> In the *Quintet* Farwell brought together the changing direction of his own creative impulse and the influences, musical and geographical, of his early professional years. . . . The music shows evidence of his European studies in the 1890's; the first movement especially suggests Pfitzner and Humperdinck, and the last movement the Guilmant/Franck idiom  of the F-Minor Quintet (as in the cyclic use of the motive of the descending melodic third throughout Farwell's Quintet). At the same time, Farwell applies a sensitivity to pitch relationships on simultaneous levels of harmony and in tonality moving from section to section which approaches the style of Richard Strauss or early Schoenberg.  His exploration of polytonality (from the very opening chords: F major/ B major) in this work leads to the piano music of his last years.  All these qualities  produce a satisfying mix between an older, derivative music and a moderately adventuresome loosening of tonal bonds. Refreshing too, is the change of the traditional balance of piano and strings to the favor of the quartet.

Farwell's *Quintet* is scored for the usual instrumentation, but he treats the piano as one of five equal voices.  The piano never dominates against the quartet as a unit, but each instrument contributes its own distinctive voice to the whole.

Although the Quintet is a late work, it still manifests some of Farwell's earlier musical interests and techniques.  His notes state that with the exception of the second movement, all of the themes were taken from his notebooks of the years 1904 to 1907 when he was traveling to the Far West.  He suggests that there will be found "something of the loneliness of the plains and the ruggedness of the mountains" in the other three movements.

However, Mr. Erickson does not find these qualities as such by themselves.  Instead, he writes:[7]

The context of the entire work, however, brings out what can be called American musical qualities in the thematic material by such means as the emphatic rhythmic pulse (largely a function of the piano as in the drumbeats at the second subject), a tendency to sectional structure with changes of movement and mood, and the tense declamatory figures, gusty exuberance, and pentatonic quality of the themes themselves.

Farwell did not quote any folksongs in his *Quintet*, but the bold and rugged themes and his expansive use of them may be his method for picturing those western scenes. The early Indianist stylistic characteristics also appear here. One finds repetition of open fourths and fifths, pentatonicism, frequent unisons, and repeated notes suggesting drumbeats, used more here than in his earlier string chamber music - *Fugue Fantasie* and *The Hako*. However, Farwell's use of these Indianist characteristics is done more subtly in the *Quintet* indicating a maturity of his style.

The *Piano Quintet* opens with a broad introduction that presents two themes used as source material for the rest of the first movement. The rhythmic first theme features a pentatonic scale and occurs bitonally. The second theme, also pentatonic, is a lyrical contrast to the ruggedness of the first theme to which it is partially related. See example 61a for samples of all the main themes for the first movement. Example 61b shows the Indianist influence in the piano found in the first movement. Example 61c demonstrates Farwell's use of imitation which builds to a strong climax at the end of the development section.

In summarizing Farwell's compositional techniques found in the first movement, Linda Richer discovered that the two themes presented in the introduction supplied motives for future themes and appeared in bridges, transitions, and the coda as well as in the development proper. She pointed out that the rhythmic relationships among themes is equally important. "This careful planning of themes and motives creates a subtle but firm cohesiveness within the movement",[8] she concludes.

Richer also felt that continuous thematic development and manipulation are an important part of Farwell's sonata-form structures. Furthermore, she notes that Farwell employs a wide

variety of developmental techniques to maintain growth and
vitality in his works. Especially in this first movement, Farwell
"adds rhythmic complexities to transform the character of a
section." Shifting accents and rhythmic ambiguity are the result
of changes from duple to triple meter. "The vibrancy and growth
created by this wide variety of developmental techniques energizes
Farwell's sonata forms."[9]

The structure of the second movement is unique and follows
a quasi-rondo form of Introduction, A B A B A coda. Everything
takes place above a steady ostinato or pedal on low C already
referred to in Lowens' review (Ex. 61d).

Farwell's skillful craftsmanship is revealed in his attention to
form and structure in this unusual movement. The constant
alteration and development of his two primary ideas take place
over the unchanging pedal. The small four-note motive of the "A"
sections grows into expanded melodies which are treated
contrapuntally and with rhythmic variation. In the "B" sections
he writes variations on a well-planned chordal progression. It is
the balance and symmetry that provides the movement with focus.

A lively delightful scherzo in the third movement is a welcome
change from the previous serious one. (See Ex. 61e for themes
"a" and "b".) Here we find exact repetitions of sections that make
it a classic example of the tripartite scherzo and trio form. One
also discovers the use of a theme from the first movement at the
end of each scherzo section which binds this movement to the
others. Here Farwell features "highly charged rhythms and
unstable harmonies" in creating a "predictable and symmetrically
balanced form."[10]

The fourth movement is another "heavy" fast one in sonata
form. (See Ex. 61f for themes in the fourth movement.) It is
very similar to the first movement in structure as we find the
introductory themes providing ideas for the remainder of the
movement. Farwell again uses a variety of developmental
techniques for growth from beginning to end. Richer is
disappointed in the total effect of the fourth movement:[11]

The fragmented and diffuse fourth movement, however, is not as concise and successful as the first movement. The structure is unable to hold the weight of the constant fragmentation in a setting of extreme harmonic ambiguity.

Richer's thorough analysis of the *Quintet* reveals Farwell's impressive use of compositional techniques that include variation, imitation, inversion, fragmentation, augmentation, retrograde, and contrapuntal combinations of melodic ideas. She also noted two trends in his choice and construction of classical forms for individual movements in his *Quintet*: 1. Farwell's experimentation with traditional forms as exemplified by expanded sonata form to include strong introductions and intensive development throughout; and 2. his use of classical forms in a predictable manner as in the scherzo movement where his adherence to tradition allowed him freedom to experiment with other elements such as harmony or rhythm.

But the real judgment of his *Quintet* lies in the totality of its sound. What beauty, interest and individuality has Farwell captured in these many pages? Thanks to Ronald Erickson and the Pacifica Chamber Players we can listen to their excellent recorded performance and decide for ourselves. The author finds the experience a rewarding one.

### Sonata for Violoncello and Piano

The *Sonata for Violoncello and Piano*, written in 1950, two years before Farwell's death, was his last chamber work. He labels his score as Op. 115, but other sources list it as Op. 116. Richard Clayton, a former student in Farwell's classes, and his wife, Kathryn, first performed the *Sonata* which Farwell had dedicated to them, in 1950. Still unpublished, it was not performed again until 1976 when Douglas Moore played it on an American Music Festival recital at the National Gallery of Art in Washington, D.C. He has also recorded it.

Many influences may be heard in this well-written work. There are Franck-like progressions in the first movement which also contains some jazz influences in Farwell's use of parallel seventh chords. The harmonic language is chromatic throughout, but quite tonal.

The sonata features a mature first-movement sonata form. The exposition includes an opening theme in D minor that is a winding chromatic one used in sequence, followed by a more lyrical second theme in E flat major. (See examples 62a and 62b.) This key relationship between the two themes is unexpected. The development section features especially the first theme group in a variety of ways: sequential development, inversions, mirroring and altered pitches. The recapitulation opens with the second theme, in D minor. The fast pointillistic, staccato notes introduced by the piano, caught up by the 'cello and the two instruments, present an interplay that builds up to the return of the second theme. Dr. Moore declares that it is difficult to tell where the development ends and the recapitulation begins. "They are overlapped so artfully as to be virtually seamless."[12] A whirlwind coda concludes the movement.

The second movement, marked "slowly", is in three-part song form. Here the lovely romantic flowing melody in 4/4 meter and key of A flat major is marked by rhythmic changes in the "A" sections. The "B" section, in faster tempo and 12/8 meter, seems turbulent by contrast with its frequent sixteenth note running figurations. In this movement, Dr. Moore discovered awkward 'cello passages that did not lie easily under his fingers, but he considered them to be "just another challenge"[13] which added to his enjoyment of the work.

The last movement written in rondo form of ABACABA, is a fast and fiery dance-like movement. One finds here the same type of continued growth within the rondo-form that was evident in the *Piano Quintet*'s second movement. The key is D major in contrast to the D minor of the first movement. Farwell marks the beginning of the second "A" section with such phrases as: "more animation", "beginning of satanic and derisive temper", and "viciously accented". Later he adds more instructions: "faster, savagely derisive", "furiously", "violently". He writes "sffz" above accented 'cello notes and the strident chords for piano. The "C" section which follows, returns to the original tempo. The piano enters "mysteriously" and the 'cello employs scordatura. Tuning the C string to B makes possible some rich and unusual chords.

The 'cello enters in soft pizzicato notes mixed with rests which offer a welcome relief from the violent preceding section. After the chordal passages, the B string is retuned to its normal C pitch for the remainder of the movement which accelerates. Again Farwell inserts directions of "with animation and energy", "violently", and "pressing forward." Dr. Moore confessed that "the last movement is the most fun to play; it gets madder and madder as it moves along!"[14]

The *Sonata* has an exotic flavor. One senses a bit of Farwell's Indianist influences in the persistent rhythmic drive and over-all feeling of pulse in the work. Farwell employs colored chromatic harmonies to avoid traditional chordal progressions. Chromatic scale passages are used especially in the piano accompaniment for the first and third movements. These tend to affect the texture and destabilize the tonal focus.

In Farwell's last chamber work, he does much experimentation with a variety of compositional techniques and it stands as an excellent example of his mature work. The *Sonata for Violoncello and Piano* deserves a more frequent hearing. Dr. Moore's impressive recording for Musical Heritage Society should stimulate other 'cellists to include the sonata in their repertoire. In fact, a performer looking for new string scores, should consider all of Farwell's chamber music as excellent sources.

**Example 57.**   *Ballade*

Respectfully dedicated to
PROFESSOR KEKULÉ von STRADONITZ.                                    3

# BALLADE

For Violin and Piano.

ARTHUR FARWELL,
Op.1.

**Example 58a.** *The Gods of the Mountain: Beggars' Dreams*

**Example 58b.**   *The Gods of the Mountain: Pinnacle of Pleasure*

**Example 58c.** *The Gods of the Mountain: The Stone Gods Come*

**Example 58d.**   *The Gods of the Mountain:* **Special Scales**

## Movement I

## Movement II

## Movement III, Dorian

## Movement IV, Phrygian

**Example 58e.   Themes using scales from *Gods of the Mountain***

**Gods of the Mountain, Movement II, measures 12-15, violin**

**Violin Sonata, Movement II, measures 2-6, violin**

**Suite for Flute and Piano, Movement I, measures 1-2, flute**

**Example 59.**     *Nocturn from Suite for Flute and Piano*

**Example 60a.**   *Land of Luthany*

To Alexander Schuster

# Land of Luthany

3

**Example 60b.** *Land of Luthany*, **measures 68-78.**

**Example 61a.** *Piano Quintet:* **Movement I, Themes**

**Measures 1-2, violin II**

**Measures 17-20, violin II**

**Measures 54-56, cello**

**Measures 60-63, viola**

**Measures 101-103, cello**

**Measures 141-144, violin I**

**Measures 157-159, violin I**

**Example 61b.** *Piano Quintet:* **Indianist influences**

**Example 61c.** *Piano Quintet:* **Measures 284-296**

**Example 61d.** *Piano Quintet:* **Movement II, cello and piano**

**Example 61e.** *Piano Quintet:* **Movement III, Scherzo themes**

**Theme A, measures 1-12, violin I**

**Theme B, measures 69-76, viola**

**Example 61f.   Piano Quintet: Movement IV, Themes**

**Measures 1-5, violin I**

**Measures 16-17, violin I**

**Measures 34-38, violin I**

**Measures 50-55, violin II**

**Transition theme 99-102, violin I**

**Measures 158-164, viola**

**Example 62a.**   *Sonata for Violoncello and Piano,* **measures 1-23.**

**Example 62b.   Themes, Movement I**

**Theme 1A, measures 1-4, cello**

**Theme 2, measures 85-91, cello**

**Theme 1A transformed, measures 268-271, piano**

# Chapter 21

# Theater and Community Music-Drama

Many experiences in Farwell's early career provided him with first hand knowledge of the essentials of good theater. He had acted in plays during high school years, then later as a supernumerary in operas produced in Boston. During his two years abroad, he witnessed many Wagnerian operas at Bayreuth, and others elsewhere in his wide travels. He was also studying with Humperdinck all during the composition of the latter's *Koenigskinder* and had witnessed its development to completion.

His later four years as Supervisor of Municipal Concerts in New York City gave him extensive opportunity to introduce theater elements with music, from lighting a pier to bringing opera into the parks. He recognized that he had seen all the elements found in the old Greek drama, which he envisioned could be fused to create a "great communal drama". (Chapter 10) Hence Farwell brought considerable background and experience to his new work in theater and community music.

A direct inspiration for Farwell's work in pageants and masques resulted from his earlier visits to the Bohemian Club's *Grove Plays* described in chapter 10. The present chapter will review chronologically, Farwell's efforts in theater, community music-drama and pageant work. We will consider these in a broad sense that include traditional professional-type performances produced in a theater building, and those productions performed by amateurs or by casts with combined professionals and amateurs. The pageants and masques, here identified as "community music-dramas" were usually performed outdoors in natural settings appropriate to the script with added stage where needed, plus a shell for the orchestra and chorus.

## East Coast Theater Works

Farwell's first real effort in writing music specifically for the theater was in composing the incidental music for Louis N. Parker's play *Joseph and his Brethren* in 1912. This seems to be the first instance in pageant-writing where the music was planned along with the script from its conception. The available orchestral score is incomplete, but the music was completed for production on Broadway in New York.[1]

In addition to composing, Farwell served as musical adviser for pageants. One noteworthy effort was the *Pageant of St. Johnsbury* at St. Johnsbury, Vermont, held August 15-17, 1912. For this event Brooks C. Peters wrote special music for the introduction, interludes, and finale, but Farwell suggested the music drawn from other sources for the main episodes and assisted at the performances.

Typically, this pageant was based on the history of the town while also commemorating its 125th anniversary. See figures 53 and 54. The author's Farwell Collection has fourteen photographs taken at this pageant, which featured nearly 700 costumed actors and had about 10,000 spectators.

Farwell wrote the music and served as music director for the *Pageant of Meriden* production in 1913. This pageant dealt with education and was prepared as a celebration of the centennial anniversary of Kimball Union Academy located in Meriden, New Hampshire. In the forward of the script written by William Chauncy Langdon, he stated, "*The Pageant of Meriden* has been written and composed on the principle that both dramatically and musically the pageant is a distinct and individual art-form, and not merely a series of historic episodes interspersed with music." The music for the pageant consisted of the Introduction, three Interludes, and the Finale. These were dramatic scenes accompanied by music for orchestra and chorus. Farwell arranged some of these pieces into what he called *A Pageant Scene*. In addition, some incidental music was interspersed through the episodes as follows: an orchestrated version by Farwell of *Arne*, three old hymns, *The Girl I Left Behind Me*, *The Battle Hymn of the Republic*, the *Class Ode*, *The Old Oaken Bucket*, *Virginia Reel*, *Oxdans* and *Tarantella*. The names of these pieces suggest the musical flavor of the pageant. The chorus was trained by Herbert E. Wood, instructor of music at Kimball Union Academy. The orchestra was the Nevers' Blaisdell's and Stewartson's orchestra of Concord, New Hampshire, directed by Farwell (Figures 55 and 56).

Typical of Farwell's philosophy, and consistent with the growing idea among pageant leaders nationally, the pageant became a community affair. Academy staff and members from

*Figure 53. Music shed at Pageant of St. Johnsbury, Vermont, in 1912, showing orchestra, chorus, and some performers. Farwell at far left in light colored suit.*

*Figure 54. Civil War episode in the Pageant of St. Johnsbury.*

*Figure 55. Music shed at Pageant of Meriden, Arthur Farwell conducting, 1913.*

*Figure 56. Entrance of "Music" (figure at right) in the Pageant of Meriden.*

nearly every family in the village took part in it. Production took place on the side of a hill looking across the valley to the hilltop on which Meriden and the Academy stood, so that the subject for celebration became veritably a part of the outdoor stage setting.

Another pageant produced at Meriden ("four miles, as the crow flies, from Cornish") on September 12, 1913, was *Sanctuary, A Bird Masque* written by Percy Mackaye whose home was in Cornish. This unusual masque served to dedicate the bird sanctuary and was promoted by the Meriden Bird Club. The music was credited to Frederick Converse, but Farwell's name was also listed in the program as composer. Whatever music he may have contributed to this pageant is not known. Again, he may have served mainly as an adviser.

Farwell wrote the music for *Pageant of Darien* in 1913, produced the same year, in the city of Darien, Connecticut. Orchestra scores for the introduction, two interludes and the finale are available in manuscript. The music from a Darien "Interlude", entitled *Principle* was performed by Clifford Demarest, F.A.G.O, on the organ at the Church of the Messiah in New York City on the program of the second annual conference of the American Pageant Association. Farwell was also one of the featured speakers, his topic being *Pageant Music*.

Benjamin Lambord recognized that Farwell was one of the first composers to write music specifically for community pageants. He praised both the *Pageant of Meriden* and the *Pageant of Darien*, for obtaining:

> . . . a remarkable success by the masterly skill with which he has welded the diffuse elements of pictorial description, folk-song suggestions, dances and choruses into a coherent and artistic whole. Equally successful along similar lines was Farwell's music for Louis N. Parker's play *Joseph and His Brethren* and Sheldon's *Garden of Paradise*.[2]

Farwell had problems composing the music for that Broadway play, *Garden of Paradise*, as the producers kept changing the script every day right up to opening night. This was an elaborate production written by Edward Sheldon with stage sets by Joseph Urban. The story was built around the Hans Christian Andersen

*Little Mermaid* tale. (Beatrice Farwell claimed it "went into a jinxed house on Columbus Circle in New York.")

Farwell worked with only two hours of sleep a night in order to meet the demands of the producers. At last when opening night came on November 29, 1914, he was so exhausted that he could not stand up and had to feel his way along the buildings as he staggered home. People thought he was just another drunk and did not bother to offer help. When he finally dragged himself into his bedroom, he collapsed on the bed where friends found him the next day running a 104 degree temperature. Noble Kreider, a close friend and Wa-Wan composer, (Figure 50) took Farwell to Bermuda to recuperate. When he returned refreshed, someone said in surprise, "I thought you went to Bermuda to die!" To which Farwell retorted, "You can't kill me! I have an iron stomach". Later, witnesses verified that remark and heard him say he drank his coffee as hot as he could possibly get it and then they watched him do it!

A critic's review of the play in the New York Times, November 30, 1914, stated:

> For sheer beauty the New York stage has never seen a picture to equal the bridal feast, with the pearl-tinted gateway,and steps leading up to a long table, the nodding heads of the happy guests outlined sharply against a distant sky of deep blue serenity, the laden board and all its people bathed in a wondrous amber light. Indeed to visit the *Garden of Paradise* is to experience something of the wonder-pleasure of looking into a strange world through those "charm'd magic casements of which the poet sang".

The review made no comments about Farwell's theater music which is missing.

Farwell never forgot his happy times of membership in DKE during college years at M.I.T. In 1914 he composed a work for his fraternity, *DKE, A Masque of Fraternity*. It contains an orchestra score for "five mystical choruses" and a fanfare plus Farwell's original texts; music has disappeared for the introduction.

Little is known about its production except that it was presented in New York City for the dedication of a new DKE building.

## Caliban

Farwell's collaboration with like-minded Percy MacKaye to produce *Caliban* in 1916 was his crowning achievement in community music-drama in the East.   Here was an opportunity that gave Farwell great visibility as a composer.   He delighted in creating a unique score that expressed democracy in action joining drama and dance with music.   The composition of the music occupied Farwell the entire winter of 1915-16 and required seven assistants in the work of orchestration.[3]

In preparing the script for *Caliban*, Percy MacKaye used Shakespeare as a jumping-off point as he explained in the preface:

> . . . the characters, derived - but re-imagined from
> . . . *The Tempest* . . . are my own conception.   Their
> words (save for a very few song-snatches and sentences)
> and their actions are those which I have given them; the
> development of their characters accords with the theme -
> not of Shakespeare's play but of this masque, in which
> Caliban's nature is developed to become the protagonist
> of aspiring humanity, not simply its butt of shame and
> ridicule.

Mackaye wanted every one working with the production to understand the message of *Caliban* and its loose relationship to *The Tempest*.   So he explained the symbolism and meaning by using questions and answers on a one page information sheet which he widely distributed.   He identified Caliban as a character living on the Yellow Sands - Prospero's magic Isle - which represented the world of Time where we all live.   Caliban's father was Setebos, "a fierce god, half tiger and half toad".   Caliban's mother was Sycorax, "A gigantic witch, a kind of earth-spirit".   Caliban was raised by three wicked teachers - Lust, War and Death - to whom he was obedient until he met Miranda.   She helped Caliban by bringing her father, Prospero - "a great Enchanter" - and his servant, Ariel, to make Caliban a better person. They introduce him to beauty as found in Shakespeare. Caliban's transformation is hindered by his old teachers of Lust, War and Death, but the Magic of Prospero, Ariel and the Spirit of Time produce a desired change in Caliban and they win in the end.

The action for this colossal undertaking took place on three stages in the Lewisohn Stadium. The Yellow Sands was the largest stage where performers acted out the history of the theater using choral singing, dance and pantomime. The three major interludes and the epilogue were also performed here. The middle stage, where much of the dialogue took place, was designed as the cave of Setebos. The third or inner stage depicting the "mind of Prospero", was where the Shakespearean vision scenes occurred.

The last scene of *Caliban* is focused on the Yellow Sands area. MacKaye describes it: "From either side enters a Pageant of the great Theatres of the world - from the ancient Theatre of Dionysus to the Comedie Francaise - in symbolic groups, with their distinctive banners and insignia . . . announced from either end of the high balcony above the inner stage by two spirit Trumpeters, the one beneath a glowing disk of the sun, the other beneath a sickle moon." The groups of War, Lust and Death that had fought with the Spirits of Ariel and captured Miranda, Prospero, and Ariel in the previous scene now "dwindle away in the background darkness."

MacKaye pictured the parade of great theatres by having famous dramatists from Thespis to Ibsen, marching through the mouths of two monumental masks on either side of the stage. These represented comedy and tragedy. Finally Shakespeare himself appears on stage and later is joined by Ariel and Miranda. Eventually Caliban slips in and speaks of how he has changed, to which Shakespeare replies now as Prospero in a quote from *The Tempest*. He concludes with "We are such stuff As dreams are made of, and our little life Is rounded with a sleep." As the lights faded, the production ended softly with the hidden choirs of Ariel's Spirits singing the same quoted lines.

A production of this magnitude required many talents. Other professionals working on *Caliban* in New York were the Viennese born artist and producer Joseph Urban; the designer Robert Edmond Jones; director Richard Ordynski from Max Reinhardt's

Deutsches Theater;    author and director Garnet Holme who
organized the community interludes; Alice and Irene Lewisohn
who worked on the Egyptian interlude; Cecil Sharp who directed
the Elizabethan Interlude and John Collier of the Peoples
Institute.

In her research on pageant history, Naima Prevots discusses
the many monetary and related problems that other composers
had in composing for some of the pageants of this period.[4]
Farwell received his commission and for once did not worry about
other business matters.  He was more concerned about giving of
*himself* through music.  (Didn't Cheiro tell Farwell that he "did
not care for money in the least and that he would always do his
work for its own sake?")  More details of the *Caliban* production
are given in Chapter 10.

This huge work to celebrate Shakespeare's Tercentenary was
performed fourteen times in Lewisohn Stadium beginning May 16,
1916.    Percy MacKaye also produced the work in Boston
beginning July 2nd through 18 the following summer at the
Harvard Stadium.    For those performances he gathered 1,400
amateur actors, dancers, and 600 singers from all over Boston and
suburbs.    Farwell served as conductor for all New York
performances and at least one at Harvard.  He described his work:

> My aim has been to carry out in the musical aspects
> of *Caliban* what I conceive to be the poet's intention in
> the poem itself, namely to present living and timely ideas
> and meanings.  I have thus been nowise concerned with
> arriving at historical musical values, except in the
> *Interludes*, which have a historical character.
>
> The master soul, Prospero, and the primitive god
> Setebos represent opposing principles.    Prospero
> commands the powers of both the higher and lower
> spheres;  his motive is a trumpet call which descends an
> octave and returns.  It is in harmony with the higher
> spheres and in dissonance in the lower.  The Setebos
> motive is the opposite - in harmony with the lower, in
> dissonance with the higher spheres.  Caliban's theme is
> uncouth, boisterous and passionate. . . .

Miranda has a theme of flowing and graceful character, heard softly through Ariel's speech . . . .

*Come unto these yellow sands,* . . . is representative of the freedom of Ariel and his spirits. It is first sung by them while they are still imprisoned in the "belly of Setebos", but on this occasion is drowned out by the roaring of Setebos' spirits. The melody occurs at various times through out the action.

A dirge of pallid and lugubrious character accompanies the coming of the puritanical aspects of the epoch standing between the Renaissance and the present time. It characterizes "Death", one of the priests of Setebos.

Compositions of large dimensions in *Caliban* are the *Roman Orgy* and *Vision of the Cross* at the end of Act I, and *War*, at the end of Act III, both of which introduce *Setebos* choruses.

For the historical Interludes the composer has in some instances composed music, as in the case of the Greek chorus, *Many are the Wonders of Time*, but in general has drawn it from various sources and epochs. There are upwards of one hundred scores, great and small.

After viewing *Caliban*, Herbert F. Peyser wrote his detailed review for *Musical America* with headlines that proclaimed "New York's First Community Masque Notable Spectacle". - "Farwell's Music a Vital and Supremely Artistic Factor" - "Two Thousand Performers Enlisted in the Most Ambitious Effort the Country Has Seen to Democratize the Arts of Drama, Music, and the Dance".

The lengthy report praised and criticized where due and then Peyser explained Farwell's work in detail:[5]

The music of Arthur Farwell was singularly excellent in that it accomplished its composer's purposes and proved itself worthy of all esteem on the basis of intrinsic qualities. Mr. Farwell understands the essentials, the potencies and limitations of community masque music as no other musician in America today. He has had

abundant previous experience in studying its problems and
he has solved them with remarkable success. To work
under the handicaps presented by the inexorable
circumstances of open-air performances in vast spaces and
yet to evolve a score in itself as interesting as that of
*Caliban* marks a distinctive achievement of artistic
creation. He has here surpassed his earlier experiments
not only in general felicity of result, but in boldness of
dimension.

The score consists of choral numbers and independent
orchestral pages. It forms a constant and indispensable
background to the most important factors of the piece,
sometimes claiming attention through its own eloquence,
sometimes only heightening the force or beauty of the
scene by its dramatically suggestive quality. It is modern
without subtle complexities and almost unfailingly direct.

Folksongs have been selected by Mr. Farwell to
accompany most of the interludes. . . . But the drama
proper . . . [uses] effects of powerful dissonance to enforce
an obvious or symbolical dramatic situation. . . . The one
number above all others which the memory treasures is
the chorus *Glory and Serenity* sung in the *Field of the Cloth
of Gold* scene - a noble, hymn-like melody, stoutly
harmonized and which one cannot hear recur without a
thrill.

Peyser believed that most of the music had been so
orchestrated that it carried readily in the open air. He pointed
out that Farwell's assistants for orchestrating the huge work
included such distinguished composers as Deems Taylor, Chester
Ide, W.H. Humiston, and Israel Amter. Members of the orchestra
were recruited largely from the Metropolitan Opera House players.
The chorus included many members of the Oratorio Society .

Isadora Duncan was the featured dancer in *Caliban*. The May
16, 1916, New York Herald praised her dancing on opening night:

One of the most effective individual incidents . . . was
the appearance of Isadora Duncan who preceded the
Grecian pageant on the sands by a solo dance in which

she crossed the entire stretch of sands followed by a soft
yellow spotlight. She seemed to be wearing only a flowing
veil which revealed every charm of her graceful figure.

An announcement of *Caliban* in the Boston *Sunday Herald* for
June 24, 1916, gives more specific details of the music:

> An orchestra of more than 100 pieces will play the
> music scored for a large orchestra, particularly in the brass
> section, which will consist of eight horns, eight trumpets,
> six trombones and four tubas. The strings are relatively
> few in number and are employed only to lend orchestral
> color. . . . One of the most impressive effects will be 20
> trumpets sounding the introduction. Two trumpets will
> sound first and others will fall in until all 20 are ringing.
> Mr. Farwell has composed new and special music for the
> pantomimes of the Roman, Germanic and Italian
> interludes. . . .
> Mr. Farwell has resorted to an Indian theme to gain
> the desired archaic effect in the Egyptian interlude in the
> chant of the priest. The other archaic number is the early
> English song *Summer is a-Cumin in*. To Mr. Mackaye's
> translation of Sophocles's *Many are the Wonders of Man*,
> the composer has set music. Another old number is the
> Gregorian chant, *Vexilla Regis* sung at the miraculous
> appearance of the cross in the Roman orgy. The hymn of
> *The Field of the Cross of Gold* is in a way typical of the
> chief motive of the drama which rears Caliban from the
> condition of a beast to a condition of friendly and
> civilized man.

Three songs from *Caliban* for medium voice are available for
study: *Come Unto These Yellow Sands*, *Under the Greenwood
Tree*, and *Many Are the Wonders of Time*. These are written to
be sung with piano accompaniment (probably used during
rehearsals), or with orchestra. Score and parts are available for
the latter.

Farwell composed these songs with the amateur singer in
mind. For example, *Under the Greenwood Tree* is scored for a

two-part male chorus.  Written in 6/8 meter, the chorus has a robust rhythmic swing propelling the melody and lower lines. Both parts are found in the accompaniment which retains the simplicity of the whole - yet maintains interest for singers and listeners.  Tessituras for these voice parts as well as for those in the other choruses are usually written in a comfortable range for the average singer.  This type of writing is characteristic of the music Farwell wrote for his pageants and masques.

In his article on pageant music written for the December 1916 *American Pageant Association Bulletin,* Farwell also described his considerations in scoring for the orchestra he used in *Caliban* (results for which Peyser praised him) and gave the following advice to other composers writing music for pageants:

> I personally strongly favor the orchestra as against the band.  The sound of continuous brass is obnoxious and pleasure destroying. . . . At *Caliban* the orchestra was employed, for an audience of 20,000 people. The orchestra numbered eighty and the brass was augmented to the point where it could be used alone for a powerful brass effect where such an effect was needed.  But in general the effect was distinctly orchestral, with strings and the lighter wood-winds, and this effect was very varied and beautiful and quite sufficient in tone, except for occasional moments of adverse wind. . . . No attempt was made to pit string tone against brass.  When the whole orchestra was used, the strings were scored high, in registers where string tone carries well out of doors, and the second violins, instead of being written on the level of the brass, where they would have had practically no weight, were scored in unison with the first violins, the wood-winds being depended upon to fill out in the register between the high strings and the brass.  The high penetrating string tones were heard very clearly, and even in fortissimo passages with all the brass, gave in the open a strong feeling of orchestra, not band.  With the orchestra, however, it is necessary to have a proper sound shell behind it. . . . In *Caliban* the entire orchestra and chorus, of about four hundred, were in a great box above the

proscenium with sufficient opening to let the sound out in the desired direction. . . .

The country is full of composers, and, many of them have already proven themselves thoroughly in this respect. The ordinary musical markets are too Europeanized to want or invite their work. The pageant movement in America should make a special point of doing this. Aside from the principle of creative progress involved, it is distracting to hear familiar music, laden with associations, used with a pageant which should direct attention wholly upon itself. . . Pageant music should be absolutely of the best. . . The composer can safely go beyond his audience. We are to look at the pageant music not as an off-shoot from the world of music in general, but as something more vital and creative than most of that which arises otherwise. . . . From the inspiration of pageants should come songs, choruses, processionals, dances, and many other forms of music of a vigorous nature, scarcely to be expected from the work of a closeted composer, who is not working in touch with the active life of the people.

Concurrently with his work on *Caliban* Farwell planned and directed the beautiful Song and Light festival concerts that concluded the 1916 season for the New York City Community Chorus. These are discussed in Chapter 10.

Farwell's music for *Caliban* earned him further recognition. He functioned as one of several distinguished professionals on what was named an "Advisory Board and Special Lectures" at the Riverdale Summer School of Pageantry in Riverdale, New York, in 1916. This was directed by the dance specialist, Mary Porter Beegle, who maintained the school at the Riverdale Country School for Boys.

Many Universities also offered special courses in pageantry and related subjects during the years 1911 - 1925. These courses met the demands of people caught up in the pageant fever of the times who felt the need for information and training. Leaders in the movement sensed that the *process* of creating a pageant was as important as either script or music; i.e. the production itself.

Many organizational skills were needed to accomplish the "Civic Engineering" which MacKaye envisioned.[6]

### Pageant Characteristics

In an address,[7] Farwell described how the pageants were written. First, a literary-dramatic form was prepared called the *Pageant Book*. Then the musical compositions, based on this book and its several episodes, were composed. These called for orchestra and chorus, and sometimes soloists, while the production itself was made by the entire community. Everything was conceived in broad outlines and large masses, and only incidentally in individual reactions as in an indoor drama. An outdoor stage was carefully selected or prepared upon which a large grandstand was built and a sound-reflecting stand for the orchestra, so participants as well as audience could hear.

The general form which William Chauncy Langdon[8] and Farwell used was that of a series of realistic, historical, dramatic episodes alternating, though not necessarily, in strict regularity, with *interludes*, and having an *introduction* and *finale* for its beginning and ending. The introduction, interludes, and finale were purely poetic conceptions - in general, "symbolistic representations of historical or romantic aspects of the history of the place which is expressing itself in the pageant." These sections are carried out through dance and dramatic movement and through chorus, the orchestral accompaniment continuing throughout these scenes as a musical support for the entire action.

In considering the history of the early American pageant, Farwell pointed out that as subject matter and themes changed, along with society's needs, the style for presentation also changed. Farwell claimed that because the masque was more flexible than the episodic pageant and more susceptible to dramatic unity, the pageant took on a style approaching drama, hence the term "pageant-drama" was used. Langdon defined the pageant as "a drama in which the place is the hero and its history is the plot".

Farwell spoke and wrote frequently and fervently about community music and its relationship to pageant-drama production. Stirred by his vision of what the "common" citizen's participation-potential was, he proclaimed it to be a "gospel of communal self-development in terms of joyous art." In trying to define this development of the pageant as community music-drama, he declared:

> Our imagination and will, with which we mould the material of this drama, is a gift from God, as we ourselves are from God. In that we all unite together in the production of this drama we realize the condition of brotherhood. Therefore as giving something approaching to a definition, I have believed that we may regard community music-drama as the most complete manifestation in living art of the fatherhood of God and the brotherhood of man".[9]

Like Langdon, Farwell believed that the pageant was an agent for social change; one became a better person by participating in it. His dream was to create a new world order through the power of community music - a dream that became his driving mission for many years. While Farwell's labors to promote the cause of the American composer and his music is often recognized, his idealistic call for the development of a democratic music in the United States is less known. He viewed the arts as playing a primary role in the evolution of universal brotherhood - a spiritual phenomenon - that could ultimately unify all mankind. As Farwell's work in community music continued, he related his hopes more to the social activists than to the on-going musical establishment. He recognized that the social mind was more concerned with the general human welfare of the people whom he longed to touch.

Taken in its broadest sense, Farwell believed that the community music-drama was potentially the logical development of music in the evolution developed by Beethoven and Wagner, and "as such, potentially, and in view of the democratic ideals of the present, may be considered as the great art form of the age." However, he considered it to be foremost a musical work and only secondly as drama. He recognized the weakness of the pageant format that alternated musical with non-musical scenes. He advocated that the dramatic conception should grow from the area of musical consciousness and at the, same time appeal to the whole person - body, mind, and soul. His goal was the use of community music drama for self-improvement which he dreamed would open a new age with music rightly related to the populace.

These then, are some of the characteristics of the pageant as it gradually developed into a vehicle for community expression.

Farwell did not compose music for any pageants with a war theme after America entered World War I. Instead he wrote patriotic music for solo voice and community choruses. Although *Caliban* had been a remarkable success, its large production requirements limited its performance. Farwell and Percy MacKaye deemed it advisable to create a smaller production for community singing. The result of their collaboration in 1917 was *The Evergreen Tree*, a Christmas masque designed with minimum requirements for staging.

### The Evergreen Tree

The text for the masque is different from the usual Christmas story. MacKaye's theology is mixed - probably because he desired not to offend any particular religious faith since the masque was designed for community presentation. The Evergreen Tree is the central character in the story. Other roles include Joseph, Ruth, Shepherds, an Elf, a Gnome, the Beasts - a Lion, a Wolf, and a Bear - Fairies, the three kings - Belshasar, Melchior, and Caspar, Claus - the Pedlar, and his mate. MacKaye's narrative implies the birth of Jesus, as the Saviour of the world, but he never uses the name of Jesus. Instead he refers to "the Child", or "Light-Child"; his Ruth seems to assume the role of Mary, the Child's mother; Mr. Claus, the Pedlar, becomes Santa Claus or Saint Claus for the Evergreen Tree. King Herod represents wickedness and its power in the world which is contrasted dramatically with the goodness and peace brought by the Child. The script contains some Christian ideas mixed with added pagan elements.

In the book of music only two scenes are mentioned: the *Place of Empire*, and the *Place of Outcasts*. Costuming is kept simple and traditional. One chorus is dressed in white. Another one wears red coverings over their white robes that later are removed in a symbolic gesture when they join the first chorus. This creates an all-white effect in the finale.

The masque features readings that tell the story between the choruses which reinforce the narrative. A few familiar carols are interspersed at appropriate places, the original text being slightly altered in some instances to fit the plot.

Some of the music deserves special recognition. Farwell's *Fairy Round* sung by the Tree, the Elf, Gnome, and Lion, has a romping rhythm that lends contrast to the more serious four-part choruses. The *Tree-Child's Lullaby* written for soprano soloist, is attractive. (Ex. 63a) The *Might of Herod* has heavy, sinister chords that build dramatic excitement with the chorus of men's voices. (Ex. 63b) When Herod speaks angrily about "who shall defeat my power?", two choruses answer him, one of mixed voices, another of all male singers. (Ex. 63c)

*The Bell, the Sword and the Laughter*, number 14 in the masque, features solos by the three kings and a trio performed by them. *The Dance of the Evergreen* which follows, (Ex. 63d) has the basses singing a two bar ostinato on the words "Ding dong" while all the higher voices sing a spirited, well accented unison melody. The three kings also combine with Claus the Pedlar in singing number 17, a short original carol in D minor. The masque ends with a triumphant chorus eulogizing the Evergreen Tree and the Christ-Child. (Ex. 63e)

The entire work is well-planned to provide variety in vocal texture, mood, and tempo, as well as movement on the stage. The music is challenging, but not too difficult for community choruses with a qualified director. Gertrude Farwell, who was trained as an actress, read the complete script as a dramatic presentation at Camp Arden when she served there as a camp counselor in 1931. Even without the addition of music, she found MacKaye's text beautiful.

Originally published by John Church in 1917, *Evergreen Tree* was acquired by Theodore Presser in 1930. Farwell wrote to Mr. Crem at Presser's on September 5, 1930 that he considered *Evergreen Tree* to be "one of the most important of his works and chorally, technically ahead of its original purpose, for the community movement."

Not having been a *commission*, like *Caliban*, but purely a labor of love, it had no guaranteed production, and has so far never had a *full* production, with *band* and *orchestra* as written. The biggest production which it ever had was in the Civic Auditorium, Denver, under Mr. Wilcox, where the organ was used. Mr. Wilcox wrote to me that it was a tremendous success.

. . . it is one of the most powerfully *creative* and joyously created works of my life, and with all the perspective which experience gives, I hold to this work and would be willing to stand or fall by it any time, *if* it were adequately heard. I know it is practical, chorally, as I have heard it excellently conducted (i.e. the choruses) and have conducted the choruses complete very successfully myself. The work has been called the "Modern Messiah".

I am writing these things to put on record now, with you, who now controls the work, my belief that the *Evergreen Tree* music is a major contribution to American music, and that it is destined one day, under the right conditions, to a very great success. The drama is one of Mr. MacKaye's best products, especially because of its simplicity of outline, and easiness of comprehension.

While the *Tree* is ostensibly a Christmas drama, it is of wider significance, and is in reality a drama of the conflict of imperial world-power (War) and the Christ spirit: i.e. a drama for *peace*, and must appeal to the great forces which are working for peace.

Farwell was hopeful that the Presser Publishing Company would do more to promote his compositions than John Church had done. Several songs also went to Presser from the Church catalogue at this time. In his letter, Farwell wrote as any composer would, to arouse fresh interest in his work. Perhaps its decline in popularity was due to the general reduction of community interest in pageant production at that time. That *Evergreen Tree* could live up to being the "Modern Messiah" is unlikely, but the masque had an acceptable place for many years and still holds potential uses.

The masque seems rather long to the author who observed that her copy has many indicated cuts. The eliminated sections are probably related to the brochure suggestions which Farwell prepared to accompany the score. He realized that some communities were not able to perform certain choruses in full. So he provided suggestions to accommodate the use of smaller groups. Farwell was able to report to Presser that "many small productions have been given in this way." He wanted to be sure that these special brochures were still available with Presser. The suggested cuts do not destroy its over-all effectiveness.

Farwell was understandably upset when two years went by without any kind of response from Mr. Crem or Presser's. So Farwell sent a registered letter to the publishing house on December 10th ordering some copies of his *Evergreen Tree* and inquired about the fate of his earlier letter. His files show no response to his inquiry, but they do have copies of his masque.

## Community Music-Drama Work in California

After Farwell moved to California in 1918, he had occasion to resume his work in community music-drama while serving as the acting head of the department of music at the University of California in Berkeley. There he produced *California*, a masque of song, in the Greek Theater on April 27, 1919. (Figures 57 and 58). It included a free verse text by Farwell with choral singing. The program lists two songs composed by Farwell, and others from a variety of sources. The inevitable audience-participation using a song-sheet, provided the "grand finale".

Farwell's temporary position at the University was concluded June 30, 1919, but he stayed on long enough to celebrate the end of the War with his *Chant of Victory* on July 4, 1919. This, too, was presented in the Greek Theater in association with the music and drama committee of the University. *The Chant of Victory* was also presented at the San Francisco Civic Auditorium. Farwell had already organized the Berkeley Municipal Community Chorus which was featured on this *Community Ceremony*. This event had narration by the "Poet", and "interpretation" by "America", as well as the usual audience-participation. Farwell wrote the free verse text and used seven songs he had composed earlier for the community chorus.

In Santa Barbara, Farwell organized another community chorus and wrote a music drama for this group. *La Primavera*, or

*Figure 57.  Rehearsal in the University of California Greek Theater, Berkeley, for the Farwell masque <u>California</u>.*

*Figure 58.  Performance, April 1919, of Farwell masque <u>California</u> in the Greek Theater.  Arthur Farwell conducted, and Gertrude Farwell was among the performers.*

"The Coming of Spring" was presented in an out-door setting in the Spring of 1920. (Figures 59)  Only the title song is known.

*Figure 59. Scenes from La Primavera (The Coming of Spring), Santa Barbara, California, April 1920 - a community music drama written and directed by Farwell.*

## The Pilgrimage Play

Farwell's biggest California effort in community music-drama was composing the music for the *Pilgrimage Play* presented in the Hollywood Bowl area in 1921. The problems Farwell encountered in preparing the score are discussed in chapter 11.

Existing music from the play includes the vocal numbers for *Manger Scene, John the Baptist, Transfiguration Scene,* and the *Ascension Chorus.* Also available are the complete scores for organ, for orchestra and for piano. Later Farwell utilized six of the themes from this play to compose his *Prelude to a Spiritual Drama.*

*Gloria in Excelsis* for mixed chorus and organ is also available in a fuller version than that used in the play. It opens with women's voices singing in four parts alone, followed by the male voices also in divisi. The organ duplicates the chorus lines in the manuals with mostly single sustained notes in the pedals, and has very few moving passages. Farwell uses rests, Handelian style, to emphasize "Glory" in the voices, then writes "peace" on a sustained soft chord to contrast with the exultant "glory" chords. He continues with frequent chromatics, but stays mostly in the originating key of F major.

A study of the program suggests the magnitude of the production. Photos of the setting and some of the characters are also impressive. (Figures 60 and 61.) The *Pilgrimage Play* was performed regularly throughout the summer beginning July 11th, 1921.

Edwyn A. Hunt, who sang bass in the chorus, described his impressions of the *Pilgrimage Play* in a letter to Edgar Kirk dated October 1, 1956.[10]

> The music he [Farwell] composed for the Pilgrimage Play, as background music essentially, was strange and difficult. We practiced it all through the winter, and when the show was over in the summer I still could not remember it, probably because I sang the bass all the time.

*Figure 60.   The Pilgrimage Play, 1921 - Scene of Jesus' invitation "Suffer the little children to come unto me, for of such is the Kingdom of Heaven."*

*Figure 61.   Palm Sunday scene from The Pilgrimage Play, 1921.*

At the time I was studying voice constantly, and hearing
a great deal of music by Ravel, Debussy, Sibelius and the great
German modernist who died a year ago in Hollywood. So I
was used to contemporary music of the day. But his music
seemed to me to be way ahead of his time; - strange
dissonances and minor strains, built symphonically rather than
lyrically. I could never feel any melody.
But Vorcho, playing the part of Mary Magdalene, said
it was wonderful to act with.

Farwell continued to write poetic texts for music-drama and
began "The Coming of Song" about this time, but only the script
is known. By 1925, he prepared another masque, *Grail Song*
which was for community singing, acting, and dancing.

**Theater of the Stars**

The development of the Theater of the Stars in 1925 has been
told in chapter 11. This project was a great challenge to Farwell
and the realization of a dream come true - the establishment of
an outdoor theater for music and drama.

In addition to the music, Farwell planned for special lighting
equipment which should reveal, in varying colors, the different
scenic aspects and unusual romantic beauties of the canyon stage.
In utilizing the lighting, he prepared the concerts with what he
considered "dramatic episodes". These consisted chiefly      of
*Prologues* involving several characters that would reveal some of
the remarkable possibilities of the natural stage.

For example, the first of these prologues was presented at the
theater with the Miniature Philharmonic Orchestra of Los
Angeles, and opened with different instruments each playing a
phrase from concealed positions in scattered parts of the forest.
First, a trumpet call blared forth from an elevated position on the
forested canyon wall. It was answered in turn by a flute and an
oboe played from different positions some distance away. Then
horns awoke, answering each other out of the darkness from their
positions nearly a quarter of a mile apart.

Finally, upon the blare of trombone and trumpet, the spirit of St. Bernard, drawn from the Old World to these San Bernardino Mountains, which have honored his memory, is revealed, and he complains of his meditations being disturbed by these "pagan" sounds. The Spirit of Life appears at a distance above him, and enlightens him with regard to the character of this new world, showing him its passing primitive race in a singing processional of Indians along the forest trail, declaring its youthful and joyous character and calling upon the new race, that comes with "music calling in the night". The concealed musicians now assemble and to the piping of one of their number, descend in procession through the forest to the spot from which the concert is to be given, while the spotlights disappear.[11]

Such an introduction to the first evening concert must have added to its interest and uniqueness. As the season advanced, further developments progressed in these incidental dramatic episodes.

Reactions to the gala opening week were unanimously favorable. The Los Angeles Miniature Philharmonic Orchestra of fourteen members performed every night and a variety of soloists were featured. A glamorous addition was "a real program of light play which followed the thought-content of the music," wrote Frances Kendig, music editor of the *Los Angeles Times*, in a July 1925 issue of *Fawnskin Folks*.[12]

A strong white beam rested against a massive rock during the rendition of a movement of stately grandeur; again the pine needles were ever so faintly lined with deep blue with the hearing of a graceful mood by Haydn, and colors mixed high on the mountain during the performance of a kaleidoscopic and richly orchestrated Rimsky-Korsakov tone picture.

Further describing the beauty of the event, Kendig claimed that it rekindled her enthusiasm for this kind of entertainment. She felt that "Arthur Farwell's inherent idealism, mixed with that practicability life needs must always bring to the poetic nature, made him fitted to carry on the project of adding the best of the art of man to that great Natural Art of God."

Intrigued, too, was Walter W. Squier who paid high tribute to Farwell in prophesying a powerful influence from the Theater of the Stars. He wrote an editorial as follows:[13]

> We cannot help feeling that, once the waves of such sheer loveliness as this sweep over one's being, they wash away some of the worship of material things, leaving not only a deeper appreciation of the truly beautiful, but a real soul hunger for it that will henceforth refuse to be denied.
>
> Such a powerful influence cannot stop with the visitors to the Theater of the Stars. Its vibrations are sure to extend on and on until the people of the whole nation will demand more of this beauty which is so soul satisfying.
>
> We dare to go to such lengths in prophesying the outcome of the movement which began at Fawnskin in June, because it seems to be inevitable, in view of the circumstances as they are:  A man - Mr. Farwell - with the desire to enrich the life of the American people, given the use of the ideal place to bring people into contact with beauty at its best and gifted with the power to make the most of that place.
>
> Whatever the future may hold for this worthy project, however, we know that it is safe with Mr. Farwell.

In another article, Squier wrote as a critic for the performances. He commented on Farwell's insistence in hiring only top quality artists which gave the new undertaking at once "a character and a name which could probably not have gained in years on any other basis." After a detailed and glowing description of events and performers at the Theater, he concluded his critique by saying:[14]

> The expression of the people, the increase in their interest and numbers up to the final night, the interest in the movement by prominent individuals as widely

separated as business man and artist, indeed every circumstance attending the productions, has stamped the opening of the Theater of the Stars with the seal of brilliant success. It will probably not be long before it will become the objective point of visitors from far and wide, whose first thought of the San Bernardino Mountains will be the Theater of the Stars.

Marjorie Dodge, an opera singer from Chicago, was a featured soloist on one of the summer concerts. She wrote to Farwell also expressing her feelings about his work:

I want to tell you what I think of your "Theater of the Stars". I have thought much about it since I appeared there for you. It impressed me greatly from many different angles. First the exquisite natural beauties - so enhanced by your ideal - and again the spell that is cast over all humans that are fortunate enough to participate in giving of music and the listeners. I, personally, think there can be no greater individual movement in the bettering of the cultural life of Southern California than you are perpetuating under the brilliance of the Fawnskin Stars.

Performers hailed the acoustic conditions of the theater as being extraordinary and phenomenal. Every nuance of a vocal or instrumental soloist was heard with perfect clarity not only from the music platform on the floor of the canyon, but from any point of the canyon wall (which constituted the "backdrop" of the stage) to its highest rim about four hundred and fifty feet above the audience. In fact, solos from this rim, rendered from the top of a monolith sixty feet high in itself, were a "highly successful feature of many of the concerts," reported Farwell. The speaking voice also carried with equal clarity and "a small orchestra of fourteen players sounded like an eighty piece orchestra," he added.[15]

For the conclusion of the first season, Farwell wrote a brief musical play, in the nature of a masque, *The March of Man*. This

was presented on four successive evenings in conjunction with a
concert following the play.  A synopsis follows:

The rocks and trees, acting as rock spirits and dryads, awaken
from their sleep only to remember the destructiveness of man.
Their existence is threatened by a woodsman cutting down a tree,
an engineer planting a blast of dynamite, and a party of revelers
who start a forest fire.  The elements create a great rain storm
which extinguishes the fire.  The World-Soul appears in the storm
and prophesies the coming of Man who shall save the Nature
Spirits.  He comes as a Seer, and opposes the operations of the
invaders - especially that of the engineer, who claims he represents
the progress of civilization - The March of Man.  The Seer,
threatened with the explosion of the dynamite, calls forth the
spirits of the rocks and the trees, and confounds the invaders.
The Seer then calls for a sign that the area shall be held sacred
and inviolate.  In response, the World-Soul sends him the Singer,
whose prayerful song reaches the heavens as tone and light,
awakening the celestial choirs and the light of the new day.[16]
The play called for about thirty-five actors, singers and
musicians.  Farwell played the role of the Seer, and his wife,
Gertrude, the leading female role.  The upper photo of figure 62
shows the Farwells in the center surrounded by this company.
The audience pictured below reveals only a small portion of the
audience seated in one of three canyons that converged upon the
largest canyon forming the "stage" area.  The orchestra for the
masque was concealed in the forest.  Figure 63 shows the setting
for musical programs where the performers were reflected in the
pool between the proscenium and amphitheater.  The lower photo
shows *March of Man* in the natural setting which used only a
fraction of the vast available stage space.  Farwell was not only
composer, actor, and general manager, but also he served as leader
of the community singing which took place during intermission.
Farwell asked the management to include funds for an extension
of lighting equipment for the new season, stating the need for the
installation of a transformer of greater capacity.  In his annual
report he summarized the possibilities of the light system as being
that of a "vast organ upon which combinations of color may be
produced instead of combinations of sound".  During the past

Figure 62. Above, company for <u>The March of Man</u>. Farwell on rock, center; Gertrude Farwell, in white, stands above him. Below, portion of the audience.

*Figure 63. Theater of the Stars. Above, stage setting for musical programs. Below, the natural setting uses a fraction of the vast stage space.*

season he had used light to make a color composition of a scene to correspond with each musical composition. Sometimes this was a fixed arrangement in the general mood of the musical work; sometimes he varied it with the changing moods of the music as Kendig reported.

Here one observes Farwell's significant contribution to the developing art of light in performance, as well as his efforts in outdoor theater. What a pity that the managers were too short-sighted to continue a project so well begun. They saw only the immediate financial burden and not the long-range potential in cultural good for the community. Hence, the following season for which Farwell had already planned expansions, was cancelled, and signaled the death of the Theater of the Stars as well as Farwell's hopes and dreams for its use.

By 1932 Farwell was ready to experiment with a different style of composing. He wrote a *Scene from the Inferno* Op. 85, from Dante's *Divine Comedy* for orchestra which features a non-singing chorus of wails, sobs, and gasps. (Ex. 64) The scene depicts the gate of Hell; first murmurings; horde driven by gadflies; Charon; the passage of Acheron; the trembling plain, and the wind. The score was to have been used with a Norman Bel Geddes production that never materialized. This is Farwell's only venture into this style, so it is interesting to observe that he was adventuresome enough to experiment with "new sounds". Work sheets reveal further experimenting and are labeled, "Results from writing the *Inferno Scene.*"

### Cartoon, or Once Upon A Time Recently

The theater work that occupied much of Farwell's last years was the completion of his only opera, *Cartoon or Once upon a Time Recently* for which the complete script and vocal score with piano accompaniment are available. Farwell's early exposure to opera in Europe and at home had convinced him that opera's formalism had affected its vitality. He believed that the Wagnerian concept of music drama brought life to the action, the drama back to life, and feeling back into the overall experience in the theater. In writing his opera, Farwell had no intention of creating a formal music drama. In a letter to George Freedley on

June 25, 1948, Farwell described his purpose in composing
*Cartoon*:

> This piece, "Cartoon", came out of my long and
> terrific struggle, from 1901 on, for the recognition of the
> American composer against the overwhelming European
> domination of the American scene, - a battle in which
> various gains have been made, but which is still   only
> partially won.
>     It was long ago that I was trying to imagine how, if
> I were a cartoonist, I could picture cartoonwise, in
> fantastic satirical fashion, for public consummation, the
> central issues of this struggle.  These imagined pictures
> "came alive" in my mind, in this work.
>     The work thus portrays the great turning point in
> American musical history, the Revolutionary War over
> again in music, and the beginning of the development of
> our native musical folk-sources.  Fantastic-satirical as it is,
> the ending may be thought to have a not inconsiderable
> serious national significance.
>     But through it all, it has been my purpose to make it
> a *show* - pictures, melody, folksongs, dances, fun, and
> American to the core.

Farwell's letter is an excellent brief description of the opera.
He wrote the scenario and with Edna Kingsley Wallace created
the text.  His wonderful sense of humor as well as his opinion of
the American musical scene is revealed in hilarious fashion.
While it is true that Farwell does have a particular bone to pick,
a viewpoint to stump, even an ax to grind about the ill treatment
of American music and composers at the hands of the "Big City
Arts" supporters and controllers, analyst Donald Ryan feels that
Farwell does this "not always with the rapier of a satirist, but
sometimes with a broadsword."[17]
    In the text, Farwell grants that American music is not as
refined as Europe's.  On the other hand he recognizes his country
is so self-assured and vibrant, that in time it cannot but give birth
to music equal to the best in the world.  For this reason he
maintains that America's music-hopefuls need to be supported,

encouraged, and cultivated. Of course these thoughts are but an echo of those he expressed in early Wa-Wan days.

One should note that *Cartoon* was "finished" in January of 1948. This was not long after the United States had shown military superiority, fueled by a strong moral purpose, in global conflicts with two of the world's great fighting forces. National euphoria was at its highest as Americans had eclipsed every other nation to become "Leader of the Free World". Farwell's patriotism had always run deeply as an integral part of his being. In his opera, he espouses these profound personal feelings. His text shows him to be a firm believer in the purpose of the United States to spread "Our Word of Liberty . . . unto all the shores that anguish to be free." He speaks of our country as "Freedom's Land".

Farwell's synopsis of the script reflects his own career - as intimated in his letter to Freedley - the American composer struggling against European domination. This is a serious enough subject to qualify its description as "opera" rather than "operetta," even though the work has many lighthearted and comical moments. Farwell's own synopsis follows:

Act I. Temple of Europus, the Music god. Impecunious young composer, *Americus*, gets raw deal at hands of Robber-Priests (powers of the musical world). He loves *Columbia*, music-loving girl of social position, who believes in him. Priests regard her rich uncle, *Samuel Stockpile*, as their meat. Love scene in Temple; *Columbia* promises to wed *Americus* when he triumphs in the Temple with his music. Society enters, witnesses Spring Ceremony (burlesque ballet). As they leave, *Americus* hides, sees Priests reveal their hypocrisy and greed. Beethoven (elevated statue) comes to life, excoriates them, tells *Americus* to go forth and gain strength from the folksongs of his people.

Act II. *Scene 1.* Spanish-California patio. Frolicking table company; guitars, songs, dance. *Americus* (secretly backed by *Stockpile*) absorbing it, inviting folkgroups East. *Scene 2.* A crypt in the Temple. Priests, suspicious, plotting against *Americus.* *Scene 3.* The plains. *Americus* at Indian dance ceremonial. He advances project.

Act III. Same as Act I, decorated for Autumn Ceremony, about to begin. Ominous knock. *Americus* rushes in with horde of shooting cowboys, whooping and dancing Indians, Spanish Californians, Negroes, Kentucky Mountaineers, etc., triumphs in the Temple with "Ceremony of the New World", leading to Indian war dance and overthrowing of Idol of Europus. *Stockpile* revealed as backer. So hailed, he is transfigured to "Uncle Sam". He exalts and blesses the lovers and extends welcome to the composers and music of America.

Farwell's score is unabashedly of the Romantic camp. It can be safely assumed that he is *for* whatever the god Europus is *against.* This is stated in the first act where melody, romance, and beauty as well as adherence to tonality, is obvious. Farwell's music is a perfect match for Edna K. Wallace, the skillful wordsmith. Together they create a boisterous first scene.

Donald Ryan thinks that "to say that the influence of the Englishmen Gilbert and Sullivan is evident here would be out and out understatement. (Ex. 65a,) It is instead, a clear copy but an excellent one. The text shows as masterful a control of the language as its British counterpart, and the music - though not typically British, is no less crafted."[18]

Another wonderful comic moment also occurs in the first act. This time it takes place at the end when the statue of Beethoven comes to life to excoriate the robber priests. Ryan sees "no Gilbert and Sullivan stuff now. Here Farwell amazingly well apes this master's style and laces the denunciation with some of Beethoven's most familiar symphonic motifs. As a musical joke this one is uproariously funny."[19]

As Ryan has indicated, the music of the first act especially, is strongly reminiscent of Gilbert and Sullivan operettas. He feels that this is the most effective act in the opera. The pacing is fast, the tunes catchy, and the satire obvious. The ballet *Pierrot's Lunacy or the Blight of Spring* is a marvelous parody on Schoenberg's *Pierrot Lunaire* and Stravinsky's *Rite of Spring.* (Ex. 65b) Ryan points out that this burlesque is one device Farwell

uses "to deride the modernist-realist trend."     Farwell's notes
suggest that the dancing may equally be a "parody of the
modernistic ballet." He provides details for the dancing in the
appendix. He also stipulates that the orchestration involves many
complexities, such as different instruments playing simultaneously
in different keys, registers, and rhythms; chromatic scales, and
other passages of several adjacent semitones, and superimposed
effects beyond the capacity of the hand in a piano arrangement.
"The present piano version is therefore but a skeleton presentation
of the actual score, preserving, in many places, only such elements
of the score as will assist the dancers in moving from piano to
orchestral rehearsals."

The style of Farwell's music purposely changes as the story
moves along. From a taste of England, the music of Columbia's
solo, *Love the Revealer* in Act one goes to the style of sentimental
salon songs of the early 1900s. (Ex. 65c) Here the lack of solid
cadences at expected points creates a mushiness that keeps one
waiting for more resolutions that never quite happen. Farwell
uses many tremolos in the accompaniment that are appropriate for
the text as well as this style of aria. Descending octave skips
occur frequently at the end of phrases which rise initially. The
melody reaches an effective climax on high $b^1$.

The second act is folk-music oriented in a setting similar to
the one Farwell visited out West in Charles Lummis's Spanish-
styled home. In this act Farwell struts his pride of country and
its heterogeneous makeup. While he might have liked to include
more ethnic groups, he limits them to the Spanish, Mexicans,
Early-Californians and Indians. Unfortunately, the pace is bogged
down by this cultural "show-off". Ryan claims that "As the bone-
picking progresses through point-stumping to ax-grinding, the
whole thing seems uncomfortably long by the end of the act." To
which the writer agrees. However, we both see scenes that can be
shortened without sacrificing the scenario.[20]

The most outstanding song is Columbia's solo at the beginning
of Act Three where she sings *Brilliant October is Here* (Complete
aria is given in example 65d.) This is not a simple aria - none of
them are - but this text is the least pretentious of them all which
makes the song more readily approachable and memorable.
Farwell's tendency to become pompous when he is serious, is not

seen here. That, plus the wholly satisfying marriage of melody and harmony makes for a "glorious effect", declares Ryan.

In analyzing the aria, one finds in the last 30 bars that in spite of all the key shifting and surprising movement, the phrasing of both the text and melody is quite metric - each four bars long. This is comforting when the text begins to be pompous again. Very satisfying is the last cadence - an authentic, with the V7 having both the 9th and 13th flatted. This particular chord is relatively rare in the opera, and as voiced here it can be a great high point for the soprano as well as the accompaniment (Ex. 74d).

The comic relief in Act Three is noteworthy. Farwell's summary of it given earlier, describes the invasion of the Temple by hordes of shooting cowboys, dancing Indians, Kentucky mountaineers and others. While previously the humor has been in words and song, here the humor is physical and potentially riotously funny.

Also in Act Three, Farwell indulges in a bit of compositional virtuosity. This is a three-song counterpoint, one of which is an unlikely choice - the *Rose of the World* duet. Ryan feels that this should be a "certain crowd-pleaser." (Ex. 65e) This moves on to the finale featuring a rousing chorus in fast-moving four-part harmony combined with the two main characters singing in unison on a sustained melody used earlier. (Ex. 65f)

An interesting comparison can be made between Farwell's use of *Rose of the World* and music bearing the same name which Horatio Parker composed for his opera *Fairyland* in 1915. Parker uses the rose as a symbol of a land where everything is good, and evil does not exist. He uses the four note motive, *Rose of the World*, in several arias where the text speaks of this wonderful place or "dreamland". The text for Farwell's *Rose of the World* is *personal* and refers to a love relationship to which the hero and heroine pledge their troth. Both composers use *Rose of the World* in the finale. Farwell's features the duet sung by the lovers and a chorus as already described. Parker's heroine, Rosamund, sings her solo based on the Rose motive, joined intermittingly by the chorus until together, they finish the finale, *Rose of the World*. Parker uses 3/4 meter and writes a quarter note for "Rose" followed by "of" as a dotted quarter note and "the" a sixteenth, which seems a less appropriate rhythmic setting for the phrase. Farwell's 6/8 setting seems better.    Parker's plot is a romantic one, but the music is academic and in these instances shows little marriage to the text.

Ryan found many of the same influences in Farwell's *Cartoon* as have other critics who reviewed earlier compositions.    He recognized that Farwell was "an avowed tonalist" who persisted in the use of key signatures.    "This is noteworthy considering Farwell's frequent forays to places far distant from the tonic."

> At this Farwell is masterful.   The writing is highly chromatic in which deceptive cadences abound. (Here his debt to the late German Romantic community - Wagner, Wolf, and their ilk - is obvious.) There are some few less inspired moments when these tonal shifts may verge on boredom or mild annoyance in *Cartoon*, but when he is "hot" - to use the vernacular, he shows a marvelous facility for sustaining tension that is at times breathtaking.
>
> In his voice leading, the French influence shows itself. The texture often has the Gallic leanness of a Franck, Fauré, or Du Parc.    The lines are never dull or hackneyed, unless intentionally so, and the bass voice movement is especially skillful.
>
> In the realm of melody, the composer shows himself an American Romanticist.   Every now and then there are heard vague links to MacDowell, and later writers of salon songs, (intentionally ?) but Farwell's place is with the top of his class.   In the arias, melodies match the harmonies with unexpected turns and twists to make them uniquely attractive.[21]

After examining the score and text, one is apt to agree with Farwell that he has succeeded in his goal to create a funny show which is "American to the core".    The opera needs to be orchestrated to add appropriate color, as Farwell died before he could do this.

Ryan states that "How well the fantasy as a whole would work on stage would depend on the director, who would have no easy task to maintain momentum.    This is because what starts out making a strong case for American composers and their music, at

the end is diverted to patriotic extollment." He also thinks that
Farwell is at his best when he is satirical. "However, when he is
pompous, or pretentious, the results are not quite up to the
stature for which he is striving." This occurs in instances where
Farwell seeks to ennoble the cause of the American composer and
raise it to an elevated position. Here an experienced director
could still make the score effective.

Although audiences at the end of World War II were used to,
and welcomed, the extensive political eulogizing Farwell projects
in the concluding scene, the passage of time has changed attitudes.
Today's audiences may not be as comfortable with such lines.
However, the 1988 presidential campaign started the pendulum
swinging back again towards a more popular national fervor and
we saw a strong reaction and response to the flag burning
episodes of the 1989 summer. National pride that developed
during and after the war to liberate Kuwait may also have altered
American response to such scenes. Any renewed patriotic interest
would ease the director's burden. However, the production must
always be viewed from its historical perspective. Ryan concludes
his analysis of the score by saying: "*Cartoon* in all respects, is not
flawless, but yet well worth experiencing. It is a marvelous mating
of text and music that gives many, many moments of pure delight."

This is a work that should have a place in a large university
music department where talented graduate students or a resident
composer would write an appropriate orchestral version for the
piano score. Students at the University of Connecticut in
Bridgeport, presented a short recital version of the opera using a
narrator and singers with piano accompaniment on April 14, 1977.
Dr. Terrence Greenawalt coordinated it on *An Evening of
American Music* with Brice Farwell as narrator.

Farwell made a list of the numbers in his opera *Cartoon* that
he considered "suitable for recording". This list is included in the
catalog of his works in section six dealing with Music for Dramatic
Forms. It is interesting here to notice that he even considered
such a project in light of his negative feeling towards recorded
music. Maybe late in life his attitude had mellowed.

In reviewing Farwell's early work for the theater and his
community music-dramas, one notes a common thread: he was
concerned about people-participation. For him, music was *not*

merely a spectator sport. He felt that there was a valuable emotional experience to be gained from participation in the pageants regardless of the part a person played or sang. His activity in the pageant and community music movement is to have been expected. Pageantry offered a culmination of all Farwell had striven for in his crusade for American music. This was a vehicle for the people, of the people, and by the people. It was Democracy in action!

By his articles, speeches, and his own compositions, Farwell strove to raise the quality of music used. He encouraged other composers to contribute to what he thought could develop into a vital new art-form. The growth and popularity of community singing was an inevitable outgrowth of the pageant movement and the war. As a result, pageants and the community singing movement were wide-spread and nationally important. Farwell was a significant leader in the movement. Again, Farwell listened and "Heard America Singing."

**Example 63a**    *The Evergreen Tree: The Tree-Child's Lullaby*

№ 6
## The Tree-Child's Lullaby
### Carol 4

Poem by
PERCY MACKAYE

Music by
ARTHUR FARWELL

**Example 63b.** *The Evergreen Tree: The Might of Herod*

Nº 8

85

The Might of Herod

Chorus B, 1: for Men's Voices

Poem by
PERCY MACKAYE

Music by
ARTHUR FARWELL

**Example 63c.**   *The Evergreen Tree: The Wrath of Herod*

## № 9
## The Wrath of Herod

**Chorus A, 4:** For Mixed Voices
**Chorus B, 2:** For Men's Voices

Poem by
**PERCY MACKAYE**

Music by
**ARTHUR FARWELL**

HEROD:

Powers of my crown and throne! Am I not Herod, Herod, the Mighty? Who shall defeat my power?

**Example 63c.**     *The Evergreen Tree: The Wrath of Herod,* cont.

**Example 63d.**  *The Evergreen Tree: Dance Carol of the Evergreen.*

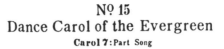

**Example 63d.** *The Evergreen Tree: Dance Carol of the Evergreen.*

**Example 63e.**    *The Evergreen Tree: Chorus of the Tree, 1-5.*

**Example 63e.** *The Evergreen Tree: Chorus of the Tree, 6-9.*

**Example 64a.** *Scene* from *The Inferno*

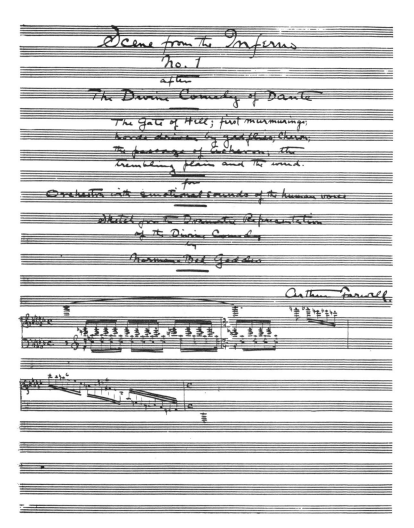

**Example 64b** *Scene* from *The Inferno*

**Example 64c.**   *Scene* from *The Inferno*

**Example 65a.  Cartoon: Act I, Chorus, *When Americus Comes With an Opus*.**

**Example 65a.    Chorus, continued.**

**Example 65b.   Act I.   *Pierrot's Lunacy - The Blight of Spring***

**Example 65b.** *Pierrot's Lunacy - The Blight of Spring,* **continued**

**Example 65c.    Act 1. Aria,** *Love the Revealer.*

**Example 65c.   Aria, *Love the Revealer,* continued.**

**Example 65d.   Act 3. Aria, *Brilliant October Is Here***

**Example 65d.** Aria, *Brilliant October Is Here*, page 2

**Example 65d.   Aria, *Brilliant October Is Here*, page 3.**

**Example 65d.**    **Aria, *Brilliant October Is Here*, page 4.**

**Example 65e.** *Rose of the World*, **Act 3, Chorus, measures 1-8.**

**Example 65e.**   *Rose of the World,* **measures 9-16**

**Example 65e.** *Rose of the World*, **measures 17-26.**

**Example 65f.    Act 3,** *Finale,* **measures 1-6.**

**Example 65f.**   *Finale,* **measures 7-12.**

**Example 65f.**    *Finale***, measures 13-18.**

# Chapter 22

# Orchestral Works

Farwell's early training in writing for the orchestra was minimal.  However, Max Wilhelm Zach, (1861-1921) who conducted the Boston Promenade Orchestra premiere of Farwell's first orchestral effort on June 19, 1896, praised him and encouraged him to continue his writing.  His only criticism was that Farwell's pieces were "too short".

### Early Works

Farwell's more promising early work was his *Suite for Grand Orchestra*.  This he planned to base on Bliss Carman's (1861-1929) *Seven Things*, an idea suggested by Gigi Hall, one of his lady friends.  Whatever happened to the other movements is unknown as the only existing score contains just the second movement and is sub-titled *Love Song*.  The work made its debut listed on the program as *Andante from a New Suite*, with Anton Seidl (1851-1898) conducting the "Metropolitan Permanent Orchestra from New York" on October 17, 1896, in Auburn, New York.  Farwell attended the rehearsal in New York City as well as the actual performance later.  Seidl also was very encouraging to the would-be composer and remarked, "How did this young man learn to score so well?"[1]

*Love Song* is scored for 2 flutes, 2 oboes, 2 clarinets, 2 bassoons, 4 horns in F, 2 trumpets, 3 tenor trombones, 1 bass tuba, kettle drums, plus the usual strings.  A notation on the score states: "I was totally self-taught at this time in orchestration."

Farwell opens his work in the key of F major with the melody in the violins.  The descending interval of a fifth is characteristic of the simple melodic development.  Often the first and second violins double on the melody and sometimes they play an octave apart.  The conductor's score shows four pages in the opening key before moving on to B flat major for nine pages and then returns to the original key of F for the concluding twelve pages.

It was the performance of *Love Song* which convinced Thomas Osborne that young Farwell should have the benefit of further study abroad. After his return from Europe, Farwell's first orchestral work was one created to honor Cornell University where he was teaching at the time.

*Academic Overture Cornell*, Op. 9, was composed in 1900. It is scored for full orchestra and "is of almost symphonic proportions".

When commenting about Farwell's style, Benjamin Lambord wrote he believed that Farwell had first 'found himself' in composing this overture. "Combining Indian themes and college songs in a sort of American academic overture, the vigor of style and effectiveness of scoring has gained for this work a permanent place in the orchestral repertoire."[2]

The opening theme, Adagio, is based on the phrase from Cornell's Alma Mater song - *Lift the Chorus, Speed it Onward*, but this is only suggested with some modifications that take on an Indian color.

The music quickly changes to an allegro theme which reappears here and there throughout the work, followed by what seems to be an Indian Dance.

After a return to the allegro movement, now treated somewhat differently, the familiar Alma Mater song is heard played softly by the oboes and woodwinds with a beautiful choral accompaniment. Next there is an abrupt swinging into the spirited *Crew Song* in which the "Stroke! Stroke!" of the oars, the click of the oarlocks, and the rush of the shell through the water are vividly brought out.

Next, Farwell uses the *Song of the Classes*, a ceremonial anthem in which each undergraduate class rises and sings its appropriate verse, followed by a chorus indicative of strenuous student life at Ithaca. First is the Freshman "who misses his bottle"; then the Sophomore "who his vile freshman ways has forsook"; then the Junior "who has not been a-wasting his time"; and finally the grave and revered Senior "who soon will be leaving this School of Cornell".[3]

This section is followed in elaborated form by the full chorale of the Alma Mater song, richly scored and "grandly conceived and the supreme moment of the overture".

The finale is worked out using the Indian theme and the Allegro as a basis for a whirlwind finish that must have impressed students and faculty alike.

*Dawn*, Op. 12, a fantasy for orchestra, was composed in 1904 and was frequently performed during Farwell's career. It was developed from his piano solo written in 1901, which was based on two Indian themes: *The Old Man's Love Song* - an Omaha melody - and a Pawnee theme as discussed in chapters 17 and 19. (See music examples in chapter 17, no. 1 & 2.) Farwell made the orchestral version after returning from his second western tour which had strengthened and broadened his interest in Indian culture. To find refuge from the hectic activities of the Wa-Wan Press in his home, he sought quiet in an old shed that he rented, where he installed an old piano. *Dawn* was the result of his labors there.

*The Domain of Hurakan*, Op. 15, is another Indian-based work arranged for orchestra in 1910 from his piano score of 1902. This composition is discussed further in chapter 17 dealing with music based on Indian themes. Piano score examples are shown in numbers 3a, 3b, 3c, and 3d. A reviewer of Farwell's works praised the orchestral version of *Domain of the Hurakan* as a "score of great impressiveness and of brilliant color." He pointed out that it has had "several conspicuous performances which have done much to win recognition for his larger gifts."[4]

Farwell insisted that this work is not to be understood strictly as a tone painting of the storm, but rather as a rhapsodic treatment of certain Indian melodies for their own sake. The first theme is a broad swinging one from Vancouver, swept in by the strings. (Orchestral Ex. 66). The second, more sprightly, is from the Pawnee; and the third is a Navajo fragment which occurs near to the end of the middle or "nocturne" section of the work. Farwell was guest conductor of this composition when it was played by the Detroit Symphony Orchestra on November 21, 1927, during his first semester at Michigan State College. Farwell's "rhapsodic treatment" of his Indian themes seems to call forth a sequence of pictures for him also as follows:

A traveller, at night, enters an Indian lodge near the Pacific ocean. . . He sees Indians singing and swaying in the animated rhythm of the game. Their ceaseless motions seem to represent to him the eternal wash and play of the waves of the ocean, and he remembers the ancient legend which tells that "Hurakan, the mighty wind, passed over the waters and called forth the earth."

The traveller goes out into the night and walks alone by the seashore, beyond the sound of the revelers. He hears the murmuring of the sea, and far-off melodies come to him . . . [until] the dim sounds die away at last into nothingness. The traveller walks back to the lodge and enters. With a shock, the sights and sounds of the boisterous game burst upon his senses once more in all their elemental rhythmic fervor. The tumult and motion rise to a climax and die away . . . As the traveller passes out of the lodge there rises before him only the black wall of the night.

The conductor's score is worn due to its frequent use in past performances. The first page bears this inscription at the top: "Over the waters passed Hurakan, the mighty wind, and called forth the earth." The tempo instruction reads, "Exultingly, with motion and swing. Accelerate greatly". The latter refers especially to the opening sweeping scale pattern in the violins that ushers in the whole orchestra. The orchestral version adds much to the original piano score.

Farwell apologized for sending "such an old war-worn score, but I never had another," when he shipped this score and others to G. L. Marshall of the British Broadcasting Corporation in Belfast, Ireland, on October 5, 1938. Mr. Marshall had met Farwell in the United States and discussed the possibilities for performance of Farwell's music on a future broadcast of American music in Ireland. Farwell's suggestions for the program were *The Gods of the Mountain* or *Domain of Hurakan* as the "best to start with over there. The first because you are in Lord Dunsany's country, the second because it is more characteristic of the United States, being on American Indian themes, and thus will have special interest as a novelty."

Mr. Marshall chose neither of these but decided to use Farwell's *Symbolistic Study No. 3* and wrote asking how much the fees would be "for its hire". This request surprised Farwell as he had not expected any remuneration for the use of his scores. He did not know how much to charge for the use of his scores and wrote a frank letter on June 4, 1939, to James Fassett, at the Columbia Broadcasting System for advice about fees.

Farwell explained that he had not the slightest idea what "I might normally ask them, without its being so little as to seem cheap or so much as to scare them! All new experience to me." Mr. Fassett suggested five pounds as a moderate figure so that is what Farwell requested and was paid. The BBC broadcast took place on June 26, 1939, from its Northern Ireland station with Mr. O'Donnell conducting the orchestra.

## Symbolistic Studies, 1901-1912

Farwell's interest in all the arts exposed him to the work of the Symbolists of his time.[5]   He used the term "Symbolistic Study" for a series of works begun in 1901, when the Symbolistic movement in literature was at its height.  The *Symbolistic Studies No. 1* and *No. 2* are piano works and were listed in chapter 19; *No. 4* on an Indian theme was not finished.   In these works Farwell explained:

> I used music frankly as a symbol of specific ideas, but avoided all close following of a program, seeking to let the music rest on the thematic presentation and development. . . . They represented, therefore, a reaction against the vitiation of music *per se* through such programmaticism, in the interests of a wholly *musical* development, in an era when the classic *tabu* against the 'picture' had been removed by a succeeding era of romanticism and symbolism.
>
> If you should ask, "Why then, if this is music *per se*, should not the picture be omitted altogether?", the answer is that pure or 'abstract' music is no longer in the content of the Time-Spirit, and the composer, in the present case, wishes to use the obvious symbolic power of music to enforce, musically, Whitman's verbally poetic concept.

*Symbolistic Study, No. 3, Once I Passed Through a Populous City*, Op.18, was suggested by lines from Walt Whitman's poem *Children of Adam* from *Leaves of Grass*:

> Once I passed through a populous city imprinting my brain
>      for future use with its shows, architecture, customs,
>      traditions'
> Yet now of all that city I remember only a woman I casually
> met there who detain'd me for love of me,
> Day by day and night by night we were together - all else
> has long been forgotten by me.
> I remember I say only that woman who passionately clung
>      to me,
> Again we wander, we love, we separate again,
> Again she holds me by the hand, I must not go,
> I see her close beside me with silent lips sad and
> tremulous.

The Whitman poem presents two sharply contrasted pictures, one on the material plane - the imposing city - and one on the psychic - the memory of an emotional experience. These two pictures are separated in time by only an instant's pause, but in the psychic level by an immeasurable abyss. Farwell's notes insist that "to this extent, but no further, the present composition follows the poem. The second part, however, contains a momentary and shadowy memory of the city, as something remote and unreal from the standpoint of the emotional experience." His notes continue as he reflects on this early work:

> This work is far from offering any challenge to ultra-modernity. It was sketched in 1905, while Wagner and Tchaikovsky were still the composer's chief enthusiasms, and undoubtedly reflects that period. The original orchestration, made about 1908, was destroyed and an entirely new orchestration made by the composer in 1921. The orchestration is therefore from a much more mature period of his life than the composition itself.

Pierre Monteux was the guest conductor of the Philadelphia Orchestra in performing the premiere of *Symbolistic Study No. 3.* on March 30 and 31, 1928. Farwell traveled to New York City and later to Philadelphia for the events. In a letter to his wife, Gertrude, Farwell wrote glowingly from New York:

> They rehearsed the *Symbolistic Study* in Philadelphia and it went simply great. I went over on the train with the Monteux's - (he had been here conducting the *L'Histoire*). He gave me a desk and seat beside him at the rehearsal and consulted me on everything. Only *one slight* mistake in all those 270 pages of parts I copied. It sounded exactly as I intended. That orchestra is a miracle - played the whole thing off at sight as if they had practiced it a long time. Not a soul missed an entry. I expect Lewis [Richards] and his daughter (up from Gaucher), Harry [Barnhart], Gena [Branscombe], will go up for Friday's performance.

After the performance in Philadelphia of this work, the *Philadelphia Public Ledger* wrote that "while it contains certain moments of great beauty, it leans too heavily upon certain earlier composers, notably Tchaikovsky and Strauss."    H. T. Craven credited the work with "Skillful orchestration", in the *Philadelphia Record.*    The *Evening Bulletin* stated that the music had "more rhythm and sound musicianship than in many modern writings for orchestra."

In an April 5th letter to Gertrude, Farwell expressed second thoughts about the Philadelphia performance of his *Symbolistic Study No. 3*:

> Beloved,
> Here are the roasts I got in Philadelphia. Well, they grant me good models anyway. I note that none of them have accused me of bad orchestration. I was indeed happy to find out that the orchestration came out so very close to what I intended, even in complex and problematical places. Nevertheless, I learned some very important things about large scale orchestration, both by many things that

"came out" and a few that didn't.  There was apparently
no point in the score that was unsatisfactory as to scoring,
but some where more emphasis could have been placed
upon this or that factor. . . .

*Symbolistic Study No. 3* was performed with Edwin McArthur
conducting the New York Civic Orchestra on March 5, 1939, and
it has had other hearings as well.

   *Symbolistic Study No. 5* was composed in 1906 but left
unfinished.  The conductor's score contains 59 completed pages
for full orchestra with four more in light pencil.  He has labeled
the work Op. 25.  This work has been favorably performed as
written and could be of interest to scholars to develop it further.

### *Symbolistic Study No. 6, Mountain Vision*

   *Symbolistic Study No. 6, Mountain Vision*, Op. 37, was begun
in the White Mountains of New Hampshire, and finished in the
Ramapos in the autumn of 1912 and written first as a piano solo.
Later it was arranged for two pianos and small orchestra in 1931.
Next it was prepared as a one movement concerto for piano,
second piano and string orchestra in 1938 to meet the
requirements of the National Federation of Music Clubs contest
in which he won first place in Division I of Class IV in 1939.
Howard Barlow, Mrs. Edgar Stillman Kelley, and Modest Alloo
were the three contest judges.

   Instead of following a story, Farwell writes a slow introduction
in this *Symbolistic Study* in which he is merely suggesting "the
boldness of mountain scenery, and the mystery of its distances."
The movement proper begins with a mood of the "joyousness of
tramping over the mountains in the crisp autumn air". (Ex. 67)
He describes the work further thus:

> Then follows the memory of experiences which have
> earlier carried the composer to the depths of failure and
> despair.  He wonders how he can again be so happy after
> such experiences!  Finally, in these memories, it is as if
> one meets a great mountain wall, which utterly blocks his
> way onward.  From this, after tentative gropings, the mood

is as if one were trying to recover himself and make a fresh start in a new direction. From this point the work gradually pulls up to the joyous mountain mood of the beginning. Except for the introduction of a third chief theme, the work is in sonata form.

The national award carried no financial reward, but did offer a national broadcast over the Columbia network, with Howard Barlow conducting the CBS orchestra, and with Karl Ulrich Schnabel and Helen Fogel as pianists. Farwell was "delighted' to learn that Schnabel would perform, as he had met his famous father, Artur Schnabel, in Lansing. The broadcast took place on May 28, 3-4, EST 1939. After the performance he received congratulatory messages from all across America and even beyond.

Karl Schnabel wrote his reactions to the performance thus in a letter to Farwell dated June 7, 1939:

I am very glad that you liked our performance of your concerto, and I thank you very much for your nice and friendly letter. We certainly tried our very best and your piece really is very difficult - so difficult, as a matter of fact, that I could not have learned it, alone. Now, as you approved of our playing, I dare to admit, that for some of the most difficult passages, we changed our parts and Miss Fogel played the first piano. However, I knew beforehand that nobody would be able to hear the difference.

Only when I got your letter I learned that the *Mountain Vision* had been composed such a long time ago. Yet I had a certain feeling it was, which does in my opinion not at all mean a negative judgment. Quite the contrary. I do not believe in the "up-to-date-" slogan that the newest must always be the best! How I feel about your piece I tried to express in my performance - and I hoped you would get the right impression. As you asked for my true opinion - I may say that there are some places, especially modulations, which I don't like so much. Also it seems to me to be slightly over-instrumentated. But this impression might have been caused by the very small hall in which the comparatively large orchestra played.

It was a great pleasure for me to perform your concerto and I hope that when you plan another performance you will think of us first, as it would mean very much to us to have more than one single performance, after we studied your work so carefully.

Helen Fogel responded eagerly to Farwell's "thank you" note:

. . . I enjoyed playing your composition very much, even though it meant hard work learning it at such short notice.  And frankly, I was both happy and relieved to discover that your work does not fall into the line of "modernism" - which music I simply cannot comprehend or even listen to.

Many of my friends remembered you and listened to the broadcast with much pleasure.

I am really glad that your work was selected for performance and hope it will have great success !

With my very best wishes to you - and hope that I shall have the pleasure of again assisting in the performance of *Mountain Vision*.

Among the many congratulatory letters Farwell received was one from a former colleague, Ralph de Golier, who had been his accompanist for community chorus work in California.  He wrote:

I just heard your delightful *Symbolistic Study No. 6* over the radio and hasten to congratulate you.  Beauty and Vision and musical values as we understand them are rare in these sterile and cacophonous times; yet I believe such music as yours will long outlive the dubious outpourings of our times.. . .   I still compose and some of my songs are occasionally performed.  My music too is delightfully out-of-date.  More success to you!

On June 19, 1947, Farwell wrote to John Kirkpatrick, concert pianist, to inform him that now he had available his "piano concerto" (*Mountain Vision*) which Kirkpatrick earlier had said was "haunting" him. Farwell's copy was the two piano version which represented a combination string orchestra and second piano, the latter covering what the winds would do if there were no second piano.

> I have always thought I would one day make a full orchestra score for it, without second piano, although it sounds good to me as it is and as it was asked for in the competition. Ethel Leginski said long ago, "Pianists will love this work!" but it was not finished then. Wonder if she were right? It's a straight romantic piece, though with a spiritual undercurrent of sinking bafflement and rising again. I have a rather persistent belief in its future.

Present day pianists are challenged to prepare this work to prove Farwell's belief in its performance value.

Farwell wrote a *Pageant Scene* (Op. 39) based on music from the Meriden pageant some time after that 1913 production. It included: *Entrance of Country Folk*, *Dance of Idleness*, *Rustic Dance*, and *Processional Exit*. Two numbers from the *Pageant Scene* were later revised and written for piano, violin, and cello. These were *Dance of Idleness* and *Rustic Dance*, first performed as a trio on March 30, 1922, at an all-Farwell concert presented by the Pasadena Music and Art Association in California.

On December 21, 1932, when Farwell corresponded with A. George Hoyen, conductor of the Massachusetts Institute of Technology Little Symphony, who requested the score and parts for Farwell's *Pageant Scene*, he expressed his fondness for the work and described its background:

> It has reference to a time when the natives, after becoming prosperous, would succumb to idleness and luxury, or turn to education. "Idleness" tries to lead them astray, by her dance, in which the country folk join. The redemption by the education part does not come into this number as adapted.
>
> It calls for one flute and one oboe, otherwise exactly your instrumentation. Special solo parts for these

instruments can be played by your first players, both entering in other parts and tuttis. I think you and your players will enjoy this work.

In a January 22, 1933, letter to Hoyen, Farwell expressed his dismay after learning that his composition would be placed between Beethoven and Mozart on the Boston program:

> I should tell you frankly that the *Pageant Scene*, fond as I am of it as a spontaneous expression, cannot be regarded as an expression of my present self, for I have grown out of recognition of myself since those days. Perhaps you will want to change your mind about it under these circumstances, and wait until I can give you something in my modern vein. Anyway, I leave this to you, and I will not be hurt by anything you decide.

Mr. Hoyen reconsidered the order of numbers on his program and placed Farwell's work as the concluding one following a Johann Strauss composition. The concert was presented at M.I.T. on March 19, 1933.

### *The Gods of the Mountain*, Op. 52

In the Spring of 1916, Stuart Walker approached Farwell about writing incidental music for his intended New York City production of the popular play, *The Gods of the Mountain*, by Lord Edward Dunsany, (1878-1957). Farwell accepted the challenge and at once began a careful study of the plot. The strange fantasy writings of the Irish writer made a strong appeal to Farwell's vivid imagination and he "set out to make some highly exotic music" which would be appropriate for this extraordinary Dunsany play. A suite was later developed from the music composed for the play and has had many successful performances.

Originally the music was written for harp, violin and 'cello. Later revisions are discussed in Chapter 20. The same musical structure appears in this suite, the most widely performed of Farwell's symphonic works. By 1928, Farwell prepared his popular orchestral version of the work listed as Op. 52, which had its premiere with the Minneapolis Symphony Orchestra, Henri Verbrugghen, conductor, on December 13, 1929. Verbrugghen repeated the performance in St. Paul on January 2, 1930. He declared that the "work was given a splendid reception" and wrote to Farwell "I have derived the greatest pleasure while working at your suite, and its orchestral technic together with its strong imaginativeness gave me a hearty thrill."

Victor Nilsson, in the *Minneapolis Journal*, wrote "this suite proves Mr. Farwell's musical talent and erudition most conclusively."

In Farwell's correspondence with conductors who planned to conduct this suite, his warning to keep the fourth movement "unbelievably slow", was as relentless as the slow tread of the "gods" themselves. Program notes for the work are included with the score which Farwell considered imperative to its correct interpretation:

1. Beggar's Dreams - Outside the gates of the city of Kongros the itinerant beggars pause and deplore their lot, finding the times "bad for beggary." They decide to enter the city and pass themselves off for the stone gods who have been seated for ages far up in the mountains, and who are worshipped in fear and awe by the people of the country. They dream of power which is to be theirs, interrupted only for a moment by a foreboding of tragical disaster.

2. Maya of the Moon - By their clever devices, and playing upon the superstitions and fears of the populace concerning the stone gods, they create the illusion that they are the gods.

3. Pinnacle of Pleasure - The beggars, as gods, are now worshipped by the people, who seek to propitiate them in every possible way with fine foods and entertainment. Suspicious individuals, however, have set on foot a plot to trap the beggars, and in the midst of their revelries disquieting forbodings again intrude.

4. The Stone Gods Come - The real gods on the mountain, enraged at the beggars' sacrilege in

impersonating them, and awful with their measured and
heavy stone tread, come down from the mountain, and in
the absence of the populace from the hall in which the
beggars are enthroned, turn them to stone, and depart.
The people entering and finding their "gods" stone,
exclaim with awe, "They were the true gods!"

Farwell describes musical aspects of his suite in detail:

The chief feature of this music is the character which
it possesses as the result of being written upon scales
other than the usual major and minor. (See Ex. 58d in
chapter 20.) This character is intensified by building the
harmony of a given movement out of the notes of the
particular scale employed, to the exclusion of all other
notes.   There are some departures from this procedure,
but not enough to destroy the characteristic color
produced in this way.  (Ex. 68a)
The forms employed are simple, and little analysis is
needed beyond that offered by the program.  The thin,
wiry theme of the first movement is suggested by the
starved nature of the beggars, followed by a motive of
determination, and is carried presently to heights of
grandeur, only to be cut off sharply by a mystical
premonition of the stony tread of the gods, followed by a
Fear motive, a sort of shudder, after which the first theme
is heard in a subdued form.
The second movement is preluded with certain strange
and mystifying effects, with important features for the
harp, which lead into the main theme, a broad cantilena
for the 'cellos.  After a short interlude on motives from
the introduction, this is stated again by the violins,
reinforced with woodwinds, being somewhat differently
developed and after a brief climax, leading to a conclusion
remote in its mood of stopped horns and muted strings.
The Phrygian mode was held by the Greeks to be
appropriate to the expression of wilder moods, and is so
employed here in the third movement, which is an
Oriental dance of somewhat orgiastic character, with a

plentiful employment of the instruments of percussion. The only interruption to the chorus of this dance is the momentary appearance, dramatically introduced, of the Fear motive.

The last movement presents the heavy tread of the approaching gods, in the low strings, pizzicato, at first distant and ominous, but soon heavily and more  near. (Ex. 68b) The Fear motive interweaves with the motive of the tread in a movement of gathering excitement. The Fear becomes realized tragedy as the gods, entering, turn the beggars to stone with the magic of a terrible gesture. As the gods make their exit in titanic, stone-heavy steps, the original pizzicato Tread has become a series of shocks by the whole orchestra. These diminish, with interspersed echoes of the Fear motive, until they have suggested the disappearance of the dread gods in the distance.

Henry Hadley (1871-1937) and Farwell were good friends and it seems only logical that he would try to help promote Farwell's work. After his return from the Orient in October 1930, Hadley began planning future programs for the Manhattan Symphony which he conducted. By February 22, 1931, he sent a telegram to Farwell announcing his scheduling of *The Gods of the Mountain* for March 15th at Carnegie Hall.

Farwell promptly shipped the parts for the music plus additional publicity material and program notes. On February 25th he wrote to Hadley as follows:

> This performance represents my re-entry into New York, in any such way, after a pretty long absence, and so is particularly interesting to me, as a sign to friends that I am still alive, and to strangers that I exist. For I have bigger intentions there for the future. But I think this work is just spicy enough to be a good re-introduction at this time, and I think you will find it not a bad little battle-horse on which to ride to victory. . . .

In a March 8th letter to Hadley, Farwell added a strong reminder about the critical slowness of the tempo in the last movement.  He also pointed out another theme that should be equally slow where it appears for a moment in the first movement. He commented on the "Fear" theme which really was a "sort of remote intuition of fear, and should always be made as *mysterious as possible* whenever it appears, until the last movement, where it becomes the theme by which the beggars are struck to stone."

Farwell felt that the "Maya" took care of itself and added "You will be quite at home in the Oriental dance - third movement."  He remembered Hadley's recent trip to the Orient.

When Farwell sent the music to Georges Barrère who planned to have his Little Symphony perform *The Gods of the Mountain*, he apologized for the condition of the percussion parts as the percussion men of the orchestras which had already played it "have made mince-meat of the original percussion parts.  I hope there is some Free-Masonry among them by which they can understand each other's cryptic and arcane marks, so that yours can comprehend these percussion parts!"

Later, Mr. Barrère reported that critics were flattering in their praise of the performance which he himself felt "went very well. And the public seemed to be impressed by the *March of the Stone Gods* which I took as slowly as I dared."

In a letter dated October 9, 1938, to Valter Poole who was scheduled to conduct the *Gods* with the Detroit Civic Orchestra, Farwell again warned about the slow tempo for the last movement and added:

> At D in this fourth movement, these two bars should be immensely large and broadened, and given with terrible force, each note beat out.  This is the climax of the movement and of the whole work for that matter. Where a foretaste of this movement is given in the first movement, at F, the same terrific slowness should be observed.  Immediately after this, 7th bar after F, at the four-four, this motive should be given with nervous hurry; it is the premonition of fear in the beggars.

In correspondence dated November 22, 1935, Pierre Monteux wrote to Farwell about also doing his *Gods of the Mountain*.

I would gladly look at it, and as you know, I am most receptive to your works and I may play it this year, especially as it lasts only 17 minutes! How wise you are not to write things that last three quarters of an hour.

I look back with great pleasure to the time when you were in Philadelphia and I would be happy to see you once again. Mme. Monteux sends you her sincere regards.

Howard Hanson performed *The Gods of the Mountain* on October 29, 1931. In his correspondence with Hanson regarding the interpretation of this work, Farwell pointed out :

There are some rather delicate retards near the end of the first movement, and they should be emphasized, and not passed over too easily - one in particular, if I remember rightly just before a 6/4 chord in A minor. The harp part at the beginning of the second movement should stand out in quite a bold solo way.

Howard Hanson recalled conducting Farwell's *Gods of the Mountain* at one of Eastman's annual Festivals of American Music. In a letter to the author on February 10, 1971, he emphasized:

It is, in my opinion, a stunning suite and worthy of inclusion on any of today's symphony programs. The final movement in the hands of a good orchestra and a good conductor can be quite overpowering. It is a sad commentary on the interest of our country in its own music that a work of such excellence is almost completely neglected.

A. Walter Kramer voiced similar enthusiasm for this particular suite. In his record jacket notes prepared for the Society for the Preservation of the American Musical Heritage recording of Farwell's work he declared:

. . . It is real Farwell. Although the plays of Lord Dunsany have virtually disappeared from today's repertoire, they were very much admired and widely

performed in the thirties, and it is easy to understand why
Arthur Farwell was attracted by the play . . . one of
Dunsany's best.

This music seems to have a character all of its own.
Never is a sumptuous treatment in the Rimsky-
Korsakoffyan manner undertaken, even in such a section
as *Pinnacles of Pleasure*.    Farwell is no extravert.
Similarly, in the opening *Beggar's Dreams*, he achieves the
mood with a musical utterance that has a mystical basis.

In conclusion, we would remark on Farwell's complete
mastery of the modern orchestra.  His scoring is rich and
remarkably balanced.  The listener is held by this music.
I say this with some knowledge, for I was present at the
performance of *The Gods of the Mountain* in the thirties,
when the late Henry Hadley conducted it with the
Manhattan Symphony in Carnegie Hall, New York.  The
audience received it with great enthusiasm.

### Symphonic Song on Old Black Joe

A work of different nature is Farwell's *Symphonic Song on Old
Black Joe*, Op. 67, composed in 1924 and written for full orchestra
and audience.    Its unique character sprang from Farwell's
association with the community chorus movement.  The audience
or community chorus enters to sing the familiar song at different
points in the score.  (Ex. 69)  The work was inspired by a
dramatic moment in Harry Barnhart's "Song and Light" Festival
in Central Park, New York, during World War I, when the huge
crowd burst into singing on the refrain of Foster's song - "I'm
coming".  This gave the impression of America's promise to join
the European allies.  In the program notes Farwell states that "the
work touches, musically, different martial moments of American
history, leading to a powerful climax at the mentioned refrain."

The theme of *Old Black Joe* is heard first in a modally
transformed form as if it were a real negro melody which is
developed into a primitive negro scene.  This leads to audience
particiption on the first verse of the song.  A Civil War episode
follows in which *Old Black Joe* and the *Battle Hymn of the
Republic* are presented in counterpoint. The audience enters again.

Then a passage suggesting the World War I is used with *Old Black Joe* and *Tipperery* in counterpoint and touches of *Over There*. For the climax, the audience rises on signal to sing *I'm coming!* There is a short quiet close with implied religious overtones.

Farwell conducted the premiere in 1924 in the Hollywood Bowl, an enterprise in which he had been intimately associated. The work was enthusiastically received there as well as later in Park concerts in New York and Brooklyn.

### Prelude to a Spiritual Drama

Farwell was concerned that the music he had composed early in 1921 for the *Pilgrimage Play* was no longer being used, so he decided to assemble some of the best themes into a new work, *Prelude to a Spiritual Drama*. This composition he labeled Op. 76, and what he sketched first in 1927 was orchestrated in 1935.

The themes which he incorporated from the original drama are these in the order of their appearance: The three opening bars are drawn from the *Transfiguration* theme followed by *The Christ*, *The Transfiguration*, *The Eternal*, *The Tomb*, *The Prayer at the Last Supper*, and after the development of these, *The Ascension*. Farwell notes that "the theme of *The Tomb*, on its first appearance, is used only in a prophetic sense, and appears later in a fuller form and orchestration."

Some of these themes are based on a scale consisting of two Oriental tetrachords with the harmonies being confined to the notes of this scale. Farwell felt that a certain unique and appropriate "color" is gained by this procedure, but the total result is not Oriental in its feeling.

Farwell had talked with Serge Koussevitsky about the possibility of having the Boston Symphony Orchestra perform the *Prelude to a Spiritual Drama* and Koussevitsky encouraged Farwell to send him the score. Farwell's letter to him dated October 28, 1932, explains his feelings about this particular composition:

I am sending the score of the *Prelude to a Spiritual Drama* to you at Symphony Hall by express today. It plays thirteen minutes.

I was entirely serious in what I said to you in Ann Arbor, that while I have had orchestral hearings all over the United States, I have waited thirty years to have a score which I felt was worthy to be proper first offering to the Boston Symphony.   I had my first musical inspiration from it, under Nikisch - later Paur, Fiedler and Muck - and was so happy to see the great tradition of the orchestra maintained so splendidly by you. . . .

I think my *Prelude* will reach the heart.  My deepest is in it, and I believe that both lyrically and dramatically you will find it will stand the test.  It was finished this year, and has been shown to no-one but you.

By November 7, 1932, Koussevitzky responded with an apology for his delay in acknowledging the receipt of Farwell's "impressive and deeply emotional *Prelude*".   He promised to look for an opportunity to include this work into one of his programs - if not the current season, then in the season to come.  Of course this pleased Farwell who replied on November 13th as follows:

I was certainly most happy to receive your kind letter saying that you would plan to give the *Prelude to a Spiritual Drama* a hearing.   And I am doubly pleased because of the words you applied to this score, which showed me that you have seen in it what I felt to be there.

It has been my very special ambition to attain a hearing with the Boston Symphony. . . .

By November 20, 1933, Farwell wrote again to Koussevitzky informing him that the parts for the *Prelude* were nearly ready, and would be sent to him that week.  His letter four days later confirmed that he had indeed sent the needed parts by express. "Well, now I can *sleep*.  Meanwhile I will await your word of the date of performance, and the most long-awaited and finest moment of my existence thus far!"

Farwell did not receive an acknowledgement of the parts he had sent to Koussevitzky, so he wrote again on February 6, 1934, to ask about them, and to compliment the conductor on his recent broadcast of Roy Harris' First Symphony. He also inquired about the intended date of performance of his *Prelude*.

Farwell's letter prompted an answer from Koussevitzky on February 10, 1934. Farwell felt the long wait was worth while as the conductor was ready to set a date for the performance of the *Prelude*. Farwell responded thus:

> I was most happy to have your letter of the 10th, and to know that you will give the *Prelude* in March. It would have a special appropriateness, coming near Easter.
>
> I cannot help feeling that this work will make an impression of some depth, not only in respect of dignity, but in its actual emotional content, rendered as I know you will do it.
>
> Beauty, above all, and the genuine reaching of the emotions are, I suppose, the things I am chiefly after. If this work holds any *new* beauty, it is likely to arise (aside from another personality at work) from the fact that it is an experiment in exotic scales, being mostly built in both melody and harmony on an Oriental scale, c d e f g b c.
>
> As soon as the date is definitely set, I will be obliged if you will let me know, so I can keep the time clear for a little Eastern trip.
>
> With many thanks for your kind letter, and with best wishes, Faithfully yours

One senses the almost child-like eagerness and anticipation which Farwell felt as he looked forward to hearing his new work ably performed. So we can empathize with him as he waited longingly and impatiently for that letter from Koussevitzky giving the exact performance date. Farwell's hopes for a Boston premiere of his *Prelude* were dashed when he belatedly received the following letter dated April 20, 1934.

> It grieves me to write you this line to say that, having tried your *Prelude* at two rehearsals, I had to give up my intention to perform it this season.
>
> I wish I could have an opportunity to see you and explain why I had to take this decision: there are some

things in the orchestration which fail to produce the effect
I expected to have from your work.

I cannot tell you how sorry I am, but I felt I must be
frank with you and that you will understand how careful
I must be in presenting a work to our discriminating
Boston audience.

    With very kind regards, believe me
        Always sincerely yours,
        Serge Koussevitzky


Farwell was too crushed and maybe even angry, at the turn of
events to make an immediate reply to Koussevitzky. He certainly
must have been uneasy when March went by without learning of
the anticipated performance date. Farwell was still waiting for
the return of his scores when he finally wrote to Koussevitzky on
October 17, of that year. (1934)

The reason I did not respond to your letter of last
April was first, that it did not call for an answer, and
second, that I was at the time in hopes of going east in
which case I would have seen you and thanked you for
what you had done, and learned in what way you found
the score of *Prelude to a Spiritual Drama* deficient. For
nothing is so important to me as an opportunity to learn.

I have no desire to *get* anything - a production, for
instance. My only desire is to give - out of my musical
impulses - and when this cannot happen with pleasure and
profit to all concerned, I would rather not be heard.

All my other works have been peculiarly successful in
just this particular respect, of orchestration, (critics have
always allowed me this even when they have objected to
my tendencies), that I am surprised to find myself failing
on this ground.

I shall manage some local opportunity to try out the
*Prelude*, and will undoubtedly discover quickly enough
where the scoring is ineffective.

You have *two* copies of the score, and the parts, as
well as a piano version, and I will be much obliged if you

will have these returned to me by American Railway Express, collect, valued at $400.00.

My sixteen-minute suite, *The Gods of the Mountain*, (after Lord Dunsany's play) has given great pleasure and met with outstanding success on every occasion, in nine symphonic hearings (including Verbrugghen, St. Paul and Minneapolis, and Hadley, New York). Perhaps you would like to let Boston hear this sometime. And I have this summer finished a symphony which I hope and believe will be among my most successful works. . . .

Farwell was trying to maintain his undaunted, positive outlook, but he had reason to be discouraged with Koussevitzky who had kept these scores for two years and then needed prodding for their return. However, he soon found a conductor interested in performing this work, once the scores were finally returned.

It was Michael Press, conductor of the Michigan State College Symphony Orchestra who chose to present Farwell's *Prelude* on his program of February 20, 1936. There it met with a warm reception. One critic friend (John Crist) of a "Baudelairish" nature wrote on the back of his program: "It is too profound and lovely, too transcendent for Christians - equal to the vision and devotion of the highly cultured Pagans and supremely refined Atheists"[6]. Theresa Shier wrote in the *Lansing State Journal*:

A feature of the very successful concert was the premiere of a work by Arthur Farwell, *Prelude to a Spiritual Drama*, which was played very well and which apparently deeply moved the audience. Silence for a long second after the last note had died away was more eloquent than the burst of applause that followed.

Mr. Farwell outlined in a brief talk the characteristics of the Christ and the episode in the well-known story that were in his mind when he wrote his *Prelude*.

There is more of the spirit than emotion suggested to the imagination by Mr. Farwell's work, more inner than outer events. By a skillful use of instruments he presented the eternal mystery of the Christ without throwing a supernatural glow over the scene, and in passages inspired by such matters as the *Struggle to Overcome Death* or in the theme of the *Tomb*, watched the beauty of his instrumentation as closely as in the lyric measures during which the sun seemed to play over the entire orchestra.

### Mountain Song

*Mountain Song*, Opus 90, was inspired by Farwell's early sojourn in the high Sierra mountains. He calls it a *Symphonic Song Ceremony* and prepared five movements for orchestra with occasional choruses.  He wrote the poetic texts as well as the music. Farwell pointed out that "It is a symphonic, *not* a choral work, as such are commonly understood." Choruses are used in and between symphonic movements. He stated that "A *symphonic conductor* (*not* a choral conductor) is required for its performance". He admitted that his symphonic song form was "suggested by the Chorale Prelude of the Reformation", where the organist developed a hymn known to the congregation, and at the conclusion brought the congregation in. However, he pointed out his form is much freer.

He explained his goal for this work: "I have sought to bring the inspiration of these great mountains, both in their scenic aspect and their inspiration to the soul, to the many who cannot reach them and participate in their beauty and grandeur."

As early as 1905, Farwell elaborated on similar thoughts in his column for the May 22, 1909, issue of *Musical America*:

> The one who lends himself sympathetically to these fresh Western inspirations will certainly be driven to new modes of expression in his endeavor to give them musical form.  They give a fillip to the imagination which shakes it out of old ruts, and leads to styles of tone painting previously unheard, and which, if developed with sufficient art - which will take time and application - will bring about worthy music of a new order, characteristic of highly poetic and picturesque aspects of our own land.

Farwell never forgot the inspiration of the Western mountains. The jottings made in his notebook carried on those western trips may well have provided themes and ideas for this major work he composed years later in the Sierras. The ideas expressed verbally after his 1905 trip remained a part of him until the time was right for musical expression. *Mountain Song* was the result: a tribute to the scenic beauty of the mountains set in a new form.

*Mountain Song* proceeds as follows:

*Introduction and Chorale of the Mountains.*

1. *From the Heights.*
2. *Depth of Pines.*
   *Chorale of the Forest.*
3. *Azure Lake.*
   *Chorale of the Lake.*
4. *Crags.*
   *Chorale of the Crags.*

Interlude: *Mystery, for Strings.*

5. *Dawn and Day.*
   *Chorale of the Mountains.*

Farwell lists the performance time for this long work as being 72 minutes. A sample of the chorales is found in Chapter 18, example 39. *Mountain Song* represents an effort to break away from old styles and create a "new" form.

The score is written for full orchestra which opens the work. The chorus enters for the first time on page seven of the conductor's score to sing *Chorale of the Mountains.* The orchestra accompanies it with a majestic straight-forward chorale, with all violins and violas playing in tremolo for the initial eight bars. Tremolo passages continue often for viola and second violins with first violins joining them in the climax. While the chorus parts are written basically for four voices, Farwell frequently has the upper three voice lines divide to create five or six parts in this chorale. This pattern he uses in other chorus sections.

In the *Depth of Pines* chorale, the orchestra continues in its supportive role, but has more to do on the interlude passages that add contrast and tension to the otherwise lyrical chorale.

The *Chorale of the Crags* is a vigorous contrast. The melody is sung in unison by all voices and doubled by some of the instruments of the orchestra to emphasize its sturdy movement.

Only four pages long, the three verses utilize the same instrumental scoring.

*Mystery* for strings is a beautiful interlude which has been performed effectively by itself. The title best describes the mood which features a very slow tempo, "with wonder", mostly played in varying degrees of pianissimo. It gradually works up to a small forte climax by page three but diminuendos for two more pages to a concluding "ppp". The music is not technically demanding and can be played by a small ensemble.

In examining the total score, one is impressed with its many possibilities. The chorus is used in various ways: sometimes it sings only a short phrase - four to eight bars long. At other times the singers perform a chorale such as those discussed. The work as a whole bears little resemblance to music written by Farwell's contemporaries. One must credit him with launching out to write something unique in style and different from his earlier compositions.

Farwell had high hopes for this work which was being considered for performance at the Minnesota 1949 centennial celebration of admission to the Union. He wrote to Mrs. Stickle[7] on January 5, 1949, about this possibility telling her he was too busy to visit her because of the "concentrated work day and night to edit the many orchestral parts, made long ago by WPA and make transparent master sheets of the chorus parts. I am told that they may be sent for at any time, and I have to have them ready." Farwell corresponded with Henry Nordlin to whom the completed parts were eventually sent. Dimitri Mitropoulos was expected to conduct the Minneapolis Symphony in the work.

There seems to be no record of the anticipated full performance. The program committee may have decided that *Mountain Song* was too long or had too many requirements. However, two of the choruses, *Depth of Pines, and Chorale of the Mountains* were presented on Legislative Day, September 2, 1949, as part of the on-going Centennial Celebration. These were performed by the St. Paul Opera Chorus, directed by Dr. Raymond Cutting. The program honored Farwell by a large footnote stating that the "The choral numbers are from the monumental *Mountain Song* of Minnesota's great composer, Arthur Farwell". In addition, Farwell was given a prominent spot on another Centennial Concert for October 4th for the presentation of his *The Lamb*, on an all-vocal program. (See Ex. 31 in chapter 18.) It was performed as a quartet arrangement by four distinguished singers and Farwell was the only composer given special recognition in the introduction to the printed program.

The program notes declared: "In this simple setting of William Blake's familiar poem, Mr. Farwell, a distinguished Minnesota-born composer and pioneer in modernism, has appropriately captured the child-like religious imagery of the text." *The Lamb* hardly stands as an example of modernism and Farwell must have chuckled at the statement, but the text was in truth "appropriately captured".

Stokowski examined the score for *Mountain Song* and wrote thus to Farwell on April 2, 1945: ". . . I have been studying new scores. I would have liked to play many more of these, but conditions made this very difficult. Thank you for giving me the opportunity of studying your score which for safety I am leaving with our librarian. . . I hope in the future to conduct your music." He never did!

Farwell's concern over the proper interpretation of his music back-fired in one instance. His former student, Roy Harris, had borrowed the music for *Mystery* for strings from *Mountain Song*, and planned to present it, but suddenly changed his mind. His letter to Farwell from Colorado Springs on August 7, 1948, suggests his reason for doing so:

> I rehearsed your work meticulously with my string quartet and had planned to put it on a nationwide broadcast, but your letter gave me such a worry that I would not do you justice according to your spiritual ideals that I decided I had better not do it. I believe the sins of omission are much easier to live down than the sins of commission.
>
> I found your work a very sensuous piece, which indicates to me that I really missed the whole spirit of it. I found it very Wagnerian and very sensuous in texture - beautiful, delicate and extremely pantheistic, exactly the opposite of what your letter said, so I fear I am too much

of a barbarian. I will have to do some more rugged work of yours I guess. I want to assure you before closing that as music it certainly has some very fine sound - colorful, rich, and warm even in its most ppppp. . . .
Affectionately, Roy

To the writer's knowledge, *Mountain Song* has not been produced in its entirety. Perhaps its musical demands and length have been the main reason. However, Farwell conceived this large work on a scale measured by the majestic Sierra Mountains. For proper appraisal, a full performance should be developed.

### Rudolph Gott Symphony

Rudolph Gott's relationship with Farwell has been told in chapter two. This eccentric, gifted musician exerted a tremendous influence on Farwell especially in his college days when they first became friends. While Farwell was making his way as a fledgling composer, Gott was "hitting the skids" and his piano career fell apart. He drifted to New York, living in Harlem, drinking, fighting, burning himself out in bouts with insanity. Eventually Gott enlisted in the army band, saw duty in the Philippines where he died of a fractured skull sustained in a fight with his superiors in 1911 just before his 39th birthday.

Farwell wrote the story of his friendship with Rudolph Gott for *Musical America* and sent a copy of it to Rudolph's brother, George, on March 31, 1931, along with this letter:

. . . My friendship with Rudolph was the greatest musical inspiration of my life. All my work is in a sense a combination of himself and myself. For the memory of his emotional quality has always remained with me to warm up my own intellectual quality. If his qualities and mine could have been rolled into one, we would have had the world by the ears. And he could have done that alone if he had succeeded in controlling his life, and not letting it go to pieces. In knowing him I feel as if I had known the soul of a Beethoven or a Wagner - for his emotional height was nothing less than that. With this knowledge of his own power (for he surely had it) and with the despair that surrounded him, I always wondered that he did not commit suicide. But this immense emotional capacity I suppose gave him a certain pleasure in life all the way through.

In writing the *Story of Rudolph Gott*, I wanted to perpetuate his memory, and draw a picture of his whole life just as it was, for whatever lessons might be learned from it. Some people who read it thought I was "making him up", that such a person never really lived! The falling of Atha Haydock's painting [of Gott] in my room only a moment after I had finished the final re-writing of the story recently, was very strange - as if he had been on the job, and knew what I was doing.

His spirit is very likely earth-bound, with a sense of not having finished his work here, or not able to get away until he had proven some further spiritual development.

Farwell's loyalty to his friends is especially notable in this instance with Rudolph. Writing his story was not enough. The memories of his friend continued to haunt him until further expression became necessary. He considered Rudolph a genius and was determined to preserve the memory of his name and worth in the best way he knew how - in music. He had rescued the music Rudolph had composed on scraps of wrapping paper intended as the opening bars of a symphony. Farwell utilized these to create the *Rudolph Gott Symphony*, Op. 95, composed during the years 1932 -1935. In notes for the symphony, Farwell has described his goals for the work, and its structure:

. . . that he was my friend and the great inspiration of my early life, together with the fact that he actually began the composition of this symphony, has provided the impulse which has led me to this effort.

This dramatic beginning consisted of about 120 bars, representing only a few pages of the first movement of the present score. (Ex. 70a) I have carried out the movement in a manner to suggest the emotions of his turbulent life and tragic death.

Wishing to embody something of his musical personality and thematic character in the second and third movements of the symphony, I drew upon a few fragments of his works which I had succeeded in preserving at the time he destroyed all his larger compositions.

The second movement is a free compound song-form extension of one of Rudolph's little pieces for piano in the character of a romance. I have added new material.

The third movement is based on his "Pastoral" for oboe and piano, which I have retained in fairly nearly its original shape, except for harmonic developments, as the first and third divisions of a binary form, to which I have contributed a middle section consisting of variations on a brief original theme of pastoral character. At one period Rudolph abandoned the piano for the oboe, gaining a considerable mastery of the instrument. This third movement commemorates Rudolph the oboist, and its orchestration favors this instrument.

The last movement is wholly original with myself, except for passing references to the "motto" motive with which Rudolph opened the symphony. (Ex. 70b) In this finale I have had in mind the suppositious state of consciousness in an after life, of a man who had not succeeded in bringing his genius to fruition during the opportunity afforded by his earthly life. Amidst the restless turmoil of his feelings, as expressed by the two regular themes of the movement, a choral - the triumphant song he would have wished to make of his life - struggles for existence, and emerges at the conclusion.

**Example 70b. Rudolph Gott's Motive.**

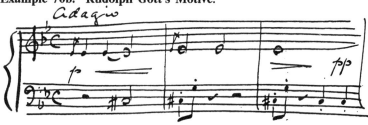

Leopold Stokowski had expressed an interest in performing the *Rudolph Gott Symphony* and Farwell shipped the conductor's score to him on May 21, 1936. Farwell commented:

> I have felt a curious destiny about this work, an important one, if I do say it, from the beginning. I was driven to do it by an overmastering feeling of the necessity to save from oblivion, if possible, the name of a great friend and inspirer of my early days, Rudolph Gott, whom after all my experience I still believe to have been the most powerful emotional genius of music born in America, or perhaps anywhere, in his time. He has been, in the long run, the great event of my life. True, his intellect could not cope with his emotions - it was an unequal struggle from the beginning - and he went to hell. He was another Cellini - a Villon - a character such as America does not believe can exist in this age. Well, in fact he could not, for long. ...I have always felt that I would never have amounted to anything without this initial inspiration of standing in such close relation of friendship to this living musical fire. I was the only friend he ever could keep - as I am now the only person alive to celebrate him. Unless I can succeed in doing this, his name dies utterly. Whether I have done it or not, I cannot say - but I have taken the gamble.
>
> I won't live forever, and I would like to get some inkling of whether or not I may have accomplished my purpose. I am nowise interested in what I can add to my name as a composer in having done this thing - I want to put the name and figure of Rudolph Gott into American musical history.

Farwell also sent Leopold Stokowski a copy of his *Story of Rudolph Gott*. When Stokowski returned the story on June 17, 1936, he wrote: "I enjoyed reading it. He was a great example of self-destruction. I had a similar experience once in my life and that helped me to understand many things."

By July 22nd arrangements were made to secure the parts of the Symphony for study through Mr. F. H. Price at the Fleisher

Collection of Orchestral Music, Free Library of Philadelphia. Farwell tried to learn exactly when the rehearsal would take place as he was eager to be present for the hearing.

Correspondence continued over the year with the rehearsal being pushed farther and farther ahead. On October 8, 1936, Marguerite Coyne, assistant to Mr. Stokowski, wrote apologizing for not being able to give Farwell an exact date. "New works are tried when time permits and we never know ahead when a particular work will be played. I hope you understand."

Eventually Farwell was informed that the rehearsal would probably take place about October 20, 1936, so he wrote to Mr. Stokowski expressing his eagerness to be present at that time:

> I do hope that you will be able to give it a thorough try-out, in all four movements. Also that you will not let any incidental features, which might be bettered or rectified by me after consulting you, stand in the way of a production. I do not know anybody who could bring through the emotional quality of the work as you could.
>
> I am just entering an inevitable and very serious crisis in my own life, and I don't know whether or not I can weather it. If I don't hear the symphony at this reading it is quite possible I will never hear it. (Though of course if I hadn't "heard" it, I couldn't have written it!)

On December 14, 1936, Marguerite Coyne wrote again about the problems Stokowski was having in trying to play the *Rudolph Gott Symphony*. The union had not only reduced the number of rehearsals, but also increased the number of concerts for the season. This left little time for reading new works. She asked what Farwell wanted done with his scores and parts.

Farwell chose to leave the score and parts in Philadelphia and did not contact Stokowski's office until the following April 5, 1937, when he sent a "Strictly Personal" note to the conductor along with a letter to Miss Coyne requesting her to please hand-deliver it. His letter to Stokowski was as follows:

> The crisis in my life, which I intimated last fall has developed to an acute and almost tragic condition. It is

deeply bound up with a general condition here, which may break at any time, and may end everything for me, even though I am standing for what is manifestly right.

I am in deep need of all the strength I can get behind me. These people here know nothing of my place and achievement.

If I could receive word at this time that you had accepted my symphony for production (even though not immediate) it would place a great strength in my hand, and might prove the saving factor in the situation.

*But* - this *only* if the symphony is artistically worth production. If not, I want nothing of it. I feel in it, I have done something near a great work. Maybe not. Congratulations on your many successes. . . .

Farwell's hopes for the scheduled rehearsal evidently did not materialize and his files show no further correspondence with Stokowski. His divorce from Gertrude took place in January 1937, and caused him many heartaches in addition to the uneasy political situation at the college. Failure to find a hearing with the Philadelphia orchestra at this time must have been another hard blow to his already pummeled spirit. Koussevitsky had rejected his *Prelude to a Spiritual Drama* in 1934 and now Stokowski did not provide the anticipated rehearsal of his Symphony. That Farwell could survive these bitter disappointments speaks well for his indomitable character. He just kept teaching and composing, plodding along the best he could. Aspiring composers continue to have similar problems getting their orchestral works performed today as they did in Farwell's time. However, some of Farwell's other compositions were widely performed in his own lifetime.

Farwell's *Rudolph Gott Symphony* had to wait until March 3, 1978, for its premiere performance. The score was brought forth by the violinist, Ronald Erickson, in his research at Berkeley where he teaches at the University. John Pereira was the daring conductor who directed his Diablo Symphony Orchestra at the Gateway Clubhouse in Rossmoor, California. They performed it a second time at St. Mary's College in Moraga and again at the Civic Arts Theater in Walnut Creek, California.

"This is a very difficult work," declared Franco Autori[8] as he listened, score in hand, to the tape of the Diablo orchestra's performance. He tended to agree with the comments made by the critics who attended the significant first performance.

The *San Francisco Examiner* critic, Michael Walsh, wrote:

. . . The symphony is a big work, heroic in its musical vocabulary, gestures and orchestration. . . . The Diablo Symphony, a community orchestra, played over its heads in the Farwell, as Pereira drew music out of it, not just sound. The Rudolph Gott Symphony, on last night's evidence, is worth further investigation.

Marilyn Tucker wrote for the *San Francisco Chronicle*:

Rudolph Gott must have been quite a guy for Arthur Farwell to write a symphony in his name that is an hour in length. . . .

The musical idioms are mostly American folk, and Farwell has developed them with the lush, romantic textures of Tchaikovsky, even Wagner.

The Gott Symphony, although certainly long, is a curiosity to be savored, and the Diablo Symphony was up to its task of its presentation.

Blake Samson had more comments for the *Contra Costa Times* on March 8th:

. . . *The Rudolph Gott Symphony* proved to be an active, imaginative piece with a multiplicity of effects. There is, after a somewhat eclectic first movement, great fertility and boldness in the work, and its more delicate moments, in particular an elegant and evocative third movement, have a unique richness of fragrance.

The symphony opens suspensefully, with definite Wagnerian bent, quickly growing to a full sweeping orchestral show. The second movement, although taken from Gott's piano piece, *Verlassen*, merges most symphonically, with a hint of Mahler and a dynamic impact all its own.

It too, is kept taut, with an equally full use of orchestral color, yet also seemed fresher and more fluid in design. Again, its moments of settling are particularly serene and melodious, yet it has an underlying feeling of intense heat, even if the overall mood is more muted than in the first movement. There is a vastness that is very much a mark of Farwell's music.

The oboe solo in the third movement is a free-spirited, songful piece soon enveloped in a particularly gentle and pleasing pastoral for strings. It moves into a stylish, debonair posture, then eases into more playful and energetic parts. A really inspired movement, it was played most eloquently.

The symphony ends with an industrious, sizable finale, full of vigor and optimism, modern in outlook and fully involving. Once again one feels the fecundity of Farwell's music, its tensile strength and suspensefulness. The closing rhythms are potent and unique.

This was not just an academic exploration in the attics of American music, but a fully exciting experience, enthusiastically received by Sunday's audience and musicians alike.

I think the composer's son, Brice Farwell, is quite correct in saying that the work captures the "internal combustion" that fired both his father and his father's best friend. Farwell also paid tribute to the innovative community orchestra.

One might suspect from his detailed review that Mr. Samson had attended more than one of the area performances. The author agrees with his analysis of the symphony and is especially fond of the pastoral quality of the third movement.

Michael Walsh had occasion to write again about the premiere in his Sunday column for the *San Francisco Chronicle* on March 19, 1978. His remarks are worth noting:

It is a large-scale work, four movements and 372 pages, taking nearly an hour in performance. [Farwell's timing was 46 minutes.] It is a very "American" work, eclectic in its idiom, heroic in its style and scored for large orchestra.

There are a great many influences at work in the symphony besides Gott's, but this should not necessarily be taken as a sign of poverty of invention. True, in the finale (wholly Farwell's) there is a distinctly Mahlerian trumpet figuration, and a horn motto that recalls Tchaikovsky's Fourth Symphony; Holst is present, probably unconsciously, and so is Ives.

Farwell was a minor composer, but his very eclecticism indicates that he was conversant with his musical surroundings and had good taste in his choice of influences, which is more than can be said about many composers today. The *Rudolph Gott Symphony* is no masterpiece of 20th-century symphonic literature, but its performance was valuable by its very nature. Farwell and other American composers of the late 19th and early 20th centuries are a part of our country's musical heritage, and to understand where we are now, and why, we must first know where we have been.

How sad that Farwell never was privileged to enjoy the premiere of his only symphony! It seems clear, upon hearing, that in being true to the passionate Gott, Farwell created a symphonic record much more expressive of grand turn-of-the century drama than of the lean intellectual works of the mid-to-late 20th century.

If Farwell's devotion to the careful presentation of Gott's memory and his music stemmed from his own musical impressions of Rudolph, that may be another instance of the Stendahl syndrome in Farwell's early, if not also lifelong, reactions to music. In any event, it is good listening music, and real American history. On that ground alone, the *Rudolph Gott Symphony* deserves a fully competent orchestral production and recording in behalf of historical scholarship, and for those who relish what music used to be. In considering the story behind the *Gott Symphony* and its musical results, Gilbert Chase calls it "A unique landmark of musical Romanticism in America."[9]

## Later Orchestral Activity

In January 1935, Dana Merriman made arrangements with Farwell for the performance of some of his music on the National Broadcasting system. Farwell chose *Dawn, The Navajo War Dance* and *A Ruined Garden* for a fifteen minute segment of the broadcast. Mr. Littau was to be the orchestra conductor. In a memo to the latter, Farwell made these comments that may still be useful to other conductors:

> *Dawn.* I have heavily underscored all those *ritards* in blue pencil. The whole thing with this work is a sufficient familiarity so that it will flow smoothly with all those tempo changes (I mean the ritards, allargandos, etc.) The mood is utter peace and restfulness. The middle part, though is strictly *guisto*.
>
> *A Ruined Garden.* The first part should move along pretty swiftly. At the first rehearsal of the work, I found that the singer simply couldn't keep up with it, and have any breath, so I made "luft-pausen" at the end of nearly every bar at the beginning of the work. I have indicated them in score and all parts, and I have no doubt you will find it necessary to observe them. The last part, 3-2 time is utterly restful, and can't be hurried.
>
> *Navajo War Dance.* The main theme here is to begin it slowly enough, and always *marcato*, an exaggerated marcato, and with almost a scratchy pressure on the strings when they enter, as the viola at the beginning. In order to get the work off today, I have had to omit doing one thing I wanted to do. This is to change the violin and viola parts in the score to correspond with the *parts*, beginning at letter B, page 7. I had to manage these portions in *divisi* to get the pulsing effect I wanted, and I never got around to fixing the score. I have boxed the beginning of these passages in red pencil and you will see

at a glance at the parts what I have done. It will be no
trouble when you understand it. (Ex. 71)

It is important that the War Dance have a severe,
stern, scratchy, *tenuto* effect, in all its earlier part, and that
it doesn't sound like a nice little pony trot, which it isn't.
Later is such a mad rush that it doesn't make much
difference. But there should always be that pressure on
the strings, and molto marcato.

Well, this is enough, and too much!

Frederick Charles Adler of the Affiliated Music Corporation,
wrote to Farwell about joining his association   for composers.
Farwell replied on May 13, 1936, thus in part:

. . . I see and know what a great and significant
enterprise this is, how much of importance it involves, and
how far it reaches. It will undoubtedly be a great and
good thing for many. The only question in my mind is
the merely personal one - is it good or a bad thing for
*me*, does my particular problem fit into the picture?

The great good it will do for systemization of many
matters, for concentrating the machinery of movement, for
many composers who are rightly circumstanced, is plain.

But myself, who is not a modernistic leftist, (though
probably all the modernistic principles will be found to
some extent in my works), . . . will not my name and my
works be swallowed up in this gigantic and necessarily
monopolistic organization, to be buried there for perhaps
a long time, and myself in the meanwhile left powerless
to accomplish much of anything in the way of hearings?
. . .

I have no doubt as to the success and appeal of my
orchestral works - every performance assures me of this.
I am inclined to think that this appeal will last after a
good many more modernistic works of the present time
have ceased to appeal. But this doesn't help me any in
the present circumstance.

My *Prelude to a Spiritual Drama* had an immense
success here this winter, in its first performance, under

Michael Press' baton. The *Gods of the Mountain* has had an outstanding success everywhere it has been played, about ten cities. The *people* everywhere give evidence of liking my stuff, even of being enthusiastic about it. It affects people's feelings and sense of beauty, rather than to cause debate over radicalisms. This is against hearings, at least until conductors come to know and care for my music, as Verbrugghen did, and as Monteux does. It seems that *these* matters can be overcome only through my personal contact with conductors - with myself conducting the negotiations. This is one of the important reasons why I can't help wondering if I fit into the picture - as regards the new association.

Farwell's files do not provide the answers to his questions nor any further information about this situation. It seems that he did not join the association. But Farwell's letter points out again the problem that some composers were having in securing a hearing of their orchestral work. Adler's organization was an attempt to meet this need.

Another letter from Adler written on January 3, 1938, told Farwell that he was preparing the 1938 Saratoga Festival and asked Farwell if he had anything new to send to him for that occasion. Evidently the friendly relationship still existed and Adler's appreciation for Farwell's work was obvious.

### The Heroic Breed

Farwell's early love, Beatrice Ayer, married George Patton Jr. who became General George Patton. After his tragic accidental death, Farwell felt moved to compose a work to honor him. The result was *The Heroic Breed* for orchestra, Op. 115, composed in 1946. Farwell's notes for the music follow:

This work is dedicated to the memory of Gen. George S. Patton, Jr.

It is based upon three military features, respectively the infantry, cavalry, and the tanks, with which latter General Patton was prominently associated. These three

aspects are represented by a march, a scene of riding, and
the heavy movement of the tanks.

The work begins with a brief heroic prelude, followed
by a march. This is followed by the contemplation of a
martial career, heard first on the brasses alone. Then the
galloping scene of riding, followed by the Theme of Love,
which is rudely interrupted by a call to war. After the
tanks, with their climax of victory, the celebrations and
enthusiasm attending the hero's return to America will be
recognized, as will also his subsequent return to Germany,
with a broken figure of *Die Wacht am Rhein*. Then, the
tragedy, relieved by the reappearance of the Theme of
Love, *Taps*, and a brief apostrophic conclusion of heroic
character.

Farwell's files include more notes on his intentions for this
score. He has listed each part of the "program" by page numbers
of the score and clue letter. Regarding Patton's death he inserted
a quote from Patton who said at the time of his accident, "This
is a hell of a way to die".

Farwell developed a correspondence with Mrs. Patton while he
was composing *The Heroic Breed*. A letter dated January 3, 1946,
written from West Point, reveals Mrs. Patton's freedom to express
her inner feelings to her former fiancé:

> Your Beatrice probably told you that I looked her up
> at the [Metropolitan] Museum the other day. She's lovely,
> and I wish I'd seen her longer, but she had an engagement
> and couldn't come to lunch.
>
> I didn't get your letter in Heidelberg; but they are
> gradually dribbling back and I probably will. The
> Sokolsky article is the only one I have ever seen that puts
> Georgie where he belongs; there in the *Heroic Breed*.
> Thank you.
>
> I am doing all right, but it is strange that Georgie
> seems so remote, so far away as almost not to belong to
> me at all. I suppose it is because he has become such a
> legend, that the Georgie I know is in a sort of theatrical
> mist, like the gauze curtains they let down one by one

when Oberon comes on the stage. I wish I could clear
them away, for my own sake. Perhaps, some day I can.
    I've never told this to anyone but you.
        As ever- Beatrice

After Farwell finished *Heroic Breed*, Mrs. Patton endeavored
to secure a hearing for the work. On August 23, 1948, she wrote
from South Hamilton, Massachusetts:

The MS is back. Do you think I should write
Stokowski first and ask him if he wants to see it, or send
it with the letter? I don't have an idea what manner of
man he is. I wish I could express to you what a
wonderful thing I feel it is that you have done to honor
Georgie. You can guess how I long to hear it played!.

Evidently Mrs. Patton's efforts were successful for she wrote
in an undated note: " Dear Arthur, - Don't worry - the address is
all right - 57th St. and everything is in order, I hope. It may take
some time to hear but let's just assume its going to be performed.
As ever, B."

And so it was! *The Heroic Breed* was played in New York
City by the Young Men's Symphony Orchestra in a rented hall for
Mrs. Patton's private party. Most of the Farwell family were
present, and Brice remembers that Mrs. Patton treated them all to
an elaborate lunch after the eventful morning performance.
Beatrice remembered her father saying, "Now that music wasn't
such 'old hat', was it?" He was concerned that his mature works
did not sound "out-of-date". Later, Beatrice told the author that
she really did not like her father's use of *Taps* in the composition,
but that he felt it belonged there.

Farwell's files reveal correspondence with Keith Merrill[10]
regarding arrangements for a hearing of *Heroic Breed* to be played
by the National Symphony Orchestra under Hans Kindler's baton.
The reading took place on February 4, 1949, but Farwell, who was
living in New York City at the time, was unable to be present and
asked Mr. Merrill to please give him an honest appraisal of this
work. His evaluation was finally sent on February 21st:

In reply to your question as to what I thought, I
purposely omitted offering a personal reaction because I
recognized it as a great work which it would be
impertinent for me to comment on, but since you ask me
for my impression, may I say that in the case of most
modern American composers, I notice the lack of melody
which I can follow in their works. Probably this is the
reaction of a fair segment of what Reginald de Koven
used to describe as the "vulgar public".

But in defense of their desires it seems to me that the
great compositions in times past have been melodic and
more melodic than those of the present; Beethoven, for
example, and Brahms.

Throughout the playing of your work, I kept
wondering if it would be possible to superimpose a
melody on what I was hearing, and that, perhaps was why
*Taps* struck so hard when it was sounded. Again my
congratulations to you, Sir, and many thanks for the
privilege of hearing your tribute to General Patton. . . .

Farwell should have been pleased to read that Mr. Merrill
considered *Heroic Breed* a "great work", but it upset him to learn
that Mr. Merrill could not recognize its melodic content. So off
went his rebuttal on March 26th as follows:

Dear Mr. Merrill:

I want to thank you for your kindness in responding
to my request for your personal reaction to *The Heroic
Breed* reading. It was of very great interest to me.

I was, however, so astonished at what you said about
*melody*, that I have been trying to think how to account
for it. I would not think of imposing anything
controversial upon you - heaven forbid! - but there are
certain thoughts I feel impelled to register with you for
what they are worth, and for what they might mean for
some possible future hearing of the work.

First, in a mere reading, neither conductor nor players
have any clear idea of what is to be brought forth and
emphasized, and may well have let the work's melodic

ideas go by casually, and without making them stand forth from the orchestra background sufficiently to impress themselves.

Second, I have often noticed that with a new and different personality, the melodic ideas pass by without being grasped by almost any hearer, very especially when the individual harmonic scheme of an unfamiliar composer presents itself, and where the richness of orchestral setting, under these circumstances, tends to monopolize the attention.

You see I am not at all an ultra-modern, and am a rather close adherent of the general scheme established by Wagner and Tchaikovsky (no invidious comparisons intended!), and am vehemently looked down upon by my younger colleagues, as a hopeless reactionary, harking back to the 19th Century, which they all despise.

Of course new concepts arise, as to what constitutes melody, as with Debussy, but I stick pretty closely to the traditional four-square pattern, AABA (letters being phrases), AABB, or sometimes ABAB.

I have set down the chief melodic ideas of the *Heroic Breed*, for you, partly to show you their simplicity and four-squareness, and partly because if in possibly hearing the work again, you might like to be a bit familiar with them beforehand.

The march, No. 1. seems to me as simple, as common, even as a march tune by Raff, as in the old Lenore Symphony, and easy to be hummed or whistled.

In No. 2, the first horse tune, the B phrase marks a greater departure from the A than is common, but returns to the A rhythm at once. Note the comparison of the phrase with the Schubert symphony phrase I have given.

The second horse theme is indeed not easily whistleable, but is very logical and direct in its melodic line, and very simple in its geometry, each A, strings, being followed by its B, flute.

The love theme 4, is wholly free in form, but I think convincing, in familiarity.

The tanks, 5 is quite a different matter, heavy, as
befits the tanks, not at all tuneful in the usual sense, but
very simple in its succession of 8-bar phrases, each a slight
variant of the preceding, and gradually increasing in the
sense of motion. The tanks wouldn't sing a very pretty
song!

There are various subsidiary themes, all on the above
traditional patterns as to form.

All the melodies *sang* themselves out to me,
emotionally, and nothing was devised merely intellectually;
to me the work *sings* throughout, and I am wondering if
it might to you, on more familiarity, and studied
performances emphasizing the melodic ideas.

Do pardon this verbose sally, please - but I had to get
it off my chest. You see there is nothing in it which you
have to bother to answer, but I have hoped that you
would find some element of interest in it. . . .

Farwell's files show no further reaction from Mr. Merrill, and
Farwell expected none. His letter is an example of how deeply
concerned he was that his music would communicate some Truth
or Beauty to its listeners. Here his hope was to provide more
understanding for Merrill who, in spite of his criticism about lack
of melody, still considered *Heroic Breed* a "great work".

* * *

Other critics who reviewed Farwell's orchestral compositions
seemed to agree that he was skillful in his orchestration. Some
thought his music showed Wagner or Tchaikovsky influences.
Others recognized a more modern style all his own. Farwell
admitted his love for Wagner and Tchaikovsky, but declared that
he tried to express what Truth and Beauty he felt in his own
original way.

A. Walter Kramer and Howard Hanson both spoke highly of
Farwell's *Gods of the Mountain* suite. Kramer said Farwell had
"complete mastery of the modern orchestra" with "rich and
remarkably balanced scoring." Hanson declared in 1971 that this
is a "stunning suite and worthy of inclusion on any of today's
symphony programs." And this was composed in 1928!

The *Gods of the Mountain* suite has been the most popular of Farwell's orchestral scores. Not only this work should be revived, but also other scores should be brought "out of the attic" for performance today. The premiere of the *Rudolph Gott Symphony* was an exciting step forward in introducing the public to more remarkable works by Farwell. This symphony and Farwell's other orchestral scores can stand on their own as historic examples of their time and provide good listening. The author regrets that more examples from these large orchestral scores could not be reduced clearly enough for reproduction here, but the original scores are generally in excellent readable condition and available.

**Example 66a.** *Domain of Hurakan,* page 1.

**Example 66b.** *Domain of Hurakan*, page 2.

**Example 66c.** *Domain of Hurakan*, **page 18.**

**Example 66d.**   *Domain of Hurakan*, page 50.

**Example 67.**    *Mountain Vision, Symbolistic Study, No. 6*

**Example 68a.** *Gods of the Mountain:* **Chord vocabulary**

**Beggar's Dream**

I.       a      Fr⁶  C⁺  It⁶    E    F    g#

**Maya of the Moon**

II.     d    Eb⁺  F⁺  G    Fr⁶  b°    It⁶

**Pinnacle of Pleasure**

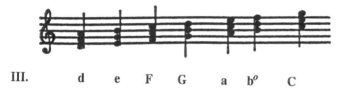

III.    d    e    F    G    a    b°    C

**The Stone Gods Come**

IV.    e    F    G    a    b°    C    d

**Example 68b.** *Gods of the Mountain:* **Tread and Fear motives**

**Tread motive**

**Fear motive**

**Example 69a.**   *Symphonic Song on Old Black Joe*

**Example 69b.**   *Symphonic Song on Old Black Joe,* **audience at D.**

**Example 70a. *Rudolph Gott Symphony:* First page**

## Example 71.    *Navajo War Dance, No. 1*

# Epilogue

*"Beating Wagner and Debussy*
*With a Yankee genius juicy . . ."*
             Cartoon   *(A. Farwell and E.K. Wallace)*

Perhaps Farwell may be best seen as a Yankee idealist caught up in a lifelong wrestling match between his art and ideals, while engaging and contending with the forces in his culture. The struggles were strengthened by an unbreakable loyalty to his values and convictions, inspired by an unflinching faith, and driven by a tireless enthusiasm and confidence in the growing power of his art. Cheiro, the palmist, was correct when he told young Farwell that he could not be discouraged in his ultimate purpose - that he would work on and on in spite of difficult circumstances.

Arthur Farwell went forth to fulfill Emerson's prophetic words that "One day we shall cast out the passion for Europe by the passion for America." Perhaps it was inevitable for Farwell's genes to heed the call of his Emersonian heritage, but who could have foreseen the scope and depth of his efforts?

When Farwell returned from his European studies and tried to have his compositions published in America, he discovered what a strong grip the music of the German masters had on American tastes - as many of his young colleagues had already learned. Publishers were reluctant to publish new serious art songs by American composers. What they did issue were the old "classics" or light sentimental songs they thought would be sure to sell.

This angered Farwell and he insisted that such a state of affairs made it intolerable for a composer in America. He vowed: "I'll not live in a country that does not accept my vocation. I will change the United States in this respect!"

The changes he wrought were unfolded in Farwell's life story as it wound through the *Wa-Wan Press* years of struggle, and his strenuous transcontinental travels to spread and strengthen the cause of American music and its composers. Farwell's lectures, the *Wa-Wan Press*, and his building of the American Music Society with its twenty "centers" nationwide, were his armaments. Farwell's "passion" for his country and his faith in its youthful cultural potential, glowed all through his life in countless essays, speeches, and in his over 116 sensitive musical compositions.

After eleven years of directing the *Wa-Wan Press* and its related campaigning, Farwell concluded that conditions for the American composer had begun to improve, and that American attitudes toward serious American music had begun to change. After the *Press* was sold to G. Schirmer, Farwell now focused his energies on music for the "common man". The "Democratization of Music" described his approach to involving all kinds of people in the vitality of music. He became a prime mover in the Community Music Movement, and also a guiding leader in the American Pageant Association.

Yet, throughout his intense public activity, Farwell continued to compose prolifically. To him composition was "the very Grail of Life". Farwell's lofty idealism ever quested what he saw as the highest in Beauty and Truth. His music shows a steady and developing expression of what he felt deep within his heart. Thus he composed in musical language he considered evocative to the human spirit. He refused to follow the experimentation of "modernists" like Stravinsky, and intellectual Schoenberg, and satirized them in his opera *Cartoon*. However, he did strike out in new tonal paths and forms of his own that resulted in what he called a more "modern" sound. He was aware of the musical trends of his time, but he built his own individualistic niche.

His diversity is seen in the wide span of compositions ranging from some short jewel-like settings for Emily Dickinson's poetry, to the long, emotionally charged *Rudolph Gott Symphony*; from folk song arrangements, to community choruses, and music for pageants and masques. His style grew from his early simple parlor-type pieces through a landmark change in his *Vale of Enitharmon* to the intricate, remorseless strength of his *Piano Sonata*. Known at first primarily as an "Indianist", Farwell became more eclectic and was labeled "the prototype of the eclectic composers in America."[1] He eventually wrote in what has been called an "idiosyncratic style" to create works of remarkable harmonic individuality, which we have only partially examined.[2]

Farwell did not see himself as an experimental composer, yet one finds him pointing forward in unexpected ways during his career. It has been noted that he was the only major American composer of his era to compose music specifically for community use. He produced the first Song and Light show experienced by

New Yorkers. He demonstrated new uses of colored lights to embellish musical episodes at the Theater of the Stars. He wrote technically abstract music such as *What's in an Octave?*, as well as Indian pieces sensitively set to the mood and original purpose they held in Indian life - a unique approach. He continually experimented with forms and harmonic vocabulary as shown in each genre of his work. His 23 *Polytonal Studies* showed creative results based on complicated charts - a disciplined new study, and another unusual effort.

In addition to his music-writing, Farwell wrote thousands of words as a crusading spokesman for an American Music. In addition to lectures on four nation-wide tours, he wrote significant essays for the *Wa-Wan Press* and its music editions, and *Wa-Wan Press Monthly*, all handsomely bound in the 1970 reprint by Arno Press. He also wrote over 100 articles in *Musical America* and elsewhere plus much material for *Music in America* (with W. Dermot Darby). David Horn's review of the latter work in *Literature of American Music* for Scarecrow Press in 1977 points out that while Darby's writing is "down-to-earth", he sees Farwell writing with vision in 1915, and with the ability to step out of an age and view it historically, thus lending the book:

> . . . a sense of some higher significance in all the activity recorded in its pages, seeing American musical history in its broader sense as "appreciation, creation and administration". . . . His chapters on "Romanticists and Neo-Romanticists" and "Nationalists, Eclectics and Ultramoderns" combine factual detail with a perceptive critical assessment that almost intuitively relates people and events to a framework of creative American culture.

Obviously, Farwell was a gifted writer and a sensitive literary critic. Furthermore, he also delighted in the visual arts. He broke away from the usual flowery style for sheet-music covers by designing simple abstract covers for the sheet-music of his Wa-Wan Press. He often carried a sketch book while traveling and some of his sketches ultimately found a place in his early articles for *Musical America*. Later, he fashioned attractive covers for his lithographed pieces, and drew the illustrations based on his "symbolic dreams" for his unpublished book *Intuition in the World-Making*. In addition to drawing, he experimented with sculpture and sent his parents a bust of Wagner, which his mother's diary reported to be a good likeness.

Although some of Cheiro's predictions did not come true, (especially one related to acquiring "plenty of money") the aware reader should have observed many of them were accurate. His life span of eighty years, and that Farwell could not be stopped in his goals and purposes - were correctly prophesied. As a result, American composers have probably gained some recognition sooner than they would have without Farwell's efforts. His work in the Community Music Movement may have found its most enduring evidence resulting from the energetic help he gave to the founding of the Hollywood Bowl, which continues to nourish musical appetites. As a teacher, Farwell's influence touched many lives of all ages from children to mature adults, his best known composition student being Roy Harris.

Farwell himself proved to be a perpetual student, thus fulfilling Cheiro's prediction to twenty year old Farwell: "Your life must be the life of a student, you must invent and create, and your work will be original and along new lines which will make your struggle for recognition all the harder." It is not surprising that he lamented early in 1893, "Oh, if only one could study *everything*; it seems so terrible that we must give up our whole life just to do one thing well!"

But Farwell did many things well, and these summarized here are just some of his varied contributions to American cultural life.

> Above all, the cross-fertilization of music, literature, and the visual arts that characterize much of his work anticipates a whole school of composers influenced by Cage. Farwell was both within the mainstream and an example of American musical experimentalism; in this he can be compared only with Ives.[3]

A. Walter Kramer declared, "Arthur Farwell is probably the most neglected composer in our history." Kramer believed that

*Figure 64. Arthur Farwell, looking back over his adventures, as he appeared in the forties.*

"at the turn of the century no one in the United States wrote music with greater seriousness, or fought harder for American music than Arthur Farwell".[4]

Others have made these same observations, and in view of the record of Farwell's public career, one may well ask "why such neglect?" The more Farwell's music has been examined and heard in recent years, the harder this question is to answer.

We know that Farwell's high-minded seriousness and spiritual idealism must have set him apart from the trends of the "Roaring Twenties". He said outright that he could not find the soul or spirit of musical beauty in the atonal and serial music that had begun to capture the fancy of those restless years. Perhaps at the time, the reactions of Koussevitsky and Stowkowski to his orchestral works were understandable. Farwell's music followed a different muse from that of his own latter days.

But the importance of Farwell's role as a trail-blazing crusader in bringing American music to the American people in the early 1900's is unmistakably clear. The music, itself, that he gave the world, we have found here to be very rewarding. Now its recognition and recovery from this noted neglect is much over due. As president of the American Music Center, Paul Sperry has said he will continue to promote Farwell's mature songs as "among the best American songs".

Beyond the effort of this writing, the scholar-musician with an ear - let him hear. The performing artist and listener will find good things to explore and share! Farwell's life and his music reflect how "He Heard America Singing"!

PART THREE

CATALOG OF MUSIC
AND
DISCOGRAPHY

# Catalog of the Musical Works
## of
## Arthur Farwell

This introductory section contains detailed guidance for the use of this catalog, including legends, keys, abbreviations and status of the music.

Arthur Farwell's musical work is classified here first into sections by the genre: vocal solo, piano, chamber and instrumental, choral and community singing, pageant and theater, and orchestral. Where he did the same work in more than one genre, the work is listed in each, with cross reference for details on the others. Because of their historical importance and musical individuality, his Indian works are listed in a separate section, as well as within the respective genre of each. These sections are:

1. Indian Music
2. Vocal Solo
   A. Piano accompaniment
   B. With Orchestra
3. Piano Music
   A. Solo
   B. With other instruments and organ music
4. Chamber and Instrumental Music
   A. Ensembles
   B. One or Two Instruments
5. Choral and Community Singing Music
6. Music for Dramatic Forms
   A. Theatrical
   B. Pageants and Masques
   C. Opera
7. Orchestral Music
   A. Orchestra Alone
   B. With Piano
   C. With Chorus
   D. Music for Dramas

Within each section, the compositions are listed in the best known chronological order of their writing. But since Farwell's opus numbering was not always consistent with chronology, an additional item numbering scheme was added here, taken from those used in *A Guide to the Music of Arthur Farwell and to the Microfilm Collection of His Work*, published in 1972 by Brice Farwell. This *Guide* Item Number is found in brackets following the title and opus number, where present.

The date first given is the date the work was completed, where known. Where records cannot be found, the date is marked "circa" with a c, when it has been approximated to the best of available current knowledge. In a few cases, "Yr ?" is stated.

A very few of the entries list compositions by Farwell that his records said had existed, but of which he left no copy in his collection, nor has one been located, or his own notes said "lost" or "destroyed". For those that have been published, even though out of print, the publisher is shown by one of the abbreviations listed below, together with year of publication. For the extensive work not yet published, a further legend defines abbreviations for the nature of the known, extant and available manuscripts.

**Publisher Abbreviations**

| | |
|-----|----------------------------------------------|
| AF | Arthur Farwell Lithograph Edition, East Lansing, MI |
| AP | Arno Press, New York, New York |
| BH | Boosey & Hawkes, New York, New York |
| CB | C. C. Birchard, NY or Boston |
| CF | Carl Fischer, New York, New York |
| CI | *The Circle* - a periodical, New York, New York |
| GF | *A Guide to the Music of Arthur Farwell*...Selected study scores herein, issued by Brice Farwell, Ashland, OR |
| GI | Ginn & Co., New York, New York |
| GM | Galaxy Music Publishers, New York, New York |
| GS | G. Schirmer, New York, New York |
| HH | Hinds, Hayden & Eldridge |
| HM | Hinshaw Music, Inc., Chapel Hill, North Carolina |
| HS | H. B. Stevens, Boston, Massachusetts |
| JC | John Church, Bryn Mawr, Pennsylvania |
| MP | Music Press |
| OD | Oliver Ditson, Bryn Mawr, Pennsylvania |
| PP | Privately printed |
| RE | Remick, New York |

SB      Silver-Burdett, Morristown, New Jersey
SP      Stevens Presser, Bryn Mawr, Pennsylvania
WW      Wa-Wan Press, Newton Center, Massachusetts

## Manuscript Legend

The music still only in manuscript form is identified as to its condition by the following:

AF Ms.      Finished manuscript in Arthur Farwell's hand.
AF Dr.      Draft, sketch or rough notes by Arthur Farwell, only.
Repr Ms.    Reproducible translucent master ms made by AF.
Var.        Manuscript by copyists or various hands.

If Manuscript legend is followed by a library code, the original manuscript is held by that library. Otherwise, it should be in the author's collection.

A library code following publication status signifies that the indicated library holds or has held a published copy.

Farwell's music, except for the recent publication of his later Emily Dickinson songs by Boosey & Hawkes, is almost entirely out of print or still unpublished. The microfilms of the composer's own collection and of his music in the New York Public Library may be examined at any of the following libraries: Library of Congress, New York Public Library (at its Research Library of Music and the Performing Arts), University of Illinois at Urbana, Eastman School of Music at Rochester, N.Y., State University of New York at Buffalo, University of Kentucky at Lexington, Arizona State University at Tempe, University of Texas at Austin, Ohio State University at Columbus, or Southwest Missouri State University at Springfield.

Libraries known to have copies of Farwell's music in their collections are listed in the following legend. The Union List code is shown in each entry for music which they hold.

## Union List Legend

CL      Los Angeles, California, Public Library
DLC     Library of Congress

MB      Boston, Massachusetts, Public Library
MH      Harvard College Library, Cambridge, Massachusetts
NNrpa   New York Public Library's Research Library of Music and
        the Performing Arts, at Lincoln Center, New York, N. Y.
PP(FC)  Edwin   A.   Fleisher   Collection,   Free   Library   of
        Philadelphia, Pa.

Published entries are presumed to have a copy in the Library of Congress. Where DLC is shown, its presence there has been verified. The rpa suffix to NN as used here may not be a formal code of Union List.

Except for those manuscripts placed by the composer in the New York Public Library or in the Fleisher Collection of the Free Library of Philadelphia, Arthur Farwell's collection of his musical life work is owned by the author. With some exceptions, it has largely been in the archival care of the composer's son, Brice Farwell. The entire collection will (in the near future) be added to the archives of the Sibley Library at The Eastman School of Music, University of Rochester, New York. There, their preservation and availability and/or reproduction for performance use, and for possible publication, as well as for scholarly research should at an early date be greatly enhanced.

Publically issued recordings are listed in a discography and are indicated in the catalog with an R following publication or manuscript and any library status.

Known privately made, or nonissued recordings are mostly of posthumous performances. These are shown in the same location, as RU. Copies of such nonissued tapes are presently held within the Farwell family archive.

One nonissued recording, of *Mountain Vision*, is in the Library of Congress and is shown as RU-DLC.

Timing of some performances was determined from these tapes for the catalog entries. Farwell specified intended time in only one or two scores, shown as AF time. Time measured from tapes is as performed, not necessarily at the composer's tempo.

Records for premieres of the composer's works are scanty. Some programs in his scrapbook or notes in his diaries have provided some entries as "first known performances." Where no performance information is shown, none was available. Some works were played by students, and a few of these are shown.

A few files of Farwell's musical work sheets and notes, not listed in the Catalog, were indicated in the published *Guide* to his music under the heading: "Collected Musical Ideas, Sketches, Drafts, Themes, Folk Tunes, Studies, Worksheets, etc." Included here are unfinished works on Indian and Spanish Californian material, some drafts of finished things not recognized for filing with their finished work, and Farwell's whimsically labelled folder: "UNFINISHE COMPOSITIONS."

Assessment cannot be wholly objective in the arts, but it is recognized that an artist's work may be found more interesting at some future time than when it was created. While a number of Farwell's works are clearly "dated", even if accidentally, and others are of routine or passing interest only, there has been significant interest discovered in Farwell's music when eventually examined. This interest has led to premiere performances, broadcasts, recordings, some publication and scholarly research.

It would be erroneous to limit exploration of Farwell to his published work, although some of this music is still or again newly interesting. This catalog provides a tentative guide to selecting music for examination and/or performance which appears to have the likelihood or some evidence of interest today. This guidance is shown in accordance with one or more of the following keys.

**Interest Key Legend**

| | |
|---|---|
| * | Played much during composer's life, or of career importance. |
| ** | Likely to have interest for professional performance today. |
| *** | Played during Farwell's career and of interest for today. |
| P | For professional or skilled amateur performers. |
| S | Suitable for students or less skilled amateurs. |
| PS | May be sensitively performed at either level of skill. |
| TD | Entry is discussed in the text of Part one or Part two and can be located in the index. |

In summary, the catalog provides the item and opus number if any, the known or approximate year of composition, a key to interest where appropriate, the title of the work and of selections within the work, the publication and/or manuscript status, known library holdings, reference to any known recording, premiere or first known performance, vocal range (shown after title) and/or instrumental scoring, known timing of recorded performance, and reference to any textual discussion.

# Catalog of Musical Works

## 1. Indian Music

Categories in Indian Section correspond with balance of catalog and Indian works may be further detailed in their respective genre classifications.

### A. Vocal Solo

1.      *American Indian Melodies*, no opus number [Guide no. 27] c1901-04 - voice and piano, harmonized from the record of original Indian melodies.    Some numbers missing or unfinished, AF Ms.
        1. "Look Up!"
        2. "Rallying Song in the Face of Death"
        3. "Thunder Consecration Ceremony No. 1"
        4. "Thunder Consecration Ceremony No. 2"
        5. "Thunder Consecration Ceremony No. 3"
        6. "Game Song"
        7. "Zonzimonde"
        8. "Omaha Tribal Prayer", SATB
        11. "Mi'Kaci"
        12. "We-Ton Song"
        15. "Victory Song"
        16. "Wate'grctu"
        18. "Second Game Song.

Unnumbered:
"Thunder Grandfather" (version of No. 16, above) AF Ms.
"Maya Song With Guitar", AF Dr. of Maya Indian usage of Spanish song "La Hamaca", Op.80 [59].
"Maya Dance", AF Dr. An Acoma Song, AF Dr.

2.  \*    *Folk Songs of the West and South* Opus 19 [31], 1905 - medium voice, Pub 1905 WW\*, loc in CL, MB, NNrpa. Main entry Vocal #35.

    P       6. "Bird Dance Song" (Cahuilla Tribe) - Perf. unknown until April 1990 by Richard Kassel at Sonneck Society Meeting, Toronto.

3.  \*\* P  *Three Indian Songs* Opus 32 [42], 1908 - medium voice, Pub 1912 GS. Main entry Song #39 and cf Piano #96.
    1. "Song of the Deathless Voice" - Loc CL, NNrpa. RU, TD.
    2. "Inketunga's Thunder Song" - loc DLC. RU, TD.
    3. A. "The Old Man's Love Song" - loc DLC.

4.  \*\* P  *Three Songs for Medium Voice*, opus 69 [95], 1924 - Indian poems by Charles O. Roos. See Song 59.
    1. "The Ravens Are Singing" - Pub 1929 GS, RU.
    2. "A Dawn Song" - Pub 1929 GS. TD.
    3. "Dark Her Lodge Door" - Pub 1927 DO, loc NNrpa, RU.

5.  S      *Invocation to the Sun God*, opus 89 [115], 1930 - baritone on poem by Charles O. Roos, AF Ms.

## B. Piano

6. **P S  *American Indian Melodies*, opus 11 [18], 1900 - Ten melodies harmonized from the original Indian, Pub 1901 WW, 1970 AP, 1977 HM; loc in CL, MB, MH; R, RU. Main entry Piano #96.

7. ***P  *Dawn*, opus 12 [21], 1908 - fantasy for piano on two Indian themes, TD.
   A. 1901 - Pub 1902 WW, 1970 AP; loc in CL, MB, NNrpa.
   B. 1940 - Arranged by John Kirkpatrick, AF Ms.
   C. 1904 - for Orchestra - See Orch. #219
   D. c1909 - Revised orchestral version: #219 D

8. * S  *Ichibuzzhi*, opus 13 [22], c1902 - based on Indian melody first harmonized by Farwell in Op.11 [18] above, Pub 1902 WW,1970 AP; loc in CL, MB, MH, NNrpa. See Piano #99.

9. ***P  *The Domain of Hurakan*, opus 15 [23], 1902.
   A. For piano - Pub 1902 WW, 1970 AP; loc CL, MB, NNrpa. RU, TD. See Piano #100.
   B. For Orchestra - See Orch. #220.

10. ***P  *Navajo War Dance No. 2*, opus 29 [28], c1904 (per AF) TD.
    A. Original AF Ms, marked with notations for
    B. 1940 - Version ed. by John Kirkpatrick, Pub 1947 MP. See Piano #101. R.

11. ***P  *From Mesa and Plain*, opus 20 [32], 1905 - for piano. Pub 1905 WW, 1970 AP; loc in CL, MB, NNrpa. Five selections, Main entry Piano #103. TD
    1A. "Navajo War Dance" (AF: "Obsolete").

1B. "Navajo War Dance (No. 1)" - new ending adds 39 bars, also pub 1905 WW, 1912 GS, 1970 AP. R.

4. "Wa-Wan Choral" - from an Omaha ceremony. See also Chamber #149.

5A. "Pawnee Horses" - from an Omaha song.

5B. "Pawnee Horses" - edited and fingered by John Kirkpatrick, Pub 1944 GS. R, TD.

12. * S    *Impressions of the Wa-Wan Ceremony of the Omahas*, opus 21 [33] - Pub 1905 WW, 1970 AP; loc in CL, MB, NNrpa. Includes 8 pieces for piano. See Piano #102

13.      *Symbolistic Study No. 4, "Wa-Wan"*, opus 24 [35] 1906. Unfinished AF Ms.

14.      *The Distant Warrior* [46], c1909 - Pub Sept. 1909 issue, *The Circle*, Loc in NN Periodicals.

15. ** P   *Indian Fugue Fantasy*, opus 44 [59], 1938 - revised for piano from early string work on Omaha theme. AF Ms loc in NNrpa. See Piano #108

## C. Chamber Music

16. ** P   *The Hako,* opus 65 [89], 1922, string quartet in A major. See Chamber #142.

## D. Choral

17. * S   *Two Indian Songs*, 1901 - Frederick Manley - SATB, adapted from #6 *Amer. Ind. Melodies* - 2 and 7, Pub 1901 CB in *The Laurel Song Book.* TD

18.      *American Indian Melodies* [27], c1901-1904 - 18 melodies in Vocal Solo main entry, #34, one has

choral arrangement: 8. "Omaha Tribal Prayer" - SATB and piano.

19. **P S   *Three Indian Songs* opus 32 [42], 1908 - Main entry in Vocal #38. 3. B. - "The Old Man's Love Song" - SATB, AF Ms. See also entry #21 below.

20. * S   *Four Part Songs For Children* opus 42 [57], 1914 - Pub 1914 SB in *The Progressive Music Series*. #169 3. "Hiawatha's Sailing".

21. **P   *Four Songs for A Capella Chorus* opus 102 [135], 1937 - Pub 1937 GS, 1st perf. by Westminster Choir with John Finley Williamson, c1937, #190, TD.
   1. "Navajo War Dance, No. 1" - SSAATTB, RU.
   2. "The Old Man's Love Song" - SSAATTBB, RU.
   3. "Pawnee Horses" - SSAATTBB.
   4. "The Mother's Vow" - SSAATTBB with soprano solo.

22. **P   *Two A Capella Choruses* opus 111 [154], 1946 - 8 parts, AF Dr, Pub 1946 PP with rehearsal piano and instructions for performing Indian vocables. Perf. on tour of Westminster Choir, 1947.
   1. "Navajo War Dance No 2." - SSAATTBB.
   2. "Indian Scene" - SSAATTBB with sop. solo. First perf. March 20, 1947 at Town Hall, NYC.

## E. Orchestra

23. * P   *Dawn - Fantasy on Two Indian Themes* opus 12 [21], 1901 - See Piano #98
   C. 1904 - Dawn - Fantasy for Orchestra - Parts and two pp. of score. In 1935, composer called this version "callow" and preferred newer version, (D, below) which he said is same as original piano work.

\*\*\* P    D. *Dawn*, c1909 - Arr. for Piano and Small Orchestra - AF Ms at PP(FC). Time: 6:20, Scoring: W - 1-1-2-1; B - 2-1-1; tmp; S - 2-1-1-1. Main entry #219, RU.

24. \*\*\* P    *The Domain of Hurakan* opus 15 [23], 1910 - Main entry Piano #100.
B. Orchestra score on 1902 piano work, AF Ms, Scoring: W 2-2-1-2-2; B 4-2-3-1; KD-BD-Cym; usual strings. Main entry #220.

25.    *Navajo War Dance No. 1* opus 110 [152], 1944 - may be part of "Indian Suite" (remainder unknown), score in Repr Ms, parts wanting. AF time: 2 min. 5 sec.; scoring: W - 3-2-1-3-2; B - 4-3-3-1; Tmp; Str. to bal. main entry #224.

## 2. Vocal Solo

### A. With Piano

26. \* S    *Thou'rt Like Unto A Tender Flower* [4], 1895 - Heine's "Du bist wie eine Blüme," Low voice, Pub 1901 OD.
27.    Early Songs without opus numbers [8] - all before 1900, Performance unknown except as shown.
   S    1. *Blow, Golden Trumpets* - Margaret Deland - SATB, composed under AF pseudonym John Francis, Pub 1897 OD.
   S    2. *The Message of the Lillies* - Margaret Deland - SATB, by "John Francis", Pub 1897, OD.
   \*\*P S    3. *In A Rose Garden* - John Bennett - Mezzo, Pub 1895 OD. First known perf. April 1990 by Judith Auer, mezzo, Alex Craig, p. Boulder, CO.
   \*\*P S    4. *Strow Poppy Buds* - A. Mary F. Robinson -High voice in C, low in A, Pub OD 1895, loc NNrpa,

First known perf. Jan 31, 1908 by Mrs. D. A.
Campbell, in Kansas City, Mo.  TD

S    5. *O Ships That Sail* - A. Mary F. Robinson - Low
voice, Pub 1897 OD.

6. *Silenced Are My Songs* - Johanna Ambrosius, AF
translation - Mezzo, Pub 1898 OD.  TD

\* P S    7. *Invocation* - W. E. Henley - Mezzo, Pub 1898
OD.

\* S    8. *Meeting* - Johanna Ambrosius, AF translation -
Soprano, Pub 1898 OD, performed July, 1975 at
Newport, R.I. Romantic Festival.  TD

\* S    9. *Wenlock Town* - A. E. Hausman - Mezzo, Pub
1902 OD.  TD

S    10. *Laddie Boy* - Mary F. Brown - medium voice,
Pub 1937 OD.

28. \*\* P S    Maedchenlieder opus 2 [9], 1897 - Four Johanna
Ambrosius Songs - medium voice, Pub 1898 HS, loc
MB.  TD

29.   S    *Three Songs*, opus 3 [10] c1897 - medium voice.
1. *Indian Serenade* - Shelley - medium voice, Pub
1899 HS, loc in DLC.
2. *To Be a Little Child Once More* - Gertrude Hall
- medium voice, Pub 1901 HS, loc NNrpa.
3. *Rosinella* - A. Mary F. Robinson - medium
voice, Pub 1901 HS, loc NNrpa.

30.    *County Guy* [12] - medium voice by Walter Scott, AF
Ms in early hand.

31.    *Transfiguration* opus 5 [14], c1899 - Mezzo on poem
by AF, AF Ms and revision dated by AF Oct. 1899,
also AF Ms.

32. \*\* P S    *Two Songs For Medium Voice* opus 59a [24] TD
1. *On A Summer Morning* - poem by Belle Willey
Gue. Ms.

2A. c1901 - *Wishing* - poem by Thomas Hood, AF Ms. First perf. 1963 Washington DC by Evelyn Davis, mezzo, with Elizabeth McCausland. 2B. Pencil rev. sketch, AF dated 1941, AF Dr.

33. *** P   *Four Songs*, Opus 14 [25]

*1. A Ruined Garden*, 1902 - High Voice on poem by Philip Bourke Marston, Pub 1902 WW, 1970 AP. First perf. Nov. 22, 1904 in Pasadena, CA by Bessie Ives Harrison, sop. with Alice Coleman, TD

\* S   *2. Love's Secret*, 1904 - William Blake - Mezzo, Pub 1904 WW, 1970 AP. First perf. Dec. 6, 1906 by a Mrs. Norton, s, Mrs. Christie, p, Detroit Fine Arts Society.

\* S   *3. Lost Love*, 1896 - Heinrich Heine - medium voice, Pub 1903 WW, 1909 CL, 1929 GS

\* P   4. *Requiescat*, 1904 - Med. voice on poem by Katherine Ruth Heyman, Pub 1904 WW, 1970 AP. First perf. Nov. 22, 1904 by Bessie Ives Harrison, sop. with Alice Coleman, p.

34.   *American Indian Melodies* [27], c1901-1904 - med. voice and piano, harmonized from the record of original Indian melodies. Some numbers missing or unfinished, AF Ms. See Indian No. 1.

35. \* P   *Folk Songs of the West and South* opus 19 [31], 1905 medium voice, Pub 1905 WW, 1970 AP; loc in CL, MB, NNrpa.

\*\* S   1. "Moanin' Dove" - First known performance April 27, 1906 by Clarence Wilson, baritone, with Heinrich Ashland, p.

\*\* S   2. "De Rocks a-Renderin'" - Perf. same as No. 1.

    **\*\*** S       3. "The Lone Prairie" - First known perf. March 28, 1906, by Bertha Cushing Child at 20th Century Club, Boston, MA.

    **\*** P       4. "The Hours of Grief" - Perf. same as No. 1.

    **\*** P       5. "The Black Face" (La Cara Negra) - First known perf. Feb. 28, 1908, by Armand Crabbe, NY Inst. of Musical Art.

    **\*\*** P      6. "Bird Dance Song" (Cahuilla Tribe) - First known perf. April 1990 by Richard Kassel at Sonneck Society Meeting, Toronto, Canada.

36. **\*** P    *Drake's Drum* opus 22 [34], 1905 - baritone on poem by Henry Newbolt, Pub 1905 WW, 1970 AP; 1st perf. March 5, 1908, by David Bispham, Omaha, NE.

37. **\*\*** P   *The Sea of Sunset* opus 26 [37], 1907 medium voice on poem by Emily Dickinson, Pub 1928 GS; first known perf. 1909 in Boston by Florence Jepperson.

38.       *Bride* opus 31 [41], 1908 - soprano song, listed by AF but unlocated.

39.    P S   *Three Indian Songs* opus 32 [42], 1908 - medium voice, Pub 1912 GS.  First known perf. 1911-1912 concert series of Edward Meade, Baritone.  See also Piano #96.

    **\*** P       1. "Song of the Deathless Voice" - loc CL, NNrpa, R, RU.

    **\***         2. "Inketunga's Thunder Song" - loc DLC, R, RU.

    **\*\*** P S   3A. "The Old Man's Love Song" - loc DLC.
               3B. Choral version, see Choral #165.
               3C. Version for soprano with orchestra, AF Ms score with parts.  Scoring: W - 2-2-2-1; B - 4-2-2-1; Tmp. Hp; Str - 6-5-3-3-3.

40.     *It Was a Long and a Tiresome Go* [43], c1908 - medium voiced cowboy folksong recorded and harmonized by AF, AF Ms.

41.     *Up on the Trail* [44] - cowboy folksong recorded and harmonized by AF, but words missing. AF Ms.

42.     *Wunct in My Saddle* [45] - medium voice, a variation of "Streets of Laredo", melody recorded by AF, still to be harmonized. Five stanzas of words.

43. * P  *The Farewell* opus 33 [47], c1909 - baritone on poem by Robert Burns, Pub 1911 WW, 1970 AP. First known performance Dec. 7, 1911, by Mr. Hermes with Mrs. M. E. Blanchard, p., at American Music Society recital in Colorado Springs.

44. **P  *Sea Vision* opus 36 [50], 1912 - High voice on poem "Duandon" by George Sterling, AF Ms and Repr Ms. See also entry #45.

45.     *Duandon* opus 34 [51], voice with orch. - unlocated except citation in The Art of Music, Vol. IV, Nat'l. Society of Music, Inc., N.Y. 1915. See #44.

46.     *Three Poems by Percy Bysshe Shelley* opus 43 [58], 1914 - Pub 1914 GS. TD
  *       1. "Bridal Song" - high voice.
  * P     2. "On a Faded Violet" - medium or high voice.
  * P     3. "Daughter of Ocean" - medium or high voice.

47. *   *Three Songs from Caliban* opus 47a [65], 1916 - for Medium Voice.
        1. "Come Unto These Yellow Sands" - Shakespeare - unknown except choral version in opus 47 [64], in Pageants #171.
        2. "Under The Greenwood Tree" - Shakespeare - as in No. 1 above. TD

3. "Many Are The Wonders Of Time" - Sophocles
- translated by Percy MacKaye, medium voice.
3A. With piano accompaniment - AF Ms.
3B. Chorus with orchestra - see #87.

48. *     *Four Songs for Community Singing* opus 51 [70] -
Main entry Choral #173.
4. Our Country's Prayer - Carl Roppel - Pub JC
1919.
4B. For low voice.
4C. For high voice.

49. * P   *Soldier, Soldier* opus 53 [72], 1919 - AF verse -
baritone, Pub 1920 JC with note: "Orchestration
may be had from publisher."

50.       *Up and Away!* [73], c1919 - H. C. Nutting - medium
voice, AF Ms. See also Choral #174

51.       *Three Songs* opus 54 [74], 1919 - medium voice, Pub
1920 JC.
  *       1. "Love's Cathedral" - James Grun.
  * P     2. "The Wild Flower's Song" - William Blake.
          3. "Cold on the Plantation" - Frank L. Stanton.

52.       *Three Songs for Soprano* opus 56 [76], poems by AF.
  * P     1. "Passion of Sunrise" c1920 - Pub 1929 GS.
          2. "By Golden Streams" c1903 - AF Ms.
          3. "Twilight Memory" - unlocated, unknown.

53. *     *Five Songs for Community Singing* opus 57 [78], 1920
- Unison or solo versions - Main entry Choral #177
1A. "We Will Be Free" - James Thompson -
Medium voice, AF Ms.
1B-1. Undated revise, AF Dr.
1B-2. Finished variant of B-1, med. voice, AF Ms.
1C. Third revise, 1946, AF Dr.
1D-1. High Voice, c1950, Pub PP, AF Repr. Ms.

1D-2. Low Voice, c1950, Pub PP, AF Repr Ms.
4. "Any Time For Singing", c1920 - poet unknown, medium voice, AF Ms.
5. "Sing Awhile Longer", c1920 - Edwin Markham, medium voice, AF Ms.

54. **\*\*\*** P S *Spanish Songs of Old California* opus 59 [80], c1922 - Pub 1923 PP, repub 1929 GS, recorded and translated by Charles F. Lummis, transcribed 1904-05 and harmonized over years through 1922 by AF. English and Spanish, good also for school and community singing; some have two parts, high and medium, others medium voice. Kept in print by, and available from, Southwest Museum, Los Angeles.
   1. "La Hamaca" TD
   2. "La Barquillera"
   3. "El Quelele"
   4. "La Noche 'sta Serena"
   5. "El Capotin"
   6. "Chata Cara de Bule"
   7. "Pena Hueca"
   8. "El Zapatero"
   9. "La Primavera"
   10. "Mi Pepa"
   11. "Es El Amor Mariposa"
   12. "La Magica Mujer"
   13. "El Charro"
   14. "Adios, Adios, Amores"

55. **\*\*** S *Song of the Holy Virgin* opus 60 [84], 1922 - M. Maeterlink - contralto, AF Ms, main entry #202

56. *Sonnet to a City* opus 64 [88], 1922 - from "Pasadena" by Celeste Turner, soprano, AF Ms.

57. 1922 - *Petal Lips* [91], 1922 by Rosalyn Martin - mezzo, AF Ms.

58. **\*\* P**     *Two Poems by Emily Dickinson* opus 66 [92] 1923, mezzo, pub 1926 GS; perf. unknown until April 16, 1975, No. 1 broadcast by David Barron, baritone with Neely Bruce, piano, from WQXR, New York, N.Y., on Robert Sherman's "The Listening Room."
1. "I Shall Know Why" TD, RU.
2. "Resurgam" TD

59. **\*\* P**     *Three Songs for Medium Voice* opus 69 [95], 1924 - Indian poems by Charles O. Roos.
1. "The Ravens Are Singing" - Pub 1929 GS. First known perf. 1963, by Evelyn Davis, mezzo, Elizabeth McCausland, piano, Washington DC. TD, RU.
2. "A Dawn Song" - Pub 1929 GS. First known perf. April 1990 by Judith Auer, mezzo, Alex Craig, piano, in Boulder, CO. RU, TD
3. "Dark Her Lodge Door" - Pub 1927 OD. loc NNrpa. First known perf. same as #58, RU.

60.            *Two Shelley Songs* opus 72 [98], 1926 - medium voice.
     **\*\* P**     1A. "Song of Proserpine" - with piano, Pub 1943 GS, loc NNrpa. TD
1B. With orchestra, see # 88.
2. "To Night" - AF Ms, with note: Revise of early student effort.

61. **\*\* P**     *Two Emily Dickinson Poems* opus 73 [99], 1926 - mezzo, Pub 1928 GS. TD
1. "Summer Shower". First known perf. 1963 by same as #59, No. 1.
2. Mine.

62.            *Three Desert Songs* opus 74 [101], 1927 - mezzo on poems of James Sheridan, AF Draft sketches only.
1. "The Desert"
2. "The Desert Flower" - music only, words missing.

3. "The Rain Cloud"

63.             *Four Children's Songs* opus 75 [102], 1927 - AF Ms.
1. "The Fairies" - William Allingham.
2. "Day's End" - Henry Newbolt.

   **        3. "Calico Pie" - Edward Lear - AF pencil draft. First known perf. June 24, 1941, Mary Frances Lehnerts, Mezzo, George Trovillo, p. in NYC.
4. "Afternoon on a Hill" - Edna St. V. Millay

   ** P S    A. Revised and Pub 1945 GM. First known perf. 1955 by Evelyn Davis, mezzo, Beth Thewlis, p, Washington DC. TD
B. AF original version, AF Ms., preferred by AF

64.             *Two Songs on Poems by William Blake* opus 88 [114], 1930 - mezzo, Pub 1936 AF. First known perf. 1963 by same as #59, 1 above. TD

   ** P S    1. A. "The Lamb" - from Blake's "Songs of Innocence". RU
1B. "The Lamb" - mixed quartet or chorus - see 5. Choral, #188.

   ** P S    2. "A Cradle Song" - from Blake's "Songs of Experience." RU

65.             *Invocation to the Sun God* opus 89 [115], 1930 - baritone on poem by Charles O. Roos, AF Ms.

66.             *Arbutus* [117], 1930 - mezzo, on poem by Will Carlton, AF Dr, pencil sketch only, words missing.

67. * S    *Grace* [122], 1931 - medium voice - AF Ms.
A. Set on anonymous verse, for evening.
B. With AF words, for Christmas.

68. ** P    *The Tyger* opus 98 [128], 1934 - Wm. Blake - mezzo, AF Ms, student perf. March 3, 1976, by Jill Feldman, s, Stephen Kelly, p. Santà Barbara, CA. TD RU

69.          *DKE Waltz* [129], 1935 - Burges Johnson - Medium
             voice.
             A. - AF arrangement of music by Lewis S.
             Thompson, AF Ms.
             B. - AF's own music, same words, AF Dr.

70..         *Fog From the Pacific* opus 99 [130], 1935 - Randolph
             Leigh - Medium voice, AF Ms.

71.    P     *The Hound of Heaven* opus 100 [131], 1935 - Francis
             Thompson - baritone. TD
             A. Voice and piano score, AF Ms.
             B. With orchestra - see entry #89, B.

72.  ** P    *Four Emily Dickinson Songs* opus 101 [134], 1936 -
             Pub 1983 BH.
             1. "Savior" - medium voice, 1st known perf. 1991,
             by Martha Peabody, sop. and Aki Shimatsu
             GIfford, p. in Cambridge, MA.
             2. "Unto Me" - medium voice, 1st known perf.
             1963 by same as #59, 1, Washington D.C. TD RU
             3. "As If the Sea" - high voice, 1st known perf.
             April 16, 1975 by David Barron, baritone, Neely
             Bruce, p. from WQXR, "The Listening Room."
             4. "Good Morning, Midnight" - high voice. TD RU

73.  ** P    *Twelve Emily Dickinson Songs* opus 105 [137], 1938-
             1941 -Pub 1983 BH.
             1. "How The Sun Rose" - medium voice.
             2. "Safe in Their Alabaster Chambers" - med., 1st
             known perf. July 29, 1975, Paul Sperry, t. Martin
             Katz, p. at Amherst, MA. Song Festival. R. TD
             3. "The Sabbath" - medium voice, 1st known perf.
             1964 by Evelyn Davis, mezzo, Elizabeth
             McCausland, p. Washington D.C. TD
             4. "These Saw Vision" - mezzo, also pub 1944 GA,
             first known perf. 1945 by Natalie Haley, contralto,
             Alice Wightman, p. in NYC. TD

5. "I Never Saw a Moor" - mezzo, 1st known perf. by same as No. 3.

6. "The Little Tippler" - mezzo, first known perf. 1985 by Judith Auer, mezzo, with Michele Schmeiding, p. at Tulsa, OK. TD

7. "Aristocracy" - medium voice, first known perf. with No. 2 above. R.

8. "The Test" - medium voice.

9. "Summer's Armies" - high voice, first known perf. with No. 2 above. R, TD.

10. "The Level Bee" - high voice, first known perf. with No. 2 above. R.

11. "With A Flower" - medium voice, first known perf. March 1966 by Linda Kiemel, sop., Daniel Grundlach, p. at U. of Illinois, Champaign.

12. "Presentiment" - medium voice, first known perf. April 16, 1975, David Barron with Neely Bruce on WQXR, N.Y. R RU

74. ** P  *Four Emily Dickinson Songs* opus 107 [144], 1941-1944 - Pub 1983 BH.

1. "On This Long Storm" - medium voice.

2. "Tie the Strings to My Life" - high voice, 1st known perf. 1965 by Evelyn Davis, mezzo, Elizabeth McCausland, p. Washington, DC. R, TD.

3. "On This Wondrous Sea" - high voice, 1st known perf. same as for No. 72, 2 above. TD

4. "Blazing In Gold" - high voice.

75.  *God of Battles* [145], 1943 - medium voice, poem by Gen. George S. Patton, Jr., AF Ms.

76. ** P  *Ten Emily Dickinson Songs* opus 108 [147], c1944 - Pub 1983 BH.

1. "Heart, We Will Forget Him" - med. voice, 1st known perf. April 22, 1974 by Winifred Black, sop., James Kosnik, p. at Buffalo, N.Y. RU. TD

2. "The Butterfly", medium voice, first known perf. July 29, 1975 by Paul Sperry with Martin Katz at Amherst MA. Song Festival. R.
3. "I Never Felt at Home Below" - medium voice.
4. "And I'm a Rose!" - high voice, first perf. same as No. 1. RU.
5. "The Sea Said, 'Come' to the Brook" - high vc.
6. "We Should Not Mind so Small a Flower" - medium voice.
7. "Ample Make This Bed" - medium voice, first known perf. same as No. 2 above. R. TD
8. "I'm Nobody, Who Are You?" - med. voice, first known perf. 1965 by Evelyn Davis, mezzo, Elizabeth McCausland, p., Washington, DC. R, RU TD.
9. "Papa Above!" - medium voice, first known perf. April 16, 1975 by David Barron with Neely Bruce on WQXR, N. Y.  R, TD.
10. "Dropped Into the Ether Acre" - high voice.

77.     *Three Patriotic Songs* [148], 1943 - medium voice, AF Ms.
1. "We Want Straight Talk"
2. "Lend a Hand"
3. "Let's Go"

78. * P     *A Soldier's Explanation* [149], c1943 - medium voice on poem by H. I. Phillips, Repr Ms.

79.     *Studies Toward a National Anthem* [150], 1944 - words and music by AF, same melody for both, AF Ms. See also Choral #192.
1A. "One World" - A. medium voice with piano.
2A. "America's Vow" - A. med. voice with piano.

80.     *Five Agnes M. Stanko Songs* [156], 1943-1948 -AF Ms. TD
1A. "Millions of Souls" - A. high voice.
2. "Soldiers Are Calling" - medium voice.

3. "Sun Song" - medium voice.
4. "Mother in Paradise" - medium voice, pencil sketch only.
5. "Light in the Darkness" - medium voice.

81.  P  *The Mouse Whose Name Is Time*, [146] 1948 - med. voice on poem by Robert Francis, AF Ms.

82.  ** P  *Three Emily Dickinson Songs* opus 112 [159], 1949 - Pub 1983 BH. TD
1. "Wild Nights! Wild Nights!" - high voice, first known perf. 1984 by Judith Auer, mezzo, Michele Schmeiding, p. at Tulsa, OK. Austrian premiere, 1985 by Melody Long Anglin, sop. Robert Theime, p. at American Institute of Musical Studies, Graz.
2. "The Grass So Little Has To Do" med. voice first known perf. July 29, 1975 by Paul Sperry, t. Martin Katz, p, at Amherst Song Festival. R
3. "An Awful Tempest Mashed the Air", high voice.

83.  ** P  *I Had No Time to Hate* [160], 1949 - medium voice on Emily Dickinson poem, Pub 1983 BH, first known perf. March 1986 by Linda Kiemel, s., Daniel Gundlach, p, at U. of Illinois, Champaign.

84.  *After All!* [165] - high or med. voice, AF Ms.

85.  *Priestess Rose*, 1940s, poem by Betty Richardson Farwell; AF Ms.

## B. With Orchestra

86.  *Duandon* opus 34 [51] - high voice with orchestra, noted in "The Art of Music," vol IV, Nat'l. Society of Music, Inc., New York, N. Y., 1915, p. 412, but unlocated. See related vocal solo op. 36 [50], #45.

87.    *Three Songs from Caliban for Medium Voice* opus 47a [65], 1916.

\*    3A. "Many Are The Wonders Of Time" - Sophocles, translated by Percy MacKaye, medium voice. With small orchestra - score AF Ms, parts Ms Var, scoring: W - 1-1-2; B - 2-2-1; Tmp; S - 8-4-1-3-2.
3C. Revised for SATB and full orchestra, see in Choral entry #171 and Pageants #208.

88.    *Two Shelley Songs* opus 72 [98], 1926 - medium voice, performance unknown.

\*\* P    1B. "Song of Proserpine" - with orchestra, score AF Ms, parts needed, scoring: W - 2-1-1-3-2; B - 2-1; Tmp; Std. Str. to balance.

89.   P   *The Hound of Heaven* opus 100 [131], 1935 - Francis Thompson - Repr Ms.

B. For tenor narrator, high baritone, and choir of 2 soprano, alto voices with orchestra - unfinished score: W - 1-1-2-1; B - 2-2-1; Tmp, Hp; voices; std. str. to bal.

### 3. Piano Music

### A. Solo

90.   S   *Regrets* [1], 1893 - "First composition of A.F." (So marked by AF. It is presumed this is the first he felt worth keeping.) - AF Ms. TD
A. Original draft, dated 7-5-1893
B. Revision, much later but undated.

91. \* S   *Tone Pictures After Pastels In Prose* opus 7 [3], 1895 - with the prose pastels, 21 pages, Pub PP, 1895. TD

92.   S   *Northern Song* [6], c1897 - pub OD, 1897.

93.  S     *Romance* [7], c1897 - pub OD, 1897.

94.        *Sonata* opus 6 [15], 1899 - "unfinished" (One mov't. done), AF Ms. Program for AF lecture-recital Mar. 25, 1903 shows "Adagio from Sonata in E Flat" by AF, played by AF, which might be from this effort. The work is in E Flat.

95. *  P S  *Owasco Memories* opus 8 [16], 1899.
            1. "Spring Moods"
            2. "By Moonlight"
            3. "By Quiet Waters"
            4. "The Casino Across the Lake"
            5. "Autumn Comes". TD
            A. For Piano, Pub. WW 1907, 1970 AP; loc in CL, MB, NNrpa. First known perf. Mrs. Robert D. Garver, Topeka, Kansas May Festival, May 3, 1909. Revived March 8, 1985, by Donald F. Reinhold playing a *Wa-Wan Press Sampler* at the Sonneck Society Conference in Tallahassee. TD
            B. Arr. for piano, violin & 'cello, 1901. See #138 Chamber Music. Premiere perf. 1922, Pasadena, CA. RU.

96. ** P S  *American Indian Melodies* opus 11 [18], 1900, harmonized from the original Indian, pub 1901 WW, 1970 AP; loc in CL, MB, MH. Premiere Fall Term, 1900 at Cornell University by AF. R RU TD
            1. "Approach of the Thunder God".
            2. "The Old Man's Love Song".
            3. "Song of the Deathless Voice".
            4. "Ichibuzzhi".
            5. "The Mother's Vow".
            6. "Inketunga's Thunder Song".
            7. "Song of the Ghost Dance".
            8. "Song to the Spirit".
            9. "Song of the Leader".
            10. "Choral".

97. * P    *Symbolistic Study No. 1, "Toward the Dream"* opus
           16 [20], 1901 - Pub 1904 WW, 1970 AP; loc in MB,
           NNrpa. First known perf. May 9, 1905, by Katherine
           Ruth Heyman at Norwalk, Conn.

98. *** P   *Dawn* opus 12 [21], 1901 - fantasy for piano on two
           Indian themes - 1901 - Pub 1902 WW, 1970 AP; loc
           in CL, MB, NNrpa. First known perf. Feb. 13, 1903
           by AF at Patria Club, New York. TD
               A. 1940 - Arranged by John Kirkpatrick, Ms,
               played by Kirkpatrick on tour 1941.
               B. 1904 - for Orchestra - See Orch. #219.
               C. Revised orchestral version, c1909 - RU.

99. * P S   *Ichibuzzhi* opus 13 [22], c1902 - based on Indian
           melody first harmonized by Farwell in opus 11 [18],
           Pub 1902 WW, 1970 AP; loc in CL, MB, MH,
           NNrpa. Perf. Feb. 13, 1903 by AF, Patria Club, New
           York. TD

100. ** P   *The Domain of Hurakan* opus 15 [23], 1902.
               A. For piano - Pub 1902 WW, 1970 AP; loc in
               CL, MB, NNrpa. First European perf. Nov. 23,
               c1902 in London by Katherine Ruth Heyman.
               She also played first known American perf. on
               Nov. 11, 1903 in Tarrytown, NY. T - 9:17, RU,
               TD
               B. For Orchestra - See Orch. #220
                   C. *Nocturne*, opus 23, 1906 - "abandoned Ms,"
               may have been arr. from *The Domain of Hurakan*,
               per program performed Nov. 13, 1906 by Lee K.
               Smith, found in AF scrapbook. *The Domain of
               Hurakan* does have a section which AF's notes
               refer to as" nocturnal" in mood.

101. ** P   *Navajo War Dance No. 2* opus 29 [28], c1904 (per
           AF). TD
               A. Original AF Ms, marked with notations.

         B. Version ed. by John Kirkpatrick 1940, Pub 1947
         MP. First perf. 1940 John Kirkpatrick. T - 2:36, R.

102. **\*\*** P    *Symbolistic Study No. 2, "Perhelion" (sic)* opus 17 [29],
         1904 - Two AF Mss with different endings. He
         noted on one that he started to orchestrate, but
         never completed it. TD

103. **\*\*** P    *From Mesa And Plain* opus 20 [32], c1905 - Piano
         version Pub 1905 WW, 1970 AP; loc in CL, MB,
         NNrpa. First known perf. of whole opus (piano
         version) Dec. 30, 1909 by Grace Lord at American
         Music Society, Colorado Springs. Selections played
         earlier.
         1A. "Navajo War Dance" (AF: obsolete) Pub WW.

   **\*\*** P    1B. "Navajo War Dance" - new ending adds 39
         bars, also Pub WW & re-issued GS 1912. (Known
         as Navajo War Dance No. 1.) AF Ms loc in
         NNrpa. First known perf. March 8, 1906 at Smith
         College. T - 2:18, R.

   **\*\*** P S    2A. "Prairie Miniature" - piano, pub WW. TD
         2B. "Prairie Miniature" - woodwind quintet, see
         Chamber #139. RU
         3. "Plantation Melody" - pub WW.

   S    4A. "Wa-Wan Choral" - piano - pub WW. RU
         4B. Choral - "Around The Lodge" - violin & piano
         - See Chamber #149.
         5A. "Pawnee Horses" - piano - pub WW. First
         known perf. Oct. 26, 1908, by Noble Kreider in
         Sargentville, ME.

   **\*\*\*** P    5B. "Pawnee Horses" - edited and fingered by John
         Kirkpatrick - pub GS 1944. First performance
         Jan. 12, 1942, New York, by John Kirkpatrick.
         R, RU, TD

104. **\*** S    *Impressions of the Wa-Wan Ceremony of the Omahas*
         opus 21 [33], 1905 - Pub 1905 WW, 1970 AP; loc

in CL, MB, NNrpa, performed by AF on his 1905
western tour.
1. "Receiving the Messenger".
2. "Nearing the Village" RU, T - 1:18.
3. "Song of Approach".
4. "Laying Down the Pipes".
5. "Raising the Pipes".
6. "Invocation".
7. "Song of Peace".
8. "Chorale". TD

105.          *Nocturne* [23], 1906 - Unknown Ms discarded by AF,
              may have been arr. from #100 - The Domain of
              Hurakan, above, per a performance program for
              Nov. 3, 1906 by Lee K. Smith in AF scrapbook,
              which listed the Farwell work, "Nocturne."

106.          *Symbolistic Study No. 4, "Wa-Wan"* opus 24 [35], 1906
              - Unfinished AF Ms.

107. *         *The Distant Warrior* [46], c1909 - Pub Sept., 1909
              issue of The Circle, loc in NN Periodicals Collection.

108.          *Fugue Fantasy* opus 44 [59], 1914.
                 A. string quintet - unfinished AF Ms -
                 Instrumental and Chamber #140.
    ** P         B. *Indian Fugue Fantasy*, 1938  - revised from A.
                 for piano - AF Ms loc in NNrpa.  Both A and
                 B versions based on an Omaha Indian theme. TD

109. ** P     *Two Poems for Pianoforte* opus 45 [60], c1915 - Pub
              singly 1923 CF.
                 1. "Treasured Deeps" - AF Ms. TD
                 2. "Flame Voiced Night" - AF Ms. TD

110. ** P     *Laughing Piece* [63], 1914 - AF Ms as revised in
              1940.

111.  P  *Modal Inventions* opus 68 [94], 1923 - AF Ms, four conceived, but 1. "Dorian" is the only one found.

112.  *Americana* opus 78 [104] - Selections dated separately.
    1. "Rarin' to Go", 1927 - AF Ms as revised in 1938.
S  2A. "Walk on de Water", 1927 - AF Ms.
S  2B. "Plantation Plaint", 1943 - rev. 2A, AF Ms.
*** P  3. "Sourwood Mountain", 1927 - Pub 1930 GS, first known perf. in 1940s by Jeanne Behrend on South American tour, R, RU; T - 4:14, TD

113. ** S  *Melody in E Minor* opus 77 [105], 1928 -
    A. For violin and piano - see Chamber #151
S  B. Piano solo version - AF Ms.

114. ** S  *Dream Flower* opus 79 [106], 1928 - Pub 1941 GS. TD

115. ** P  *Two Poems for Pianoforte* opus 82 [109], 1929 - Premiere by Seta Kashakarian, Merkin Hall, New York, June 3, 1986.
    1A. "Dream Tides" - AF Ms.
    1B. "Lyric Tides" - AF Ms.
    2. "Thwarted Current" - AF Ms. T - 4:46, RU TD

116.  *Pastorale* opus 83 [110], 1930 - lost, unknown listed piano work.

117. ** P  *What's In an Octave?* opus 84 [111], 1930 - AF Ms. First known perf. April 16, 1975 by Neely Bruce, WQXR live broadcast from "The Listening Room," New York, N.Y. T - 8:06, RU, TD.

118. ** P  *In the Tetons, Suite* opus 86 [112], 1930 - AF Ms, Selections 1 -5 Loc in NNrpa, and 1 - 9 in author's collection.

1. "Granite and Ice" (Time 4:10).
2. "Lonely Camp Fire" (4:45).
3. "Arduous Trail" (3:31).
4. "Wild Flower" 3:18).
5. "The Peaks at Night" (4:07).
6. "Wind Play" (2:29).
7. "Northern Lights" (AF draft sketch only).
8. "Big Country" (4:46).
9. "Mountains and Clouds" (unfinished). Conceived to become two suites, but if merged, composer suggests No. 6 should precede No. 5. Premiere Nov. 16, 1990 by David Vayo at Connecticut College, New London, Conn. for all numbers except "Peaks at Night" which was perf. Jan.2, 1939, by Frances Schmidt in Allentown, PA. RU.

**S          A. *Purple Lupine* [113], 1930 - Version of 4. *Wild Flower* of opus 86 [112] as Pub 1941 GS. Transposed, simplified piano version pub GS in "Piano Pieces from the Early Grades."
B. Arranged for Vc & Piano. See Instr.#153 C.

119. ** P          *Vale of Enitharmon* opus 91 [116], 1930 - Pub AF 1935, also draft Ms with revision notes. First known perf. by Noble Kreider c1936. TD

120. ** P          *Two Compositions for Piano* opus 93 [124], 1932 - AF Ms.
1. "Emanation".
2. "Fire Principle".

121. ** P          *Four Meditations* opus 97 [127], 1934 - AF Ms numbered without titles. A student perf. 1948 of No. 1, by Florence Vantella at Juilliard School of Music, NYC.

122. ** P          *Altar Gift* [132], c1930s - AF Ms.

123. **P  *Prelude and Fugue* opus 94 [121], 1936 - AF Ms of Fugue dated 1931 and of Prelude dated 1936. TD

124. **P  *Two Tone-Pictures for Piano* opus 104 [133], 1936 - AF Ms.
    1. "Pastel".
    2. "Marine".

125. **S  *Line Study* [139], 1939 - AF Ms. TD

126. **S  *Happy Moment* [140], c1939 - AF Ms  TD.

127.  *Pastorale* [141], 1940 - on two themes written by AF in 1895, AF pencil Ms. (No indication whether this relates to lost and unknown opus 83 [110] of same title in 1930, #116 above.)

128. **S  *Two Little Poems for Piano* opus 106 [142], 1942.
    1. "Girl Singing" - Pub 1944 GS.
    2. "Strange Dream" - AF Ms.  TD

129.  S  *For Cynthia* [143], 1942 - AF Ms.

130. **P  *Polytonal Studies* opus 109 [151], 1940-1952 - etudes with treble clef in a key other than in bass clef. AF draft study of abstract key relations preserved; 46 relations planned, 23 completed. First known perf. Oct. 29, 1941 by Hazel Griggs at Carnegie Chamber Music Hall, New York, of Nos. 2, 9 and 26. Neely Bruce has played others, much later. ($^T$ indicates the tonic)
    1. $I^T$ - $V^T$ in keys of C and G. TD
    2. $I^T$ - $IV^T$ in G and C.
    3. $I^T$ - $VI^T$ in C and A.
    4. $I^T$ - $III^T$ in A-flat and C. TD
    5. $I^T$ - $II^T$ in G-flat and A-flat. TD
    6. $I^T$ - $VII^T$ in C and B.  TD
    7. $I^T$ - $II^T$ in C and D-flat.

8. $I^T$ - flat $III^T$ in C and E-flat. TD
9. $I^T$ - flat $V^T$ in G and D-flat.
10. $I^T$ - flat $VI^T$ in D and B-flat. TD
11. $I^T$ - flat $VII^T$ in F and E flat.
12. $I^T$ - $V^T$ in C minor and G minor.
13. $I^T$ - $IV^T$ in C minor and G minor. TD
14. $I^T$ - flat $VI^T$ in B minor and G minor.
15. $I^T$ - flat $III^T$ in C minor and E-flat minor. TD
16. $I^T$ - $II^T$ in D minor and E minor.
17. $I^T$ - $VII^T$ in F minor and E minor. TD
18. $I^T$ - $II^T$ in F minor and F-sharp minor.
19. $I^T$ - maj. $III^T$ in G minor and B-natural, minor. TD
20. $I^T$ - plus $V^T$ in E-flat minor and A minor. TD
21. $I^T$ - maj. $VI^T$ in B-flat minor and G minor.
26. Keys of D-flat major and F minor.
34. Keys of E-flat major and E-flat minor.

131. ** P S    *Melody in D Minor* [157], 1948 - AF Ms. TD

132. ** P    *Sonata for Piano* opus 113 [161], 1948 - in one movement - Repr Ms, first known public perf. April 16, 1975, by Neely Bruce in WQXR broadcast from "The Listening Room," NYC. T - 11:30. RU, TD.

133. ** S    *Palm Tree Daughters,* AF Ms. Versions in two keys (same sound). "Inspired by a poem in Mark Van Doren's *World Anthology*." Probably early work. TD

134.    *Fantasie on a Turkish Air* [166] - AF Ms, probably an early work. TD

## B. Piano with Other Instruments and Organ Music

135. ** P    *Symbolistic Study No. 6 opus 37 [52], 1912-1938 - Mountain Vision.*
A. Piano solo, 1912 - AF Ms.

B. Two piano revision with unscored orchestra arrangement, 1931 - concerto form, AF Ms.

**P     C. Arrangement for two pianos with string orchestra, 1938 - Details in Orch. #226. Premiere broadcast from Columbia network, May 26, 1939, as prizewinning work in N.F.M.C. competition. Howard Barlow conducted the Columbia Orchestra, Karl Ulrich Schnabel, 1st p., Helen Vogel, 2nd p. T - 16:52, RU-DLC, TD

136.   P    *The Pilgrimage Play* opus 58 [79], 1920-1921 - Main entry Pageant #199 for complete organ score, integrated with orchestra and vocal elements of this production.

137.**P    *Quintet in E Minor for piano and strings* opus 103 [136], 1937. Main entry Chamber #145. R, TD

### 4. Chamber and Instrumental Music

## A. Ensembles

138.**P S    *Owasco Memories,* opus 8 [16], 1901. B. Arr. for piano, violin and 'cello, AF Ms. Premiere perf. March 13, 1922, by Sarah Coleman Bragdon, P., Reginald Bland, V., Axel Simonsen Vc., at Pasadena, CA. Other performances unknown until May 1, 1976, Berkeley, CA, by Ronald Erickson, V., Julie Steinberg, P., Amy Radner, Vc. See Piano #95. RU; T - 9:02, TD.

139.**P S    *From Mesa and Plain* opus 20 [32], 1905 - No. 2. "Prairie Miniature" - woodwind quintet, Repr Ms. See also entries in Piano #103 and #149 for two instr., RU; T - 1:30, TD.

140.     *Fugue Fantasy* opus 44 [59], 1914 - string quintet, AF Ms, unfinished. See Piano #108, Indian #15.

141. ** P   *The Gods of the Mountain* opus 52 [68], 1917 -
            Incidental music for the play by Lord Dunsany. TD
            A. Original trio version, Harp, V and Vc, AF Ms,
            premiere at Portmanteau Theatre, Carnegie Hall,
            New York, 1917.
            B. Revised 1917 for V, Vc and P, AF Ms.
            Premiere perf. March 13, 1922, by same group as
            #138 in Pasadena, CA. TD
            C. See main entry in Orch. #232.

142. ** P   *The Hako* opus 65 [89], 1922 - String quartet in A
            major, AF Ms at NNrpa, premiere by Zoellner
            Quartet at Ojai, CA, Music Festival 1923. TD

143.        *Symphonic Song on Old Black Joe* opus 67 [93], 1923
            Main entry in Choral #184.
            C. Trio arrangement - AF unfinished draft.

144. ** P   "Mystery for Strings" opus 90 [119], 1931 - An
            Interlude in *Mountain Song*, also appropriate for
            independent program use.  Premiere Sept. 1937, at
            the Spa Theater, Saratoga Springs, NY, by 24 strings
            of the NY Philharmonic.  Main entry Orch. #229.

145. ** P   *Quintet in E Minor* opus 103 [136], 1937 - For piano
            and strings - AF Ms at NNrpa, first known perf.
            Dec. 13, 1939 by Composer's Forum Quartet and
            Erich Weill, p. in NYC. T - 36:16, R, TD

## B. One or Two Instruments

146.  S     *Ballade for Violin and Piano* opus 1 [11], 1898 - Pub
            1899 HS.

147. *      *American Indian Melodies* opus 11 [18], 1900 - Main
            entry Piano #96.  Programs from Wa-Wan years
            show several of these 8 melodies played by AF on
            violin with piano accompaniment.  Selection titles

not given, nor is there music preserved for these
versions.

148.   S   *To Morfydd* [26], 1903 - Oboe and Piano - Pub 1903
WW, 1970 AP.   TD

149.   S   *From Mesa and Plain* opus 20 [32], 1905 - No. 4.
"Wa-Wan Choral, Around the Lodge" - V-P, AF Ms.
No. 2 of this opus in Ensembles #139; Main entry
Piano #103.   TD

150.   P S   *Song Flight* opus 61 [85], 1922 - V-P, Pub CF 1923.
First known perf. Nov. 16, 1922, Sol Cohen in Los
Angeles.   TD

151. * S   *Melody in E Minor* opus 77 [105], 1928.
A. V-P, pub 1936 AF, first known perf. Feb 21,
1938 by Harold Smith, V, at concert of Peoples
Symphony Orchestra, Lansing, Mich. TD
B. Piano solo version - AF Ms, #113.

152. ** P   *Sonata for Violin and Piano* opus 80 [107], 1927, rev.
1935 - AF Ms 1927 at NNrpa, Repr Ms 1935,
premiere 1936, Morris Hochberg, V, Sylvia Hochberg
p, Mich. State College, E. Lansing.   TD.

153. ** P S   *Purple Lupine* opus 86 [113], 1930 (a variant version
of *Wild Flower*, in opus 86 [112].   See Piano #118)
- B. Arr. for Vc-P by Richard Clayton, Ms. Var.,
premiere by Richard Clayton, date unknown.

154. ** P   *Land of Luthany* opus 87 [118], 1931 - 'cello and
piano, pub 1933 AF.   First perf. Dec. 28, 1931 by
Alexander Schuster, vc., Archie Black, p. R, RU, TD

155. ** P   *Eothen* opus 92 [120], 1931 - V-P, AF Ms. TD

156. ** P    *Sonata in G Minor* opus 96 [126], 1934 - V Solo, 4
             movements, AF Dr, Premiere c1938, Morris
             Hochberg, U. Mich., May 1, 1976, Ronald Erickson,
             Berkeley, CA, T - 16:15 RU, TD.

157. ** P    *Suite for Flute and Piano* opus 114 [162], 1949.
             1. "Woodland Colloquy"
             2. "Nocturn" - Repr Ms pub GF 1972, first known
             perf. Feb. 22, 1987 by Patricia Harper, fl, Leander
             Dean, p, Conn. College, New London, T - 9:59,
             RU, TD

158. ** P    *Sonata for Violoncello and Piano* opus 116 [163] 1950
             - Repr Ms, first known perf. April 28, 1950 by
             Richard Clayton, Vc, Kathryn Clayton, P, Artist
             Concert Series, Lafayette, Ga, T - 22:39, R, TD


## 5. Choral and Community Singing Music

        Included are a capella, orchestra, and piano or organ
accompaniment forms.

159. * S     *Two Choruses* opus 10 [19], 1901 - Pub 1901 CB.
             1. "Build Thee More Stately Mansions" - Oliver
             W. Holmes, SATB, loc at NNrpa, DLC., Pub 1901
             CB in The Laurel Song Book.
             2. "Daybreak" - loc unknown, not in collection.

160. * S     *Two Indian Songs*, 1901 - Frederick Manley - SATB,
             adapted from *Amer. Ind. Melodies* #96, 2 and 7, Pub
             1901 CB in *The Laurel Song Book*.  TD

161.         *American Indian Melodies* [27], c1901-1904 - 18
             melodies in Vocal Solo main entry, #34, one has
             choral arrangement: 8. "Omaha Tribal Prayer" -
             SATB and piano.

162. S      *Wanderer's Night Song* opus 27 [38], 1907 - Longfellow tr. (Goethe), male quartet, AF Ms.

163. S      *Keramos* opus 28 [39], 1907 - Longfellow.
         A. Male quartet, AF Ms. AF noted he must revise this to correspond with improvements made in doing it as a mixed chorus.
    P      B. *Keramos* c1949 - SATB with S & T solos, pub 1952 RE.

164.      *How Beautiful Is Night* opus 30 [40], 1907.
         A. Mixed chorus on poem attributed to Robert Southey, Pub 1907 SB.
         B. *Night in the Desert* - Choral version of same song, SATB, Pub 1923 SB in A Book of Choruses, G. W. Chadwick et al., eds. Copy not located.

165. **P S      *Three Indian Songs* opus 32 [42], 1908 - Main entry in Vocal #39, 3. B. - "The Old Man's Love Song" - SATB, AF Ms. See also entry #190 opus 102 [135]

166. *      *Hymn to Liberty* opus 35 [48], 1910 - AF verse - SATB, Pub 1911 WW, premiere at NYC. July 4 City Celebration, 1911 by United German Singers. Loc in NNrpa. TD
    * P      A. Orchestra and SATB version, c1910 - AF Ms. Scoring: W - 3-2-1-2-2; B - 4-3-3-1; Tmp, LD, Cym; std. str., Score AF Ms, parts Ms Var.

167. P      *O Captain, My Captain* opus 34 [49], 1912 - Walt Whitman, SATB, Pub 1918 JC, loc in DLC. TD

168. * S      *The Christ Child's Christmas Tree* opus 41 [56], 1913 - Jean Dwight Franklin.
         A. SATB with piano or organ, Pub 1913 GS.
         B. c 1913 - Orchestra and SATB version of above - AF Ms. Scoring: W - 2-2-2-2; B - 4-2-3-1; Tmp;

std str; SATB. Score AF Ms, parts not located.
First perf. c1913, NYC.

169. * S   *Four Part Songs For Children* opus 42 [57], 1914 -
Pub 1914 SB in *The Progressive Music Series*.
1. "Spring Song".
2. "Hoof Beats".
3. "Hiawatha's Sailing".
4. "Morning".

170. * S   *Caliban* opus 47 [64], 1915 - Shakespeare
Tercentenary Masque by Percy Mackaye, choruses
and incidental music. Main entry Pageants #208.
See also 3 C. in #171, below.

171. * P S   *Three Songs from Caliban for Medium Voice* opus
47a [65], 1916.
1. "Come Unto These Yellow Sands" -
Shakespeare - unknown except choral version in
opus 47 [64], above.
2. "Under The Greenwood Tree" - as No.1 above.
3. "Many Are The Wonders Of Time" - Sophocles,
translated by Percy MacKaye.
A. With piano accomp. AF Ms, see Vocal #47.
B. With orchestra, Caliban vers. see Vocal #87.
C. Revised for SATB and full orchestra, scoring:
W - 3-2-3-2; B - 4-3-3-1; Tmp, BD, Cym; Std.
Str.

172. * S   *Three Songs for Community Singing* opus 48 [66],
1916.
1. "March! March!" - AF words. Unison, piano
acc. in E Flat - Pub 1916 GS, TD.
A. Unison, piano acc. in D Flat - AF Ms.
B. SATB
1. piano acc. in E Flat - Pub 1916, GS.
2. in E Flat, 2 trumpets, 2 trombones, AF Ms
3. with Orch. (E Flat), score AF Ms, parts
Ms Var, Scoring: W - 2-2-1-2-2; B -

4-2-3-1; Tmp, BD, Cym, SmD; Std Str. First perf. Song and Light Festival, Central Park, NYC, Sept. 13, 1916. TD

2. "Joy! Brothers, Joy!" - words and music by A.F.

A. Piano prelude - AF Ms.
B. SATB
1. with piano acc. - Pub 1916 GS.
2. with Orch., score AF Ms, parts Ms Var, Scored: W - 2-2-1-2-2; B - 4-2-3-1; Tmp, BD, Cym; Std. Str. 1st perf. as #1D. TD
C. Prelude - orchestra parts only, AF Ms.
3. "After The Battle", 1917 - words and music by Arthur Farwell, Pub 1917 GS.

173. * P S *Four Part Songs for Community Chorus* opus 51 [70], 1918.
1A. "Hosanna" - SATB, piano acc., Pub 1918 JC, First perf. 1918, Third Street Music Settlement School, NYC.
1B. Orch. score, AF MS, Scoring: W - 2-2-2-2; B - 4-2-3-1; Tmp, SmD, Cym; Std. Str. Perf. 1918 by Third Street Music School Settlement Chorus and Orchestra in Carnegie Hall, NYC.
2. "Breathe On Us, Breath of God" - SATB, piano acc., Pub 1919 JC.
3. "Watchword" - SATB, piano acc., Pub 1919 JC, loc in DLC.
4. "Our Country's Prayer" - A. SATB, piano acc., Pub 1919 JC. B and C, Low and high voice versions - see Vocal #48.

174. *Up and Away!* [73], 1919 - medium or mixed voices, on poem by H. C. Nutting, AF Ms, unison until finale SATB.

175. *Defenders* [75], 1919 - SATB, piano acc., Pub 1920 JC.

176. *    *La Primavera* opus 56a [77], 1920 - Santa Barbara Community Music Drama, title song Spanish California folksong harmonized by AF, SATB, piano acc., AF Ms. Other 9AF arrangements on song sheets. TD

177. *    *Five Songs for Community Chorus* opus 57 [78], 1920 - unison, choral and later, also solo. See Vocal #53.
       1A. - "We Will Be Free" - Poem by James Thompson. - unison or solo, with piano acc.,
       1B-1. c1938 or later, pencil revision, AF Dr.
       1B-2. Finished var. of 1B-1 - med. voice, AF Ms.
       1C. Third Revision, 1946, AF Dr.
       1C-1. Male Chorus or Quartet, c1950, 2T,2B, piano acc. optional, Repr MS.
       1C-2. Eight Voice Mixed Chorus, c1950, piano acc. optional, Repr Ms
       1D-1. High voice, c1950, Pub PP.
       1D-2. Low voice, c1950, Pub PP.
       2. "On A Summer Morning" - unlocated,
       3. "Sing! Brother, Sing!" c1920 - unlocated.
       4. "Any Time for Singin'"c1920 - poet unknown, medium voice, unison or solo, AF Ms.
       5. "Sing Awhile Longer" - Edwin Markham, medium voice, unison or solo, AF Ms.

178. ** P    *Gloria in Excelsis* opus 58 [79], c1921 - adapted from music for *The Pilgrimage Play*, opus 58 [79] #199 in Pageant and Dramatic - Full *Gloria*, more than used in production, SATB with orch. score and piano acc. Scoring: W - 3-2-2-2; B - 4-3-3-1; tym, cym; harp; std. str., chorus.

179. ** P S    *Spanish Songs of Old California* opus 59 [80], c1922 - Pub 1923 PP, and 1929 GS, recorded and translated by Charles F. Lummis, transcribed 1904-05 and harmonized over years through 1922 by AF. English and Spanish, suitable for community singing; some have two parts, high and medium, others

medium.   Titles in Vocal #54. Kept in print by Southwest Museum, Los Angeles.

180. * P     *Symphonic Hymn on March! March!* opus 49 [81], 1921 - AF verse, for orchestra with or without chorus.  See Orchestra #228, also cf. #170, D.

181.     *Three School Choruses* opus 62 [86], c1922?- Pub c 1922 GI but publ. copies unlocated.  AF Ms only, in collection.
>   1. "The Daffodils" - Wordsworth, SATB with piano.
>   2. "Pippa's Song" - Robert Browning, SATB with piano.
>   3. "New Year's Bell" - girl's voices with piano.

182.     *Two School Choruses* opus 63 [87], 1922 - Pub c 1922 HH, but copies unlocated, no Mss in collection.
>   1. "Out in the Fields".
>   2. "Beautiful Things".

183. *     *La Golondrina* [90], 1922 - Spanish California folksong harmonized by AF for Pasadena Community Music Meeting, on Song Sheet No. 1, for mixed voices in unison.

184. * P     *Symphonic Song on Old Black Joe* opus 67 [93], 1924, for orchestra and audience - with composer's program notes, Orch. score AF Ms and Repr Ms, parts Ms Var, Scoring: W - 3-2-1-3-2; B - 4-3-3-1; Tmp, SD, Tri, BD, Cym, TamTam, Hp; audience in unison; Std. Str.   Performance Aug. 22, 1924, in Hollywood Bowl.   Trio version, see #143.

185.     *America The Beautiful* [100], 1927 - SATB, entry in contest for "A truly noble setting" of Katherine Lee Bates' hymn.  (The judges made no award.)  AF Ms.

186.            *Our Country* - opus 81 [108], 1929 - SATB, AF Ms
                on poem by Minna Irving.

187.            *For America* [163], c1929? - SATB, AF Ms on poem
                by Arthur Guiterman.  He set #186 and #187 on
                prizewinning poems in a national anthem contest,
                probably at same time, but AF separated them in
                his files, and left #187 without date or opus no.

188. *          1. B. *The Lamb* opus 88 [114], 1930 - by William
                Blake, SATB for chorus or quartet, accompanied or
                a capella, AF Ms.  Main entry in Vocal #64.

189. ** P       *Mountain Song* - opus 90 [119], 1931 A symphonic
                song ceremony of the High Sierras, in five
                movements, for orchestra with occasional choruses.
                SATB, details at main entry in Orch. #232.

190. ** P       *Four Songs for A Capella Chorus* opus 102 [135],
                1937 - Pub 1937 GS, First performance by
                Westminster Choir with John Finley Williamson,
                c1937.  TD
                    1. "Navajo War Dance, No. 1" - SSAATTBB. R,
                    RU
                    2. "The Old Man's Love Song" - SSAATTBB. R,
                    RU
                    3. "Pawnee Horses" - SSAATTBB.
                    4. "The Mother's Vow" - SSAATTBB with s. solo.

191.            *Cathedral Scene, (Finale, Part I)* [138], 1938 -
                Arranged SATB with sop. solo, for two pianos, AF
                Ms.  Evidently a part of an unknown larger work
                (373 bars, including incidental passages with voices
                tacet).

192.            *Studies Toward a National Anthem* [150], c1945 -
                words by AF for both on his setting of "Glory and
                Serenity" in Caliban, #171, AF Ms.  See also #79
                in Vocal Solo .

1B. "One World", SATB with piano.

2B. "America's Vow", SATB with piano, 2 sets of verses.

193.   *United Nations Anthem* [156], 1946 - Sidney T. Cooke.

  A. - SATB, piano acc., Repr Ms. TD

  B. - SATB, orch score repro Ms. Scoring: W -2-2-3-2; B - 4-4-3-1; Tmp; Chorus; Std. Str.

194. ** P   *Two A Capella Choruses* opus 111 [154], 1946 - 8 parts, AF Dr, Pub 1946 PP with rehearsal piano and instructions for performing Indian vocables. Perf. on tour of Westminster Choir, 1947.

  1. "Navajo War Dance No 2." - SSAATTBB.

  2. "Indian Scene" - SSAATTBB with sop. solo. First perf. March 20, 1947 at Town Hall, NYC.

## 6. Music for Dramatic Forms

### A. Theatrical

195.   *Cinderella* [13], c1911? - incidental and background music, unfinished, but marked for use with opus 46 [61], #197, AF Ms.

196. * P   *Joseph and His Brethren* opus 38 [53], 1912 - incidental music for a pageant play by Louis N. Parker, orchestra score, incomplete in collection. Perf. New York, 1912.

197. *   *Garden of Paradise* opus 46 [61], 1914 - Incidental music for play by Edward Sheldon, music unknown except for references in AF writings and in margins of draft AF Ms of #195, above. Perf. NYC, 1914.

198. ** P   *The Gods of the Mountain* opus 68 [52], 1917 - Incidental music for the play by Lord Dunsany. TD

A. Original trio version, Harp, V and Vc, AF Ms, premiere at Portmanteau Theatre, Carnegie Hall, New York, 1917.
B. Revised 1917 for V, Vc and P, AF Ms. Premiere perf. March 30, 1922, by Sarah Coleman Bragdon, P., Reginald Bland, V., Axel Simonsen, VC. in Pasadena on an all-Farwell program. TD.
C. Orchestra version. Main entry Orch. #232, TD.

199. * P     *The Pilgrimage Play, the Story of the Christ* opus 58 [79], 1920-1921, by Christine Wetherill Stevenson, conducted by the composer at original production, near the Hollywood Bowl, 1921. 20 musical numbers. Available materials microfilmed: TD
A. Vocal numbers: 2. "Manger Scene" 4. "John The Baptist" 7. "Transfiguration Scene" 20. "Ascension Chorus"
B. Complete scores for organ, piano, and orchestra using organ in lieu of strings, with voices. Scores AF Ms, parts wanting.

*** P     C. "Gloria in Excelsis", full version, more than used in production, SATB with piano and with orchestra. AF Mss. Scoring: W - 3-2-2-2; B - 4-3-3-1; Tmp, Cym, Hp; str. to balance; SATB. See also Choral #178. TD

200. *     *The Coming of Song* [82], c1921, A music drama by Arthur Farwell - complete prologue and poetic text. Music only begun: pencil sketches, and AF ink Ms of first 28 measures of No. 1. "Out of the Night", the prologue by the celestial choir, SATB with piano.

201. * S     *Songs for Baby's First Christmas Tree* opus 55 [83], c1920 - play by Gertrude Brice Farwell, Pub 1922 CB.

202. * S     *Sister Beatrice* opus 60 [84], 1922 - Songs and incidental music for Pasadena Community Playhouse production, 1922, only music found is *Song of the Holy Virgin*, contralto on Maurice Maeterlink poem, AF Ms. Listed also in Vocal #55.

203.   P     *Scene from the Inferno* opus 85 [123], 1932, of Dante's *Divine Comedy* for orchestra and non-singing chorus of wails, sobs, gasps; pencil draft, studies, and sketches for a Norman Bel Geddes production - that did not occur. TD

## B. Pageants and Masques

204. * S     *Pageant of Meriden, N. H.* opus 39 [54], 1913, by William Chauncey Langdon - Introduction, three interludes, and finale, scores, parts, and some various arrangements, with book of words. AF Ms. Performance June 24-25, 1913 at Meriden.

      P     A. Pageant Scene opus 39 [54a] - Arrangement for orchestra. See Orch. #231.

205. * S     *Sanctuary, A Bird Masque*, 1913 by Percy MacKaye - composed in collaboration with Frederick S. Converse, music not in collection. First performance September 11, 1913 at Meriden, N. H.

206. * S     *Pageant of Darien, Conn.* opus 40 [55], 1913 by William Chauncey Langdon - Orchestra scores for introduction, two interludes and finale. AF Ms. Perf. August 30, September 1, 6, 1913 at Darien.

207.      *DKE, A Masque of Fraternity* [62], c1914 - Words and music by AF for dedication of his fraternity building in New York. AF Ms of "Fanfare" and draft orchestra scores for choruses. TD

208. * S    *Caliban, the Shakespeare Tercentenary Masque* opus
            47 [64], 1915 by Percy MacKaye - music by AF,
            choruses Pub 1916 GS, Loc in MH, NNrpa.  Cf with
            Vocal #87 and Choral #171.  TD
    1. "Choirs of Setebos and Ariel", SA, antiph. TB.
    2. "Ariel's Choirs Silenced by Setebos", SA, antiph.
       TB.
    3. "Spirits of Ariel", S1, S2, A.
    4. "Spirits of Ariel and Setebos in Conflict",
       SATB, in canonic chorus.
    5. "Liberation of Ariel", S1, S2, A.
    6. "Come Unto These Yellow Sands", S1, S2, A.
    7. "In The Same Abode And Cell", S1, S2, A.
    8. "Roman Orgy and Vision of the Cross",Un, TB
    9. First stamza of "Dirge", No. 11, SA and TB.
    10. "The Field of the Cloth of Gold", SATB.
    11. Dirge - "Gray - Gray - Gray", SA and TB.
    12. "Under The Greenwood Tree", TB.
    13. Second stanza of No. 12.
    14. Designated part of first stanza of No. 12.
    15. "Fie on Sinful Fantasy", Unison all voices.
    16. "Acclaim of Caliban", Unison TB.
    17. "War" - pub separately, GS.  Unison TB.
    18. "Glory and Serenity", same as No. 10.
    19. "We Are Such Stuff As Dreams Are Made
        On", SATB.
            Orchestra, fanfare and solo scores are not in
            collection, nor is "War."  Performance Lewisohn
            Stadium, NYC, May 23-27, 1916, and Harvard U.
            Stadium, June 28 - July 21, 1917.

209. *** P S *The Evergreen Tree* opus 50 [67], 1917, a Christmas
            Masque for community singing and acting, by Percy
            Mackaye - Playscript With 21 singing works, carols
            and choruses, intended for production on any scale.
            Microfilm collection includes:  TD
            A. "Book of Music" - Piano and SATB, Pub 1917
            JC, Loc in CL, MB, NNrpa.  Book suggests to
            inquire of Pub JC re orchestra material.

B. No. 6, "The Tree Child's Lullaby" - AF Ms.
C. Orchestra scores for all the choruses except Nos. 8 and 10, and for the carols Nos. 5, 6 and 15 - AF Ms.
D. Band scores for Nos. 8, 9, 10, 20, and 21 - Ms Var.
E. Some parts, for some Nos. - Ms Var.

210. *    *California, a Masque of Song* [69], 1918 - Given in the Greek Theater, University of CA at Berkeley, 1918. Free verse text by AF with choral singing of some University and Farwell songs. Text, with audience song sheet microfilmed with prose material.

211. *    *Chant of Victory, a "Community Ceremony"* [71], 1919 - Given July 4, 1919 at San Francisco Civic Aud. Free verse by AF, some existing AF music, some other, microfilmed with prose material. TD

212. *    *La Primavera* opus 56a [77], 1920, Santa Barbara Community Music Drama - Title song, only, found, 4 voices and piano. TD

213. * S    *Grail Song* opus 70 [96], 1925 - A masque for community singing, acting and dancing, all by Arthur Farwell - Complete text, pianist's rehearsal copy of choral numbers (to be reproduced for the voices), full orchestra score and score with parts for small orchestra of flute, piano and strings. Full scoring: W - 2-1-2-1; B - 2-1-1-0; Tmp, BD, SmD, Cym, Hp; Std. Str., SATB. Much of the music based on modes other than the usual major and minor, as marked on score. Premiere April 23, 1925, for Two Scenes: *Dance of the World*, and *Dance of the Soul* performed by J. J. Gilbert, FL., Umberto Sistarelli, V. Mary Tyner Novis, VC. and Raymond McFeeters, P. in Los Angeles. TD

214. *      *The March of Man* opus 71 [97], 1925 - A masque
           for the dedication of the Theatre of the Stars,
           Fawnskin, Big Bear Lake, California, by Arthur
           Farwell - materials are only the text of production
           script, string parts for the number, *World Soul*, and
           the strings, piano and voice for the *Prayer*.  TD

## C.  Opera

215. ** P    *Cartoon or Once Upon a Time Recently* [158], 1948
           -an Operatic Fantasy of Music in America, in three
           acts with a burlesque ballet.  Text by Edna Kingsley
           Wallace and Arthur Farwell, on a scenario by the
           composer.  TD
              1. Text, with production notes, in two or three
              versions, one indicated to be final, in typed Ms.
              2. Vocal score, with piano arrangement, AF Ms.
              3. Repr Ms of opening chorus, *Robbers, We*.
              4. AF Ms of burlesque ballet - *Pierrot's Lunacy,
              The Blight of Spring*.  Orchestration and parts need
              to be made, throughout.  First known perf. of
              Aria, *Love the Revealer*, sung March 30, 1922, by
              Mrs. Norman Hassler, sop. in Pasadena.   A
              shortened version of the opera was presented
              April 14, 1977, by music students at the U. of
              Conn. in Bridgeport on "An Evening of American
              Music".  Dr. Terrence Greenawalt was coordinator
              with Brice Farwell as narrator.
           Farwell listed the following numbers from *Cartoon*
           as being "suitable for recording:"
           Act I.
              Chorus, "Robber Priests of Europus", (with special
                 ending from p. 36)
              Sop. Aria, "Love the Revealer"
              Bar. solo, "I Don't Know Much of Music"
              Duet, "Life is a Rose"
              Ballet, "Pierrot's Lunacy or the Blight of Spring"
              Bass aria, "Beethoven's Speech"

Act II.

Prelude. (Cowboy, Indian and Spanish Californian themes)

Spanish Californian and Mexican Folksongs of Scene 1

Bar. solo, "Robber Song" (What is a Robber without his Wine?)

Indian Ceremonial Dance

Act III.

Sop. aria, "Brillian October is Here"

Priests' Chant and Entrance of the Daughters of Immigrantus. (Two melodies simultaneously in 2nd part.)

Entrance of Americus with followers, and Americus' Prologue, (Cowboy and Indian themes) leading into

The New World Ceremony, (The concluding Indian War Dance would make a separate recording.)

Chorus with Americus and Columbia

Finale, (Chorus with 3 principle melodies sung simultaneously)

## 7. Orchestral Music

### A. Orchestra Alone

216.     *The Death of Virginia* opus 4 [2], 1894 - Fantasy for Orchestra - AF score, 19 pp, needs parts. Scored: W - 2-1-2-1-3-2; B - 4-3-3-1; Tmp-BD-Cym-Gong; each string voice divided. TD

217. * P     *Suite for Grand Orchestra* [5], 1896, second movement only, titled "Love Song" - AF Ms score 26 pp, parts missing. Performance Oct. 17, 1896, by Anton Seidl and Metropolitan Permanent Orchestra of New York, N.Y., at Auburn, N.Y., then titled Andante

from a New Suite. Scored: W - 2-2-2-2; B - 4-2-3-2-1; Tmp; Std Str. TD

218. * P    *Academic Overture, "Cornell"* opus 9 [17], 1900 - parts only, needs score, perf. 1900 by Cornell University Orchestra, Ithaca, N.Y., 12 min. Scoring: W - 2-2-2-1; B - 2-2-3-1; Tmp; Str. TD

219. * P    *Dawn - Fantasy on Two Indian Themes* opus 12 [21], 1901 - See Piano #98.

       C. 1904 - Dawn - Fantasy for Orchestra - Parts and two pp. of score. Perf. 1904 at St. Louis Exposition and 1909 at concert of American Music Society in New York, N.Y. conducted by AF. In 1935, composer called this version "callow" and preferred newer version, (D, below) which he said is same as original piano work.

*** P    D. *Dawn*, c1909 - Arr. for Piano and Small Orchestra - AF Ms at PP(FC), 1st perf. April 18, 1909 by Peoples Symphony at Carnegie Hall, New York, conducted by AF. Time: 6:20 , Scoring: W - 1-1-2-1; B - 2-1-1; tmp; S - 2-1-1-1. RU TD

220. *** P    *The Domain of Hurakan* opus 15 [23], 1910 - Main entry Piano #100.

       B. Orchestra score on 1902 piano work, AF Ms, premiere Aug. 24, 1910, by Volpe Symphony Orchestra, Cental Park Mall, New York, conducted by AF, Scoring: W - 2-2-1-2-2; B - 4-2-3-1; KD-BD-Cym; usual strings. TD

221. *** P    *Symbolistic Study No. 3, "Once I Passed Through A Populous City"* opus 18 [30], 1921 - AF Ms at PP(FC), re-orchestrated from 1908 version based on original sketch composed in 1905. Perf. March 30, 1928, by Pierre Monteux with Philadelphia Orchestra, AF T - 16 min., scoring: W - 3-2-1-3-3; B - 4-3-3-1; Tmp-BD-TT-Cym-Hp; S - 10-10-8-6-5. TD

222.             *Symbolistic Study No. 5* opus 25 [36], 1930 -
                unfinished score on 1905 themes, AF Ms.

223. ** P       *Rudolph Gott Symphony* opus 95 [125], 1934 -
                Complete score and parts at PP(FC) and score in
                author's collection with original sketches and piano
                version, built on composition fragments by Rudolph
                R. Gott, saved by AF from turn of century.
                Premiere Mar. 3, 1978, Diablo Symphony Orchestra
                at Walnut Creek, CA, John Periera, cond.; AF time:
                46 min., Scoring: W - 3-2-1-3-3; B - 4-4-3-2; Tmp-
                BD-SmD-Cym-TT; S - 12-12-5-5-4. RU, TD.

224.            *Navajo War Dance No. 1* opus 110 [152], 1944 - may
                be part of "Indian Suite" (remainder unknown), score
                in Repr Ms, parts wanting.  AF time: 2 min. 5 sec.;
                scoring: W - 3-2-1-3-2; B - 4-3-3-1; Tmp; Str. to bal.

225. ** P       *The Heroic Breed* opus 115 [155], 1946 - in memory
                of Gen. George S. Patton, Jr., score AF Ms, parts
                Repr Ms.  Premiere by Young Men's Symphony
                Orchestra, NYC. in 1946. Scoring: W - 3-2-1-3-3; B
                - 4-4-3-1; Tmp, GD, Cym, SD, T-T, Chimes; Std.
                Strings to balance.  TD

## B. With Piano

226. *** P      *Symbolistic Study No. 6, "Mountain Vision"* opus 37
                [52], 1938 for piano with string orchestra and second
                piano ("replacing winds" - AF), concerto arrangement
                revised   from   1912   piano   solo   after   earlier
                orchestrated development.   AF Ms and parts at
                PP(FC).  Time, 16:52.  Premiered as NFMC prize
                broadcast on Columbia Broadcasting System May 26,
                1939, Karl Ulrich Schnabel and Helen Vogel,
                pianists, Howard Barlow conducted the Columbia
                Orchestra. Scoring: 12-10-6-6-2.  RU TD.

## C. With Chorus

227. * P   *Three Songs from Caliban for Medium Voice* opus 47a
[65], 1916 - Main entry in Choral #39. 3. "Many Are
The Wonders Of Time" - Sophocles, translated by
Percy MacKaye.
C. Revised for SATB and full orchestra, scoring:
W - 3-2-3-2; B - 4-3-3-1; Tmp, BD, Cym; Std. Str.

228. * P   *Symphonic Hymn on March! March!* opus 49 [81],-
Op.49 [8] 1921, orchestra with or without chorus,
original piano version AF Ms, orchestra score AF
Ms, and Mss of parts, performance Mar. 18, 1923, by
Pasadena Philharmonic Orchestra, conducted by
Arthur Farwell. Scoring: W - 2-2-1-2-2; B - 4-3-3-1;
Tmp-BD-SmD-Tri-Glock; Str - 8-7-5-5-4. SATB. TD

229. ** P   *Mountain Song, A Symphonic Song Ceremony of the
High Sierras opus 90 [119], 1931*, in five movements,
for orchestra with occasional choruses. Complete
score at NNrpa, complete orchestra parts in author's
collection, choral parts wanting, except 1. and 3. in
author's collection. AF's time: 72 min., scoring: W -
3-2-1-3-3; B - 4-3-3-2; Tmp, BD, SmD, SnD, TT,
Tri, Cym, Cel, Hp; chorus; S - 8-7-5-5-4. TD. First
perf. Sept. 2, 1949, by St. Paul Civic Opera Chorus
for Commemorative Centennial Ceremony at MN.
State Fair.   Performed works*:
1. "Introduction" and "Chorale of the Mountains"*
2. "From the Heights"
3. "Depth of Pines"*
4. "Chorale of the Forest, Deep, Deep"
5. "Azure Lake"
6. "Chorale of the Lake"
7. "Crags"
8. "Chorale of the Crags"
9. "Mystery" (string interlude) See Chamber #142.
10. "Dawn and Day", 1935.

230.       *The Hound of Heaven* opus 100 [131], see Vocal #89

## D. Music for Dramas

231. * P    *Pageant Scene* opus 39 [54a], 1913 - for small orchestra, adapted from music for the Pageant of Meriden, N. H., AF Ms at PP(FC), first known performance Feb. 21, 1938 by Peoples Symphony Orchestra, Lansing Mich., Frederick Lewis, conducting. AF time: 10 min., Scoring: W - 1-1-2-1; B - 2-2-1; tmp; Std. Str. TD

232. *** P   *The Gods Of The Mountain* opus 52 [68], 1917 - Incidental music for play of same title by Lord Dunsany. See also Chamber #141.

    PS      A. Trio for harp, violin & 'cello.
    PS      B. Revised for violin, 'cello & piano.
    P       C. 1928 P - Revised for orchestra - AF Ms loc in PP(FC). Premiere Henri Verbrugghen with Minneapolis Symphony Orchestra Dec. 13, 1929; 17 min. Scoring: W - 2-2-1-3-3; B - 4-3-3-1-0; Tmp, BD, OrD, Tb, TT, Cym, Tri, Hp; Str - 8-6-5-5-4. *(Farwell's most popular orchestral work.)* R TD

233. ** P   *Prelude to a Spiritual Drama* opus 76 [103], 1935 - sketch developed in 1927 from Op. 79 [58] *The Pilgrimage Play* - AF Ms loc NNrpa, premiere 1937, East Lansing, by Michigan State College Syɪ phony Orchestra, composer conducting. AF time: 13 min., scoring: W - 3-2-1-3-2; B -4-4-3-1; Tmp, BD, Cym, Hp; Str-10-9-8-6-5. TD. See also Dramas #199.

# Discography

Although Arthur Farwell used recordings in his classes to illustrate his teaching, he deplored these devices. The spirit of the music, he strongly felt, was conveyed importantly, in part, by the expressive passion of the performers - and conductor - as visual cues added to the sound. Farwell's own playing or speaking was never recorded. He may have heard the earliest "long-playing" recordings, but never knew or heard of stereophonic high-fidelity. Despite his convictions, Farwell was resigned to the necessity and opportunity of recordings to bring music into the lives of many who do not have access to the concert hall.

This discography has two sections. First, the publically issued recordings, which are shown by an R in the Catalog, and then a second list of privately made or otherwise non-issued tapes of Farwell's music that have been acquired by his family as an archive. These are marked with RU in the Catalog. Most of them would require permission by the performer(s) for duplicates to be dubbed, or for them to be played in public, or for use other than to assess suitability for further performance programming. They represent a partial spectrum of the Farwell works that have attracted performance interest over the last twenty-five years.

Nearly all the works and their recordings in both sections are posthumous performances as their datings should show. The listings are generally ordered by composition date in both lists. It cannot be certified that either list is exhaustive.

## Recording Companies

Golden Crest  (GC)
Gregg Smith Singers Production  (GSS)
Magellan
Musical Heritage Society  (MHS)
New World Records  (NW
Nuova Era  (NUO)
RCA Victor Masterpiece Series  (RCA-Victor)
Society for the Preservation of the American Musical Heritage
    (MIA)

## I. Compositions on Issued Recordings

1. *Song of the Deathless Voice* - 1900, (Op.11, No.3) Leo Smit, pianist, on *A Crazy Quilt of American Piano Music.* Musical Heritage Society, MHS 7534, 1986.

2. *American Indian Melodies* - 1900, Op.11. from *American Indian Music,* Dario Muller, pianist, Nuova Era, NUO 6821, CD 1990.

3. *Navajo War Dance, No. 1* - 1905 (Op. 20. No. 1.B) Jeanne Behrend, pianist - RCA Victor Masterpiece Series, M-764, *Piano Music by American Composers,* c 1944.

   *Navajo War Dance, No. 1.* Peter Basquin, pianist - from *The Music of Arthur Farwell, Preston Ware Orem, and Charles Wakefield Cadman.* New World Records, NW 213, Stereo, 1977.

4. *Pawnee Horses* - 1905 (Op. 20, No. 5.B) Peter Basquin, pianist, from - *The Music of Arthur Farwell, Preston Ware Orem, and Charles Wakefield Cadman.* New World Records, NW 213, Stereo, 1977.

5. *Navajo War Dance No. 2* - c1904 (Op. 29 B), edited with John Kirkpatrick in 1940. Grant Johannesen, pianist - Golden Crest, S-4065, *Encores From A Russian Tour,* c 1960.

6. *Song of the Deathless Voice* - 1908 (Op. 32, No. 1) William Parker, baritone; William Huckaby, piano. *Three Indian Songs* from *The Music of Arthur Farwell, Preston Ware Orem and Charles Wakefield Cadman.* New World Records, NW 213. Stereo, 1977.

7. *Inketunga's Thunder Song* - 1908 (Op. 32, No. 2) Parker and Huckaby as recorded in #6.

8. *The Old Man's Love Song* - 1908 (Op. 32, No. 3) Parker and Huckaby as recorded in #6.

9.  *Sourwood Mountain* - 1927 (Op. 78, No. 3) - Jeanne Behrend, pianist - RCA Victor Masterpiece Series, M-764, *Piano Music by American Composers,* c 1944.

10. *The Gods Of The Mountain* - 1928 (Op. 52 C), Karl Krueger conducting the Royal Philharmonic Orchestra, London - Society For The Preservation Of The American Musical Heritage, MIA-128, 1965.

11. *Land of Luthany* - 1931 (Op. 87) Douglas Moore, cello; Paula Ennis-Dwyer, piano - Musical Heritage Society, MHS Stereo 4348, 1981.

12. *Quintet in E Minor for piano and strings* - 1937 (Op. 103) The Pacifica Chamber Players - Ronald Erickson, v1; Celia Rosenberger, v2; Elizabeth Kissling, viola; Wanda Warkentin, cello; Aileen James, piano - Musical Heritage Society, MHS 3827, 1978;   Re-issued by Magellan, S-3827, 1989.

13. *Navajo War Dance No. 1 for a capella chorus* - 1937 (Op. 10, No. 1) *The Music of Arthur Farwell, Preston Ware Orem and Charles Wakefield Cadman.*  The New World Singers, John Miner, conductor - New World Records NW 213 Stereo, 1977.

14. *The Old Man's Love Song for a capella chorus* - 1937 (Op. 102, No. 2)  On same recording as #13.

15. *Safe In Their Alabaster Chambers* - Emily Dickinson - 1938-1941 (Op. 105, No. 2)   Paul Sperry, tenor; Irma Vallecillo, piano - Gregg Smith Singers, GSS 105, Paul Sperry: *Romantic American Songs*, 1985.

16. *Aristocracy* - Emily Dickinson - 1938-1941 (Op. 105, No. 7) Same recording as #15.

17. *Summer's Armies* - Emily Dickinson - 1938-1941 (Op. 105, No. 9) Same recording as #15.

18. *The Level Bee* - Emily Dickinson - 1938-1941 (Op. 105, No. 10) Same recording as #15.

19. *Presentiment* - Emily Dickinson - 1938-1941 (Op. 105, No. 12) Same recording as #15.

20. *Tie The Strings To My Life* - Emily Dickinson - 1941-1944 (Op. 107, No. 2) Same recording as #15.

21. *The Butterfly* - Emily Dickinson - c 1944 (Op. 108, No. 2) Same recording as #15.

22. *Ample Make This Bed* - Emily Dickinson - c 1944 (Op. 108, No. 7) Same recording as #15.

23. *I'm Nobody, Who Are You?* - Emily Dickinson - c 1944 (Op. 108, No. 8) Same recording as #15.

24. *Papa Above!* - Emily Dickinson - c 1944 (Op. 108, No. 9) Same recording as #15.

25. *The Grass So Little Has To Do* - Emily Dickinson c 1944 (Op. 112, No. 2) Same recording as #15.

26. *Sonata for Violoncello and Piano* - 1950 (Op. 116) Douglas Moore, cello, Paula Ennis-Dwyer, piano, Musical Heritage Society, MHS Stereo 4348, 1981.

## II. Compositions on Non-issued Recordings

1. *American Indian Melodies* - 1900 (Op. 11)    Dale Arndt, pianist, at Maine Federation of Music Clubs Concert, February 11, 1975.

2. *Owasco Memories* - 1901 (Op. 8 B)    Ronald Erickson, v; Amy Radner, c; Julie Steinberg, p; Berkeley, CA, May 1, 1976.

3. *The Domain of Hurakan* - 1902 (Op. 15 A)    Frank Wasko, pianist, at California State U., Sacramento, Feb. 27, 1974.

4. *Love's Secret* - William Blake - 1902 (Op. 14, No. 2 A)    Jill Feldman, soprano; Stephen Kelly, piano; University of California, Santa Barbara, March 3, 1976.

5. *Navajo War Dance, No. 1* - 1905 (Op. 20, No. 1 B)    Frank Wasko, pianist, California State U., Sacramento, Feb. 27, 1974.

6. *Wa-Wan Chorale* - 1905 (Op. 20, No. 4)    Frank Wasko, pianist, at California State U., Sacramento, February 27, 1974.

7. *Pawnee Horses* - 1905 (Op. 20, No. 5)    Frank Wasko, pianist, at California State U., Sacramento, February 27, 1974.    Max Morath, pianist, New York, c September, 1990.

8. *Impressions of the Wa-Wan Ceremony*, No. 1, Nearing The Village - 1905 (Op. 21, No. 1) Frank Wasko, pianist, at California State University, Sacramento, February 27, 1974.

9. *Song of the Deathless Voice* - 1908 (Op. 32, No. 1)    David Barron, baritone; Neely Bruce, piano; broadcast from WQXR, New York on "The Listening Room," April 16, 1975.

10. *Inketunga's Thunder Song* - 1908 (Op. 32, No. 2)    Barron and Bruce as in #9.

11. *Dawn, a Fantasy on Indian Themes* - c 1909 (Op. 12 D) Ensemble of faculty and students conducted by Daniel

Kingman, California State University, Sacramento, February 27, 1974.

12. *Symbolistic Study No. 6, "Mountain Vision"* - 1912, revised orchestration 1938 (Op. 37 C)  Karl Ulrich Schnabel, piano, Helen Vogel, second piano, Howard Barlow conducting Columbia Orchestra in NFMC prize broadcast, New York, May 26, 1939, recorded over the air, loc DLC.

13. *I Shall Know Why* - Emily Dickinson - (Op. 66, No. 1) Barron and Bruce as in #9.

14. *The Ravens are Singing* - Charles O. Roos - 1924 (Op. 69, No. 1) Barron and Bruce as in #9.

15. *Dark Her Lodge Door* - Charles O. Roos - 1924 (Op. 69, No. 3)  Barron and Bruce as in #9.

16. *Sourwood Mountain* - 1927 (Op. 78, No. 3)  Marianne Scialdo and Camille Budarz, pianists in a two piano arrangement by the performers, Scarborough, New York, c 1980.

17. *Thwarted Current*, Poem for Pianoforte - 1929 (Op. 82, No. 2) Seta Karakashian, pianist, broadcast from WQXR, New York on "The Listening Room," c May 29, 1986.

18. *What's In an Octave?* - 1930 (Op. 84)  Neely Bruce, pianist, broadcast from WQXR, New York on "The Listening Room", April 16, 1975.

19. *In The Tetons*, suite for piano - 1930 (Op. 86) Nos. 1-7. David Vayo, pianist,  Connecticut College, November 16, 1990.

20. *The Lamb* - William Blake - 1930 (Op. 88, No. 1)  Jill Feldman, soprano; Stephen Kelly, piano; University of California, Santa Barbara, March 3, 1976.

21. *A Cradle Song* - William Blake - 1930 (Op. 88, No. 2)   Jill Feldman, soprano; Stephen Kelly, piano; University of California, Santa Barbara, March 3, 1976.

22. *Land of Luthany* - 1931 (Op. 87) Tigran Makarian, cellist; Seta Kashakarian, pianist, broadcast from WQXR, New York on "The Listening Room," c May 29, 1986.

23. *The Rudoph Gott Symphony* - 1932-1934 (Op. 95)   The Diablo Symphony Orchestra conducted by John Periera at Walnut Creek, CA, March 3, 1978.

24. *Sonata in G Minor*, for solo violin - 1934 (Op. 96)   Ronald Erickson, violinist, Berkeley, CA, May 1, 1976.

25. *The Tyger* - William Blake - 1934 (Op. 98)   Jill Feldman, soprano, Stephen Kelly, piano, U. of California, Santa Barbara, March 3, 1976.

26. *Unto Me* - Emily Dickinson - 1936 (Op. 101, No. 2)   David Barron, baritone; Neely Bruce, piano, broadcast from WQXR, New York, on "The Listening Room," April 16, 1975.

27. *As If The Sea* - Emily Dickinson - 1936 (Op. 101, No. 3) Barron and Bruce as in #26.

26. *Navajo War Dance No. 1*, for a capella chorus - 1937 (Op. 102, No. 1)   The Paul Hill Chorale, conducted by Paul Hill at the Kennedy Center, Washington, DC, March 10, 1973.

28. *The Old Man's Love Song*, for a capella chorus - 1937 (Op. 102, No. 1)   Same performers as #26.

29. *Presentiment* - Emily Dickinson - 1938-1941 (Op. 105, No. 12) David Barron, baritone; Neely Bruce, piano; broadcast from WQXR, New York on "The Listening Room," April 16, 1975.

30. *Tie The Strings To My Life* - Emily Dickinson - 1941-44 (Op. 107, No. 2)   Barron and Bruce as in #29.

31. *Papa Above!* - Emily Dickinson - 1944 (Op. 108, No. 9) Barron and Bruce as in #29.

32. *Heart, We Will Forget Him* - Emily Dickinson 1944 (Op. 108, No. 1) Winifred Black, soprano; James Kosnick, piano; State University of New York at Buffalo, April, 1974.

33. *And I'm A Rose* - Emily Dickinson - 1944 (Op. 108, No. 4) Black and Kosnick as in #32.

34. *I'm Nobody, Who Are You?* - Emily Dickinson - 1944 (Op. 108, No. 8) Same performers as #32.

35. *Sonata for Piano* - 1949 (Op. 113)   Neely Bruce, pianist, broadcast from WQXR, New York on Robert Sherman's "The Listening Room," April 16, 1975.

    Ruth Anne Rich, pianist, Merkin Hall, New York, September 15, 1986.

36. *Suite for Flute and Piano, No. 1, Woodland Colloquy* - 1950 (Op. 114, No. 1)   Claire Vining, flute; Frances Grasso, piano; at concert of Maine Federation of Music Clubs, Portland, Me., February 11, 1975.

37. *Suite for Flute and Piano*, complete - 1950 (Op. 114)   Patricia Harper, Flute; Leander Bean, piano; Connecticut College, New London, February 22, 1987.

END PAPERS

End Notes by Chapter

Appendices

Bibliography

Indexes

# Chapter Notes for Part I

## Introduction

1. Ralph Waldo Emerson developed the ideas of Transcendentalism as it flourished in New England in the quarter century before the Civil War. It was more of an intellectual and spiritual movement than a strictly reasoned body or doctrine. Basically eclectic in their philosophy, American transcendentalists borrowed generously not only from contemporary German philosophers, but also from religious books of the Orient, especially the *Bhagavadgita*. Transcendentalism maintains that man has ideas, that come not through the five senses or the powers of reasoning, but are either the result of direct revelation from God, his immediate inspiration, or his presence in the spiritual world. It asserts that man has something besides the body of flesh -a spiritual body, with senses to perceive what is true and right. This spiritual body within man's physical body, transcendentalists termed the oversoul, the conscience, or the inner light. Emerson's emphasis on the innate worth of the individual was a logical extension of the theory that man knows by intuition what is true and real.

   See also, Octavius Brooks Frothingham, *Transcendentalism in New England*. Farwell developed his ideas on "Intuition" into a book, *Intuition in the World-Making*. Emerson's doctrine of self-reliance which sought to arouse courage and authenticity of thinking in his countrymen, was also fundamental to Arthur Farwell's philosophy. Also: Ralph Waldo Emerson, *American Scholar,* See vol. 1, pp. 82-83 in Ralph Waldo Emerson, *The Complete Works of Ralph Waldo Emerson* ed. Edward Waldo Emerson, 12 volumes, Boston: Houghton Mifflin Co. 1903.

2. Evelyn Davis, Dissertation, *The Significance of Arthur Farwell as an American Music Educator*. College Park: University of Maryland, 1972.

3. Evelyn Davis Culbertson, "Arthur Farwell's Early Efforts on Behalf of American Music, 1899-1921", *American Music* Vol. 5, No. 2, Summer 1987.

4. Barbara Zuck, *History of Musical Americanism*. Ann Arbor, MI: UMI Research Press, 1980, p. 65.

5. Daniel Kingman, *American Music: A Panorama*. NY: Schirmer Books, 1979, p. 371.

## Chapter 1

1. Much of the material in this chapter and those following that deal with Arthur Farwell's early years are based on information derived from diaries and journals written by his mother, Sara Wyer Farwell, or his own that are in the author's Farwell collection.

2.  George Farwell's father, Lyman, is listed in the *Farwell Genealogy* as item #1997, page 340, as having married Eliza Ann Adams. For an extended biography of Lyman Farwell see Holton, *Farwell Ancestral Memorial*, 1879.

3.  Information supplied by Ernestine Wyer in a letter to Brice Farwell, dated Jan. 26, 1955.

4.  Ibid.

5.  Ibid.

6.  Ibid.

7.  See annual *Carnival Brochure* prepared and published by the St. Paul Carnival Committee, St. Paul, Minnesota.

8.  Ibid.

# Chapter 2

1.  In later years, Sidney was involved with the government in the building of the Panama Canal, after which he was engaged in business and agriculture in upstate New York and New England where he owned large apple orchards. Sidney married the sister-in-law of Louise Homer, the Metropolitan Opera singer, but otherwise was not closely associated with music after leaving college. They had no children.

2.  Arthur Farwell. "Wanderjahre of a Revolutionist", *Musical America*, IX (Jan. 23, 1909), p. 5.

3.  Letter written by L. B. Buchanan to Edgar Kirk, June 2, 1955. This is part of a collection of letters Kirk received when he was doing research for his doctoral dissertation, *Toward American Music*, at Eastman School of Music. Upon completion of his study, he gave the collection to Brice Farwell who loaned it to the author.

4.  Ibid. Letter to Kirk from Howard R. Barton, June 11, 1955.

5.  Farwell's daughter, Sara, suspects it was the number 5, the sum of the digits in his birthday, 2 and 3. He told her early in life that the number 4 would be important to her, her digits being 1 and 3. Such interests led him eventually to a study of the *Cabbala* and its relationship to sonata form as explained in chapter 16.

6.  Later in life, Farwell composed *Heroic Breed*, an orchestral poem, in memory of General Patton and dedicated it to his widow, Beatrice Ayer Patton.

Farwell also named his oldest daughter "Beatrice" after Miss Ayer, his first "real love".

7.  George Lyman Kittredge, 1860-1941, was an American educator and an authority on Shakespeare and early English literature. He taught at Harvard for 48 years. He was interested in music and wrote books on English and Scottish ballads and folk songs.

8.  Farwell, *Wanderjahre,* ibid.

## Chapter 3

1.  Farwell, "Wanderjahre", *Musical America* IX (Jan. 23, 1909) p. 5.

2.  Farwell. "Wanderjahre", *Musical America*, IX (Jan. 30, 1909) p. 11.

3.  Ibid.

4.  Ibid.

5.  Thomas Mott Osborne was a wealthy business man, noted for his humane penologist work at Sing Sing prison. Sidney's specific position with Osborne is unknown, but probably was in some kind of business administration work.

6.  Farwell, "Tribute to Thomas Mott Osborne" in *The New York Times*, n.d., where Farwell wrote glowingly about this man as he had come to know him intimately.

7.  Mrs. Farwell's diary for August 4, 1893, records a visit from a Mr. Minster, a Norwegian nephew of Ole Bull. He played 'cello and guitar for some Norwegian songs during an evening of music-making. Arthur performed on the violin with Mrs. Horn, piano. It is possible that this contact was the start for a later friendship with Mrs. Ole Bull, or the visit could have been the result of an already existing friendship. This is her first reference to the Ole Bull family.

8.  Swami Saradananda was a religious teacher in the Ramakrishna movement whose purpose was to bring the Hindu spiritual wisdom to the West. Swami Vivekananda was its principal leader in America. His colleague, Swami Saradananda, concentrated his teachng on the East coast and New England area.

    Modern Hinduism is highlighted by the teachings of Shri Ramakrishna (1836-1886), who is considered "one of the most remarkable Hindu mystics of recent history". After a period of intense spiritual discipline when he made a profound study of several other religions, notably Christianity and Islam, he experienced ecstatic visions and trances. He lived and taught in the precincts of a Hindu temple. Hindus by the millions have followed Ramakrishna, because "he clearly spoke from the depths of a profound religious experience" and he was credited with a number of miracles. His followers founded the Ramakrishna Mission, which has more than a hundred teaching stations (Vedanta Centers) throughout the world, including twelve in the United States. These are active in medicine, education, publishing, and charity, as well as in spiritual matters. (Life Magazine editorial staff, *The World's Great Religions*, New York: Time Incorporated, 1963, vol. 1 of three, p. 46.) See also *Encyclopedia of Occultism and Parapyschology*, Leslie A. Shepard, ed. Vol. 2, Detroit, MI: Gale Research Co., 1978. pp. 763-64.

9.   Farwell, "Wanderjahre", *Musical America* IX (Feb. 6, 1909) p.
     21.   For listing of these early compositions, see catalogue of Ditson publications for 1897.

## Chapter 4

1.   Farwell, "Wanderjahre of a Revolutionist", *Musical America*, IX (Feb. 6) 1909, p. 21.

2.   Farwell Journal, Book VI.

3.   Farwell, "Wanderjahre", *Musical America* IX (Feb. 6, 1909) p. 21.

4.   Farwell Journal, Book VI.

5.   Ibid.

6.   Farwell,"Wanderjahre", *Musical America* IX (Feb. 13, 1909) p. 21.

7.   Farwell,"Wanderjahre", *Musical America* IX (Feb.20, 1909) p. 21.

8.   Ibid.

9.   Ibid.

10.  Farwell Journal, Book VI.

11.  Farwell, "Wanderjahre", *Musical America*, IX (Feb. 27, 1909) p. 28.

12.  Ibid.

13.  Farwell, "Wanderjahre", *Musical America*, IX (March 6, 1909) p. 23.

14.  Ibid.

15.  Ibid.

16. Alan Howard Levy, *Musical Nationalism, American Composer's Search for Identity*. Westport, Conn.: Greenwood Press, 1983, pp. 46-47 and 51-52.

17. A letter dated Feb. 18, 1899, tells Arthur "I can see you next Friday at 9:A.M. Please let me know as soon as possible by writing me at Meudon, as I must count on you to be there for I will go to my house in Paris especially for your lesson. I am very busy and I do not want to make a special trip for nothing."

18. Levy, Ibid, pp. 46-47. When the report prepared by César Franck and Vincent d'Indy to improve the curriculum at the prestigious Paris Conservatory was rejected, d'Indy and his sympathizers, notably Charles Bordes and Guilmant, formed their own school in 1894 where Guilmant taught organ. However, Guilmant's calling card still retained the Conservatoire connection in 1898. (One notes also that his calling cards and all of his personalized stationery were trimmed with wide black borders at the time when he corresponded with Farwell.)

19. Levy, Ibid, p. 51. Levy gives no source for this information which is obviously wrong to include Farwell.

20. Farwell, "Wanderjahre", *Musical America*, IX (March 13, 1909) p. 14.

21. Ibid.

## Chapter 5

1. *This Fabulous Century 1900-1910*, by the editors of *Time Life Books*, Vol.1, 1969, p. 29.

2. Frederick Jackson Turner, *The Significance of the Frontier in American History*. A paper read at the World's Columbian Exposition in Chicago, in 1893.

3. Harvey Wish, *Contemporary America*. New York: Harper and Brothers, 1945, p. 3.

4. *This Fabulous Century*, p. 6.

5. Ibid, p. 30.

6. Oscar Handlin, *The History of the United States*, Vol.II. New York: Holt, Rinehart, and Winston, 1968, p. 47.

7. Harold Faulkner, *American Political and Social History*, 6th ed. New York: Appleton-Century-Crofts, Inc., 1952, p. 514.

8.   Irving Sablowsky, *American Music*. Chicago: The University of Chicago Press, 1969, p. 97.

9.   David Ewen, *Music comes to America*. NY: Thomas Crowell, 1942, pp. 96-7.

10.  Rose Yont, *Status and Value of Music in Education*. Published doctoral dissertation, University of Iowa, 1916, p. 220.

11.  David Ewen, *Music Comes to America*. NY: Thomas Crowell, 1942, p. 101.

12.  Ibid, pp. 74-77.

13.  Faulkner, p. 624.

## Chapter 6

1.   Farwell, "Wanderjahre", *Musical America*, (March 20, 1909) p. 26.

2.   Ibid.

3.   Ibid.

4.   Ibid.

5.   Farwell, "Wanderjahre", *Musical America,* IX (Mar 27, 1909) p. 19.

6.   Ibid.

7.   Francis Brancaleone, "Edward MacDowell and Indian Motives", *American Music* Vol. 7, No. 4, (Winter 1989) p. 363. Brancaleone's article sheds new light on MacDowell's use of Indian motives and is recommended reading. He shows 15 musical examples using Indian motives. Included is a Dakota tune as harmonized by J. C. Fillmore, compared with one by Farwell.

8.   Farwell, "Wanderjahre", *Musical America* IX (March 27, 1909)  p. 19.

## Chapter 7

1.   Farwell,"Wanderjahre", *Musical America* IX (April 3, 1909) p. 19.

2.   Gilbert Chase, *American Music: From the Pilgrims to the Present*, 2nd rev. ed. New York: McGraw-Hill, 1966, p. 392.

3.   As quoted by Edward N. Waters in "The Wa-Wan Press: An Adventure in Musical Idealism", published in *A Birthday Offering to Carl Engel*, ed. Gustav Reese. New York: G. Schirmer, 1943, p. 217.

4.   Ibid, p. 215.

5.   Ibid, pp. 215-216.

6.   Farwell, "Wanderjahre", Ibid.

7.   Waters, p. 218.

8.   Alan Howard Levy, *Musical Nationalism, American Composer's Search for Identity*. Westport, Conn.: Greenwood Press, 1983, p. 20.

9.   Farwell, "Wanderjahre", *Musical America* IX (April 10, 1909).

10.  Waters. p. 219.

11.  Daniel Kingman, *American Music: A Panorama*. New York: Schirmer Books, 2nd ed. 1990, p. 444.

12.  Adrienne Fried Block, "Amy Beach's Music on Native American Themes", *American Music*, 8, No. 2 (Summer 1990): 142-145. Block points out that 43 percent of the U.S. population attended the Fair, which made it a strong source for molding public opinion and attitudes.

13.  Gilbert Chase, *The Wa-Wan Press, A Chapter in American Enterprise*. Introduction to the re-issue by Arno Press, New York, 1970, p. x.

14.  Kingman. Ibid, pp. 444-445.

15.  Joseph A. Musselman, *Music in the Cultured Generation. A Social History of Music in America, 1870 -1900*. Evanston, Ill.: Northwestern University Press, 1971, pp. 114-115.

16.  Reginald de Koven, "Nationality in Music and the American Composer", *Music of the Modern World* Vol.I, edited by Anton Seidl. New York: D. Appleton Press, 1895, p. 192.

17.  Zoltan Roman, "Music in Turn-of-the-Century America: A View from the 'Old World'". *American Music*, Fall 1989, pp. 320-321.

18.  Ibid, p. 22.

19.  Frédéric Louis Ritter, *Music in America*, [2d ed.] 1890 reprint, New York: Johnson Reprint Co. 1970, pp. 426, 437.

20.  Louis C. Elson, *The National Music of America and Its Sources* (Boston: L.C. Page and Co. 1900) quoted by Roman, Ibid, p. 322.

21. De Koven, Ibid, p. 193.

22. Farwell, *A Letter to American Composers*. Quoted by Gilbert Chase in his introduction to the reissue of the *Wa-Wan Press: A Chapter in American Enterprise*, New York: Arno Press, 1970, pp. xvii-ix.

23. Mussulman, Ibid, pp. 116-117. Quotes from an article written by Emma Bell Miles, "Some Real American Music" for *Harper's* CIX (June, 1904), p. 118.

24. A. Davidoff's letter to Farwell, March 31, 1903, was written in French, trans. by Dr. James Shelton of Oral Roberts University. "Je dois avouer que tout ce que j'ai connu jusqu'à présent de la musique d'outre mer ne m'était nullement sympathique de sorte que je me suis mis à étudier vos éditions avec beaucoup de méfiance, mais j'ai éprouvé un vif plaisir de me voir forcé à changer mon opinion sur la musique américaine qui est évidemment trop peu connue chez nous, et je ne peux plus me contenter d'un simple compte-rendu des quelques lignes. Je serais heureux si je parviens à intéresser les musiciens et le public russes à votre musique.... Agréez, cher monsieur, mes remerciements pour tout ce que vous trouverez possible de faire, ainsi que l'expression de mes sentiments les plus distingués."

25. Lawrence Gilman, "Some American Music", *Harper's Weekly*, (March 7, 1903) p. 394.

26. Juliet Danziger, "Altruistic Music Publishing in America", *Musical Mercury* (Oct.-Nov. 1934) pp. 92-96.

27. Quaintance Eaton, "The Red Man Sings for his Paleface Brothers", *Better Homes and Gardens*, Aug. 1936, pp. 46-49.

28. Kingman, *American Music*, Ibid, p. 445.

## Chapter 8

1. Farwell, "Wanderjahre", *Musical America* IX (April 17, 1909) p. 21.

2. Ibid.

3. Ibid, p. 31.

4. Charles F. Lummis (1859-1928) archaeologist, historian and explorer, city librarian of Los Angeles, and an Indian specialist. He was a classmate, adviser and speech writer for President Theodore Roosevelt, a friend of famous painters, writers, politicians and actors at the turn of the century. He helped organize the Landmarks Club in 1895 to preserve the old missions and the Southern California Historical Society credits him with saving four of them from decay. He also fought for Indian rights. He was the author of a series

of books on the cultural heritage of the Southwest for which he received knighthood from the King of Spain. See Charles Lummis Memorial Association for current information on the famous house which Lummis built that became an historical cultural monument. See also Dudley Gordon's book: *Charles F. Lummis: Crusader in Corduroy*, Cultural Assets Press, 1973.

5.  Farwell, "Wanderjahre, *Musical America* X (May 1, 1909) p. 21.

6.  Pages from Lummis's guest book are illustrated in the book by Turbesé Lummis Fiske and Keith Lummis, *Charles F. Lummis, The Man and His West*, Norman, OK: University of Oklahoma Press, 1975. See Plate IV.

7.  The Bohemian Club created a special musical presentation each year, called the "High Jinks" to afford their members a great time of entertainment and relaxation in their hideaway where they celebrated "the slaying and burial of Care". Farwell gives details of this two weeks' experience in *Musical America* (May 8, 1909).

8.  Farwell, "Wanderjahre", *Musical America*, X (May 1,1909) p. 21.

9.  Farwell, "Wanderjahre" *Musical America*, X (May 8, 1909) p. 23.

10.  *Musical Courier*, Farwell Scrapbook. n.d.

11.  At that time, the A.T.& S.F. Railroad was endeavoring to attract travelers to see the Grand Canyon area and gave Farwell passes as part of their promotional efforts. The expenses were in support of the archeological transcription work, not just a private philanthropy of the railroad. Fred Harvey, head of the A.T.& S.F., was a supporter of Lummis's work for these same promotional reasons.

12.  From a pamphlet in Farwell's Scrapbook.

13.  Farwell, "Wanderjahre", *Musical America* X (May 22, 1909) p. 22.

14.  Farwell "Wanderjahre", *Musical America* X (May 29, 1909) p. 19.

15.  These lectures were entitled: 1) *Myth and Music of the American Indians and Its Relation to the Development of American Musical Art* and 2) *A National American Music*.

16.  Farwell, "Wanderjahre", *Musical America* X (June 12, 1909) p. 19.

# Chapter 9

1.  Farwell, "Wanderjahre", *Musical America* X (June 5, 1909) p. 22.

2. Ibid.

3. Ibid.

4. *Wa-Wan Press Monthly*, Vol.VI. No. 51, Nov. 1907, p. 44.

5. *WWP Monthly*, Vol. VI. No. 52, Dec. 1907, p. 47.

6. *WWP Monthly* Nov. 1907, p. 43.

7. Farwell, "Wanderjahre" *Musical America* X (June 12, 1909) p. 19.

8. Ibid.

9. Farwell, "Wanderjahre", *Musical America* X (June 19, 1909)  p. 19.

10. Ibid.

11. Details of these concerts are described in the same installment of "Wanderjahre" for June 19, 1909.

12. Farwell, "Wanderjahre", *Musical America* X (June 12, 1909)  p. 19.

13. Ibid.

14. Farwell prepared a printed brochure for promoting his new "school" entitled, *Home Life and Music Study*. The title implies the purpose of the school. Farwell felt that "we should spend our life, not alone in studying for life, but in living it while we study." His plan was to provide living quarters for some girls in the Farwell home under the supervision of his mother, and arrange accommodations for boys and others in the immediate neighborhood. It had already been a custom every Wednesday evening to have a social gathering in the Farwell home of composers, musicians, and music lovers from the Boston area .

Arthur Shepherd reported playing four hand duets with Olin Downes at one of these evening affairs. Pupils would have the advantage of these gatherings at which they would hear new music as well as "old", thus experiencing the "double foundation" of home and an established art-life. Courses of study included: Harmony and Counterpoint, Piano, Voice, History of Music, and Coaching in Vocal Repertoire. Farwell, Arthur Shepherd, and Boston teachers, (by special arrangement) were listed as staff. John Beach was later added as another piano teacher. Farwell also provided the option of study in composition by correspondence for those who lived too far away to come to Newton Center. For further description, see Evelyn Davis dissertation *The Significance of Arthur Farwell as an American Music Educator*, University of Maryland, College Park, MD, 1972, pp. 44-46.

15. Farwell, "Wanderjahre", *Musical America*, X (July 3, 1909) p. 19.

16. In the information that Farwell supplied David Ewen for his entry in *American Composers of Today*, he listed the number of centers as being 20 in 1909.

17. Information provided by Carol Walden, Librarian at the New England Conservatory of Music in a letter to Edgar Kirk, April 25, 1956.

18. Farwell, "Wanderjahre", ibid.

## Chapter 10

1. Farwell, Address, "Music for the People" delivered in Ottawa, Canada, to the Canadian Club meeting on March 21, 1914.

2. Theodora Bean, "Audiences on Piers and in the Parks", clipping in Farwell Scrapbook, n.d.

3. Farwell, "When Thou Makest a Feast", an essay published in pamphlet form with some revisions after publication in *Musical America*, XXII (1916) 89. Its purpose was to give suggestions for the meaning of community music.

4. Rose Yont, *Status and Value of Music in Education*. Doctoral dissertation, University of Nebraska. Lincoln, Neb.: Woodruff Press, 1916, pp. 225-6.

5. From the author's taped interview with Gertrude Farwell, May 1965.

6. *Berkeley Times*, Sept. 9, 1919, p. 1.

7. Edward Wagenknecht, *The Seven Worlds of Theodore Roosevelt*, New York: Longmans, Green and Co., 1958, p. 80.

8. From Gibran correspondence, Southern Historical Collection, University of North Carolina.

9. Claude Bragdon, *More Lives Than One*, N.Y.: Alfred A. Knof, 1938, p. 70.

10. Ibid, p. 71.

11. *Berkeley Times*, ibid.

12. Ibid.

13. Henry L. Perry, in charge of membership records for the Bohemian Club, supplied this information. He also proudly added he was a professional singer until his retirement and sang with Farwell during his time at UCLA.

14. The Russell Sage Foundation was organized in 1907 for the improvement of social and living conditions in the U.S.

15. Quoted by Naima Prevots in *American Pageantry: A Movement for Art and Democracy*, Ann Arbor: UMI Research Press, 1990, p. 90.

16. Farwell, "Community Music-Drama: Will Our Country People in Time Help Us to Develop the Real American Theater?" *The Craftsman*, XXVI/4 (July 1914) pp. 418-24.

17. Prevots, Ibid, pp. 47-48.

18. Farwell, "The Pageant and Masque of St. Louis", *Review of Reviews*, L, 1914 pp. 187-193.

19. Prevots, Ibid, p. 72.

20. Prevots, Ibid. p.75.

21. *Berkeley Times*, Sept. 9, 1919.

22. Myrle Wright, "The New York Comunity Chorus." Boston: *National Magazine*, (Nov. 1916) p. 227.

23. See biography on Arthur Farwell in *The New Grove Dictionary of American Music*, eds. H. Wiley Hitchcock & Stanley Sadie. London: Macmillan 1986, p. 102.

24. Claude Bragdon, *More Lives Than One*. N.Y.: Alfred A. Knof. 1938, p. 72. Bragdon and his his wife, Eugenie, determined to "give a party to end all parties". Harry Barnhart was called in to provide "eloquent music" with a chorus hidden among the trees at the foot of the spacious grounds. Bragdon designed and made multicoloured lanterns and used powerful lamps shielded with glass-covered circular screens made to look like rose-windows of a cathedral as featured decorations. The unusual party provoked much talk and news of it finally reached members of the city Park Board. The result was that Bragdon and Barnhart were asked to organize a big civic festival with similar format. The "Festival of Song and Light" took place on September 30, 1915 and was repeated the following year on August first. Farwell's Festival was not until September 23, 1916. These were so successful that other Festivals of Song and Light were staged under Bragdon and Barnhart's direction at Syracuse and Buffalo in 1917.

25. Kenneth Clark, "New York Carried on Tidal Wave of Community Music", *Musical America* XXIV/21 (Sept. 23, 1916) pp. 1, 3-4.

26. Clark, Ibid.

27. Address by Farwell to the Music Teachers National Association, *Community Music and the Music Teacher* as published in the *Volume of Proceedings 1916,* p. 197.

28. *Berkeley Times,* Sept. 9, 1919.

29. Farwell letter to Mr. Crem at Presser Pub. Co., Sept. 5, 1930.

30. National Conference on Community Music, *A Call to a National Conference on Community Music,* New York City, April 7, 1917.

31. Some of the distinguished supporters were: Cabot Ward, President of the Park Board and Park Commissioner of N.Y. City; William G. Willcox, President of the Board of Education, N.Y. City; Mrs. Edward MacDowell; Mrs. Howard Mansfield, President of the National Association of Music School Societies; Mrs. V.G. Simkovitch, President of the National Federation of Settlements; Harry Barnhart, Director of the N.Y. Community Chorus; Franz Kneisel, and John Collier, Secretary of the National Community Conference.

32. Reported by Walter R. Spaulding in "Community Music Conference", Music Teachers National Association, *Volume of Proceedings, 1918,* p. 267.

33. Edward Bailey Birge, *History of Public School Music in the United States.* Reprint. Washington, D.C.: Music Educators National Conference, 1966, pp. 201-202.

34. David Ewen, *Music Comes to America,* New York: Thomas Crowell, 1942, p. 155.

# Chapter 11

1. From a newspaper clipping found in Farwell's files.  No name.

2. Alfred Metzger, "Music Teachers Honor Their New President, Arthur Farwell", *Pacific Coast Musical Review,* Vol. 35, No. 17, January 25, 1919, p. 4.

3. Edgar Lee Kirk, *Toward American Music,* doctoral dissertation  at Eastman School of Music, University of Rochester, Rochester, New York, 1958, p.55. The wife of Rev. Mears was Ernestine Wyer, Farwell's cousin.  It was she who provided information about her childhood experiences with the Farwell boys for Chapter one.  Her early love for George Farwell would have urged her husband to help her elderly uncle.

4. Brice Farwell report as told him by his father.

5. *Musical America,* XXXI/13 (January 24, 1920,) p. 13.

6. Charles Lummis, "Flowers of Our Lost Romance", *Spanish Songs of Old California*. Los Angeles: Charles Lummis, 1923.

7. Farwell, "Notes", *Spanish Songs of Old California*.

8. Kirk, Ibid, p. 56. Also author's interview with Gertrude Farwell.

9. Kirk, Ibid.

10. H. Russell Stimmel, a letter to Edgar Kirk, June 18, 1956.

11. Kirk, Ibid.

12. Edwyn Hunt's letter to Kirk, Oct. 1, 1956.

13. Kirk, Ibid, p. 60.

14. Ernest Batchelder, a letter to Kirk, Jan. 14, 1955.

15. Isabel Morse Jones, *Hollywood Bowl*. Los Angeles: G. Schirmer, Inc. 1936, p. 35.

16. Ibid, p. 60.

17. *Fawnskin Folks* was a magazine devoted to news about the people and events at the real estate development on Big Bear Lake operated by Thompson and Waybright. See also a reprint from *Fawnskin Folks* of a Farwell article concerning the "Theater of the Stars" in *A Guide to the Music and to the Microfilm Collection of His Work*, Brice Farwell, ed. pp. 86-88.

18. Farwell,"Dramatic Ceremony and Symphonic Song Visioned as New Form in Development of True American Art," *Musical America* 45 (Mar 26. 1927): 3.

19. Thomas Stoner, "The New Gospel of Music: Arthur Farwell's Vision of Democratic Music in America", *American Music*, Vol. 9, No. 2 (Summer 1991) pp. 202-203.

## Chapter 12

1. Theresa Shier, "Lansing Forces Unite in New Institute", *Musical America*, (March 31, 1928) p. 29.

2. Edgar Lee Kirk, *Toward American Music - A Study of the Life and Music of Arthur George Farwell*, doctoral dissertaion at Eastman School of Music, Rochester, NY, p. 70.

3. Brice Farwell report to the author.

4. Farwell met Joseph Clark when he went to the Tetons to compose one summer in the 1930s. Clark was his landlord at the Double Diamond Ranch, but also practiced law. He was a U.S. senator from Pennsylvania, and at one time had been mayor of Philadelphia. Brice Farwell told the author that when he visited the Tetons in 1972 that Clark remembered his father very vividly from his summer sojourn and spoke "very highly of him and his music".

5. Farwell letter to Tom Weigle, a former composition student, Dec. 9, 1933.

6. John W. Crist letter to Edgar Kirk, 1956.

## Chapter 13

1. Author's interview with Gertrude Farwell May 1965.

2. Farwell, "Roy Harris" *Musical Quarterly*, (Jan. 1932) .

3. Dan Stehman, *Roy Harris, An American Pioneer*. Boston: Twayne Publishing Co., 1984, p. 13.

4. Edgar Lee Kirk, *Toward American Music*, doctoral dissertation at Eastman School of Music, Rochester, NY, p. 87.

## Chapter 14

1. Brice Farwell provided taped interviews with other members of his family. He also gave the writer much further information in personal interviews, by telephone and by letters. Sara and Emerson Farwell supplied special information and letters. This chapter is largely the result of these contacts.

2. The writer questioned Brice Farwell about the fate of his father's own full-size violin. He responded that he never heard what had happened to it, nor did he recall ever seeing it in the house. He suspects that his father may have finally sold the violin when in desperate financial need. However, Brice had seen and heard his father play someone else's violin when they were visiting Sara at Nyack. "He did a lively job of *Sourwood Mountain*".

3. Farwell, "When Thou Makest a Feast", *Musical America*, Oct. 1916, later published in pamphlet form.

## Chapter 15

1. One such student was Mae Nelson Stewart who arranged for a day's teaching-session with Farwell in the summer of 1939. She had won first prize in the

song cycle category of the National Federation of Music Club's competition. This was in the same contest where Farwell's *Symbolistic Study No. 6* had won a prize, so she was eager to meet him. She told the author of that long lesson which she hoped would be the first of many more. She was impressed by Farwell's energy and boyish enthusiasm, his wonderful sense of good humor, and genuine helpful interest in her work, as well as the work of other students he mentioned. One warning he gave her was "Be careful about repeating a sequence too many times." Farwell's move to New York prevented further lessons. The paths of Mae Stewart and the author eventually crossed in Ocala, Florida, where Mrs. Stewart became her excellent piano accompanist for her Farwell lecture-recitals there.

2. Anthroposophists were believers of a spiritualistic and mystical doctrine, derived mainly from the philosophy of Rudolph Steiner (1861-1925). He taught an occult philosophy relating man to his natural environment, with special emphasis on the significance of color and rhythm. Anthroposophy covers a wide range of activity - education , music, painting, eurhythmy, biodynamic farming, medicine, and architecture. There are about 70 anthroposophical schools throughout the world and the Society has many branches.

3. The Rudolph Steiner School in New York City was one of several established by Steiner, a seer, who founded the Anthroposophist movement. It places great emphasis on color, form, rhythm and the life of nature. These schools were noted for their sensitivity and secured remarkable results in their special schools for retarded children. *Encyclopedia of Occultism and Parapsychology*, Leslie A. Shepard, ed. Vol. 2, Detroit. MI: Gale Research Co. pp. 882-83.

4. Farwell's Symbolic Dreams were a vital part of his inner life. These were unusual vivid dreams that held special meaning for him. Even those he experienced before 1900, he could recall clearly enough many years later so he was able to draw them on paper in every detail.

5. *The Villager*, New York Aug. 1, 1940.

6. Noble Kreider was a life-long friend and a Wa-Wan composer. Farwell knew that Kreider was a great lover of Japan and Japanese culture because he had traveled to Japan several times. Sara also knew Kreider's Japanese interests. Hence the meaning of the "surprise story" in Farwell's letter.

7. Farwell's handwriting is unclear for this item.

8. The fate of the recordings to which Farwell refers, is unknown. They are not found in the family archives.

# Chapter Notes for Part II

## Chapter 16

1. Farwell, "Wanderjahre of a Revolutionist", *Musical America* IX Feb. 27, 1909, p. 19.

2. I visited the Brice Farwell home in Briarcliff Manor, New York, in May 1965, where Brice had gathered members of the Farwell family for me to interview. I recorded these conversations on tape also during this time. Beatrice, Sara, Emerson, and Gertrude Farwell as well as Mr. and Mrs. Brice Farwell were present and provided information. I interviewed Jonathan and his wife, Joerle, in my Maryland home. Further interviews with members of the family continued to take place until the completion of this book.

3. Ibid.

4. In 1937, Brice Farwell visited the pension where his father had lived in Boppard. He talked with the son and daughter (now elderly) of Arthur's pension keeper there, who remembered his father, and gave this report.

5. The Stendahl Syndrome is a phenomenon discovered by Dr. Graziella Magherini, chief of psychiatry at the Santa Maria Nuova Hospital in Florence. While her studies of 107 cases dealt with disoriented art-lovers, the symptoms seem applicable to music-lovers as well. See also an editorial in the Spanish newspaper *Hoy*, for Jan. 3, 1990, "El síndrome de Stendahl", written by Alfredo Bryce Echenique, Santo Domingo, Dominican Republic.

6. Farwell, "Sonata - Only Possible Form", *Musical America*, XVI?6 (June 15, 1912), p. 21.

7. Farwell, "Musical Form Under New Human Conditions", *Musical America*, XXII/1 (May 8, 1915) p. 34.

8. Farwell, "Sonata Form and the Cabbala"," *Musical Quarterly*, XXVII/1 (January 1941), pp. 26-37.

9. Arnold Schoenberg, *Structural Functions of Harmony*. New York: Norton, 1954, pp. 76-113.

10. Linda Richer, *Arthur Farwell's Piano Quintet: Aspects of Form and Thematic Development*, M.M. thesis at San Francisco State University, 1987, p. 59.

11. To place Farwell's harmonic style into context of his times, see Jim Samson, *Music in Transition: A Study of Tonal Expansion and Atonality, 1900-1920*. New York: Norton, 1977, pp. 1-3.

12. Kirk, Edgar, *Toward American Music - A Study of the Life and Music of Arthur Farwell*, p. 247.

13.  Chase, Gilbert. *America's Music*, second edition, p. 571

14.  Quoted from K. Robert Schwartz's review of Ned Rorem's book *Settling the Score* as found in the Book Nook II column page 6 of the *I.S.A.M. Newsletter* for Volume XVIII, No. 1: Nov. 1988.

## Chapter 17

1.  Gilbert Chase, *America's Music*, 3rd ed. Ch. 22.

2.  Ibid, p. 410.

3.  Alice Fletcher, *Indian Story and Song from North America* (Boston: Small, Maynard and Co., 1900)  The well-worn copy in the author's Farwell Collection attests to its former frequent use. Fletcher, who was holder of the Thaw Fellowship, Peabody Museum, Harvard University, worked for twenty years to preserve the folklore and song of the American Indian.

4.  Rough translation from old German script by Dr. Seigfried Schatzmann of Oral Roberts University.

5.  *Laurel Song Book Manual*, C.C. Birchard, 1903, pp. 12-13; pp. 92-93.

6.  Ibid, p. 57.

7.  Ibid, pp. 58-60.

8.  Another letter from Humperdinck to Farwell also written in old German script translated by Dr. Siegfried Schatzmann. The spelling for the name "Stonuss" is unclear.  This letter and others from Humperdinck are in the Farwell Collection for further viewing if desired.

9.  Benjamin Lambord, *Music in America*, Vol. 4 of *The Art of Music*. Farwell and Darby, eds.  New York: The National Society of Music, 1915, p. 411.

10.  Chase devotes an entire chapter on the Indian's cultural life in his new edition of *America's Music* as noted above in no.1.

11.  Lambord, Ibid, p. 412.

12.  Translation by Dr. Seigfried Schatzmann of Humperdinck's letter to Farwell written in old German script.

13.  David Ewen, *American Composers Today*. New York: The H.W. Wilson Co. 1949, p. 92.

14. Edgar Kirk, *Toward American Music*, unpublished doctoral dissertation, Eastman School of Music, University of Rochester, 1957, p. 209.

15. Lambord, Ibid, p. 412.

16. Kirk, Ibid, p. 209.

17. Angie Denbo, *Geronimo*. Norman, OK: University of Oklahoma Press, 1976, pp. 400-407.

18. Lambord, *Music in America*, ibid, pp. 311-312.

19. Farwell, "Wanderjahre of a Revolutionist", *Musical America* X (May 22, 1909) p. 22.

20. *The International Cyclopedia of Music and Musicians*, Oscar Thompson, ed.-in-chief, 9th ed. Robert Sabin. New York: Dodd, Mead and Co. 1964, p. 715.

21. Mark Fenster,"Preparing the Audience, Informing the Performers: John A Lomax and *Cowboy Songs and Other Frontier Ballads*", *American Music* Vol. 7, No. 3, Fall 1989, p. 267.

22. *The International Cyclopedia*, ibid. Quoted by Anne Masters, p. 715.

23. Ibid, p. 715.

24. Lombard, *Music in America*, p. 312.

25. Lombard, Ibid, p. 413.

26. Gustav Reese (1899-1977) was head of the publication department for the firm of G. Schirmer at this time and from 1945 to 1955 held the same post at Carl Fischer. He was a founding member of the American Musicological Society and active in its administration. He set the standards for scholarly writing with his *Music in the Middle Ages* and *Music in the Renaissance*.

27. For further information on Indian music see Bruno Nettle's detailed account in *North American Indian Musical Styles*, especially pp. 24-37 and 42-48, "Memoirs of the American Folklore Society", Vol. 45, Austin: University of Texas Press, 1954. An excellent article entitled "Navajo Music" by David P. McAllister and Douglas F. Mitchell, is found in *Handbook of North American Indians*, Vol. 10 "Southwest", Smithsonian Institution, 1983, pp. 605-623. Other informative volumes in this well-documented series are: Vol. 8, *California*, 1978, "Music and Musical Instruments", by William J. Wallace, pp. 642-648; Vol. 11, *Great Basin*, 1986, "Music" by Thomas Vennum, Jr., pp. 682-704. These books are part of a planned series of 20 volumes which the Smithsonian Institute publishes whenever a volume pertaining to a particular group of

Indians is completed.  Presently, volumes 5, 6, 8, 10, 11, and 15 are known available.

## Chapter 18

1.  "Of Songs, Contests, and Publishers" *The Sonneck Society Bulletin*, Summer 1988, Vol. XIV, No. 2, p. 83.

2.  Benjamin Lambord, *Music in America*,  Vol. 4 of *The Art of Music*, ed. Farwell and Darby.  New York: The National Society of Music, 1915, pp. 412-413.

3.  Farwell's *Thirty-four Songs on Poems of Emily Dickinson*, published by Boosey and Hawkes in two volumes.

4.  Nathan Broder was a music editor at G. Schirmer publishers.

5.  Farwell used two related poems in setting *The Little Tippler*.

6.  Quoted by Ruth C. Friedberg in *American Art Song and Poetry*, Vol. I, 1981, Metuchen, NJ: Scarecrow Press Inc., p. 110.

7.  Daniel Pinkham's lecture, *Putting Emily Dickinson's Poems to Music* given on the Cambridge Forum Radio program, Sept. 23, 1988. The writer secured a taped copy of the lecture.

8.  Elizabeth Phillips, *Emily Dickinson. Personae and Performance*. University Park, Pennsylvania: Pennsylvania State University Press, 1988, p. 2.

9.  Richard B. Sewell, ed., *Introduction to Emily Dickinson.  A Collection of Critical Essays*.  Englewood Cliffs, New Jersey: Prentice Hall, 1963, p. 6.

10. From a letter David Leisner wrote April 14, 1989, to Carlton Lowenberg who was gathering data for his bibliography: *Musicians Wrestle Everywhere, Emily Dickinson and Music*.

11. See Farwell essay on *Emily Dickinson* in Appendix B, p. 6.

12. Ibid, pp. 2-3.

13. Edgar Kirk, *Toward American Music - A Study of the Life and Music of Arthur George Farwell* unpublished Ph. D. dissertaton, Eastman School of Music, U. of Rochester, 1957, p. 116.

14. William Treat Upton, *Art-Song in America*, Boston: Oliver Ditson, 1930, p. 156.

15. Upton, *Supplement, Art-Song in America, 1930-1938*.  Boston: Oliver Ditson, 1938, p. 19.

16. Richard B. Sewell, *The Life of Emily Dickinson*, Vol. 2, New York: Farrar, Straus, and Giroux, 1974, p. 485.

17. Karl Kroeger, "Word Painting in the Music of William Billings", *American Music* Vol. 6, No. 1, Spring 1988, p. 45. Kroeger presents some history of the use of word painting and the "doctrine of affections". He quotes Thuringus' three types from "Word painting" in the *New Harvard Dictionary of Music* ed. Don Michael Randel (Cambridge Belknap Press of Harvard University Press, 1986) p. 935.

18. Ruth C. Friedberg, *American Art Song and American Poetry*, Vol. I, Metuchen, NJ: Scarecrow Press, 1981, p. 16.

19. T. H. Johnson, *Emily Dickinson, An Interpretive Biography*, Cambridge, MA: Belknap Press of Harvard University Press, 1955, pp. 107-108.

20. *Getting to Heaven* was commissioned by the Unitarian Universalist Association and the Unitarian Universalists Musicians' Network on the occasion of the "Concert for the Hymnbook" held in Faneuil Hall, Boston.

21. Author's telephone interview with Daniel Pinkham March 28, 1989.

22. Thomas W. Ford, *Heaven Beguiles the Tired*, University, Alabama: University of Alabama Press, 1966, pp. 9?-100.

23. Pinkham radio lecture. See item 7.

24. Carlton Lowenberg has been compiling lists of composers who have made settings of Dickinson's works for his bibliography: *Musicians Wrestle Everywhere, Emily Dickinson and Music, to be published by Fallen Leaf Press.* He has located 270 composers who have set Dickinson's poetry and letters.

25. Ibid.

26. Gilbert Chase, *America's Music*, 3rd ed. p. 356.

27. See Paula Bennett, *My Life a Loaded Gun, Female Creativity and Feminist Poetics*, Boston: Beacon Press, 1986, p. 61. Also T. H. Johnson, *Emily Dickinson, An Interpretive Biography*, pp. 98-99.

28. Ruth Miller, *Poetry of Emily Dickinson*, Middletown, Connecticut: Wesleyan Press, 1968, pp. 91-92.

29. Jo Ann Sims *Capturing the Essence of the Poet: A Study and Performance of Selected Musical Settings for Solo Voice and Piano of the Poetry of Emily Dickinson*, unpublished doctoral dissertation, University of Illinois at Urbana-Champaign, 1987. See pages 182-190

30. A. Farwell, Wa-Wan Press, 1902, in his introduction n.p. preceding *Helen,* by Arthur R. Little, p. 5.

31. Upton, *Art Song in America*, p. 156.

32. Brice Farwell, "More Than Music Composed After Blake by Arthur Farwell" in *Blake, an Illustrated Quarterly*, 42 (Fall 1977), pp. 86-103.

33. Upton, Ibid, p. 153.

34. Donald Fitch, *Blake Set to Music* Berkeley: University of California Press, 1989, p. 260.

35. Upton, Ibid, pp. 155-156.

36. Lambord, *Music in America*, p. 413.

37. Thomas Bullfinch, *The Golden Age of Myth and Legend*, London: George G. Harrap & Co. 1915, pp. 65-69.

38. Donald Ivey, *Song, Anatomy, Imagery, and Styles*, NY: Free Press, 1970, p. 95-96.

39. Quoted by James Husst Hall, in *The Art Song*, Norman, Oklahoma: University of Oklahoma Press, 1953, p. 184.

40. Ibid, p. 75.

41. Vernon H. Moeller has made an excellent analysis of some of Farwell's songs in his study, *Theoretical Aspects of Arthur Farwell's Musical Settings of Poems by Emily Dickinson* for his M. M. degree at the University of Texas in Austin, May 1979. See pages 54 and 58.

42. Ibid, p. 72.

43. Ibid, pp. 96-98.

44. Susanne Langer, *Feeling and Form*, New York: Scribner's, 1953, p. 51.

45. Discussed in chapter 10.

46. *Soldier, Soldier.* Dramatic ballad for baritone. Text also by Arthur Farwell.
   Arouse! Arouse! "Arouse and beware!"
   Life for life, the fight is on, Land and sea and air;
   Ten million men a-marching To set the world aright,
   The flag of the Union in the thickest of the fight.
   Where's the corner of the land Deaf to the call?

Where's the friend of liberty Will not give his all?
North, South, East and West, One forevermore,
Arouse! Arouse! Arouse and beware!
Who's for the war, the war!

"Soldier, soldier, tell me, Where are you going,
Singing so gaily in the morning? "
"I'm off to do my bit Where the trench fires are lit,
Singing so gaily in the morning."

"Soldier, soldier, there's no war in the land,
"Say where would you be fighting?"
"Over there, across the sea,
Where my brother calls to me
There's where I would be fighting." . . . .

"Drummer, drummer, what do I hear?
That falls so heavy on the morning? "
"The dead march, the dead march, trumpet and drum,
Falling so heavy on the morning."
"Gunner, gunner, what do you bear
On your caisson so slow in the morning?"
"A soldier, a soldier, slain across the sea,
On my caisson so slow in the morning."

The poem continues for many more verses building up in tension and patriotic fervor. The Spirit of War speaks to claim his power. Then fast, agitated music speaks to the dead soldier to awake and "sing your song again" until a united America is "uprisen and united" to answer the call. The first verse is repeated, "Arouse!" etc. to conclude the song. This is a major dramatic ballad covering 25 pages of music.

47. Michael Tippett, *A History of Song*, Denis Stevens, ed. New York: W. W. Norton & Co. 1960, p. 463.

48. Sidney T. Cooke was minister of the Church of the Holy Apostles in New York City. Farwell's files include several letters from Rev. Cooke regarding the promotion of the United Nations Anthem that the two had created. Rev. Cooke was active also in the American Theosophical Society, serving as its vice president in 1946.

49. *New Songs For New Voices*, David Mannes and Louis Untermeyer, editors, New York: Harcourt and Brace, 1928.

## Chapter 19

1. Brice Farwell, letter to the writer in which he recalled that his father made this claim of influence on Griffes.

2. *The New Grove Dictionary of American Music*. Edited by H. Wiley Hitchcock and Stanley Sadie, London: Macmillan, 1986, p. 102.

3. Ibid, p. 102.

4. Ibid, p. 103.

5. The reaction from David Hall, critic for *Stereo Review*, after seeing the piano score and listening to a taped performance of the Sonata. He was very favorably impressed with the music.

## Chapter 20

1. Brice Farwell's *Guide to the Music of Arthur Farwell and to the Microfilm Collection of His Work* lists 1901 as the year of completion.

2. Linda Richer, *Arthur Farwell's Piano Quintet: Aspects of Form and Thematic Development*, M. M. thesis at San Francisco State University, 1987, p. 74.

3. Ibid, pp. 74-75.

4. Ibid, p. 78.

5. Morris Hochberg attended Michigan State College where he studied violin with Michael Press, head of the violin department. Press considered Hochberg to be one of his best students. In later years, Hochberg concertized with his wife, Sylvia, who was an excellent pianist.

6. Irving Lowens, "Arthur Farwell: Rediscovering an American Original," *High Fidelity Magazine*, 28/11 (November 1978), pp. 100-102.

7. Ronald Erickson's program notes for the record jacket of the *Piano Quintet*.

8. Richer, p. 97.

9. Ibid, p. 99.

10. Ibid, p. 109.

11. Ibid, p. 117.

12. Douglas Moore, Program notes for record jacket, *Music for Cello and Piano, Arthur Farwell and Charles Cadman*, Musical Heritage Society, #4348.

13. Moore's comments from a telephone conversation with author, Oct. 15, 1988.

14. Ibid.

## Chapter 21

1. It is possible that a copy might be available in the Arthur W. Tams library as the Tams logo is on the existing score.

2. Benjamin Lambord, *Music in America*, Vol. IV, p. 412, of the *Art of Music*. Farwell and Darby (ed). New York: The National Society of Music, 1915.

3. Interview for *The Berkeley Times*, Sept. 9, 1919.

4. Naima Prevots, *American Pageantry: A Movement for Art and Democracy*, Ann Arbor: UMI Research Press, 1990, pp. 157, 205-210.

5. Herbert Peyser, *Musical America*, XXIV/5 (June 3, 1916) pp. 1, 3-4.

6. Quoted by Gertrude Farwell in 1965 interview.

7. Farwell address at a Canadian Club meeting No. 24, in Chateau Laurier, Ottawa, March 21, 1914.

8. William Chauncey Langdon was an early prominent leader in the American Pageant Association. See Chapter 10.

9. Farwell, Address, *Music for the People*, March 21, 1914.

10. Hunt's letter was one of many which Kirk received while doing research for his doctoral dissertation, *Toward American Music*.

11. Farwell, Report to the Management of the Theater of the Stars, first season, 1925. Courtesy of UCLA Library, Special Collections.

12. *Fawnskin Folks* was a magazine devoted to news about the people and events at Waybright and Thompson's real estate development on Big Bear Lake.

13. Walter W. Squier, "Appreciation and a Prophecy", *Fawnskin Folks*, July 1925, p. 18.

14. W. W. Squier, "Opening of the Theater of the Stars", *Fawnskin Folks*, July 1925, pp. 22-28.

15. Farwell's Report to Management.

16. Ibid.

17. Donald Ryan, a colleague, was engaged to study the score of *Cartoon* to give the author a second opinion of Farwell's only opera. Distinguished as concert pianist and teacher, Ryan is well qualified to do so.

18. Ryan, "Analysis of Arthur Farwell's opera *Cartoon*," Spring 1989, unpublished report.

19. Ibid.

20. Some of the folk music scenes in act two can be cut as they only lend color to the opera without contributing much to the total story.

21. Ryan, ibid.

## Chapter 22

1. Farwell journal entry, Book VI.

2. Benjamin Lambord, *Music in America*, Vol. IV, p. 411 of *The Art of Music*, Farwell and Darby, (ed.), New York: The National Society of Music, 1915.

3. Program notes, Rochester Symphony Orchestra concert, Feb. 24, 1925.

4. Lambord, ibid.

5. The Symbolists were part of a literary movement that originated in France in the late 19th century. They were a reaction against realism and naturalism. These writers and artists concerned themselves with general truths instead of actualities, exalted the metaphysical and the mysterious, especially the mystical power and charm of music, and aimed to unify and blend the arts and the functions of the senses. Symbolism is defined as the practice of investing things with a symbolic meaning by expressing the invisible, intangible, or spiritual by means of visible or sensous representation in literature and the fine arts. (Webster's New International Dictionary) William Fleming states that the art of the symbolist is one of the fleeting moment; everything rushes past in an accelerated panorama. "With the metaphor as a starting point, a symbolist prose poem flows by in a sequence of images that sweeps the reader along a swift current of words with a minimum of slowing down to ponder their meaning." (William Fleming, *Arts and Ideas*. NY: Holt, Rinehart and Winston, Inc. 3rd ed. pp. 496-97). Composers adopted some of these ideas in their creations. The quotation from Farwell explains his position.

6. Brice Farwell, *Guide*, p. 42.

7. Mrs. Stickle was a friend who lived in Pennsylvania and frequently invited Farwell to be her guest.

8. Franco Autori, composer and distinguished co-conductor with Arturo Toscanini of the New York Philharmonic Orchestra for ten years and conductor of other well-known orchestras, was invited to the author's home for this occasion when Brice Farwell shared his copy of the Rudoph Gott Symphony taped performance. The beautifully prepared score is part of the writer's Farwell Collection.

9. Gilbert Chase. *America's Music* 3rd ed., Chicago: University of Illinois Press, 1987, p. 353.

10. Keith Merrill evidently handled publicity and work connected with the National Symphony Orchestra while Hans Kindler was the conductor.

## Epilogue

1. *The New Grove's Dictionary of American Music*. Edited by H. Wiley Hitchcock and Stanley Sadie, London: Macmillan, 1986, p. 103.

2. Ibid, p. 102.

3. A. Walter Kramer made these statements on the record jacket of Farwell' *Gods of the Mountain* recording by The Royal Philharmonic Orchestra, Karl Krueger, conducting.

# Appendix I.

## A Partial List of Articles
## by Arthur Farwell

1. "Aspects of Indian Music," *Southern Workman* XXXI (1902), 211-17.
2. "A Letter to American Composers," *Wa-Wan Press* 1903.
3. "The Music of the American Indians," *American Art Journal* LXXXII (1903), 386.
4. "The Influence of Folk Song Upon Classical Music," *International Quarterly* VII (1903), 32-4.
5. "An Affirmation of American Music," *Musical World* III Jan. 1903, p. 11.
6. "Music in the Abstract," *Musical World* III (1903), 93.
7. "The Search for the Present," *Musical World* III (1903), 164-166.
8. "A Brief View of American Indian Music," *The Messenger* IV (1903), 266.
9. "Artistic Possibilities of Indian Myth," *Post Lore* I (1904), 46-61.
10. "Toward American Music," *Out West* XX (1904).
11. "The Darling of Music," *Musical Student* I (1906), 4-7.
12. "Struggle Toward a National Music," *North American* CLXXXVI 1907), 565-70.
13. "Harmony, Psychology, and Folksongs," *The New Music Review* VI (1907).
14. "A National Movement for American Music," *Review of Reviews* XXXVIII (1908), 721-724.
15. "Society and American Music," *Atlantic Monthly* CI (1908), 232-236.
16. "The Basis of Chromatics," *The New Music Review*, Oct. 1908.
17. "What Teachers and Pupils Could Do for American Music," *Etude*, Dec. 1908.
18. "The Relation of Folksong to American Musical Development," *MTNA Proceedings, Series 2*, 1907.
19. "National Work Versus Nationalism," *The New Music Review* VIII (July, 1909).
20. "Wanderjahre of a Revolutionist," *Musical America* IX (1909), 12-16 and 16-26.

21. "How to Become a Judge of Good Music," *The Circle*, Jan. 1909.
22. "American Theater for Opera in English," *Review of Reviews* XXXIX (1909), 493-94.
23. "How the Midsummer High Jinks' Came into Existence," *Musical America* X (July 17, 1909), 3.
24. "The Bohemian Club High Jinks of 1909," *Musical America* X (Oct. 6, 1909), 3-8.
25. "On the Grave Danger of a Composer Being Natural," *The New Music Review* IX, Feb. 1910.
26. "New York Leads Way to New Era in Municipal Music," *Musical America* XII, (Oct. 8, 1910), 92.
27. "American Opera on American Themes," *Review of Reviews* XLIII, (1911), 441-48.
28. "New York's Municipal Music: Two Years Advance," *Review of Reviews* XLIV, (Oct. 1911), 451-58.
29. "Significance and Progress of Municipal Music, and Its Power to Develop the Festival Spirit," *The Craftsman* IX, (Nov. 1910) 179-185.
30. "Noted Composers Honored at Norfolk Festival," *Musical America*, June 17, 1911.
31. "Noted 'World Hymn' for July Fourth Celebration," *Musical America* XIV, July 1, 1911.
32. "Keeping in Touch with the World's Musical Problems," *Musical America* XIV, May 20, 1911.
33. "Keeping in Touch with the World's Musical Growth through the Piano," *Musical America* XIV, Sept. 5, 1911.
34. "A Glance at Present Musical Problems in America," *Musical America* XIV, Oct. 14, 1911.
35. "Oscar Hammerstein," *Review of Reviews* XLV (1912), 183-86.
36. "Promotor of American Music," *Hampton* XXVIII (1912), 75.
37. "Ragtime and Symphony," *The International*, Sept., 1912.
38. "The Incubus of American Culture," *The International*, July, 1912.
39. "Leadership in Contemporary Music," *Musical America* XV, Jan. 6, 1912.
40. "Preparing Oneself to Meet Intense Competition in Musical World Today," *Musical America* XV, Jan. 13, 1912.
41. "What Is Personality?" *Musical America* XV, Jan. 20, 1912.

42. "A Word About Brahms," *Musical America* XV, Jan. 27, 1912.
43. "The Poem of 'Mona'," *Musical America* XV, Feb. 3, 1912.
44. "Symphonic Apostasy of America," *Musical America* XV, (1912), 31.
45. "The Debussy of 'Saint Sebastian'," *Musical America* XV, Feb. 24, (1912).
46. "Music - A Sick Art," *Musical America* XV (Mar. 9, 1912), 30.
47. "Personality or Not," *Musical America* XVI, (1912), 18.
48. "American Librettos--Aspect One," *Musical America* XVI, March 16, 1912.
49. "Maecenases in American Music," *Musical America* XVI, March 23, 1912.
50. "Futurism in America," *Musical America* XVI, March 30, 1912.
51. "Music and the Subjective Mind," *Musical America* XVI, (1912) 20.
52. "Music and the New Fourth," *Musical America* XVI, April 13, 1912.
53. "The Wagner of Parsifal," *Musical America* XVI, April 20, 1912.
54. "Parsifal Revisited," *Musical America* XVI, April 27, 1912.
55. "Retrospect and Vista," *Musical America* XVI, April 27, 1912.
56. "Retrospect and Vista," *Musical America* XV, May 4, 1912, 26.
57. "Sonata - Only Possible Form," *Musical America* XVI, (June 15, 1912), 24.
58. "A Singer Who Understood," *Musical America* XVI (July 20, 1912), 28.
59. "An Eleven Year's Adventure," *Musical America* XVI, Oct. 14, 1912.
60. "The Minor Artist's Salvation," *Musical America* XVI, No.22, 17.
61. "A Call for the Times," *Musical America* XVII, (Nov. 9, 1912), 17.
62. "Municipal Music in New York," *MTNA Proceedings*, Series 8, 1913.
63. "Pageantry and the Composer," *Musical America* XVII, (Feb. 1913), 18.
64. "Youth and Composition," *Musical America* XVII (Feb. 8, 1913), 14.

65. "Revolutionary Portents," *Musical America* XVIII, (Apr. 26, 1913).
66. "Overtones and Sanity," *Musical America*, XVII, May 3, 1913.
67. "Meriden N.H. Tests Musical Possibilities of the Pageant," *Musical America* XVIII, (July 12, 1913), 3, 31.
68. "Individual Advancement - I," *Musical America* XIX, (Dec. 20, 1913), 18.
69. "Individual Advancement - II," *Musical America* XIX, (Dec. 27, 1913), 32.
70. "Individual Advancement - III," *Musical America* XIX, (Jan.3, 1914), 32.
71. "Examples of Creative Experience," *Musical America* XIX, (Jan. 10, 1914), 37.
72. "The Ideal of the Artist," *Musical America* XIX, (Feb. 14, 1914), 40.
73. "Music in the New Age," *Musical America*, XIX, (Mar. 21, 1914), 3.
74. "Music in the New Age - II," *Musical America*, XIX, (Mar. 28, 1914), 32.
75. "The New Gospel of Music," *Musical America* XIX, (Apr. 4, 1914), 32.
76. "The New Gospel of Music - II," *Musical America* XIX, (Apr. 14, 1914), 36.
77. "A New Art of the People," *Musical America* XIX, (Apr. 18, 1914), 32.
78. "A New Art of the People - II," *Musical America* XIX, (Apr. 25, 1914), 32.
79. "Music in the Pageant," *Musical America* XX, (May 30, 1914), 32.
80. "Community Music Drama: Will Our Country People in Time Help Us to Develop the Real American Theater?" *Craftsman* XXVI (1914), 418-24.
81. "The Content of Community Music-Drama," *Musical America* XX, (June 13, 1914), 14.
82. "The Pageant and Community Auto-Suggestion," *Musical America* XX, (June 27, 1914).
83. "Pageant and Masque of St. Louis," *Review of Reviews* L (1914), 187-93.

84. "The Three Camps," *Musical America* XXI, (Mar. 27, 1915), 14.
85. "The Coming Composer," *Musical America* XXI, (Apr. 10, 1915), 28.
86. "The Camp of the Servers", *Musical America* XXI, (Apr. 17, 1915), 14.
87. "The Composer and the Second Commandment," *Musical America* XXI, (May 1, 1915), 10.
88. "The Camp of the Conservers," *Musical America* XXII, (May 22, 1915), 34.
89. "Antichrist in Art," *Musical America* XXII, (May 29, 1915), 34.
90. "Servers, Conservors, and AntiChrists in Music," *Musical America* XXII (1915), 1.
91. "Musical Forms under New Harmonic Conditions," *Musical America* XXII (1915), 2-4.
92. "Recent Object Lessons for an American Music Drama," *Musical America* XXII, (July 10, 1915), 10.
93. "Final Considerations as to a National Music Drama," *Musical America* XXII, (July 17, 1915), 10.
94. "American Music After 15 Years," *Musical America* XXII, (July 31, 1915), 10.
95. "Community and the Music Teacher," *MTNA Proceedings*, Series 11, 1916.
96. "The Shadow of War," *Musical America* XXII, (Oct. 16, 1915), 47.
97. "Arthur Farwell States Case of the Community Chorus in Reply to Frank Damrosch's Criticism," *Musical America* XXIII, Mar. 4, 1916).
98. "Song and Light Festival Reveals a New Art Form," *Musical America* 24 (August 12, 1916): 6
99. "When Thou Makest a Feast," *Musical America* XXIV (Oct. 14, 1916), 89.
100. "Giving the People What They Want," *The Touchstone* , May, 1917.
101. "Community Chorus," *New Magazine*, March, 1917.
102. "Music as a Form of Public Recreation," *Association Seminar*, April, 1917.
103. "The Riddle of the Southwest," *The Los Angeles Times*, Sept. 26, 27, and 29, 1926.

104. "Music and the People," *Touchstone* I (1926), 88-93.
105. "Dramatic Ceremony and Symphonic Song Envisioned as New Form in Development of True American Art," *Musical America* XLV, No. 23 (1927), 3.
106. "Evolution of New Form Foreseen for America's Music," *Musical America* XLV, (Mar. 19, 1927), 13.
107. "The Zero Hour in Musical Evolution," *Musical Quarterly* XVIII (Jan. 1927), 85-99.
108. "Roy Harris," *Musical Quarterly* XVIII (1932), 18-32.
109. "Let Us Play," Scribner's XC (1934), 145-50
110. "Pioneering for American Music," *Modern Music* XII, March 1935.
111. "Composer Lithographs Own Music," *Musical America* LVII, No.10, (1937), 25.
112. "Sonata Form and the Cabbala," *Musical Quarterly* XXVII (Jan. 1941), 26-37.
113. "Science and Intuition," *Tomorrow* IV, August, 1943.
114. "Hidden Race," *Tomorrow*, August, 1943.
115. "America's Gain from a Bayreuth Romance: The Mystery of Anton Seidl," *Musical Quarterly* XXX (1944), 448-57.
116. "Hitler's Intuition," *Tomorrow* IV, No. 1, Sept., 1944.
117. "Freedom to Not Worship God," *Tomorrow* IV, No. 6. Feb. 1, 1945.
118. "Katherine Ruth Heyman--A Tribute," *Etude* LXVI (1945), 46.

### Addenda

Thirty thousand words in *The Art of Music*, (New York: The National Society of Music, Inc., 1915), Vol. IV.

Contributed articles to *The International Cyclopedia*, (New York: Dodd, Mead Co., 1946).

*Intuition in the World-Making*, an unpublished book, written c. 1935-1945.

Monthly articles in *Fawnskin Folks* 1925-26.

# Appendix II.

## Emily Dickinson
by
### Arthur Farwell

Poe remarked the fact that a poem exhibiting genius, if too brief, is likely to be overlooked and not given its proper due. Following this thought a little further, it may perhaps be said that the output of a poet of genius, if not quantitatively impressive, and especially if delicate and fragile in form, will, as a whole, be similarly neglected and underrated. This reflection is prompted by a rereading of the poems of Emily Dickinson, which like certain other profitable writings, as the Bible or Tom Sawyer, will well bear such a test. And Emily Dickinson, above all, would be selected as the classic example in America of the point in question. America needs to be reminded of her existence from time to time. And her strangely unique life and work are a still very inadequately tilled field, as regards the possible harvest of thought and content to be raised upon them.

Emily Dickinson needs no literary advocate, especially at this date. Genius, like an axiom, is its own argument. You can not prove what proves itself. Anybody dull enough to wish Emily Dickinson different would wish the same of a star. Such exquisiteness as hers, such poignancy of intuition, we approach with a species of awe. That which awes us we can scarcely criticize, we can merely accept. But it is the character of her adventure in life that must interest us equally, and its relation to her achievement, and to that too little attention has been given.

In the monastic and non-divorcing ages, if a properly brought up and high-minded maiden fell upon what was in those unemancipated days regarded as a "hopeless" love, she straightway renounced the world and immured herself in a nunnery. We might expect an action so unequivocal and dramatically complete to give us the thrilling sense of perfection. It does not, because it is an action constrained from without, dictated by an artificial code. It was the usual thing; no other course, under the circumstances, would be *comme il faut*. Its heroism is meager, its originality nil.

How vastly different the great adventure of Emily Dickinson comes before us! An American girl, a genius, high-spirited, modern beyond her period, comes upon the great experience, under similar "impossible" conditions. It may well be that she is moved by consideration for another woman's happiness, and that she is by no means free of moral constraints, both external and internal. But we see that she responds to something far above these obvious considerations. These motives admit a tincture of the negative, but she, impelled by a restless universe of latent creative genius within herself, knows life only as positive. She is phenomenally sensitive, but nowise morbid. Her experience reveals to her, within herself, the perfection of perfections. She will not see it marred or dimmed, she will keep it eternally whole and clear, dwell with it in spiritual perfection, to the end. That this may be, she enters her father's house, her father's garden, at twenty-three, never, in virtual effect, to leave it again except in death, thirty-three years after.

But here the story is only half told. With any ordinary mortal this sequestration is where blurring, dimming, aberration, shrinking of the vision would begin. But we are reckoning with one of the most original geniuses which America has produced. By a veritably providential intuition, Emily followed faithfully the higher law of her particular being. For in this act she entered into the eager and waiting universe of her creative imagination, illuminated now, and expanded to its heights and depths by the experience of experiences.

Now follows one of the most extraordinary of recorded cases in which the outward experiences and impressions of an environment no greater than a single house with its garden served to fecundate amply, luxuriantly, an imagination of veritably cosmic scope. We are to bear in mind that Emily did not view her environment with any monastic eye. Rather was it with one riotously and mischievously pagan. Of all that occurred or penetrated within, or impinged upon this little world of her choosing, she availed herself as freely as she desired. Stupid visitors, to be sure, were fled from, but not spring, summer, autumn, winter, daffodils, foxglove, bees, robins, bobolinks, sunlight, books, correspondence, birth, death, children, human relations, thought. It was indeed a richly and intensely populated world.

Emily's family was thoroughly religious in the old true to type New England way. But in spite of "family prayers" and all that term implies of nineteenth century theological environment in Amherst, Massachusetts, Emily was impervious to its usual and characteristic influence. It would appear that her family never became aware of the definitely neo-pagan character of her none the less high spirituality (although she shocked them not infrequently), especially as the bulk of her amazing poetry remained wholly unknown to them, as to the world, until her death. Others may "keep the Sabbath going to church," but she "keeps it staying at home,

> With a bobolink for a chorister,
> And an orchard for a dome,"

and the sermon is preached by "God, a noted clergyman", and is moreover, "never long". She jests in similar vein frequently with ecclesiastical and Biblical terminology, often with sly mischief and always inoffensively, or plays with it as legitimate artistic material, but we never feel that she accepts it in the same sense as those about her. She has her little laugh, we guess, at the manner in which these about her use the traditional expressions, but at the same time we feel that she has her own private versions of the same concepts, no less beautiful (being a true poet) and vastly more penetrating.

What Emily Dickinson gleans from her spatially restricted environment (if we admit only three dimensions) fills us at every moment with surprise and delight. Seldom does any poet habitually make such big use of such little things. She often enough enjoys what she sees for no more than it is, as a robin "drinking a dew", or the "punctual snow". But while she is the very soul and genius of service to all about her, her life is lived chiefly in the fourth dimension, in her spiritual consciousness, of which the phenomena of the three-dimensional world present but suggestive symbols. The "long shadow on the lawn, indicative that suns go down," offers itself massively as a somber image of "presentiment", and in swinging us by an inspired plural to star-systems beyond our own, lifts the most casual incident of nature to a suggestion of cosmic tragedy.

An amazing juxtaposition of words, concepts, ideas, is continually animating this intractable and bound-defying poetry.

Surprising and unprecedented as this juxtaposition is in itself, it is thrown into still bolder relief by the terseness of its setting. There is no room in these hyper-concentrated lines for anything but their wonder. The "level! bee," who moves like trains of cars on tracks of plush;" the sunshine that "threw his hat away;" the "divine majority" of the soul, in electing her own society - the closing of the "valves of her attention"; the newly-realized possession of love as comforted by a "delirious charter"; the second bridal festivity of lovers "born everlasting now" in heaven, with "a paradise" for a host, the odd appearance of one's own girlhood as seen from behind the "soft eclipse" of marriage; the rose being "out of town" in the autumn; the "distance" on "the look of death;" "clouds, like listless elephants," straggling down horizons; the "trembling sun" of "time" sinking in "human nature's west;" God permitting "industrious angels" to play afternoons; after a death in the house, the "sweeping up the heart" and putting away of love that will not need to be used "until eternity;" Christ explaining "in the fair schoolroom of the sky", each separate anguish of the life of earth. Such daring and arresting expressions engage us at every turn in Emily Dickinson's poetry. But it is the use to which she puts them that matters. And this is, to reveal to us in new colors and exhaustless and compounded symbolism to bring us home to the awe and wonder of the boundless universe which our spiritual selves inhabit.

And when we have finished our first encounter with the poetry of this elusive and unclassifiable neo-pagan paradox of puritan New England, we have the ample delight of her letters, with their new harvest of pungent and aromatic expressions to gather. At random - "there is no first or last in Forever. It is Center there all the time" (how this mode of thought harmonizes with the great mystics!); "Great hungers feed themselves but little hungers ail in vain;" "to live is so startling, it leaves but little room for other occupations."

Where does such a time-and-place-escaping soul fit in the New England scene in the middle of the last century? Presumably exactly where we find it, in a poet's self-created cloister, driven there at last by the event which gave her to herself, that she might give herself to the world. Life offered her the opportunity of her supreme adventure. She accepted the challenge highly and heroically, and, while not seeking her reward, nevertheless could not escape it - not the fame and place which posterity has given her, but the vision and the power of expression given her of the Spirit. If I mistake not, she places herself through spiritual stature and sheer literary originality not far from the five or six greatest American poets.

# Bibliography

**Primary Sources**

CULBERTSON FARWELL COLLECTION

**Journals**

Arthur Farwell:  Book II, July 6 - Nov. 8, 1893; Book VI, June 5, 1897 - March 11, 1898.
Sara Wyer (Mrs. George Farwell):  1) April 5, 1865 - Feb. 22, 1867;  2) Oct. 5, 1886 - Nov. 25, 1888;  3) Nov. 28, 1889 - Feb. 20, 1892;  4) Feb. 23, 1892 - June 22,1893;  5) June 23, 1893 - Oct. 27, 1899.  (Sara Wyer was Arthur Farwell's mother.  Diary No. 1 was written before her marriage.)

**Correspondence**

Personal correspondence with over 75 persons includes such notables as:  Lawrence Gilman, Charles Griffes, Alexandre Guilmant, Henry Hadley, Reynaldo Hahn, George Hale, Howard Hanson, Hedwig and Engelbert Humperdinck, Serge Koussevitsky, Edward MacDowell, Carl Sandburg, Arthur Shepherd, Frank Lloyd Wright, and 25 letters and cards from Roy Harris.

**Writings**

Unpublished essays as well as original copies of published ones. Copies of lectures given on Farwell's four transcontinental tours. Class lectures given at UCLA and addresses for various clubs and music teachers' organizations.  Some chapters for his unpublished book, *Intuition in the World-Making*; flyers prepared by Farwell and original poems.

**Photographs and Drawings**

Photos of pageants and individual cast members; community music productions; drawings Farwell prepared from dreams or visions he experienced, along with their interpretation as he used them for his lectures on *Intuition*.

## Manuscripts, Scores

Manuscripts of Farwell's unpublished compositions; annotated scores of his published works; music by Farwell's contemporaries, some with comments; notebooks with theme jottings; autographed copies of six compositions by Charles Griffes; multiple copies of music prepared on Farwell's lithograph press.

## Miscellaneous

Accounts; books - including Troward, *Edinburgh Lectures on Mental Science*, W. M. H. Milner, *The Royal House of Britain, An Enduring Dynasty*; Alice Fletcher, *Indian Music, Indian Ceremonies (autographed), and The Import of the Totem*; John C. Fillmore's *Harmonic Structure of Indian Music* and three monographs by R. A. Millikan; files resulting from Farwell's research on American Indian music and cowboy songs of the West and the Plains; magazine clippings on subjects which particularly concerned Farwell, such as Jung's psychology; notes from Farwell's study of ancient history and related subjects he used in the preparation for certain pageants or masques; press clippings; programs where his works were performed, with notes and personal comments; and a collection of programs from the Bohemian Club.

## Taped Interviews

Gertrude (Mrs. Arthur) Farwell
Brice and Ruth Farwell
Emerson Farwell
Beatrice Farwell
Sara Farwell Milbert
Jonathan and Joearle Farwell

## Essays and Lectures (some published)

"The Artist as a Man of Destiny" (Written at Los Angeles)
"America's Gain from a Bayreuth Romance. The Mystery of
    Anton Seidl." (original essay, later somewhat revised.)
"American Indian Song"

"Business Man and Artist"
"Clement Harris"
"Finding a National Musical Life"
"Freedom to Not Worship God"
"'Gasoline', and Other New Music"
"A Hidden Race"
"Indian Mythology and American Music"
"Indian and Negro in American Music a Reversal of Prophecy"
"The Influence of Spengler"
"Jazz and the Fourth Dimension"  (written at Pasadena, CA)
"Music and Myth of the American Indians" (Lecture tour)
"Music for the People", address to Canadian Club Meeting No. 24, Chateau Laurier, Ottawa, March 21, 1914.
"A National American Music" (Lecture Tour)
"The New National Movement for Community Music"
Opera Lectures for classroom use
"Outline of Music History" (a diagram)
"Safe and Sane Fourth of July" (c. 1914)
"The Southwest" (possibly 1926)
"Spiritual Interpretation of American Musical History in the Twentieth Century"
"To the Guild of American Organists"
"Wa-Wan Press and the Ceremony of the Omahas"
"The Zero Hour in Music"

### Selected Secondary Sources Consulted

**Books**

Anderson, Charles. *Emily Dickinson's Poetry: Stairway of Surprise.* New York: Holt, Rinehart & Winston, 1960.

Bacon, Ernst. *Words on Music.* Syracuse, NY: Syracuse University Press, 1960.

Barzun, Jaques. *Music in American Life.* Bloomington, Indiana: Indiana University Press, 1962.

Bennett, Paula. *My Life A Loaded Gun, Female Creativity and Feminist Poetics*, Boston: Beacon Press, 1966.

Birge, Edward Bailey. *History of Public School Music in the United States*. Reprint. Washington, D.C.: Music Educators Conference, 1966.

Blegen, Theodore C. *Minnesota. A History of the State.* 2nd ed., Minneapolis: University of Minnesota Press, 1975.

Bowen, Ezra, (ed.) *This Fabulous Century, 1900-1910*, Vol. 1, New York: Time Life Books, 1969. Reprinted 1970.

Bowers, Faubion. *The New Scriabin.* New York: St. Martin's Press, 1973.

Bragdon, Claude. *More Lives Than One.* New York: Alfred A. Knopf, 1938.

Brown, Calvin. *Music and Literature.* A Comparison of the Arts. Athens, Georgia: University of Georgia Press, 1948.

Bulfinch, Thomas. *The Golden Age of Myth and Legend.* London: George G. Harrap & Co., 1915.

Chase, Gilbert. (ed.) *The American Composer Speaks.* (Historical Anthology, 1770-1965). Baton Rouge: Louisiana State University Press, 1966.

_____. *America's Music.* 2nd. ed. New York: McGraw-Hill, 1966.

_____. *America's Music.* 3rd ed. Chicago: Univ. of Ill. Press, 1987.

_____. *The Wa-Wan Press, A Chapter in American Enterprise.* *The Wa-Wan Press*, Vol. I. Edited by Vera Brodsky Lawrence. Five volumes. New York: Arno Press, 1970. Reissue of original Wa-Wan series, 1901-12, edited by Arthur Farwell.

Churchill, Allen. *Remember When.* New York: Ridge Press, 1967.

Commager, Henry Steele. *The American Mind.* New Haven: Yale University Press, 1950.

Copland, Aaron. *The New Music. 1900-1950.* Revised & enlarged. New York: W. W. Norton & Co., 1968.

Cowell, Henry.(ed.) *American Composers on American Music.* Originally, Palo Alto: Stanford University Press, 1933. New York: Frederick Ungar, 1962.

Curti, Merle. *The Growth of American Thought.* 3rd ed. New York: Harper and Row, 1964.

Davis, Ronald L. *A History of Music in American Life.* Vol. II, The Gilded Years, 1865-1920. Huntington, New York: Robert Krieger Publishing Co., 1980.

Denbo, Angie. *Geronimo.* Norman, OK: University of Oklahoma Press, 1976.

Deutsch, Karl W. *Nationalism and Social Communication.* Cambridge, MA: The M.I.T. Press, 1933.

Dobrin, Arnold. *Aaron Copland. His Life and Times.* New York: Thomas Y. Crowell Co., 1967.

Elson, Louis C. *The National Music of America and Its Sources.* Boston: L. C. Page & Co. 1900.

Emerson, Ralph Waldo. *American Scholar.* Vol. 1 in Emerson's *The Complete Works of Ralph Waldo Emerson*, 12 Volumes. Boston: Houghton Mifflin Co., 1903.

*Encyclopedia of Occultism and Parapyschology*, Leslie A. Shepard, ed., Vol. 2. Detroit, MI: Gale Research Co., 1978.

Ewen, David. *American Composers Today*. New York: The H. W. Wilson Co., 1949.

_____. *Music Comes to America*. New York: Thomas Y. Crowell Co., 1942.

Farwell, Arthur. "Community Music and the Music Teacher". Music Teachers National Association, *Volume of Proceedings*, 1916.

_____. "Introduction," *The Art of Music: Vol. 4. Music in America*. New York: The National Society of Music, 1915.

Farwell, Brice. ed. *A Guide to the Music of Arthur Farwell and to the Microfilm Collection of His Work*. Privately printed, Briarcliff Manor, NY. 1972.

Faulkner, Harold. *American Political and Social History*, 6th ed. New York: Appleton-Century Crofts, Inc., 1952.

Federal Works Agency. *Los Angeles, A Guide to the City and Its Environs*. New York: Hastings House, 1941. Revised, 1951.

Ferris, Anthony R. (ed. and translator). *Kahlil Gibran: A Self-Portrait*. New York: Citadel Press, 1959.

Fillmore, John Comfort. *The Harmonic Structure of Indian Music*. New York: G. P. Putnam's Sons, 1899.

Finck, Henry T. *Songs and Song Writers*. New York: Scribners, 1900.

Fitch, Donald. *Blake Set to Music*. Berkeley: University of California Press, 1989.

Fleming, William. *Arts and Ideas*. 3rd ed. New York: Holt, Rinehart and Winston, Inc., [1968].

Fletcher, Alice. *The Import of the Totem. A Study from the Omaha Tribe.* Salem, MA: The Salem Press, 1897.

_____. *Indian Ceremonies.* Salem, MA: The Salem Press, 1884.

_____. *Indian Story and Song from North America.* Boston: Small, Maynard and Co., 1900.

Ford, Thomas W. *Heaven Beguiles the Tired.* University, Alabama: University of Alabama Press, 1966.

Friedberg, Ruth C. *American Art Songs and American Poetry*, Vol. 1. Metuchen, New Jersey: Scarecrow Press Inc., 1981.

_____. *American Art Songs and American Poetry*, Vol. 2. Metuchen, New Jersey: Scarecrow Press Inc., 1984.

Gibran, Kahlil and Jean. *Kahlil Gibran, His Life and World.* Boston: New York Graphic Society, 1974.

Green, Janet M. *Musical Biographies*, W. L. Hubbard, ed. Vol. 1. New York: Irving Squire, 1908.

Hall, James Husset. *The Art Song.* Norman, OK: University of Oklahoma Press, 1953.

Handlin, Oscar. *The History of the United States.* Vol. 2. New York: Holt, Rinehart, & Winston, 1968.

Hitchcock, H. Wiley. *Music in the United States: A Historical Introduction.* Englewood Cliffs, NJ: Prentice-Hall, 1969.

Hitchcock, H. Wiley, and Stanley Sadie, eds. *The New Grove Dictionary of American Music.* 4 vols. London: Macmillan, 1986.

Horn, David. *Literature of American Music.* Metuchen, New Jersey: Scarecrow Press Inc., 1977.

Howard, John Tasker. *Our American Music*. New York: Thomas Y. Crowell, 1929.

_____. *Our Contemporary Composers*. New York: Crowell Co. 1941.

Hughes, Rupert. *American Composers*. Boston: The Page Co., 1914.

Ivey, Donald. *Song, Anatomy, Imagery, and Styles*. New York: Free Press, 1970.

Jackson, Richard. *U.S. Music, Sources of Bibliography & Collective Bibliography*. Brooklyn, New York: Institute for Studies in American Music, 1976.

Johnson, T. H. *Emily Dickinson, An Interpretive Biography*. Cambridge, MA: Belknap Press of Harvard Univ. Press, 1955.

Jones, Isabel Morse. *Hollywood Bowl*. Los Angeles: G. Schirmer, Inc., 1936.

Kingman, Daniel. *American Music: A Panorama*. New York: Schirmer Books, Division of Macmillan Publishing Co., Inc., 1979. Also second edition, 1990.

Kirk, Elise K. *Music at the White House. A History of the American Spirit*. Chicago: University of Illinois Press, 1986.

Koopal, Grace G. *The Miracle of Music: The History of the Hollywood Bowl*. Los Angeles: W. Ritchie, Golden Jubilee Edition, 1972.

de Koven, Reginald. *Music of the Modern World*. Vol. 1, "Nationality in Music," edited by Anton Seidl. New York: D. Appleton Press, 1895.

Lambord, Benjamin. *Music in America*, Vol. IV of *The Art of Music*. Arthur Farwell and Dermot Darby, editors. New York: The National Society of Music, 1915.

Lahee, Henry Charles. *Annals of Music in America*. Boston: Marshall Jones Co., 1922.

Lang, Paul Henry. *One Hundred Years in America*. New York: G. Schirmer, Inc., 1961.

Langer, Suzanne. *Feeling and Form*. New York: Scribner's, 1953.

Levy, Alan Howard. *Musical Nationalism, American Composer's Search for Identity*. Westport, CT: Greenwood Press, 1983.

Lowenberg, Carlton and Territa A. *Musicians Wrestle Everywhere, Emily Dickinson and Music*. Berkeley, CA: Fallen Leaf Press, pre-publication copy, 1992.

MacKaye, Percy. *Annals of an Era*. Hanover: Dartmouth College Press, 1932.

Martin, Wendy. *An American Triptych: Anne Bradstreet, Emily Dickinson, Adrienne Rich*. Chapel Hill, North Carolina: University of North Carolina Press, 1984.

Mason, Daniel Gregory. *Music in My Time and Other Reminiscences*. Westport, CT: Greenwood Press, 1938.

_____. *Tune in, America*. New York: Alfred A. Knopf, 1931.

McCue, George (ed.) *Music in American Society. 1776-1976. From Puritan Hymn to Synthesizer*. New Brunswick, New Jersey: Transaction Books, 1977.

Mellers, Wilfrid. *Music in a New Found Land*. New York: Alfred A. Knopf, Inc. 1965.

Miller, Ruth. *Poetry of Emily Dickinson*. Middleton, CT: Wesleyan Press, 1968.

Mussulman, Joseph A. *Music in the Cultured Generation. A Social History of Music in America, 1870 - 1900*. Evanston, IL: Northwestern University Press, 1971.

Nettle, Bruno. *North American Indian Musical Styles*. Vol. 45, "Memoirs of the American Folklore Society". Austin: University of Texas Press, 1954.

Phillips, Elizabeth. *Emily Dickinson. Personae and Performance*. University Park, PA: Pennsylvania State Univ. Press, 1988.

Prevots, Naima. *American Pageantry: A Movement for Art and Democracy*. Ann Arbor, MI: UMI Research Press, 1990.

Reis, Claire R. *Composers in America*. NY: Macmillan, 1947.

Ritter, Frédéric, Louis. *Music in America*. 2nd ed. 1890 reprint, New York: Johnson Reprint Co. 1970.

Rublowsky, John. *Music in America*. New York: Crowell-Collier Press, 1967.

Ryan, Thomas. *Recollections of an Old Musician*. New York: E. P. Dutton & Company, 1899.

Sablowsky, Irving. *American Music*. Chicago: University of Chicago Press, 1969.

Salazar, Adolfo. *Music in Our Time*. New York: W. W. Norton, 1946.

Samson, Jim. *Music in Transition: A Study of Tonal Expansion and Atonality, 1900-1920*. New York: W. W. Norton, 1977.

Schauffler, Robert Haven and Sigmund Speath. *Music as a Social Force in America*, Vol. 19. *Fundamentals of Musical Art*,

Edward Dickinson, ed. New York: The Caxton Institute, Inc. 1927.

Scholes, Percy A. *The Oxford Companion to Music*, 9th edition. New York: Oxford University Press, 1955.

Schönberg, Arnold. *The Lives of the Great Composers*. New York: W. W. Norton & Co, 1981.

_____. *Structural Functions of Harmony*. New York: W. W. Norton, 1954.

Schwab, Arnold T. *James Gibbons Huneker, Critic of the Seven Arts*. Stanford, CA: Stanford Univ. Press, 1963.

Sessions, Roger. *Reflections on the Musical Life in the United States*. New York: Merlin Press, 1956.

Sewell, Richard, ed. *Introduction to Emily Dickinson. A Collection of Critical Essays*. Englewood Cliffs, NJ: Prentice Hall, 1963.

_____. *The Life of Emily Dickinson*. Vol. 2. New York: Farrar, Straus, and Giroux, 1974.

Siegmeister, Elie. *Music and Society*. New York: Haskell House Publishers, Ltd., 1974.

Sherman, John K. *Music and Maestros, The Story of the Minneapolis Symphony Orchestra*. Minneapolis: University of Minnesota Press, 1952.

Slonimsky, Nicolas. *Music Since 1900*. 3rd ed. New York: Coleman-Ross, Inc., 1949.

Smith, Catherine Parsons, and Cynthia S. Richardson. *Mary Carr Moore, American Composer*. Ann Arbor: University of Michigan Press. 1987.

Spaulding, Walter R. "Community Music Conference," *Volume of Proceedings*, Music Teachers National Association, 1918.

Stehman, Dan. *Roy Harris, An American Pioneer*. Boston: Twayne Publishing Co., 1984.

Stevens, Denis, ed. *A History of Song*. New York: W. W. Norton & Co., 1960.

Surette, Thomas Whitnew. *Music and Life*. Boston: Houghton Mifflin Co., 1917.

Swan, Howard. *Music in the Southwest*. San Marino, CA: Huntington Library, 1952.

Tawa, Nicholas. *Serenading the Reluctant Eagle: American Musical Life, 1925-1945*. New York: Schirmer Books, a division of Macmillan, Inc., 1984.

_____. *A Sound of Strangers: Musical Culture, Acculturation, and the Post-Civil War Ethnic American*. Metuchen, New Jersey: Scarecrow Press Inc., 1982.

Tischler, Barbara L. *An American Music. The Search for an American Musical Identity*. New York: Oxford University Press, 1986.

Thompson, Oscar, ed.-in-chief. *The International Cyclopedia of Music and Musicians*. 9th ed. Edited by Robert Sabin. New York: Dodd, Mead & Co., 1964.

Thomson, Virgil. *American Music Since 1910*. New York: Holt, Rinehart, & Winston, 1971.

Upton, William Treat. *Art-Song in America*. Boston: Oliver Ditson, 1930.

_____. *Supplement, Art-Song in America, 1930-1938*. Oliver Ditson, 1939.

Wagenknecht, Edward. *The Seven Worlds of Theodore Roosevelt.* New York: Longmans, Green and Co. 1958.

Waters, Edward. "The Wa-Wan Press, An Adventure in Musical Idealism". In *A Birthday Offering to Carl Engel*, edited by Gustave Reese. New York: G. Schirmer, Inc., 1943.

Wish, Harvey. *Contemporary America.* New York: Harper & Bros., 1945.

Yerbury, Grace D. *Song in America from Early Times to About 1850.* Metuchen, NJ: Scarecrow Press, Inc., 1971.

Zuck, Barbara. *History of Musical Americanism.* Ann Arbor, MI: UMI Research Press, 1980.

**Articles**

"Arthur Farwell," *The Berkeley Times*, Berkeley, California, September 9, 1919.

"Arthur Farwell Continues Good Work," *Pacific Coast Musical Review*, XXXVII, Oct. 25, 1919.

"Arthur Farwell Elected President of Music Teachers Association," *Pacific Coast Musical Review*, Vol. 35, No. 11, Dec. 14, 1918.

"A Berkeley Municipal Community Chorus," *Pacific Coast Musical Review*, XXXV/24, March 15, 1919.

Bispham, David. "The American Idea in Music, and Some Other Ideas," *The Craftsman*, Feb. 9, 1909.

Block, Adrienne Fried, "Amy Beach's Music on Native American Themes," *American Music*, 8, No. 2, Summer 1990.

Brancaleone, Francis. "Edward MacDowell and Indian Motives," *American Music*, Vol. 7, No. 4, Winter 1989.

"Celebrated Actors in Cast for Masque," *New York Times*, May 17, 1916.

Clark, Kenneth S. "New York Carried on Tidal Wave of Community Music," *Musical America*. Vol. XXIV, No. 21, Sept. 23, 1916.

"Composer Lithographs Own Music," *Musical America*, LVII/10, May 25, 1937.

"Composer-Printer," *New York Times*, May 16, 1937.

"Concert Review of Berkeley Community Chorus," *Musical Review*, Vol. 35, No. 24, March 15, 1919.

Culbertson, Evelyn Davis. "Arthur Farwell's Early Efforts on Behalf of American Music, 1899-1921," *American Music*, Vol. 5, No. 2, Summer 1987.

Danziger, Juliet. "Altruistic Music Publishing in America," *Musical Mecury*, Oct.-Nov., 1954.

Devries, Rene. "America Comes of Age as a World Power in Music," *Musical Courier*, Feb. 1955.

Duke, John. "The Significance of Song," *Ars Lyrica*, I (1961)

_____. "Some Reflections on the Art-Song in English," *The American Music Teacher*, XXV: 4 (1976).

Dvořák, Antonin. "Music in America," *Harper's Monthly*, XC, No. 537, March 1895.

Eaton, Quaintance. "The Red Man Sings for his Paleface Brothers," *Better Homes and Gardens*, Aug. 1936.

Edwards, George Boosinger. "Farwell Describes the Community Chorus," *Pacific Coast Musical Review*, Vol. XXXVI, No. 1, April 5, 1919.

Farwell, Arthur. "Announcement," *Wa-Wan Press Monthly*, Vol. VII, No. 53, Jan. 1908.

_____. "Aspects of Indian Music," *Southern Workman*, XXXI/4, April 1902.

_____. "A Call for the Times," *Musical America*, XVII/1 Nov. 9, 1912.

_____. "Community Music-Drama: Will Our Country People in Time Help Us to Develop the Real American Theater?" *The Craftsman*, XXVI/4, July 1914.

_____. "Dramatic Ceremony and Symphonic Song Visioned as New Form in Development of True American Art," *Musical America*, XLV/23, March 26, 1927.

_____. Editorial, "American Music Study" column, *Wa-Wan Press Monthly*, Vol. VI, No. 51, Nov. 1907.

_____. Editorial, "How to Study American Music," *Wa-Wan Press Monthly*, Vol. VI, No. 44, April 1907.

_____. "Editorial," *Wa-Wan Press Monthly*, Vol. V, No. 43, March 1907.

_____. "Editorial," *Wa-Wan Press Monthly*, Vol. VI, No. 53, Dec. 1907.

_____. "An Eleven Years' Adventure," *Musical America*, XVI/19, Sept. 14, 1912.

_____. "Evolution of New Forms Foreseen for America's Music," *Musical America*, XLV/22, March 19, 1927.

_____. "Extremists in Paint and Tone," *Musical America,* XVII/23 (April 12, 1913).

_____. "Giving the People What They Want - Music and the People," *The Touchstone*, 1 May 1917.

_____. "Introduction," *Wa-Wan Press*, Sept. 1903.

_____. "Municipal Music in New York," in *Music Teachers National Association, Papers and Proceedings of the Thirty-Fifth Annual Meeting*, College of Music, Cincinnati, Ohio, Dec. 29, 1913 - Jan. 1, 1914. Hartford, CT: The Association, 1914.

_____. "Music and the New Fourth," *Musical America*, XV/23, April 13, 1912.

_____. "Musical Form Under New Human Conditions," *Musical America*, XXII/1, May 8, 1915.

_____. "Nationalism in Music," *The International Cyclopedia of Music and Musicians*. Oscar Thompson, ed.-in-chief; 10th edition, Bruce Bohle, ed. New York: Dodd, Mead, & Co. 1975.

_____. "National Work Vs. Nationalism," *The New Music Review*, 8/92, July 1909.

_____. "New York Concert of the Wa-Wan Society," *Wa-Wan Monthly*, Vol. VII, No. 54, Feb. 1908.

_____. "New York's Municipal Music: Two Years' Advance," *Review of Reviews*, XLIV/4, Oct. 1911.

_____. "The Pageant and Masque of St. Louis," *The American Review of Reviews*, L/2, Aug. 1914.

_____. "Pioneering for American Music," *Modern Music*, XII/3, March-April 1935.

_____. "Roy Harris," *Musical Quarterly*, XVIII/1, Jan. 1932.

_____. "Science and Intuition," *Tomorrow*, April 1942.

_____. "Society and American Music," *Atlantic Monthly* CI, 1908

_____. "Sonata Form and the Cabbala," *Musical Quarterly* XXVII/1, Jan. 1941.

_____. "Sonata - Only Possible Form," *Musical America*, XVI/6, June 1912.

_____. "Song and Light Festival Reveals a New Art Form," *Musical America* XXIV, Aug. 12, 1916.

_____. "The Struggle Toward a National Music," *North American*, CLXXXVI, 1907.

_____. "Toward an American Music," *Boston Transcript*, May 20, 1916.

_____. "Tribute to Thomas Mott Osborne," *New York Times*, n.d.

_____. "Wanderjahre of a Revolutionist," *Musical America*, IX, Jan. 23, 30; Feb. 6, 13, 20, 27; March 6, 13, 20, 27; April 3, 10, 17, 24; May 1, 8, 15, 22, 29; June 12, 19, 26; July 3, 1909.

_____. "When Thou Makest a Feast," *Musical America*, XXII, Oct. 1916.

_____. "The Zero Hour in Musical Evolution," *Musical Quarterly*, XIII/1, Jan. 1927.

"Farwell Extension Lectures," *Pacific Coast Musical Review*, XXXV/24, March 15, 1919.

"Farwell's 'Hymn to Liberty' to be sung at Peterboro Pageant," *Musical America*, XIV, Aug. 12, 1911.

Farwell, Brice. "More Than Music Composed After Blake by Arthur Farwell," *Blake, An Illustrated Quarterly*, 42, Fall 1977.

Fenster, Mark. "Preparing the Audience, Informing the Performers: John A. Lomax and Cowboy Songs and Other Frontier Ballads," *American Music*, Vol. 7, No. 3, Fall 1989.

"First Performance of 'Cello Sonata," *Violins*, XI (1950).

Gilman, Lawrence. "The New American Music", *The North American Review*, Vol. 179, Dec. 1904.

_____. "Some American Music," *Harper's Weekly*, March 7, 1903.

Gould, John A. "(Emily) Dickinsinging and the Art Thereof," *Andover Alumni Bulletin*, Vol. 78, No. 34, Spring 1985.

Harvey, John. "Harvey Offers a Birthday Salute to Arthur Farwell," *St. Paul Pioneer Press*. May 4, 1947.

Ingraham, Henry. "A Recent Development in American Music," *The Chautauquan*, 50/1, March 1908.

Kendig, Frances. "Fawnskin and the Theater of the Stars," *Fawnskin Folks*, July 1925.

de Koven, Reginald. "Nationalism in Music". *The North American Review*, Vol. 189, March 1909.

Lowens, Irving. "Arthur Farwell: Rediscovering an American Original," *High Fidelity Magazine*, 28/11, Nov. 1978.

Mathews, W. S. "Editorial Bric-a-Brac," *Music* XXII (1902).

Metzger, Alfred. "Music Teachers Honor Their New President, Arthur Farwell," *Pacific Coast Musical Review*, Vol. 35, No. 17, Jan. 25, 1919.

"Minnesota Honors A Notable Musician," *Musical America*, LXIX, 1949.

"New American Hymn to Liberty Launched," *Musical America*, XIV/10, July 15, 1911.

"New National Hymn to be sung Here on the Fourth," *New York Times*, July 2, 1911, Section 5.

Newman, William S. "Arthur Shepherd," *Musical Quarterly*, Vol. XXXVI, No. 2, April 1950.

Nilssohn, Victor. "Applaud Premiere of American Work," *Musical America*, L/1, Jan. 10, 1930.

Peyser, Herbert F. "New York's First Community Masque Notable Spectacle," *Musical America*, XXIV/5, June 3, 1915.

"Promoter of American Music," *The Hampton Magazine*, XXVIII (1912).

Roman, Zoltan. "Music in Turn-of-the-Century America: A View from the 'Old World'," *American Music*, Vol. 7, No. 3, Fall 1989.

"Santa Barbara Joins in Brilliant Concert by Mr. Farwell's Choristers," *Musical America*, XXXI/13, Jan. 24, 1920.

Schwartz, K. Robert, "Book Nook II," *I.S.A.M. Newsletter*, Vol. XVIII, No. 1, Nov. 1988.

Seidl, Anton. "The Development of Music in America," *Forum* 13, May 1892.

"Settlement Turns Out Its Thousand," *New York Times*, March 3, 1918, Section V.

Shier, Theresa. "Lansing Forces Unite in New Institute," *Musical America*, March 31, 1928.

Slonimsky, Nicolas. "Roy Harris," *Musical Quarterly* 33, 1947.

Squier, Walter. "Appreciation and a Prophecy," *Fawnskin Folks*, July 25, 1925.

_____. "Opening of the Theater of the Stars," *Fawnskin Folks*, July 1925.

Straus, Noel. "John Kirkpatrick in Piano Recital," *New York Times*, Jan. 15, 1942.

Weil, Irving. "The American Scene Changes," *Modern Music*, Vol. 6, No. 4 (1928-29) 3-9.

Wright, Merle. "The New York Community Chorus," *National Magazine*, Nov. 1916.

**Unpublished Dissertations**

Aborn, Merton Robert. "The Influence on American Musical Cultures of Dvořák's Sojourn in America." University of Indiana, 1965.

Davis, Evelyn (Culbertson). "The Significance of Arthur Farwell as an American Music Educator." University of Maryland, College Park, 1972.

Kelly, Stephen K. "Arthur Farwell and the Wa-Wan Press." Rutgers University, 1969. (Master's thesis).

Kirk, Edgar Lee. "Toward American Music: A Study of the Life and Music of Arthur George Farwell." Eastman School of Music, University of Rochester, 1958.

Loucks, Richard. "Arthur Shepherd." Eastman School of Music, University of Rochester, 4 vols. 1960.

Moeller, Vernon. "Theoretical Aspects of Arthur Farwell's Musical Settings of Poems by Emily Dickinson." University of Texas at Austin, May 1979. (M.M. thesis)

Richer, Linda. "Arthur Farwell's Piano Quintet: Aspects of Form and Thematic Development." San Francisco State University, 1987. (M. M. thesis).

Rider, Merton Robert. "The Musical Thought and Activities of the New England Transcendentalists." University of MN, 1965.

Sims, Jo Ann. "Capturing the Essence of the Poet: A Study and Performance of Selected Musical Settings for Solo Voice and Piano of the Poetry of Emily Dickinson." University of Illinois at Urbana-Champaign, 1987.

Yont, Rose. *Status and Value of Music in Education.* Published thesis, University of Iowa, Woodruff Press, 1916.

**Obituaries**

*Instrumentalist.* Vol. VII. Sept., 1952, p. 63

*Musical America.* Vol. LXXII. February 1952, p. 274.

*Musical Courier.* Vol. CLXV. February 1952, p. 15.

*New York Times.* January 21, 1952.

*School and Society.* Vol. LXXXV. January 26, 1952, p. 63.

*Variety.* Vol. CLXXXV. Jan. 23, 1952, p. 63.

# Index

Bold numbers represent illustrations.

Huneker, James 392, 418, 502, 552
Hunt, Edwyn A. 211, 609
Huss, Henry Holden 83

*I hear America singing* 87, 92, 123, 182
*Ici bas* (J. P. Beach) 93, 94
Ide, Chester 597
Impressionism 512, 507
Indian 78, 80-82, 85, 86, 99, 100, 111,
   356, 359, 392, 654, 711
Indian music 78, 106, 109, 111, 119
*Indian Story and Song from North
   America* 77, 357
International Institute 151
Intuition 252
Irwin, Will 166
*Israfel* (Gilbert) 86, 105
Ives, Charles 426, 712

Johannesen, Grant 382, 509
John Church Publishing Company 605
Journal of the St. Petersburg Society of
   Musical Assemblies 102

Kagen, Sergius 440
Keith, William 114
Kelley, Edgar Stillman 82, 83, 86-88,
   105, 145
Kelley, Mrs. Edgar Stillman 660
Kelsey, Mrs. Charles 156-157, 160
Kempf, Paul M. 143
Kendig, Frances 612
Kernochan, Marshall 347
Kimball Union Academy 587
Kindler, Hans 693
Kingman, Daniel xxvi, 91, 110
Kirk, Brice 186
Kirk, Edgar 202, 212, 232, 288, 384
Kirk, Elise 356
Kirkpatrick, John 211, 319, 367, 382,
   384, 662
Kittredge 29
*Koenigskinder* 63, 66
Koussevitzky, Serge 671, 673-675
Kramer, A. Walter 347, 669, 712
Kreider, Noble 138, 164, 240, 299, 325,
   **344**, 445, 510, 512, 592
Krishnamurti, J. 229, 308,

Kroeger, Ernest R. 112, 128, 133
Kuntz, George F. 153

La Trinité 68
Lake Owasco 48, 80
Lambord, Benjamin 399, 400, 419, 451,
   591, 654
Landormy, Charles Rene 237
Langdon, William Chauncy 153, 166,
   168-170, 587, 601
Lansing Civic Players Guild 296
Lansing State Journal 231
Laurel Song Books 82, 84, 364
Lawrence, Vera Brodsky 109
Le Centre de Premieres Auditions, 392
Leginski, Ethel 663
Levy, Alan 70, 90
*Lilac* (J. P. Beach) 93
Lilienthal, Joseph L. 141
Listening Room, WQXR 520
Lithographic hand press 245-250, 251,
   269, 311, 313, 511
Little, Arthur Reginald 104
Lloyd, Frank 223
*Lochinvar* (Chadwick) 143
Loeffler, Charles Martin 88, 128, 141,
   141, 382
Lomax, John A. 396
Loomis, Harvey Worthington 83, 104,
   403
Los Angeles Miniature Philharmonic
   Orchestra 609, 610
*Lost Colony* 390
Louisiana Purchase Exposition 116
Lowenberg, Carlton 440
Lowens, Irving 563
Lummis, Charles F. 113, 115, 203, 219,
   400-402

Massachusetts Institute of Technology
   Little Symphony 663
MacKaye, Percy 166, 171-174, 184, 593
Mahler, Gustav 99
Mallery, Winslow 43, 51, 116
Manhattan Symphony orchestra 667,
   670
Manley, Frederick 82, 83, 364
Mannes, David 153, 461

# Farwell Compositions Discussed in Text

# About the Author

Evelyn Davis Culbertson (B.A. Concordia College, M.M. Syracuse University, Ph.D. Maryland University) is Professor Emerita, former Director of the Music Education program she developed at Oral Roberts University. She received her first piano lessons at age five from her mother and continued musical studies at Concordia College Music Conservatory. She won highest awards in college as a scholar and later received scholarships towards her Master's degree. In 1972 she received a Doctoral Grant from the Mu Phi Epsilon Memorial Foundation. She has been active in state and national M.E.N.C. as well as local music circles. In addition to college teaching in several areas, her past experiences include positions as choral director, church organist, and both performer and teacher of voice and piano. She specializes in lecture-recitals on "The Life and Music of Arthur Farwell" and "The Vocal Music of Norway". The latter was researched with the assistance of the Norwegian government and has been performed in native costume and language. She has presented numerous papers on various aspects of the life and music of Arthur Farwell and has published several articles in professional journals such as *American Music* and *Oklahoma School Music News*.